Introduction to Cybersecurity in the Internet of Things

This book addresses the security challenges facing the rapidly growing Internet of Things (IoT) industry, including the potential threats and risks arising from its complex architecture.

The authors discuss the overall IoT architecture, covering networking, computing, and security threats and risks to hardware such as sensors, actuators, and portable devices, as well as infrastructure layers. They cover a range of technical concepts such as cryptography, distributed storage, and data transmission, and offer practical advice on implementing security solutions such as authentication and access control.

By exploring the future of cybersecurity in the IoT industry, with insights into the importance of big data and the threats posed by data mining techniques, this book is an essential resource for anyone interested in, or working in, the rapidly evolving field of IoT security.

Keke Gai is a professor at the School of Cyberspace Science and Technology, Beijing Institute of Technology, China. With over a decade of experience serving on editorial boards, publishing books, and writing peer-reviewed journal and conference papers, he has developed a passion for various research areas, including cybersecurity, blockchain, the Internet of Things (IoT), privacy-preserving computation, centralized identity, and cloud computing.

Jing Yu is an associate professor with the Institute of Information Engineering, Chinese Academy of Sciences. She is an expert in cutting-edge fields of cybersecurity, including AI security, visual question answering, visual dialogue, and cross-modal information retrieval.

Liehuang Zhu is a full professor with the School of Cyberspace Science and Technology, Beijing Institute of Technology. He is an academic explorer in a few frontier areas, such as blockchain, space network, and advanced cryptographic applications.

Introduction to Cybersecurity in the Internet of Things

Keke Gai,
Jing Yu, and
Liehuang Zhu

CRC Press
Taylor & Francis Group
Boca Raton London New York

CRC Press is an imprint of the
Taylor & Francis Group, an **informa** business

Designed cover image: © BeeBright

First edition published 2024
by CRC Press
2385 NW Executive Center Drive, Suite 320, Boca Raton FL 33431

and by CRC Press
4 Park Square, Milton Park, Abingdon, Oxon, OX14 4RN

CRC Press is an imprint of Taylor & Francis Group, LLC

© 2024 Keke Gai, Jing Yu and Liehuang Zhu

ISBN: 978-1-032-69039-1 (hbk)
ISBN: 978-1-032-69488-7 (pbk)
ISBN: 978-1-032-69481-8 (ebk)

DOI: 10.1201/9781032694818

Typeset in Latin Modern font
by KnowledgeWorks Global Ltd.

Publisher's note: This book has been prepared from camera-ready copy provided by the authors.

Contents

Part II Major Cybersecurity Issues

Chapter   4 ∎ Security in Cloud Computing and Cyber-Physical
Systems   137

Part IV Next Generation of Cybersecurity in the
　　　　Internet of Things

Chapter　10 ▪ Digital Twin Optimization in the Internet of Things 543

Preface

This book focuses on cybersecurity in the realm of mobile computing. The content is designed explicitly to instruct audiences on the knowledge of cybersecurity in mobile computing from various dimensions. Reading this book facilitates students, professionals, and educators in refining and reshaping their knowledge scaffold. This book aims to educate people with updated knowledge in the security field and assist learners in upgrading their techniques to match the security requirements in the era of mobile computing.

Next, this book covers many requisites for having a holistic view of cybersecurity in the mobile environment. A few security issues in mobile computing are distinct from that of on-premises. Advanced security techniques require solid fundamental support. Thus, it is necessary and important for researchers to have a concrete understanding of relevant basic topics in the field, such as mobile privacy issues, wireless security, and distributed secure data storage. This book is a perfect fit for those researchers who need a book offering a panoramic view of mobile cybersecurity and who intend to explore their work in a specific direction.

Moreover, the content of this book follows a well-organized, reader-friendly writing style, which starts with a few easily-digestible chapters and explores advanced-level techniques given in the latter chapters. The main content in this book is formed by four parts. The first part provides learners with basic information about cybersecurity in mobile computing from three perspectives, including basic concepts, fundamental cyber issues in mobile computing, and relevant knowledge about the *Internet-of-Things* (IoT) and cloud computing. The next part, Part II, further pictures the significant cybersecurity issues. Three dimensions involved in this part include privacy categorizations, security matters in *Cyber-Physical System* (CPS) and mobile cloud systems, and network threat models. Next, Part III addresses the advanced security techniques and shows a few solutions to major threats/issues referred to in the precedent chapters. This part is the main body of this book. A number of crucial aspects include cryptography techniques, intrusion detections, infrastructure and hardware security, and distributed data storage protections. Finally, Part IV introduces a few emerging cybersecurity technologies in mobile computing. This book also offers some supplementary documents for educators in appendices, such as project and test samples.

Furthermore, this book may attract distinct groups of people who are interested in the domain of mobile cybersecurity. The book encompasses fundamental knowledge and state-of-the-art techniques, such that this book may engage the attention of beginner learners and senior researchers. For instance, the wireless security component will introduce a novel data encryption strategy technique. Additionally, the design of this textbook follows constructivism, which facilitates readers to construct their knowledge scaffold. Studying chapters in this book can aid readers in completing a learning-for-use or a learning-for-research process. Both theoretical content and hands-on experiences will be offered to readers.

In addition, the main benefits deriving from reading this book are threefold. First, this book is a higher-education-focused textbook which offers a comprehensive vision of cybersecurity in contemporary technological settings. Reading this book can facilitate newcomers in constructing their knowledge structure and enlighten senior researchers' insights and exploration intentions. Second, this book is good learning material for different levels of learners. The book is designed to deliver knowledge in a learner-friendly manner. Each chapter offers exercises and a glossary section to help readers to review the key contents. Finally, this book is an updated teaching material for higher-education educators. The structure and organization of this book follow a way of curriculum design. Instructors can determine partial or full contents for their teaching activities.

There is no specific prerequisite for understanding most of the contents of this book. Some mathematical backgrounds are required in some chapters. The contents of this book are organized into ten chapters within four parts, including Part I (Basic Concepts and Mechanisms of Cybersecurity in the Internet of Things), Part II (Major Cybersecurity Issues), Part III (Security Solutions in the Internet of Things), and Part IV (Next Generation of Cybersecurity in the Internet of Things).

In Part I, we include Chapters 1–3. To be specific, Chapter 1 (**Introduction to Cybersecurity**) guides readers in the realm of cybersecurity from basic concepts and discusses a few characteristics of cybersecurity. This chapter provides learners with a fundamental knowledge presentation about key facets of cybersecurity so that learners can start their study journey from this chapter on. Chapter 2 (**Basic Concepts of Cybersecurity in the Internet of Things**) discusses an overview of cybersecurity concepts and challenges in the context of the Internet of Things (IoT). The contents include the history of IoT, architecture of IoT, security challenges, as well as descriptions of fundamental solutions. In Chapter 3 (**Privacy Issues Categorizations in the Internet of Things**), we outline the infrastructure security for OSI layers (i.e., network, host, and application layers), protection methods in distinct scenarios of data storage, and explain the importance of data privacy regarding data management.

Part II is comprised of Chapters 4–6. In detail, Chapter 4 (**Security in Cloud Computing and Cyber-Physical Systems**) discusses the security issues and threat taxonomy in IoT. This chapter also addresses major security challenges in cyber-physical systems. Chapter 5 (**Threat Models and Network Security**) focuses on security issues and principles in networks. Chapter 6 (**Cryptography and Cryptosystems**) introduces basic concepts, terminology, and notation in cryptography and presents relevant concepts and characteristics of symmetric cipher model and asymmetric cipher model. A few common attack methods have been covered as well.

Next, in Part III, we have described security solutions in IoT from Chapter 7 to Chapter 9. Chapter 7 (**Wireless Network Security**) mainly covers security measures and technologies in wireless networks, devices, and data from unauthorized access, theft, and malicious attacks. Threats in wireless networks are detailedly discussed. Chapter 8 (**Infrastructure and Hardware Security**) discusses the threats and solutions in computer infrastructure concerning various dimensions of IoT. A series of measures have been explained in this chapter. Chapter 9 (**Secure Distributed Data Storage and Processing**) exhibits a few security measures in distributed systems, from data storage to processing in IoT. The chapter presents an overview of the latest techniques and practices in secure distributed computing, including secure Moore's Law, heterogeneous CMP, distributed computing algorithm, and distributed data storage algorithm.

Finally, Part IV presents an example of future generation of cybersecurity in IoT. Chapter 10 (**Digital Twin Optimization in the**

Internet of Things) provides audiences with a relevant recent exploration in adopting distributed ledger technologies for enabling digital twins in IoT. This scheme describes an approach that increases the efficiency of task allocation in the scenario of IoT.

Keke Gai
Jing Yu

Beijing,
2023

Liehuang Zhu

Acronyms

This section provides audiences with a list of acronyms. The abbreviations in the list are unified in this book. Most selected abbreviations are broadly accepted concepts in the computing domain.

2FA Two-Factor Authentication

ABAC Attribute-Based Access Control

ACL Access Control Lists

ADAS Advanced Driver Assistance Systems

AE Authenticator Entity

AES Advanced Encryption Standard

AI Artificial Intelligence

ALU Arithmetic Logic Unit

AP Access Point

API Application Programming Interface

APPI Act on the Protection of Personal Information

APT Advanced Persistent Threats

AR Augmented Reality

ASE Authentication Service Entity

ASSA Accuracy-Based Smart Swapping Algorithm

ASU Authentication Service Unit

ASUE Authentication SUpplicant Entity

AT Allocation Table

AWS Amazon Web Services

B8ZS Bipolar with 8-Zero Substitution

BSS Basic Service Set

BSSID Basic Service Set Identifier

CAN Controller Area Network

CCA Chosen Ciphertext Attack

CDPA Consumer Data Protection Act

CISC Complex Instruction Set Computer

CNII Critical National Information Infrastructure

COA Ciphertext Only Attack

COPPA Children's Online Privacy Protection Act

CP Control Plane

CPA Chosen Plaintext Attack

CPPA Canada Privacy Protection Act

CPS Cyber-Physical Systems

CPSs Cloud Service Providers

CPU Central Processing Unit

CRC Cyclic Redundancy Check

CRM Customer Relationship Management

CSMA Carrier Sense Multiple Access

CSMA/CA Carrier Sense Multiple Access/Collision Avoidance

CTA Chosen Text Attack

DAC Discretionary Access Control

DARPA Defense Advanced Research Projects Agency

DBSS DataBase Security Services

DES Data Encryption Standard

DDoS Distributed Denial of Service

DDPA Distributed Data Processing Algorithms

DDSA Distributed Data Storage Algorithms

DGA Distributed Graph Algorithms

DH Dieffie-Hellman

DI Distributed Identity

DLC Data Life Cycle

DLM Data Lifecycle Management

DLP Data Loss Prevention

DMLA Distributed Machine Learning Algorithms

DNS Domain Name System

DoS Denial-of-Service

DRAM Dynamic Random Access Memory

DSA Distributed Sorting Algorithms

DSL Data Security Law

DSM Distributed Shared Memory

DSS Distributed System Service

DSSS Direct-Sequence Spread Spectrum

DT Digital Twins

DTE2AI Digital Twin-Enabled Edge AI

DTN Digital Twins Network

DWH Data Warehouse

EAN European Article Numbering Association

EATA Efficiency-Aware Task Assignment

ECC Elliptic Curve Cryptography

ECT Energy Consuming Table

EHR Electronic Health Records

EPC Electronic Product Code

EPCIS EPC Information Services

ERP Enterprise Resource Planning

ESS Extended Service Set

ESSA Energy-Based Smart Swapping Algorithm

ESSID Extended Service Set Identifier

ETL Extract, Transform, Load

EU European Union

FDMA Frequency Division Multiple Access

FedRAMP Federal Risk and Authorization Management Program

FHSS Frequency-Hopping Spread Spectrum

FMI Functional Mock-Up Interface

FP Forwarding Plane

FTC Federal Trade Commission

GDPR General Data Protection Regulation

GLBA Graham-Leach-Bliley Act

GPDL General Data Protection Law

GPS Global Positioning System

HDB3 High-Density Bipolar3-zero

HDL Hardware Description Language

HIPAA Health Insurance Portability and Accountability Act

HLA High-Level Architecture

HMI Human-Machine Interface

HomeRF Home Radio Frequency

HR Human Resources

HR-WPAN High-Speed WPAN

HSM Hardware Security Module

IaaS Infrastructure-as-a-Service

IAM Identity and Access Management

IdAM Identity Access Management

IdM Identity Management

IdPs Identity Providers

IDS/IPS Intrusion Detection/Prevention System

IIoT Industrial Internet-of-Things

IoT Internet-of-Things

IP Internet Protocol

IP Initial Permutation

IPFS InterPlanetary File System

IPSec Internet Protocol Security

IR Instruction Register

IrDA Infrared Data Association

ISM Infrastructure Security Management

ISM Industrial, Scientific, Medical

ISMS Information Security Management Systems

IT Information Technology

ITS Intelligent Transportation Systems

IDS Intrusion Detection System

KPA Known Plaintext Attack

KSI Keyless Signature Infrastructure

LAOR On-Demand Routing Protocol

LiDAR Light Detection and Radar

LQR Linear Quadratic Regulators

LR-WPAN Low-Speed WPAN

M2M Machine to Machine

MAC Mandatory Access Control

MANET Mobile Ad-Hoc Network

MBSE Model-Based Systems Engineering

MBWA Mobile Broadband Wireless Access

MD Message Digest

MFA Multiple-Factor Authentication

MITM Man-in-the-Middle

ML Machine Learning

MPC Model Predictive Control

MPI Message-Passing Interface

MRAM Magnetoresistive Random Access Memory

MTJ Magnetic Tunnel Junction

NICs Network Interface Cards

NLOS Non-Line-of-Sight

OFDM Orthogonal Frequency-Division Multiplexing

ONS Object Naming Service

OpenSSH Open Secure Shell

PaaS Platform-as-a-Service

PACL Port Access Control List

PAM Privileged Access Management

PAYG Pay-as-You-Go

PC Program Counter

PCI-DSS Payment Card Industry Data Security Standard

PHI Protected Health Information

PII Personal Identifier Information

PID Proportional-Integral-Derivative

PIN Personal Identification Numbers

PIPL Personal Information Protection Law

PISS Personal Information Security Specification

PIV Personal Identity Verification

PKI Public Key Infrastructure

PMP Point-to-Multipoint

PSK Pre-Shared Key

PSU Power Supply Unit

RADAR Radio Detection and Ranging

RAM Random Access Memory

RBAC Role-Based Access Control

RC Rivest Code

RC4 Rivest Cipher

RECT Relative Energy Consuming Table

RFID Radio Frequency Identification

RISC Reduced Instruction Set Computer

PLCs Programmable Logic Controllers

ROM Read-Only Memory

RSA Rivest–Shamir–Adleman

RTCT Relative Time Consuming Table

RTU Remote Terminal Units

SaaS Software-as-a-Service

SAML Security Assertion Markup Language

SCADA Supervisory Control and Data Acquisition

SCP Secure Copy Protocol

SDN Software-Defined Network

SDV Self-Driving Vehicles

SFTP Secure File Transfer Protocol

SHA Secure Hash Algorithm

SIEM Security Information and Event Management

SMOR Multi-Path On-Demand Routing

SMP Symmetrical Multiprocessing

SP Service Provider

SRAM Static Random Access Memory

SRP Security Routing Protocol

SSA Smart Swapping Algorithm

SSD Solid-State Drive

SSH Secure Shell Protocol

SSID Service Set Identifier

SSL Secure Sockets Layer

SSO Single Sign-On

STT Spin-Transfer Torque

TAC Transaction Authorization Code

TAT Training Accuracy Table

TCO Total Ownership Costs

TCP Transmission Control Protocol

TCT Time Consuming Table

TDMA Time Division Multiple Access

TDS Tag Data Standard

TECAMP Time and Energy-Constraint Accuracy Maximum Problem

TKIP Temporal Key Integrity Protocol

TLS Transport Layer Security

TMA Task Mapping Algorithm

TOTP Time-Based One-Time Password

TRA Table Relativization Algorithm

TSRP Trusted Secure Routing Protocol

TSSA Time-Based Smart Swapping Algorithm

UCC Uniform Code Council

UDP User Datagram Protocol

UMA Uniform Memory Access

USM Unified Security Management

UTMI Unified Threat Management

UVP Unified Virtualization Platform

UWB Ultra-Wideband

V2I Vehicle-to-Infrastructure

V2P Vehicle-to-Pedestrian

V2V Vehicle-to-Vehicle

V2X Vehicle-to-Everything

VAPs Virtual Access Points

VR Virtual Reality

VPN Virtual Private Network

VV Verification and Validation

WAF Web Application Firewalls

WAI WLAN Authentication Infrastructure

WAPI Wireless LAN Authentication and Privacy Infrastructure

WBAN Wireless Body Area Network

WDS Wireless Distributed System

WEP Wired Equivalent Privacy

WLAN Wireless Local Area Network

WPA WiFi Protected Access

WPA2 WiFi Protected Access 2

WPAN Wireless Personal Area Network

WPI WLAN Privacy Infrastructure

WPS Wheel Position Sensor

WSN Wireless Sensor Network

WWAN Wireless Wide Area Network

XP Extreme Programming

XSS Cross-Site Scripting

ZTAC Zero Trust Access Control

Acknowledgments

We are very grateful to all contributors for their input and support in creating this book. We highly appreciate Weilin Chan, Yue Zhang, Tianxiu Xie, Jinbo Gao, Yihang Wei and all students and faculty members from OAK Lab (Beijing Muguo Tech Ltd. - School of Cyberspace Science and Technology of Beijing Institute of Technology, BlOckchAin and Future NetworKs Joint Laboratory) for their efforts in producing this work. We also sincerely appreciate the support given by the School of Cyberspace Science and Technology at the Beijing Institute of Technology and the Institute of Information Engineering, Chinese Academy of Sciences. We would like to acknowledge those editors and scholars who provide insights and recommendations for improving and correcting this work. We also dedicate this work to all the authors' families. Without their love, support, trust, and encouragement, none of this would have happened.

I

Basic Concepts and Mechanisms of Cybersecurity in the Internet of Things

CHAPTER 1

Introduction to Cybersecurity

This chapter mainly guides readers in the realm of cybersecurity from basic concepts and discusses a few characteristics of cybersecurity. Reading this chapter will be a good start for learners to have an essential picture showing the major aspects of cybersecurity. The objective of studying this chapter is to provide learners with a fundamental knowledge presentation about key facets of cybersecurity so that learners can start their study journey from this chapter on. Notations and terms defined/presented in this chapter will be used in the succeeding chapters. Meanwhile, learners will understand the following concepts or knowledge points after reading this chapter: the concept of cybersecurity, main perspectives of cybersecurity, major impacts in cybersecurity, need of cybersecurity, Internet-based criminals, cyberspace and cyber warfare, cyber attacks, and basic defending malware. A number of safety tips will be given at the end of this chapter.

1.1 BASIC CONCEPTS IN CYBERSECURITY

1.1.1 Cybersecurity

Contemporarily, cybersecurity has become a popular term in the world of *Information Technology* (IT) along with the swift development of Internet technologies. The concept of cybersecurity is considered a broad-ranging term since it is hard to have a standard definition. The reason for the difficulty of defining cybersecurity is that it covers so many aspects of computing and has a twisted relationship with the Internet/Intranet. It implies that cybersecurity exists in the implementation of all computing

DOI: 10.1201/9781032694818-1

approaches and lives at all communication layers over the network. In fact, there may be millions of cybersecurity concepts, which are defined by distinct organizations/individuals for various purposes, intentions, or usage.

In order to have a good understanding of the concept of cybersecurity, this chapter presents three characteristics that a basic cybersecurity concept should possess. The characteristics are listed as follows:

- Shall have humans involved.

- Shall have activities take place in a networking environment, either using wired or wireless networks.

- Shall have a purpose that it protects objectives from unexpected actions. Objectives can be networks, infrastructure, humans, computers, applications (software), data, information, business operations, or any entities participating in a computing-related activity. An unexpected action can be an attack, abuse, spoofing, jamming, phishing, monitoring, unauthorized access, or any activity against the rule/regulation/law settled by the developer or the government.

The concept typically involves three keywords, according to the listed fundamental characteristics of cybersecurity. They are humans, networks, and protections. It indicates that humans must participate in the activity of cybersecurity so that the concept cannot be a pure machine-to-machine interaction. Next, a network also is a must-have element in cybersecurity, no matter whether it is wired or wireless. Thus, cybersecurity is different from security since a complete on-promises security issue generally is not counted as a cybersecurity problem. Finally, "protection" is always a theme in cybersecurity. The protection subject is the purpose of cybersecurity. A protection subject can be anything valuable for people or organizations. The core is the design of the protection approach that is needed against one or several attacks.

As the presentation above, we shall observe that cybersecurity is a cross-disciplinary term that describes a socio-technical system. There may be a few misunderstandings about the concept of cybersecurity. For example, some individuals may think that cybersecurity is another presentation of cryptography. In fact, cryptography is a type of data protection method, which can be used as an approach for data protection. However, cryptography sometimes is an encryption technique

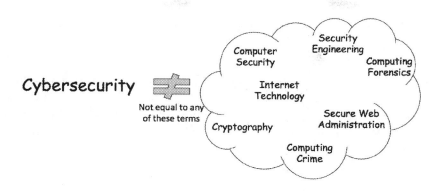

Figure 1.1 Cybersecurity is not equal to some terms.

without a network. It means that cybersecurity and cryptography are not in a dependency relation, but they do have some overlaps. This phenomenon is often applied in the relationship between cybersecurity and other highly hierarchized computing terms. Fig. 1.1 exhibits a few common computing terms that cannot be equally considered a presentation of cybersecurity.

1.1.2 Why Cybersecurity is Necessary

It is widely acknowledged that cybersecurity is a pivotal aspect of all network-related activities, ranging from educational instruction to e-commerce and telecommunications to modern financial e-services. Irrespective of the application scenario, safeguarding data and systems represent two primary tenets of cybersecurity protection. As such, a successful cybersecurity solution must establish a baseline that guarantees data security and system protection from a broad range of threats.

Furthermore, the ubiquity of networked environments means that cybersecurity issues are prevalent and pervasive. These issues may manifest as either long-standing challenges or novel concerns. Despite the pressing need for solutions, many conventional security problems in networking remain unresolved. In addition, emerging network-based techniques introduce new security vulnerabilities, some of which arise from novel paradigm designs, while others stem from inherent weaknesses in the networking infrastructure. Recent high-profile attacks serve as a stark reminder that cyber threats can rapidly upend people's lives despite the manifold benefits afforded by web technologies. For instance, hackers can compromise vehicles, smart home security systems, and even entire aircraft, emphasizing the critical importance of cybersecurity.

The question naturally arises: "Where should we begin in comprehending cybersecurity?" This is a salient query, as a clear roadmap is crucial for initiating one's understanding of the subject. To this end, the following section will elucidate several pivotal cybersecurity perspectives, with the aim of acquainting audiences with the fundamental structure of the cybersecurity discipline.

1.1.3 Cybersecurity Perspective

As we discussed, cybersecurity could be treated as a big concept that covered a broad range. There should be an easier way for us to start learning this subject rather than looking into overlaps and a wide range. One approach for us to comprehend cybersecurity is to know distinct perspectives in this field. In general, the cybersecurity discipline has at least five perspectives, which are threat management (TM), cybersecurity insurance, infrastructure secure management, cyber operations/manipulations, and cyber integrations. It is possible to have some other perspectives because of different priority concerns. We select these five *Cybersecurity Perspectives* due to their representativeness and present a concise description for each perspective.

Threat Management

TM is a category of the approach to network security that deals with various types of malware or adversarial actions. The implementation of the TM embraces both hardware and software, such as computers, networks, servers, firewalls, or anti-virus software. With the increase of online applications, threats are becoming varied due to various systems and numerous involvers in an online operation. A TM offering a comprehensive security service is an expected solution in the industry.

A Unified Threat Management (UTM) describes a single system that provides an integrative platform for encompassing multiple security products and achieving multi-functions in security. In most situations, the concept of UTM is exchangeable with *Unified Security Management*. The UTM system mainly involves a comprehensive list of security products, including traditional firewalls and specific-purpose security tools. A few examples of specific-purpose security tools are Intrusion Detection System (IDS) [1], Virtual Private Network (VPN), and Content Filter.

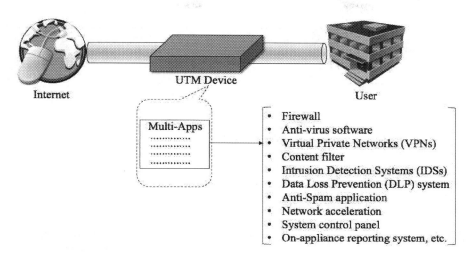

UTM Device

User

Multi-Apps
....
....
....

- Firewall
- Anti-virus software
- Virtual Private Networks (VPNs)
- Content filter
- Intrusion Detection Systems (IDSs)
- Data Loss Prevention (DLP) system
- Anti-Spam application
- Network acceleration
- System control panel
- On-appliance reporting system, etc.

Figure 1.2 Fundamental architecture of the Unified Security Management.

Fig. 1.2 exhibits the fundamental architecture of the UTM. The UTM device offers multiple security products in an integration style over a channel supported by the Internet. The major benefit of using a UTM solution is that users obtain a simplified control interface for all security tools or components. Due to its one-stop service style, UTM systems are widely accepted by small/medium businesses.

Cyber Insurance

Cyber Insurance, also called Cybersecurity Insurance, is a type of insurance product that is designed for protecting/preventing businesses or individuals and their possessed IT-related infrastructure or activities from Internet-related threats [2]. This business is becoming hot due to the great needs. According to the report from US Department of Homeland Security, cyber insurance "is designed to mitigate losses from a variety of cyber incidents, including data breaches, business interruption, and network damage" [3].

The primary objective of implementing cyber insurance is to reduce the rate of successful cyber attacks [4]. Enterprises also expect to reduce the financial budget by lowering the risk of cyber risks. The inspiration of spreading cyber insurance will benefit both enterprises (policy-holders) and insurance companies. A promoted level of the secure mechanism facilitated by the enterprises can lead to more insurance coverage. This win-win paradigm encourages enterprises to adopt better self-protection secure mechanisms. Data loss or breach sometimes cannot be counted financially after all, even though an insurance coverage can cover the partial loss.

Moreover, cyber insurance product is in great demand in the market because of the continuously growing online products and emerging vulnerabilities in both old and new systems, even though cyber insurance is still at its early stage yet. Despite a few observable benefits, there are many challenges in practice. Before we discuss its challenges, we need to know the basic workflow of cyber insurance from a technical perspective. Fig. 1.3 presents a typical business process for cyber insurance, which shows several important operations during the process of service formulation. Two crucial tasks need to be highlighted in this process. First, cyber insurers must fully perceive potential cyber incidents, such as understanding attack methods, network vulnerabilities, and potential defense solutions. The other important task is to categorize cyber incidents in an insurance-friendly way based on the understanding [5]. For example, an insurance company shall know a lot of information about a cyber incident, such as its reason, scenario, harmful level, estimated defense cost, successful defense rate, coverage cost, and attack probability.

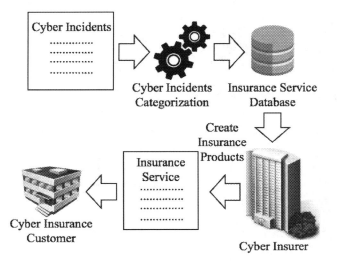

Figure 1.3 A typical business process for cyber insurance.

The insurance company needs a database to store all the information derived from investigations, probes, and syntheses.

There are some open research questions in security within this series of procedures [6, 7].

The first question addresses the establishment of the data repository for sharing cyber incident data. A Data Repository is a safe data storage space in which anonymous cyber incident data are shared [8] and processed for the purpose of supporting risk analyzes. The purpose of data sharing in cyber insurance is to assist cyber insurers to have a better understanding on cyber incidents via real-world investigations. An analysis of actual data generally cannot be replaced by a theoretical analysis, considering the serious consequence, even though a theory-oriented report is an important component in building up the database. The challenge part is to find out a method that can effectively protect users' privacy in the data repository. Currently, data security is ensured by regulations and laws; however, it is far from making a secure data repository from a technical perspective. Attacking on data repository is always a great concern.

The next urgent question is to resolve information asymmetry. The problem of Information Asymmetry describes a failure in linking stakeholders, such as insurers, insureds, and brokers, in cyber insurance business operations. It also can be considered a matching selection problem between insurers and insurance customers. The core issue is the obstacle to differentiating cyber incidents in insurance operations. Most contemporary cyber insurers offer fixed insurance service offerings, but cyber incidents are varied in distinct environments. Insurance customers may have different priority concerns based on the risks they are mainly facing. Many studies have addressed this issue recently. As a knowledge representation method, a semantic approach can effectively describe complex relationships between ontologies [5]. Each cyber incident or element in insurance operations can be formulated into an ontology [9–11]. Using a knowledge graph [12, 13] can create a comprehensive knowledge mapping for all objectives in cyber insurance, such as cyber incidents, cyber coverage, IT environment, etc.

The last question we intend to discuss is about cyber insurance services in operations. Insurers claim a bunch of coverage items; however, the boundary of the service scope is hard to define. A typical cyber insurance covers the data breach notification, personal data restoration, data recovery, or damage repair. Before the insured receives compensation, it needs an investigation on relevant aspects, such as responsibilities, context, and incident processes. This problem is far more complicated than categorizing cyber incidents since a knowledge graph may fail in pointing out the scope. A relation map can tell the relationship between entities but is insufficient to define how much relationship is there.

The next section will talk about security management in the perspective of the infrastructure.

Infrastructure Security Management

In cybersecurity, an effective management on infrastructure is another significant aspect that requires support from different departments/organizations. An Infrastructure Security Management (ISM) refers to a wide scope of essential operations for managing/governing IT infrastructure and ensuring its effectiveness and implementation in an organization. As mentioned in the concept, it covers a wide extent throughout the domain of IT, from security policies, business process modeling, human resource management to equipment maintenance, technical supports, and information lifecycle analyzes.

The core of ISM is data protection, the same as other perspectives in cybersecurity. In the mobile context, the activities of ISM need to consider data security in both storage and transmission. On one side, data storage includes on-premises and remote databases. With the growing deployment of cloud systems, distributed data storage is becoming a popular way for mobile computing. Data centers make the computation more centralized. This virtualization-based technology is bringing a technical revolution to the IT industry. But, there are many challenges raised by using remote cloud servers due to the uncertainty of the third-party service providers and masked technical operations in the cloud. More details about mobile cloud computing will be discussed in Chapter 2 and latter chapters.

The other side of infrastructure security addresses networks. Data have a chance of being attacked during data transfers. An IP-based security problem is a typical problem in a networked environment. Each networking node can be a potential adversarial target, of which monitoring, spoofing, or jamming attacks. Thus, maintaining networking infrastructure is a major duty for an ISM operator who needs to ensure infrastructure is physically secure. Fig. 1.4 illustrates a sample of ISM service list for a simplified data lifecycle. Any physical components in a networking communication can be a service target for an ISM technician. Google also lays out its infrastructure security design for its cloud

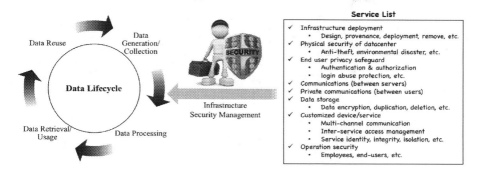

Figure 1.4 A service list sample of ISM for a simplified data lifecycle.

product, "Google Cloud Platform" [14]. Its design consists of 6 layers, which are operational security, Internet communication, storage services, user identity, service deployment, and hardware infrastructure. This deployment design considers the operation security the higher-level and the hardware security the lower-level. More information about security in mobile cloud computing will be discussed in latter chapters, such as Chapters 4 and 9. The next section will talk about cyber operations.

Cyber Operation

A Cyber Operation describes cyber capabilities for one or a series of applications to achieve certain mission objective(s) in cyberspace. A cyberspace is a conceptual term that describes a networking environment where communications and networked activities take place. The cyber operation is an inter-discipline consisting of computing operations and activities in cyberspace, which can be observed from its literature. A cyber operation can be either a technical or non-technical move. We mainly consider technical operations in this book.

In a general situation, network operations form the main body of technical cyber operations. Today's network systems are dramatically growing and turn into large cyberspaces. The Network Operation Center is a type of core node in cyberspace that offers management and governance functions. Most cyber operations are implemented by the network operation center. The deployment of the network operation center can locate one or multiple physical locations.

Next, the management scope of the network operation center mainly includes monitoring networks, controlling data transfers, and other

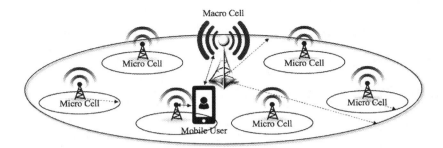

Figure 1.5 Mechanism of the heterogeneous network.

networking management activities. It attracts many research attentions when novel mechanisms of networks are introduced, such as Heterogeneous Network and Software-Defined Network (SDN). We briefly introduce the operating mechanisms of these two novel networks in the following paragraphs in order to understand how the network operation center works and where vulnerabilities can be located.

First, the heterogeneous [15, 16] network is a type of network setting that uses different operating systems and/or different protocols to build up web connections between devices. Fig. 1.5 presents a basic operating mechanism of the heterogeneous network. The mobile user has two choices of the network, a macro cell and a micro cell. Currently, many scholars are working on this novel network setting to make it safer and more efficient. For instance, securing data in various communication channels and optimizing the utilization of transmission resources are two essential research questions. Thus, establishing and deploying a heterogeneous network needs a large number of cyber operations due to selective communications among various network cells.

Meanwhile, the SDN is a technical approach for networks that supports network administrators in programmable networking configuration, controls, and governance on an open interface. Fig. 1.6 provides the high-level architecture of an SDN deployment. Basically, an SDN consists of three layers, namely, application [17], control, and infrastructure layers. Applications connect to the SDN controller via an Application Programming Interface (API). In many practical cases, an SDN controller is responsible for Control Plane (CP) operations. A Management Plane can configure the CP. Meanwhile, the SDN controller communicates the infrastructure layer with a data plane interface. Physical

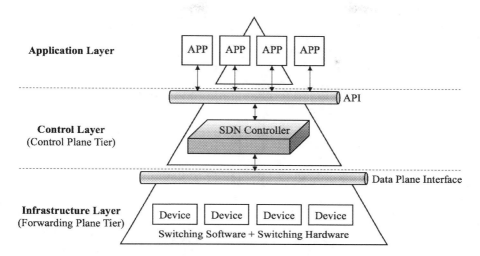

Figure 1.6 High-level architecture of the Software-Defined Network.

devices are interconnected via Forwarding Plane (FP) operations. The layer-based setting requires a great volume of communications between layers.

It is perceptible that vulnerabilities can exist in numerous communications. Comparing with traditional networks, both heterogeneous networks and SDNs have more complicated networking architecture designs. The increased communications between networking nodes can provide adversaries more opportunities of launching attacks. The network operation center can be fooled by any attacked networking node in the system, even though its deployment offers monitoring functions. Spoofing and jamming attacks are common adversarial actions that can result in communication trouble. Currently, securing cyber operations in advanced networks is still an ongoing research topic. We also will discuss the solution in the future chapters. The next section will address cyber integration issue in cybersecurity.

Cyber Integration

As a new discipline in computing, Cyber Integration is a technical term describing the operations implemented by the cyber integration center, which allows data transfers and synchronization among multiple processes or components of a solution in both development and operation periods. Two crucial aspects in cyber integration are data transfers and

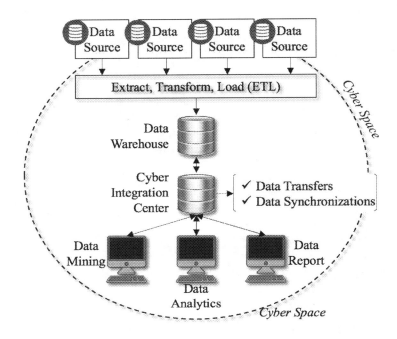

Figure 1.7 High-level architecture of the Cyber Integration.

data synchronizations. Similar to cyber operations, the cyber integration also covers both technical and non-technical activities. The literature "integration" can refer business operations in some situations. This book mainly talk about its meaning in the technical domain.

The context of implementing cyber integration is a cyberspace as well. Conceptually speaking, the cyber integration can be considered a cyberspace integration. The involvement of the cyber integration includes application and infrastructure, of which the interoperability is emphasized. Thus, the cyber integration plays an interconnection role who connects cyberspace operations with integrated management for multiple systems. The core component is the cyber integration center that connects data warehouse with various functional systems.

Fig. 1.7 presents the high-level architecture of the cyber integration. As shown in the figure, there are multiple data sources. An Extract, Transform, and Load (ETL) layer is needed to make these various data sources work together. The integrated data are stored in the data warehouse. This is a typical paradigm of the data integration. The Data Warehouse (DWH) is a centralized data repository that stores data from various sources and is used for data-oriented functions. Moreover, on one side, the cyber integration center communicates with the DWH for data retrievals and updates; on the other side, the center connects to distinct components/functions systems to ensure them efficient transfers and synchronizations.

The major benefit of deploying a cyber integration center is increasing the efficiency and reliability of data transfers as well as synchronizations. However, vulnerabilities also exist in this setting as the weaknesses in other web-based techniques. For instance, frequent data transfers in the network context generally increase the chance of adversaries, since attackers will have more opportunities to monitor communications. Another example is that the implementation of cloud computing moves the data warehouse to the remote uncontrolled cyberspace. Any hacked infrastructure in the cloud may release the configuration of the cloud resource, such as infrastructure mapping. The data security during the transmission process is crucial in cyber integration. More discussions will be presented in the latter chapters.

1.2 IMPACTS OF CYBERSECURITY

1.2.1 Major Impacts

This section talks about the major impacts brought by cybersecurity. As cybersecurity problems can exist everywhere in a cyberspace, its impacts have penetrated numerous fields. From a perspective of humans, the impacts of cybersecurity are threefold:

1. Impacts on personnels: All users of the networked computers can be potential victims of cyber crimes. A single attack on a personal computer sometimes can result in not only personal loss but also the entire/partial system down. Various impacts in this dimension may include financial losses, reputational damage, or legal issues. For example, the identity theft may take place when a user's personal information (e.g., name, date of birth, phone number, zip codes) is obtained by an attacker who uses the identity information to apply for credit cards or make e-commerce frauds.

2. Impacts on business: Many modern enterprises highly rely on benefits obtained from adopting network-based solutions, e.g., retrieving massive updated information from the Internet for data mining/ analytics as well as building up interconnections between the

enterprise and customers throughout the network. It also implies that current business is vulnerable to one or multiple types of cyber attacks. Similar to impacts on personnels, the impacts may cover financial, reputational, and legal issues; however, the extent of the impact can be much larger. The scope of the business and the number of involved individuals can amplify the level of the damage. For example, considering financial losses, cybersecurity issues may cause sensitive information leakage (commerce contract, corporate information, trading disruption, etc.). A reputation damage on a corporation is even worse than a direct damage on financial losses in may cases. Either losing loyal customers or loss in sale is a common consequence caused by cyber attacks.

3. Impacts on officials: There are at least two dimensions concerning impacts on officials. On one hand, officials will attempt to continuously modify the business process in order to avoid emerging risks. Redefining business rules is one of common methods for risk mitigation.

Solving cybersecurity issues is a necessary task for most contemporary IT systems due to the demands of securing data from threats and safeguarding systems. It is observable that cybersecurity issues can be found everywhere throughout the cyberspace world, including both old and emerging issues. In individuals' daily lives, many examples are showing the necessity of concerning cybersecurity. For instance, a hacked car running on the road is seriously threatening people's life safety; a hacked smart home alarm system can cause a serious privacy leakage.

1.2.2 Cyber Crime

Cybercrime is any criminal activity on the internet or other digital technologies. It includes many illegal activities, including hacking, identity theft, cyberstalking, online fraud, and phishing scams. In the Internet of Things (IoT) environment, cybercrime poses unique challenges due to the complexity and interconnections of these systems.

IoT devices are vulnerable to cyber attacks, which can have serious consequences. For example, hackers can gain control of IoT devices and use them to attack other systems or steal sensitive data from them. Cyber attacks can also cause physical damage or disrupt critical infrastructure systems such as power grids or transportation networks.

The growing number of devices connected to the internet and the increasing complexity of IoT systems have made them an attractive target for cybercriminals. To address these challenges, developing robust, erode-resistant and secure IoT systems that can withstand cyber attacks is essential. This requires a coordinated effort from technology developers, policymakers, and cybersecurity professionals to ensure that these systems are designed with security in mind and regularly updated and maintained to address emerging threats. Additionally, it is essential to educate users on cybercrime risks and encourage them to take steps to protect their devices and data.

1.3 INTRODUCTION TO CYBER ATTACKS

1.3.1 Cyberspace and Cyberwarfare

Cyberspace

In the computer field, the network uses physical links to connect separate workstations or hosts together to form data links, so as to achieve resource sharing and communication. Cyberspace is the environment where communications over computing networks [18]. Three main characteristics of cyberspace are as follows:

- Cyberspace exists objectively. It does not refer to the objective existence of computer terminals, cables and programs that constitute the external conditions of the network, but refers to the objective existence of independent information dissemination and derived space supported by these external conditions.

- Cyberspace is global and ubiquitous. Since the birth of the network, the connection has crossed national and regional borders.

- Cyberspace is managed in a decentralized manner. Since each machine on the network can act as a server for other machines, there is no absolute center or centralized power in the cyberspace.

Cyberwarfare

Cyberwarfare is becoming an increasingly important combat style of technological warfare. In a narrow sense, cyberwarfare refers to a series of network offensive and defensive actions taken to disrupt the enemy's network information system and to ensure the normal operation of one's own network information system. In a broad sense, cyberwarfare refers to a new form of warfare that integrates physical space and cyberspace. It is not just a hacker attack in cyberspace or a war that uses the network as an offensive weapon. Contemporary cyberwarfare is an offensive and defensive contest that uses the Internet and even the *Internet of Things* (IoT) as the war space, with countries, interest groups, and even individuals as participating parties.

Cyberwarfare takes computers and computer networks as main objectives, and uses network communication technology as the basic means [19]. Cyberwarfare generally includes cyber reconnaissance, cyber attack, and cyber defense. Cyber reconnaissance refers to obtaining information from the enemy's network that is conducive to network attacks. A cyber attack is a malicious action that weakens and destroys the enemy's computer network system. The main goal of network defense is to protect our own network system against network attacks.

An important feature of network warfare is that it has a wide range of combat forces, which can cover all personnel proficient in network technology. In addition, the rapid update of cyberwarfare technology requires the continuous learning and accumulation of network warfare participants. Moreover, the openness of the Internet obscures combat objectives, and the combat space is easy to extend to the whole world. Last but not the least, the combat mode of cyberwarfare is naturally asymmetric, and the combat process is abrupt. Now that the 5G era has arrived, the threats of network security and network warfare are closely related to the lives of every netizen. The ability of cyberspace warfare has become more and more significant, so that a strong cyber defense force is needed to protect against cyber attacks.

1.3.2 Cyber Attacks and Hackers

Cyber Attack

Cyber attacks refer to malicious offensive actions carried out on computer information systems, infrastructure, computer networks or personal computer equipment using digital technologies. For example, acts such as destroying software or services, stealing or accessing computer data without authorization, etc. are all regarded as cyber attacks. Attackers generally take advantage of the vulnerabilities and security defects of network information systems to attack systems and resources, which usually cause data leakage, property loss, and other severe consequences. The threats faced by network information systems come from many aspects and change over time.

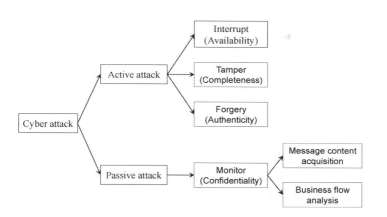

Figure 1.8 Classification of cyber attacks according to the information destruction effect.

Cyber attacks can be divided into external attacks and internal attacks according to the location of the attack [20]. The external attack means that an adversary destroys the system from outside of the subnet. The internal attack refers to the attack launched by the enemy from the inside of the subnet by capturing nodes or injecting malicious nodes into it. Internal attacks mainly include notorious Sybil Attack, Replication Attack, Tunnel Attack, etc. These attacks consume node resources, thereby reducing the span of network, while the more serious can steal secret data, and even publish false malicious information, which interferes with the normal operation of the network.

As we can see from Fig. 1.8, cyber attacks can also be divided into active attacks and passive attacks in terms of their destructive effects on information [21]. Active attacks are characterized by tampering with data streams or generating fake data streams. Active attacks are generally divided into data tampering, message forgery, and terminal denial of service, which are introduced as follows.

1. Message tampering means that certain parts of the legal message are changed, deleted or delayed to produce an unauthorized message.

2. Message forgery means that an entity pretends to be another entity and sends out data containing the identity information of other entities, so as to obtain the rights and privileges of legitimate users by deception.

3. Denial of service usually destroys the entire network, causing communication equipment to be unconditionally terminated.

The main technical method to combat active attack is detection and timely recovery from the damage caused by the attack. Specific measures include automatic auditing, intrusion detection and integrity recovery, and so on. Detection also has a certain deterrent effect, so it can also play a role in preventing attacks to a certain extent.

In passive attacks, the attacker does not make any modification to the data information, but adopts attack methods such as eavesdropping, traffic analysis, and cracking of weakly encrypted data streams.

1. Eavesdropping means that an attacker obtains information or relevant data without the consent and approval of the user. Data transmission on the local area network is based on broadcast, which makes it possible for a host to receive all the information transmitted on this subnet. When the message is not encrypted, the entire content of the communication can be fully grasped through protocol analysis.

2. The traffic analysis attack method is suitable for certain special occasions. For example, sensitive information is confidential, and the attacker cannot know the real content from the intercepted message. However, attackers can observe the patterns of these datagrams, analyze and determine the location of the communicating parties, the number of communications, and the length of the message, thereby obtaining relevant sensitive information.

Since passive attacks do not modify the attacked information, it is very difficult to detect, so the focus of combating such attacks is prevention. Specific measures include using virtual private network VPN, encrypting transmission information, and adopting switched network equipment.

Hacker

Hackers refer to people who break into the other party's system without permission to obtain control authority for a specific purpose [22]. Main types of hackers are listed below.

- Script kiddies are hackers who maliciously damage the system by downloading and using programs developed by other hackers. Script kiddies may not know how to hack a system, but they know how to use programs and tools written by hackers and exploit some known program vulnerabilities.

- White hats are ethical hackers who study information security technology and network defense, identify security vulnerabilities in computer systems or network systems, and help to repair vulnerabilities and eliminate viruses. White hats are the main force to maintain cyberspace security.

- Black hats often use technology to maliciously break into websites to steal resources or crack charged software to achieve profit. Black hats specifically look for system or network vulnerabilities to launch attacks.

- Grey hats refer to those hackers who understand defensive techniques and have the ability to break through these defenses, although they generally do not do that. Grey hats hope to discover network or system vulnerabilities and achieve the purpose of warning through their hacking actions.

1.3.3 Common Cyber Attacks

Malware Definition and Classification

The word "malware" is a combination of "malicious" and "software". Malicious software refers to software that is forcibly installed and operated on a terminal without a consent, which infringes the legitimate rights and interests of the user [23]. Malicious software includes any software that harms the interests of users. Malware not only affects the infected computer or device, but may also affect other devices that communicate with the infected device. For instance, ransomware extorts money from users through harassment, intimidation, and even kidnapping of user files. Generally speaking, ransomware executors will also set a payment time limit, and the ransom amount will also increase over time. In addition, a keylogger is a type of malware that can record keyboard operations. When typing with the keyboard, the keylogger can record the input strings and upload them to the remote server. By analyzing these strings, the server can guess private information such as the user's username and password.

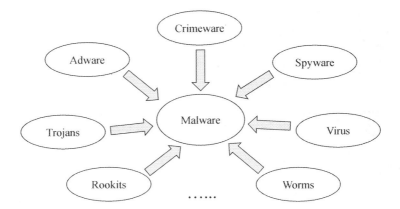

Figure 1.9 List of common types of malware.

Fig. 1.9 enumerates several common malicious software and we introduce their attack execution methods as well as hazards.

1. A worm is an independent malicious program that can run, replicate and spread through a computer network without the aid of a host program. Once the worm invades the system, it will immediately create multiple copies on its own and spread through the network connection, infecting any computers and servers on the network that are not fully protected. Each subsequent copy of the worm can also replicate itself, so the infection can spread very quickly through computer networks.

2. Computer virus is a man-made malicious program that destroys computer information or system. Its characteristics are destructive, infectious and latent. Unlike worms, viruses do not exist independently, but hidden in other executable programs. After the virus invades the system, it will remain dormant until the infected host file or program is activated, which in turn activates the virus so that it can run and replicate on the system. Viruses can affect the speed of the computer, damage files or systems, which causes great losses to users.

3. Spyware is a kind of malware that can install a backdoor on the user's computer and collect information without awareness. Private data and important information can be captured by backdoor programs and sent to hackers, commercial companies, etc. These backdoor programs can even remotely manipulate the user's computer to form a huge "botnet" to launch a Distributed Denial of Service attack.

4. Crimeware is a kind of malware that can invade the computer browser program, and unknowingly redirect the surfer to a disguised website to defraud personal information. The classic example of crimeware is the aforementioned keylogger. Virus makers, hackers and spammers have all increased their power to steal information to make huge profits, so that the development of crimeware is very rapid.

5. Adware refers to malware that is installed on a user's computer without permission to seek commercial benefits through pop-up advertisements and other forms. Such software is not only mandatory to install and cannot be easily uninstalled, but also frequently pops up advertisements, consuming system resources. In addition, adware usually collects user information in the background for profit.

6. Rookit is a special malware that resides in the target computer for a long time without knowing it, manipulates the system, and collects data through secret channels. The three elements of rootkit are hiding, manipulating, and collecting data. The purpose of a rootkit is to hide itself and not be discovered. In addition, rootkit can hide almost any software, including file servers, keyloggers, botnets, and remailers. Therefore, rookit is generally used in conjunction with other malicious programs.

7. Trojan Horse refers to an unauthorized remote control program that resides in a computer. It can open system permissions, leak user information, and even steal the entire computer management and use permissions without being discovered by the computer administrator. It is known as one of the most commonly used tools by hackers. Trojans disguise themselves as other useful software in order to persuade unsuspecting users to install them. A common strategy is to trick users into opening files or web links that contain malware.

With the development of network technology, the classification of malware is becoming more and more detailed. Some new kinds of rogue software are constantly emerging [24], and the classification standards will inevitably be adjusted accordingly.

Basic Methods Defending Malware

First, we introduce the infection and spreading methods of malicious software, which will facilitate the adoption of appropriate preventive measures.

Malicious code writers generally use three types of methods to spread malware: exploiting software vulnerabilities, deceiving users, or a mixture of the two. Some malicious codes are self-starting worms and embedded scripts, which have no requirements for user activities. Some malicious codes such as Trojan horses and email worms need to analyze the victim's psychology and manipulate them to execute unsafe codes. Others are tricking users into turning off protection measures to install malicious code.

As mentioned above, vulnerabilities are defects in the specific implementation of hardware, software, protocols or system security policies, which can enable an attacker to access or damage the system without authorization. According to the situation that vulnerabilities are mastered, vulnerabilities can be divided into the following three types.

1. Known vulnerabilities refer to public vulnerabilities that have been discovered and widely spread. The causes and utilization methods of vulnerabilities have been mastered by many security organizations, hackers and hacker organizations. Security organizations or manufacturers can add protection methods for corresponding types of vulnerabilities in their security protection products or security service items according to the published causes and utilization methods of vulnerabilities.

2. Unknown vulnerabilities refer to vulnerabilities that already exist but have not been discovered yet. The characteristic of this type of vulnerabilities is that although they have not been found, they already exist objectively. When they are found out by hackers intentionally or unintentionally, they will pose a huge threat to computer network security.

3. The 0 day vulnerabilities refer to vulnerabilities that have been discovered but have not been widely spread. In other words, this

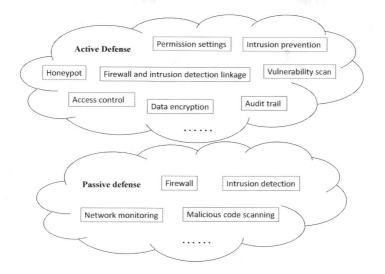

Figure 1.10 Common techniques for active and passive defense.

type of vulnerability may be in the hands of a very few people. Hackers may use this time gap to attack targets before the information of this type of vulnerability has been widely spread. Since the majority of users have not obtained the relevant vulnerability information, it is difficult to carry out effective defense.

All computer systems have vulnerabilities, and this is exactly what malware developers have been trying to find and exploit. Therefore, defending malware is an unstoppable theme.

Network security technology can be divided into active defense technology and passive defense technology, as illustrated in Fig. 1.10.

Active defense [25] is a security measure that can promptly and accurately warn before the intrusion has a bad impact on the computer system, so as to build a flexible defense system in real time to avoid, transfer and reduce the risks. Active defense is also a disguised offensive security measure, which focuses on making attackers lose their intrusion ability or destroying their intrusion actions. Active defense is mainly to monitor the entire computer system in real time, so as to quickly capture changes in network traffic and analyze program behaviors, achieving the purpose of protecting the security of the computer system. At the same time, the active defense system will also collect suspicious ways of connecting to the computer (potential intrusion behavior) and useful information about other intruders. Through the collected information, users can adopt certain "attack" means to resist intruders, making it difficult to invade. Several common active defense technologies include: data encryption, access control, permission settings, vulnerability scanning technology, honeypot technology, audit trail technology, intrusion prevention technology, firewall and intrusion detection linkage technology, etc.

Passive defense [26] is a security measure taken after a computer is attacked. For example, the security audit tool (firewall or anti-virus software) detects the presence of Trojan horses or virus files in the computer system, and then kills or deletes them permanently. Repairing system vulnerabilities or bugs is also a passive defense. Passive defense technologies mainly include the following types: firewall technology, intrusion detection technology, malicious code scanning technology and network monitoring technology, etc.

Password Cracking and Securing Password

Password cracking refers to recovering plaintext without knowing the encryption key. Frequently employed cryptanalysis techniques include attacks such as analyzing only the ciphertext, exploiting known plaintext, selecting specific plaintext, manipulating ciphertext, and manipulating text. Then, we introduce the above password cracking methods [27, 28] with an example.

As shown in Fig. 1.11, Alice and Bob conduct encrypted communication, where P_i represents plaintext, C_i represents the ciphertext, E_k represents the encryption function, and D_K represents the decryption function. The messages generated in the communication process are three groups of plaintext-ciphertext pairs, namely (P_1, C_1), (P_2, C_2), and (P_3, C_3).

1. *Ciphertext only attack.* The ciphertext-only attack is a password-cracking method that only analyzes the intercepted ciphertext to obtain the plaintext or the key. It is assumed that the cryptanalyst already knows the encryption algorithm and the statistical properties of the plaintext in advance. After analyzing the intercepted one or more ciphertexts encrypted with the same key, the plaintext or key may be obtained. Passwords that cannot withstand ciphertext-only attacks are considered insecure. In the above example, a ciphertext-only attack means that the adversary only

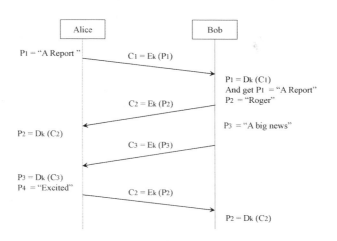

Figure 1.11 The encrypted communication process between Alice and Bob.

knows the ciphertext (that is, one or more of C_1, C_2, and C_3), and then uses statistical characteristics to infer the plaintext and secret key.

2. *Known plaintext attack.* Known plaintext attack refers to the password cracking method in which an attacker has mastered a certain piece of plaintext P and the corresponding ciphertext C to infer the secret key. Known plaintext attack in the above example is that the adversary obtains some given plaintext and the corresponding ciphertext, where it can be any non-empty subset of (P_1, C_1), (P_2, C_2), (P_3, C_3).

3. *Chosen plaintext attack.* The adversary in chosen plaintext attack has access to the encryption function E_k and can construct the ciphertext corresponding to any plaintext. The adversary selects the specific plaintext and its corresponding ciphertext to solve the key beneficial to the attack or the corresponding plaintext from the intercepted ciphertext. In addition to the above-mentioned basis, the attacker can create a plaintext, such as "Excited", and obtain the encrypted ciphertext.

4. *Chosen ciphertext attack.* Chosen ciphertext attack is a password-cracking method that solves the key or the corresponding plaintext by selecting the specific ciphertext and its corresponding plaintext that are beneficial to the attack. The adversary has access to the decryption function D_k, and can select the ciphertext for decryption. Choosing the ciphertext attack method is stronger than known plaintext attacks. The adversary has the ability to choose or control the ciphertext and can choose any ciphertext and its corresponding plaintext that is beneficial to the attack. In the above example, the attacker can arbitrarily create or select some ciphertext to obtain its decrypted plaintext. Specifically, the adversary can forge the message to replace the real message in the communication process and then steal the result obtained and decrypted by the receiver. It is possible to find that the decrypted result of the forged ciphertext is meaningful.

5. *Chosen text attack.* Chosen text attack can create any plaintext/ciphertext and get the corresponding ciphertext/ plaintext, a combination of the above two.

The order of strength of the above password cracking methods is as follows: ciphertext only attack- known plaintext attack- chosen plaintext attack-chosen ciphertext attack- chosen text attack. While the difficulty of attack implementation is the opposite.

When setting the password, users can take corresponding measures to prevent the password from cracking, such as using a strong password, avoiding using the same password at different sites (preventing credential stuffing attacks), etc.

Cyber Accidents

Cyber accidents refer to accidental events that cause harm to the network and information systems or the data in them due to human causes, software and hardware defects or faults, natural disasters, etc. Cyber accidents usually include harmful program events, cyber attack events, information destruction events, equipment and facility failure events, catastrophic events, and other events. To further reduce the impact caused by cyber accidents and ensure the network system's safe, stable and efficient operation, we introduce various protection methods.

First, perform safe backup and data recovery on time to achieve physical security. The security and integrity of data are of the utmost importance in network security, so a comprehensive backup strategy should be developed. Second, install the latest anti-virus software on the network for real-time monitoring and regular scans to prevent the latest malware attacks, such as network viruses and worms. Next, use firewall technology to separate the internal and public access networks. An access control standard implemented in the two network communications can prevent most network hackers. In addition, the formulation of cyberspace security strategy not only considers how to prevent external attacks but also how to prevent internal attacks, that is, personnel management issues. To a certain extent, the latter is far more complex and difficult than the former. Personnel management, such as identification of sensitive positions, security training, and security inspections, are all important links in cyber security.

Different areas receive different levels of cyber attacks, so the formulation of network security strategies is also different, restricted by convenience, efficiency, funding, and legal systems. Therefore, different security strategies should be considered according to the actual situation.

1.4 SUMMARY

This chapter starts with certain basic concepts and provides a systematic introduction to basic knowledge about cybersecurity.

First, cybersecurity is introduced in Section 1.1 to guide readers in understanding the field. Among them, we focus on five perspectives of network security, including thread management, cyber insurance, infrastructure management, cyber operations and cyber integration. Second, in Section 1.2, we summarize the impact of cybersecurity on personnel, business and official, thus leading to the requirements for cybersecurity. Then, we state the concept of cyberspace and the cyberwarfare of the current era in Section 1.3.1 . Moreover, in Section 1.3.2, we are illiterate about a cyber attack and divide the types of hackers. In Section 1.3.3, we further focus on the classification and defense methods of common network malware and password cracking and protection. After reading the content of this chapter, we have provided some exercises in Section 1.5 to facilitate readers to consolidate and self-check.

1.5 EXERCISES

After completing this chapter, please answer the following questions. Suggested answers are also listed below.

1. What the meaning of cyber attack? List several cyber attacks you are familiar with.

   Cyber attacks refer to malicious offensive actions carried out on computer information systems, infrastructure, computer networks or personal computer equipment using digital technologies. Cyber attacks can be divided into active attacks and passive attacks in terms of their destructive effects on information. Active attacks generally include data tampering, message forgery, and terminal denial of service, which are introduced as follows. Passive attacks usually include eavesdropping, traffic analysis, and cracking of weakly encrypted data streams.

2. What is a hacker? What types of hackers can be classified according to their behaviors?

   Hackers are individuals who break into the other party's system without permission to obtain control authority for a specific purpose. They possess advanced technical skills and knowledge to exploit computer systems, networks, or software vulnerabilities. Their motivations can vary, including curiosity, activism, or criminal intent. According to the behaviors, hackers can be classified into script kiddies, black hats, white hats and gray hats, etc.

3. Can you list several kinds of malware that you are familiar with? In what ways did they conduct malicious activities?

   - Spyware is a kind of malware that can install a backdoor on the user's computer and collect information without awareness. Private data and important information can be captured by backdoor programs and sent to hackers, commercial companies, etc. These backdoor programs can remotely manipulate the user's computer to form a huge "botnet" to launch a Distributed Denial of Service attack.

   - Crimeware is a kind of malware that can invade the computer browser program and unknowingly redirect the surfer to a disguised website to defraud personal information. The classic example of crimeware is the aforementioned keylogger. Virus makers, hackers and spammers have all increased their power to steal information to make huge profits so the development of crimeware is very rapid.

- Adware refers to malware installed on a user's computer without permission to seek commercial benefits through pop-up advertisements and other forms. Such software is not only mandatory to install and cannot be easily uninstalled but also frequently pops up advertisements, consuming system resources. In addition, adware usually collects user information in the background for profit.

- Trojan Horse is an unauthorized remote control program in a computer. It can open system permissions, leak user information, and even steal the entire computer management and use permissions without being discovered by the computer administrator. It is known as one of the most commonly used tools by hackers. Trojans disguise themselves as other useful software to persuade unsuspecting users to install them.

4. What is the difference between a virus and a worm?

- A worm is an independent malicious program that can run, replicate and spread through a computer network without the aid of a host program. Once the worm invades the system, it will immediately create multiple copies on its own and spread through the network connection, infecting any computers and servers on the network that are not fully protected.

- Unlike worms, viruses do not exist independently but are hidden in other executable programs. After the virus invades the system, it will remain dormant until the infected host file or program is activated, which activates the virus to run and replicate on the system. Viruses can affect the computer's speed, and damage files or systems, which causes great losses to users.

5. Please briefly describe the concept and difference between active defense and passive defense.

- Active defense is a security measure that can promptly and accurately warn before the intrusion has a bad impact on the computer system, so as to build a flexible defense system in real time to avoid, transfer and reduce the risks. Active defense is mainly to monitor the entire computer system in real time, so as to quickly capture changes in network traffic and analyze program behaviors, achieving the purpose of protecting the security of the computer system.

- Passive defense is a security measure taken after a computer is attacked. For example, the security audit tool (firewall or anti-virus software) detects the presence of Trojan horses or virus files in the computer system, and then kills them or deletes them permanently. Repairing system vulnerabilities or bugs is also a passive defense.

6. What types of cryptanalysis attacks can be divided into? What are their characteristics?

Commonly used cryptanalysis attacks include ciphertext only attack, known plaintext attack, chosen plaintext attack, chosen ciphertext attack, and chosen text attack.

- The ciphertext only attack is a password cracking method that only analyzes the intercepted ciphertext to obtain the plaintext or the key. It is assumed that the cryptanalyst has already known encryption algorithm and the statistical properties of the plaintext in advance. After analyzing the intercepted one or more ciphertexts encrypted with the same key, the plaintext or key may be obtained.

- Known plaintext attack refers to the password cracking method in which an attacker has mastered a certain piece of plaintext and the corresponding ciphertext in an attempt to infer the secret key.

- The adversary in chosen plaintext attack has access to the encryption function E_k and can construct the ciphertext corresponding to any plaintext. The adversary selects the specific plaintext and its corresponding ciphertext to solve the key that is beneficial to the attack, or solves the corresponding plaintext from the intercepted ciphertext.

- Chosen ciphertext attack is a password cracking method that solves the key or the corresponding plaintext by selecting the specific ciphertext and its corresponding plaintext that are beneficial to the attack. The adversary has access to the decryption function, and can select the ciphertext for decryption. The adversary has the ability to choose or control the ciphertext, and can choose any ciphertext and its corresponding plaintext that is beneficial to the attack.

- *Chosen text attack.* Chosen text attack can create any plaintext/ ciphertext and get the corresponding ciphertext/ plaintext, which is a combination of the above two.

7. How to protect against cyber attacks?

First, perform safe backup and recovery of data on time to achieve physical security. Second, install the latest anti-virus software on the network for real-time monitoring and regular scans to effectively prevent the latest malware attacks such as network viruses and worms. Next, use firewall technology to separate the internal network from the public access network. In addition, the formulation of cyberspace security strategy not only considers how to prevent external attacks, but also how to prevent internal attacks, that is, personnel management issues. Finally, different security strategies should be considered according to the actual situation.

GLOSSARY

Application Programming Interface: is a set of defined routines or methods for ensuring different software components a successful communication.

Content Filter: is a category of the content-control software that determines what content can be available or be blocked from the source of the Internet.

Control Plane: is a component of the router architecture that determines the method of forwarding the incoming packets.

Cyber Insurance: is a type of the insurance product that is designed for protecting/preventing businesses or individuals and their possessed IT-related infrastructure or activities from the Internet-related threats.

Cyber Integration: is a technical term describing the operations implemented by the cyber integration center that allows data transfers and synchronization among multiple processes or components of a solution in both development and operation periods.

Cyber Operation: describes cyber capabilities for one or a series of applications to achieve certain mission objective(s) in the cyberspace.

Cyber Space: is a conceptual term that describes a networking environment where communications and networked activities take place.

Forwarding Plane: also called the Data Plane or User Plane, is a component of the router architecture that receives information from the arriving packet on the inbound interface and determines its path to the destination address.

Heterogeneous Network: is a type of network setting that uses different operating systems and/or different protocols to build up web connections between devices.

Data Repository: is a safe data storage space in which anonymous cyber incident data are shared and processed for the purpose of supporting risk analyzes.

Information Asymmetry: describes a failure in linking stakeholders, such as insurers, insureds, and brokers, in cyber insurance business operations.

Infrastructure Security Management: refers to a wide scope of essential operations for managing/governing IT infrastructure and ensuring its effectiveness and implementation in an organization.

Intrusion Detection System: is a group of hardware or software that monitor the network(s) or system(s) for the purpose of preventing/detecting adversarial behaviors or violations

Management Plane: is a part of networking system that provides methods for device configuration, monitoring, and management functions.

Network Operation Center: is a type of core node in the cyberspace that offers management and governance functions.

Software-Defined Network: is a technical approach for networks that supports network administrators in programmable networking configuration, controls, and governance on an open interface.

Threat Management: is a category of the approach to network security that deals with various types of malware or adversarial actions.

Unified Threat Management: describes a single system that provides an integrative platform for encompassing multiple security products and achieving multifunctions in security.

Virtual Private Network: is a networking setting method that allows users to extend a private network to be deployed over a public network in order to enable their devices to virtually connect the private network for security concerns.

CHAPTER 2

Basic Concepts of Cybersecurity in the Internet of Things

This chapter discussed an overview of cybersecurity concepts and challenges in the context of the Internet of Things (IoT). The IoT is a rapidly growing network of interconnected devices that are capable of collecting and processing data in real-time. However, this interconnectedness also creates new security challenges in this digital realm, as these devices can be vulnerable to cyber-attacks. The first section begins by introducing the history of IoT and it started the attention of various parties, including governments. The IoT architecture and design are highly complexity and require multiple technologies to store, process and retrieve the data captured from portable devices. It then explores the unique security challenges posed by the IoT, such as device heterogeneity, data privacy, and distributed denial of service attacks. Later, an overview of the various cybersecurity solutions that can be used to protect IoT devices and networks has been discussed, including encryption, access control, and threat detection. It discusses the importance of risk assessment and security audits in ensuring the effectiveness of these solutions.

2.1   ABOUT THE INTERNET OF THINGS

2.1.1   Overview of IoT History

In this section, we take a short history journey of the concept of IoT to explain where IoT comes from and why it is needed.

                                        DOI: 10.1201/9781032694818-2

IoT [29–31] is not a new term for the current digital industry. The concept of IoT probably derives from 1995 or earlier, for example, when Bill Gates provided a series of predictions about the future IT industry's development in his book *The Road Ahead* [32]. In this book, Gates made a foreseen big picture in which digital devices were expected to be connected in the networking context. Even though a great digital world was pictured, the prediction made by Gates was not paid much attention by the public then due to the technical restriction of the network and sensor technologies. A few years later, Auto-ID Center was launched by European Article Numbering Association (EAN) and Uniform Code Council (UCC), which started to develop Electronic Product Code (EPC) following the standards of GS1 (a non-profit organization for developing/maintaining business communications global standards), in 1999. EPC is a typical identifier technology that uses a numerical code for identifying objects, e.g., commodities. Introducing EPC to the cyber world provided a low-cost approach for identifying physical objects. Along with wireless/wired network technologies, establishing a cyber world that supported object-object interconnections became possible.

In 2005, series report *ITU Internet Reports* [33] showed a convinced concept of IoT [34] in its 7*th* edition, "ITU Internet Reports 2005: The Internet of Things" [35]. The report emphasized the role of the "connections" between digital products in the upcoming digital era. Mobility was explicitly involved in the proposed definition, with a statement of "from anytime, any place connectivity for anyone, have connectivity for anything". It also was deemed to be a representative milestone that officially introduced IoT to the public as a term. From then on, as an emerging technical concept, IoT had been inspiring a variety of new applications, products, and even ecosystems. Individuals have become used to enjoying the achievements of developing this technical concept, for example, from remotely controlling appliances to vehicular networks, from educational technology to smart grids.

The official statement about IoT concept has successfully attracted attention from governments, industries, and even academia. For instance, IBM announced its Smarter Planet plan in 2008, inspired by the IoT technology, which emphasized three crucial dimensions that powered up the rise of IoT technology, including instruments, interconnectivity, and intelligence [36]. A wishing list on IoT development was given in the project, which had a great impact in multiple areas, including infrastructure development in the US. We can observe that most goals or expectations have been changing people's lives and today's society, i.e., intelligent systems, power grids, food supplies, environmental protections, financial systems, telecommunications, healthcare, etc. Many nations noticed the vital role of IoT in the economy and proposed various development plans, such as the USA, China, and Japan.

Now, we start with smartphones to have a glance at contemporary IoT development and its security and privacy concerns. Today's smartphone is a type of mobile device that generally possesses strong capabilities in computation, communication, and even storage, in which an extensive mobile operating system is deployed for executing various mobile apps. In other words, to make a normal mobile phone smart, we usually highly combine multiple technologies, including both hardware and software, to establish a mobile multi-function platform. For example, a smartphone maybe a combination of sensors, cameras, graphic processing systems, Global Positioning System (GPS), multi-core processing system, wireless connection system, mobile operating system, wireless data services, mobile apps, mobile call & messages service, personal digital assistant, wireless network protocols, and storage management software.

In fact, from the complex combination above, we can observe that it is hard to define a modern smartphone due to its multi-role characteristic. Individuals may use a smartphone in different ways, e.g., making a call, listening to music, scheduling an alarm, making a reminder, writing a diary, taking a note, or shooting a picture. Meanwhile, a smartphone also knows its owner's geographic movements, credit card information, and even exercises or hobbies. This fact raises the concern of using smartphones, as any malicious behaviors on personal information may result in security and privacy issues.

More examples/scenarios about IoT devices' security and privacy concerns are given in the followings.

- *Wearable Devices:* Due to the demand of functions offered by most wearable devices, e.g., location services, mobile payment, or heart rate display, data concerning personal information (identities, credit cards, health data, etc.) and environments/surroundings (location, temperature, etc.) are generally collected. Data leakage becomes a common concern as the wearable device may encounter either physical or virtual threats.

- *Smart Home:* This scenario covers most networked appliance or digital products at home, such as tablet, fridge, microwave oven, television, dryer, or toilet. The issue often is raised by those devices that have a lower-level capability in data protections. Adversaries may target at the "weak nodes" in the network of smart home, such that a successful attack on a single node may cause a big loss throughout the whole network. Potential threats include leaking users' behaviors or stealing personal information.

- *Telehealth Systems:* Telehealth system, on one hand, is deemed to be one of significant advances benefiting from the development of the network. The advantage of telehealth system has been further proved in the recent COVID-19 pandemic. On the other hand, as telehealth system needs to collect patients' sensitive information (identities, diagnose information, etc.) for the purpose of health-care service offerings, privacy leakage may take place during the implementation, such as data storage, communication, and processing. Moreover, some mobile apps and healthcare equipment are attached to telehealth systems, so that data collected by the third-party app/equipment may release users' privacy (e.g., behaviors). Malicious activities are varied, such as directly stealing data or data mining-based attacks.

- *Smart Cars:* Smart cars have become a buzzy word over years, due to its advanced and attractive customer experience. A smart car also can be considered a combination of multiple technologies, including not only mechanic engineering, but also a pool of digital technologies. Acting as a multi-role in smart cars, IoT technology (i.e., networked sensor supports) contributes to data collections, communications, storage, analysis/mining, and even partial mechanic controls. The significance of using IoT in smart cars is noticeable, but the concern is co-exist. Any adversaries or errors to IoT devices/equipment can incur serious consequences (s), especially for a moving vehicle.

Discussions above display a few examples of IoT applications, which also provides hints of security and privacy issues when IoT technologies are deployed. The purpose of showing examples here is to assist audiences to obtain a basic picture about security and privacy issues in IoT. To be specific, audiences need to have an understanding why we need to protect IoT devices/data and where potential threats come from. A key problem addressed by this book is *"How can we protect data security and privacy in IoT?"* We will have opportunities to address each scenario and explain threat sources and corresponding solutions in successive chapters,

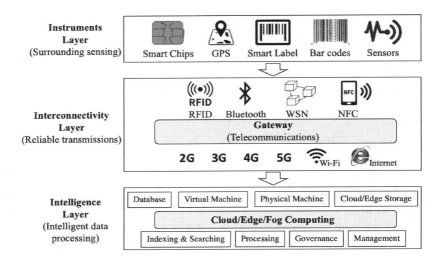

Figure 2.1   Architecture of key characteristics of IoT.

2.1.2   Definition of IoT

We provide a unified definition of IoT below in this book. Internet of Things is a type of network in which physical objects with sensors, software, or other technologies are connected via (a) certain communication protocol(s) for achieving one/multiple functions over the Internet.

One of major missions of sensors in IoT is collecting data. Besides sensors, some common technologies used in data collection include Radio Frequency Identification (RFID) [37], GPS, and laser scanners. In order to achieve data exchanging/sharing [38], physical objects need to be interconnected through communication protocol(s) over the Internet. The expected function scope may include but is not limited to pattern recognitions, location-based services, tracking, supervision, and management. On the whole, IoT is an information-oriented platform that utilizes Internet and telecommunication networks to connect all free-running addressed physical objects. As mentioned in IBM report, three key features of IoT include *instruments* (surrounding sensing), *interconnectivity* (reliable transmissions), and *intelligence* (intelligent data processing). We present a high-level architecture of IoT's key characteristics in Fig. 2.1.

- Internet of Things is a type of network in which physical objects with sensors, software, or other technologies are connected via

(a) certain communication protocol(s) for achieving one/multiple functions over the Internet.

- Radio Frequency Identification: is a technology that uses radio waves to read and capture information retrieved from tags attached to objects. RFID technology is widely used to track supply chain items and other scenarios needing verified identities.

- Global Positioning System: is a satellite-based navigation system funded by the US Department of Defense, which provides positioning and timing services for global users.

Electronic Product Code

As mentioned in Section 2.1.1, EPC is a fundamental technology for enabling IoT. The concept of EPC derives from the development of RFID and network technologies. RFID technology can identify an untouched object in various scenarios, for example, when the object is in a fast-moving state with multiple labels. The original purpose of building up EPC system is to establish a global open standard for labeling each commercial object. A typical EPC system generally comprises multiple technologies, such as the digital label(s) [39], reader, bar codes, information processing system, encoding system, addressing system, information service system, and the Internet. Fig. 2.2 shows a technical framework of the EPC system.

As displayed in Fig. 2.2, a typical EPC system consists of three fundamental components, namely, EPC encoding format standard, RFID, and network system. EPC encoding format standard mainly refers to the EPCglobal Tag Data Standard (as known as EPC Tag Data Standard (TDS)), which is designed for identifying physical objects. A typical EPC is a URI. A sample format of EPC URI is given as follows:

`urn:epc:id:scheme:component1.component2. ...`

More details about EPC TDS can refer to the "EPC Tag Data Standard" [40] issued by GS1. In addition, RFID is not exclusively designed for EPC systems, while it plays a crucial role in the system. Two key parts are involved in a RFID system, which are EPC tags and EPC readers. EPC tags are used for making digital labels attached to or embedded into a physical object. EPC readers are used for identifying those digital labels. Finally, network system refers to the network infrastructure for achieving connections between components of EPC system. Three major parts of EPC network system include EPC middleware, Object

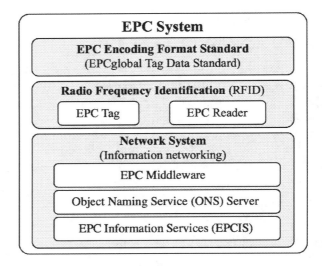

Figure 2.2 Technical framework of EPC system.

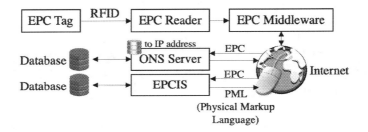

Figure 2.3 Fundamental workflow of EPC system.

Naming Service(ONS) Server, and EPC Information Services(EPCIS). In Fig. 2.3, we display a typical workflow of EPC system, aligning with major technical components given in Fig. 2.2.

2.1.3 IoT Deployments

IoT has become integral to our daily lives, facilitating interconnectivity among various devices, ranging from household appliances to industrial equipment. While IoT deployments offer immense benefits such as convenience, efficiency, and cost savings, they also present a host of security concerns that must be addressed.

IoT deployments include implementing and integrating IoT devices and systems into various environments. The IoT is a network of interconnected physical devices, vehicles, buildings, and other items embedded with sensors, software, and network connectivity, which enables them to collect and exchange data. IoT deployments can be found in various sectors, such as healthcare, manufacturing, transportation [41], agriculture, and smart cities. Implementing these deployments can enhance effectiveness, output, and convenience. Nevertheless, they also present notable security concerns. Several primary security issues arise in IoT deployments.

1. Insecure Devices and Networks

   IoT devices often come with default usernames and passwords, making them susceptible to unauthorized access. Many manufacturers prioritize ease of use and cost over security, leading to devices with weak or non-existent security measures. IoT networks are often connected to the internet without proper security controls, leaving them vulnerable to cyberattacks.

2. Data Privacy

   IoT devices gather and transmit extensive volumes of data, encompassing personal and sensitive details. Unauthorized retrieval of such data can result in grave repercussions for both individuals and entities. Ensuring data privacy requires robust encryption and access control mechanisms, often lacking in IoT deployments [42].

3. Lack of Standardization

   Various devices, protocols, and platforms characterize the IoT landscape. The lack of standardization in the industry creates challenges in implementing uniform security measures across different devices and networks. This fragmentation makes it difficult for security professionals to maintain a consistent security posture.

4. Insufficient Authentication and Authorization

   IoT devices often have weak or non-existent authentication and authorization mechanisms, allowing unauthorized users to access devices and networks. Attackers can leverage these weaknesses to exploit devices, disrupt services, or obtain unauthorized access to sensitive data. Ensuring appropriate authentication and authorization protocols are in place becomes crucial to preserve the security, confidentiality, and integrity of IoT systems.

5. Vulnerable Firmware and Software

   IoT devices run on firmware and software that may contain vulnerabilities which cybercriminals can exploit. Furthermore, many IoT devices do not have the capability to receive firmware or software updates, leaving them permanently exposed to known vulnerabilities. Addressing this issue requires manufacturers to prioritize security during the development process and provide timely updates to their devices.

6. Denial of Service Attacks

   IoT devices can be targeted by Denial of Service (DoS) attacks, where an attacker overwhelms the device with excessive traffic, rendering it unresponsive. IoT deployments with weak security measures are particularly vulnerable to such attacks, which can disrupt critical services and cause financial and reputational damage to organizations.

7. Physical Security

   Physical access to IoT devices can enable attackers to tamper with or extract sensitive data. This risk is particularly high for devices in public spaces or unsecured locations. Physical security involves preventing unauthorized access to devices, such as tamper-proof casings and secure mounting.

8. Supply Chain Attacks

   Supply chain attacks involve compromising a device or software during its development, manufacturing, or distribution. Attackers can introduce vulnerabilities into IoT devices or software, which can later be exploited to compromise systems. Addressing this risk requires robust supply chain security practices, including secure manufacturing processes and third-party vendor assessments.

9. Inadequate Security Awareness and Training

   The rapid adoption of IoT devices often outpaces users' understanding of the associated security risks. This lack of awareness can result in poor security practices, such as using weak passwords or ignoring software updates. Sufficient emphasis on security awareness and comprehensive training initiatives are imperative to ensure that users possess a deep understanding of the potential risks and adhere to established best practices, thereby safeguarding their devices and data effectively.

10. Legal and Regulatory Challenges

The IoT landscape is evolving rapidly, and the legal and regulatory frameworks governing security and privacy have struggled to keep pace. This lack of clear guidance creates challenges for organizations seeking to comply with security requirements and can result in uneven security practices. Developing comprehensive legal and regulatory frameworks that address IoT security concerns is crucial to mitigate risks and ensure consumer protection.

2.1.4 Cyber-Physical Systems

Cyber-Physical System (CPS) is mostly deemed to be an advanced deployment of IoT, which has been permeating a broad range of applications, from nanorobots to critical infrastructure. It integrates a variety of information technologies, e.g., sensors, embedded computing, and network communications, to achieve intelligent manufacturing operations through a higher-level collaboration on computation, communication, and control. The objective of CPS essentially is to construct a powerful manufacturing service system via multi-dimensional technical supports. A wide scope of technologies is involved in the technical fundamental of CPS, such as sensing, standardized communications, protocols, API, security, automatic control, and data processing.

Meanwhile, CPS emphasizes the instant information feedback and dynamic circling processes between cyber and physical spaces. In the field of manufacturing, for example, the production system receives responses/feedback while it is operating mechanical sectors; hence, in this case, connections between the physical and cyber worlds are built up. Upload and Download actions are two general manners for instant information/commands deliveries. Compared to other IoT deployments, CPS contributes more to science research, as the system fuses physical objects into a cyber world in which consists of a mixed group of IT systems. A holistic view created by CPS is helpful for better decision-making or business process improvements. Sometimes, as fundamental IT systems for next-generation industry, CPS is also called Industrial IoT (IIoT).

☐ Cyber-Physical System is a type of IoT deployment that integrates a variety of information technologies, e.g., sensors, embedded computing, and network communications, to achieve intelligent manufacturing operations through a higher-level collaboration on computation, communication, and control.

Wireless Sensor Network

Wireless Sensor Network (WSN) is a type of wireless network that interconnect sensor nodes in an Ad Hoc and distributed manner for monitoring/analyzing physical or surrounding conditions. This type of network emphasizes the role of sensor nodes in data collection. A variety of data can be collected following the demand of data usage, such as temperature, movement speed, frequency, radio signals, humidity, etc. The collected data are transferred to the party that observes the target environment. In some WSN contexts, sensor nodes can complete simple data pre-processing and inter-communication jobs before the data are transferred.

Meanwhile, even though sensor nodes logically can have various offerings, those sensors deployed in WSN are not designed for playing a multi-role. Most nodes in WSN are low-cost sensors that offer few functions with a limited capability in memory, computing, communication, and energy supply. The primary purpose of WSN is data collection and transmission. A pure WSN system is not responsible for interconnecting physical objects so control systems are not involved in the function list of WSN. In most situations, WSN is deemed a junior manner of IoT as it does not offer resource control functions that are considered one of the core offerings of IoT. Therefore, WSN offers less reliability than CPS.

Cloud computing introduces a new service model to WSN. Sensing-as-a-Service is a type of cloud computing service model that offers flexible on-demand sensing services or on-demand WSN assets management services. Sensing-as-a-Service model has all key features of cloud computing, such as pay-as-you-go and resource pools. The model regards sensors as computing resources for selling. A typical Sensing-as-a-Service model consists of four layers, as shown in the figure, namely, sensors and sensor owners, sensor publishers, extended service providers, and sensor data consumers.

☐ Wireless Sensor Network is a type of wireless network that interconnect sensor nodes in an Ad Hoc and distributed manner for monitoring/analyzing physical or surrounding conditions.

☐ Sensing-as-a-Service is a type of cloud computing service model that offers flexible on-demand sensing services or on-demand WSN assets management services.

Machine to Machine

Machine to Machine (M2M) is a term for describing a group of technologies that intelligently interconnect or inter-communicate machines. Interconnections and intercommunications in M2M generally take place among humans, devices, and IT systems. The fundamental of M2M is deploying intelligent devices that possess communication capabilities. The core of M2M is constructing networks for providing reliable connections between network nodes. A practical M2M solution may include multiple tele-communication technologies. The primary purpose of M2M is to meet the demand of data transmissions. In general, M2M is considered one of fundamental technologies supporting IoT.

Rather than a simple connection between machines, the concept of M2M emphasizes intelligent and interactive communications. The original idea of M2M is to enable those machines without communication module to possess communication capabilities with other devices or IT systems through wireless network. The idea derived from humans' communication networks, e.g., mobile phone network, which was proposed to achieve machine-based networking. Some extended concepts of M2M covered, for example, *Man-to-Machine* and *Machine-to-Man*.

Since term M2M emphasizes the functionality of communications, network plays a vital role in its deployments. Establishing a reliable connection for constructing an end-to-end communication is an essential goal of M2M. Wireless network also becomes a common method for the networking establishment. We can deem M2M to be a fundamental of IoT, as IoT applications are available only when the network is available.

With the development of IoT, M2M technology is offering a large scope of services. There are many different methods for categorizing M2M services. We provide a sample of M2M service architecture in Table 2.1 in order to help audiences to have a fundamental cognition on its service coverage.

2.2 KEY ISSUES IN IOT SECURITY

Security issues can be found in all aspects of IoT systems, in most situations, considering either traditional security threats (e.g., data breach) or emerging risks (e.g., linkage attacks or privacy mining). Since an IoT system logically can consist of millions of devices, it provides messy attacking opportunities for adversaries. Any hacked devices can be utilized for triggering attacks as an adversarial node, which may further threaten

Table 2.1 Service Architecture of M2M

Service Sectors	Application Fields	Scenarios Locations	Devices Equipment
IT & Networks	Either public or private/community services	Data warehouse, e-commerce, datacenter, etc.	Most edge devices, storage, network equipment, etc.
Security & Safety	Security monitoring, movement tracking, critical infrastructure, public surveillance, emergency services, etc.	Covers a wide scope, from military to individual scenes; from critical infrastructure to foods, healthcare, etc. Applications may not only address data security but also safety issues.	Home appliance, critical infrastructure, military facility/equipment, digital devices, etc.
Manufacturing & Supply Chain	Involves a great range of applications. From the perspective of production, some examples include auto-controls, oil & gas, process management, distributions, etc. from the purpose of services, examples include hospitality, entertainment, and retails.	Covers most mobile sensing aspects, such as pipelines, conveyance, producing activities (e.g., mining, irrigations, etc.), assembly, retailing, and tests. Service locations are varied, e.g., gas stations, hotels, restaurants, supermarkets, entertainment places, agriculture, oil/ mining fields, etc.	Includes a broad scope of functionality-oriented equipment, e.g., assembly/packaging, vehicles, vessels, tanks, motors, production machines, oil wells, robots, etc.
Individual Service/ Assistant	Entertainment, transportation, healthcare, smart home, and research.	Personal entertainment devices, public entertainment facilities, personal healthcare assistant, home monitoring systems, hospital, clinic, healthcare labs, medicine research, diagnostics, traffic management, road construction, intelligent transportation system, etc.	Home appliance, personal digital devices, wearable devices, healthcare equipment (e.g., pumps, monitors), road-side units, vehicles, etc.

the whole network system. Moreover, interconnections between IoT devices also bring attackers opportunities for stealing sensitive information through the "network bridges". Most network-related threats also exist in the IoT context. In addition, even though API supports communications between hardware and software, lack of standard may result in security issues as well. Therefore, an IoT security solution needs to deal with multi-dimensional threats.

IoT Security mainly refers to those technologies or solutions that guarantee the IoT system (including bot hardware and software) can be protected from either deliberate attacks or accidental damages in order to make the system/service consistent, reliable, and maintainable. The principal protection objective is data, which are facing multiple threats, such as data breach, leakage, or distortion. The major purpose of IoT security is to prevent data/information carried on the IoT network from illegal operations or unexpected usage.

Fig. 2.1 shows key characteristics of IoT that consists of three layers. In the line with the three layers, IoT security also contains three dimensions, which are sensing system, transmission system, data process system security. Sensing system security refers to protecting data collected by sensors from leakage and unexpected operations. In this dimension, data security and location-related privacy [43] protections are two basic protection objectives. Transmission system security means protecting in-transit data over IoT [44] network from any malicious actions, e.g., illegal monitoring. Data processing security [45] means the system needs to guarantee data can be safely used while fully considering the requirement of data security and privacy protections [46]. For example, malicious data tracing and user ID mining shall be prevented in this dimension.

Three common threats exist in most IoT security, which are data/information leakage, data/information damage, and DoS.

- Information leakage: Information leakage refers to information security incidents caused by the exposure of confidential, sensitive, personal privacy and other information in the information system to unauthorized persons.

- Information damage: Information damage refers to an information security incident caused by the tampering or counterfeiting of information in an information system through a network or other technical means. Tampering refers to information security problems caused by the unauthorized replacement of information in an information system with the information provided by attackers, such as web page tampering.

- DoS attack: A Distributed Denial of Service (DDoS) attack occurs when multiple assailants situated in various locations simultaneously target one or more specific entities, or when a single attacker manages multiple machines located in diverse places to orchestrate a synchronized assault on the victim. The name "Distributed Denial of Service" stems from the fact that the attack originates from multiple locations, involving the collaboration of multiple attackers.

2.3   SECURITY THREATS IN THE INTERNET OF THINGS

The Internet of Things (IoT) represents a network where physical devices, vehicles, structures, and other objects are integrated with sensors, software, and network connectivity. This interconnectedness has revolutionized convenience and productivity, yet it has concurrently introduced a host of security vulnerabilities that necessitate attention. IoT devices facilitate the collection and exchange of data, enabling intelligent automation and control across numerous domains. Nevertheless, as the IoT landscape expands, so too does the magnitude of security risks associated with it.

One of the biggest security threats in IoT is the lack of security measures in IoT devices. Many IoT devices are designed with functionality and cost in mind, rather than security. As a result, these devices often lack the necessary security protocols and features to protect against cyber-attacks. This makes them easy targets for cybercriminals who can exploit vulnerabilities in the devices to gain access to sensitive information, such as personal data or financial information.

Another security threat in IoT is the lack of encryption in data transmission. IoT devices often transmit sensitive information over unsecured networks, which makes it easy for cybercriminals to intercept and steal data. Without proper encryption, IoT devices are vulnerable to a range of attacks, including man-in-the-middle attacks, where attackers intercept data between two devices and steal information.

In addition to these technical vulnerabilities, human error is also a major security threat in IoT. Many IoT devices are operated by non-technical users who may not be familiar with best practices for securing their devices. This can lead to situations where devices are left unsecured or passwords are easily guessable, leaving them vulnerable to attack.

One specific example of a security threat in IoT is botnets. Botnets are networks of devices that have been infected with malware, and are controlled remotely by a cybercriminal. Botnets can be used for a variety of malicious activities, such as DDoS attacks, where a website or service is overwhelmed with traffic, rendering it unavailable. In the case of IoT devices, botnets can be created by infecting vulnerable devices, such as routers, webcams, and smart home appliances. Once infected, these devices can be controlled remotely to carry out attacks on other devices or networks.

Another example of a security threat in IoT is ransomware. Ransomware is a type of malware that encrypts a user's files or data, rendering them inaccessible. The attacker then demands a ransom in exchange for the decryption key. In IoT, ransomware attacks can be particularly devastating as they can target critical infrastructure systems, such as those used in hospitals or power plants. This can result in significant disruption to services and even loss of life.

Finally, privacy is also a major concern in IoT. As IoT devices become more prevalent, the amount of personal data being collected and transmitted is increasing. This data can include sensitive information, such as health records or financial information, which can be used for identity theft or other malicious purposes. In addition, IoT devices can be used for surveillance, either by governments or malicious actors. This can lead to a range of privacy concerns, including violations of personal freedoms and civil liberties.

To mitigate these threats, it is important to design IoT devices with security in mind, including encryption, secure network protocols, and regular software updates. Additionally, users must be educated on best practices for securing their devices and data. Governments and industries must work together to develop regulations and standards for IoT security to ensure that users are protected from the growing number of threats.

2.4 SUMMARY

This chapter takes a short history journey of the concept of IoT to explain where IoT comes from and why it is needed. In Section 2.2, we discussed three common threats in most IoT security: data/information leakage, data/information damage, and DoS. Section 2.3 explained some security threats in IoT, such as the lack of security measures in

IoT devices, encryption in data transmission, human error, botnets, ransomware, and privacy. Overall, this book chapter is a valuable resource for anyone seeking to understand the basic concepts of cybersecurity in the context of the Internet of Things. It provides a comprehensive overview of the challenges and solutions involved in securing IoT devices and networks and highlights the importance of implementing robust cybersecurity measures to protect against cyber attacks.

2.5 EXERCISES

1. What is the meaning of Distributed Denial of Service (DDoS) attack? What methods can be used to implement the DDoS attack? A DDoS attack involves the simultaneous assault on one or more targets by numerous assailants located in diverse regions, or when a single attacker manipulates multiple machines spread across different locations to collectively target the victim. Due to the dispersed nature of the attack's origin, it is classified as a Distributed Denial of Service attack, which can involve multiple attackers.

2. What is a hacker? What types of hackers can be classified according to their behaviors?

   Hackers refer to people who break into the other party's system without permission to obtain control authority for a specific purpose. According to the behaviors, hackers can be classified into script kiddies, black hats, white hats and gray hats, etc.

3. Can you list several kinds of malware that you are familiar with? In what ways did they conduct malicious activities?

   - Spyware is a kind of malware that can install a backdoor on the user's computer and collect information without awareness. Private data and important information can be captured by backdoor programs and sent to hackers, commercial companies, etc. These backdoor programs can even remotely manipulate the user's computer to form a huge "botnet" to launch a Distributed Denial of Service attack.

   - Crimeware is a kind of malware that can invade the computer browser program, and unknowingly redirect the surfer to a disguised website to defraud personal information. The classic example of crimeware is the aforementioned keylogger.

Virus makers, hackers and spammers have all increased their power to steal information to make huge profits, so that the development of crimeware is very rapid.

- Adware refers to malware that is installed on a user's computer without permission to seek commercial benefits through pop-up advertisements and other forms. Such software is not only mandatory to install and cannot be easily uninstalled, but also frequently pops up advertisements, consuming system resources. In addition, adware usually collects user information in the background for profit.

- Trojan Horse refers to an unauthorized remote control program that resides in a computer. It can open system permissions, leak user information, and even steal the entire computer management and use permissions without being discovered by the computer administrator. It is known as one of the most commonly used tools by hackers. Trojans disguise themselves as other useful software in order to persuade unsuspecting users to install them.

4. What is the difference between a virus and a worm?

- A worm is an independent malicious program that can run, replicate and spread through a computer network without the aid of a host program. Once the worm invades the system, it will immediately create multiple copies on its own and spread through the network connection, infecting any computers and servers on the network that are not fully protected.

- Unlike worms, viruses do not exist independently, but hidden in other executable programs. After the virus invades the system, it will remain dormant until the infected host file or program is activated, which in turn activates the virus so that it can run and replicate on the system. Viruses can affect the speed of the computer, damage files or systems, which causes great losses to users.

5. Please briefly describe the concept and difference between active defense and passive defense.

- Active defense is a security measure that can promptly and accurately warn before the intrusion has a bad impact on the computer system, so as to build a flexible defense system in real time to avoid, transfer and reduce the risks. Active defense is mainly to monitor the entire computer system in real time, so as to quickly capture changes in network traffic and analyze program behaviors, achieving the purpose of protecting the security of the computer system.

- Passive defense is a security measure taken after a computer is attacked. For example, the security audit tool (firewall or anti-virus software) detects the presence of Trojan horses or virus files in the computer system, and then kills them or deletes them permanently. Repairing system vulnerabilities or bugs is also a passive defense.

6. What types of cryptanalysis attacks can be divided into? What are their characteristics?

Frequently employed cryptanalysis techniques encompass various types of attacks, such as attacks based on ciphertext only, known plaintext, chosen plaintext, chosen ciphertext, and chosen text.

- The ciphertext only attack is a technique used for cracking passwords, wherein the intercepted ciphertext is examined to deduce the corresponding plaintext or key. This method assumes that the cryptanalyst possesses prior knowledge of the encryption algorithm and statistical characteristics of the plaintext. By analyzing one or more intercepted ciphertexts encrypted using the same key, it becomes possible to derive the plaintext or key.

- Known plaintext attack refers to the password cracking method in which an attacker has mastered a certain piece of plaintext and the corresponding ciphertext in an attempt to infer the secret key.

- The adversary in chosen plaintext attack has access to the encryption function E_k and can construct the ciphertext corresponding to any plaintext. The adversary selects the specific plaintext and its corresponding ciphertext to solve the key that is beneficial to the attack, or solves the corresponding plaintext from the intercepted ciphertext.

- Chosen ciphertext attack is a password cracking method that solves the key or the corresponding plaintext by selecting the specific ciphertext and its corresponding plaintext that are beneficial to the attack. The adversary has access to the decryption function, and can select the ciphertext for decryption. The adversary possesses the capability to exercise control over the ciphertext, enabling them to selectively choose any ciphertext and its associated plaintext that serves their objectives during the attack.

- Chosen text attack can create any plaintext/ ciphertext and get the corresponding ciphertext/ plaintext, which is a combination of the above two.

7. How to protect against cyber attacks?

First, perform safe backup and recovery of data on time to achieve physical security. Second, install the latest anti-virus software on the network for real-time monitoring and regular scans to effectively prevent the latest malware attacks such as network viruses and worms. Next, use firewall technology to separate the internal network from the public access network. In addition, the formulation of cyberspace security strategy not only considers how to prevent external attacks, but also how to prevent internal attacks, that is, personnel management issues. Finally, different security strategies should be considered according to the actual situation.

GLOSSARY

Cyber-Physical System: is a type of IoT deployment that integrates a variety of information technologies, e.g., sensors, embedded computing, and network communications, to achieve intelligent manufacturing operations through a higherlevel collaboration on computation, communication, and control.

Electronic Product Code: is a typical identifier technology that uses a numerical code for identifying objects, e.g., commodities.

Global Positioning System: is a satellite-based navigation system funded by the US Department of Defense, which provides positioning and timing services for global users.

Internet of Things: is a type of network in which physical objects with sensors, software, or other technologies are connected via (a) certain communication protocol(s) for achieving one/multiple functions over the Internet.

Machine to Machine: is a term for describing a group of technologies that intelligently interconnect or inter-communicate machines.

Radio Frequency Identification: is a kind of technology that uses radio waves to read and capture information retrieving from tags attached to objects.

Sensing-as-a-Service: is a type of cloud computing service model that offers flexible on-demand sensing services or on-demand WSN assets management services.

Wireless Sensor Network: is a type of wireless network that interconnect sensor nodes in an Ad Hoc and distributed manner for monitoring/analyzing physical or surrounding conditions.

CHAPTER 3

Privacy Issues Categorizations in the Internet of Things

This chapter outlines the infrastructure security for OSI layers, focusing on network, host, and application layers. Furthermore, detailed discussions explain protection in three different scenarios of data storage, which consist of data-at-rest, data-in-transit, and data-in-motion. The discussion extended to cover a few standards and mechanisms available in the industry to protect data, especially in cloud storage, against different security threats. Data privacy is the current nation's primary concern and even a global issue due to its capability to handle Personal Identifier Information (PII) for the digital perimeter. A proficient system for identity management, which effectively manages and regulates user access, plays a critical role in mitigating data breaches and preventing unauthorized access to sensitive information. This chapter will provide an overview of identity management involvement's fundamental concept and historical progression. The chapter also addresses and examines the implications of privacy breaches and their significant repercussions on individuals and organizations. To safeguard against privacy breaches, individuals and organizations must adopt robust security measures and exercise utmost care when handling confidential data. Finally, the chapter explains the importance of data privacy regarding data management.

DOI: 10.1201/9781032694818-3

3.1   INFRASTRUCTURE SECURITY

The popularity of IoT computing is rising due to its connectivity, advancements, and the vast amount of data it generates, which can be utilized for big data analytics, automation, and control. This enables the generation of valuable insights into trends, forecasting, predictions, pattern recognition, and other related areas. It is seen as a viable option to achieve superior performance due to its improved abilities in managing systems, distributing resources, sharing data, and adapting flexibility [47, 48]. Some prominent IoT systems that could be relatively popular but gaining privacy concerns are Self-Driving Vehicles (SDV), smart cities, water supply systems, oil pipelines, medical care, and grid system across multiple regions [49]. A microgrid is a smaller-scale power grid operating autonomously or coordinating with a larger power grid. The microgrid concept can be broadly categorized into simple, multi-DG, and utility microgrids. Its primary objective is to deliver dependable, efficient, and sustainable energy to local communities, buildings, or industrial facilities [50]. While Supervisory Control and Data Acquisition (SCADA) is a system used to monitor and control industrial processes and infrastructure on a large scale, for instance, for power plants, transportation systems, water treatment plants, and vehicle manufacturing facilities [51–53]. It comprises of five main components: supervisory control, data acquisition, Human-Machine Interface (HMI), Remote Terminal Units (RTU) or Programmable Logic Controllers (PLCs), and Communication Infrastructure. SCADA able to improve operation efficiency by providing real-time monitoring, data visualization, data analytics, and useful reporting to assist operator in optimizing process performance [54].

The underlying hardware and software to support the connectivity and secure the reliability performance is a challenge due to its large capacity of electronic devices within a network or across. Resource allocations in a high-complexity ecosystem require a specific mechanism and approach to obtain high performance and efficiency. Infrastructure security for IoT refers to the protection of the underlying hardware and software infrastructure that supports the IoT operations.

3.1.1   Network Level

Infrastructure security at the network level refers to the measures and practices used to protect the underlying network infrastructure that enables communication between different devices and systems. This includes protecting physical devices such as routers, switches, servers, and other networking equipment and the data that flows through them.

Some common practices and techniques used for infrastructure security at the network level include:

1. **Access Control** is the process of controlling who has access to the network infrastructure. This involves setting up user accounts with appropriate permissions, implementing authentication mechanisms such as passwords or biometrics, and monitoring access logs to detect unauthorized access attempts.

2. **Network Segmentation** involves partitioning a network into smaller sub-networks, known as segments or zones, with controlled access between them. This approach restricts the repercussions of security breaches and hinders attackers from traversing the network horizontally.

3. A **Firewall** is a critical network security device that plays a vital role in supervising and controlling the movement of incoming and outgoing network traffic, meticulously adhering to well-defined security rules. It can be implemented as software or hardware, acting as a robust barrier to impede any unauthorized access attempts from known malicious IP addresses. By effectively preventing unauthorized entry into sensitive systems, a firewall diligently enforces rigorous security policies, ensuring the integrity and confidentiality of network communications.

4. **IDPS** is a advanced security device that diligently monitor network traffic, actively seeking out indications of malicious activity and promptly taking preventive measures against potential attacks. These robust systems excel at detecting and obstructing known attack signatures, while also demonstrating exceptional proficiency in recognizing and responding to emerging threats or previously unidentified vulnerabilities.

5. **VPNs** facilitate the establishment of secure and encrypted connections between remote devices and corporate networks, bolstering data protection during transit by mitigating interception and eavesdropping risks. Additionally, VPNs serve as a reliable mechanism to grant secure access to remote workers and contractors,

ensuring their connections remain safeguarded and impervious to unauthorized access.

6. **Network Monitoring** involves collecting and analyzing data from network devices to detect security incidents, performance issues, and other problems. This can include monitoring network traffic, device logs, and system metrics and using tools such as intrusion detection systems, network analyzers, and packet sniffers to identify and respond to security threats.

Achieving robust security necessitates a holistic approach that encompasses both the physical and logical dimensions of network security. This comprehensive strategy entails the integration of diverse security technologies and practices, effectively safeguarding against a broad spectrum of threats. By harmonizing these elements, organizations can fortify their defenses and establish a resilient security posture capable of countering evolving and multifaceted risks.

3.1.2   Host Level

The host-level measures and practices used to protect individual computing devices, such as servers, workstations, laptops, and mobile devices, shall include protecting the underlying hardware, operating systems, applications, and data on the device. Some common practices and techniques used for infrastructure security at the host level include:

1. **Vulnerability management:** involves identifying and addressing vulnerabilities in the infrastructure components, such as software patches, firmware updates, and configuration changes.

2. **Network security:** measures such as firewalls and network segmentation prevent unauthorized access to the infrastructure components and limit the impact of security incidents.

3. **Encryption** : protects data stored on the infrastructure components and transmitted between them. This may include encrypting data at rest, such as on hard drives or in databases, and by encrypting data in transit, such as over the network. Data encryption can help to protect sensitive data on the host by converting it into an unreadable format that can only be decrypted with a key. This can be achieved through software or hardware-based encryption, such as self-encrypting drives.

4. **Disaster recovery:** plans are implemented to ensure critical infrastructure components can be recovered during a disaster or outage.

5. **Patch Management:** is paramount in mitigating the risk of known vulnerabilities being exploited, necessitating the regular updating of the operating system and applications on each host with the latest security patches. This critical practice entails proactive measures such as consistent monitoring for and prompt application of security updates and hotfixes. To streamline and enhance the process, configuring automatic updates wherever feasible ensures a seamless and efficient approach to keeping systems up to date, further bolstering resilience against potential exploits. By diligently adhering to these practices, organizations can fortify their security posture and proactively safeguard against emerging threats.

6. **Antivirus and Anti-Malware:** installing and maintaining an antivirus and anti-malware solution on each host can help to prevent, detect, and remove malicious software that may attempt to compromise the host or steal sensitive data.

7. **Host-Based Firewalls:** refer to software-based firewalls that operate on individual hosts, effectively thwarting unauthorized access to and from the host. These firewalls meticulously regulate incoming and outgoing network traffic based on pre-established rules, granting or denying access accordingly. By implementing host-based firewalls, organizations can fortify the security of their individual hosts and ensure that only authorized network communication takes place.

8. **User access control:** using mechanisms, such as password policies, two-factor authentication, and role-based access control, plays a pivotal role in guaranteeing that only authorized users have the ability to access sensitive data and resources on the host. These measures contribute to maintaining the integrity and security of the system by enforcing strict controls and verifying the identity and permissions of individuals seeking access.

9. **Host-based Intrusion Detection and Prevention:** solutions function as powerful security measures that carefully observe and analyze the activities occurring on individual hosts. They

proactively identify potential signs of malicious behavior, including unauthorized access attempts, suspicious network traffic, and unauthorized alterations to important files. By closely monitoring host activity, HIDP solutions empower organizations to promptly detect and respond to security breaches, strengthening their overall defensive capabilities and fortifying resilience against emerging threats.

3.1.3 Application Level

In today's digital world, many systems are driven by IoT or the Internet of Things, where data are collected automatically or by pulling from devices. Infrastructure security at the application level refers to the measures and practices used to protect the applications and software systems that run on top of the underlying infrastructure. For example, Application Programming Interfaces (API) is a great tool to establish connections and communication between all objects to exchange information. Hence, security at the application level shall include protecting the application code, data, and user interfaces from attacks, vulnerabilities, and unauthorized access.

Some common practices and techniques used for infrastructure security at the application level include:

1. Developing secure code is essential to application security. This involves following **Secure Coding Practices**, such as input validation, error handling, and secure data storage, to prevent common vulnerabilities such as injection attacks, buffer overflows, and cross-site scripting.

2. An **Application Firewall** serves as a robust security device that actively monitors and governs the flow of incoming and outgoing traffic to an application. It plays a crucial role in shielding the application from various types of attacks, including SQL injection, cross-site scripting, and other vulnerabilities at the application layer. By effectively mitigating these threats, an application firewall strengthens the overall security posture of the application, safeguarding it from unauthorized access and potential exploitation.

3. **Encryption** can protect sensitive data within the application and communication between the application and other systems. This

includes using HTTPS to secure web traffic and encryption for data at rest and in transit.

4. **Authentication and Authorization** mechanisms play a pivotal role in guaranteeing that only authorized users can gain access to an application and its associated data. This involves the implementation of robust user authentication procedures and the application of role-based access control. The concept of user authentication using a one-time password (OTP) was initially introduced by Lamport in 1981. This authentication scheme relies on the utilization of hash functions and pre-shared keys to verify the identity of users. By leveraging these mechanisms, organizations can establish a secure and controlled environment, ensuring that only authenticated individuals with appropriate privileges can interact with the application and its sensitive data.

5. **Vulnerability Scanning and Penetration Testing** are essential tools for identifying vulnerabilities and weaknesses in the application. This includes performing regular scans to identify security weaknesses and conducting penetration testing to simulate real-world attacks and identify areas for improvement.

6. **Secure Configuration Management** involves ensuring that the application is configured securely and that all components are updated with the latest security patches. This includes configuring security settings for the application and all supporting components and regularly checking for and applying updates and patches.

Ultimately, by implementing secure coding practices, using application firewalls, encryption, authentication and authorization, vulnerability scanning, and secure configuration management, organizations can help ensure their applications' security and protect against a wide range of threats.

3.2 DATA SECURITY AND STORAGE

A vast amount of data have been generated in this digitization ecosystem, either from various equipment like IoT devices and sensors or social media posts, which has turned big data, artificial intelligence, and machine learning become trending [55]. Data drives operational efficiency and determines the quality of an organization's products or services by setting performance goals. Data plays a vital role in decision-making,

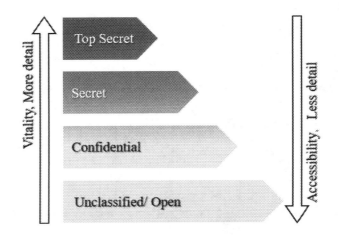

Figure 3.1 Document classification.

analysis, improving procedures, and getting to know the customer better. Therefore, data must be protected and prevented from being stolen, tampering, and modified by unauthorized parties. Data security protects digital assets from unauthorized access, theft, modification, or destruction. The main reason for the protection is to ensure data are kept safely and securely with various techniques and tools available. For example, access control, firewall, intrusion prevention/detection system, policies and procedures, encryption, and auditing.

In comparison, data storage stores digital assets on various media types, such as hard drives, cloud storage, or portable USB drive. Such data can include documents, images, videos, recordings, log files, and metadata. Both data security and storage are critical aspects of information technology and contain different degrees of confidentiality. Due to the working environment and type of data collected or stored, it could be classified and labeled as *TOP SECRET*, *SECRET*, *SENSITIVE*, *CONFIDENTIAL*, or *OPEN* or *UNCLASSIFIED*.

TOP SECRET refers to data that requires the highest degree of protection. The data contains sensitive information, and unauthorized disclosure would cause harm and damage to the organization or even national security. For example, government and military organizations protect information related to security and defense policies that could be potentially damaging to the parties who have the interest.

A *SECRET* document is information or material intended to be kept confidential and hidden from unauthorized individuals or groups. It may contain sensitive or confidential information, such as classified government documents, private business information, or personal data. These documents are often labeled with various classification levels, indicating the degree of sensitivity and the level of protection they require. Classifying a document *SECRET* is to protect national security interests, maintain confidentiality in business operations, safeguard personal privacy, or protect intellectual property. Such documents are prohibited from disclosure to unauthorized parties, which may cause significant harm to individuals, organizations, or countries.

Government secret documents may include classified military strategies, intelligence reports, diplomatic cables, or confidential financial information. Businesses may keep secret documents such as trade secrets, proprietary technology, or financial statements. Personal secret documents may include medical records, tax returns, or personal identification information.

Protecting document secrecy requires a lot of effort. Various security measures are put in place, including physical security measures such as locked cabinets, safes, and restricted access areas, as well as digital security measures such as encryption and password protection. Individuals with access to secret documents must undergo background checks, sign non-disclosure agreements, and receive regular security training.

A *CONFIDENTIAL* document is a document that contains sensitive or private information that is intended to be kept secret or limited to a selected group of people. This document is often marked with a confidentiality notice or label to indicate that it will not be shared with anyone authorized to view it. Examples of confidential documents include contracts, financial statements, medical records, legal documents, and trade secrets. Maintaining the confidentiality of these documents is essential to protect the privacy and interests of the individuals or organizations involved. Breaches of confidentiality can result in legal action, loss of reputation, and financial damages. These documents typically contain information that could be used to harm individuals or organizations if it were to fall into the wrong hands.

Confidential documents require a secure storage system, restricted access, and careful dissemination. Those authorized to view confidential documents should be trained on the proper handling and protection of these documents to prevent unauthorized disclosure.

SENSITIVE data refers to any information that could cause harm or damage to an individual or organization if it falls into the wrong hands. This type of information can include PII, financial information, health records, intellectual property, trade secrets, and other confidential data. This classification is very similar to *SECRET* document classification in that it involves categorizing information according to its level of sensitivity and implementing appropriate security measures to protect it. The process typically involves identifying the types of sensitive data an organization handles, assessing the associated risks, and implementing appropriate safeguards to protect it.

Sensitive data can be classified into different categories, such as public, internal, confidential, and restricted. The level of protection required for each category depends on the potential harm or damage that could result from unauthorized access or disclosure of the data.

Organizations typically implement various security measures to protect sensitive data, including access controls, encryption, firewalls, and intrusion detection systems. They may also conduct regular security audits and assessments to identify vulnerabilities and ensure their security controls work effectively.

UNCLASSIFIED is the lowest category of document classification in the document pyramid. Unclassified does not contain sensitive or classified information that requires protection and control but can be freely distributed, shared and accessed by the public. Documents under this category cover a wide range of information, from the public report, academic papers, research reports and statistic reports. However, even though unclassified documents do not contain sensitive or classified information, they may still contain proprietary or confidential information that an organization may want to protect from unauthorized disclosure. In such cases, an organization may choose to implement security controls to limit access to the information.

When we think of a strategy and design to protect the data against attacks for each class of data based on the vitality, accessibility, and granularity of the data, we need to understand the different states of data to apply effective countermeasures. There are three states of data identified: *data-at-rest*, *data-in-motion*, and *data-in-use*.

Data security refers to the process of safeguarding information from unauthorized access, modification, disclosure, or destruction. It is a critical aspect of information technology, ensuring the confidentiality, integrity, and availability of data stored, transmitted, or processed across various digital platforms. The growing reliance on technology and the internet has made data security an essential component of personal, corporate, and governmental operations.

Data breaches can lead to significant financial losses, reputational damage, and legal consequences. Consequently, organizations employ various measures to protect their information assets. Data security practices include encryption, strong authentication, firewalls, intrusion detection systems, access control, and regular software updates.

Data Leakage

Data leakage is a situation that occurs when sensitive or private information is disclosed to unintended or unauthorized parties [56]. It can happen in many ways, such as through deliberate or accidental actions, cyber attacks, system failures, and even human error.

Data leakage can occur at any stage of data processing, from data collection to data storage, analysis, and transmission. For example, if a company collects customer data and stores it in an unsecured database, it may be vulnerable to data leakage if the database is hacked or accessed by unauthorized personnel. Similarly, if a data analyst accidentally includes sensitive information in a data set that is shared with others, it may lead to data leakage. There are a few common reasons that caused data leak.

1. *System mis-configuration:*
   Data leak could happen either caused by digital (USB drive, network, portable devices) or non-digital source (human being). The remote access function available at tools and databases settings could leave a security breach and being a backdoor to the system that might lead to serious security problems.

2. *Unintentional data leak:*
   An employee could have unintentionally sends or reveals a sensitive or confidential information to the wrong person or unauthorized parties due to human error, technical issues, or other unforeseen circumstances. Such leaks can occur in various ways, including:

   - Emailing sensitive information to the wrong person or group

   - Uploading files with sensitive data to a publicly accessible server or cloud storage

   - Failing to properly secure devices or networks, leaving them vulnerable to attacks or data breaches

- Misconfigured software or systems that expose sensitive information to unauthorized access

- Employees or contractors accidentally sharing sensitive information on social media or public forums.

In each case, the unintended release of sensitive information can have severe consequences, including financial losses, legal liabilities, and reputational damage. Once confidential data is out in the open, it can be difficult, if not impossible, to retrieve, and the harm may already have been done.

3. *Intentional data leak:*
   This type of data leak occurs when an individual or group in an organization intentionally shares sensitive information with unauthorized parties. The incidents could be one of below:

   - Insider Threats: One of the most common ways intentional data leaks happen is through insider threats. This is when an employee, contractor, or third party with access to sensitive information leaks the data to an unauthorized party.

   - Cyber Espionage: Cyber espionage is a form of an intentional data leak that involves the theft of sensitive information by foreign governments or other groups. This can happen through hacking, phishing, or other cyber attacks.

   - Social Engineering: Social engineering is a tactic cyber criminals use to manipulate individuals into sharing sensitive information. This can happen through phishing emails, phone calls, or in-person interactions.

   - Malicious Software: Malware can be used to gain unauthorized access to a computer system and steal sensitive information. This can happen through viruses, trojan horses, or other types of malicious software.

   - Careless Employees: Sometimes intentional data leaks can happen because employees are careless with sensitive information. For example, an employee might accidentally send an email containing sensitive information to the wrong person or leave a laptop containing sensitive information unattended.

Data leakage can have significant ramifications for both individuals and organizations, encompassing detrimental effects such as financial

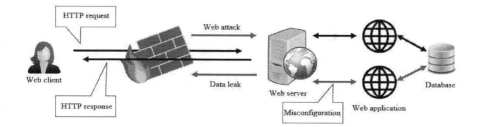

Figure 3.2 Data leakage in web application.

losses, identity theft, reputational harm, and potential legal liabilities. Consequently, it becomes crucial for organizations to adopt proactive measures to safeguard their data and avert any instances of data leakage. These protective measures may involve the implementation of robust security protocols, fostering employee awareness about data protection, vigilant monitoring of data access, and periodic review and enhancement of security measures. By diligently adhering to these practices, organizations can bolster their defenses, mitigate risks, and ensure the integrity and confidentiality of their valuable data.

Organizations need to take steps to prevent intentional data leaks, such as implementing strict access controls, conducting regular security awareness training for employees, and implementing technologies like Data Loss Prevention (DLP) solutions. There are a few techniques used to countermeasure data leakage:

1. **Watermarking** is a technique that can be used to track and identify the source of data leakage. Watermarking involves embedding a unique identifier into a document or piece of data that is not visible to the naked eye but can be detected using specialized software. It can be used in two ways to prevent data leakage:

   - *Deterrence:* By informing users that the document they are accessing is watermarked, they may be deterred from leaking it. Knowing that their actions can be traced back to them can discourage employees or third-party vendors from sharing confidential data.

   - *Detection:* Watermarking can also be used to detect when a document has been leaked. When a watermarked document is leaked, the unique identifier can be used to trace the source of the leak. This can help organizations quickly identify the employee or vendor responsible for the leak and take appropriate action to prevent future leaks.

2. **Fingerprinting** [57] is a technique used in data leakage prevention to detect and prevent the unauthorized transfer of sensitive information outside an organization. It is a content-based method used for detecting data leakage by creating a unique digital signature or "fingerprint" of the data, which can be used to identify and track the data wherever it goes.

To create a fingerprint, software tools analyze the content of the data and generate a mathematical representation of it. This representation can include file size, file type, and unique text strings. Once the fingerprint is created, it can be added to a database and used to monitor the transfer of sensitive data. When a file or document is being transmitted outside the organization, the fingerprinting software can compare the file's digital signature to the database of known fingerprints. If a match is found, it can trigger an alert and prevent data transfer.

Fingerprinting is an effective technique for preventing data leakage because it can detect and prevent the transfer of sensitive information, even if the data is disguised or altered somehow. However, it's important to note that fingerprinting is not foolproof and may only be effective in some situations. Additionally, it's crucial to balance data security with employee privacy concerns, as some individuals could see fingerprinting as intrusive.

3. **Scrambling** is a technique used in countermeasure data leakage to protect sensitive information from being leaked or intercepted by unauthorized parties. In this method, the original data is encrypted using a scrambling algorithm to make it unreadable to anyone who does not have the decryption key. Scrambling involves altering the original data so that it is still useful for analysis and processing but no longer contains identifiable information. This can be done through various methods, such as replacing identifiable data with random values, using encryption or hashing techniques, or substituting certain values with similar but different values. The

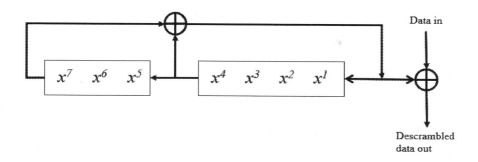

Figure 3.3   Scrambling technique for data leakage.

scrambling algorithm can be a simple substitution cipher or a more complex encryption algorithm, depending on the level of security required.

Scrambling is often used with other data protection measures, such as access controls, authentication, and encryption, to provide a layered approach to data security. By scrambling sensitive data, organizations can ensure that even if the data is intercepted or leaked, it will be of no use to anyone who does not have the decryption key.

There are two types of scrambling techniques:

- Bipolar with 8-zero substitution (B8ZS)
- High-density bipolar3-zero (HDB3)

4. **Interleaving** is used to prevent or reduce the impact of data leakage. Interleaving involves mixing or shuffling the order of data in a way that makes it difficult for someone to reconstruct the original data without knowledge of the interleaving scheme. It can be used in a variety of contexts to prevent data leakage, such as:

- *Communication Systems:* In communication systems, Interleaving can prevent errors caused by bursty noise or interference. By interleaving the transmitted data, the effects of noise or interference can be spread over time, reducing the likelihood of errors.

- *Error Correction:* In error correction codes, Interleaving can improve the error correction performance. By interleaving the data before encoding it with an error correction code, errors that affect adjacent bits are spread out, allowing the error correction code to correct more errors.

5. **Perturbation** as highlighted in previous research, is an additional approach that can effectively mitigate or minimize the detrimental effects of data leakage [58]. This technique involves altering the original data in a manner that renders it challenging for unauthorized individuals to discern the original values or patterns within the data. Perturbation techniques can be applied to diverse categories of sensitive data, including personal information, financial data, and confidential business secrets. By implementing perturbation methods, organizations can enhance the privacy and security of their data, decreasing the risk of unauthorized exposure and preserving the confidentiality of valuable information. It can be used in multiple contexts to prevent data leakage, for example:

   - **Privacy Preservation:** encompasses the utilization of perturbation techniques to safeguard the privacy of sensitive data, all while enabling the extraction of valuable information. By introducing random noise or making slight alterations to the values, the original data can be effectively camouflaged, thereby rendering it arduous for unauthorized individuals to identify sensitive information. This approach strikes a balance between data utility and privacy protection, allowing organizations to extract meaningful insights while ensuring the confidentiality of sensitive data. Perturbation serves as a valuable tool in preserving privacy, fortifying the security of data, and mitigating the risks associated with unauthorized disclosure.

   - **Machine Learning:** In machine learning, perturbation can prevent overfitting, which occurs when a model learns the specific details of the training data and performs poorly on new, unseen data. The model can learn more general patterns by perturbing the training data, improving its performance on new data.

     Machine Learning: Perturbation plays a vital role in machine learning by mitigating overfitting, a phenomenon in which a model excessively focuses on the specific details of the training data, leading to subpar performance on new and unseen data. By applying perturbation to the training data, the model can learn more generalized patterns, enhancing its ability to perform well on new and unseen data. Perturbation acts as a regularization technique, promoting improved generalization and preventing the model from becoming overly specialized to the training set. This approach enhances the model's adaptability and ensures its efficacy in handling diverse and real-world data scenarios.

- **Data Security:** Within the realm of data security, perturbation serves as a valuable tool to uphold the confidentiality of data. By applying perturbation techniques prior to data transmission or storage, the original values or patterns inherent in the data are intentionally altered, rendering it considerably more challenging for unauthorized individuals to discern sensitive information. Perturbation acts as an effective barrier, obscuring the original data and heightening the protection of confidential information against potential threats or unauthorized access. This approach fortifies data confidentiality and bolsters overall data security measures, ensuring the privacy and integrity of critical information.

Data Breach

A data breach occurs when an unauthorized person or group gains access to confidential or sensitive data, such as personal information like names, addresses, social security numbers, credit card numbers, and medical records. Data breaches can happen due to various reasons, including hacking, social engineering, phishing, malware, and physical theft of electronic devices or storage media. Once the data is compromised, it can be used for identity theft, financial fraud, or other malicious activities.

In the context of IoT, data breaches can occur through different impact vectors, with vulnerabilities exploitation in IoT devices being one of the most common issues. IoT devices are often targeted by hackers due to their limited storage capacity and capabilities to take precautionary measures compared to other devices.

The consequences of a data breach can be severe for individuals and organizations. Individuals may face financial losses or damage to their credit scores, while organizations may face legal liabilities, financial penalties, loss of reputation, and decreased customer trust.

To prevent data breaches, organizations must implement robust security measures, such as data encryption, access controls, strong authentication, firewalls, intrusion detection systems, network security, regular software updates and patches, and employee training programs. Individuals can also take steps to protect their personal information, like using strong passwords, avoiding phishing scams, and monitoring their accounts for suspicious activity.

3.2.1 Security in Data-in-Transit

This data type is also addressed as ***data-in-transit*** because it transfers from one end to another across the internet or private network outside the original organization's peripheral. Such movement could get the data exposed to various types of risks and many unpredicted possibilities. This kind of data is vulnerable to attacks as it is less secure than other inactive data, especially network attacks, eavesdropping, ransomware, and data theft, where hackers may intercept data packets along the transmission channel via the internet, causing data breaches. This data's biggest challenge is determining the *threat, likelihood,* or *frequency* of the data at risk, the users who have *rights* to access it, and the *capability* of existing safeguards. More importantly, this kind of data holds the latest updated information, for instance, email, social media updates, new applications, instant messages, WiFi and mobile network, file sharing that is synchronized by collaboration tools or cloud storage, copying a file from local storage to cloud storage, uploading file into cloud storage, sending an email to partner, or even data synchronization with offsite storage. Fig 3.4 shows how email is transit from sender to receiver in the network.

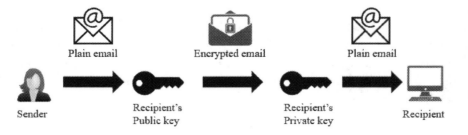

Figure 3.4 Email as one of the Data-in-Transit.

Data protection is required before this data is traveling, while it is traveling, and after receiving it. Therefore, it needs to be remediated by identifying the correct points of the transit and the medium passing by so that the most effective solution can be applied. To remediate data that may expose to the risk of getting attacks, many solutions have been proposed to ensure proactive actions to prevent or avoid security breaches or sensitive data leakage, which often may trigger other severe matters to the organization, such as malfunction of internal operations, financial loses, brand and reputation damage, and losing customer trust. Currently, there are a few renowned security controls applied to protect **data-in-transit** including:

- secured protocol for networking: Transport Layer Security (TLS), Secure Sockets Layer (SSL)

- data encryption mechanisms: Advanced Encryption Standard (AES), Data Encryption Standard (DES), Rivest–Shamir–Adleman (RSA) and Elliptic Curve Cryptography (ECC).

- backup and restore: full backup, incremental backup and differential backup

- antivirus and malware protection

- VPN

- DLP

- Steganography

- hashing: Secure Hash Algorithm (SHA) and Message Digest (MD)

Data protection for **data-in-transit** needs to ensure the endpoints can detect and track any action of an unauthorized copy of file and folder events, for instance, using USB devices and other portable storage devices. The control of user access rights to access the secure encrypted transmission channel also need to be monitored, react promptly for an attempt of access, and suspend a connection once various activities are detected.

The actual cost of a breach is outstanding, especially if it leads to compensation, court cases, and even sanctions and fines resulting from a breach of intellectual property on an organization. The consequences of data loss for **data-in-transit** may severely impact the organization.

Once data breaches or losses are detected in an organization may lead to substantial non-compliance penalties and image and reputation issues due to loss of trust. The hackers may hold for ransom the vast amount of data, and organizations may put halted due to the incidents.

3.2.2 Security of Data-at-Rest

This type of data refers to non-actively moving data or stored in a non-volatile state, for instance, archive data or data stored in the database but was not frequently accessed or referred to. The data stayed stagnantly in the hard disk, flash drive, in a perimeter-based defense such as a firewall, Intrusion Detection/Prevention System (IDS/IPS) and antivirus-protected environment, and not moving across a network or nodes in the web for a while. Security protection is only taken effective if the data remains at the periphery. Sometimes, it poses vulnerabilities whereby users forget the existence of the data and loosen the defense. However, such data are still the target of hackers to steal or ransom for the purpose, although the vulnerability to attacks is relatively low compared with ***data-in-transit***.

Although these files are not transferring over the network, it is still vulnerable to cyber-criminal's attention and being the target of malicious insiders as well because any damage or missing of these data will still affect the company's reputation. The security protection barrier was enlarged during the COVID-19 pandemic whereby many office equipment were taken out the office space to continue the business operation during the movement control. The sudden change of lifestyle of *work from office* to *work from home* was put on a debate where most of the companies were at the state of *somewhat prepared* and *not at all prepared* for such an outbreak. The condition had given them no choice but to put human life at their top priority, and slowly adapt to the change of working environment and then only protect their data from possible cyber attacks.

Data-at-rest requires measures to safeguard the data from unauthorized access, theft, destruction, or alteration while it is stored. Therefore, encryption added another layer to the data to protect stored data that is not moving through networks, notably in cloud backups, where it is always the attackers' target. Access to these data may be restricted by applying the authorization rights to the highest level to ensure the data maintains its confidentiality, integrity, and availability of sensitive or precious information.

3.2.3 Security of Data-in-Use

Data-in-use or data processing is all operational data recently generated, accessed, deleted, appended, or altered regularly in an organization and used by the system, staff, students, vendors, partners and other related parties. These data include weekly log files, daily log files, and event logs, which users actively read, write and execute.

The *data-in-use* must be protected from two primary perspectives. The first is to protect the access control of the data with strict rules. Next is to integrate with some verification process to authenticate a person's identity as they claim they are. The data will only be limited to the "need to have access" condition and not everyone in the organization or even all administrator group members. Therefore, Two-Factor Authentication (2FA) [59,60] or Multiple-Factor Authentication (MFA) shall be applied as an additional layer of security to verify users before they gain access to the data.

organizations must also deploy trace and tracking systems to instantly detect suspicious users and activities. The design should be able to analyze the current condition by referring to the number of attempts gathered while giving recommendations on improving the security in which warning and alert messages are received. This will help the organization diagnose better, understand the environment, and take precautions against any potential threat.

3.2.4 Compliance Standard for Securing Data

Compliance standards for securing data are guidelines, best practices, and regulations that organizations must adhere to ensure the confidentiality, integrity, and availability of sensitive information. Compliance standards are implemented to help protect against data breaches, identity theft, and other forms of cybercrime.

The following are some common compliance standards for securing data:

1. General Data Protection Regulation (GDPR): This directive is applicable to all entities that handle the personal information of individuals within the European Union (EU). Organizations are obligated to adopt suitable technical and organizational safeguards to safeguard personal data, which encompasses implementing measures such as encryption and access controls.

2. Payment Card Industry Data Security Standard (PCI DSS): This set of guidelines is applicable to any organization that accepts

credit card payments. It establishes a framework for ensuring the security of cardholder data, encompassing measures such as maintaining secure networks and systems, encrypting cardholder information, and conducting regular monitoring and testing of security systems. The primary objective of this standard is to mitigate the risk of credit card fraud by delineating specific requirements for merchants and service providers involved in processing, storing, or transmitting credit card data. These requirements also emphasize the necessity of utilizing secure payment channels for transmitting credit card information.

3. Health Insurance Portability and Accountability Act (HIPAA): This regulation applies to healthcare providers, insurance companies, and other entities that handle Protected Health Information (PHI). Organizations must implement physical, technical, and administrative safeguards to protect PHI's privacy, confidentiality, integrity, security and availability [61].

4. ISO 27001: This international standard outlines best practices for Information Security Management Systems (ISMS). It provides a framework for organizations to develop and implement policies and procedures to protect their information assets.

5. Federal Risk and Authorization Management Program (FedRAMP): This program is used by the US government to assess and authorize Cloud Service Providers (CSPs) for use by federal agencies. It requires CSPs to implement stringent security controls and undergo regular security assessments.

6. Graham-Leach-Bliley Act (GLBA): This federal law in the United States mandates that financial institutions prioritize the security and confidentiality of their customers' non-public personal information. Compliance with this law necessitates that financial institutions establish and execute a comprehensive written information security program. This program serves as a blueprint, delineating the necessary procedures and protocols for safeguarding customer information effectively. By adhering to this law, financial institutions demonstrate their commitment to protecting customer data and maintaining robust information security practices.

Adhering to these standards enables organizations to mitigate the potential risks associated with data breaches and adhere to the industry's recommended practices for safeguarding sensitive information. It is crucial to acknowledge, however, that compliance alone does not guarantee absolute security. Therefore, organizations should consistently implement supplementary measures to enhance data protection and augment their overall security posture.

3.2.5   Determining Security Mechanisms

Determining security mechanisms is a critical step in securing any system or network. Security mechanisms are the tools and techniques used to protect against threats and vulnerabilities that may compromise the confidentiality, integrity, and availability of information or resources. Several factors must be considered to determine the appropriate security mechanisms, including the nature of the system, the assets being protected, the level of risk, and the potential impact of a security breach.

One of the primary and foundational steps in establishing effective security measures is to conduct a *risk assessment*. This crucial process involves the identification of potential threats and vulnerabilities, followed by a comprehensive evaluation of the likelihood and potential impact associated with each threat. Additionally, the assessment aims to determine the level of risk posed by each vulnerability. By conducting a thorough risk assessment, organizations can gain valuable insights into the specific areas of their system that require heightened attention and focus. These insights, in turn, guide the selection of appropriate security mechanisms that effectively mitigate the identified risks.

Once the risk assessment is completed, the subsequent step involves *identifying the most suitable security mechanisms* to address and minimize the identified risks. A wide range of security mechanisms are available, including access controls, encryption, firewalls, intrusion detection and prevention systems, antivirus software, and more. The selection of security mechanisms should be based on the risks identified during the risk assessment and the assets that need protection. Careful consideration and alignment between the identified risks and the chosen security mechanisms are crucial in establishing a robust and comprehensive security framework.

Access controls are security mechanisms that control who can access a system or resource and what actions they can perform. Encryption is a mechanism that protects data by converting it into a code that can only be deciphered with a key. Firewalls protect a network by controlling access to and from the web. Intrusion detection and prevention systems monitor network activity and identify and prevent malicious activity.

Antivirus software is a mechanism that protects against malware and other malicious software.

Ensuring the appropriateness of selected security mechanisms for the particular system and assets safeguarded is of utmost importance. Regular testing and evaluation of these mechanisms are necessary to confirm their continued efficacy in providing adequate protection against the identified risks. Furthermore, it is crucial to stay abreast of the latest security threats and trends to ensure that the implemented security measures remain effective in countering new and emerging threats. By staying proactive and up to date, organizations can maintain robust security practices and continuously adapt their security mechanisms to address evolving risks effectively.

3.2.6   Key Mechanisms for Protecting Data

Authentication, access control, and auditing are the key mechanisms for data protection available. Together, the trio form a powerful set of mechanisms for data protection.

- **Authentication:** involves the process of confirming the identity of an individual or system that seeks access to data or a resource. This verification typically relies on credentials, such as a combination of username and password, or more sophisticated techniques like biometric authentication. The purpose of authentication is to establish trust and ensure that only authorized entities are granted access to the desired data or resource. By confirming the identity of users or systems, organizations can uphold security measures and protect sensitive information from unauthorized access.

  Authentication plays a crucial role in safeguarding data and resources by ensuring that only authorized users or systems are granted access. By meticulously verifying the identity of users and systems, organizations fortify their security measures and effectively deter unauthorized access and potential data breaches. This robust authentication process acts as a defensive barrier, preventing malicious actors from compromising sensitive information and upholding the integrity and confidentiality of valuable data assets.

- **Access control:** is the process of determining what level of access a user or system has to a particular resource or set of resources. Access control is often determined by the user's organization role or specific permissions.

Access control serves as a critical mechanism in guaranteeing that users are granted access solely to the data or resources for which they possess authorized permissions. Through the implementation of access control measures, organizations effectively restrict access to data and resources, thereby mitigating the risks associated with accidental or intentional data breaches. This robust control framework enables organizations to maintain the integrity and confidentiality of their valuable information by preventing unauthorized individuals from gaining entry to sensitive data and resources.

- **Auditing:** involves monitoring and recording access to data and resources. This can include logging user activity, access attempts, and data changes.

  Auditing helps to provide a record of who accessed what data when they accessed it, and what changes were made. This can be useful in identifying potential security breaches and compliance purposes, especially for cloud infrastructure, whereby it could ensure the deployment and compliance of cloud strategies in an organization [62].

3.2.7   Data Lineage

Data lineage is the process of tracking and managing the flow of data from its source to its destination throughout its lifecycle. Organizations must understand data lineage to ensure data accuracy, quality, and governance. It provides a comprehensive view of the entire data journey, starting from its origin, transformation, and processing and culminating in its final destination. It involves capturing metadata such as the data source, conversion, storage, and consumption. This information is important for many reasons, such as compliance, quality control, troubleshooting, and data governance. From Fig. 3.5, we can see that the data starts at the source, a database, a file system, or a data lake. From there, it goes through a series of processes or transformations. These transformations could include data cleansing, enrichment, or aggregation. The arrows between each stage represent the data flow, with the arrows pointing from the source to the destination. Each arrow could represent a single data point or a batch of data. Finally, we see the destination: another database, a data warehouse, an analytics platform or even a report. The data lineage diagram helps us understand how data

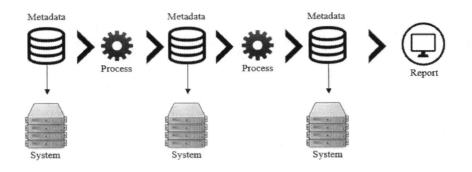

Figure 3.5 Data lineage diagram.

flows through the pipeline and allows us to trace any issues or errors that may occur along the way.

Data lineage helps organizations in several ways, such as:

1. Data Accuracy: Data lineage ensures that data is accurate by tracing the data to its source and tracking any changes made through different systems.

2. Data Quality: Data lineage helps identify the data quality issues by tracking the data movement, transformation, and processing. It allows organizations to pinpoint the cause of any quality issues and address them promptly.

3. Compliance: Data lineage helps organizations comply with data regulations and standards. It allows organizations to trace the data's lineage to ensure it meets regulatory requirements.

4. Data Governance: Data lineage is integral to data governance. It provides transparency and accountability in data management, allowing organizations to ensure data is used ethically and responsibly.

There are several techniques used for capturing data lineage. The choice of technique for capturing data lineage depends on the complexity of the data flow, the resources available, and the level of accuracy required. A combination of techniques may also be necessary to provide a complete picture of data lineage.

1. Manual documentation: manually recording the data lineage information using spreadsheets, documents, and other tools. It is time-consuming and prone to errors.

2. Automated data lineage: using software tools to capture and document the data lineage information automatically. It is efficient and accurate and helps in reducing the risk of errors. However, they can be expensive and require customization to suit specific needs.

3. Metadata extraction: Many data integration tools can automatically extract metadata, such as data sources, transformations, and destinations, to generate a data lineage. This technique is useful for complex data flows, but it can be limited by the capabilities of the tool.

4. Code profiling: This involves analyzing the source code of data integration jobs to identify the data flows. It is useful for custom-built data integration solutions but requires technical expertise and can be time-consuming.

5. Hybrid approach: combines manual documentation with automated data lineage to ensure accuracy and completeness.

6. Reverse engineering: This technique involves analyzing the data in the destination system to trace its lineage back to the source. It can be useful for troubleshooting or validating data, but it can be challenging for complex data flows.

3.2.8 Data Provenance

Data provenance tracks data's origins, ownership, and movement throughout its lifecycle, from creation to deletion. In cybersecurity [63], data provenance is essential to ensuring data integrity, authenticity, and security. By establishing a clear and complete record of a data object's history, organizations can better understand how the data has been used, who has accessed it, and whether it has been modified or tampered with.

Computational accuracy refers to the accuracy of the computational steps taken to produce a particular piece of data. In data provenance, computational accuracy relates to the actions taken to create a specific amount of data. Data provenance is to ensure computational accuracy, it is essential to document the details of the computational steps taken to produce the data, including the specific algorithms and parameters used. This documentation ensures that the computational steps can be reproduced and validated by others, increasing the reliability and trustworthiness of the data.

In the context of security, data provenance can be used to achieve several important goals, including:

1. Data provenance can help **detect and prevent unauthorized changes** to data by providing a complete audit trail of all changes made to the data. By tracking the origin of each shift and the individuals responsible, data provenance can help organizations quickly identify unauthorized modifications and take appropriate action to address the issue.

2. Data provenance can **help forensic analysts trace the source** of a data breach or cyber attack. By tracking the movement of data throughout an organization, data provenance can provide valuable insights into how an attacker may have gained access to sensitive data and what data they may have accessed or modified.

3. Data provenance can help **ensure the quality and accuracy** of data by providing a complete history of the data object. Organizations can ensure that data is of the highest quality and integrity by tracking the data source, any transformations or processing that has occurred, and the individuals responsible for those activities.

4. Data provenance can help organizations **meet regulatory and compliance requirements** by providing a complete record of data usage and access. This can be critical for demonstrating compliance with GDPR, HIPAA, and PCI-DSS regulations.

There are several techniques and tools used in data provenance, including:

1. **Metadata** is data that describes the characteristics and context of a data object, including its origin, content, and usage. Organizations can create a complete record of its history and use it by attaching metadata to a data object.

2. **Digital signatures** can be used to verify the authenticity of a data object and ensure that it has not been tampered with. By attaching a digital signature to a data object, organizations can ensure that any modifications to the data will be detected.

3. **Hashing** is a technique to create a unique digital fingerprint for a data object. By hashing the data and storing the resulting hash value, organizations can ensure that any modifications to the data will be detected.

4. **Provenance capture tools** are software applications that capture and record data provenance information. These tools can automatically capture provenance information during data processing and storage.

Data provenance is an essential aspect of cybersecurity that can help organizations ensure their data's integrity, authenticity, and security. By tracking the origins, ownership, and movement of data throughout its lifecycle, organizations can better understand how it has been used, who has accessed it, and whether it has been modified or tampered with. This can help improve security, enhance forensic analysis, improve data quality, and meet regulatory and compliance requirements. Techniques and tools such as metadata, digital signatures, hashing, and provenance capture tools can capture and record data provenance information.

3.2.9   Managed and Unmanaged Cloud Storage

Cloud storage has become famous for businesses and individuals looking to store and manage their data. Cloud storage offers several advantages over traditional on-premises solutions, including scalability, accessibility, and cost-effectiveness. However, there are two main types of cloud storage: managed and unmanaged, which differ in terms of who is responsible for managing and maintaining the storage infrastructure. This article will explain the differences between managed and unmanaged cloud storage.

Managed Cloud Storage refers to a cloud storage solution fully managed by a service provider. In managed cloud storage, the service provider manages the infrastructure, hardware, and software required to store and manage data. The service provider typically offers various services and features to help users manage their data, such as provisioning, configuring, securing, monitoring, automated backups, replication, and disaster recovery.

Managed cloud storage solutions are typically more expensive than unmanaged solutions, as the service provider is responsible for managing the infrastructure and ensuring the availability and reliability of the service. A few Service Providers (SP) prominent in providing managed services are Google Cloud, Amazon Web Services, Oracle, etc. However, managed cloud storage solutions offer several advantages, including:

1. Easy to use: Managed cloud storage solutions are typically easy to use and require minimal setup and configuration. Users can sign up for the service, create an account, and start storing data.

2. High availability: Managed cloud storage solutions are designed to be highly available, with redundant hardware and software systems to ensure that data is always available.

3. Scalability: Managed cloud storage solutions generally exhibit remarkable scalability, enabling users to effortlessly adjust their storage capacity according to their specific requirements. This inherent scalability feature empowers organizations to easily and flexibly expand or reduce their storage capabilities as the need arises, ensuring optimal resource allocation and efficient management of storage needs.

4. Security: Managed cloud storage solutions commonly offer cutting-edge security functionalities, such as encryption and access controls, to safeguard data against unauthorized access. These advanced security features are designed to fortify the protection of data, ensuring that only authorized individuals or systems can access and interact with the stored information.

Such services allow users to tap into the 'cloud' concept, where they can choose packages, services, or IT functions according to their needs on a Pay-as-You-Go (PAYG) basis. NIST [64] defined cloud computing or simply just *cloud*, as a model that *able is to provide ubiquitous, on-demand, convenient to a shared pool of resources (e.g., services, rack space, computing power, storage, and networks) that can be provisioned on a self-service basis*. A cloud service has to meet five essential characteristics: rapid provisioning, resource pooling, on-demand services, measured service, and broad network access.

There are three basic service models [65–68].

1. Infrastructure-as-a-Service (IaaS) is a cloud computing service that provides virtualized computing resources over the internet. It allows organizations to rent and manage computing resources, such as servers, storage, and networking, from a cloud service provider instead of owning and maintaining physical hardware.

Figure 3.6   Cloud characteristics.

With IaaS, customers can access a wide range of quickly provisioned and scaled computing resources to meet their needs. This enables organizations to avoid the upfront costs and ongoing maintenance associated with physical infrastructure while still being able to customize and manage their computing resources as if running on their hardware. Some examples of IaaS providers include Amazon Web Services (AWS), Microsoft Azure, and Google Cloud Platform. These providers offer various services and pricing options to meet the needs of different organizations, from small startups to large enterprises.

2. Platform-as-a-Service (PaaS) is a cloud computing service model that provides a platform and environment for developers to build, run, and manage their applications over the internet.

In contrast to IaaS, which provides virtualized computing resources, PaaS offers a higher level of abstraction and focuses on providing developers with a complete software development environment, including tools, libraries, frameworks, and runtime environments for developing, testing, deploying, and scaling applications. PaaS empowers developers to construct and launch applications without the burden of managing the underlying infrastructure, including servers, storage, and networking components. This liberates developers to concentrate on coding and creating inventive applications, while the PaaS provider assumes responsibility for the underlying infrastructure and associated tasks. These responsibilities encompass essential activities such as patching, updates, and security measures, allowing developers to offload these operational concerns and dedicate their efforts towards driving innovation and delivering high-quality applications.

Various PaaS (Platform as a Service) providers, such as Heroku, Google App Engine, and Microsoft Azure App Service, exemplify the range of options available in the market. These providers offer diverse services and pricing models tailored to cater to the requirements of developers and organizations, spanning from fledgling startups to expansive enterprises. Each PaaS provider brings its unique set of offerings, enabling users to select the platform that best aligns with their specific needs and objectives.

3. Software-as-a-Service (SaaS) refers to a software distribution model where an application is hosted by a provider and made accessible to customers via the internet. In contrast to traditional methods of software installation on individual computers or servers, customers can conveniently access the software through a web browser or a mobile application. This cloud-based approach eliminates the need for local installations and allows users to leverage the software's functionalities directly through their preferred online platform.

In a SaaS model, customers typically pay a subscription fee on a monthly or annual basis to use the software rather than purchasing and installing it outright. The provider is responsible for maintaining and updating the software and providing technical support to customers.

SaaS is a popular model for delivering a wide range of software applications, including Customer Relationship Management (CRM), Enterprise Resource Planning (ERP), Human Resources (HR) management, and productivity tools like word processing and project management. SaaS has become increasingly popular in recent years due to its cost-effectiveness, scalability, and flexibility.

Unmanaged Cloud Storage refers to a cloud storage solution not managed by a service provider. In unmanaged cloud storage, users manage their storage infrastructure and data. This includes setting up and configuring the hardware and software required to store and manage data and implementing backups, replication, and disaster recovery solutions.

Unmanaged cloud storage solutions are typically less expensive than managed solutions, as users are responsible for managing their infrastructure, as well as configuring, securing, monitoring, and backing up the storage. However, unmanaged cloud storage solutions require more technical expertise and effort to set up and manage. It is a service where the users are responsible for managing and maintaining the storage infrastructure. Some advantages of unmanaged cloud storage solutions include the following:

1. **Customizability** Unmanaged cloud storage solutions offer more incredible customizability and control over the storage infrastructure and data.

2. **Cost-effective** Unmanaged cloud storage solutions can be more cost-effective than managed solutions, especially for organizations with the technical expertise to manage their storage infrastructure.

3. **Flexibility** Unmanaged cloud storage solutions are typically more flexible, allowing users to customize and configure their storage infrastructure to meet their needs.

4. **Choice of storage provider** With unmanaged cloud storage solutions, users can choose their storage provider and customize their storage infrastructure as needed.

Both managed and unmanaged cloud storage solutions offer advantages and disadvantages, depending on the specific needs and requirements of the organization. Managed cloud storage solutions are typically easier to use, more highly available, secure, and expensive. Unmanaged cloud storage solutions are typically more customizable, cost-effective, and flexible but require more technical expertise to set up and manage. Organizations should carefully evaluate their needs and requirements before choosing a cloud storage solution and consider factors such as ease of use, scalability, security, cost, and customization options.

3.2.10 Compliance Standards and Guidance

Data compliance refers to best practices, acts, standards, rules, and regulations that an organization must follow and put into practice to deliver the best for the organization to keep data secure and compassionate data, and prevent data loss, theft, and misconduct. These data compliance rules and regulations encompass different countries, regions, and industries. Ultimately, this legislative purpose is to protect consumers and residents by looking after their own mandated data.

A. International Standards

There are a few international standards that provide guidelines and techniques to demonstrate and explain how data privacy should be preserved by using available identity management techniques for the enterprise. A list of frameworks is being proposed to assist companies in getting certified with the identity-related components of the documents to gain customer trust and confidence in the services provided. A few of the published standards are as below:

1. ISO/IEC 24760-1:2019/Amd 1:2023 IT Security and Privacy – A framework for identity management – Part 1: Terminology and concepts – Amendment 1

2. ISO/IEC DIS 24760-2 IT Security and Privacy – A framework for identity management – Part 2: Reference architecture and requirements [Under development]

3. ISO/IEC TS 29003:2018 Information technology – Security techniques – Identity proofing

4. ISO/IEC WD 24760-4 IT Security and Privacy – A framework for identity management – Part 4: Authenticators, Credentials and Authentication [Under development]

5. ISO/IEC 24760-3:2016 Information technology – Security techniques – A framework for identity management – Part 3: Practice

6. ISO/IEC 24760-2:2015 Information technology – Security techniques – A framework for identity management – Part 2: Reference architecture and requirements

7. ISO/IEC 24760-1:2019 IT Security and Privacy – A framework for identity management – Part 1: Terminology and concepts

8. ISO/IEC 23220-1 Card and security devices for personal identification – Building blocks for identity management via mobile devices – Part 1: Generic system architectures of mobile eID systems [Under development]

9. ISO/IEC 24760-3:2016/Amd 1 Information technology – Security techniques – A framework for identity management – Part 3: Practice – Amendment 1: Identity Information Lifecycle processes [Under development]

10. ISO/TR 23249:2022 Blockchain and distributed ledger technologies – Overview of existing DLT systems for identity management

11. ISO/IEC TR 29144:2014 Information technology – Biometrics – The use of biometric technology in commercial Identity Management applications and processes

12. ISO/IEC AWI TS 23220-2 Cards and security devices for personal identification – Building blocks for identity management via mobile devices – Part 2: Data objects and encoding rules for generic eID systems [Under development]

13. ISO/IEC TS 29003:2018 Information technology – Security techniques – Identity proofing

B. National Institute of Standards and Technology

National Cybersecurity of Excellence under the purview of NIST also released a few publications on digital identity best practices and guidelines to accommodate the ever-changing digital era to reduce risk and security concerns related to digital identity.

1. NIST SP 800-63, Digital Identity Guidelines [Under review]

2. Digital Identity Guidelines: Authentication and Lifecycle Management

3. Securely Connecting the World with Cybersecurity Standards

4. A Taxonomic Approach to Understanding Emerging Blockchain Identity Management Systems

5. Derived Personal Identity Verification (PIV) Credentials

6. Identifying Public Safety's Security Requirements for Mobile Apps

C. National Acts

Several laws and regulations have captured the urgency of establishing models in data handling. Nevertheless, a few of these regulations contain specific target groups such as children, healthcare, or the financial industry, which require special safeguards and measurements.

D. General List

1. United States: Children's Online Privacy Protection Act (COPPA)

2. European Union – GDPR: General Data Protection Regulation, 2016

3. China – CL: Cyber Law, 2016

4. China – Personal Information Security Specification (PISS), 2017

5. Japan – Act on the Protection of Personal Information (APPI), 2017

6. Brazil – General Data Protection Law (GPDL), 2018

7. United States – CCPA: California Consumer Privacy Act, 2020

8. Canada – Canada Privacy Protection Act (CPPA), 2020

9. China – Civil Code: Book IV Personality Rights, 2020

10. China – Personal Information Protection Law (PIPL), 2021

11. China – Data Security Law (DSL), 2021

12. United States: Virginia Consumer Data Protection Act (CDPA), 2023

E. Specific List

1. Health Insurance Portability and Accountability Act (HIPAA)

2. Payment Card Industry Data Security Standard (PCI DSS)

3. Graham-Leach-Bliley Act (GLBA)

4. Federal Trade Commission (FTC)

3.3   IDENTITY AND ACCESS MANAGEMENT

Identity Management (IdM), Identity and Access Management (IAM), or Identity Access Management (IdAM) are used interchangeably. IAM refers to the framework enterprises adopt in their business process to recognize users, protect their identity from dispute, and, most importantly, grant permissions to access services [69]. SP such as Google, Facebook, Microsoft, and LinkedIn, or organizations like companies, universities, and insurance companies to grant permission for accessing different services or modules using IAM based on other attributes carried by the user - roles, responsibilities, subscriptions, and credentials [70]. IAM is not a new concept, but a framework believed to have been introduced to the world since the first computer system was introduced. The aim was to authenticate and authorize user access to storage, design, application, or data. It has evolved significantly recently to meet the transformation based on the derived digital requirements. The IdM model, starting as a centralized and isolated IdM to federated IdM, and the latest trend is Distributed Identity (DI), which is a hype in the digital world.

Large enterprises like universities, multinational enterprises, oil and gas companies, and government agencies provide secured tunneling for remote employees to access the company's internet network and systems using VPN. Usually, usernames and passwords are used as an identifier to allow access to the company's communication platform, such as email, storage, collaborative application, sensitive files, and information, which is only available for staff with the proper credentials.

IAM is critically important in the digital realm for various reasons. As organizations increasingly rely on digital technologies [71], effective IAM becomes essential for ensuring security, privacy, and regulatory compliance. Here are some of the key reasons why IAM is important:

1. Security: IAM helps protect sensitive data and digital assets by controlling who has access to them, and under what conditions. This minimizes the risk of unauthorized access, data breaches, and other security incidents.

2. Authentication and Authorization: IAM provides mechanisms for verifying the identity of users (authentication) and determining what they are allowed to do within the system (authorization). This ensures that only authorized individuals can access specific resources and perform certain actions.

3. Access control: IAM empowers organizations to establish and enforce precise access control policies, considering user roles,

responsibilities, and additional attributes. By implementing IAM, organizations can ensure that users are granted access to the resources essential for their job functions. This meticulous control over access privileges helps mitigate the risk of insider threats, as users are restricted from accessing resources beyond their operational requirements. IAM is vital in maintaining the integrity and security of organizational systems and data by minimizing unauthorized access and potential internal risks.

4. Auditing and Compliance: IAM solutions can help organizations monitor and track user activities, which can be invaluable for meeting regulatory requirements, conducting internal audits, and investigating security incidents.

5. Productivity and User Experience: By streamlining the process of granting and managing access to resources, IAM can improve the overall user experience and increase productivity. For example, Single Sign-On (SSO) allows users to authenticate once and access multiple applications, reducing the need to remember multiple usernames and passwords.

6. Scalability: As organizations grow and evolve, IAM solutions can help manage increasing numbers of users, devices, and applications, ensuring that access control remains consistent and manageable.

3.3.1   IAM in Networks

Several unique challenges are associated with IAM for networks [72]. Some of these challenges include:

1. Complexity of network infrastructure: Network infrastructure can be complex, with multiple devices and endpoints, different operating systems and platforms, and various levels of access required for other users. Managing and securing access to these resources can be challenging, especially in large and distributed networks.

2. Lack of visibility: As networks grow larger and more complex, it can become challenging to maintain visibility into all the devices, endpoints, and users accessing network resources. Proper visibility makes identifying potential security threats easier and ensures access controls are adequately enforced.

3. Dynamic environments: Network environments constantly change, with new devices, applications, and users being added and removed regularly. This can make it challenging to track who has access to what resources and ensure that access controls are being correctly updated and enforced.

4. User behavior: IAM for networks can be complicated because users are only sometimes predictable. For example, users may share login credentials, use weak passwords, or try to circumvent access controls to access resources they shouldn't have access to.

5. Compliance: Different area has different regulations and industry standards, such as HIPAA, GDPR, and PCI·DSS, which require significant effort to plan, deploy and maintain quality [61].

6. Integration with other systems: IAM for networks may need to be integrated with other methods, such as identity providers or Security Information and Event Management (SIEM) systems. Ensuring these integrations work seamlessly can be challenging, mainly if different systems use different protocols and formats for exchanging data.

Identity theft is a grave form of cybercrime that revolves around the illicit acquisition of an individual's personal information, including their name, social security number, credit card particulars, or login credentials, with the intention of perpetrating fraudulent activities. In the realm of network IAM, identity theft can transpire when an attacker successfully obtains a user's login credentials through various malicious techniques such as phishing attacks, keylogging malware, or similar means. Subsequently, the attacker utilizes these stolen credentials to assume the identity of the legitimate user, thereby gaining unauthorized access to the network or system. This unauthorized access poses significant risks, potentially leading to data breaches, unauthorized data manipulation, or other malicious activities that can inflict substantial harm to individuals and organizations alike.

Once an attacker gains access to a network or system using stolen credentials, they can perform various malicious activities, such as stealing sensitive data, manipulating or deleting data, or launching further attacks on other systems within the network. Identity theft can be particularly devastating in the context of IAM. It can compromise the entire system and allow an attacker to access multiple accounts and resources with a single set of stolen credentials.

Organizations can adopt diverse security measures to prevent identity theft in network IAM. These measures include implementing stringent password policies, enabling two-factor authentication, monitoring user activity for any unusual behavior, and implementing role-based access control. These measures collectively ensure that users are granted access solely to the resources necessary for their job functions, thereby minimizing the risk of unauthorized access and potential identity theft incidents [73]. Additionally, user education and awareness training can help users identify and avoid phishing attacks and other tactics attackers use to steal login credentials. Regular security audits and assessments can also help identify and mitigate vulnerabilities that attackers may exploit to steal credentials and compromise network security.

3.3.2 Concept of IAM

IAM, based on the specific identities of individuals or entities, plays a pivotal role in managing and governing access to critical resources, including systems, applications, data, and physical spaces. By accurately controlling access privileges, IAM aims to thwart unauthorized users from gaining entry to these resources, while simultaneously guaranteeing that only authorized individuals or organizations possess the necessary access rights. Through this meticulous access management framework, IAM acts as a formidable safeguard, preserving the integrity, confidentiality, and availability of essential resources, and reinforcing the overall security posture of the organization.

IAM involves several key components and processes, including:

1. **Identity management** This involves creating, managing, and maintaining digital identities for users or entities that need access to resources. This includes defining and assigning user roles, permissions, and access controls.

2. **Access management** This involves controlling access to resources based on user identity and monitoring and managing access to ensure it remains appropriate over time. Access management involves managing user authentication and authorization and enforcing policies on accessing and using resources.

3. **Authentication and authorization** Authentication is verifying a user's identity, usually through a combination of a username and password or other authentication factors such as biometrics,

smart cards, or tokens. Authorization involves determining what resources a user can access based on their identity and the policies and rules defined for that resource.

4. **Privileged access management** This involves controlling access to privileged accounts that can change or access sensitive information, such as administrator accounts. This is especially important for preventing unauthorized access and for ensuring accountability in case of a security incident.

5. **User provisioning and de-provisioning** User provisioning creates, updates, and disables user accounts. In contrast, de-provisioning removes access to resources when a user no longer needs them. This is critical for ensuring access remains appropriate and only authorized users can access help.

IAM is important for organizations to ensure security and compliance while enabling users to access the resources they need to do their jobs. By implementing effective IAM practices, organizations can improve their security posture, reduce the risk of unauthorized access, and simplify the management of access to resources [74]. Additionally, IAM solutions can help organizations comply with regulatory requirements such as HIPAA, PCI-DSS, and GDPR.

3.3.3 Terms in IAM

IAM refers to managing digital identities and controlling access to resources in a computing environment, allowing organizations to manage who has access to their systems and data. IAM involves creating and managing user accounts and the access privileges associated with those accounts. This includes determining who has access to what data or systems, setting permissions and policies, and enforcing security protocols to ensure that only authorized users can access sensitive information. To fully understand IAM, familiarity with the various terms used in the field is important. This article will provide an overview of the key terms used in Identity and Access Management.

Identity is a digital representation of an individual or entity used to manage access to resources and systems. Identity is a critical component of IAM, as it is used to authenticate and authorize users.

Authentication is verifying the identity of a user, system, or application. This can be done through various means, such as passwords, biometric scans, or smart cards. Authentication aims to ensure that only authorized users can access resources.

Authorization is the process of determining what resources an authenticated user can access. This is typically done through role-based access control, where users are assigned roles based on their job functions or responsibilities.

SSO is a feature of IAM solutions that allows users to access multiple systems and applications thanks to the SSO capability of IAM solutions. Users' authentication procedures are made easier, and by not having to remember as many passwords, security may be increased.

Federated identity is a way of sharing identity information between organizations. This allows users to access resources in other organizations using their own identities [75]. This can be useful for organizations that collaborate with partners or customers. The federated identity on confidentiality as third parties should have no access permission to read plaintext. It is a single set of digital credentials to access multiple online services across different organizations and countries. It involves creating a trusted network of identity providers, such as government agencies or financial institutions, for instance, the Estonian Government using eID systems to verify a user's identity and provide access to relevant services. The federated identity simplifies and secures online transactions while ensuring user privacy and control over personal data. It is integral to the European Union's efforts to create a more unified and secure digital single market.

Privileged Access Management (PAM) refers to the set of practices, technologies, and policies used to control, monitor, and audit access to sensitive resources and information within an organization. In particular, PAM is concerned with managing and securing the access privileges of privileged users, such as system administrators, network engineers, and other personnel with elevated levels of access to critical systems and data. It typically involves using specialized software tools and platforms that provide a range of capabilities, including password management, access control, session monitoring and recording, and reporting and analysis.

Directory Services store and manage identity information. This includes user accounts, group memberships, and access permissions. Popular directory services include Active Directory and LDAP.

MFA enhances the security of resource access by requiring users to provide multiple forms of identification. This multifaceted approach encompasses various factors, including something the user physically does (such as a biometric scan), something they possess (like a smart card or a unique token), or something they are knowledgeable about (like a password or a PIN).

Attribute-based Access Control (ABAC) is a method of authorization that uses attributes to determine access. Attributes can include information about the user (such as job function or location), the resource being accessed, and the environment in which the access occurs.

PAM is a subset of IAM that focuses on managing access to privileged accounts. This includes accounts that have administrative access to systems or applications. PAM solutions ensure that only authorized users can access these accounts.

User Provisioning is creating and managing user accounts. This includes creating new accounts, modifying existing accounts, and deleting them when no longer needed. User provisioning is a critical component of IAM, ensuring only authorized users can access resources.

IAM is a complex and ever-evolving field that requires a solid understanding of the various terms and concepts used. By becoming familiar with the terms and concepts outlined in this article, organizations can improve their IAM practices and ensure that only authorized users can access their systems and data.

3.3.4 Design Access Management

Access management is critical to any design process, particularly in the digital realm. It refers to controlling access to resources, information, and systems within an organization to ensure that only authorized individuals are allowed access.

In a design context, access management controls access to design assets, including designs, prototypes, and other materials. This is important because design assets often contain sensitive information, such as proprietary intellectual property, that unauthorized individuals could misuse or leak. There are several components of access management that designers should be familiar with. These include authentication, authorization, and auditing.

Authentication is the process of verifying the identity of a user. This can be done through various means, such as passwords, biometric data, or two-factor authentication. By ensuring that only authorized users can access design assets, authentication helps to prevent data breaches and other security incidents. Authentication is vital in preserving personal privacy information, especially in healthcare and finance institutions. It is also critical to authenticate users from outsiders to gain access to the cloud resources (e.g., compute, network, and storage).

While *Authorization* determines what resources a user can access. This involves defining user roles and permissions, which can be assigned based on factors such as job function, seniority, or project involvement. By limiting access to only the resources that users need to do their jobs, authorization helps to reduce the risk of accidental or intentional data breaches. Authorization determines an account's boundaries on what a user can access and use.

Auditing tracks and logs access to design assets. This helps to ensure accountability and transparency, as well as to identify any unauthorized access attempts. Auditing also helps designers track changes to design assets and ensure they are used appropriately.

Effective access management requires a combination of technical controls, such as password policies and access controls, as well as organizational policies and procedures. Designers should work closely with their organization's IT and security teams to ensure access management policies and practices are in place and followed.

In addition to protecting sensitive information, access management can help improve collaboration and productivity within design teams. By ensuring that only authorized team members can access design assets, designers can work more efficiently and securely without worrying about unauthorized access or data leaks.

Access management is an essential aspect of design security and should be a top priority for all designers. By implementing strong authentication, authorization, and auditing practices, designers can protect sensitive design assets and ensure they are used appropriately.

3.3.5 Create Strong Authentication

The three fundamental functions of IAM are authentication, authorization, and auditing. *Authentication* was defined as a process that can affirm the source and the integrity of the exchange or store information or the person responsible for the process [76] via a claimed identity, which is a valid credential. Two parties are involved, the principal, who act as the claimant, and a verifier, who is the source of information [77].

Other than that, using retina or iris scans is getting popular for enterprises, especially in handling high-sensitivity documents—such as inherent authentication factors. When systems can effectively identify users based on their biometrics data, inherent can be one of the most secure authentication factors. Despite the fact that the biometrics method is helpful for the identification and authentication of users, the scheme is not suitable for CPS for a few reason [78]:

1. CPS is a machine-to-machine network, and each device communicates with each other in multiple interactions seamlessly without human intervention.

2. Biometrics authentication requires additional components and software to support identification. Herefore, it is hard to complete the identification process in resource-constrained devices.

3. The number of portable devices increased tremendously, making consolidating devices with biometrics harder.

The fundamental of authentication mechanisms can be classified into three main categories. In general, the authentication mechanism refers to *"Something you have"* [79] to claim who you are by showing one or more of the following evidence:

1. ***Knowledge-based authentication*** refers to the pairing of username and password where it is the most commonly seen authentication mechanism, also known as **information** or **password authentication**. By providing the exact matched of information, the system will compare the hash value of the data inserted by the user with the previously stored data in the internal repository. Once verified, handshaking between the SP and the User will be established, and access to the account will soon be granted.

   The username is mostly public, but the password should be confidential and well-protected from exposure to the public. Because it is easy to implement, someone may have or steal the information and could impersonate you and grant access to the system. Some password attacks can be listed in Fig. 3.7. The ultimate goal is to obtain a user's password and gain access to the system or network without the consent or knowledge of the authorized user. Password attacks can be performed in various ways, such as:

   (a) Brute force attack: With this technique, an attacker attempts each and every conceivable character combination in search of the right password. If the password is weak, this method can be time- and resource-consuming yet is often successful.

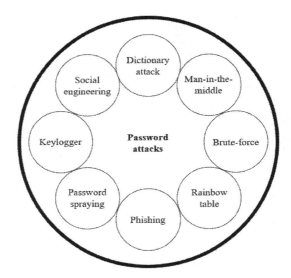

Figure 3.7 Possible password attacks.

(b) Dictionary attack: In this method, attackers try to guess the password using a pre-built list of widely used words, phrases, or passwords. If the password is a well-known word or phrase, this method may be quicker than a brute force attack and more effective.

(c) Phishing: Phishing attacks involve tricking users into giving away their passwords by sending them fraudulent emails or links that appear legitimate.

(d) Social engineering: In this method, attackers use psychological manipulation to obtain user passwords. For example, they may trick a user into revealing their password by posing as a legitimate authority figure or using other methods of deception.

Password attacks can be used for malicious purposes, such as stealing personal information, accessing sensitive data, or gaining unauthorized access to computer systems. Using strong passwords and protecting them appropriately is essential to prevent password attacks. Therefore, password policies and password strength should be enforced. A strong password with high complexity is necessary to ensure it is impossible to guess, either using a dictionary attack or a brute attack.

This method would require a user to show the SP that *"Something you know"* [80] about the service they are trying to access. Typically, it refers to a series of code (numeric) or Personal Identification Numbers (PIN), a pattern, an answer to a secret question, or a password that the user pre-set during registration, all named as memorized secret authenticator [81]. However, due to different deployment standards, users must maintain multiple IdM systems with multiple identities to manage for other purposes. Soon, users must face password fatigue due to too many usernames and passwords to maintain.

2. ***Possession-based authentication*** or **device** is another way to authenticate users. By sending a text message to the phone or by phone call to verify user identification, which acts similarly to key cards where only authentic users will have the credentials to enter the building or perform an activity.

   Two common types of tokens are available in the market. The first type is using ***hard tokens*** which can be a device which is physically connected, for example, a dongle, a Bluetooth tokens, a USB tokens, or a smart card, to conduct and run the authentication process. There is a screen to authenticate a user via secure PIN, fingerprints [82], cryptographic key or biometric data [83]. These codes could have expiration times or only use-once tokens to avoid brute force guessing.

   Another type of token is ***soft tokens*** where no physical tokens are needed but just a piece of code to be stored on electronic devices, for example, a desktop, laptop, or mobile phone.

3. ***Inherent-based authentication*** or **factor recognition**, or user authentication credentials that are integral to an individual. It is unique to the user and in the form of biometric data. The most popular methods available to answer *"something you are* are" fingerprints, thumbprints, vein, retina, iris, and palm or hand prints. Other options for authentication methods are voice, speech, and facial recognition, which have gained popularity since the pandemic for contactless access (Fig. 3.8).

Nevertheless, face recognition, iris and fingerprint are among the most usable modalities found in common for authentication. However, NIST pointed out a few considerations that may affect the accuracy of the biometric activation [81].

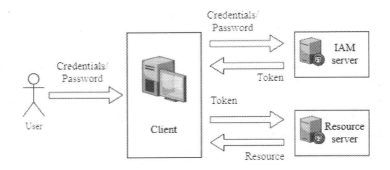

Figure 3.8   Token-based authentication.

1. user needs to remember which finger or wearing any artefacts or mask during enrolment.

2. fingerprint capture for certain people may be impossible due to the quality degraded after the user is exposed to some chemical.

3. eyes color when wearing colored contact lenses, different levels of brightness or sickness, which may result in recognition difficulties.

OAuth, OpenID Connect and Security Assertion Markup Language (SAML) [84] are three common mechanisms responsible for user authentication and authorization to reduce security breaches like data leaks, identity theft, information breaches, and other security problems related to web application security [85]. OpenID Connect is built atop OAuth to complement OAuth, which use for authorization, by addressing the lack of an authentication mechanism, especially in handling sensitive information. However, all these three protocols are incompatible with each other.

OAuth or Open Authentication [86] is not an authentication protocol but rather an authorization framework for the authentication of digital assets. An application can take access on behalf of a user after getting approval from the user without them sharing their credentials. The IdP will issue tokens to third-party applications automatically once the user grant permission to agree to let them take access to resources from the server on behalf of the user, for example, contacts. It appears in two versions and provides secure delegated access. Comparatively, OAuth 1.0 and other existing protocols, such as Microsoft Live ID and OpenID, are not web-based. OAuth 1.0 doesn't isolate the role of the resource server and authentication server. Therefore, OAuth 2.0 has better security separation regarding roles and user experience. It is widely used on the internet today and consists of four roles: client, resource server, authentication server, and resource owner.

Let's use the example of Alice, who is trying to access Yelp using her Google account, to explain the following terminologies.

- **Resource Server** is the API or the system that holds the resources (actions or data) owned by *Resource Owner* (Alice) that the *Client* (Yelp) wants to get, which is the Google contacts API. The server will only allow a client to use Alice's data if Alice approves it. However, a client can prove to *Resource Server* that Alice's approval has also been obtained from the Authorization server.

- **Authorization Server** is the system, in this case, accounts.google.com, where Alice could log in to access her Google account and click 'Yes' to grant permission for Yelp to get her Google contacts. The server provides Yelp with a way to prove that Alice approved it to work with her data. This is also called the Google contacts API. When the *Authorization Server* gives access to a client on behalf of *Resource Owner*, a token will be issued, which is needed to show to *Resource Server* as a prove. Sometimes, *Authorization Server* and *Resource Server* are on the same machine.

- **Client** refers to the application, which can be an app or a web application. In this case, Yelp is the client who wants to get Alice's contact.

- **Resource Owner** refers to the party who owns the data and has the authority to grant access to a resource. For example, Alice is the resource owner with the right to click to allow Yelp to access her contacts in her Google account upon request by the application. A *Resource Owner* uses a username and password to identify themselves.

Single Sign-On [87, 88] was introduced to solve problems mostly related to the increasing numbers of credentials in our daily activities. The idea behind SSO was to reduce the hectic of remembering too many usernames/passwords as the applications increased, which resulted in

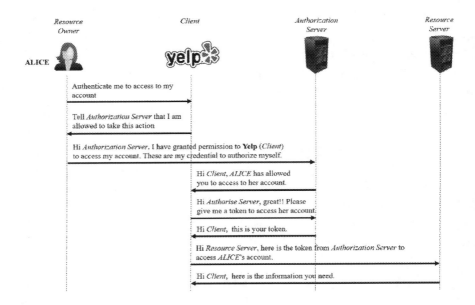

Figure 3.9 OAuth 2.0 Permission Graph.

losing or forgetting, especially with the enforcement of password policy: password should be changed every 90 days, each password should not be reused, a password must consist of at least eight characters and with combinations of numbers, letters and symbols – such policies irritating users, especially if forcing users to change passwords too often. Hence, the OAuth-based SSO system was designed and applied widely in large enterprises like Google, Microsoft, and Meta (Facebook) to take down problems due to massive numbers of web users [89–91]. They also function as SSO IdP for other websites by providing identity services to other applications.

OpenID Connect [92] is another open standard organizations use to authenticate users using IdP, such as Google or Facebook. It is a decentralized authentication protocol that eliminates the organization's webmaster to prepare their login system but gets users to authenticate using a relying party. It is also convenient and easy management for the user as they can create multiple accounts without having to create a username and password for each separately, but rather all via one single relying on IdP. OpenID Connect filled up some gaps or weaknesses that

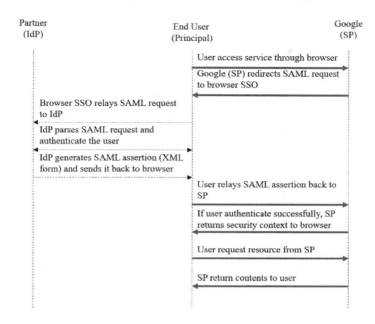

Figure 3.10 SAML authentication.

OAuth has in dealing with authentication, where it seems low on some details requiring a dedicated solution.

Security Assertion Markup Language [93] is an open standard for authentication and authorization between two parties. It is an XML-based markup language that acts between SPs and Identity Providers (IdPs) for security by verifying user identity and permissions before they are granted or denied their attempts to access the services. It is commonly applied to a corporate working environment where Human Resource Department or employer-enabled staff can log in to their intranet and access numerous services, for instance, Salesforce, SharePoint, Exchange server, cloud storage or communication platform, without having to key in your credentials every time trying to access. *Service Provider* is the party that will trust IdP as the authentication party and grant permission to the user to obtain the services once IdP verifies the identity of the user. *Identity Provider* is the party to perform authentication upon user request to access services provided by SP. IdP parses the user's credentials to SP with authorization level.

Passwordless is a method to authenticate users with email addresses or mobile phone numbers [94, 95]. The idea is to simplify the

Table 3.1 SAML, OAuth, and OpenID Connect Comparison

	SAML 2.0	**OAuth 2.0**	**OpenID Connect**
Founder	OASIS 2001	Google 2010	OpenID Foundation 2005
Category	Open	Open	Open
Client type	Web based	Web based	Web based
Scenario	SSO for enterprises	API authorization	End user apps
Supporting	XML, HTTP, SOAP and any protocol that using XML	HTTP	HTTP, XRDS
Tokens	SAML assertion	Access tokens (RFC6750)	Id token - JSON web token (JWT)
Type	Federated identity	Federated identity	Federated identity
Format	XML	JSON	JSON
Usage	Authorization and authentication - allow user from a corporate or partner to access intranet or services using SSO	Authorization - provide temporary resource access to 3rd-party apps on behalf of user	Authentication - to authenticate user for a web or apps without need to create a new account

authentication process and improve user experience by associating with the user's familiar attributes. Users also do not need to memorize many passwords, which portrays a considerable vulnerability, for instance, reuse, weak, or password sharing. Research has shown that user gets frustrated when the frequency of authentication increases. Without using a password, FIDOv2's (Fast IDentity Online v2) open authentication protocol may confirm a user's identity. Fig. 3.11 shows the significance of user responses relative to the level of authentication. Enterprises also may reduce investment in password policy and establish a team to implement and monitor complex password policies such as password length, expiration, salting, and hashing to store in the database, and procedures to prevent password theft [96].

2FA and MFA are security measures to protect user accounts and data from unauthorized access. However, there are differences between the two that are important to understand.

3.3.5.1 Two-factor authentication

While the basic authentication using a username and password form refers to single-factor authentication, another method to deploy a two-factor password is called 2FA [97]. The idea of 2FA implementation

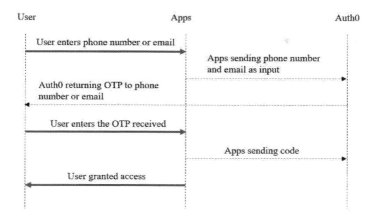

Figure 3.11   Passwordless authentication.

was to improve online internet security and address the lack of conventional authentication protocol using usernames and passwords. Individuals, governmental agencies, and companies are among the common target of malicious attackers to gain access and increase the risk of web security, such as data breaches, website defacement, system down, virus attacks, and being phished. There is a requirement for a web portal to add another layer of security to minimize the attack by associating it with passwords. By establishing a distinct form of additional identification, accessing something becomes harder. This is to avoid attacks from the attacker and cause disruption to the system by adding another factor (or evidence) as an authentication program. 2FA is a mechanism to prevent hackers from taking over an account if they can guess the password correctly and grant access to the report [98,99]. Still, the additional credential layer could keep your account safe and protect personal information from being disclosed. Somebody can steal the combination of username-password, but the second factor adds a layer of security beyond a password that will keep the data safe as they will need to pass through another layer of the verification process, making it more difficult for an attacker to gain access to an account. Online banking usually uses 2FA, apart from email accounts and other sensitive applications.

There are a few methods to deploy for 2FA by using a combination of any two of below [81]:

- something that you know (*knowledge-based authentication*): the password or PIN created by you during registration, verification

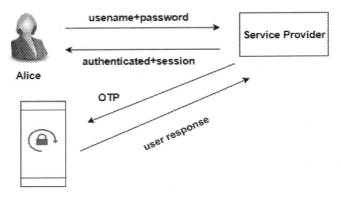

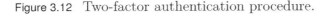

Figure 3.12 Two-factor authentication procedure.

code that was sent to you by the system via SMS, or security questions

- something that you have (*possession-based authentication*): software token or hardware token via USB or dongle or a text or code that will send to your phone number or email address, or a Transaction Authorization Code (TAC) number, security code, PIN or authenticator apps such as Microsoft Authenticator, Google Authenticator and Authy

- something that you are (*inherent-based authentication*): biometrics like fingerprint, face recognition, retina scan or palm scan

To generate 2FA codes in your code, you can use the Time-based One-Time Password (TOTP) algorithm. Here are the general steps:

1. Install a TOTP library. Several TOTP libraries are available for different programming languages, such as Python, Java, and JavaScript. For example, the PyOTP library is a popular TOTP library for Python.

2. Generate a secret key. A secret key is a random string of characters to generate 2FA codes. You can use a cryptographically secure random number generator to generate a secret key and store it securely in your application's configuration.

3. Generate a TOTP code. Using the secret key and the current time, you can generate a TOTP code using the TOTP library. The code is typically a 6-digit number that changes every 30 seconds.

4. Verify the TOTP code. Once the user enters the TOTP code, you can verify it by generating a TOTP code using the same secret key and comparing it with the code entered.

5. Set up the user's 2FA. When a user enables 2FA, you need to provide them with a unique secret key, which they can use to generate the TOTP code. This secret key can be communicated to the user using a secure channel, such as an encrypted email or a QR code that scans with mobile apps.

6. Store the user's 2FA information. When the user sets up 2FA, you should store their TOTP secret key and user account information. You can keep this information securely in your database, using encryption or hashing to protect it.

7. Verify the user's 2FA. When the user logs in, you must prompt them for their TOTP code and then generate a TOTP code using their secret key. You can then compare the TOTP code entered by the user with the TOTP code generated by your code to verify the user's identity.

An example in Python using the PyOTP library is as below:

```
1  import pyotp
2  import time
3
4  # Set up the TOTP generator with a secret key
5  # This key should be kept secret and only known to the user
       and the server
6  totp_secret = 'JBSWY3DPEHPK3PXP'  # Example secret key,
       should be replaced with a random value
7  totp = pyotp.TOTP(totp_secret)
8
9  # Generate a TOTP code and print it
10 # This code will be valid for the current time window (30
       seconds by default)
11 totp_code = totp.now()
12 print("TOTP code:", totp_code)
13
14 # Wait for 5 seconds and generate another code
15 time.sleep(5)
16 totp_code = totp.now()
```

```
17 print("TOTP code:", totp_code)
18
19 # Verify a user-entered TOTP code against the current valid
       code
20 user_input = input("Enter TOTP code: ")
21 if totp.verify(user_input):
22     print("Code is valid!")
23 else:
24     print("Code is invalid.")
```

Listing 3.1 TOTP

3.3.5.2 Multi-factor authentication

More complex mechanisms are available to deploy security to protect data from being compromised [100]. MFA is similar to the 2FA method which the user will only be granted access to an account after verifying themselves for the application with more than one piece of evidence. Fig. 3.13 demonstrates how 2FA implements with a combination of knowledge-inheritance, knowledge-possession, or inheritance-possession factors. Users must provide at least two of these factors to authenticate using MFA [101, 102]. For example, a user may be required to enter a password and then provide a one-time code generated by a mobile app. Alternatively, they may be required to use a fingerprint and enter a PIN. The 2FA is the most frequently used MFA to place an extra layer of security to the identification through authentication.

MFA aims to provide an additional layer of security to traditional password-based authentication by requiring users to provide additional evidence to prove their identity [103,104]. MFA creates a situation where attackers become hard to gain access or break through the multiple security barriers. With multiple authentication factors, even if attackers can obtain a user's password, they can still not authenticate and access the system or resource.

3.4 PRIVACY

3.4.1 Concept of Privacy

Data privacy is a subset of data security but is more concerning properly handling data. It is a type of data governance that focuses on how users can protect their PII from misuse and keep their data confidential under the protection of legal and regulations. Data protection requires tools and policies to control the usage of data. For instance, following

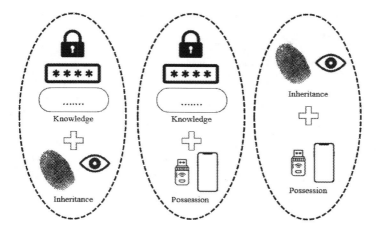

Figure 3.13 Two-factor authentication combination.

industries' standards and best practices could help enterprises comply while minimalizing data breaches and other damages to the organization.

The GDPR enforced by the EU in 2018 has become one of the most crucial and discussed topics in the industry as it claims as the world's most robust set of data privacy laws for all of its member countries. The focus of GDPR is to better protect individuals and their rights in this data-heavy lifestyle [105, 106]. GDPR is about protecting the personal data of EU citizens, including a person's name, residential address, login details, IP addresses, and sensitive data, like political opinions, race, monthly salary, health information, etc. GDPR has seven fundamental principles in Article 5 of the legislation that organizations must follow when processing personal data. These principles are as below:

1. **Lawfulness, fairness, and transparency**: Personal data must be processed lawfully, fairly, and transparently. Each individual must know how their data is collected, used, and shared, and the processing must base on a legitimate purpose.

2. **Purpose limitation**: It is necessary to acquire personal data for clear, explicit, and legal purposes and not to process it inconsistently. Organizations must have a legitimate, clear, and justifiable basis for collecting and processing personal data.

3. **Data minimization**: Personal data must be sufficient, pertinent, and kept to a minimum required for its processes. Organizations

should only gather and use the minimal personal information required for legitimate reasons.

4. **Accuracy**: Personal data must be kept current and correct whenever necessary. The accuracy, completeness, and currentness of the personal data that reasonable measures must guarantee organizations process.

5. **Storage limitation**: For no longer than is required for the purposes for which the personal data has been processed, personal data must be kept in a form that allows the identification of data subjects. This means businesses are only required to preserve personal data as long as it takes to fulfil their legitimate goals.

6. **Integrity and confidentiality**: Personal data processing must be done securely, protecting against unauthorized or unlawful processing as well as accidental loss, deletion, or damage. Organizations must implement the necessary organizational and technical safeguards to prevent unauthorized access to or disclosure of personal data.

7. **Accountability**: The controller is in charge of upholding these values and must be able to prove them. Organizations must take responsibility for their processing operations and be able to prove that they are abiding by GDPR guidelines.

The seven fundamental principles of GDPR in Article 5 require organizations to process personal data lawfully, fairly, and transparently for specific and legitimate purposes, using only the minimum necessary data and ensuring the accuracy and security of the data while limiting its storage to only the time required. The most crucial part of GDPR is giving individuals the right to get their identity data erased or when it no longer needs to be collected. Organizations must also be accountable for their processing activities and be able to show that they are following the principles. By following these principles, organizations can protect EU citizens' privacy and personal data and avoid costly penalties for non-compliance with GDPR.

3.4.2 Data Life Cycle

A Data Life Cycle (DLC) consists of a series of phases, and each phase comes with policies to govern the value of the data along the life cycle.

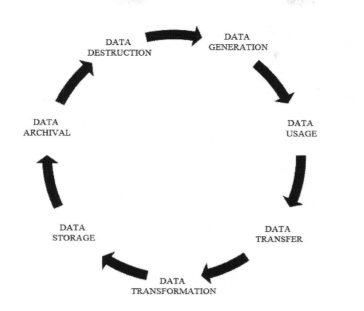

Figure 3.14   7-Step data lifecycle management.

Data Lifecycle Management (DLM) is increasingly important when the volume of data incorporated with enterprises is growing tremendously, and the importance of data is getting more precious as an enabler for sound decision-making in enhancing business strategy [107, 108]. Good quality data can be a good storyteller and interpret the business quickly. It could also visualize a company's current scenario and provide recommendations for actions to take to improve the operations. Marketing campaigns help a business visualize the present business scenario and inspire. There are seven steps in DLM.

The data life cycle is a framework that describes the different stages that data goes through from its creation to its eventual retirement [109]. This framework can be helpful for organizations and individuals who want to manage their data better, ensure its quality, and use it effectively for decision-making. The data life cycle. There are various ways to conceptualize the data life cycle, and the version presented here typically includes the following stages:

1. **Data Generation** is the first stage of the data life cycle, which involves the creation or acquisition of data. Data can be generated

in various ways, such as through sensors, surveys, experiments, or from third-party sources. Ensuring the data is accurate, complete, and relevant to the project's goals is important. Data quality is critical at this stage, as poor quality data can negatively impact subsequent stages of the data life cycle.

2. **Data Usage** comes after data is generated, which involves the application of data to solve a problem or answer a question. Data usage can take various forms, such as descriptive, predictive, or prescriptive analytics. Data usage may also involve the creation of reports, dashboards, or other visualizations to communicate insights to stakeholders. Ensuring that the data is used ethically and responsibly and that any insights generated are accurate and relevant to the problem is vital.

3. **Data Transfer** involves moving data from one location to another and may occur for various reasons, such as sharing data with collaborators, moving data to a cloud-based platform, or transferring data from one system to another. It is essential to ensure that data transfer occurs securely and that any data privacy or security concerns are being addressed.

4. **Data Transformation** is required to make it more stable once data has been transferred to a new location. This stage involves various activities, such as data cleaning, integration, or enrichment. Data transformation is critical for ensuring that data is of high quality and in a format usable for subsequent stages of the data life cycle.

5. **Data Storage** The next stage is data storage, which involves storing data in a secure and accessible manner. This can apply various technologies like databases, data warehouses, or cloud-based storage. It is essential to ensure that data is stored securely and that any data privacy or security concerns are addressed. Data should also be stored in a way that is easily accessible to those who need it.

6. **Data Archival** Over time, data may become less valuable or need to be retired for other reasons. The next stage, data archival, involves moving data to long-term storage or deleting it altogether. This stage is essential for managing data storage costs and maintaining data privacy and security. It is essential to ensure that data

is archived securely and that any data privacy or security concerns are addressed.

The data life cycle is a framework that helps to describe the various stages that data goes through from its creation to its eventual retirement. Understanding the data life cycle is important for effective data management [110], as it helps to ensure that data is of high quality, is used ethically and responsibly, and is stored securely and in a way that is accessible to those who need it. By following the 7 stages of the data life cycle, organizations and individuals can better manage their data and use it effectively for decision-making.

3.4.3 Privacy in Data Storage

Privacy in data storage refers to the protection of personal and sensitive information that is stored in various forms, such as databases, servers, and cloud storage systems. Data storage is an essential component of any organization's data management system, and it is critical to ensure that personal information is kept secure and protected from unauthorized access, misuse, and theft.

One of the main challenges of privacy in data storage is a large amount of personal information collected and stored by organizations. Personal information can include names, addresses, phone numbers, email addresses, financial information, health information, and other sensitive data. This information is often stored in various systems and databases, making it vulnerable to cyber-attacks and other security threats.

To ensure privacy in data storage, organizations must take several steps to protect personal information. These steps include:

1. **Encryption** converts plain text into a code to prevent unauthorized access. Encryption is a critical component of data storage security, and it can be used to protect data at rest and in transit.

2. **Access control** refers to controlling who has access to data and what actions they can perform with that data. Access control systems can include password protection, multi-factor authentication, and role-based access control.

3. **Regular backups** of data is essential to ensure that data can be recovered in case of a security breach or loss. Backups should be

stored in a secure location and regularly tested to ensure that data can be restored promptly.

4. **Data retention policies** should be implemented to ensure that personal information is only stored for as long as necessary. This can help to reduce the risk of data breaches and misuse.

5. **Compliance with regulations** Organizations must comply with various regulations and standards related to data privacy, such as the GDPR and the CDPA. Compliance with these regulations can help ensure that personal information is stored and managed responsibly and ethically.

Privacy in data storage is essential for protecting personal information and maintaining the trust of customers and stakeholders. Organizations that fail to protect personal information face serious consequences, including legal action, reputational damage, and financial losses. By implementing effective data storage and management practices, organizations can ensure that personal information is kept secure and protected from unauthorized access and misuse.

3.4.4 Privacy in Data Retention

Privacy in data retention refers to the management and storage of personal information over a specified period. Data retention policies dictate how long personal information is kept, how it is stored, and how it is ultimately destroyed or deleted. This is important for ensuring the privacy of an individual's personal information and complying with relevant regulations and laws.

Data retention is a method, including policy and management, of how long a corporate should keep its content for future use. However, the longer the data is kept, the more storage media and space are needed to ensure the data can be stored, which may recur long-term costs. Different types of data require different lengths of data retention. The same principle applies to industry standards where different retention policies are prepared for divergent business requirements. For instance, HIPAA is for health care and HIPAA-related documents, and the data retention requirements are for a minimum of 6 years from the document was created.

Data retention policies should be available and updated according to needs as it is a valuable document that deals with the issue of maintaining essential documents in the organization where it poses how we should keep the information.

Data retention policies vary by organization, and they are often influenced by factors such as the type of data being collected and the purpose for which it is being collected. For example, some organizations may retain personal information for extended periods if it is necessary for legal or regulatory reasons. In contrast, others may delete data as soon as it is no longer needed.

To ensure privacy in data retention, organizations must take several steps to protect personal information. These steps include:

1. Establishing clear data retention policies: Data retention policies should be established and communicated clearly to all stakeholders. These policies should outline what data is being retained, how long it will be retained, and how it will be destroyed or deleted.

2. Implementing technical and organizational measures: Technical and organizational measures should be implemented to ensure that personal information is kept secure and protected from unauthorized access, misuse, and theft. These measures can include data encryption, access controls, and regular data backups.

3. Complying with relevant regulations and laws: Organizations must comply with relevant regulations and laws related to data privacy, such as the GDPR and the CCPA. Compliance with these regulations can ensure that personal information is retained and managed responsibly and ethically.

4. Limiting access to personal information: Access to personal information should be limited to only those with a legitimate need to access it. This can help to reduce the risk of unauthorized access and misuse.

5. Regularly reviewing and updating retention policies: Data retention policies should be regularly reviewed and updated to ensure they are still relevant and effective. This helps ensure that personal information is kept secure and protected over time.

Privacy in data retention is important for several reasons:

1. It helps protect individuals' privacy by ensuring that personal information is not retained for longer than necessary.

2. It can help to reduce the risk of data breaches and unauthorized access to personal information.

3. It can help organizations to comply with relevant regulations and laws related to data privacy.

Privacy in data retention is an important aspect of data management that organizations must take seriously. By establishing clear data retention policies, implementing technical and organizational measures, complying with regulations and laws, limiting access to personal information, and regularly reviewing and updating retention policies, organizations can ensure that personal information is kept secure and protected over time. This helps maintain the trust of customers and stakeholders, reduce the risk of data breaches and misuse, and ensure compliance with relevant regulations and laws.

3.4.5 Privacy in Data Destruction

Data destruction refers to the process of *securely and permanently deleting data* from storage devices such as hard drives, solid-state drives, and flash drives in a way that the data cannot be recovered by any means. Data destruction is typically performed when sensitive or confidential data needs to be removed from a device, such as when a device is being repurposed, recycled, or disposed of.

The purpose of data destruction is to *prevent unauthorized access* to the data, to ensure *compliance with legal or regulatory requirements* related to data privacy and security, and to *protect sensitive information* from falling into the wrong hands. Various methods of data destruction are available, including physical destruction (e.g., shredding or pulverizing a storage device), degaussing (using a powerful magnetic field to erase the data), and overwriting (writing random data over the existing data multiple times to make it unrecoverable). The method used depends on the *sensitivity of the data* and the *level of security* required. For instance, to destruct ***SECRET*** documents will require dedicated technical and skilled methodology compared to ***CONFIDENTIAL***to ensure the data is completely clean with no dust or debris.

The key privacy concern in handling data destruction is to ensure that sensitive and confidential data is securely and permanently deleted from storage devices so that it cannot be recovered by any means. This is particularly important when handling personal or sensitive data, such as financial information, medical records, and other PII.

To address privacy concerns in handling data destruction, organizations should implement appropriate policies and procedures to ensure that data destruction is carried out securely and complies with *legal and regulatory requirements*. This may include using secure data destruction methods, such as physical destruction or overwriting with random data multiple times, to prevent unauthorized access to the data.

Organizations should enforce *strict and firm policies* and ensure that only authorized personnel have access to the data and receive adequate training on handling and disposing of sensitive data securely. Maintaining an audit trail of all data destruction activities, including the date, time, and method used, is also important to ensure accountability and compliance with regulations.

Overall, privacy concerns in handling data destruction highlight the importance of protecting personal and sensitive data throughout its lifecycle, from collection to destruction, to ensure that it is not misused or abused.

3.4.6   Privacy Breaches

A privacy breach occurs when there is unauthorized access to sensitive or confidential information. This can happen in various ways, including hacking, theft, or human error. When someone gains access to information that they should not have, it can lead to a breach of privacy that can have severe consequences for the individuals whose information has been compromised.

Privacy breaches can occur in many contexts, including healthcare, finance, and social media. For example, a healthcare privacy breach might occur when a hacker gains access to patient records, including sensitive information like medical histories, treatment plans, and social security numbers. In finance, a privacy breach might occur when a financial institution loses track of customer data, resulting in identity theft or other financial fraud. Finally, a privacy breach in social media might occur when a user's personal information is shared without their consent or when their account is hacked.

The consequences of a privacy breach can be severe. Individuals with compromised information may experience identity theft, financial loss, or other harm. Additionally, companies and organizations that experience privacy breaches can face legal and regulatory consequences, damaging their reputation and losing customer trust. Therefore, companies and individuals must take steps to protect sensitive information and prevent privacy breaches from occurring.

3.4.7 Data Responsibility and Risk Management

A privacy breach occurs when sensitive, confidential, or personal information is accessed, used, disclosed, or compromised without the consent or knowledge of the individuals affected. Privacy breaches can occur in various forms, including data theft, hacking, human error, or social engineering. The consequences of a privacy breach can be severe and may include identity theft, financial loss, reputation damage, and legal liability.

One of the most common forms of privacy breach is *data theft*. This occurs when an unauthorized person or entity gains access to sensitive information stored on electronic devices, such as computers, servers, or mobile phones. Data theft can occur through hacking, malware, phishing, or other cyber attacks. For example, a hacker may gain access to a company's database containing personal information, such as names, addresses, Social Security numbers, and credit card information, and use this information for fraudulent purposes.

Another common form of privacy breach is *human error*. This occurs when an individual accidentally or intentionally discloses sensitive information to unauthorized parties. For example, an employee may email sensitive information to the wrong person or leave confidential documents unsecured in a public place.

Social engineering is another form of privacy breach. This occurs when an attacker manipulates or deceives individuals into revealing sensitive information or granting access to restricted areas. For example, a hacker may impersonate a trusted authority figure, such as a bank representative or IT support, and ask the victim for their login credentials or personal information.

A privacy breach may have serious and far-reaching repercussions. Due to the breach, individuals may suffer from identity theft, financial loss, and reputational harm. The breach may expose organizations to legal liability, regulatory penalties, a loss of client confidence, and reputational harm. Privacy violations must be avoided through a multifaceted strategy. Firewalls, antivirus software, and encryption are just a few of the *robust security measures* organizations must implement to safeguard their computer systems and data against cyber-attacks.

Organizations must implement these measures to safeguard their computer systems and data against cyberattacks. They also need to ***establish policies and procedures*** to manage personal information gathering, use, and disclosure. The risks of privacy violations should be explained to employees during training on these rules.

Individuals can also take steps to protect their privacy, such as being ***cautious about sharing personal information online*** and ***monitoring their credit reports*** for any suspicious activity. They should also use strong passwords, avoid public Wi-Fi for sensitive transactions, and enable two-factor authentication wherever possible. To mitigate the risks of privacy breaches, individuals and organizations should implement strong ***security measures***, such as using complex passwords, encrypting sensitive data, and conducting regular security audits. In addition, individuals should be cautious when sharing personal information online or in person, and organizations should train their employees on best practices for protecting sensitive information.

3.5 SUMMARY

This chapter introduced network, host, and application security by explaining the attributes to protect against CNII. Section 3.2 further discussed the importance and requirement to classify data by label: top secret, secret, sensitive, confidential and open. This was for organizations to apply different security measures based on the sensitivity of the data. The three different states specifically for data-at-rest, data-in-motion and data-in-transit are discussed to further effective countermeasures. The Section further discussed data leakage and data breach, which occur at any stage of the data, from the collection, storing and process, followed by the mechanisms to prevent it. In Section 3.3, we explained the concept of IAM and how IAM is deployed in different scenarios to achieve authentication, authorization and auditing. Finally, in Section 3.4, we discussed data privacy in terms of concept, life cycle, and solutions to resolve privacy issues in different conditions: storage, duration of keeping and destruction of data after obsolete.

3.6 EXERCISES

After completing this chapter, please answer the following questions.

1. How important of IAM in the digital realm?

   With the increase of digitization with more and more data generated from the system, data plays a crucial role in assisting organizations in making decisions and forecast enterprises' road map for short-term and long-term planning in a trajectory means. IAM plays a vital role in infiltrating intruders and safeguarding sensitive data, meeting compliance requirements, enhancing productivity, and minimizing security risks. Some of the key reasons are as below:

(a) Security: It helps protect sensitive data and digital assets by controlling who can access them and under what conditions.

(b) Authentication and Authorization: It provides mechanisms for verifying the identity of users and determining what they are allowed to do within the system.

(c) Access control: IAM empowers organizations to establish and enforce precise access control policies, considering user roles, responsibilities, and additional attributes. By implementing IAM, organizations can ensure that users are granted access to the resources essential for their job functions. This meticulous control over access privileges helps mitigate the risk of insider threats, as users are restricted from accessing resources beyond their operational requirements. IAM is vital in maintaining the integrity and security of organizational systems and data by minimizing unauthorized access and potential internal risks.

(d) Auditing and Compliance: It helps organizations monitor and track user activities, which can be invaluable for meeting regulatory requirements, conducting internal audits, and investigating security incidents.

(e) Productivity and User Experience: By streamlining the process of granting and managing access to resources, IAM can improve the overall user experience and increase productivity. For example, Single Sign-On (SSO) allows users to authenticate once and access multiple applications, reducing the need to remember multiple usernames and passwords.

(f) Scalability: As organizations grow and evolve, it helps manage increasing numbers of users, devices, and applications, ensuring that access control remains consistent and manageable.

2. What solutions are available to overcome security matters at the host level?

There are a few host-level measurements and practices that serve the security of infrastructure, including:

(a) Vulnerability management where vulnerabilities are identified at the infrastructure components, such as patches, firmware updates, and configurations.

(b) Network security where appliances like firewall, IDS/IPS at the network segment are used to set a boundary to restrict access to the network.

(c) Encryption is commonly used to protect data-in-transit and data-at-rest. This method can protect data especially sensitive data at the host by converting it into an unreadable format and only be able to decrypt it with a key.

(d) Disaster recovery is vital to ensure that critical infrastructure components can recover back to normal as soon as possible to reduce financial losses and retain the organization's reputation in the industry.

(e) Patch management ensures the system and applications are always equipped with the latest security patches to reduce the risk of exploitation due to vulnerabilities.

3. List several standard practices used for application security.

There are a few standard practices which commonly used.

(a) Input validation: Verify and validate all user inputs to prevent any malicious code from entering the system.

(b) Authentication and Authorization: Ensure only authorized and authenticated users can access the application's resources.

(c) Password policies: Enforce strong password policies, including complexity requirements and regular password updates.

(d) Encryption: Use encryption to protect sensitive data in transit and at rest.

(e) Access control: Implement access control measures to limit access to sensitive data and functionality only to authorized users.

(f) Error handling: Implement proper error handling and logging to prevent the disclosure of sensitive information.

(g) Security testing: Find and fix any security issues, conduct routine security testing such as penetration testing and vulnerability scanning.

(h) Code review: Conduct regular code reviews to identify and address any security vulnerabilities in the application code.

(i) Secure coding practices: Train developers on secure coding practices, such as avoiding common security pitfalls and using secure coding frameworks.

(j) Patch management: Ensure all software and systems are regularly patched and updated to address known security vulnerabilities.

4. How do we choose the suitable authentication mechanism for my application?

A suitable authentication mechanism is chosen depending on various factors.

(a) Security requirements: The level of security needed for your application will determine the authentication mechanism you should choose. For example, if your application handles sensitive data, you may need to implement two-factor or multifactor authentication to ensure higher security.

(b) User experience: The authentication mechanism you choose should also be user-friendly and easy to use. Users may avoid using your application altogether if the authentication process is too complex or time-consuming.

(c) Integration with existing systems: If your application needs to integrate with existing authentication systems, such as LDAP or Active Directory, you may need to choose an authentication mechanism compatible with those systems.

(d) Cost: Some authentication mechanisms may be more expensive than others. You should consider the cost of implementing and maintaining the authentication mechanism and any licensing fees that may apply.

(e) Regulatory compliance: Depending on the nature of your application and the industry you operate in, you may need to comply with certain regulations, such as HIPAA or PCI DSS. You should choose an authentication mechanism that meets these regulatory requirements.

5. What is the difference between hard tokens and soft tokens?

Hard tokens and soft tokens are two types of authentication mechanisms used to verify the identity of users in secure systems. The main difference between hard tokens and soft tokens lies in their physical form and how they are generated.

Hard tokens are physical devices that generate a unique one-time password (OTP) for each authentication attempt. These devices can be in the form of a key fob, USB drive, or smart card. Hard tokens are often used in high-security environments, such as banks or government agencies, where the risk of a cyber attack is high.

Soft tokens, on the other hand, are generated by software applications that run on a user's mobile device or computer. Soft tokens are typically generated using a time-based algorithm and expire after a certain amount of time. Soft tokens are often used in lower-security environments like online banking or social media sites.

The advantages of hard tokens include their high level of security, as they are not susceptible to malware or hacking attempts. However, hard tokens can be expensive to produce and distribute, and users may need to carry them around at all times.

On the other hand, soft tokens are more convenient for users, as they can be generated using a mobile device or computer. They are also less expensive to produce and distribute than hard tokens. However, soft tokens are vulnerable to malware and hacking attempts, which can compromise their security.

Which token to choose depends on the level of security required and the organization's or application's specific needs.

6. Do you think controlling system access is only applicable for CNII? Please explain why you say so.

No, controlling system access is not only applicable to Critical National Information Infrastructure (CNII). Controlling system access is a basic security measure that applies to all systems, whether critical infrastructure or not.

Controlling system access refers to limiting and managing who has access to a computer system or network. This can include requiring strong passwords, multi-factor authentication, limiting user privileges, and monitoring user activity. By controlling system access, organizations can prevent unauthorized individuals from accessing sensitive data, performing malicious actions, or disrupting system operations.

While it is true that controlling system access is particularly important for CNII systems due to the potential impact of a security breach, all systems can benefit from these security measures. Many cyber attacks target smaller organizations with less robust security measures precisely because they are seen as easier targets.

7. What is the key significant difference between data-at-rest, data-in-motion, and data-in-use?

Data-at-rest refers to the information stored on a device or system, such as a hard drive, flash drive, or cloud storage. This data is typically not actively being used or transmitted at the time and is considered to be in a static state.

On the other hand, data-in-motion refers to data actively transmitted over a network or between systems. This can include data being sent over the internet, between servers, or between devices on a local network.

Data-in-use refers to data actively accessed and manipulated by an application or user. This can include data being processed by a computer program, viewed on a screen, or edited in a document.

The key difference between these three data types is their state: data-at-rest is stored and not actively being used, data-in-motion is being transmitted over a network, and data-in-use is actively being accessed and manipulated. Each data type requires different security measures to protect it from unauthorized access, theft, or manipulation.

8. Explain in brief how 2FA is being applied.

The traditional username and password authentication procedure is made more secure using two-factor authentication (2FA). Users must supply two identity factors when logging into an account or system. The goal is to make it more difficult for unauthorized people to get access since even if one factor is compromised, the other still needs to be known to or acquired by an attacker.

2FA can be applied using various combinations of the following factors:

(a) Something you know (knowledge): This includes passwords, PINs, or secret questions that must enter by the user to get authenticated.

(b) Something you have (possession): These are physical items, such as a security token, a mobile device, or a smart card, that generate a one-time code or a biometric factor such as a fingerprint or face recognition.

(c) Something you are (inherence): Biometric information, such as fingerprints, retina scans, facial recognition, or voice recognition that uniquely belongs to an individual.

Here's how 2-factor authentication might be applied in a typical scenario:

(a) The user enters their username and password (first factor) on a website or app.

(b) Upon successful entry of the first factor, the system requests the second factor. The second factor could be a one-time passcode (OTP) sent via SMS or email, a push notification to a smartphone app, or a code generated by a hardware token or authenticator app.

(c) The user provides the second factor by entering the code, approving the push notification, or scanning their fingerprint, for example.

(d) If both factors are correct, the user can access their account or the protected resource.

Two-factor authentication is widely used to secure online accounts, such as email, banking, and social media, and in corporate environments to protect sensitive data and systems. It significantly reduces the risk of unauthorized access, even in cases where a user's password has been compromised.

9. Explain data lifecycle management in general. DLM refers to managing data throughout its entire lifespan, from creation to destruction. The data lifecycle typically consists of several stages,

including data generation, usage, transfer, transformation, storage, archival, and destruction. In this answer, we will discuss each of these stages in detail.

Data Generation: This stage involves the creation of new data, which can be generated through various sources such as sensors, surveys, customer interactions, etc. The data generated must be properly labeled and recorded with relevant metadata, such as timestamps, location data, and data source information.

Data Usage: This stage involves processing and analysing data to generate insights or make decisions. Data usage can be done in real-time or batches, typically involving applying statistical or machine-learning models to the data. It's important to ensure that the data used for analysis is accurate and consistent.

Data Transfer: This stage involves moving data from one location to another, such as from a sensor to a data center, or from one application to another. Data transfer must be done securely to prevent data breaches and properly documented to maintain an audit trail.

Data Transformation: This stage involves converting data from one format to another, such as converting raw data into a structured format suitable for analysis. Data transformation may involve cleaning, filtering, or merging data from multiple sources.

Data Storage: This stage involves storing data in a secure and reliable manner. It's important to choose the right storage technology and architecture that meets the data's requirements. The data should be regularly backed up to prevent data loss in case of hardware failures or disasters.

Data Archival: This stage involves moving data not actively used to a long-term storage location, such as tape or cloud storage. Archiving helps to free up storage space and reduce costs while ensuring that data is still accessible if needed.

Data Destruction: This stage involves securely erasing data no longer needed, such as when data retention policies require it or when sensitive data needs to be protected. Data destruction must be done to prevent the data from being recovered by unauthorized parties.

In summary, data lifecycle management is critical for organizations that handle large amounts of data. It ensures that data is properly managed throughout its entire lifespan, from creation to destruction, while maintaining accuracy, security, and accessibility.

10. What is the difference between OAuth, SAML and OpenID Connect?

OAuth, SAML, and OpenID Connect are all protocols that allow users to authenticate and authorize access to resources in a distributed environment, but they differ in their technical implementation and use cases.

OAuth is primarily used for authorization, allowing a user to grant a third-party application access to their protected resources without revealing their credentials. OAuth 2.0 is the most widely used version, and it uses access tokens to provide limited access to a user's resources. OAuth 2.0 does not provide authentication but relies on other protocols such as OpenID Connect or SAML for authentication.

SAML (Security Assertion Markup Language) is an XML-based protocol for exchanging authentication and authorization data between parties. It is primarily used for single sign-on (SSO) in enterprise environments, allowing users to log in once and access multiple applications without re-entering their credentials. SAML uses a central identity provider (IdP) to issue assertions to service providers (SPs) after a user has authenticated, providing a secure way to share identity information across different applications and systems.

OpenID Connect is a simple identity layer built on the OAuth 2.0 protocol. It provides a standard way for users to authenticate and authorize access to resources across different applications and platforms. OpenID Connect uses a central authorization server to issue ID tokens to clients containing user identity information such as name, email, and profile picture. OpenID Connect also supports

SSO, allowing users to log in once and access multiple applications without re-entering their credentials.

Generally, OAuth is a protocol for authorization, SAML is a protocol for exchanging authentication and authorization data, and OpenID Connect is a simple identity layer built on top of OAuth for authentication and authorization. While they share some similarities and can be used together in some cases, they have different technical implementations and use cases.

GLOSSARY

Access Control: is the process of controlling who has access to the network infrastructure. This involves setting up user accounts with appropriate permissions, implementing authentication mechanisms such as passwords or biometrics, and monitoring access logs to detect unauthorized access attempts.

Application Firewall: is a security device that monitors and controls incoming and outgoing traffic to the application.

Data Leakage: is a situation that occurs when sensitive or private information is disclosed to unintended or unauthorized parties.

Data lineage: is the process of tracking and managing the flow of data from its source to its destination throughout its lifecycle.

Determining security mechanism: is critical in securing any system or network. Security mechanisms are the tools and techniques used to protect against threats and vulnerabilities that may compromise the confidentiality, integrity, and availability of information or resources.

Digital signatures: can be used to verify the authenticity of a data object and ensure that it has not been tampered with.

Fingerprinting: is a technique used in data leakage prevention to detect and prevent the unauthorized transfer of sensitive information outside an organization.

Firewall: is a network security tool that keeps track of and manages incoming and outgoing network traffic in accordance with pre-established security rules.

Identity and Access Management: refers to the framework enterprises adopt in their business process to recognize users, protect their identity from dispute, and, most importantly, grant permissions to access services.

Infrastructure-as-a-Service: is a cloud computing service offering online access to virtualized computing resources.

Metadata: is data that describes the characteristics and context of a data object, including its origin, content, and usage.

Network Monitoring: involves collecting and analyzing data from network devices to detect security incidents, performance issues, and other problems.

Network Segmentation: divides a network into smaller sub-networks, called segments or zones, and controls access between them.

Platform-as-a-Service: is a cloud computing service model that provides a platform and environment for developers to build, run, and manage their applications over the internet.

Privileged Access Management: refers to the practices, technologies, and policies used to control, monitor, and audit access to sensitive resources and information within an organization.

Scrambling: is a technique used in countermeasure data leakage to protect sensitive information from being leaked or intercepted by unauthorized parties.

Secure Configuration Management: ensures that the application is configured securely and that all components are updated with the latest security patches.

Software-as-a-Service: is a provider that hosts an application and makes it accessible to clients online.

Vulnerability management: involves identifying and addressing vulnerabilities in the infrastructure components, such as software patches, firmware updates, and configuration changes.

Watermarking: is a technique that can be used to track and identify the source of data leakage. Watermarking involves embedding a unique identifier into a document or piece of data that is not visible to the naked eye but can be detected using specialized software.

II

Major Cybersecurity Issues

CHAPTER 4

Security in Cloud Computing and Cyber-Physical Systems

As mobile devices and CPS become increasingly prevalent, ensuring their security is paramount. The rise of CPS or IoT has been widely used in the digital-driven computing environment. The infrastructure to support the innovation and development of CPS becomes a vital element to ensure business insights and communications with multi-channel facilities can operate seamlessly. This chapter explores the security problems in IoT [111] computing. It discusses a few of the taxonomy of threats commonly in data management, introducing the basic concept of cyber-physical systems and their usage in the industry. Finally, the chapter also examines CPS's security challenges and its primary issues in deploying in a real scenario.

4.1 SECURITY PROBLEMS IN MOBILE CLOUD SYSTEMS

Mobile cloud systems are becoming increasingly popular due to their convenience and flexibility. However, they also present several security challenges that need to be addressed. Some of the common security problems in mobile cloud systems are as below.

4.1.1 Customers' Loss of Control

With the adoption of mobile cloud systems, customers often store their data on cloud servers managed by third-party CSPs. This means that customers rely on the CSP to maintain the security and privacy of their data. Hence, CSPs like Amazon Web Services have published a shared responsibility model to explain to customers their responsibility for maintaining security in the cloud. The model extended to IT controls to differentiate the responsibility in operating IT resources depending on the type of services, including management control and security configuration.

The loss of control over data can also result in a lack of transparency regarding how the data is being used and accessed. The cloud service provider may have access to the customer's data, which can be a concern for customers who want to ensure the confidentiality and integrity of their data.

Moreover, customers may need more control over mobile cloud systems' software applications. The cloud service provider may provide the software, and the customer may need help to customize or modify the software. This can result in customers relying on the cloud service provider to ensure the security of the software applications.

4.1.2 Lack of Trust in the Cloud

The cloud refers to using remote servers to store, manage, and process data. Cloud computing [112–114] has become increasingly popular due to its scalability, flexibility, and cost-effectiveness. However, despite these benefits, many people still need more trust in the cloud [115] This essay will explore why people need more trust in the cloud [116].

Security Concerns

Security concerns are among the primary reasons people hesitate to trust the cloud [117]. Although cloud service providers are in charge of protecting the data kept on their servers, security breaches are always a possibility. Sensitive data, such as private information, financial data, and intellectual property, may be taken or destroyed due to a breach.

Additionally, the data stored remotely can lead to concerns about data privacy. Users may worry that their data is accessed or viewed by unauthorized parties or not protected from third-party access. These concerns can be especially pronounced for businesses and organizations that deal with sensitive information, such as healthcare providers, financial institutions, and government agencies.

Data Sovereignty

Another factor that can contribute to a lack of trust in the cloud is the issue of data sovereignty. Data sovereignty refers to the concept that data is subject to the laws and regulations of the country or region where it is stored. It concerns businesses and organizations operating in multiple jurisdictions or with customers in different countries.

For example, if a business stores data in the cloud subject to a foreign country's laws, it may be subject to different regulations or legal processes than if the data were stored locally. It creates uncertainty and legal risk, contributing to a lack of trust in the cloud.

Downtime and Reliability

Another factor that can contribute to a lack of trust in the cloud is the issue of downtime and reliability. Cloud providers typically offer high uptime and reliability, but interruptions or outages are always risky. If the cloud provider experiences downtime, users may be unable to access their data or applications, which can be costly and disruptive.

Furthermore, if a cloud provider experiences a significant outage or data loss can result in widespread disruption and loss of productivity. This can be especially problematic for businesses and organizations relying heavily on cloud services.

Lack of Control

Finally, a lack of trust in the cloud can be driven by a lack of control. When data store on local servers, businesses and organizations have a high degree of control over how that data is managed, accessed, and secured. However, control is transferred to the cloud provider when data is stored in the cloud.

This lack of control can be problematic for businesses and organizations with specific data management or security requirements. It can also create a sense of uncertainty and lack of transparency, as users may need to learn exactly how their data is being managed or secured by the cloud provider.

While cloud computing can offer many benefits, it is essential for businesses and organizations to carefully consider these factors when deciding whether or not to use cloud services. By taking these concerns into account and working with trusted cloud providers, it is possible to use the cloud safely and effectively.

4.1.3 Multi-Tenancy Issues in the Cloud

Multi-tenancy refers to multiple users or tenants sharing a common computing infrastructure, such as a cloud environment. Multi-tenancy in cloud computing refers to the ability of a single instance of a software application or service to serve multiple customers or tenants, each with its own isolated data and configuration settings. This approach allows for greater efficiency, cost savings, improved resource utilization, and scalability for the provider and the customers. Apart from benefits, it also presents several challenges that must be addressed. Multi-tenancy signifies multiple cloud service customers sharing the same pool of resources. Although it is an instance of software architecture to serve several groups concurrently, each data is kept separate and safe. Some of the common multi-tenancy issues in cloud computing include:

1. Data security: Multi-tenancy can raise security concerns, as tenants share the same physical infrastructure, and there is a risk of data leakage or unauthorized access. Since multiple tenants share the same physical resources, there is a risk that one tenant's data could be compromised or accessed by another tenant. To mitigate this risk, cloud providers must implement strong security controls, encryption, and isolation measures to prevent unauthorized access and ensure that data is only accessible to authorized users.

2. Resource allocation: The same resources, such as CPU, memory, and storage, are shared by several users in a multi-tenant system. As a result, there are problems with resource allocation and contention, where a single user may monopolise resources and negatively affect the performance of other tenants. To address this, cloud service providers must implement resource allocation policies with just processes and monitoring tools to guarantee that each tenant gets their fair amount of resources and that performance is stable.

3. Performance and availability: Multi-tenancy can impact application performance and availability as multiple users compete for the same resources. Cloud providers must implement performance monitoring and load-balancing mechanisms to ensure that resources are distributed efficiently and that users receive the expected level of service.

4. Compliance and regulatory: Multi-tenancy can make it challenging to comply with regulatory requirements and industry standards,

as there may be concerns around data privacy and security. Different tenants may have different compliance requirements or regulations that must be adhered to, which can be challenging for cloud providers to manage. Cloud providers must ensure their services comply with relevant regulations and standards and provide tenants with the necessary controls to manage their data securely.

5. Tenant isolation: Tenants in a multi-tenant environment must be isolated from each other to prevent interference and data leakage. Cloud providers must implement robust isolation mechanisms to keep each tenant's data and resources separate from others.

Overall, multi-tenancy in the cloud presents various challenges that must be addressed to ensure users can access secure, high-performance cloud services that meet their needs.

4.2 TAXONOMY OF THREATS/FEAR

A comprehensive taxonomy of threats is built to identify various categories that may impact the organizer by clustering and structuring it at a granular level. As listed below, threats are listed as the most commonly discussed issues. The taxonomy was a framework for each threat for a more detailed study.

The US Federal Code Title 44 Section 3542 [118] defined *confidentiality, integrty* and *availability* below.

4.2.1 Confidentiality

Confidentiality is about protecting the data and information have restrictions and only on limited access and exposure so that it could prevent the data from unauthorized access and data breach. The idea of protection is to protect an organization's proprietary information and intellectual property, including means for protecting personally identifiable information and sensitive information, from being stolen or misused by other parties. The impact of data leakage could be severe depending on the level of data confidentiality.

Supervisory Control and Data Acquisition and Data Acquisition or better known as *SCADA* system, is a fully computer-based production control system that is commonly used in a wide range of industry applications, for instance, in monitoring and controlling of electrical power, oil and gas industry, utilities, mining, chemical industry, railway, shipping, and other heavy industrial activities. The system can monitor, gather and control real-time data whereby human inventions are minimized.

SCADA systems are essential for industrial organizations to maintain efficiency, process data for wiser decisions, and communicate system problems to help minimise downtime. Only authorized parties will have access to the information. Its functions mainly focus on four aspects: a real-time collection of production data, process monitoring of production equipment, abnormal alarm of production equipment, data analysis, data report, and dashboard display, and its characteristics mainly reflect the following aspects.

Confidentiality is critical in healthcare according to [119] where Public Health Systems need to take extra measurements against personal health records due to the need to comply with the HIPAA by encrypting the data during transmission, as well as limited to the location where it could be stored. While in the CPS environment, confidentiality is necessary to protect the sensors and actuators from being compromised and inferring the physical system's state.

4.2.2 Integrity

Integrity is defined as the protection of information and information system from improper alteration or eradication, along with non-repudiation and accuracy of the information. In the information security environment, data integrity refers to maintaining completeness, correctness, consistency, and credibility, whereby safeguards are applied to ensure no modification or alteration by any unauthorized party. The most common fund methods to meet such requirements are encryption, a user control list, backup and recovery, and secure tunneling to communicate and exchange information.

4.2.3 Availability

Data availability means the data must always be accessible to authorized users. Availability is related to system up-time and response time. Therefore the system should react in stealth against malicious software, which may cause hardware failure, unscheduled system downtime, cyber threats, human errors, and insider threats. The whole system, including the network, should be backed up and have full redundancies so that users can access essential data and applications.

Backups and recoveries are the most critical processes in an organization to reduce the risk of system failure and ensure business continuity. It can safeguard data loss by ensuring the organization has enough copies of redundancies to the original copy in case it gets destroyed by malicious activities or human error.

There are three types of backup available, full backup, incremental backup, and differential backup.

1. **Full backup** is a complete full backup made over to files and folders. The process is time-consuming as the data size is getting bigger, and the time required to duplicate will be longer. In addition to that, the process will put a strain on the network as well as server resources (including storage, memory, and computing power) to run the operation. However, a copy of the full backup is the best to restore if a disaster happens, as it contains the same content as the original.

   This backup copy is the most important of all backup copies and must be well protected. The data required a strong encryption mechanism to prevent it from being stolen or falling to an unauthorized party.

2. **Incremental backup** requires at least one **full backup** is available. Although it takes the least space and does not put a strain on the network, it is the most time-consuming to restore a full system.

3. **Differential backup** is compromising among both regular **full backup** and **incremental backup**. It has the longest time to restore a full system than **full backup** but shorter time compared with **incremental backup**.

4.2.4 Massive Data Mining

Massive data mining is extracting valuable insights and knowledge from large datasets using advanced data analysis techniques. However, the vast amounts of data being processed and analyzed also pose significant risks and threats that can compromise data privacy, security, and ethics. Below are a few of the problems that are faced by massive data mining:

- Data Breaches occur when unauthorized parties access sensitive information such as customer records, credit card numbers, or personal identifying information. It happens due to inadequate

Table 4.1 Backup Types Comparisons

	Full Backup	**Incremental Backup**	**Differential Backup**
Utilization of resources	strain the network, need a lot of resources during backup job scheduled	low network utilization, memory, storage and resources	low network utilization, memory, storage and resources
Size of backup file	huge but good practices for SME	small	smallest
Resource consumption	strain the network time-consuming during backing up	will not strain the network	will not strain the network, server or other resources
Recovery	fast	slow and need at least one full backup	slow and need at least one full backup
Frequency of backup	once a week	daily or every 4 hour, may change based on Recovery Time Objective (RTO)	minutes or hourly, subject to changes

security measures, such as weak passwords, unsecured data storage, or phishing attacks.

- Privacy Violations: This occurs when data mining practices violate users' privacy rights, such as collecting data without consent, tracking behavior without permission, or using data for unintended purposes. It can lead to reputational damage, loss of trust, and legal penalties.

- Bias and Discrimination: Data mining can also perpetuate or amplify existing biases and discrimination, leading to unfair treatment of certain groups or individuals. It happens due to biased data sampling, flawed algorithms, or human biases influencing data analysis and decision-making.

- Inaccurate or Misleading Results: Data mining techniques can produce results that are inaccurate or misleading, either due to faulty data sources, flawed analysis, or incorrect assumptions. It leads to incorrect decisions, wasted resources, or even harm to individuals or groups.

- Intellectual Property Theft: Data mining can also pose risks to intellectual property, such as copyrighted materials, trade secrets, or patents. It can happen due to data breaches, insider threats, or cyber-attacks that steal or misuse valuable information.

- Regulatory Non-Compliance: Data mining practices must comply with various regulations and standards, such as GDPR, HIPAA, or PCI-DSS. Failure to comply can result in legal penalties, fines, or other consequences.

4.2.5 Attack Interfaces

In computer security, an attacking interface is any entry point or interaction between an attacker and a system. Attack interfaces can take many forms, including network interfaces, web interfaces, APIs, input validation routines, and more. Attack interfaces can be a significant threat to the security of a system for several reasons.

First, attack interfaces often expose sensitive information or functionality to potential attackers. For example, a web interface might provide access to sensitive data or allow an attacker to execute arbitrary code on the system, such as Cross-Site Scripting (XSS). This information and functionality can carry out a wide range of attacks, from stealing sensitive data to taking control of the system.

Second, attack interfaces are often the primary entry point for attacks against a system. Attackers frequently use attack interfaces to gain initial access to a system, from which they can launch more sophisticated attacks. For example, an attacker might use a web interface to gain access to a system, where a communication link would be the most popular channel, and then use that access to launch a more targeted attack against a specific system component.

Third, attack interfaces can be difficult to secure, especially in multiple-layer environments. Attack interfaces are often complex and may have a large attack surface, making them difficult to understand and secure fully. Additionally, many attack interfaces are designed to be open and accessible to a wide range of users, making it challenging to implement effective access controls [120] and other security measures. The condition becomes more serious when data are stored in a shared environment like a cloud service, and the source of vulnerabilities could be the cloud employees themselves.

It is essential to take a holistic approach to system security to mitigate the threat posed by attack [121] interfaces. This approach should include network segmentation, access controls, regular security testing, and software patching. It is also critical to maintain awareness of the latest security threats and vulnerabilities and update security measures to protect against them regularly.

4.2.6 Auditability and Forensics

Auditability and forensics are important aspects of threat taxonomy, as they help to identify, investigate, and prevent security incidents.

Auditability refers to the ability to track and analyze security-related events and activities in a system or network. It includes logging of user activity, monitoring of system events, and the ability to audit security configurations and settings. Auditability is important for detecting and investigating security incidents, as well as for compliance and regulatory purposes.

Forensics refers to collecting, analyzing, and preserving digital evidence to determine the cause of a security incident and identify the responsible parties. This includes examining logs, system files, and other digital artifacts to reconstruct the events leading up to the incident. Forensics is important for identifying an attack's source, determining the incident's scope, and developing remediation strategies.

Both auditability and forensics are often considered cross-cutting concerns that apply to all types of threats. For example, in network security, auditability and forensics might be relevant to threats such as malware infections, unauthorized access, and data exfiltration. In order to effectively address these threats, security controls such as logging and monitoring must be implemented to support auditability and forensics.

4.2.7 Legal Issues

Legal issues can arise in cloud storage when there are concerns about data privacy, security, and ownership. These issues can affect the cloud storage provider and the user storing data on the cloud.

Cloud storage providers may be held responsible for data breaches or other security incidents that result in the loss, theft, or unauthorized access of data. This responsibility may depend on the terms of the service agreement between the provider and the user and applicable laws and regulations. Providers may also be required to comply with data protection regulations such as the GDPR in the European Union or the CDPA in the United States.

Users who store data on the cloud may also have legal responsibilities related to the data they store. For example, they may be responsible for ensuring that the data they store does not infringe on intellectual property rights or violate data protection regulations. Users may also be responsible for ensuring that their cloud storage use complies with applicable laws or regulations, such as data retention or localization.

In cloud services related to cross-country data privacy, some concerns are raised by agencies like government institutions and medical care. The main concerns include the following:

1. Data residency: Data residency is the least restrictive concept compared with data sovereignty and data locality, where it only specifies the geographical location of a government body to store its data. It depends on how data is stored and accessed within the system and how close the data is to the processes that use it.

2. Data sovereignty: Data sovereignty refers to the concept that data should be subject to the laws and regulations of the country where it is stored. When data is stored in a cloud server in a different country, there is a risk that the data may be subject to different laws and regulations, leading to privacy violations or other legal issues [61].

3. Data localization: All data, including sensitive and personal data, must be stored within the country's geographical area. The main idea is to ensure the relevant government may have access to and audit the data of its citizen and do not require to apply for special permission by involving bilateral or multi-lateral procedures where it may content to other countries' privacy laws. It mainly refers to the legal and regulatory requirements around where data can be stored and processed. Depending on the jurisdiction and the nature of the data being processed, specific laws or regulations may dictate where the data can be stored or processed. For example, some countries have tight data localization laws that require specific types of data to be stored within the country's borders or that prohibit certain types of data from being stored or processed outside the country, for instance, Russia's On Personal Data Law.

4. Data breaches: Data breaches can occur in any cloud environment, but cross-border data privacy raises additional concerns. If a cloud service provider stores data in multiple countries, there may be different security requirements in each country, making it harder to maintain consistent security across all locations. In addition, if

a data breach occurs in a country with less stringent data privacy regulations, it may be easier for cybercriminals to access sensitive data.

5. Access controls: Access controls ensure only authorized individuals can access sensitive data. However, cross-border data privacy concerns can access data stored in a different country. For example, if a CSP stores data in a country with less stringent data privacy laws, there may be a risk that unauthorized individuals could access the data.

6. Compliance: Compliance with data privacy regulations can be challenging in a cross-border cloud environment. Different countries have different data privacy regulations, and complying with them can be complex and time-consuming. In addition, ensuring that all data processing activities are fully compliant with all relevant regulations can be challenging.

In cases where legal issues arise in cloud storage, responsibility may be shared between the provider and the user, depending on the specific circumstances. It is essential for both providers and users to understand their legal responsibilities and to take steps to mitigate risks related to data privacy, security, and ownership. It includes implementing strong security measures, establishing clear policies and procedures for data management, and seeking legal advice when necessary.

4.3 INTRODUCTION TO CYBER-PHYSICAL SYSTEMS

What is Cyber-Physical System?

The term "Cyber-Physical System" was first coined by the United States National Science Foundation in 2006 and then by Dr. Helen Gill. CPS consist of physical processes and cyber systems [119]. A CPS-based system integrates physical processes and computation components by embedding computer management and governance into the physical processes. It covers computation, control, and communication into one platform, as shown in Fig 4.1. The goal of research on cyber-physical [122] systems is to combine expertise and engineering principles from various fields, such as networking, control, software, human interaction, learning theory, electrical engineering, mechanical engineering, chemical engineering, biomedical engineering, materials science, and other engineering

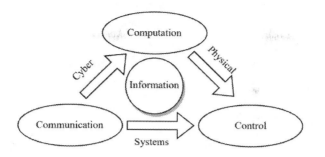

Figure 4.1   Cyber-physical systems.

disciplines. The aim is to create innovative CPS science and technology that supports these systems [123].

CPS is crucial in facilitating efficient decision-making and forecasting business trajectories in detail. In CPS, physical systems are monitored and controlled through computer systems, which allow for real-time feedback and automated decision-making [124]. CPS can be found in various applications, including manufacturing, transportation, healthcare, energy systems, and smart cities. It is based on three core components: decentralized sensors, physical processes, actuators, and a network that initiates the connections [125, 126]. However, people always found the name had high similarity with another term, *"cyberspace"*, due to both being originating from *"cybernetics"*, which was coined in 1948 by Norbert Wiener, a mathematician.

CPS vs IoT: What are the differences?

CPS is very similar and interrelated with the IoT, as both have complex platforms and networked systems and sometimes share the same infrastructure and technology setups. Both technologies make a crossover between cyber and physical components, as shown in Fig 4.2, in which both mechanisms depended entirely on computer-based algorithms to operate.

The development of CPS involves expertise from multiple disciplines, such as electrical engineering, computer science, mechanical engineering, and control theory. CPS typically involves sensors, actuators, communication networks, control algorithms, and data processing tools to achieve

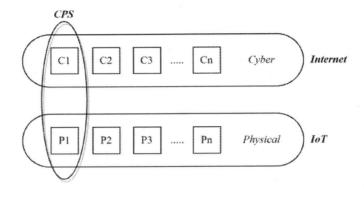

Figure 4.2 CPS vs IoT.

its goals. The primary objective of CPS is to improve efficiency, accuracy, safety, and productivity while reducing costs and human effort.

IoT and CPS are sometimes used interchangeably, but they are distinct concepts with some crucial differences. CPS and IoT will likely express their preference in their community, where each would express its uniqueness and should not be named interchangeably. CPS is commonly used in engineering communities (e.g., mechanical engineering, aerospace engineering, and even computer science) that work on embedded systems with sensors and associated technologies for testing, verification, and verification. The USA more frequently refers to the term CPS. While IoT is more commonly used in telecommunication, networking, and computer scientists working in the next-generation networking industry. The term IoT is more commonly used in the EU.

Today, the world is intensely moving towards an ecosystem that entirely connects the physical devices that we own, e.g., sensors, actuators, and embedded appliances, to be integrated and communicated with the information that we have to form a few terms which we are familiar with, like Industrial Revolution 4.0 (IR4), IoT, and M2M. IoT has the highest degree of overlapping with CPS, where CPS cover a more comprehensive range of ecosystems than IoT [127, 128]. CPS is the intersection of physical and digital. Such intersection required an environment where apparatus devices, communication, software, and physical processes could harmonize but be dynamic.

IoT refers to the interconnectivity of devices, objects, and sensors over the internet. These devices can be anything from a smart thermostat to a wearable fitness tracker or connected car. IoT devices are typically designed to collect and transmit data and can be remotely controlled and monitored via the Internet. The goal of IoT is to make our lives more convenient, efficient, and automated [129].

On the other hand, CPS refers to integrating physical systems with computing systems, aiming to achieve a high level of automation and control. CPS involves using sensors, actuators, and other physical devices to monitor and control physical processes, such as manufacturing or transportation systems [130, 131]. CPS systems are designed to optimize performance, reduce energy consumption, and improve safety.

Here is a brief comparison:

1. **Scope:** IoT generally refers to devices and systems connected to the internet and can be accessed and controlled remotely, often for consumer or home use. Conversely, CPS refers to systems involving physical and digital components designed to monitor and control physical processes in real-time, often in industrial or manufacturing settings.

2. **Integration:** IoT devices are often standalone objects or systems that can be connected to the internet through wireless or wired networks. On the other hand, CPS involves integrating physical components (such as sensors and actuators) with digital components (such as software and algorithms) to create a unified system that can control physical processes.

3. **Complexity:** CPS systems tend to be more complex than IoT systems because they involve the integration of physical and digital components and must be designed to operate in real-time with high reliability and safety. CPS systems often require sophisticated control and optimization algorithms, as well as specialized hardware and software components.

4. **Security:** IoT and CPS systems are vulnerable to cyber attacks, but the risks may be higher for CPS systems because they often involve the control of physical processes that can have serious safety implications. CPS systems must be designed with security and safety in mind and may require specialized security measures such as intrusion detection, authentication, and encryption.

Overall, while there is some overlap between IoT and CPS, they represent different types of systems with different design requirements, applications, and security risks. Both fields are rapidly evolving and are likely to significantly impact a wide range of industries and applications in the future. CPS systems typically have more stringent reliability, safety, and security requirements due to the critical nature of the physical processes they control [47]. IoT devices, however, are often less critical and have fewer safety requirements.

CPS vs DT vs DTN

Despite the comparisons with IoT, CPS can be differentiated from DT technology and DTN. In DT, data flow between a physical object and its virtual twin should be bi-directional. It is a one-to-one comprehensive simulation in a shared intelligence and cooperation condition. While in DTN, the relationship between physical and virtual is many-to-many mapping constructed by multiple one-to-one DTs using advanced communication technologies. Physical items and their digital counterparts, known as virtual twins, can exchange messages, cooperate, exchange data, accomplish tasks together, and create a network for sharing information by linking various DT nodes [124]. The DT focuses on creating a virtual representation of a single physical object, while the DTN involves the cooperation of several DTs to simulate a collection of objects. DTN is an extension of DTs with greater capacities and advances in data processing, computing, and physical data processing technologies.

4.3.1 Cloud Computing and Edge Computing in Cyber-Physical Systems

CPS has become increasingly important in today's world as they enable the development of intelligent systems that can interact with their environment in real-time. With the growing popularity of IoT devices, the number of CPS is expected to increase rapidly in the coming years. A few CPS examples include smart homes, smart cities, autonomous vehicles, and industrial control systems. These systems generate and process large amounts of data, which require advanced computing resources. Cloud computing and edge computing are two computing paradigms that can be used to manage and process the data generated by CPS.

The distribution of computing services via the Internet is called cloud computing. Therefore, by providing scalable, flexible, and affordable computing resources, the significance of cloud computing in providing infrastructure to handle the integration of physical and digital systems has also expanded. Services, including on-demand access to storage,

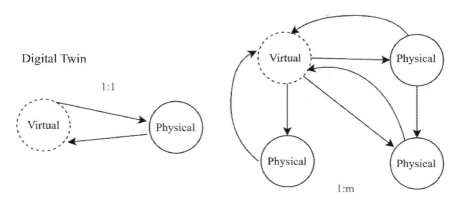

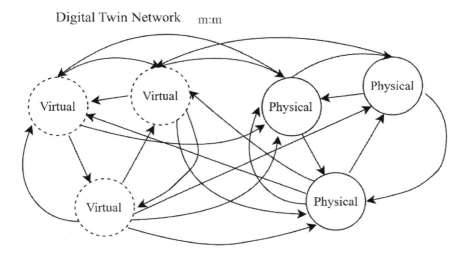

Figure 4.3 DT, DTN differences with CPS.

processing, and networking resources, are provided by cloud computing companies. Applications for CPS benefit greatly from cloud computing.

It offers flexible computing resources that may be scaled up or down in response to demand. This is particularly helpful for CPS applications whose workload may change. Its capacity for handling and storing enormous volumes of data. CPS produces enormous volumes of data, which may be examined to learn more and improve system performance. To gain insights from the data produced by CPS, advanced analytics capabilities offered by cloud computing can be leveraged. Last but not least, cloud computing may provide high availability and fault tolerance, essential for CPS applications that must run continuously.

Fig. 4.4 shows the importance of cloud computing for CPS implementation. Apart from the benefits mentioned earlier, cloud computing allows CPS to access computational resources from anywhere in the world without being restricted by geographical boundaries. Owners or organizations do not need to invest in capital expenditure to own and manage their own resources locally. Still, they may able to subscribe to the service providers to get the necessary resources, including computational power, instantly. This ensures that the system can handle peaks in demand without experiencing performance issues. Cloud computing also allows for the use of advanced machine learning algorithms, which can improve the performance of CPS. For example, autonomous

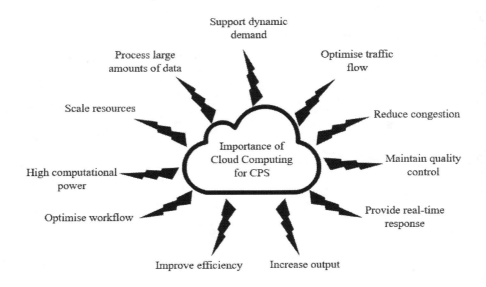

Figure 4.4 Importance of cloud computing for CPS.

vehicles can use cloud computing to access real-time traffic data to optimize their routes. Cloud computing also offers improved security for CPS. By storing data and applications in the cloud, security measures can be centralized and standardized, reducing the risk of vulnerabilities and improving overall security posture.

However, cloud computing also has some limitations for CPS applications. One of the main limitations is latency. Latency refers to the delay between the time a request is made and the time a response is received. Low latency is critical for ensuring safe and efficient operation in CPS applications such as autonomous vehicles. However, cloud computing introduces additional latency due to the time required to send data to and from the cloud. This latency can be unacceptable for some CPS applications.

Edge computing is an alternative computing paradigm that can address some of the limitations of cloud computing for CPS applications. Edge computing refers to the processing and analysis of data at or near the data source. In edge computing, processing and analysis are done locally rather than in the cloud. Edge computing has several advantages for CPS applications. First, it can reduce latency by processing data locally, improving the system's responsiveness. Second, edge computing can reduce the amount of data that needs to be sent to the cloud, reducing bandwidth requirements and lowering costs. Finally, edge computing can improve privacy and security by keeping data local. Edge computing has been well-known as an excellent solution to security problems by preserving privacy, reducing latency, energy, and cost savings, and improving reliability.

However, edge computing also has some limitations for CPS applications. One of the main limitations is limited computing resources. Edge devices such as sensors and controllers may have limited processing power and memory, limiting the applications that can be run locally. In addition, edge devices may have limited connectivity, limiting their ability to communicate with other devices and the cloud.

Therefore, a hybrid approach can be used to overcome the limitations of both cloud computing and edge computing. In this approach, processing and analysis are done both at the edge and in the cloud. For example, edge devices can perform some basic processing and filtering of data before sending it to the cloud for more advanced analytics. This approach can combine the low latency and privacy of edge computing with the advanced analytics and scalability of cloud computing.

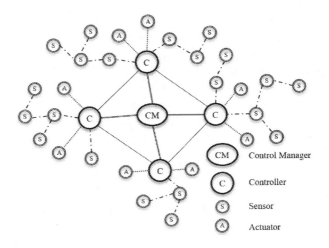

Figure 4.5 CPS-based system configuration.

4.3.2 Concepts and Motivation of CPS

CPS or IoT has presented its benefits to various industries that significantly impact global manufacturing growth. However, while enjoying the development and innovation brought by CPS, the market is also facing some challenges that hinder the nation or even the globe. CPS devices are resource constraint equipment. Therefore, there need to be more resources like computing power, storage, network capability, and even the size of the battery to maintain the security and privacy of data. A simple CPS-based system configuration is shown in Fig 4.5.

4.3.3 Importance of Cyber-Physical Systems

As technology continues to advance exponentially, we are witnessing the emergence of new, innovative systems that are changing how we live and work. One such system that has gained increasing attention over the years is the CPS. CPS refers to a system that combines physical components, such as sensors and actuators, with computational and communication capabilities to create a network of interconnected devices that can interact with the physical world in real-time.

CPS is becoming increasingly important in our modern world because it is the backbone of the IoT. With billions of devices being connected to the internet, CPS is the driving force behind the interconnectivity and interoperability of these devices, enabling them to communicate and work together seamlessly.

The importance of CPS lies in its ability to bridge the gap between the physical and digital worlds. By bringing together the physical and digital realms, CPS can enable a new level of **automation and control**, making it possible to optimize and streamline a wide range of processes. For instance, CPS can be used in manufacturing to create smart factories, where machines can communicate with each other and humans in real-time to optimize production and reduce downtime.

Another area where CPS can significantly impact is **transportation**. With the advent of autonomous vehicles, CPS can be used to create intelligent transportation systems that can communicate with each other and traffic management systems to optimize traffic flow, reduce congestion, and improve road safety.

CPS is also playing an increasingly important role in healthcare. With wearables and other smart devices, CPS can monitor patients in real-time, enabling doctors and other healthcare professionals to detect health issues early and intervene before they become more serious.

One of the most significant advantages of CPS is its ability to enhance efficiency and productivity. By automating processes and reducing human error, CPS can help businesses and organizations operate more efficiently, reducing costs and improving profitability.

However, with great power comes great responsibility, and CPS has challenges. One of the most significant challenges of CPS is security. With so many devices connected to the internet, the potential for cyber-attacks and data breaches is a real concern. As such, it is essential to implement robust security measures to protect these systems from cyber threats.

Another challenge of CPS is the complexity of the systems. CPS involves the integration of multiple technologies and components, making it challenging to design, develop, and maintain these systems. As such, it is essential to have skilled professionals with the expertise to design, develop, and maintain these systems effectively.

Characteristics of CPS

CPS has gained a good reputation by proven tremendous achievements in application emerged as a vital application, especially since the focus on autonomous and self-service machinery has gained attention and taken on a more significant role in manufacturing and construction works. CPS portrays several significant characteristics that enable it to integrate physical and computational components and allow communication with each other seamlessly to perform multiple tasks.

Cyber-Physical Systems are systems that integrate physical components with computational elements. The fundamentals of CPS are as follows:

1. Control Theory: CPS involves designing and implementing control systems that can interact with physical systems. Control theory is essential for understanding how to design controllers that can achieve the desired behavior of a CPS.

2. Real-time Systems: CPS often involves systems that operate in real-time, meaning that they must respond to events and stimuli in a timely manner. Real-time systems are critical to ensure that the physical and computational systems can interact in a coordinated and efficient way.

3. Sensor Networks: CPS often relies on sensor networks to collect data about the physical environment. Sensor networks provide information that can be used to control and optimize the behavior of a CPS.

4. Communication Networks: Communication networks are critical for enabling the exchange of information between the physical system and the computational system. CPS must be able to handle the challenges of communication over wireless networks, which can be subject to interference and delay.

5. Embedded Systems: CPS often involves designing and implementing embedded systems, which are computer systems integrated into physical devices. Embedded systems are critical for controlling and monitoring physical systems in real-time.

6. Security: CPS must be designed with security in mind to ensure that the physical system and computational systems are protected against cyber-attacks. Security is critical to prevent malicious actors from disrupting the behavior of a CPS and causing physical harm.

The Architecture of Cyber-Physical Systems

A CPS is an integrated network of physical processes, computational elements, and communication infrastructure. The rise of IR4 in the industry has paved the way for a drastic deployment of CPS to have more systematic and detailed monitoring of the physical peripheral. These systems combine embedded computing, sensing, and control to interact with the physical world in real-time. The architecture of a CPS typically consists of several layers that interconnect and interact with each other to ensure proper functioning.

Physical Layer: The physical layer consists of the physical entities or processes that the system interacts with or monitors. This layer can include devices, machinery, sensors, actuators, and other physical components. The physical layer is responsible for collecting data from the environment and performing actions based on instructions received from the cyber layer.

Sensing and Actuation Layer: This layer comprises sensors and actuators facilitating the interaction between the physical and cyber layers. Sensors gather data from the physical layer, while actuators perform actions in response to instructions from the cyber layer. Examples of sensors include temperature, pressure, and proximity sensors, while actuators can range from simple motors to complex robotic arms.

Communication Layer: The communication layer ensures the efficient transfer of data between different components of the CPS. This layer is responsible for connecting the sensing and actuation layer with the cyber layer, enabling the exchange of information between them. Depending on the system's requirements, communication can be wired or wireless and may use various protocols such as Zigbee, Wi-Fi, or Ethernet.

Cyber Layer: The cyber layer comprises the computational elements responsible for data processing, decision-making, and control. This layer hosts various software components, including data processing algorithms, machine learning models, and control algorithms. The cyber layer processes the data received from the sensing and actuation layer and generates instructions for the actuators based on the desired outcomes or goals.

Application Layer: The application layer is the topmost layer in the CPS architecture, focusing on the specific goals or functionalities the system aims to achieve. This layer encompasses the user interfaces, data analytics, and other software applications that utilize the information processed by the cyber layer. The application layer defines the overall purpose and behavior of the CPS.

Security and Privacy Layer: As CPSs often deal with sensitive data and critical operations, security and privacy are essential to their architecture. This layer ensures the system remains protected from external threats and maintains user data privacy. Techniques such as encryption, secure communication protocols, and access control mechanisms are employed to achieve these goals.

The architecture of Cyber-Physical Systems involves multiple interconnected layers that work together to achieve a specific goal or functionality. Each layer plays a crucial role in the system's overall functioning, from data collection and communication to processing and actuation. Ensuring the security and privacy of these systems has become a critical aspect of their design.

Technologies for Cyber-Physical Systems

CPS refers to integrating computation, networking, and physical processes to enable smart, autonomous systems capable of interacting with the real world. In CPS, physical components are connected to computational components through sensors, actuators, and other devices. The computational components control the physical components, gather sensor data, and make decisions based on that data.

Fig. 4.5 is a graphic showing a CPS's component view. This figure demonstrates the CPS's three main components:

1. Computational Components: These are the components responsible for processing data, making decisions, and sending commands to the physical components. They can be implemented as software, hardware, or a combination.

2. Sensors: These components detect and measure physical phenomena such as temperature, pressure, or motion. They provide input to the computational components.

3. Actuators: These components convert the output of the computational components into physical actions such as moving a motor, opening a valve, or turning on a light.

This seamless integration of physical and virtual systems has revolutionized various industries, such as manufacturing, transportation, healthcare, and energy management. Key technologies that facilitate

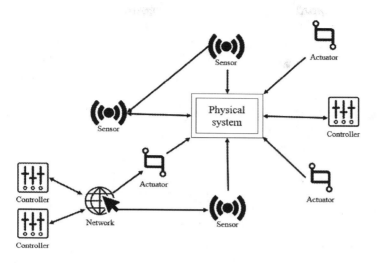

Figure 4.6 CPS component view.

CPS include the IoT, Artificial Intelligence (AI), cloud computing, wireless sensor networks, and cybersecurity. CPS relies on various technologies as below to achieve desired performance with enhanced functionality.

1. Sensor and actuator networks: These networks consist of a collection of sensors and actuators distributed across the CPS to detect and control physical processes. These networks can be wired or wireless and enable the exchange of data between the physical world and computational systems.

2. WSNs: WSNs consist of spatially distributed sensors that communicate wirelessly to collect and transmit data about their environment. These networks are crucial for monitoring and controlling physical processes in CPS. WSNs can be used to detect changes in environmental conditions, monitor equipment performance, and provide feedback for control systems. WSNs enable real-time data collection and analysis, making them ideal for use in CPS applications.

3. IoT: IoT forms the backbone of CPS, allowing for the interconnection of physical devices, vehicles, buildings, and other objects. IoT devices gather data from their environment using sensors and actuators, and communicate with one another through embedded

computing systems and wireless networks. The data collected by IoT devices are essential for enabling CPS to make intelligent decisions and optimize system performance. IoT refers to a network of devices, sensors, and objects that are connected to the internet and can communicate with each other. In the context of CPS, IoT technology enables the collection of data from sensors and other components in the physical world and their integration with computational systems.

4. Cloud Computing and Edge Computing: Cloud computing provides on-demand access to shared computing resources, such as servers, storage, and applications, over the internet. Edge computing, on the other hand, involves processing data at the edge of the network, close to the source of the data, rather than sending it to a centralized cloud. Cloud computing supports the real-time processing and analysis of data collected by IoT devices, allowing CPS to make informed decisions quickly. Both cloud computing and edge computing can be used in CPS to provide computational resources for processing data and enabling real-time responses.

5. AI: AI plays a critical role in CPS by providing the capability to analyze large volumes of data generated by IoT devices, identify patterns, and make predicted decisions based on that data. Machine learning (ML), a subset of AI, is especially useful for processing, analyzing, and interpreting the data collected by IoT devices in real-time. Additionally, AI/ML can be used to automate decision-making processes and optimize system performance.

Finally, the Physical Components refer to the parts of the CPS that perform the physical work. Depending on the application, they can include mechanical, electrical, or chemical systems. The component view of CPS shows us how physical and computational components work together to achieve a specific goal.

System View of Cyber-Physical Systems

A system view of CPS provides a holistic perspective that encompasses the various interconnected components and processes that make up these complex systems. This perspective is crucial for understanding, designing, and managing CPS effectively. A CPS can be viewed as a network of interacting components categorized into three layers: physical, cyber, and human. The physical layer consists of the processes the CPS is

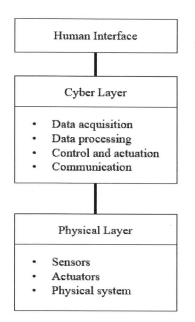

Figure 4.7 Three layers of CPS.

designed to control or monitor. The cyber layer consists of the computational and communication systems that gather and process data from the physical layer and control the physical processes. Fig. 4.7 shows the three layers of the CPS briefly. The human layer comprises the human operators and stakeholders interacting with the system.

A few of the key aspects of a system view of CPS include:

1. Integration of physical and cyber components: CPS combines physical processes, such as sensors and actuators, with cyber components like computation and communication. A system view of CPS recognizes the interdependencies and interactions between these elements and aims to optimize their integration for efficient and reliable performance.

2. Multi-scale and multi-domain: CPS often span multiple scales, from nano- and micro-scale devices to large-scale infrastructure systems. They also operate across various domains, such as transportation, healthcare, and energy. A system view acknowledges

these varying scales and domains and strives to address their specific requirements and constraints.

3. Heterogeneity: CPS typically involves diverse components, technologies, and standards. A system view considers this heterogeneity and focuses on developing interoperability and seamless integration of these disparate elements.

4. Real-time and dynamic operation: Many CPS operate under strict real-time constraints and respond dynamically to changing conditions. A system view takes into account the need for real-time performance and adaptability and designs systems that can meet these requirements.

5. Human interaction: CPS often interacts with human users or operators, either directly or indirectly. A system view acknowledges the importance of human factors, such as usability, safety, interface design, user experience, and the impact of automation on human roles and skills. These criteria are critical considerations in CPS design.

6. Networking and communication: CPS consists of physical systems and computational systems that are highly interconnected. The physical system includes sensors, actuators, and other hardware components, while the computational system includes software and communication networks. The efficient exchange of information between CPS components is essential for system performance. A system view emphasizes the design of effective communication protocols, architectures, and networking technologies that support reliable, secure, and energy-efficient data exchange.

7. Security and privacy: Ensuring the security and privacy of CPS is critical, given their potential vulnerabilities to cyber-attacks and the sensitive data they handle. A system view addresses these concerns by incorporating security and privacy measures into system design and management.

8. Resilience and reliability: A system view of CPS prioritizes the resilience and reliability of the system in the face of component failures, software bugs, or external disturbances. This involves designing fault-tolerant and self-healing mechanisms that can maintain system functionality even under adverse conditions.

9. Energy efficiency: A system view also considers the energy consumption of CPS, aiming to minimize energy usage through the development of energy-efficient hardware, software, and communication protocols.

10. Legal, ethical, and regulatory aspects: A system view of CPS takes into account the broader legal, ethical, and regulatory contexts in which these systems operate, addressing challenges related to safety, liability, and data protection.

The physical layer consists of processes monitored and controlled by sensors and actuators. The data from the physical layer is acquired by the cyber layer through sensors and then processed by the computational systems. Based on the data and control inputs, the cyber layer generates control signals sent to the physical layer through actuators. The human layer interacts with the system through a human interface that provides information about the state of the physical processes and allows human operators to give input to the system.

The cyber-physical interface is the layer that connects the cyber and physical space. It includes hardware and software components allowing communication and control between the two spaces.

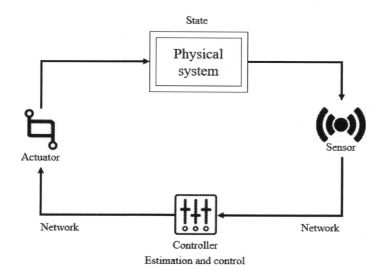

Figure 4.8 CPS system view.

Wang et. al (2010) [119] described the general workflow of CPS into four steps:

1. **Monitoring**: To ensure the upcoming events of the essential CPS function may achieve the goal of CPS based n the response received.

2. **Networking**: All sensors and actuators in the network need to communicate with each other to generate dissemination and assemblages in real-time.

3. **Computing**: Sensors are used to collect and analyze the condition of the environment to ensure it is working well in normal circumstances and meeting the minimum criteria.

4. **Actuation**: This step takes necessary actions against the *Computing* phase by reacting to the change in the physical process. For instance, a water sprinkler may turn on to water the crop.

4.3.4 Cyber-Physical Systems Design Principles and Methodologies

CPS represents the integration of computation, communication, and control technologies, seamlessly linking the physical world with the cyber realm. The fusion of these technologies underpins the functioning of numerous application domains, such as autonomous vehicles, smart grids, robotics, and healthcare systems. As such, CPS's design is essential for these systems' successful operation. In this subsection, we will explore the fundamental design principles and methodologies of Cyber-Physical Systems.

Design Principles

The design of CPS is guided by several principles to ensure that the systems achieve the desired performance, reliability, and robustness level. The key principles are as follows:

- **Holistic Design:** CPS design requires a holistic approach that accounts for the interdependencies and interactions between the cyber and physical components. This entails the integration of various disciplines, including computer science, engineering, and mathematics, to address the complex challenges posed by the integration of computation, communication, and control technologies.

- **Scalability:** CPS must be designed to accommodate the increasing scale of interconnected devices and systems, which can lead to increased complexity and communication overhead. Scalability is achieved through modular and hierarchical architectures, efficient algorithms, and communication protocols that can handle large nodes and connections.

- **Adaptability:** Given the dynamic and uncertain nature of the environments in which CPS operates, adaptability is a critical design principle. CPS must be capable of modifying their behavior in response to environmental changes, including the ability to learn and adjust to unforeseen circumstances.

- **Resilience:** Ensuring the resilience of CPS is essential due to its critical role in various application domains. This involves designing the systems to tolerate and recover from failures, whether hardware, software, or communication-related. Techniques such as redundancy, fault tolerance, and error correction are employed to enhance the resilience of CPS.

- **Security and Privacy:** CPS faces many cybersecurity threats, given their interconnected nature and reliance on communication networks. Therefore, security and privacy must be integral to the design process. This encompasses encryption, authentication, access control, and secure communication protocols to protect against unauthorized access, data breaches, and cyberattacks.

Design Methodologies

The complex nature of CPS necessitates using systematic design methodologies encompassing the entire development lifecycle, from requirements analysis and specification to implementation, verification, and validation. Key methodologies for CPS design include:

- **Model-Based Systems Engineering (MBSE):** MBSE is a methodology that relies on creating and manipulating system models to represent the structure, behavior, and interactions of CPS. This approach enables engineers to analyze and simulate the system's behavior under various scenarios and conditions, facilitating early detection and resolution of design issues. MBSE promotes interdisciplinary collaboration and allows for efficient and accurate communication between stakeholders.

- **Formal Methods:** Formal methods involve the use of rigorous mathematical techniques for the specification, design, and verification of CPS. These methods provide a high level of assurance regarding the correctness and reliability of the system, reducing the risk of failures and vulnerabilities. Examples of formal methods include model checking, theorem proving, and formal verification.

- **Co-Design and Co-Simulation:** Given the tight integration between CPS's cyber and physical components, co-design and co-simulation methodologies are essential. These approaches enable the concurrent design of hardware and software components, as well as the simulation and testing of the system in a unified environment. This facilitates identifying and resolving design issues and ensures seamless interaction between the cyber and physical components.

- **Component-Based Design:** Component-based design is a modular approach that emphasizes developing and assembling reusable software and hardware components. This methodology facilitates the rapid and efficient development of CPS by enabling the reuse of proven components and reducing the complexity of system design. By leveraging existing components, engineers can focus on developing novel functionalities, enhancing the overall efficiency and effectiveness of the design process.

- **Iterative and Incremental Development:** To address the evolving requirements and complexity of CPS, iterative and incremental development methodologies are employed. These approaches involve the progressive refinement and extension of the system through a series of iterations, allowing for incorporation of new features and improvements based on feedback and evaluation. Examples of such methodologies include Agile, Scrum, and Extreme Programming (XP).

- **Verification and Validation (V & V):** Ensuring CPS's correctness, reliability, and safety is paramount. Verification and validation methodologies are employed throughout the design process to assess whether the system meets the specified requirements and functions as intended. Verification focuses on checking the consistency and correctness of the design, while validation involves evaluating the system's performance and behavior under real-world conditions. Techniques for V&V include simulation, testing, formal methods, and model checking.

The design of Cyber-Physical Systems demands a thorough understanding of the intricate interdependencies between the cyber and physical components. By adhering to essential design principles such as holistic design, scalability, adaptability, resilience, and security and utilizing systematic methodologies like MBSE, formal methods, co-design, component-based design, iterative development, and V&V, engineers can develop robust, efficient, and reliable CPS that can cater to the ever-growing demands of today's interconnected world.

4.3.5 Cyber-Physical Systems Modeling and Simulation

CPS are complex, interconnected networks of physical processes and computational components that seamlessly integrate the physical world with the digital realm. These systems have become ubiquitous in modern society, powering applications such as autonomous vehicles, smart grids, robotic systems, and healthcare. Due to their inherent complexity and the critical nature of many of their applications, it is essential to accurately model and simulate CPS to ensure optimal performance, safety, and reliability. In this section, we will discuss the modeling and simulation of CPS.

CPS modeling focuses on capturing the dynamic interactions between physical processes, computational elements, and communication networks that define the system's behavior. This multidisciplinary approach necessitates integrating knowledge from various fields, including control theory, computer science, and communication systems. The primary goal of CPS modeling is to develop accurate, computationally efficient representations of system components and their interactions, enabling the evaluation of design choices, predicting system behavior, and optimizing performance.

On the other hand, simulation is the process of using these models to virtually replicate the real-world behavior of a CPS under various conditions. This allows researchers and engineers to test, validate, and refine system designs, identify potential issues, and explore new ideas without needing costly and time-consuming physical prototypes. Simulation can also be employed for operator training, maintenance planning, and understanding the impact of unexpected events on system performance.

There are several challenges in CPS modeling and simulation. One of the most significant is the **heterogeneous nature** of the systems, which often consist of diverse components with distinct characteristics, such as continuous dynamics in the physical domain and discrete dynamics in the cyber domain. This necessitates the developing of **hybrid modeling techniques** that can effectively capture the interactions between these disparate elements. Additionally, the large-scale nature of many CPS and the presence of distributed components with **complex communication patterns** further complicate the modeling process.

To overcome these challenges, various modeling and simulation approaches have been proposed. One common approach is using **multi-domain modeling languages**, such as Modelica and SysML, which facilitate the representation of diverse components and their interactions. Another technique is the development of **co-simulation frameworks** that enable the integration of multiple simulation tools, each specialized for a particular domain, to simulate the overall system behavior. Such frameworks include the Functional Mock-up Interface (FMI) and the High-Level Architecture (HLA). Furthermore, formal methods, such as **model checking and theorem proving**, can be employed to verify the correctness of CPS models and ensure their adherence to safety and performance requirements.

4.3.6 Communication and Networking in Cyber-Physical Systems

CPS represents a new paradigm in computing, where the physical world and the digital realm are tightly interconnected. These systems consist of sensors, actuators, and computing devices, which collaborate to monitor, control, and optimize processes in various sectors, such as transportation, healthcare, energy, and manufacturing. A key aspect of CPS functionality is the seamless communication and networking among its components, which ensures real-time and precise decision-making, efficient resource utilization, and enhanced resilience.

Communication and networking in CPS play a critical role in achieving the desired level of interoperability, responsiveness, and reliability. The complex interplay of heterogeneous [132, 133] devices, diverse communication protocols, and stringent latency requirements necessitates a robust communication infrastructure that can support the efficient exchange of information across various system layers.

Communication Protocols and Technologies

Multiple communication protocols and technologies have been developed to facilitate data exchange among CPS components. These protocols can be broadly classified into wired and wireless categories, with the latter gaining more prominence due to their scalability and flexibility.

- Wired Protocols: These include Ethernet, Controller Area Network (CAN), and MODBUS, extensively used in industrial automation systems. These protocols offer deterministic communication with low latency, making them suitable for time-sensitive applications.

- Wireless Protocols: Some widely adopted wireless protocols include ZigBee, Bluetooth, Wi-Fi, and 5G/6G. These protocols cater to various CPS requirements, such as low power consumption, high data rates, and long-range communication. For instance, ZigBee is ideal for low-power, low-data-rate applications, while 5G/6G offers high-speed data transfer, ultra-reliable low-latency communication, and massive machine-type communications.

Network Architectures and Topologies

The network architecture and topology play a vital role in determining the performance and scalability of a CPS. Common network topologies include star, mesh, and hybrid configurations. Star topology has a central hub through which all devices communicate, while a mesh topology allows direct communication between devices, improving fault tolerance and network resilience. Hybrid [134] topologies combine the advantages of different architectures to create an optimized network [135].

In recent years, edge computing has emerged as a promising approach to address traditional cloud-based architectures' latency and bandwidth limitations. By pushing computation and decision-making closer to the data source, edge computing reduces the data transfer overhead and enables real-time processing.

Communication and networking are essential for the efficient functioning of Cyber-Physical Systems. The choice of communication protocols, network architectures, and topologies significantly influences the system's performance, scalability, and resilience.

4.3.7 Control and Optimization of Cyber-Physical Systems

CPS are complex, integrated networks of physical and computational processes designed to enable advanced monitoring, control, and optimization of real-world systems. These systems are increasingly prevalent in various sectors, such as transportation, healthcare, energy, and manufacturing, where they are responsible for critical infrastructures that impact our daily lives. The seamless integration of the cyber and physical domains in CPSs allows for increased efficiency, adaptability, and scalability but also brings forth new challenges in terms of control and optimization. This section provides an in-depth overview of the key aspects related to the control and optimization of CPSs, including the fundamentals, challenges, techniques, and applications.

Fundamentals of CPS Control and Optimization

The primary goal of control and optimization in CPSs is to achieve desired performance levels while considering system constraints, uncertainties, and disturbances. The underlying processes involve monitoring physical variables, processing data, making decisions, and executing actions in the physical domain. These processes necessitate the use of advanced control and optimization algorithms, which can be broadly classified into *centralized, decentralized,* and *distributed approaches.* Centralized algorithms rely on a single decision-making entity, while decentralized and distributed methods allow for decision-making at multiple levels, enabling greater flexibility and adaptability.

Challenges in CPS Control and Optimization

There are several challenges inherent in CPS control and optimization, which can be broadly grouped into four categories:

- Complexity: CPSs are typically large-scale, non-linear, and interconnected systems, making it difficult to develop accurate models and control strategies.

- Uncertainty: Inherent physical and cyber-domain uncertainties can lead to unpredictable behavior and performance degradation. These uncertainties include sensor noise, communication delays, and unpredictable disturbances.

- Security: The interconnected nature of CPSs makes them vulnerable to cyber-attacks, which can compromise their functionality and performance. Ensuring security while maintaining optimal control is a significant challenge.

- Scalability: As CPSs grow in size and complexity, the computational and communication requirements for control and optimization algorithms can become prohibitively expensive, necessitating scalable and efficient solutions.

Techniques for CPS Control and Optimization

CPSs are widely used in transportation, healthcare, energy management, and manufacturing domains. Various control and optimization techniques are employed in the design and operation of CPSs to ensure efficiency, robustness, and resilience. To address the aforementioned challenges, researchers have developed a variety of control and optimization techniques for CPSs, including:

- Model-Based Control: Model-based control techniques rely on mathematical models of the system's dynamics to develop controllers that can efficiently regulate the system's behavior. Examples of model-based control techniques include Linear Quadratic Regulators (LQR), Proportional-Integral-Derivative (PID) controllers, and Model Predictive Control (MPC). These techniques require accurate models of the system, which may not always be available or easy to obtain.

- Data-Driven Control: Data-driven control techniques leverage the power of machine learning and artificial intelligence to develop controllers based on the data collected from the system. These techniques can be particularly useful when accurate system models are unavailable or when the system's behavior is too complex to be captured by traditional model-based approaches. Examples include reinforcement learning, adaptive control, and neural network-based control.

- Hybrid Control: CPSs often exhibit continuous and discrete behaviors, requiring a mix of continuous and discrete control actions. Hybrid control techniques combine the strengths of continuous and discrete control methods to handle these mixed behaviors effectively. Examples include hybrid automata, mixed-integer optimization, and switching control.

- Adaptive Control: Adaptive control techniques can automatically adjust their parameters to account for system dynamics, uncertainties, or operating conditions changes. This enables the controller to maintain the desired performance as the system evolves over time. Examples include gain scheduling, self-tuning regulators, and adaptive model predictive control.

- Resilient or Robust Control: Uncertainties and disturbances can severely affect the performance of a CPS. Robust control techniques are designed to provide satisfactory performance even in the presence of uncertainties and disturbances. Examples include H-infinity control, robust model predictive control, and sliding mode control.

Various control and optimization techniques can be applied to CPSs to achieve desired performance objectives. The choice of the appropriate technique depends on factors such as the availability of accurate system models, the level of uncertainty and disturbances, the desired performance criteria, and the complexity of the system's behavior.

4.3.8 Cyber-Physical Systems in Different Domains

The main objective of a CPS is to ensure the efficient, reliable, and safe operation of physical processes. CPS has become increasingly prevalent in many areas, including manufacturing, transportation, healthcare, agriculture, and energy. They are expected to play a critical role in the future of smart cities and the IoT. CPS is beneficial in today's modern lifestyle, where everything is connected by the Internet and communicated using devices. CPS has the most significant impact on Critical Infrastructure like healthcare, smart grid, manufacturing, transportation, defense system, aerospace, building design, environmental quality, robotics, surveillance systems, and large-scale infrastructure like constructions and utilities [126, 136]. CPS technologies have changed how people react to engineering. Comparatively, the internet changed how people react to information.

Medical Health Care

Researchers have more interest in improving device performance through modeling and analysis. There are a lot of biomedical sensors for better monitoring and control of a patient, from portable wearable devices to smart monitoring systems that track how patients react to a specific medication. Technological breakthroughs in portable medical devices with embedded sensors at a more affordable price have gained the interest of healthcare professionals and caregivers for better understanding and monitoring of an individual's health condition in real-time, for example, a cardiac detector for arterial and ventricular fibrillation. Lately, there has been a significant advancement in utilizing smart devices or apparatus in healthcare: smart capsules to detect cancer, pulse rate, infusion pumps, accelerometer sensor, hearing aids, blood glucose monitoring, pulse oximeter for oxygen reading, and medical and biomedical sensors [137].

The term *Telehealth* or *telemedicine* are used interchangeably, especially during the outbreak Coronavirus period. It was due to its promising cost-effectiveness and treatment for patients without physical human contact, which happened to be the cause of Covid-19 spreading worldwide. However, although both refer to remotely treating patients, telehealth has broader coverage than telemedicine as it refers to remote non-clinical services, such as administrative meetings, health care, and continuing medical education. It is also gaining popularity in rural areas where access to physical health treatment is complex and troublesome [138]. The platform has introduced a new experience to the public, besides being more convenient than meeting a doctor physically at a clinic, according to patients' feedback. It is also not restricted by time; patients may make appointments at their own pace. Patients may also choose and pick their favorable doctors and specialists according to the area they want to seek consultations. Here are some examples of how CPS could be used in medical healthcare:

1. **Remote Patient Monitoring:** CPS can monitor patients remotely using sensors, wearables, and other devices. This enables healthcare providers to track patient health and well-being in real-time and respond quickly to any changes or emergencies.

2. **Personalized Medicine:** CPS can be used to develop personalized treatment plans for patients based on their unique characteristics, such as genetic makeup, lifestyle factors, and medical history. This can help doctors and other healthcare providers deliver more effective treatments with fewer side effects.

3. **Predictive Analytics:** With the help of CPS, large amounts of data from medical records, clinical trials, and other sources to predict the likelihood of disease could be analyzed, as well as identify high-risk patients and develop more effective treatment plans.

4. **Medical Robotics:** CPS can be used to develop medical robots that perform various tasks, such as surgery, drug delivery, and rehabilitation. This can help reduce the risk of human error, improve precision, and increase efficiency.

5. **Asset Management** CPS can be used to track and manage medical supplies, medications, and other materials to ensure they are delivered on time and in the right quantity. This can help reduce waste, minimize costs, and improve patient care. The need to protect the privacy and security of a patient in telehealth is always the top priority in the healthcare environment. Besides holding Electronic Health Records (EHR), telehealth refers to the extensive use of EHR along with PII, such as name, home address, blood type, treatment records, and medicine consumed, both clinical and administrative.

Fig. 4.9 shows how CPS was deployed in the healthcare system and benefited its stakeholders conceived from multiple researchers [139–143]. Process 1 shows how data is collected from households and hospitals using various sensors and sent to the cloud for storage. In Process 2, data is sent to a cloud server, and queries are processed in real-time. Process 3 shows how historical data is processed in response to query replies. In Process 4, computation in the cloud has been completed.

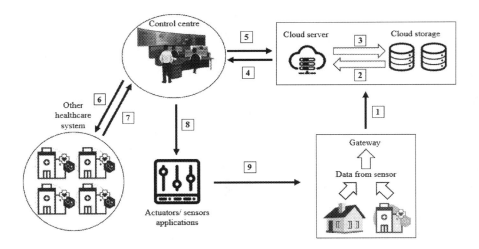

Figure 4.9 CPS in healthcare system.

There is a need to generate and deliver alarms and deliver to the control center. The data will access by other clinical staff via the observation center, as shown in Process 5. The clinical consultations as input may be needed from other healthcare systems, as in Process 6 and get replies from them as in Process 7. Specialists and clinicians from the control center will give decisions to the actuators/sensors as in Process 8 and the necessary actions needed will be delivered back to the sensors on the patients as in Process 9.

Telehealth captured health information in mobile devices, including wearable products like a smartwatch, and the data grew exponentially over the past five years. With the advent of smart devices, many applications were created to capture data from these devices for further analysis. Such devices have gained users' attention by having attractive features, e.g., measuring and monitoring sleeping patterns, heart rate, respiration rate, activity identification, and calories burnt. However, this information is collected from users, but users have no access and control over their own. Researchers proposed a healthcare CPS assisted by cloud computing and big data analytics to improve the quality of healthcare services by enabling real-time monitoring of patients and detecting early diseases [144]. A vast amount of data is collected from medical sensors and health devices, stored in the cloud and analyze by analytics to produce meaningful patient outcomes. The same goes for a data-driven closed-loop for manufacturing complex biomedical devices [145]. The proposed system leverages cyber-physical systems and data-driven techniques to enable real-time monitoring and control of the manufacturing process. The system collects data from various sensors and uses machine learning algorithms to analyze the data and make real-time decisions to optimize production.

Overall, CPS has the potential to revolutionize medical healthcare by improving patient outcomes, increasing efficiency, and reducing costs. However, it is crucial to ensure that these systems are designed, developed, and implemented to prioritize patient safety, security, and privacy.

Supply chain management

SCM has the most prominent potential use of smart sensors to run logistics and ensure product delivery arrives at the customer on time while providing real-time stock control on warehouse and store inventory. By leveraging CPS, businesses can enhance supply chain efficiency, visibility, resilience, sustainability, performance, robustness, stability, and reliability [146,147]. CPS can be used in SCM in several ways and gain benefits as below.

- **Improved Efficiency** CPS can optimize supply chain operations by providing real-time monitoring and control of various processes, such as manufacturing, transportation, and warehousing. This enables businesses to streamline operations and minimize delays, reducing lead times and costs [148]. Additionally, these systems can facilitate better decision-making by analyzing historical data to predict future trends and requirements, allowing companies to adjust their strategies proactively.

- **Enhanced Visibility:** Cyber-physical systems facilitate transparency throughout the supply chain by connecting stakeholders, suppliers, manufacturers, and customers, through a centralized platform. This allows for seamless information sharing, tracking goods and shipments, and monitoring inventory levels. By providing real-time access to this data, businesses can identify potential bottlenecks or inefficiencies, enabling them to take corrective actions and ensure the smooth flow of goods from suppliers to customers.

- **Increased Resilience:** Supply chain disruptions, such as natural disasters, political instability, or pandemics, can have severe consequences for businesses. CPS can help mitigate these risks by monitoring the supply chain in real-time and using advanced analytics to detect potential disruptions early. By identifying these risks, companies can develop contingency plans, diversify their supplier base, and reroute shipments to avoid affected areas. This way, CPS can help businesses maintain their operations even during challenging situations.

- **Sustainable Supply Chains:** As concerns about climate change and environmental degradation grow, businesses increasingly focus on sustainable supply chain management. Cyber-physical systems can play a vital role in achieving sustainability by enabling companies to monitor and control energy consumption, emissions, and waste. By leveraging data from CPS, businesses can identify opportunities to reduce their environmental footprint, such as optimizing transportation routes, implementing energy-efficient manufacturing processes, and adopting circular economy principles.

- **Enhanced Collaboration:** Cyber-physical systems provide a platform for all stakeholders to collaborate and share information, fostering a more integrated and connected supply chain. By breaking down silos between different departments and organizations, businesses can leverage the collective intelligence and resources of their entire supply chain network. This collaborative approach can lead to more innovative solutions, better risk management, and improved overall performance.

- **Better Customer Experience:** CPS can help businesses meet customer expectations by providing real-time information about product availability, shipment status, and estimated delivery times. Companies can enhance customer satisfaction and loyalty by offering more accurate and up-to-date information. Furthermore, businesses can use data from CPS to analyze customer preferences and tailor their offerings accordingly, enabling them to deliver more personalized and relevant products and services.

Manufacturing

Firstly, CPS can enable real-time monitoring and control of manufacturing processes. CPS can gather performance, quality, and energy usage data by integrating sensors and other monitoring devices into machines and equipment. This data can then be used to optimize manufacturing processes, identify potential issues, and prevent downtime. Secondly, CPS can support predictive maintenance. By analyzing data collected from sensors and other sources, CPS can detect when equipment will likely fail and schedule maintenance before it disrupts production. Thirdly, CPS can support automation and robotics. By using software to control machines and robots, manufacturers can reduce the need for human labor and increase the speed and accuracy of production processes. Finally, CPS can enable greater flexibility in manufacturing [149]. By using software to control production lines and supply chains, manufacturers can quickly adapt to changing market demands, such as customization and personalization. Implementing CPS in manufacturing can improve efficiency, productivity, quality, and agility.

Moreover, CPS can enable better communication and collaboration among different systems, machines, and even different facilities within the manufacturing process. It helps manufacturers to optimize their operations, reduce costs, and improve overall performance [150]. Additionally, CPS can enhance the safety and security of the manufacturing process. For example, sensors and cameras can monitor employee safety, while cybersecurity measures can be implemented to protect against data breaches and cyber-attacks [151].

Furthermore, CPS can also provide manufacturers with new opportunities for innovation and product development. Using data analytics and artificial intelligence, manufacturers can gain insights into consumer preferences, identify new trends, and develop new products that meet customer needs. Finally, implementing CPS can also contribute to sustainability and environmental goals. By optimizing energy usage, reducing waste, and minimizing the use of harmful materials, manufacturers can minimize their impact on the environment and contribute to a more sustainable future.

In summary, cyber-physical systems can offer significant benefits to manufacturing, from real-time monitoring and control to improved efficiency, safety, and sustainability. By integrating advanced technologies into their operations, manufacturers can optimize their processes, reduce costs, and enhance their competitive advantage.

Agricultural

CPS has the potential to improve farming operations, enhance crop yields, and reduce waste. The integration of CPS in agriculture can take many forms, from autonomous tractors and drones to sensor-based irrigation and livestock monitoring systems. Below are some examples of how CPS can be used in agriculture [152–154].

- **Precision agriculture** is a farming technique that uses technology to optimize crop yields and reduce waste. CPS can play a significant role in precision agriculture by providing real-time data about soil conditions, weather, and plant growth. By using sensors and actuators, farmers can monitor and control the irrigation, fertilization, and pesticide application in real-time based on the specific needs of each plant.

- CPS can also be used to **monitor the health and behavior of livestock**. Farmers can collect animal movement data, feeding habits, and overall well-being using sensors and cameras. This information can help farmers identify potential health issues, such as disease outbreaks or injuries, and take appropriate action to prevent further damage.

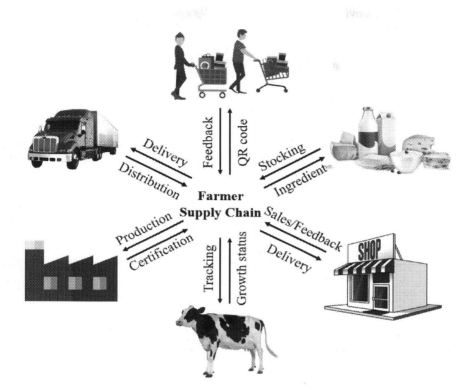

Figure 4.10 Farmer's supply chain system.

- **Autonomous farming** is a growing trend in agriculture. CPS can be used to develop autonomous tractors, drones, and other farming equipment. Without human intervention, these devices can be programmed to carry out specific tasks, such as planting, weeding, or harvesting. It saves farmers time and labor costs, increasing efficiency and reducing waste.

- CPS can also be used to optimize **supply chain management** in agriculture. Farmers can track their crops from the field to the market using sensors and RFID tags, ensuring they are delivered in optimal conditions. It helps reduce waste and increase the quality of the produce.

- CPS can be used to **monitor the environment** in which crops are grown. By collecting data on soil moisture, temperature, and air quality, farmers can adjust their farming practices to ensure that the crops are grown in optimal conditions. It leads to higher yields and better quality crops while reducing waste and minimizing environmental impact.

- CPS can be used to control pests and diseases in crops. By using sensors and actuators, farmers can **detect and control pests and disease** in real-time before they cause significant damage to the crops. It helps reduce the need for pesticides, leading to healthier crops and a more sustainable farming operation.

CPS has the potential to revolutionize agriculture by improving efficiency, increasing crop yields, and reducing waste. By using sensors, networks, and software to interact with the physical world, farmers can optimize their farming practices, reduce labor costs, and minimize their impact on the environment [155]. With the growing demand for sustainable farming practices and the need to feed an increasing global population, CPS in agriculture is a promising solution for the future of farming.

Transportation

CPS in **transportation** refers to integrating physical systems, such as vehicles, roads, and infrastructure, with computer-based systems that collect and analyze data and provide real-time information to drivers and transportation agencies. Although the integrated systems are complex, using CPS in transportation is seen as a way to improve safety, reduce congestion, and increase efficiency [156].

One of the primary applications of CPS in transportation is the development of autonomous vehicles. These vehicles use a combination of sensors, cameras, and artificial intelligence to navigate roads and make driving decisions. Transportation infrastructure, inclusive of the terrestrial and aerial systems, has been impacted by CPS, where the later vehicles emerged. This technology is seen as a way to reduce accidents caused by human error and increase transportation efficiency by reducing traffic congestion and improving fuel efficiency. However, the future of transportation is confronted with the obstacle of incorporating autonomous vehicles into the conventional traffic flow. Self-driving vehicles are equipped with multiple sensing technologies, for instance, Light Detection and Radar (LiDAR), Radio Detection and Ranging (RADAR), ultrasonic sensors, GPS, and Wheel Position Sensor (WPS). These

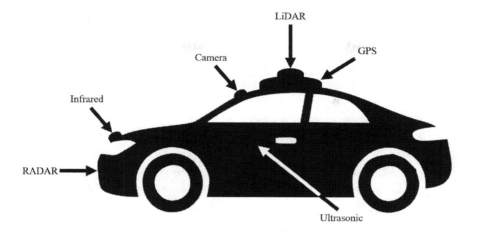

Figure 4.11 Self-driving car sensors.

sensors are used in various combinations, depending on the specific self-driving car model and its level of autonomy. The combination of sensors to perceive and interpret their surroundings, make decisions, and navigate safely [157].

Another application of CPS in transportation is the development of smart traffic management systems. These systems use data from sensors and cameras to monitor traffic flow, predict congestion, and adjust traffic signals in real-time to improve traffic flow and reduce delays [158]. This technology also improves safety by alerting drivers to hazards such as accidents or road closures.

CPS is also used to develop Intelligent Transportation Systems (ITS) designed to integrate different modes of transportation, such as cars, buses, trains, and bicycles, into a seamless transportation network. This technology improves mobility and sustainability, reduces congestion, and improves safety by providing real-time information to travellers about traffic conditions, transit schedules, and other transportation-related information [159].

Transportation is a multifaceted industry that involves the movement of people and goods through various modes, such as air, land, and sea. On the other hand, fleet management focuses specifically on managing a company's fleet of vehicles. With the advent of cyber-physical systems (CPS), fleet management has been transformed to include real-time monitoring of vehicle condition and performance, optimization of fuel consumption with recommended routes, and proactive monitoring of driver behavior to ensure safety. By providing advance cautions and alerts, CPS can significantly reduce the likelihood of accidents, and fleet managers can take corrective action based on real-time data and insights before any serious issues occur. As a result, CPS has become an essential tool for improving the efficiency, safety, and sustainability of fleets in today's transportation industry.

Overall, using CPS in transportation can significantly improve the safety, efficiency, and sustainability of transportation systems [160]. However, there are concerns about the potential for cybersecurity threats and the need to ensure that these systems are designed with privacy and security in mind. As CPS continues to evolve and become more integrated into transportation systems, it will be important to carefully consider these issues to ensure that they are safe, secure, and effective.

Environment and sustainability

CPS could build a data-rich ecosystem that makes automation possible in the environmental area. The fourth industrial revolution has played a significant role in improving sustainability and creating new opportunities for industries to adapt to the urgent needs of society for competitive and sustainable manufacturing. One crucial strategy for achieving this is energy efficiency, a key aspect of sustainable and carbon-neutral production [161]. Below are some methods and solutions that can benefit the overall efficiency of processes in terms of energy consumption using CPS.

1. Resource Optimization: Sensors installed at premises could optimize the use of resources by monitoring and controlling physical processes in real-time. For example, in a smart building, CPS can regulate lighting, humidity and temperature, and HVAC systems to reduce energy consumption.

   Besides that, CPS enables real-time monitoring and control of energy consumption in various systems such as buildings, transportation, and manufacturing. This real-time monitoring allows for more efficient use of energy resources, reducing waste and costs associated with unnecessary energy consumption. For example, smart buildings equipped with CPS technology can automatically adjust heating, ventilation, regulate lighting, humidity and temperature, and HVAC systems based on occupancy levels, thereby reducing energy waste and lowering operating costs.

2. Environmental Monitoring: CPS can collect real-time data on environmental parameters such as air quality, water quality, and weather conditions. This information can help manage natural resources, detect environmental hazards, and take necessary precautions to minimize the impact of pollution.

3. Energy efficiency: CPS can be used to optimize energy consumption in buildings, factories, and other infrastructure. For example, smart thermostats can monitor and adjust heating and cooling systems based on occupancy and weather data, reducing energy waste. It may reduce carbon emissions from traditional vehicles and factories and optimise logistics and transportation processes, reducing fuel consumption and greenhouse gas emissions.

4. Precision Agriculture: CPS can optimize agriculture practices by real-time monitoring soil moisture, nutrient levels, and other variables. This information can help farmers to optimize crop yield while minimizing the use of fertilizers and pesticides.

5. Sustainable transportation: CPS have the potential to enhance traffic flow, alleviate congestion, and boost transportation efficiency. Intelligent traffic management systems, as an instance, can dynamically modify traffic signals to minimize delays and enhance fuel efficiency. Moreover, CPS can contribute to sustainability efforts by enabling predictive maintenance. By constantly monitoring physical systems and analyzing data, CPS can accurately predict maintenance needs, thereby reducing the likelihood of unexpected breakdowns and the necessity for urgent repairs. This proactive approach minimizes waste associated with replacing damaged components and extends the lifespan of equipment and machinery.

6. Sustainable agriculture: CPS offer valuable applications in enhancing crop yields, conserving water resources, and reducing the reliance on pesticides and hazardous chemicals. Precision agriculture systems serve as an example, utilizing sensors and analytics to continuously monitor factors such as soil conditions, weather patterns, and crop growth. This wealth of data enables farmers to make well-informed decisions regarding irrigation, fertilization,

and pest management. By leveraging CPS technology, agricultural practices can be optimized to maximize productivity while minimizing environmental impact.

7. Waste reduction: CPS can be used to improve waste management processes and lower landfill waste. Smart waste management systems, for instance, can monitor the volume of waste produced in real-time and improve waste pickup routes to cut down on emissions and fuel use.

8. Smart Transportation: CPS can optimize the movement of goods and people, reducing emissions and improving efficiency. Smart traffic management systems can reduce congestion, while electric and hybrid vehicles can reduce carbon emissions.

9. Renewable Energy: CPS can help integrate renewable energy sources, such as solar and wind power, into the grid by integrating them with traditional energy sources like fossil fuels. CPS can monitor energy generation from renewable sources and dynamically adjust power usage and storage to ensure that the energy produced is used efficiently and effectively.

Automotive Telematics

The CPS technology can be used to improve the safety, efficiency, functionality, and overall performance of the system with the capability to work together to perform a specific task. Automotive telematics refers to integrating telecommunications and information technologies with vehicles, allowing for the remote monitoring and control of various vehicle systems [162]. In this context, CPS involves seamlessly coordinating advanced data-driven solutions with real-world systems. In automotive telematics, this fusion of digital and physical realms enables improved vehicle connectivity, monitoring, and decision-making capabilities [163].

- **Vehicle Connectivity and Communication:** The emergence of connected vehicles has paved the way for innovative telematics solutions. By utilizing CPS, vehicles can now communicate with other vehicles, infrastructure, and cloud-based services, sharing information in real-time. This level of connectivity promotes Advanced Driver Assistance Systems (ADAS), such as adaptive cruise control, lane departure warnings, and collision avoidance systems. By processing data from various sensors and cameras, vehicles can make informed decisions, anticipating potential hazards and adjusting their behavior accordingly.

Moreover, CPS-enabled automotive telematics supports Vehicle-to-Everything (V2X) communication, which encompasses Vehicle-to-Vehicle (V2V), Vehicle-to-Infrastructure (V2I), and Vehicle-to-Pedestrian (V2P) interactions. These technologies ensure enhanced road safety and improve traffic flow [164], traffic management, and environmental sustainability, and reduce congestion and accidents. For instance, traffic signal information can be transmitted to vehicles, allowing them to adjust their speeds to reduce fuel consumption and emissions.

- **Fleet Management and Optimization:** CPS-based telematics systems significantly improve fleet management, allowing operators to monitor and optimize the performance of their vehicles remotely. Real-time data on fuel consumption, vehicle health, driver behavior, and location can be collected and analyzed to identify potential inefficiencies and areas for improvement. This information can then be used to plan effective maintenance schedules, optimize routes, and reduce operational costs.

  Additionally, incorporating predictive analytics and machine learning, CPS-based telematics can foresee potential component failures and schedule preventive maintenance. This proactive approach helps minimize downtime, extend vehicle lifespan, and reduce maintenance costs.

- **Enhanced Safety and Security:** CPS plays a crucial role in enhancing vehicle safety and security. Advanced driver assistance systems rely on sensor fusion and real-time data processing to detect and mitigate potential risks. For example, CPS can enable features like blind-spot detection, forward-collision warnings, and pedestrian detection, alerting drivers and even initiating autonomous emergency braking to prevent accidents.

  Furthermore, CPS-based telematics can improve vehicle security by employing advanced monitoring and intrusion detection systems. In the event of unauthorized access or theft, these systems can notify the vehicle owner or authorities and track the vehicle's location in real-time.CPS can be used to improve the security of vehicles. It can help prevent theft by tracking the vehicle's location and alerting the owner or law enforcement if it is moved without authorization. CPS can also help protect against cyber-attacks by implementing secure communication protocols and software updates.

- **Personalized Driving Experience:** CPS enables the development of personalized driving experiences through telematics. By analyzing driver behavior, preferences, and driving habits, vehicles can automatically adjust settings, such as seat position, climate control, and infotainment preferences. Additionally, connected vehicles can leverage cloud-based services to access real-time information on weather, traffic, and nearby points of interest [165], providing personalized guidance and recommendations to drivers.

Smart Grid

A smart grid is a modern electrical power grid infrastructure that utilizes advanced technologies to manage and distribute electricity efficiently. Smart grids use advanced communication, control, and monitoring technologies to manage the flow of electricity in real-time, optimizing the efficiency and reliability of the grid. Integrating CPS using sensors, actuators, embedded controllers, and communication networks into smart grid systems has revolutionized the energy industry, offering numerous benefits, such as optimizing energy consumption, reducing waste, and increasing efficiency, reliability, and security [166, 167]. Some examples of how CPS can be used in smart grids include:

1. Monitoring and control: CPS can monitor the flow of electricity through the grid and control power distribution to different areas, ensuring that the grid operates efficiently and effectively.

2. Predictive maintenance: CPS can be used to monitor the health of equipment and predict when maintenance or repairs are needed, minimizing downtime and maximizing the lifespan of the equipment.

3. Demand response: CPS can be used to manage the electricity demand, reducing the strain on the grid during periods of high demand and reducing the need for new power plants.

4. Distributed energy resources: CPS can integrate renewable energy sources, such as solar and wind power, into the grid, ensuring that these energy sources are used efficiently and effectively.

One of the primary applications of CPS in a smart grid is the integration of renewable energy sources such as solar and wind power. Renewable energy sources are highly variable and dependent on environmental conditions, which makes them challenging to integrate into the energy grid. However, using CPS, renewable energy sources can be intelligently integrated into the grid, allowing for efficient and reliable energy distribution.

Obviously, using CPS in smart grids can help increase the grid's efficiency, reliability, security, and sustainability while reducing costs and minimizing environmental impact [168]. By utilizing advanced sensing, communication, and control technologies, CPS can efficiently monitor and manage power generation, distribution, and consumption. This allows for better load balancing, improved fault detection and isolation, and more efficient energy distribution, reducing energy wastage.

CPS improves the reliability of smart grid systems by providing real-time data on system performance and the ability to respond quickly to changes in demand or supply. The integration of advanced analytics algorithms and machine learning techniques allows CPS to predict potential system failures and take proactive measures to prevent them, improving the power grid's reliability and reducing the likelihood of blackouts.

Another critical application of CPS in a smart grid is the use of advanced analytics and machine learning algorithms to predict energy demand and supply. With the integration of CPS, energy providers can collect real-time data from sensors and use this information to optimize energy production and distribution. This helps to reduce energy waste and improve the efficiency of the grid, resulting in lower energy costs for consumers.

Furthermore, CPS enhances the security of smart grid systems by providing robust cybersecurity measures to protect against cyber-attacks. Integrating advanced encryption algorithms and secure communication protocols ensures that the data transmitted within the system is protected from unauthorized access or tampering. This protects against attacks that can compromise the power grid's operation, leading to loss of power or even physical damage to the infrastructure [169, 170].

In addition to these benefits, integrating CPS in smart grid systems enables the implementation of demand response programs. These programs allow utilities to incentivize consumers to reduce energy consumption during peak periods, reducing the strain on the power grid and increasing system stability. Implementing demand response programs also allows for more efficient energy usage and a reduction in consumer electricity costs.

4.3.9 Challenges in Cyber-Physical Systems

CPS integrates computation, networking, and physical processes, enabling complex and innovative applications. However, these systems face various challenges. Security and privacy is crucial, as breaches can lead to disastrous consequences.

Security Challenges in Cyber-Physical Systems

The benefits of CPS that it brings to industries are undeniable. However, the growth of sensor adoptions and the wide spread of users could be the loophole for many information and instructions transferring around. The high frequency of device interactions would increase the risk of failure or other cyber threats. While they offer several benefits, such as improved efficiency and enhanced safety, they also pose several challenges, including:

- *Security:* CPS systems are vulnerable to cyber attacks, which can lead to the theft of sensitive information or the malfunctioning of physical components. Cybersecurity threats can affect the integrity and availability of CPS systems and the critical infrastructure they support. These attacks can cause physical damage or even harm human life, and as such, security is a critical challenge for CPS. There are a couple of attacks have been identified that may harm CPS:

  1. **Eavesdropping** refers to an attack where the attacker intercepts information during transmission through a network passively, not interfering with the system at all. The attacker must only observe the system's behavior while sensors transfer data via the network. Such an attack compromises the integrity and privacy of the data, especially if sensitive or personal information is being transmitted.

  2. **Compromised-key attack** A key is a confidential code necessary to interpret secure information. If an unauthorized

person gains access to the key, it is considered compromised. With a compromised key, an attacker can get access to secured communication without detection by the sender or receiver. The attacker can perform all the roles and responsibilities as granted and perform actions on the resources and communications.

3. **Man-in-the-middle attack** The attacker sends false messages to the operator, resulting in either a false positive or a false negative. It causes the operator to take unnecessary actions or not take necessary actions. The attack may lead the operator to take corrective action that could result in an undesirable event. There are numerous ways that control data can be modified or replayed in such attacks, which can affect the system's operations.

4. **Denial of Service** is a type of network attack that aims to disrupt the processing or response of legitimate traffic or requests for network resources. These attacks involve overwhelming the network with a large amount of data to consume its resources and prevent regular services from being provided. Such an attack can prevent the system from functioning normally, and once the attacker gains access to the network of cyber-physical systems, they can perform various actions, including:

    (a) Flooding the controller or the entire sensor network with traffic until it overloads and shuts down.

    (b) Sending invalid data to controller or system networks, causing abnormal termination or behavior of the services.

    (c) Blocking traffic results in authorized elements of the system losing access to network resources.

- *Safety:* CPS systems operate in real-time and control physical systems, which can result in significant consequences in case of malfunctions or failures. The safety of CPS systems must be ensured to avoid catastrophic events, not even malfunction or faulty the system, as it could result in significant consequences. For instance, safety is the paramount and top priority in power grids, transportation systems, and medical care services. The impact is a life-threatening situation, economic loss, or property damage.

To ensure the safety and stealth of a system, going through rigorous repeating tests, verification, and validation of the design and operation is a must while ensuring compliance with international and industry standards and regulations to meet a certain quality of control and reduce the risk. The safety of CPS systems is a significant challenge that requires a multidisciplinary approach that integrates engineering, computer science, mathematics, and social sciences expertise.

- *Complexity:* CPS systems involve a large number of components and interactions that make it difficult to design, implement, and maintain. The complexity arises from integrating several components, such as sensors, actuators, control systems, and communication networks. This complexity also increases the likelihood of

- *Interoperability:* CPS systems often need to communicate and exchange information with other systems, which may use different technologies or protocols. CPS consists of multiple components, such as sensors, actuators, controllers, and software systems, developed by different vendors with varying standards and protocols. These components must work seamlessly together for the CPS to function correctly. Achieving interoperability between these components is a significant challenge.

- *Scalability:* CPS systems are designed to operate in dynamic and changing environments, and as such, they need to be scalable to accommodate new requirements, devices, and applications. As the system keeps developing and growing, the quantities of connected devices will also grow in size and complexity, and it becomes challenging to manage and synchronize the communication. Issues like delays, throughput, performance, speed, and response time may lead to bottlenecks or downtime. Furthermore, CPS requires rapid and real-time response time with zero downtime and low latency to perform and achieve at scale. Researchers are working hard to address the scalability problem by innovating in edge computing [171], fog computing [172,173], distributed control, and machine learning-based optimization approaches.

- CPS often involves *human users or operators*, so it's essential to address human factors such as usability, user experience, and the potential impact of automation on human jobs and skills.

- Reducing the energy consumption of CPS is vital for their widespread adoption, especially in energy-constrained environments. This necessitates the development of *energy-efficient* algorithms, communication protocols, and hardware components.

- Many CPS require real-time or near-real-time performance, which imposes strict *real-time constraints* on system response times. Meeting these requirements can be challenging, especially when dealing with complex, large-scale systems.

- CPS systems raise several *ethical and legal issues*, such as privacy, data protection, liability, and accountability. All our alerts of how CPS is vulnerable to cyber-attacks could result in *privacy* compromising of individuals and an organization's security. Ensuring that CPS systems comply with legal and ethical standards can be challenging, especially given their complexity and real-time nature. It was due to the capability of sensors and actuators to collect and store personal data, which raises public concerns about how the data is used, protected, and shared.

- Another issue related to ethics is *accountability and transparency* whereby CPS is all computer-based algorithm controlled, which may create a lack of transparency and bias in the decision-making process. When CPS starts rolling out to the public, issues related to legal may also arise. CPS may get involved in accidents or incidents resulting in harm, property damage, or injury. It raises legal actions to be taken over the reliability and liability for any damage that happened.

- The other issue of concern will be on *intellectual property rights and ownership* of data generated by CPS. CPS generates massive data that may involve valuable intellectual property, such as trade secrets, patents, or copyrights. As CPS often involves the integration of hardware and software from multiple parties with data, it will make it difficult to determine the owner of the collected data. For instance, wearable smart devices generate data from the end-user while the software to collect belongs to the company or the analyst. The data belongs to the end user. Hence they have no control and access to the data. Meanwhile, competitors or unauthorized parties could easily steal the data, which may lead to infringement or business loss. The worst case is that it is hard to trace and track where the infringement occurred and who is responsible for the loss.

Addressing these challenges requires a multidisciplinary approach integrating expertise from computer science, engineering, mathematics, and social sciences.

Main Privacy Issues and Solutions in Cyber-Physical Systems

The network is the most vulnerable component of CPS as attackers may use the control system channels by using denial of service and cause delays in getting a response. Technologies are taking over our daily lives, and more operations are moving towards automation and self-service. Almost all businesses are driven by technology. Therefore, security plays a vital role. Traffics are being sent as input and output via an electronic device. There is a need to protect these data from being manipulated and altered by the wrong parties intentionally or unintentionally.

Apart from facing security challenges, as mentioned above, CPS also poses significant privacy concerns, specifically due to the vast amount of data generated by these systems. These systems can collect, store, and process personal data such as location, health information, and biometric data. The misuse of this data can lead to significant harm to individuals, including identity theft, financial loss, and reputational damage. Therefore, it is essential to address the privacy issues related to CPS.

1. ***Data Breaches*** has become one of the main privacy concerns in CPS. Data breaches occur when unauthorized individuals gain access and steal personal data. Due to the interconnected nature of CPS, a single vulnerability in the system can lead to a widespread data breach. For instance, a vulnerability in a single sensor can allow hackers to access the entire system. Furthermore, data breaches can occur due to human error, malicious attacks, or software vulnerabilities.

2. CPS collects vast amounts of data, including personal information such as location, health information, and biometric data. Although this data is necessary for the system's functioning, it can also be collected unintentionally and become ***Unintended Data Collection***. For instance, a smart home system can collect data on the habits and routines of its occupants without their knowledge or consent. The collection of this data can violate an individual's privacy and lead to the misuse of their personal information.

3. The **Lack of Transparency** in CPS is another significant privacy concern. Due to the complex nature of these systems, it can be challenging to understand how they operate and use personal data. Multiple sensors, actuators, and edge nodes [174,175] are interconnected via a wired or WSN, which makes the integrity of the data become the top priority to ensure the system results are high in trustworthiness. This lack of transparency can make it difficult for individuals to make informed decisions about how their data is used.

4. **Unauthorized Access** to personal data is another significant privacy issue in CPS. Due to the interconnected nature of these systems, a single vulnerability in the system can allow hackers to gain access to personal data. Furthermore, unauthorized access can occur due to human error or insider threats.

5. The **Misuse of Personal Data** is a significant concern in CPS. The vast data these systems collect can be used for various purposes, including advertising and targeted marketing. However, this data can also be used for malicious purposes like identity theft or financial fraud. Therefore, it is essential to ensure that personal data collected by CPS is used only for its intended purpose.

6. **Third-party access** Many CPS are designed and maintained by third-party vendors. This can pose a risk to privacy if these vendors do not properly secure the system or collect and share sensitive data without authorization. To address this, organizations can implement contractual obligations and audit requirements to ensure that vendors comply with privacy and security regulations.

7. **Network security** CPS rely on network connectivity to communicate with other systems and devices. This can make them vulnerable to DoS attacks or Man-In-The-Middle (MITM) attacks. CPS designers can use secure communication protocols and implement intrusion detection and prevention systems to address this.

A few of the solutions have been addressed to solve the issues in CPS:

1. **Encryption** is one of the primary solutions to address privacy concerns in CPS. Encryption involves converting data into code, which can only be decrypted using a key. This process ensures

that data is protected and cannot be accessed by unauthorized individuals. Furthermore, encryption can secure communication between different system components, ensuring data is transmitted securely.

2. ***Access Control*** is another essential solution to address privacy concerns in CPS. Access control involves restricting access to sensitive data to authorized individuals only. This process ensures that personal data is protected and cannot be accessed by unauthorized individuals. Furthermore, access control can restrict access to different system components, ensuring authorized individuals access only data.

   Several access control models are available to regulate the process of authorization and authorization for the system.: Access Control Lists (ACLs), Role-based Access Control (RBAC), and ABAC. Which model to use depends on the purpose of computer networking and security protection. For instance, RBAC is based on roles, and access is only granted based on the roles assigned, with every permission associated with specific resources. ABAC is a model to grant permission based on user attributes, such as user identification, job position, department, location, and other metadata related to the user. ABAC seems more flexible as it could take account of both user and resource attributes.

3. ***Privacy by Design*** is a design approach that considers privacy issues at the beginning of the system's design. This process ensures that privacy is incorporated into the system's design rather than added as an afterthought. Furthermore, privacy by design help ensures that the system is transparent and data collection is limited to only what is necessary for the system's intended purpose. This approach can also ensure that privacy is considered throughout the system's lifecycle, from design to decommissioning.

4. ***Data Minimization*** involves collecting only the minimum amount of data necessary for the system's intended purpose. This approach can help reduce the risk of unintended data collection and minimize the risk of data breaches. Furthermore, data minimization can help reduce the risk of the misuse of personal data, as there are fewer data available to be misused.

5. ***Regular Security Audits*** can help identify vulnerabilities in the system and address them accordingly before hackers can exploit them. Furthermore, security audits can help ensure that the

system operates as intended and that personal data is protected. Conducting security audits may ensure the organization always complies with international and industry standards, which might preserve the quality of products and services. Regular security audits can also help ensure the system complies with relevant privacy regulations.

6. *Training and Awareness* are essential in addressing privacy concerns in CPS. Employees and system users should be trained to identify and respond to security threats. Furthermore, individuals should be informed of their privacy rights and how their data is used. This approach can help ensure that individuals are informed and make informed decisions about how their personal data is used.

7. *Data Masking* is a technique used to protect sensitive or confidential data by replacing the original data with a masked or obfuscated version. This technique solves privacy issues by preventing unauthorized access to sensitive data, even if it is accidentally or maliciously disclosed. The process to implement data masking in solving data privacy issues is as below:

   (a) The first step is to **identify the sensitive data** that needs to be protected. This can include PII such as names, addresses, social security numbers, and financial data.

   (b) There are different levels of data masking, and the **appropriate level of masking required** depends on the sensitivity of the data and the intended use of the masked data. For example, some data may require full masking, while others only need partial masking.

   (c) There are several **data masking techniques** available, including substitution, shuffling, and encryption. The chosen technique will depend on the level of masking required and the intended use of the masked data.

   (d) Once the appropriate data masking technique has been chosen, it can be **implemented to mask the sensitive data**. This can be done using automated tools or manual processes, depending on the size and complexity of the data set.

   (e) It is important to **test and validate the masked data** to ensure that it is accurate and usable for its intended purpose. This can involve checking for data consistency, comparing the masked data to the original data, and testing the masked data in the same environment where the original data was used.

(f) **Monitor and maintain the masked data** are important to ensure that it continues to provide the necessary level of privacy protection. This can involve implementing access controls and audit trails to track who has accessed the masked data and how it has been used.

8. ***Privacy Regulations*** such as the GDPR and the CCPA are essential in protecting individuals' privacy rights in CPS. These regulations require organizations to protect personal data and ensure that individuals have control over it. Furthermore, privacy regulations can help ensure that organizations are transparent about their data collection practices and that individuals are informed about how their data is used.

The misuse of personal data collected by CPS can lead to significant harm to individuals. Therefore, it is essential to address privacy concerns in CPS. Encryption, access control, privacy by design, data minimization, regular security audits, training and awareness, and privacy regulations are some solutions to address privacy concerns in CPS. By implementing these solutions, organizations can ensure that personal data is protected and individuals' privacy rights are respected.

4.3.10 Emerging Trends in Cyber-Physical Systems

- CPS has come a long way since its inception, with advances in information and communication technology revolutionizing various domains. As we move towards a more interconnected world, new and innovative applications of CPS are emerging across diverse industries. There are some of the most notable trends in the field of Cyber-Physical Systems.

- One of the most significant trends in CPS is the proliferation of **IoT** devices. IoT refers to a network of physical objects embedded with sensors, software, and connectivity to exchange data. With billions of IoT devices predicted to be in use in the coming years, they will play an integral role in creating smarter CPS by enhancing data collection, processing, and communication.

- **Machine Learning and Artificial Intelligence** are becoming increasingly important in CPS. These technologies enable the analysis of vast amounts of data generated by IoT devices and facilitate real-time decision-making. By incorporating AI and ML, CPS can better adapt, optimize, and predict potential issues, leading to increased efficiency and reduced downtime.

- **Edge Computing** is another emerging trend in CPS, addressing the challenges of data volume, latency, and security. Instead of transmitting data to a centralized cloud, edge computing processes data closer to the source, reducing the need for bandwidth and minimizing latency. This enables CPS to respond faster and more effectively, providing real-time insights and actions. The edge computing and IoT integrated model are specifically designed to cater to the requirements of a scalable and controllable IoT system. It effectively leverages the benefits of edge computing to establish a robust mechanism while also considering cost savings.

- The rollout of **5G networks** and their successors will dramatically impact the capabilities of CPS. Faster data transmission, lower latency, and enhanced connectivity will enable the rapid exchange of information between devices and systems. This will allow for more complex and demanding applications, such as autonomous vehicles and remote surgeries, to become a reality.

- **Digital Twins** are virtual replicas of physical assets, processes, or systems, which serve as a bridge between the physical and digital worlds. By simulating real-world conditions, digital twins enable the optimization of processes, identification of potential issues, and testing of new designs. The growing adoption of digital twins in CPS allows for improved system monitoring and predictive maintenance, leading to increased efficiency and cost savings.

- As CPS become more interconnected and critical to our daily lives, the need for robust **cybersecurity** measures has never been greater. Emerging trends in cybersecurity include advanced encryption techniques, blockchain technology, and AI-powered threat detection, all aimed at securing these systems from malicious attacks.

- As CPS evolve, **human-machine collaboration** is becoming increasingly important. By incorporating technologies such as Augmented Reality (AR), Virtual Reality (VR), and haptic interfaces, CPS can provide intuitive and interactive experiences that enhance human decision-making and performance. This collaboration will be essential in areas such as healthcare, manufacturing, and transportation.

- CPS has the potential to contribute significantly to **environmental sustainability** by optimizing resource usage, reducing waste, and minimizing emissions. For example, smart grid systems can balance energy production and consumption, while precision agriculture can optimize water and fertilizer usage. As climate change concerns grow, the development of sustainable CPS solutions will become even more crucial.

- **Industry 4.0** also known as the Fourth Industrial Revolution, is characterized by the increasing digitalization and automation of manufacturing processes. CPS plays a central role in this transformation, enabling real-time monitoring and control of production, predictive maintenance, and increased collaboration between humans and machines. This leads to greater efficiency, flexibility, and reduced production costs.

- **Autonomous Systems** is a critical component of the future of CPS. Self-driving vehicles, drones, and robots are just a few examples of autonomous systems that rely on CPS for navigation, decision-making, and control. As technology advances, we can expect to see increased adoption of autonomous systems in areas such as transportation, agriculture, and warehousing, leading to improved safety, efficiency, and productivity.

- **Smart Cities** leverage CPS to optimize urban infrastructure, services, and resource management. By incorporating IoT devices, advanced analytics, and automation, smart cities can improve traffic management, waste disposal, energy efficiency, and public safety. As the global urban population continues to grow, the demand for smart city solutions will only increase.

- CPS is transforming the healthcare industry by enabling remote monitoring, diagnostics, and treatment. Wearable devices and sensors can track vital signs and alert healthcare providers of potential issues, while telemedicine and remote surgeries can bring expert care to patients in rural or remote areas. As the need for accessible and cost-effective healthcare solutions grows, we can expect to see increased adoption of CPS technologies in the **healthcare and remote medicine** domain.

Cyber-Physical Systems have shown its emerging trends in shaping the future of various industries, with the potential to revolutionize the way we live and work. From smart cities to healthcare, these trends highlight the importance of continuous innovation and the need for interdisciplinary collaboration to address the challenges and seize the opportunities presented by an increasingly connected world. As we move forward, it is essential that we harness the power of CPS to create a more sustainable, efficient, and productive future for all.

4.3.11 Future Trends and Opportunities in Cyber-Physical Systems

CPS are systems that integrate physical processes with computation, communication, and control. They are becoming increasingly prevalent in our daily lives, from autonomous vehicles to smart homes and factories. The future challenges and opportunities in CPS are numerous and varied. The challenges that arose in CPS are discussed in Subsection 4.3.9. Therefore, a few opportunities have been promoted to overcome such situations.

CPS has helped in increasing the efficiency of physical processes by integrating computation and human control, This evolution lead to significant cost reduction, improved performance, prevention of bias, and better quality control over the production line. In addition, CPS help improves the safety of applications, from autonomous vehicles to smart homes and factories. This also helps in reducing accidents, saving lives, and increasing fault detection. Meanwhile, CPS may improve our quality of life by automating tedious tasks, monitoring our health, and making our homes and workplaces more comfortable and convenient. CPS may also help in ensuring robustness and resilience in the face of hardware failures, software bugs, and cyber attacks is a critical research challenge for CPS in the near future. Finally, CPS can enable new business models and revenue streams, such as subscription services for smart home automation or usage-based insurance for autonomous vehicles.

4.4 SUMMARY

This chapter discussed mobile cloud systems and cyber-physical systems. In Section 4.1, the security problems from the customer's perspective, the lack of trust in the cloud due to the cloud's characteristics, and the problems brought by multi-tenancy in the cloud. Followed by Section 4.2 which discusses the taxonomy of threats, focusing on confidentiality, integrity, and availability. Finally, Section 4.3 explained the importance of cyber-physical systems, from concept, component view, and system view, up to the challenges of CPS and the main privacy issues faced by the industry. A few outstanding examples of CPS implementation are also listed.

4.5 EXERCISES

After completing this chapter, please answer the following questions.

1. What are the concepts and motivations of Cyber-Physical Systems?

   - Cyber-physical systems (CPS) are integrated systems that tightly couple physical and cyber components, creating a seamless interface between the physical and digital worlds. CPS integrates physical and computational resources to improve the efficiency and effectiveness of a wide range of systems, including transportation, manufacturing, and healthcare.

   - The concept of CPS is motivated by the growing need to address the complexity, heterogeneity, and interdependence of modern engineering systems. These systems are becoming increasingly complex, with a growing number of interacting components, sensors, and actuators. As a result, the design, operation, and maintenance of these systems require a comprehensive understanding of their physical, cyber, and social aspects.

   - CPS has three main components: physical systems, cyber systems, and the interface between the two. Physical systems refer to the hardware, such as sensors and actuators, that interact with the physical world. Cyber systems include software, networks, and computing resources that enable the processing, analysis, and control of physical systems. The interface between the two components enables communication and coordination between the physical and cyber components.

   - The motivation behind CPS is to improve the performance and efficiency of engineering systems by using real-time feedback and control mechanisms. For example, CPS can be used to optimize traffic flow in cities by using sensors to detect traffic patterns and adjust traffic lights accordingly. In manufacturing, CPS can be used to improve the quality and efficiency of production processes by using sensors to monitor machines and adjust their settings in real-time. CPS has the potential to revolutionize many industries by enabling the development of new technologies and systems that are more responsive, adaptable, and efficient.

2. What are the common issues and challenges faced by Cyber-Physical Systems?

Cyber-Physical Systems (CPS) combine physical systems with cyber technologies to achieve efficient and effective system control and monitoring. As with any technology, CPS presents issues and challenges that must be addressed to ensure optimal performance and security. Here are some of the most common issues and challenges in CPS:

- Security: One of the biggest challenges in CPS is ensuring its security. Since these systems are connected to the internet, they are vulnerable to cyberattacks. A breach in security can cause much damage to the physical system, making it crucial to have robust security protocols in place.

- Safety: CPSs are designed to manage and control physical systems, which makes safety a critical concern. Any malfunction in the system can cause accidents and injuries, so safety must be built into the system design.

- Complexity: CPS is a complex system requiring multiple technologies to work in tandem. This complexity can make it challenging to design, develop, and maintain CPSs.

- Interoperability: CPS integrates various technologies and systems often designed to work separately. Interoperability issues can arise, and it can be challenging to resolve these issues.

- Scalability: CPS often requires integrating multiple physical systems, making it difficult to scale the system as the business grows.

- Privacy: CPS generates a vast amount of data, which can include personal information. It is important to protect this data from unauthorized access and use.

3. What are the component views of CPS?

Cyber-Physical Systems (CPS) are integrations of computational, networking, and physical components that enable intelligent and autonomous decision-making. CPS has a wide range of applications, from robotics and autonomous vehicles to smart cities and energy management. To understand the technical implementation of CPS, it is essential to examine its key component views:

- Computational Components: These are the algorithms, software, and hardware that enable data processing, analysis, and control in CPS. They include embedded systems, microcontrollers, processors, and high-performance computing platforms. Computational components execute various tasks, such as sensor data processing, decision-making, and control of physical processes, based on mathematical models and algorithms.

- Networking Components: Communication infrastructure plays a crucial role in CPS, as it enables data exchange between the computational and physical components. Networking components, such as wired and wireless communication technologies, protocols, and middleware, ensure reliable and secure data transmission among sensors, actuators, and computational units. This communication is crucial for real-time monitoring, control, and coordination of distributed CPS elements.

- Physical Components: The physical components of a CPS include sensors, actuators, and other devices that interact with the environment. Sensors collect data from the physical world, such as temperature, pressure, or position, while actuators perform actions based on computational decisions, like controlling motors or adjusting valves. Physical components are essential for CPS to monitor and control processes, maintain safety, and ensure optimal performance.

- Cybersecurity: As CPS becomes increasingly interconnected, the risk of cyber-attacks grows. Ensuring the security of data, communication, and control systems is paramount for the safe and reliable operation of CPS. Security measures include encryption, authentication, intrusion detection, and secure software development practices, all of which aim to protect the system from unauthorized access, manipulation, or disruption.

- System Integration and Interoperability: The successful implementation of CPS relies on the seamless integration of its diverse components. Standardization, open architectures, and modular design approaches facilitate the interconnection of different elements, allowing for interoperability and scalability. This enables the development of more complex and adaptive systems, as well as the possibility of integrating legacy systems and emerging technologies.

- Human-Machine Interaction: As CPS often involves complex decision-making and control tasks, user-friendly interfaces and effective human-machine interaction are critical. Visualization tools, virtual and augmented reality, and natural language processing techniques help users better understand and interact with CPS, enabling more informed decisions and efficient system management.

4. What are the key aspects of a system view of Cyber-Physical Systems?

- Heterogeneity: CPS typically involves diverse components, technologies, and standards. A system view considers this heterogeneity and focuses on developing interoperability and seamless integration of these disparate elements.

- Networking and communication: CPS consists of physical systems and computational systems that are highly interconnected. The physical system includes sensors, actuators, and other hardware components, while the computational system includes software and communication networks. The efficient exchange of information between CPS components is essential for system performance. A system view emphasizes the design of effective communication protocols, architectures, and networking technologies that support reliable, secure, and energy-efficient data exchange.

- Security and privacy: Ensuring the security and privacy of CPS is critical, given their potential vulnerabilities to cyber-attacks and the sensitive data they handle. A system view addresses these concerns by incorporating security and privacy measures into system design and management.

- Real-time and dynamic operation: Many CPS operate under strict real-time constraints and respond dynamically to changing conditions. A system view takes into account the need for real-time performance and adaptability and designs systems that can meet these requirements.

- Human interaction: A system view acknowledges the importance of human factors, such as usability, safety, interface design, user experience, and the impact of automation on human roles and skills. These criteria are critical considerations in CPS design.

- Resilience and reliability: Being the top priority of the system in the face of component failures, software bugs, or external disturbances. This involves designing fault-tolerant and self-healing mechanisms that can maintain system functionality even under adverse conditions.

5. How cyber-physical systems beneficial to healthcare, manufacturing, transportation and automotive telematics?

- Healthcare: CPS can improve patient care by enabling real-time monitoring of vital signs, medication adherence, and other health parameters. For example, wearable devices that use CPS technology can track a patient's heart rate, blood pressure, and oxygen saturation levels, and alert medical professionals if any abnormalities are detected. This can help doctors make more accurate diagnoses and provide better treatment.

- Manufacturing: CPS can improve manufacturing efficiency by enabling real-time monitoring of production processes, inventory levels, and equipment performance. For example, CPS technology can be used to monitor the performance of machines and equipment, detect defects in products, and optimize production schedules to minimize downtime.

- Transportation: CPS can improve transportation safety and efficiency by enabling real-time monitoring of traffic patterns, weather conditions, and other factors that affect travel. For example, CPS technology can be used to optimize traffic flow, predict accidents, and provide real-time information to drivers about road conditions and alternate routes.

- Automotive telematics: CPS can improve vehicle safety and efficiency by enabling real-time monitoring of vehicle performance, driver behavior, and road conditions. For example, CPS technology can be used to monitor engine performance, detect maintenance issues, and provide real-time feedback to drivers about their driving habits.

6. What are the challenges faced by Cyber-Physical Systems in handling privacy issues?

- CPS often collects and processes massive amounts of data, including personal information such as location, health information, and other sensitive data. Ensuring that this data is collected, stored, and aggregated in a privacy-preserving manner is a significant challenge. It could become unintended data collection due to collection by habits and routines without their knowledge and consent.

- Users need to have control over their data, know what data is being collected, and can provide informed consent for its use is a crucial aspect of privacy protection. Achieving this in the context of complex CPS is challenging due to the technical complexity and the multitude of stakeholders involved.

- As the system keeps developing and growing, the quantities of connected devices will also grow in size and complexity, and it becomes challenging to manage and synchronize the communication. As the number and complexity of interconnected CPS grow, privacy protection mechanisms must be able to scale accordingly, without sacrificing performance or security. Issues like delays, throughput, performance, speed, and response time may lead to bottlenecks or downtime. Furthermore, CPS requires rapid and real-time response time with zero downtime and low latency to perform and achieve at scale. Many works have been carry on to address the scalability problem by innovating in edge computing, fog computing [176], distributed control, and machine learning-based optimization approaches.

- Preserving user privacy often requires anonymizing or de-identifying the collected data. However, it can be challenging to achieve true anonymization without sacrificing the utility of the data, especially in the context of interconnected systems.

● There is a need to balance privacy and functionality, which can be challenging. Overemphasis on privacy can hamper the efficiency and effectiveness of these systems, while inadequate privacy protection can lead to breaches and loss of trust.

GLOSSARY

Attack Interfaces: is any entry point or interaction between an attacker and a system in computer security.

Auditability: refers to the ability to track and analyze security-related events and activities in a system or network.

Availability: means the data must always be accessible to authorized users. Availability is related to system up-time and response time.

Confidentiality: is about protecting the data and information have restrictions and only on limited access and exposure so that it could prevent the data from unauthorized access and data breach.

Data Sovereignty: refers to the concept that data is subject to the laws and regulations of the country or region where it is stored.

Forensics: refers to collecting, analyzing, and preserving digital evidence to determine the cause of a security incident and identify the responsible parties.

Integrity: is defined as the protection of information and information system from improper alteration or eradication, along with non-repudiation and accuracy of the information.

Massive Data Mining: is extracting valuable insights and knowledge from large datasets using advanced data analysis techniques.

Multi-Tenancy: refers to multiple users or tenants sharing a common computing infrastructure, such as a cloud environment.

Supervisory Control and Data Acquisition: is a fully computer-based production control system that is commonly used in a wide range of industry applications.

CHAPTER 5

Threat Models and Network Security

This comprehensive chapter delves into threat modeling and its pivotal role in fortifying network security. It provides a clear and concise definition of threat modeling and its main components, followed by an in-depth discussion of the key issues and threat models in IoT computing, with a detailed examination of various attack types. The subsequent section focuses on network security, particularly Web Services, shedding light on the advantages and disadvantages of SOAP and REST API. In addition, the chapter covers fundamental network security principles, such as access control, and emphasizes the importance of implementing them for robust network security.

5.1 INTRODUCTION TO THREAT MODEL

5.1.1 Concept of Threat Model

The security of information system involves various aspects, which is to be planned comprehensively for the security of the whole system and covered in the whole life cycle of the system. The security of information system involves various aspects, which is to be planned comprehensively for the security of the whole system and covered in the whole life cycle of the system. As a whole, it includes two parts, namely theory and practice. At the theoretical level, it is necessary to design the system architecture, form the overall framework, expand, refine and improve in the framework, and form a methodology that can guide practice. At the practical level, it is necessary to face the application scenarios and give specific application measures according to the specific business

DOI: 10.1201/9781032694818-5

characteristics, vision planning, mission and target strategy, etc., and in combination with the business needs.

A **Threat** [177] is a potential breach of system security that could have some negative impact on the system. From the moment a system is created, it is exposed to various forms of security threats.

Security Threat Modeling (or **Threat Modeling**) is a cyclical process for information system security threats that includes identification, documentation, and mitigation processes. In this process, a threat model describing the potential attack of the system will be generated. This model can be used to understand the implementation of the attack and calculate the level of security risk brought by the security threat. According to the risk level of the threat attack, the order and strength of the system to deal with the threat and the security treatment scheme adopted by the system will be determined. The threat modeling is to find the possible security [178] vulnerabilities of the system from the perspective of the attacker, detect the internal state and workflow of the system, and help the security personnel understand the security state of the system. These aspects or factors help us evaluate the advantages, disadvantages and threats of any given situation, and provide us with feasible solutions or measures to prevent security vulnerabilities.

The first step in threat modeling is to find out the valuable resources that need to be protected in the system, that is, the security targets. A clear safety goal is helpful to clarify the work purpose and formulate the work plan. This process should ensure that the system is fully understood and that the correct security goals are set.

The **Threat Model** is basically a conceptual tool for understanding and improving network security. The threat model has many aspects: attack surface (which technology or system they use as the potential "entry point" of the attack), adversary (who may be interested in attacking their security), attack medium (attack means or attack means) and mitigation methods (possible solutions or preventive measures to reduce the risk of attack). A threat model typically includes:

- Description of the subject to be modeled.

- Assumptions that can be checked or challenged in the future as the threat landscape changes.

- Potential threats to the system.

- Actions that can be taken to mitigate each threat.

- A way of validating the model and threats, and verification of success of actions taken.

5.1.2 Main Components of Threat Model

- The system is owned by the **Key Stakeholders**. They want a system that operates effectively and has little risk. To lessen the hazards to an asset, owners will take precautions.

  For each asset, there could be a wide variety of stakeholders. Executives, product owners, and the development and security teams are a few examples. Owners or stakeholders within an organization are generally those who place value in a specific asset and stand to lose if it is undermined.

- An **Asset** is something under the control of an owner or stakeholder and is valued by them. Examples of assets can be computing systems, data or anything that, if compromised, causes damage to the owners.

  Choosing the assets that should be represented in the threat model is an important first step. The potential security risks and threats to these assets can be determined based on this asset identification.

- **Security risk** quantifies the likelihood that something could go wrong with a specific item. It is determined by adding together the likelihood that a specific danger will materialise and its potential effects.

  Risk assessments and threat modeling are closely related. The possible hazards to a certain asset are identified through threat modeling exercises. The probability and impact of each threat are determined using the list of detected threats in a risk analysis. The outcomes of this study are used to identify and rank potential countermeasures that might be utilized to lower asset risk.

- **Threat agents** are separate but related ideas from **security threats**. A threat agent is an actor who has the intent to misuse or harm an asset. The Advanced Persistent Threats (APTs) and other similar organizations fall under this category. Based on their level of sophistication, objectives, relationship to the system (insider versus external threat), and level of trust in the system, threat actors can be categorized.

Threats are the results of actions by threat actors. Threats are the combination of three factors:

- Hostile intent: In order for there to be a danger, the threat actor must want to misuse or harm some asset.
- Capability: An attacker must have the necessary skills, equipment, knowledge, and other resources to carry out a potential threat in order for it to be realized.
- Opportunity: In order for a possible threat to be taken seriously, an attacker must have a chance to accomplish their goal.

When hostile intent, capability, and opportunity converge, a threat actor becomes capable of posing a substantial risk to a system. To effectively mitigate threats, it is crucial to address and eliminate one or more of these three fundamental components. By targeting the hostile intent, reducing the capability, or removing the opportunity, the overall risk to the system can be significantly reduced.

- A **Security vulnerabilities** is an example of a realized threat to a system. They are possible attack points that, if used maliciously, could cost the organization (time, money, resources, and so on).

The main goal of countermeasures like security controls and mitigations is to reduce vulnerabilities. Threats, vulnerabilities, and countermeasures should all have one-to-one relationships since countermeasures lessen the risk to an organization's assets.

- **Security controls and mitigations** are preventative procedures created to get rid of or lessen risks and vulnerabilities. These remedies lessen the possibility that a threat materialises into a weakness, which an attacker can then utilise to damage assets.

Countermeasures might be put into practise as business decisions or technical mitigations. Technical mitigation aims to lower the risk brought on by a potential hazard or weakness. When the possibility and/or impact of a prospective danger or vulnerability are deemed to be sufficiently low, a business decision is made to accept the risk. A threat model connects the risks that have been discovered with the solutions that address them.

5.1.3 Main Issues and Threat Models in IoT Computing

Computing refers to the use of computing technologies to enable the connection and communication of physical devices or objects over the Internet. This involves the integration of hardware, software, and networking technologies to create intelligent and interconnected systems that can collect, analyze, and act on data in real time. IoT computing involves various technologies and components, including sensors, actuators, microcontrollers, wireless networks, cloud computing, and data analytics. These technologies work together to collect and process data from physical devices and objects and communicate that data to other devices or systems over the Internet. Some of the main issues and threat models in IoT can be used to identify and mitigate potential security risks and threats, including:

1. Device theft or loss: IoT devices are small and portable, making them easy to misplace or steal. This can result in sensitive information being accessed by unauthorized individuals.

2. Data interception: IoT devices rely on wireless networks to transmit data, which attackers can intercept. This can result in sensitive information, such as login credentials or financial data, being stolen.

3. Malware and viruses: IoT devices are susceptible to malware and viruses, which can compromise the security of the device and the data stored on it.

4. Rogue applications: Applications downloaded from untrusted sources can contain malware or spyware that can compromise the security of the device and the data stored on it.

5. Phishing attacks: Phishing attacks can be used to trick users into giving up sensitive information, such as login credentials or financial data, by posing as a legitimate entity.

6. Unauthorized access to cloud services: IoT devices often rely on cloud services to store and access data. As the device's internal storage is relatively small, many applications switch to edge computing or fog computing to process the data collected by the devices. This has introduced another loophole whereby data breaches may occur at the low-security features edge and hackers get access

easily. Unauthorized access to these services can result in sensitive information being accessed by unauthorized individuals.

7. Insecure communication protocols: Mobile devices rely on a variety of communication protocols to transmit data, which can be vulnerable to interception and tampering.

5.1.4 Introduction to Attack Types

- **Replay Attack** refers to the attacker sending a packet that has already been received by the target host to deceive the system, mainly used in the identity authentication process to undermine the correctness of the authentication. The Replay attack can be carried out by the initiator or the enemy who intercepts and retransmits the data. Attackers use network monitoring or other methods to steal authentication credentials, and then resend them to the authentication server. Replay attacks may occur during any network communication.

- **Man-in-the-middle attack** is an indirect intrusion attack, which involves using various technical means to virtually place a device controlled by the intruder between two communication devices in a network connection. This device is called a "man in the middle" in IoT.

- **Inflection Attack** When a subject sends a message to its intended subject and requests a response, the attacker intercepts the message and returns it directly to the sender, thereby breaking the protocol.

- **Fragment Overlap Attack** execute simultaneously in two or more consecutive steps, causing duplication between protocol steps and achieving the desired results.

5.2 NETWORK SECURITY IN THE INTERNET OF THINGS

With the prevalence of smartphones, tablets, and other mobile devices, mobile computing has become an essential part of our daily routines, allowing us to communicate and access information from anywhere at any time. Nevertheless, the extensive use of mobile devices has given rise to security threats, including malware attacks, data theft, and unauthorized access. Therefore, it is crucial to adopt effective network security measures to safeguard mobile devices and protect the sensitive data transmitted over wireless networks. This book chapter offers a comprehensive examination of network security in mobile computing, covering common vulnerabilities and threats, security standards and protocols, and best practices for securing mobile devices. By gaining a thorough understanding of these topics, both individuals and organizations can secure their networks and minimize the risk of security breaches.

In this section, we will study the use of Web Services with IoT to create advance and interconnected communicate among the devices for data exchange purpose. For example, IoT devices can be connected to Web Services that provide data storage, analytics, and other services. This enables the devices to share data and functionality with other applications and systems, creating new opportunities for innovation and automation.

5.2.1 Web Service Overview

Web Services are a software architecture that enables communication between different applications over the Internet. They provide a standardized way for applications to exchange data and functionality, regardless of the programming languages or platforms used to develop them.

Web Services are typically categorized into two main types: SOAP (Simple Object Access Protocol) and REST (Representational State Transfer) [179].

Simple Object Access Protocol (SOAP) Web Services

SOAP Web Services utilize a standardized messaging system based on XML to exchange data between applications. These services are often described using a WSDL file and are commonly used in enterprise environments where reliability and security are critical. SOAP Web Services provide a standardized way of exchanging data between applications and support advanced features such as message queuing and transaction processing. Furthermore, SOAP is an official protocol maintained by the World Wide Web Consortium (W3C).

SOAP Web Services follow a client-server architecture, where the client sends a SOAP request message to the server, and the server responds with a SOAP message. The SOAP message contains the details of the request or response, such as the method to be executed, the input parameters, and the output data.

SOAP Web Services are primarily used in enterprise environments where reliability, security, and advanced features such as message queuing and transaction processing are essential. Industries such as finance, healthcare, and government commonly use SOAP Web Services for their critical applications.

There are several reasons why organizations may choose SOAP Web Services over RESTful APIs:

1. Reliability: SOAP Web Services are known for their reliability as they have built-in error handling and message validation capabilities, making them suitable for mission-critical applications.

2. Security: SOAP Web Services have built-in security features such as WS-Security, which provides message-level security, making them suitable for applications that deal with sensitive data.

3. Transaction Processing: SOAP Web Services support transaction processing, which allows multiple requests to be grouped together as a single unit of work, ensuring data integrity.

4. Legacy Systems: Organizations with legacy systems that use SOAP Web Services may choose to continue using them to maintain compatibility with existing systems.

5. WSDL: SOAP Web Services are typically described using a WSDL file, which provides a standardized way of describing the service, making it easier for developers to understand and use.

As a major player in the technology industry, Microsoft has incorporated SOAP Web Services into many of its services to promote secure and reliable communication between applications [180]. Among the frameworks and technologies that leverage SOAP Web Services are ASP.NET Web Services[1], Windows Communication Foundation (WCF)[2], and BizTalk Server[3].

---

[1] Microsoft, https://learn.microsoft.com/en-us/aspnet/overview

[2] Microsoft, https://learn.microsoft.com/en-us/dotnet/framework/wcf/whats-wcf

[3] Microsoft, https://learn.microsoft.com/en-us/biztalk/core/introducing-biztalk-server

ASP.NET Web Services, for instance, is a framework that facilitates the development and consumption of SOAP Web Services using the .NET framework. It provides developers with a plethora of tools and libraries to create and use SOAP Web Services and supports WSDL for the description and discovery of SOAP Web Services.

Similarly, WCF is a technology that eases the development of service-oriented applications that utilize SOAP Web Services. It provides a single programming model for creating distributed applications that can interoperate across different platforms and technologies. On the other hand, BizTalk Server is an enterprise integration server that enhances messaging, business process management, and service-oriented architectures. It supports SOAP Web Services, enabling organizations to create and consume SOAP Web Services in their enterprise applications.

Microsoft also employs SOAP Web Services in its cloud services, including Azure[4] and Office 365[5]. Azure allows the creation and use of SOAP Web Services using WCF, making it possible to develop reliable and secure cloud applications. Azure's WCF support offers developers numerous tools and features to create, host, and manage SOAP Web Services in the cloud. It supports various deployment models like virtual machines, cloud services, and containers.

Furthermore, Azure's WCF support also includes several features to ensure the reliability and security of SOAP Web Services hosted in the cloud. For example, it provides message-level security using standards like WS-Security to encrypt and sign SOAP messages, safeguarding their confidentiality and integrity.

An exemplary case of how Azure employs SOAP Web Services is through its support for the Microsoft Dynamics 365 Customer Engagement Web Services API. This API allows developers to extract and manipulate data from the Microsoft Dynamics 365 customer relationship management platform using SOAP Web Services. In addition, Office 365 employs SOAP Web Services to enable integration with other Microsoft services, facilitating user access to data and services from different applications.

5.2.1.1   What are the elements of SOAP messages?

A SOAP (Simple Object Access Protocol) message is an XML-based message to exchange structured data between client and server applications. The elements of a SOAP message include:

---

[4]Microsoft, https://azure.microsoft.com/en-us

[5]Microsoft, https://www.office.com/

1. Envelope: This is the top-level element of a SOAP message and contains the entire message. It acts as an XML identifier, defines the SOAP message's namespace and indicates the SOAP version being used.

2. Header: This element contains additional header information about the SOAP message, which is optional for SOAP XML Messages, such as authentication data, routing information, or transaction identifiers. This information is not essential for processing the message but can provide additional context.

3. Body: This element contains the data being exchanged between the client and server applications. It defines the content of the request or response message, including the method being called and any parameters or data being passed. This element is mandatory.

4. Fault: This element is used to report errors that occur during the processing of a SOAP message. It contains information about the error, such as an error code and message, and is nested under the response message's body.

These elements work together to define the structure and content of a SOAP message. The envelope and header provide context and information about the message, while the body contains the data being exchanged. The fault element is used to report errors that occur during the processing of the message.

What is WSDL?

A WSDL (Web Services Description Language) is an XML-based language used to describe and specify the functionality of web services. The major elements of a WSDL include:

1. Types: This element defines the data types used in the web service. It specifies the structure of the request and response messages and the data types of the parameters and return values.

2. Messages: This element defines the format of the messages exchanged by the web service. It specifies the input and output messages and the data types of the message parts.

3. Port Type: This element defines the web service's operations. It specifies the input and output messages for each operation and the order in which they are sent.

4. Binding: This element defines the protocol and data format for exchanging messages with the web service. It specifies the SOAP version, transport protocol, and encoding style.

5. Service: This element defines the location of the web service and the binding used to access it. It specifies the endpoint address where the service can be accessed and the binding used to communicate with it.

There are two types of WSDL: abstract and concrete WSDL.

1. Abstract WSDL

It describes the interface of a web service without specifying how it is implemented. It defines the operations, associated messages, input and output messages, and data types. An abstract WSDL only describes the structure of the messages and does not provide any implementation, binding or transport details. Its purpose is to use the server side to define a standard interface that can be implemented by different service providers, allowing clients to access the service without knowing the underlying implementation details. This Top-Down approach defines only what functionalities Web Services should be but not how to contact them.

2. Concrete WSDL

It provides all the implementation details of the Web Services, including the transport protocol, endpoint address, and binding. It specifies how the service is accessed and how messages are exchanged between the client and server applications. A concrete WSDL includes all the elements of an abstract WSDL and adds the implementation details necessary for a client to access the service.

What are the advantages and disadvantages of using SOAP Web Services?

SOAP web services provide a reliable, secure, and standardized way for applications to communicate and exchange data over the Internet,

1. Language and platform independence: SOAP web services use XML to format data and messages, making them usable across different programming languages and platforms. It is application protocol neutral and supports multiple protocols: HTTP/HTTPS,

JMS, STP, etc. This means that SOAP web services can be used by applications written in different programming languages and running on different platforms.

2. Standardization: SOAP web services have a standardized structure consisting of an envelope, header, and body. It uses XML as its core. This makes it easier for applications to communicate and exchange data with each other, as they can have great control over data types and understand the structure of the messages being exchanged.

3. Security: SOAP web services can use a variety of security mechanisms to protect the confidentiality, integrity, and availability of the data being exchanged. These mechanisms include digital signatures, encryption, and authentication.

4. Reliability: SOAP web services provide reliable communication between client and server applications. They can guarantee message delivery and ensure that messages are delivered in the correct order.

5. Compatibility: SOAP web services can be used with various transport protocols, including HTTP, HTTPS, SMTP, and FTP. This makes them compatible with a wide range of network environments and technologies.

6. Tool support: SOAP web services have extensive tool support, including libraries, frameworks, and development tools using a WSDL file. This makes it easier for developers to create, test, and deploy SOAP web services.

While SOAP Web Services encountered many advantages, they also have a few disadvantages, including:

1. Complexity: SOAP web services can be more complex to implement and use compared to other web services such as REST (Representational State Transfer) web services. The standardized structure of SOAP messages can make them difficult to read and understand, and the additional layers of security and reliability can add complexity to the system.

2. Performance: SOAP messages are often larger and more complex than other messages, impacting performance and increasing network latency. The payload size is larger in SOAP compared with

REST. Additionally, the additional layers of security and reliability can add overhead to the system and reduce performance.

3. Compatibility: While SOAP web services are designed to be platform- and language-independent, there can be compatibility issues between different implementations. SOAP is purely based on XML and doesn't support another format like JSON. This can lead to interoperability problems between different systems and applications.

4. Tool support: While SOAP web services have extensive tool support, some tools can be expensive and require specialized knowledge to use effectively.

5. Tight coupling: A tight coupling between the client and server makes it harder to make any changes.

6. Limited browser support: SOAP web services are not directly supported by web browsers, which can limit their use for web-based applications. SOAP relies very much on specific client applications.

5.2.1.2 What are RPC and Document Style in SOAP Services?

RPC (Remote Procedure Call) and Document style are two different styles of designing SOAP (Simple Object Access Protocol) web services. **RPC style** involves designing web services that behave like remote procedure calls, where the client sends a request with one or more parameters, and the server returns a response with a result. RPC-style web services typically have a WSDL (Web Services Description Language) that defines the operations that can be performed by the service, the input and output parameters of each operation, and the data types used. RPC-style web services are often used for simple, stateless operations where the client needs to call a specific method on the server.

While **document style**, on the other hand, involves designing web services that exchange XML documents instead of remote procedure calls. In document style, the client sends an XML document as a request and the server returns an XML document as a response. Document style web services typically have a WSDL that defines the format and structure of the request and response messages, but not the operations that can be performed. Document style web services are often used for more complex, stateful operations where the client needs to send or receive a large amount of data.

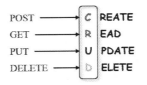

Figure 5.1 CRUD.

Representational State Transfer (REST) API

A REST API, also referred to as a RESTful API, State Transfer is a type of web API or application programming interface that adheres to the principles of the REST architectural style and permits communication with RESTful Web Services [181]. REST was developed by a computer scientist named Roy Fielding.

RESTful Web Services, on the other hand, use HTTP (Hypertext Transfer Protocol) as the communication protocol and are typically delivered in one of these formats via HTTP: JSON (JavaScript Object Notation), HTML (Hypertext Markup Language), Python, plain text, or XML (eXtensible Markup Language). However, JSON is the most popular as it is a human-readable format besides machines. RESTful Web Services are designed to be lightweight and flexible, making them well-suited for use in web-based applications and mobile apps. They are often used to build APIs (Application Programming Interfaces) that enable applications to access data and functionality from other applications or services.REST Web Services use URIs (Uniform Resource Identifiers) to identify resources and HTTP methods (GET, POST, PUT, DELETE) to perform operations on those resources. Fig. 5.1 demonstrates the CRUD which stands for Create, Read, Update, and Delete. It refers to the four basic functions that can be performed on data in a web service or database.

Web Services are implemented using various technologies, including XML, JSON (JavaScript Object Notation), and HTTP. XML is commonly used as the message format for SOAP Web Services, while JSON is used as the message format for REST Web Services. HTTP is the communication protocol for both SOAP and REST Web Services.

To be considered RESTful, an API (Application Programming Interface) must conform to architectural principles and constraints. Here are the six key criteria that an API must meet to be considered RESTful:

1. Client-Server Architecture: The API must have a client-server architecture, where the client and server are separated from each other and can evolve independently.

2. Statelessness: The API must be stateless, meaning that each request contains all the information required to complete the request. The server stores no information about the client's state between requests.

3. Cacheability: The API must be designed to support caching, which can improve performance by reducing the number of requests that need to be made to the server.

4. Layered System: The API must be designed as a layered system, where each layer has a specific function and can be replaced or modified without affecting the other layers.

5. Uniform Interface: The API must have a uniform interface, which means that all resources are identified by a unique URI (Uniform Resource Identifier) and can be manipulated using a standard set of HTTP methods, such as GET, POST, PUT, and DELETE.

6. Code-on-Demand: This optional constraint allows the server to send code to the client to be executed. This can be used to implement custom features or manipulate data on the client side.

The benefits of using Web Services for application development are numerous. Web Services provide a standardized way for applications to communicate with each other, regardless of the programming languages or platforms used to develop them. This makes integrating different applications and systems easier, reducing development time and costs. Web Services also enable applications to access functionality and data from other applications without replicating that functionality or data within the application itself. This can help to improve application performance and reduce the amount of data that needs to be transmitted over the network.

An application must first locate the service and its methods to use Web Services. This is typically done using a service registry or discovery mechanism [182], such as UDDI (Universal Description, Discovery, and Integration) or WSDL. Once the application has located the service, it can use the methods provided by the service to exchange data and functionality. The data is typically exchanged using XML or JSON, and the communication is secured using encryption and authentication mechanisms, such as SSL (Secure Sockets Layer) or OAuth (Open Authorization).

What are the components of REST API?

A REST API (Representational State Transfer Application Programming Interface) is an architectural style for developing Web Services. It defines a set of constraints that must be followed to create scalable and interoperable Web Services. The components of a REST API are:

1. Resource: A resource is the core component of a REST API and represents an object or entity that can be accessed through a unique URI (Uniform Resource Identifier). Resources can be physical entities such as files or databases or abstract entities such as user accounts or orders.

2. URI (Uniform Resource Identifier): A URI is a string of characters identifying a resource. In a REST API, each resource is identified by a unique URI used to access and manipulate the resource. The URI should be designed to be easy to read, understand, and use.

3. HTTP Methods: REST APIs use HTTP methods to perform operations on resources. The details of this part are explained at 5.2.1.2.

4. Representation: A representation is the data format in which a resource is returned to the client. REST APIs support a variety of representation formats, such as JSON, XML, and HTML. The client can specify the desired representation format using the Accept header in the HTTP request.

What are the common rules for REST API?

REST API is an architectural style for building Web Services, and it follows a set of rules or constraints to ensure interoperability and scalability. These rules are commonly known as the REST constraints or principles, and they include the following:

1. Client-Server Architecture: A REST API's client and server components should be separated to improve scalability and simplicity. The client component should only deal with the user interface,

and the server component should only deal with data storage and manipulation.

2. Statelessness: A REST API should be stateless, meaning the server should not store client context between requests. Each request should contain all the necessary information to complete the request, and the server should not rely on any previous requests.

3. Cacheability: A REST API should support caching to improve scalability and performance. Responses should be marked as cacheable or non-cacheable, and the client should be able to cache responses when appropriate.

4. Layered System: A REST API should be designed as a layered system to improve scalability and flexibility. The client should not know or care about the server's internal architecture, and the server should be able to scale by adding or removing layers.

5. Uniform Interface: A REST API should have a uniform interface to improve interoperability. The interface should be simple, consistent, and well-defined and should include the following four constraints: URI, HTTP methods,

6. Code on Demand (Optional): A REST API may allow clients to download and execute code on demand, such as JavaScript, in a web browser. This constraint is optional and not commonly used.

How are REST API stateless?

An application API or Web Services that is considered stateful stores data from the client on its own servers. For instance, a server store username and password when the pair is passed from the client to the server [183]. In this case, the web server is stateful. For REST API, each request made by the client must comply with all necessary information for HTTP methods: *POST*, *PUT*, *DELETE*, *PATCH* and *GET*. Developers should choose the appropriate HTTP method based on the desired action and the state of the resource on the server [184].

1. *GET*: The *GET* method retrieves information about a resource. When a *GET* request is made, the server returns the requested resource in the response body. *GET* requests are considered safe, as they do not modify the state of the resource on the server.

2. *POST*: The *POST* method creates a new resource on the server. When a POST request is made, the server creates a new resource using the data in the request body and returns the created resource in the response body. POST requests are considered unsafe, as they modify the resource's state on the server.

3. *PUT*: The *PUT* method is used to update an existing resource on the server. When a PUT request is made, the server updates the resource using the data in the request body and returns the updated resource in the response body. *PUT* requests are considered idempotent, meaning that multiple identical requests will have the same effect as a single request.

4. *DELETE*: The *DELETE* method is used to delete a resource on the server. When a *DELETE* request is made, the server deletes the resource and returns a success status code in the response.

5. *PATCH*: The *PATCH* method is used to update a part of an existing resource on the server. When a *PATCH* request is made, the server updates the specified part of the resource using the data in the request body and returns the updated resource in the response body.

What is HTTP status code?

HTTP status codes are three-digit numbers a server returns in response to a client's HTTP request. They provide information about the status of the requested resource and help the client understand the request's outcome [185,186]. There are five categories of HTTP status codes, each with its own range of status codes.

- **1xx (Informational)**: These status codes indicate that the server has received and is processing the request. For example, 100 (Continue) indicates that the server has received the initial part of the request and is waiting for the client to send the rest.

- **2xx (Successful)**: These status codes indicate that the server has successfully received, understood, and processed the request. For example, 200 (OK) indicates that the request was successful, and the server is returning the requested resource in the response body.

- **3xx (Redirection)**: These status codes indicate that the client needs to take additional action to complete the request. For example, 301 (Moved Permanently) indicates that the requested resource has been moved to a new location, and the client should update their request to the new location.

- **4xx (Client Error)**: These status codes indicate that the client has made an error in the request. For example, 404 (Not Found) indicates that the requested resource could not be found on the server.

- **5xx (Server Error)**: These status codes indicate that the server has encountered an error while processing the request. For example, 500 (Internal Server Error) indicates that the server encountered an unexpected condition that prevented it from fulfilling the request.

HTTP status codes are an essential aspect of web architecture and design [187]. They provide a standardized mechanism for communicating the status of HTTP requests and responses, enabling interoperability between different systems and applications. HTTP status codes are an essential aspect of web architecture and design. They provide a standardized mechanism for communicating the status of HTTP requests and responses, enabling interoperability between different systems and applications. Moreover, HTTP status codes play a crucial role in designing RESTful APIs, as they help developers to define the behavior of resources in response to different types of requests. Fig. 5.2 shows how REST API works and communication established between client-server.

REST API features

Pagination is a technique used in REST APIs to limit the amount of data returned in response and improve performance. Pagination allows clients to retrieve data in smaller chunks or pages rather than all the data simultaneously [188, 189]. This can be useful when dealing with large datasets, as it reduces the amount of data transferred and improves response times.

In a REST API, pagination is typically implemented using query parameters in the URL. The two most common query parameters used for pagination are:

- limit: This parameter specifies the maximum number of items to be returned in a single response. For example, if the limit is set to 10, the server will return a maximum of 10 items in each response.

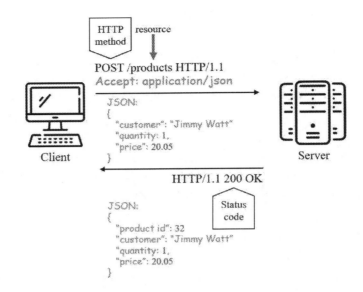

Figure 5.2 How REST API works.

- offset: This parameter specifies the starting point of the data to be returned in the response. For example, if the offset is set to 20, the server will skip the first 20 items and return the next set starting from the 21st item.

Both the limit and offset parameters allow clients to retrieve data in smaller chunks or pages. For example, if a client wants to retrieve data in chunks of 10 items, it can request a limit of 10 and an offset of 0 to retrieve the first 10 items. To retrieve the next 10 items, the client can request a limit of 10 and an offset of 10.

In addition to the limit and offset parameters, REST APIs may also return metadata in response to provide information about the total number of items available, the current page, and the number of pages. This metadata can be useful for clients to implement pagination controls such as the next and previous buttons. Here is an example URL for a REST API that uses pagination:

`https://example.com/api/items?limit=10\&offset=0` This URL requests the first 10 items from the "items" resource. The server will return a maximum of 10 items in the response, starting from the first item.

What's the similarity and difference between APIs and Web Services?

Web Services and APIs are used for communication between client applications and servers, but they have different purposes and characteristics [190, 190]. The choice of protocols deployed depends on the specific requirements of the system. However, REST APIs are commonly used for IoT computing due to their lightweight nature and ability to handle large amounts of data.

REST, representing Representational State Transfer, is an architectural style for building Web Services that use HTTP or HTTPS for data exchange. REST APIs interact with resources through simple HTTP methods like *GET*, *POST*, *PUT*, and *DELETE*. They are stateless, meaning each request contains all the information required to complete it. In IoT computing, REST APIs are well-suited for handling large amounts of data that sensors and other IoT devices generate. REST APIs can retrieve data from IoT devices, send commands to IoT devices, and trigger actions based on data received from IoT devices.

In contrast, Web Services are used to integrate web applications using open standards over an Internet protocol backbone. Web Services use XML (Extensible Markup Language) to tag and transport data, SOAP (Simple Object Access Protocol) to transfer data, WSDL (Web Services Description Language) [191] to describe the availability of Web Services, and UDDI (Universal Description, Discovery, and Integration) [192] to discover Web Services. In IoT computing, Web Services can integrate different IoT systems and devices with one another, share data between them, and provide a standardized way for IoT devices to access and interact with cloud-based services.

However, Web Services are less commonly used for IoT computing than REST APIs due to their heavier nature and more complex architecture. REST APIs are more lightweight, simpler to implement, and better suited to handle the large amounts of data generated by IoT devices.

Nevertheless, Web Services and APIs (Application Programming Interfaces) are related concepts that have several things in common:

1. Both are used for communication: Web Services and APIs enable communication between software systems or applications. They provide a standardized way for systems to interact with each other, regardless of the programming languages, platforms, or devices used.

2. Both use standard protocols: Web Services and APIs use standard protocols such as HTTP, XML, and JSON to communicate

between systems. These protocols ensure the systems can understand each other's requests and responses.

3. Both are designed for interoperability: Web Services and APIs are designed to be interoperable, meaning they can work with different systems and platforms. This allows developers to build applications that can interact with each other seamlessly.

4. Both expose functionality: Web Services and APIs expose functionality or services that other systems or applications can use. This functionality can include retrieving data, performing calculations, or executing actions.

5. Both can be accessed over a network: Web Services and APIs can be accessed over a network, such as the Internet, making them accessible from anywhere in the world. This allows developers to build distributed systems that users can use in different locations.

What are the benefits of using Web Services?

Web Services provide a standardized way for different applications and systems to communicate with each other, regardless of the platform or programming language they are built on. Several benefits have been discovered for using Web Services.

1. Improved Interoperability

   One of the main benefits of using Web Services across different platforms is improved interoperability. Web Services use standard web technologies such as HTTP, XML, and SOAP, widely supported by different platforms and programming languages [193]. This means that applications built on different platforms can easily communicate with each other using Web Services, without the need for complex integration or custom code.

2. Increased Flexibility

   Another benefit of using Web Services across different platforms is increased flexibility. Web Services provide a layer of abstraction between different applications, allowing them to interact with each other without needing to know the underlying details of the system. This makes building and maintaining complex distributed systems easier and allows applications to be added or removed from the system without disrupting the overall architecture.

3. Reduced Development Time and Costs

Using Web Services across different platforms can also help to reduce development time and costs. By providing a standardized way for applications to communicate with each other, Web Services eliminate the need for custom integration code or proprietary protocols [194]. This can save developers time and effort and reduce the risk of errors or inconsistencies in the system.

4. Improved Interoperability

One of the main benefits of using Web Services across different platforms is improved interoperability. Web Services use standard web technologies such as HTTP, XML, and SOAP, widely supported by different platforms and programming languages [195]. This means that applications built on different platforms can easily communicate with each other using Web Services without the need for complex integration or custom code. They have the ability to facilitate integration between different systems and applications. They can be used to integrate legacy systems with modern applications or to connect different applications across different departments or organizations.

5. Increased Flexibility

Another benefit of using Web Services across different platforms is increased flexibility. Web Services provide a layer of abstraction between different applications, allowing them to interact with each other without needing to know the underlying details of the system. This makes building and maintaining complex distributed systems easier and allows applications to be added or removed from the system without disrupting the overall architecture.

6. Reduced Development Time and Costs

Using Web Services across different platforms can also help to reduce development time and costs. By providing a standardized way for applications to communicate with each other, Web Services eliminate the need for custom integration code or proprietary protocols. This can save developers time and effort, and reduce the risk of errors or inconsistencies in the system.

In addition to these benefits, there are several other advantages of using Web Services across different platforms, including:

1. Scalability: Web Services can be used to build distributed applications that can scale to handle large amounts of traffic or data.

2. Security: Web Services can be secured using standard web security protocols such as SSL (Secure Sockets Layer) or HTTPS (Hypertext Transfer Protocol Secure), ensuring that data is protected during transmission.

3. Reuse: Web Services can be designed to be reusable, allowing different applications to access the same services or functionality without needing to duplicate code or data.

4. Integration: Web Services can be used to integrate different applications or systems, allowing data or functionality to be shared across different parts of the organization or with external partners.

5.2.2 Concept and Types of Denial-of-Service Attacks

A Denial-of-Service (DoS) attack is a type of cyber attack designed to disrupt website, server, or network access by overwhelming it with traffic or other malicious activity [196]. The goal of a DoS attack is to make a system or service unavailable to legitimate users, either temporarily or permanently [197].

The concept of a DoS attack is based on the idea of resource exhaustion. Every system or service has a finite amount of resources, such as bandwidth, processing power, and memory. By flooding a system with traffic or other malicious activity, an attacker can exhaust these resources, making the system unavailable to legitimate users.

DoS attacks can take many different forms, including:

1. Network-based attacks involve flooding a network or server with traffic, such as a Distributed Denial-of-Service (DDoS) attack. DDoS attacks involve multiple devices or systems, known as a botnet [198], coordinating to flood a target with traffic.

2. Application-based attacks target specific applications or services like web servers or email servers. Application-based attacks can exploit vulnerabilities in the application or overload it with requests.

3. Protocol-based attacks: These attacks exploit vulnerabilities in network protocols, such as TCP/IP or DNS, to flood a target with traffic or disrupt communication.

Distributed Denial of Service (DDoS)

Distributed Denial of Service (DDoS) attacks have compromised the availability of information security. Attackers utilize a large amount of traffic to consume the network or service resources of the target server, preventing legitimate users from accessing resources and causing significant financial losses for the victims. DDoS attacks can cause paralysis of network equipment and infrastructure, which not only seriously affects personal life and economic development, but also poses a serious threat to national security.

Currently, DDoS attacks are common on the Internet, and the number of attacks is increasing year by year. A report indicates that in the first half of 2020, there were as many as 4,000 attacks of over 100 Gbps, an increase of 45% compared to the same period in 2019. Three reasons can be summarized for the frequent occurrence of DDoS attacks with high attack intensity:

Firstly, DDoS attack tools are easily obtainable. In the early days, attackers needed to manually construct specific data packets and manipulate many hosts to launch DDoS attacks. However, with the development of the Internet, fully automated attack tools have become common and easily accessible. This has greatly reduced the cost and threshold for launching attacks, making it possible for even a novice computer user to successfully launch a DDoS attack.

Secondly, attackers are driven by money or interests to launch DDoS attacks. They use DDoS attacks as a threat to extort victims and achieve illegal profits. Some even establish dedicated attack platforms to rent out DDoS attack traffic for illegal profits [199]. For example, Webstresser, Europe's largest DDoS attack rental platform, launched as many as 40 million DDoS attacks between 2015 and 2018.

Thirdly, DDoS attacks evolve through the integration of new technologies. The continuous emergence of new technologies has led to the evolution of DDoS attacks into more diverse attacks. For example, DDoS attacks combined with IoT infect many IoT devices to launch attacks with a traffic volume of up to 1TB per second. Previous attacks were unable to reach such a high volume. A thorough analysis of the development of DDoS attacks is essential for studying defense against DDoS attacks. This article studies the evolution process and defense methods of DDoS attacks, first introducing the classification of DDoS attacks. Then, based on the characteristics of DDoS attacks during different periods, it divides them into three periods: the early DDoS period, the Botnet era, and the application layer era, providing a detailed discussion of the attack methods and defense measures for each period.

DDoS attacks can be classified into two types based on the attack methods. The first type exploits vulnerabilities in systems or services to launch a denial-of-service attack. For example, the vulnerability of the CVE-2019-0708 allows an attacker to shut down a Windows Server by sending a carefully crafted RDP packet [200]. The second type of attack involves flooding the victim's resources with many useless packets, making it impossible for legitimate users to access the service. Defending against the first type of attack can be achieved by patching the system, while the second type requires accurately distinguishing legitimate traffic from DDoS traffic, which is a research focus in academia. This chapter focuses on the second type of attack.

DDoS attacks can be classified into two categories based on their objectives: network-layer attacks and application-layer attacks. Network-layer attacks aim to consume the target's bandwidth or network device resources. Examples of such attacks include TCP SYN flood [201] and UDP flood attacks [201]. Application-layer attacks use application-layer protocols to consume the server's resources. Examples of such attacks include HTTP slow attacks and CC attacks.

DDoS attacks can be classified into two types based on their methods: direct and reflected. **Direct attacks** require attackers to interact directly with the target host. They are often combined with network-layer attacks to flood the victim with a large number of packets. **Reflected attacks** involve intermediate servers, where attackers send a large number of packets to the intermediate server by spoofing the source IP address as the target host. The intermediate server then returns a large number of packets to the target host. Examples of such attacks include DNS reflection attacks and SSDP reflection attacks. Because the ratio of response packets to request packets is much greater than 1, these attacks are also known as DDoS amplification attacks. By classifying DDoS attacks based on their objectives and methods, they can be divided into four types.

1. Network-layer attacks: These attacks aim to consume the victim's network bandwidth or device resources. Examples include TCP SYN flood and UDP flood attacks.

2. Application-layer attacks: These attacks use application-layer protocols to consume the victim's server resources. Examples include HTTP slow attacks and CC attacks.

3. Direct attacks: These attacks require attackers to interact directly with the victim host. They are often combined with network-layer attacks to flood the victim with a large number of packets.

4. Reflected attacks: These attacks involve intermediate servers that are used to amplify the attack traffic. Attackers spoof the source IP address as the victim host and send a large number of packets to the intermediate server. The intermediate server then returns a large number of packets to the victim host, amplifying the attack traffic. Examples include DNS reflection attacks and SSDP reflection attacks.

How does DDoS launch an attack?

The first known DDoS attack occurred in 1996 when attackers flooded a target host with many TCP SYN packets, causing the host to become paralyzed. In the early days of the Internet, network devices and protocols were designed without sufficient security awareness, which made it easy for attackers to exploit their vulnerabilities and launch DDoS attacks. This section summarizes three characteristics of DDoS attacks in the early days:

1. Network-layer flooding attacks were the main attack type: Attackers mainly used TCP flooding and ICMP flooding, which were simple and practical methods to quickly consume the target's network resources. Since bandwidth on network devices was limited in the early days and effective defense mechanisms were lacking, network-layer flooding attacks were very effective and became the mainstream attack method.

2. Attackers manually infected hosts: To successfully paralyze a target host, attackers needed many network resources. More zombie hosts meant more IP addresses, traffic, and bandwidth, making hosts with security vulnerabilities a prime target for attackers. In the early days, attackers manually infected hosts and used them to launch DDoS attacks. This also led to the slow growth of zombie hosts.

3. Attackers tended to spoof IP addresses: Due to the deficiencies in early network infrastructure, attackers could easily spoof IP addresses, indirectly increasing the attack traffic. By spoofing source IP addresses, the victim would mistakenly believe that many hosts

were communicating with it. The cost of launching an attack by spoofing IP addresses was much lower than that of building zombie hosts, and the technical requirements were low, making IP address spoofing a popular method for launching DDoS attacks in the early days.

How to protect ourselves from being a zombie in a DDoS attack?

DDoS attack is a cyber attack that floods a website or network with traffic from multiple sources, rendering it inaccessible to legitimate users. One of the ways attackers achieve this is by using a botnet, a network of compromised devices, to launch the attack. A compromised device, or zombie, can send traffic to the victim without the owner's knowledge. To protect yourself from being a zombie in a DDoS attack, there are several steps you can take:

1. Keep your software up-to-date: Attackers often exploit vulnerabilities in software to compromise devices. Keeping your operating system, web browser, and other software up-to-date with the latest security patches can help prevent attackers from exploiting known vulnerabilities.

2. Use antivirus software: Antivirus software can help detect and remove malware that can be used to turn your device into a zombie. Ensure that your antivirus software is up-to-date and set to scan your device regularly.

3. Use a firewall: A firewall can block unauthorized access to your device and prevent malware from communicating with the attacker's command and control servers. Make sure your firewall is enabled and configured properly.

4. Use strong passwords: Use strong and unique passwords for all your accounts to prevent attackers from gaining access to your device through brute force attacks. A strong password should be at least 12 characters long and include a mix of uppercase and lowercase letters, numbers, and symbols.

5. Enable two-factor authentication: Two-factor authentication adds an extra layer of security by requiring a second form of authentication, such as a code sent to your phone, in addition to your password. Enable two-factor authentication for all your accounts that offer it.

6. Be cautious of suspicious emails and links: Do not click on links or download attachments from suspicious emails or websites. These may contain malware that can turn your device into a zombie.

7. Monitor network traffic: Use network monitoring tools to monitor network traffic and detect any unusual activity that may indicate a DDoS attack. If you notice any suspicious activity, disconnect your device from the network and contact your IT department or a cybersecurity professional.

8. Use a VPN: A virtual private network (VPN) encrypts your internet traffic and routes it through a secure server, making it more difficult for attackers to monitor your online activity and compromise your device.

9. Disable unnecessary services: Disable any unnecessary services, such as file sharing or remote desktop, to reduce your device's attack surface.

What is Botnet, and how can we detect it?

A Botnet refers to a network of compromised hosts controlled by malicious programs. With the development of the internet, hosts have grown rapidly, but people's awareness of network security is relatively weak, which has provided opportunities for attackers [202]. The disclosure of vulnerability information and the ease of obtaining hacker tools have significantly increased Botnet hosts in cyberspace. During this period, the majority of attack traffic was generated by Botnets [203, 204].

The attack characteristics of this period are as follows [205–207]:

- High volume of traffic

  The significant attack characteristics during this period included a rapid increase in attack traffic. Botnets can generate a high traffic volume, typically used in DDoS attacks to overwhelm the target system or network. The traffic can be generated using various techniques, such as UDP floods, SYN floods, or HTTP GET floods. The traffic volume can range from a few megabits per second to several gigabits per second. Botnets can also use amplification techniques, such as DNS amplification or NTP amplification, to increase traffic volume by sending small requests to public servers that return large responses to the victim. The high traffic volume makes it difficult for the target to handle legitimate traffic and can cause service disruptions or downtime. On the other hand, as the hardware cost decreased, target hosts had more network and computing resources, requiring more attack traffic to achieve the denial of the server effect.

- Wide range of attack sources: Botnets can use various attack sources, including computers and other devices from different geographic locations and internet service providers. This makes it difficult for the target to block the traffic, as it can come from many different sources. Botnets can also use compromised servers or cloud-based services to generate traffic, making it more difficult to identify and block the attack sources.

- Long attack duration: Botnets can carry out attacks for long periods, ranging from hours to days or even weeks. This makes it more difficult for the target to mitigate the attack and resume normal operations. The long attack duration can also cause additional damage, such as increased bandwidth usage, data loss, or reputation damage.

- Randomized attack patterns: Botnets can use randomized attack patterns, making detecting and blocking traffic more difficult. This can involve changing the type of attack, the source IP addresses, or the attack frequency. Botnets can also use spoofed IP addresses or domain names to disguise the attack traffic or make it appear legitimate.

- Hidden command and control infrastructure: Botnets can use hidden command and control (C&C) infrastructure to communicate with compromised devices. This can make it more challenging to locate and shut down the botnet. The C&C infrastructure can use various techniques to evade detection, such as encrypted communication, peer-to-peer communication, or dynamic DNS services. Botnets can also use fast-flux techniques to rapidly change the IP addresses of the C&C servers, making tracking and blocking them more difficult.

- Adaptive behavior: Botnets can adapt to changes in the attack environment, such as changes in the target defenses or the network topology. This can involve changing the attack strategy, the attack frequency, or the attack sources. Botnets can also use machine learning or artificial intelligence techniques to optimize the attack parameters or evade detection.

• Persistence: Botnets can remain active even after the initial attack has been mitigated. This can involve using compromised devices for other malicious activities, such as spamming or phishing. Botnets can also use stealth techniques, such as rootkits or backdoors, to remain undetected on compromised devices or regain control after removal.

During this period, defenders needed to accurately identify normal and attack traffic to defend against and mitigate DDoS attacks. A feature-based detection method was proposed by extracting attack traffic features and building detection models to identify traffic accurately.

Defense method using a feature-based detection method This method requires extracting features from the dataset, building detection models, and evaluating the goodness of the models using test samples [204]. Under normal circumstances, the ratio of TCP incoming to outgoing packets is stable [208]. MULTOPS detects DDoS attacks based on the difference in packet rate between incoming and outgoing subnets [209]. This method can adjust the detection granularity in real time according to changes in traffic but consumes large amounts of memory. In response to DDoS attacks, the statistical distribution of packet header information differs from normal conditions. A DDoS detection method based on IP packet entropy (IPSE) was proposed, which detects attacks by observing the time series of packet entropy. TCP traffic and RTT exhibit strong periodicity during communication processes. A method based on spectral analysis was proposed to identify DDoS attacks [210, 211]. It estimates the power spectral density of the signal by using the number of packet arrivals in the RTT interval as the signal to detect TCP flooding attacks. During the Botnet era, attackers were more focused on the size of attack traffic and tended to launch network layer attacks to consume target bandwidth resources. Defense methods focused on extracting attack features and identifying attack traffic. When attackers focused more on consuming host resources, DDoS attacks entered the next era.

Application Defense

Compared to network layer protocols, application layer protocols are more numerous and complex, making each application layer protocol a potential attack surface. During the application layer period, attackers focused on the quality of attacks due to developing defense methods, achieving better results than network layer attacks through carefully crafted application layer DDoS attacks. The attack characteristics of the application layer period are as follows:

1. Attackers tend to launch application layer attacks. Reports show that application layer attacks were the three most frequent DDoS attacks from 2017 to 2019. The proportion of application layer attacks continues to grow, with SSDP reflection attacks and DNS reflection attacks reaching the top in 2018 and 2019, respectively. However, network layer attacks are still active, and for hosts lacking defense, the impact of network layer attacks is still significant.

2. Attacks tend to become more complex and diversified. Attackers no longer settle for a single type of attack, but instead use a combination of multiple attacks. These mixed attacks are more destructive and more difficult to defend against. Compared to network layer DDoS attacks, the traffic of application layer attacks at the network layer is completely normal, and the differences between different application layer protocols are significant, making it difficult to detect using feature extraction methods. Based on the complexity of application layer protocols, researchers have proposed test-based identification methods and behavior-based detection.

Defense methods for application layer attacks can be categorized as follows:

1. **Test-based identification:** The core of test-based identification methods is the Turing test. CAPTCHA and AYAH are the most commonly used methods, distinguishing between humans and automated machines based on recognizing images or answering certain questions. They block requests that fail the test from accessing the service. However, this type of method can affect users' normal access to the service, and a balance needs to be found between test strength and user experience. Golle has proposed a seamless integration test method to enhance the strength of the Turing

test [212]. This test requires users to play games online, ensuring user experience while increasing test intensity. A system based on the Turing test has been proposed in the literature to analyze the implicit browsing patterns of human users when browsing web pages to determine whether the current user's browsing pattern is normal. This method does not require direct human interaction, unlike CAPTCHA.

2. **Behavior-based detection:** Behavior-based detection first requires establishing a baseline behavior model. By analyzing user behavior over a period of time and comparing it with the baseline behavior model, users whose behavior deviates from the model are identified as illegal users. Literature has proposed calculating a behavior score based on statistical attributes of each connection, such as request rate, access time, and click depth, and identifying connections with low scores as malicious connections. Xie et al. have proposed a semi-Markov model based on implicit information to identify abnormal user browsing behavior. By modeling HTTP requests using information entropy, users whose behavior deviates from the model are identified as attackers. Literature has also proposed mining log systems to establish baseline models for user logs to identify malicious behavior. This method can detect DDoS attacks and other types of attacks against the application layer. Recent reports show that the number of application layer attacks still ranks first, and we are still in the application layer period. We do not know what the next stage will be like or its characteristics. However, DDoS attacks will certainly continue to evolve in conjunction with new technologies.

5.2.3   Methods to Resist Denial-of-Service Attacks

Denial-of-Service (DoS) attacks are a type of cyberattack that intends to disrupt the normal operations of computer networks or websites by overwhelming them with an excessive volume of traffic or requests. Designing and deciding on methods to resist Denial of Service (DoS) attacks can be a complex and ongoing process, as attackers constantly evolve their methods and techniques. However, some general steps can be taken to help mitigate the impact of DoS attacks. Here are some steps to consider:

1. Identify potential attack vectors: The first step in resisting DoS attacks is to identify the potential attack vectors that an attacker

could use to target your system. This may include network-level attacks, such as flooding the network with traffic, or application-level attacks, such as overwhelming a web server with requests.

2. Monitor and analyze traffic: Once potential attack vectors have been identified, it is important to monitor and analyze network traffic to detect any anomalies or suspicious patterns. This can be done using tools such as network intrusion detection systems (IDS) [213] or security information and event management (SIEM) solutions [214, 215].

3. Implement traffic filtering and rate limiting: To prevent malicious traffic from overwhelming your system, it is important to implement traffic filtering and rate limiting measures. This can include blocking traffic from known malicious sources, limiting the rate of incoming traffic, and prioritizing traffic from trusted sources.

4. Use load balancing and redundancy: Load balancing and redundancy can help distribute traffic across multiple servers or systems, reducing the impact of a DoS attack on any one system. This can also help ensure the system remains available even if some components are offline.

5. Implement caching and content delivery networks (CDNs) [216]: Caching and CDNs can help reduce the load on the system by serving frequently accessed content from a cache or proxy server. This can also help improve performance and reduce the impact of DoS attacks.

6. Test and update defenses regularly: It is important to test and update your defenses regularly to ensure they are effective against new and evolving DoS attack techniques. This can include penetration testing, vulnerability scanning, and regular updates to security software and configurations.

Several popular methods are being discussed to resist such attacks, including traffic filtering, rate limiting, IP blocking, Content Delivery Networks (CDNs) [217], and Cloud-Based Protection Services [218].

- The traffic filtering method involves using firewalls, intrusion detection systems (IDS), or load balancers to detect and filter out traffic that appears to be part of a DoS attack [219]. This can be achieved through proactive or reactive actions against malicious IP addresses or by analyzing traffic patterns to identify anomalous behavior.

- Blocking traffic from known malicious sources: Firewalls can be configured to block traffic from known malicious IP addresses or ranges of addresses. This can be done using threat intelligence feeds or blacklists of known malicious IP addresses.

- Filtering traffic based on protocol and port: Firewalls can be configured to filter traffic based on the protocol and port used. For example, a firewall can be configured to block all traffic on port 80, which is commonly used by web servers, if it exceeds a certain rate or if it originates from suspicious sources.

- Implementing rate limiting: Firewalls can be configured to limit the rate of incoming traffic to prevent overwhelming the target system. For example, a firewall can be configured to limit the number of requests per second from a particular IP address or range of addresses.

- Blocking traffic based on packet size: Firewalls can be configured to filter traffic based on the size of packets. This can help prevent attacks such as ping floods, where an attacker sends too many ping requests with large packet sizes to overwhelm the target system.

- Using stateful packet inspection: Firewalls can use stateful packet inspection to examine incoming traffic and determine whether it is part of a legitimate connection or a DoS attack. This can help prevent attacks that involve sending a large number of incomplete or malformed packets.

- Implementing traffic prioritization: Firewalls can be configured to prioritize traffic from trusted sources, such as customers or partners, over traffic from unknown or suspicious sources. This can help ensure that DoS attacks do not block critical traffic.

• Rate limiting involves restricting the number of requests or connections that can be made to a server within a specific time frame, thereby preventing a server from being overwhelmed by a flood of requests. IP blocking involves blocking traffic from specific IP addresses that are known to be part of a DoS attack. This can be performed manually or automatically by employing tools that monitor network traffic for signs of a DoS attack.

- CDNs can assist in resisting DoS attacks by distributing traffic across multiple servers and data centers, making it more difficult for a DoS attack to overwhelm a single server. Cloud-Based Protection Services, such as DDoS protection, can provide additional resistance against DoS attacks by supplementing bandwidth and processing power to absorb the attack.

- Machine learning-based (ML) approaches are not new to deploy as the shield to resist DoS attacks. Machine learning-based approaches involve training algorithms to detect and mitigate DoS attacks by analyzing network traffic and identifying patterns of attack behavior. Application-layer defenses involve strengthening applications and servers to resist common DoS attack vectors, such as SYN floods and HTTP floods. Below are a few commonly seen methods available back-ended by ML techniques.

  - Anomaly detection: ML algorithms can be trained to detect anomalous traffic patterns and identify potential DoS attacks in real time. These algorithms can detect attacks that traditional signature-based methods may miss by analyzing network traffic and identifying patterns that deviate from normal behavior.

  - Deep learning: Deep learning algorithms, such as neural networks, can be used to analyze large amounts of data and identify patterns that may be indicative of a DoS attack. These algorithms can be trained on historical data to detect similarities between current traffic patterns and past attacks.

  - Ensemble methods: Ensemble methods, such as random forests and boosting, can combine multiple ML algorithms to improve the accuracy of DoS attack detection. By combining the strengths of different algorithms, these methods can provide a more robust and effective defense against DoS attacks.

    Another possible method for an ensemble with ML is heuristic methods. Although heuristics do not involve ML algorithms, they can be combined with ML to improve the accuracy and effectiveness of DoS systems. For example, heuristic methods can be used to identify known attack patterns, which can be used to train ML algorithms to detect new and emerging attack patterns. Similarly, ML algorithms can be used to analyze traffic patterns and identify suspicious behavior that may not be detected by heuristic methods.

- Reinforcement learning: Reinforcement learning algorithms can dynamically adjust network configurations and policies in response to DoS attacks. By learning from past attacks and adjusting policies in real time, these algorithms can help mitigate the impact of attacks and improve the resilience of the network.

- Hybrid approaches: Hybrid approaches that combine ML algorithms with traditional signature-based methods can provide a more comprehensive defense against DoS attacks. These approaches can detect known attacks using signature-based methods while also detecting new and emerging attacks using ML algorithms.

5.3 MAIN SECURITY SOLUTIONS TO NETWORKING THREATS

Security threats can have a significant impact on our lives, both personally and professionally. These threats can result in the loss or theft of sensitive data, service disruptions, and reputational damage. They can also lead to financial losses, identity theft, and legal action. In some cases, security threats can even pose a risk to physical safety, such as in the case of cyber-physical attacks that target critical infrastructure. It is important to take network security seriously and implement strong security controls to protect ourselves and our businesses from the potential consequences of a successful attack.

Security threats can have a wide range of impacts on our lives. The most significant will be financial losses, whereby security threats, such as cyber-attacks or fraud, can result in financial losses for individuals and businesses. In some cases, these losses can be severe and long-lasting. the consequences of financial loss would be damage to individuals' and businesses' reputations, leading to a loss of trust and credibility. It can impact an organization's ability to attract customers and partners. A high-profile security breach can damage an organization's reputation and result in lost business. This can have long-term consequences, including loss of business and difficulty attracting new customers or employees.

The next important item would be the effect of personal information theft, as it can be used for identity theft or other types of fraud. This can have serious consequences for individuals, including damage to credit scores and financial stability. DDoS or DoS attacks can cause service disruptions or downtime, impacting businesses, individuals, and critical infrastructure. This can result in lost productivity, revenue, and reputation damage. Legal action, including fines, penalties, and lawsuits. This can be particularly damaging for businesses, which may face significant financial and reputational consequences. The legal consequences of a security breach can vary depending on the type and severity of the attack, the type of data or information that was compromised, and the laws and regulations that apply to the industry or organization affected. Security breaches can result in lawsuits from individuals or groups affected by the breach. These lawsuits can seek damages for financial losses, identity theft, or other damages resulting from the breach.

Physical safety is an important aspect of network security that is often overlooked. While many security threats are focused on data or information theft, there are also threats that can pose a risk to physical safety. These threats are known as cyber-physical attacks and can target critical infrastructure, such as power grids, transportation systems, or manufacturing plants. Cyber-physical attacks involve using computer systems to target physical infrastructure, causing damage or disruption. These attacks can have severe consequences, including loss of life, property damage, and economic disruption. One example of a cyber-physical attack is the Stuxnet worm, which was discovered in 2010 [220]. The Stuxnet worm targeted industrial control systems used in nuclear facilities, including those in Iran. The worm was designed to modify the behavior of industrial control systems, causing physical damage to centrifuges used in nuclear fuel enrichment [221]. In this case, regular training and awareness programs can help to educate employees about the risks of cyber-physical attacks and how to identify and respond to them.

The design of a secure network is critical to protecting against various network security threats. There are several design principles that can be used to develop a secure network architecture. Below are some of the key design principles of a secure network:

1. Defense in depth: The principle of defense in depth involves implementing multiple layers of security controls to protect against

network security threats. This approach involves building multiple layers of security controls such as firewalls, intrusion prevention systems, and malware detection systems to provide multiple barriers against potential attacks. This principle assumes that no single security control is enough to protect against all types of threats and ensures that if an attacker breaches one layer of security, there are additional layers of protection in place.

2. Least privilege: The principle of least privilege involves granting users and processes only the minimum level of access required to perform their job functions. This approach helps to minimize the risk of unauthorized access to sensitive data or systems and reduces the impact of any successful attack.

3. Separation of duties: The principle of separation of duties involves dividing critical functions and responsibilities among multiple individuals or teams. This approach helps to prevent a single point of failure and ensures that no single individual has complete control over the network.

4. Network segmentation: Network segmentation involves dividing a network into smaller, isolated subnetworks. This approach helps to limit the spread of malware or attacks by containing them to a specific segment of the network. Network segmentation can also help to improve network performance by reducing the amount of broadcast traffic and limiting the number of devices that need to be managed.

5. Secure remote access: Secure remote access involves implementing secure ways for users to access the network remotely. This can include using virtual private networks (VPNs) or multi-factor authentication (MFA) to ensure that only authorized users can access the network remotely.

6. Redundancy: The principle of redundancy involves building duplicate systems or resources to ensure that there is no single point of failure in the network. This approach can help to improve network availability and reduce the impact of any hardware or software failures.

7. Monitoring and logging: Monitoring and logging involve collecting and analyzing network traffic and system logs to identify potential

security threats. This approach can help to detect and respond to security incidents more quickly and effectively.

8. Regular updates and patches: Regular updates and patches involve keeping software and firmware up-to-date to ensure that known vulnerabilities are addressed promptly. This approach helps to prevent attackers from exploiting known vulnerabilities in the network.

By following these design principles, organizations can build a secure network architecture that is better equipped to defend against a wide range of network security threats, including DDoS and DoS attacks. However, it is essential to remember that network security threats are constantly evolving, and security controls must be regularly updated to keep up with the latest threats.

5.3.1 Minimizing Lack of Trust

The **Language Policy** is a set of guidelines that outlines the standards and expectations for language use within an organization. Language policy is an essential element of organizational communication as it ensures everyone understands language use and communication expectations. Here are some of the key rules that can be included in a language policy to be deployed for network security:

1. Standard Language Use: A language policy should specify the use of standard language, a common language widely understood and accepted. Standard language promotes effective communication and ensures that everyone understands the exact meaning of words and phrases. For example, using standard English grammar and spelling in written communication.

2. Validation: Validation is verifying the accuracy and correctness of language use. A language policy should include guidelines for validating language use, such as using grammar and spell-checking tools to ensure that language use is correct. Validation also includes ensuring that language use is culturally sensitive and appropriate, particularly when communicating with international customers and partners.

3. Machine-Friendly Language: Machine-friendly language refers to language easily understood by machines and can be used for automated processing. This is particularly important in industries

that rely heavily on automation, such as finance and healthcare. A language policy should specify guidelines for machine-friendly language use, such as using standard machine-readable formats for data and avoiding ambiguity in language use. This is particularly important in industries that rely heavily on automation, such as finance and healthcare.

4. Convey policies and expectations: A language policy should convey the policies and expectations for language use within the organization. This includes guidelines for tone, style, formality, and expectations for appropriate language use in different contexts.

5. Represent SLA: A language policy should represent the Service Level Agreement (SLA) agreed upon by all parties. This includes specifying the level of language proficiency required for employees and contractors and guidelines for language use in customer service and support.

6. Agreed by all parties: A language policy should be agreed upon by all parties, including employees, contractors, and customers. This ensures that everyone understands the organization's language use and communication expectations.

7. Training and support: A language policy should provide training and support for employees and contractors to improve their language skills and ensure they meet the required language proficiency levels. This includes providing access to language courses, language proficiency tests, and language tools such as translation software.

8. Accessibility: A language policy should ensure that language use is accessible to all employees and customers, including those with disabilities. This can include guidelines for using plain language, providing alternative formats for written communication, and using assistive communication technologies.

5.3.2   Minimizing Loss of Control

In today's digital age, network security is more critical than ever before. With the increasing number of cyber threats and attacks, it is essential for organizations to take proactive measures to secure their networks and minimize the risk of security incidents. One way to achieve this is by minimizing loss of control in network security. Minimizing loss of control involves implementing measures that help detect and prevent security incidents before they escalate into major events. This can include early detection of threats, rapid response to security incidents, compliance with regulations and standards, improved network performance, and prevention of data loss. By minimizing loss of control in network security, organizations can ensure that their networks are secure and resilient against cyber threats and attacks.

5.3.2.1 Monitoring

Monitoring is an essential aspect of minimizing loss of control in network security. It involves the regular and ongoing observation of network activity to identify and respond to threats and vulnerabilities. By monitoring network activity, organizations can detect and respond to security incidents promptly, minimizing the loss of control. There are several ways in which monitoring can achieve this.

Early detection of threats is one of the most critical ways monitoring can help minimize loss of control in network security. By analyzing network activity, organizations can identify abnormal behavior and suspicious activity, which can indicate a security threat. Early detection of these threats allows organizations to take appropriate action to prevent security incidents from occurring or escalating.

Rapid response to security incidents is another way monitoring can help minimize loss of control. By detecting and analyzing security incidents in real time, organizations can take immediate action to minimize the impact of the incident and restore normal operations. This can include disabling compromised accounts, removing malware, and patching vulnerabilities.

Compliance with regulations and standards is also an essential aspect of network security. Monitoring can help organizations comply with regulations and standards related to network security. By monitoring network activity, organizations can ensure that they meet the requirements of regulatory bodies and industry standards. This can include monitoring for unauthorized access, data breaches, and other security incidents.

Improved network performance is another benefit of monitoring. Organizations can identify bottlenecks and other performance issues by analysing network activity, which can be addressed to improve network speed and efficiency. This can include optimizing network configurations, upgrading hardware, and implementing performance monitoring tools.

Data loss prevention is another critical way in which monitoring can help minimize loss of control in network security. Monitoring can help prevent data loss by detecting and responding to security incidents that could result in the loss of sensitive data. Organizations can identify and address vulnerabilities in their security infrastructure by monitoring network activity to prevent data loss. This includes monitoring for data exfiltration, unauthorized access to sensitive data, and malware infections.

Before-attack monitoring

Before-attack monitoring is a critical aspect of network security that involves analyzing network activity to identify potential vulnerabilities and threats before attackers exploit them. This type of monitoring allows organizations to take proactive measures to secure their networks and prevent security incidents from occurring.

Before-attack monitoring involves several key steps, including:

1. Baseline Network Activity: The first step in before-attack monitoring is establishing a baseline of normal network activity. This involves monitoring network traffic over a period of time to identify typical patterns of network behavior. This baseline can then be used as a reference point for detecting abnormal activity.

2. Identify Potential Vulnerabilities: Once a baseline of normal network activity has been established, the next step is to identify potential vulnerabilities that attackers could exploit. This can include software vulnerabilities, misconfigured network settings, and weak passwords.

3. Threat Intelligence Gathering: Before-attack monitoring also involves gathering threat intelligence information from various sources, such as security blogs, forums, and other online sources. This information can help organizations identify new and emerging threats that may target their network.

4. Analyze Network Traffic: Before-attack monitoring involves analyzing network traffic to identify potential threats and vulnerabilities. This can include monitoring for unusual traffic patterns, unexpected network connections, and suspicious user behavior.

5. Proactive Measures: Based on the analysis of network activity, organizations can take proactive measures to secure their networks

and prevent security incidents from occurring. This can include patching vulnerabilities, updating security configurations, and implementing new security measures.

By implementing before-attack monitoring, organizations can identify potential threats and vulnerabilities before attackers exploit them. This type of monitoring allows organizations to take proactive measures to secure their networks and prevent security incidents from occurring. This approach is instrumental in preventing zero-day attacks, which exploit vulnerabilities the software vendor or security community does not know. A zero-day attack is a type of cyber attack that exploits a previously unknown vulnerability or weakness in software or hardware that is not yet known to the software vendor or the security community [222]. Zero-day attacks are a challenging type of cyber attack to prevent, as they exploit vulnerabilities that are not yet known to the software vendor or security community. This makes zero-day attacks particularly difficult to detect and prevent, as there is no known fix or patch available to protect against the vulnerability. Cybercriminals can launch zero-day attacks to steal data, conduct espionage, or disrupt operations. They can compromise networks, steal sensitive information, or install malware on the victim's system.

5.3.2.2 *Access control*

Access control refers to controlling access to IoT devices and data. With the increasing number of connected devices in IoT networks, access control becomes critical to ensuring the security and privacy of the network and its users.

IoT access control involves several aspects, including authentication, authorization, and accountability. Authentication is the process of verifying the identity of a user or device, while authorization is the process of determining what actions a user or device is allowed to perform. Accountability is the ability to track and trace actions performed by users and devices.

IoT access control can be implemented at multiple levels, including device level, network level, and application level. At the device level, access control can involve physical security measures such as encryption, secure boot, and firmware updates. At the network level, access control can involve firewalls, intrusion detection and prevention systems, and network segmentation. At the application level, access control can involve user authentication and authorization mechanisms, such as passwords, biometrics, and two-factor authentication.

Access control prevents unauthorized users from accessing resources with restricted operation permissions or authorized users from performing operations beyond their authorized scope. The basic access control concepts include subject, object, operation, and environment. The subject refers to the user who requests access to a resource to perform a certain operation. The object refers to the resource the subject requests access to, including files, applications, servers, APIs, etc. The operation refers to the action the subject wants to perform on the object, such as read, write, execute, modify, copy, delete, etc. The environment refers to the contextual information of each access request, such as the time, location, communication protocol, communication encryption method, etc.

Classification of traditional access control mechanisms (based on different access control policies): Discretionary Access Control (DAC), Mandatory Access Control (MAC), and Role-Based Access Control (RBAC) [223].

1. DAC is a type of access control mechanism used in computer systems to regulate access to resources such as files, folders, or applications. In DAC, the owner or administrator of a resource has complete control over who can access it and what level of access they are granted. The owner of a resource can grant or revoke access to the resource at their discretion, hence the name "discretionary".

   DAC works by assigning permissions to individual users or groups of users based on their identity. These permissions include read, write, execute, and delete, among others. The owner or administrator of a resource can specify which users or groups are allowed to access the resource and what level of access they are granted. For example, the owner of a file might grant read-only access to a group of users while granting write access to a select few individuals.

   One of the advantages of DAC is that it allows for flexibility in managing access to resources. The owner or administrator of a resource has complete control over who can access it and can grant or revoke access as needed. However, this flexibility also means that managing access to resources in large organizations with many users and resources can be challenging.

Most systems implement DAC using an access control matrix. This method can control direct access by subjects to objects but cannot control indirect access. When the access control matrix is relatively large, access control linked lists and capacity tables are often used to implement it. The authorization relationship is the union of these two, representing the access control matrix. Each relationship represents the access permission of a subject to an object, and the access matrix is stored in a database.

2. MAC was developed as DAC could not effectively defend against Trojan virus attacks. MAC is a type of access control mechanism used in computer security that restricts access to resources based on a set of rules defined by a central authority. In MAC, the operating system enforces rules that determine what level of access users or processes can have to resources such as files, folders, or applications. The system administrator or security policy typically defines these rules and cannot be modified by individual users. MAC is commonly used in government and military environments, where strict control over access to sensitive information is necessary.

   - Unlike DAC, MAC does not allow ordinary users to manage access controls. MAC uses a centralized management mode to control all information flows within the system.
   - MAC suits strict security requirements, e.g., military or governments. MAC determines whether a subject can access the object by measuring the security attributes of the subject and the object
   - Security attributes: can be assigned by security admins or automatically by the system to each entity, which cannot be tampered with.
   - When the system regards that a subject with a specific security attribute cannot access an object with a certain security attribute, then there is no way to make the subject access the object
   - MAC guarantees that the information flow strictly follows the security attributes, even though a Trojan virus exists. (DAC issue is solved in this case)
   - Representative examples: Bell-LaPadula model and Biba model

3. RBAC is a type of access control mechanism used in computer security that regulates access to resources based on user roles or job responsibilities within an organization. RBAC provides a flexible and scalable way to manage access to resources in large organizations with many users and resources.

In RBAC, access to resources is assigned based on users' roles or job functions within an organization. A role is a collection of permissions defining the user's access level to a particular resource. Users are assigned roles based on their job responsibilities within the organization, and access to resources is granted based on their assigned roles.

RBAC provides several benefits over other access control mechanisms, such as Discretionary Access Control (DAC), where the owner or administrator of a resource controls access. RBAC provides a more centralized and controlled way to manage resource access, as permissions are assigned based on roles rather than individual users. This makes it easier to manage access to resources in large organizations with many users and resources.

RBAC also provides a more secure way to manage access to resources, as it reduces the risk of unauthorized access or privilege escalation. By assigning permissions based on roles, RBAC ensures that users only have access to the resources they need to perform their job functions and nothing more.

DAC, MAC and RBAC comparison

Discretionary Access Control (DAC), Role-Based Access Control (RBAC), and Mandatory Access Control (MAC) are three different access control mechanisms used in computer security. Each of these mechanisms has its own advantages and disadvantages [224].

DAC provides flexibility in managing access to resources, as the owner or administrator of a resource has complete control over who can access it and what level of access is granted. However, this flexibility also means that it can be challenging to manage access to resources in large organizations with many users and resources, and it can lead to a higher risk of unauthorized access or privilege escalation.

RBAC provides a more centralized and controlled way to manage access to resources, as access is assigned based on users' roles or job functions within an organization. This makes it easier to manage access to resources in large organizations with many users and resources. However, RBAC can be more complex to implement than DAC, and it may not be suitable for smaller organizations or environments with high user turnover.

MAC provides a high level of security, as access to resources is controlled by a central authority based on a set of rules. This makes it ideal for environments where strict control over access to sensitive information is necessary, such as in government or military environments. However, MAC can be complex to implement, and it may not be suitable for environments where users need a high degree of flexibility in accessing resources.

Customer-Managed Access Control

Customer-Managed Access Control (CMAC) is an access control mechanism used in cloud computing that gives customers more control over the security and management of their resources and data in the cloud [225]. With CMAC, customers can manage access to their resources and data directly without relying solely on the cloud service provider.

CMAC provides several benefits to customers, including increased control over their data and resources, improved security, and greater flexibility in managing access to their resources. Customers can set their own security policies, manage resource access, and monitor access activity.

CMAC is typically implemented through security tools and services the cloud service provider provides, such as identity and access management (IAM) tools, security groups, and network security features. Customers can use these tools to manage access to their resources and data, including setting user permissions, defining security policies, and monitoring access activity [226].

One of the key advantages of CMAC is that it gives customers more control over their security posture and enables them to meet their own regulatory and compliance requirements. CMAC can also help customers reduce their risk of security incidents and data breaches by enabling them to implement more granular security policies and controls.

However, implementing CMAC can also be complex and require high technical expertise. Customers must thoroughly understand the security tools and services provided by their cloud service provider and be able to configure and manage these tools effectively.

5.3.2.3 AWS, Google, and Microsoft

Tech giants like Amazon Web Services (AWS), Alphabet (Google), and Microsoft are three of the leading cloud service providers, each of which has its approach to access control management [227–229].

AWS provides customers with a range of access control tools and services, including Identity and Access Management (IAM), which enables customers to manage access to AWS resources, and AWS Key Management Service (KMS), which helps customers control access to their data encryption keys. AWS also provides various security and compliance services, such as AWS Shield, which provides DDoS protection, and AWS Artifact, which provides access to compliance reports.

Google Cloud Platform (GCP) provides customers access control tools and services, including Cloud Identity, which enables customers to manage user accounts and access GCP resources, and Cloud IAM, which enables customers to manage access to GCP resources based on roles. GCP also provides various security and compliance services, such as Cloud Security Command Center, which provides vulnerability scanning and threat detection, and Cloud Audit Logs, which provide access to activity logs.

Microsoft Azure provides customers with a range of access control tools and services, including Azure Active Directory (AAD), which enables customers to manage user accounts and access to Azure resources, and Azure Role-Based Access Control (RBAC), which enables customers to manage access to Azure resources based on roles. Azure also provides various security and compliance services, such as Azure Security Center, which provides threat detection and vulnerability management, and Azure Policy, which provides access to compliance reports.

5.3.3 Minimizing Multi-Tenancy

Multi-tenancy refers to a software operational mode where multiple independent instances of one or multiple applications run in a shared environment. In a multi-tenant environment, each user or organization has its own set of resources, but they all share the same underlying infrastructure. This can be an efficient and cost-effective way to use computing resources, particularly for cloud-based systems. The instances (tenants) are logically isolated but physically integrated. While logical isolation must be complete, the degree of physical integration may vary. The more physical integration, the more difficult it is to maintain logical isolation. The tenants (application instances) can represent organizations that have access to multi-tenant applications (as this is the scenario when ISVs offer application services to multiple customer organizations). The tenants may also be multiple applications competing for shared underlying resources (as this is the private or public cloud scenario where multiple applications are provided in a public cloud environment). In a cloud environment, multiple customers share the same physical infrastructure, such as servers, networks, and storage.

Multi-tenancy can also introduce security risks, as users or organizations may have different security requirements or levels of trust. The security challenges in multi-tenant environments arise from multiple tenants sharing the same resources, which can create opportunities for data breaches and unauthorized access. Therefore, multi-tenancy security solutions must incorporate measures such as access control, data encryption, and network segmentation to ensure that each tenant's data and resources are secure and isolated from other tenants. Here are some steps that can be taken to minimize the risks associated with multi-tenancy:

1. Use virtualization or containerization: Virtualization or containerization can be used to isolate each user or organization's resources and data. This can help to prevent unauthorized access and ensure that users or organizations can access only their own resources and data.

2. Implement access controls: Access controls should be implemented to ensure that users or organizations can access only their own resources and data. This can help to prevent unauthorized access and limit the impact of a security breach.

3. Encrypt data: Data should be encrypted in transit and at rest to prevent unauthorized access. This can help to protect against data breaches and ensure the confidentiality of sensitive data.

4. Regularly monitor and review access logs: Access logs should be regularly monitored and reviewed to detect suspicious activity. This can help to identify potential security threats and allow for timely response.

5. Conduct regular security audits: Regular security audits should be conducted to identify and address security risks. This can help to ensure that security controls are effective and up-to-date and that potential vulnerabilities are identified and addressed.

Segmentation is an important technique that can be used to reduce the risks associated with multi-tenancy. Segmentation involves dividing a network into smaller segments or subnets, each with its own security policies and controls. This can help to limit the impact of a security breach and prevent unauthorized access to sensitive data.

- Network segmentation: Network segmentation can be used to create separate network segments for each tenant. This can help to prevent unauthorized access to tenants' data and resources and limit the impact of a security breach [230]. Each tenant can have its own security policies and controls, such as firewalls, intrusion detection systems, and access controls [231].

- Application segmentation: Application segmentation can be used to separate applications used by different tenants. Each tenant can have its own set of applications and data, which are isolated from other tenants [232]. This can help to prevent unauthorized access to sensitive data and limit the impact of a security breach.

- Data segmentation: Data segmentation can be used to separate data used by different tenants. Each tenant can have its own set of data, which is isolated from other tenants. This can help to prevent unauthorized access to sensitive data and limit the impact of a security breach [233].

Increasing **isolation** between tenants in a multi-tenant environment is an important step towards improving network security. It is an essential aspect of multi-tenancy that ensures the security and privacy of each tenant's data and resources. Isolation can be achieved through physical, logical, and administrative controls.

1. Physical isolation involves physically separating the infrastructure and resources different tenants use. This can be done by using data centers in different regions worldwide or physical barriers such as cages and cabinets to isolate the infrastructure used by different tenants.

2. Logical isolation involves creating separate instances of operating systems and applications for each tenant. This can be achieved using virtualization and containerization technologies to ensure that tenants' data and resources are isolated from other tenants. Network segmentation can also create separate network segments for each tenant.

- Use virtualization or containerization: Virtualization or containerization can create separate instances of an operating system and applications for each tenant. This can help to ensure that each tenant's data and resources are isolated from other tenants.

- Implement network segmentation: Network segmentation can create separate network segments for each tenant. This can help to prevent unauthorized access and limit the impact of a security breach.

- Implement access controls: Access controls should be implemented to ensure that each tenant can access only their own resources and data. This can help to prevent unauthorized access and limit the impact of a security breach.

3. Administrative isolation ensures only authorized personnel can access tenants' data and resources. This can be done by implementing strict and role-based access controls to limit access to sensitive data and resources. Regular security audits and vulnerability assessments can also be conducted to identify and address potential vulnerabilities.

   - Regularly monitor and review access logs: Access logs should be regularly monitored and reviewed to detect suspicious activity. This can help to identify potential security threats and allow for a timely response.

   - Conduct regular security audits: Regular security audits should be conducted to identify and address security risks. This can help to ensure that security controls are effective and up-to-date and that potential vulnerabilities are identified and addressed.

4. Encryption: This method is also used to protect data in transit and at rest. Transport Layer Security (TLS) is used to encrypt data in transit, and BitLocker encryption is used to encrypt data at rest. Azure Key Vault is used to manage encryption keys. Data should be encrypted in transit and at rest to prevent unauthorized access. This can help to protect against data breaches and ensure the confidentiality of sensitive data.

   Kumar et. al [234] proposed a hybrid data encryption approach based on Elliptic Curve Cryptography (ECC) to enhance the security of multi-tenancy in cloud computing. The encryption approach used in the research paper involves a combination of symmetric and asymmetric encryption. The symmetric encryption algorithm is used to encrypt the data, and the asymmetric encryption algorithm is used to encrypt the key used for symmetric encryption. The use of ECC in the asymmetric encryption algorithm provides several benefits, including smaller key sizes, faster processing times, and greater resistance to attacks. The hybrid encryption approach used in the research paper provides an additional layer of security to multi-tenancy in cloud computing by ensuring that data is encrypted both in transit and at rest.

Microsoft[6] implements a variety of measures to achieve isolation in their cloud services and ensure that each tenant's data and resources are protected. They use a combination of physical, logical, and administrative controls to achieve this [235]. For physical isolation, Microsoft separates the infrastructure and resources used by different tenants using data centers located in different regions worldwide. They also use physical barriers such as cages and cabinets to isolate the infrastructure used by different tenants. For logical isolation, Microsoft creates separate instances of operating systems and applications for each tenant using virtualization and containerization technologies. They also use network segmentation to create separate network segments for each tenant. Administrative isolation is achieved by ensuring that only authorized personnel can access tenants' data and resources. Microsoft uses strict access controls and role-based access control to limit access to sensitive data and resources [236]. They also conduct regular security audits and vulnerability assessments to identify and address potential vulnerabilities. Encryption is used to protect data both in transit and at rest. Microsoft uses Transport Layer Security (TLS) to encrypt data in transit and BitLocker encryption to encrypt data at rest. Azure Key Vault is used to manage encryption keys. Finally, Microsoft undergoes regular third-party audits to ensure that their cloud services comply with industry standards and regulations such as ISO 27001, SOC 1, SOC 2, HIPAA, and GDPR. These certifications demonstrate that Microsoft has implemented appropriate security controls and practices to protect tenants' data and resources.

---

[6] Azure, https://learn.microsoft.com/en-us/azure/security/fundamentals/isolation-choices

5.4 SUMMARY

This chapter introduced the concept and main components of the threat model. In Section 5.2, we make an overview of web security in IoT-of-Things. Meanwhile, the concept and types of the Web Services and RESTful API are being discussed and compared to get a clearer picture of pros and cons for each mechanism. DoS are introduced. Some methods can be used to resist Denial-of-Service Attacks. Section 5.3 explained the main security solutions to networking threats, such as minimizing lack of trust, minimizing loss of control, and minimizing multi-tenancy.

5.5 EXERCISES

1. Explain what SOAP Web Services is.

   SOAP (Simple Object Access Protocol) is a protocol used to exchange structured data between applications over the Internet. SOAP web services use this protocol to facilitate communication between client and server applications. These web services use XML to format data and messages, which makes them usable across different programming languages and platforms.

   The structure of SOAP web services is standardized and consists of an envelope, header, and body. The envelope contains information about the message being exchanged, while the header contains optional information such as authentication data. The body contains the actual data being exchanged between client and server applications.

   SOAP web services are frequently used in enterprise environments where standardized communication between systems and applications is essential. They provide a reliable and secure method for exchanging data over the Internet. However, they can be more difficult to implement compared to other web services, such as REST web services.

2. What are the elements of SOAP message?

   A SOAP (Simple Object Access Protocol) message is an XML-based message to exchange structured data between client and server applications. The elements of a SOAP message include:

- Envelope: This is the top-level element of a SOAP message and contains the entire message. It acts as an identifier for XML, defines the namespace for the SOAP message and indicates the version of SOAP being used.

- Header: This element contains additional header information about the SOAP message, which is optional for SOAP XML Messages, such as authentication data, routing information, or transaction identifiers. This information is not essential for processing the message but can provide additional context.

- Body: This element contains the data being exchanged between the client and server applications. It defines the content of the request or response message, including the method being called and any parameters or data being passed. This element is mandatory.

- Fault: This element is used to report errors that occur during the processing of a SOAP message. It contains information about the error, such as an error code and message, and is nested under the response message's body.

3. What are the major elements of a WSDL?

There are four types of elements of a WSDL:

- Types: This element defines XML Sheme and the data types used in the web service. It specifies the structure of the request and response messages and the data types of the parameters and return values.

- Messages: This element defines the format of the request and response messages exchanged by the web service. It specifies the input and output messages and the data types of the message parts. It also defines the fault message elements for each operation.

- Port Type: This element defines the web service's operations. It specifies the input and output messages for each operation and the order in which they are sent.

- Binding: This element defines the protocol and data format specifications for exchanging messages with the web service. It specifies the SOAP version, transport protocol, and encoding style.

● Service: This element defines the location of the web service and the binding used to access it. It specifies the endpoint address where the service can be accessed and the binding used to communicate with it.

4. What are the advantages of using SOAP Web Services?

SOAP web services provide a reliable, secure, and standardized way for applications to communicate and exchange data over the Internet,

● Language and platform independence: SOAP web services use XML to format data and messages, making them usable across different programming languages and platforms. It is application protocol neutral and supports multiple protocols: HTTP/HTTPS, JMS, STP, etc.

● Standardization: SOAP web services have a standardized structure consisting of an envelope, header, and body. It uses XML as its core. This makes it easier for applications to communicate and exchange data with each other, as they can have great control over data types and understand the structure of the messages being exchanged.

● Compatibility: SOAP web services can be used with various transport protocols, including HTTP, HTTPS, SMTP, and FTP. This makes them compatible with a wide range of network environments and technologies.

● Tool support: SOAP web services have extensive tool support, including libraries, frameworks, and development tools using a WSDL file. This makes it easier for developers to create, test, and deploy SOAP web services.

5. Describe the main difference between REST API and SOAP Web Services.

In general, all Web Services are APIs, but not all are Web Services. The choice between REST and SOAP depends on the requirements of the application and the type of operations that need to be performed.

The main difference between REST API and SOAP web services lies in their design philosophy and the way they handle data exchange. REST API is designed around the concept of resources and uses HTTP (Hypertext Transfer Protocol) methods such as GET, POST, PUT, and DELETE to interact with these resources. REST APIs focus on the transfer of data, and the data is sent and received in a lightweight format such as JSON (JavaScript Object Notation) or XML (Extensible Markup Language). REST APIs are stateless, meaning each request contains all the necessary information to process the request and cannot rely on previous requests. REST APIs are lightweight, and resource-based.

On the other hand, SOAP web services are designed around the concept of remote procedure calls (RPC) and use XML to format the data being exchanged. SOAP web services have a standardized structure consisting of an envelope, header, and body and use a variety of protocols and transport mechanisms to exchange messages. SOAP web services are often used in enterprise environments where there is a need for standardized communication between different systems and applications.

GLOSSARY

Asset: is something under the control of an owner or stakeholder and is valued by them.

Botnet: refers to a network of compromised hosts controlled by malicious programs.

Denial-of-Service: is a type of cyber attack designed to disrupt website, server, or network access by overwhelming it with traffic or other malicious activity.

HTTP status codes: are three-digit numbers a server returns in response to a client's HTTP request.

Man-in-the-middle attack: is an indirect intrusion attack, which involves using various technical means to virtually place a device controlled by the intruder between two communication devices in a network connection.

Replay Attack: refers to the attacker sending a packet that has already been received by the target host to deceive the system, mainly used in the identity authentication process to undermine the correctness of the authentication.

Representational State Transfer: is a type of web API or application programming interface that adheres to the principles of the REST architectural style and permits communication with RESTful Web Services.

Security risk: measures the potential for something to go wrong with a particular asset.

Simple Object Access Protocol: is an XML-based message to exchange structured data between client and server applications.

Threat: is a potential breach of system security that could have some negative impact on the system.

Threat Agent: is an actor that is motivated to abuse or cause damage to an asset. This includes cybercriminals, Advanced Persistent Threats (APTs) and similar groups.

Threat Modeling: is a cyclical process for information system security threats that includes identification, documentation, and mitigation processes.

Uniform Resource Identifier: is a string of characters identifying a resource. In a REST API, each resource is identified by a unique URI used to access and manipulate the resource.

Web Services: are a software architecture that enables communication between different applications over the Internet.

Web Services Description Language: is an XML-based language used to describe and specify the functionality of web services.

CHAPTER 6

Cryptography and Cryptosystems

This chapter begins with frequent cybersecurity incidents and introduces the importance of cybersecurity. Then, basic concepts, terminology, and notation in cryptography are introduced. Moreover, this chapter focuses on the concepts, characteristics of symmetric cipher model and asymmetric cipher model, as well as their typical algorithms and respective application scenarios. Specifically, in the symmetric cipher model, the principles, examples and code implementations of DES and AES are introduced in detail. In addition, in the asymmetric cipher model, relevant contents of typical *Dieffie-Hellman* (DH) and RSA algorithms are selected for specific introduction. Furthermore, this chapter covers the concepts, elements, and common types of access control mechanisms. Finally, we outline five commonly used attack methods in modern cryptography and introduce the security of cryptosystems. Reading this chapter will lay a good foundation for learners to have an essential picture of showing major aspects of cybersecurity.

6.1 INTRODUCTION TO CRYPTOGRAPHY

The situation facing cyberspace security is complex and changeable, and frequent information security incidents pose serious threats to enterprise and national security. Listed below are several recent major global network information security incidents. In June 2020, BlueKai, the data management platform of technology giant Oracle Corporation, leaked the data records of billions of people because the data was not password-protected. Tesla had 11 suspected out-of-control accidents in China in

DOI: 10.1201/9781032694818-6

	14	04	13	01	02	15	11	08	03	10	06	12	05	09	00	07
S_1	00	15	07	04	14	02	13	01	10	06	12	11	09	05	03	08
	04	01	14	08	13	06	02	11	15	12	09	07	03	10	05	00
	15	12	08	02	04	09	01	07	05	11	03	14	10	00	06	13
	15	01	08	14	06	11	03	04	09	07	02	13	12	00	05	10
S_2	03	13	04	07	15	02	08	14	12	00	01	10	06	09	11	05
	00	14	07	11	10	04	13	01	05	08	12	06	09	03	02	15
	13	08	10	01	03	15	04	02	11	06	07	12	00	05	14	09
	10	00	09	14	06	03	15	05	01	13	12	07	11	04	02	08
S_3	13	07	00	09	03	04	06	10	02	08	05	14	12	11	15	01
	13	06	04	09	08	15	03	00	11	01	02	12	05	10	14	07
	01	10	13	00	06	09	08	07	04	15	14	03	11	05	02	12
	07	13	14	03	00	06	09	10	01	02	08	05	11	12	04	15
S_4	13	08	11	05	06	15	00	03	04	07	02	12	01	10	14	09
	10	06	09	00	12	11	07	13	15	01	03	14	05	02	08	04
	03	15	00	16	10	01	13	08	09	04	05	11	12	07	02	14
	02	12	04	01	07	10	11	06	08	05	03	15	13	00	14	09
S_5	14	11	02	12	04	07	13	01	05	00	15	10	03	09	08	06
	04	02	01	11	10	13	07	08	15	09	12	05	06	03	00	14
	11	08	12	07	01	14	02	13	06	15	00	09	10	04	05	03
	12	01	10	15	09	02	06	08	00	13	03	04	14	07	05	11
S_6	10	15	04	02	07	12	09	05	06	01	13	14	00	11	03	08
	09	14	15	05	02	08	12	03	07	00	04	10	01	13	11	06
	04	03	02	12	09	05	15	10	11	14	01	07	06	00	08	13
	04	11	02	14	15	00	08	13	03	12	09	07	05	10	06	01
S_7	13	00	11	07	04	09	01	10	14	03	05	12	02	15	08	06
	01	04	11	13	12	03	07	14	10	15	06	08	00	05	09	02
	06	11	13	08	01	04	10	07	09	05	00	15	14	02	03	12
	13	02	08	04	06	15	11	01	10	09	03	14	05	00	12	07
S_8	01	15	13	08	10	03	07	04	12	05	06	11	00	14	09	02
	07	11	04	01	09	12	14	02	00	06	10	13	15	03	05	08
	02	01	14	07	04	10	08	13	15	12	09	00	03	05	06	11

Figure 6.1 Details of the eight S-boxes.

2020, and the owner and Tesla failed to reach a consensus on the authenticity and reliability of the data information. In August 2018, Tencent Cloud, a subsidiary of Tencent, was claimed 11 million for data loss due to errors in data migration operations. In December 2018, Blizzard Entertainment and NetEase services were interrupted for more than 24 hours, and the direct revenue loss was estimated to be in the millions. With the increasing harm caused by computer viruses, the increasing number of computer crimes, and the increasing frequency of hacker attacks, cyber security has become a problem that people have to face [237].

Essentially, cyber security [238] involves safeguarding the hardware, software, and data within a network system from potential damage, alteration, or unauthorized disclosure caused by accidental or malicious factors. The primary objective is to ensure the smooth functioning of the system and uninterrupted provision of network services. In a broader sense, network security research encompasses various technologies and theories focused on maintaining the confidentiality, integrity, availability, authenticity, and controllability of information on the network.

- **Confidentiality.** Ensure that information is not exposed to unauthorized entities, that is, leak-proof.

- **Integrity.** Ensure that the received data is exactly the same as the sent data, including complete data content, complete data sequence, correct time, etc., that is, tamper-proof.

- **Availability.** Ensure that the service is available and the response time delay is within the allowable range, that is, interrupt-proof.

- **Authenticity.** Ensure the true identity of the participants. It is impossible for a participant to deny actions and commitments that have been done, that is, non-repudiation.

- **Controllability.** Ensure the ability to control the dissemination and content of network information.

Above properties are called cyber security attributes, which are one of the information elements for security situation assessment in the field of cyber security. In the assessment of cyber security situation, information such as historical records and operating conditions of cyber security attributes are used to judge the current security state and development trend of security in the cyberspace. Furthermore, cyber security properties are not always constant. With the development of offensive and defensive technologies in cyberspace, the demand for security attributes needs to be updated in real time.

Cryptography is the core technology for ensuring the security of cyberspace (including the cyberspace of the Internet of Things). Cryptography, derived from the Greek words krypt's (meaning hidden), and graphein (meaning writing), is the study of how to transmit information secretly. Ron Rivest, a famous cryptologist and winner of Turing Prize, explained that "Cryptography is about how to communicate in the environment where the enemy exists". Based on the above-mentioned cyber security properties, the role of cryptography is summarized as follows.

- Provide confidentiality. Encryption and decryption are performed through cryptographic techniques, and data is stored, transmitted and processed in ciphertext.

- Used for authentication and authentication to resolve identity spoofing (often combined with message authentication codes). The receiver of the message can confirm the source of the message, and the sender cannot pretend to be someone else. The sender must also be able to confirm whether the receiver is who he claims to be, and the receiver cannot pretend to be someone else.

- Provide integrity to address tampering. The recipient of the message should be able to verify that the message was not modified during delivery.

- Prevent denial. It is not possible for the sender or receiver to falsely deny the messages they sent or received afterwards.

In order to facilitate the reading of the subsequent content of this chapter, the basic terminology of cryptography is first introduced.

- **Plaintext.** Plaintext refers to messages waiting to be disguised or encrypted, and in communication systems may be bit streams, such as text, bitmaps, digitized speech, images, and video, etc. In general, plaintext can be simply thought of as a meaningful set of characters or bits, or a message that can be obtained through some public encoding standard.

- **Ciphertext.** Ciphertext refers to the messages and signals generated by the cryptosystem, which are output through some kind of disguise or transformation of the plaintext. When the ciphertext

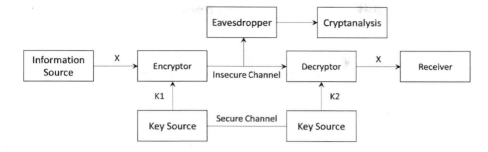

Figure 6.2 Schematic diagram of the encrypted communication model.

is not decrypted by the recipient, others cannot understand the content of the ciphertext, which ensures the confidentiality of the sent information.

- **Encryption.** [239] Encryption refers to processing the original plaintext information into incomprehensible ciphertext according to a certain algorithm or rule, so as to protect the data from being illegally stolen and read.

- **Decryption.** Decryption refers to the process of restoring ciphertext to plaintext using the corresponding algorithm or key.

- **Key.** Obtaining the ciphertext corresponding to the plaintext relies on an additional parameter, called the key. The receiver of the ciphertext needs another key to perform reverse operations to complete the decryption and recover the plaintext.

- **Cryptographic Algorithm.** Cipher algorithm refers to a set of operational rules or procedures that describe the cryptographic processing (encryption and decryption), which is the basis of a cryptographic protocol.

Fig. 6.2 shows the schematic diagram of the encrypt communication model.

Generally speaking, the encryption and decryption process of data is controlled by the cipher system and the key. The cipher system refer to algorithms that perform encryption and decryption. The cipher system need to be easy to use, especially on personal computers. The security of cipher systems depends on the security of keys. Modern cryptography does not pursue the confidentiality of encryption algorithms, but the

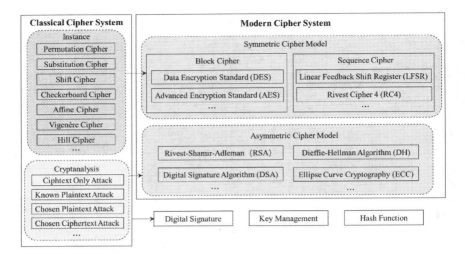

Figure 6.3 Classification of cipher systems.

completeness of encryption algorithms. It means that the attacker has no way to find a breakthrough from the algorithm without knowing the key. Cipher systems usually adopt methods such as shift, substitution and algebra to perform transformations of encryption and decryption. In addition, one or a combination of several methods can be used as the basic module of data transformation. Definition 6.1 presents a formal definition of the cipher system.

Definition 6.1 *A cipher system is a quintuple (P, C, K, E, D) that satisfies the conditions::*

- *P is a finite set of possible plaintexts (plaintext space).*

- *C is a finite set of possible ciphertexts (ciphertext space).*

- *K is a set of possible keys (key space).*

- $\forall k \in \boldsymbol{K}$, *there is an encryption algorithm, $e_k \in \boldsymbol{E}$, and the corresponding decryption algorithm $d_k \in \boldsymbol{D}$, such that $e_k \colon \boldsymbol{P} \to \boldsymbol{C}$ and $d_k \colon \boldsymbol{C} \to \boldsymbol{P}$ are the encryption and decryption functions respectively, satisfying $d_k(e_k(x)) = x$, where $x \in \boldsymbol{P}$.*

In the following, the classification of cryptosystems is introduced in conjunction with Fig. 6.3, and the content of the figure is also the focus of this chapter. According to the development process of the cipher system, it can be divided into classical cipher system and modern cipher system. Cipher systems that appeared before the advent of computers are collectively referred to as classical cipher system. In general, plaintext and ciphertext in classical cipher systems consist of a unified alphabet, such as the English alphabet. Common classical cryptosystems include permutation cipher, substitution cipher, shift cipher, checkerboard cipher, affine cipher, Vigenere cipher, Hill cipher, etc.

Core methods of these classical cipher models can be summarized as permutation and substitution. Whether it is permutation or substitution, the core idea is derived from the ancient cyclic shift. Permutation means that the letters in the plaintext are still used in the ciphertext but the order is rearranged. Substitution fundamentally changes the basic characters used in the plaintext, substituting other characters for the characters in the plaintext. Substitution ciphers can be divided into column substitution and periodic substitution, and substitution ciphers are divided into single-table substitution and multi-table substitution. Classical ciphers are relatively simple and easy to decipher. Knowing these ciphers and their analysis method is very beneficial for understanding modern cipher system.

With the rapid development of computer technology, computer systems are widely used in various industries as a common tool, and the requirements for information security and data encryption are getting higher and higher. At the beginning of the 20th century, with the continuous enrichment and improvement of cryptography theory, cryptography was upgraded from the "art" to the "science", and modern cryptography was born with its unique cipher system. It is extremely dangerous that the classical cryptographic algorithm places its security hopes on the attackers' ignorance of the internal mechanism of the algorithm. In contrast, the security of modern cryptographic algorithms is based on key security, and the details of the algorithm can be disclosed.

6.2 SYMMETRIC CIPHER MODEL

Symmetric encryption [240, 241] , also known as shared key encryption, means that the sender and receiver use the same key to encrypt and decrypt data. Note that the key must be distributed using a secret channel. Even if the ciphertext encrypted by the symmetric encryption algorithm is stolen by illegal users, the information in it cannot be understood, which can realize the confidentiality of the data. Fig. 6.4 illustrates the

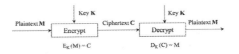

Figure 6.4   Encryption and decryption under symmetric cipher model.

principle of the symmetric cipher model as well as the encryption and de-cryption process. Symmetric encryption [111, 242, 243] is generally used in scenarios where a large amount of data needs to be encrypted and de-crypted, such as service data in *Internet Protocol Security* (IPSec) and VPN.

Diffusion and confusion are major factors that affect password se-curity [244]. Diffusion refers to rearranging or spreading each bit in a message, applying the influence of each bit of plaintext or key to more bits of output ciphertext as quickly as possible. The easiest way to gener-ate diffusion is to perform permutation. Confusion refers to complicating the relationship between the key and the ciphertext, thereby increasing the difficulty of attacking through statistical methods. Confusion can be easily achieved by using a substitution algorithm. In various symmet-ric cipher algorithms, efforts are being made to increase the degree of diffusion and confusion to enhance the cryptographic strength.

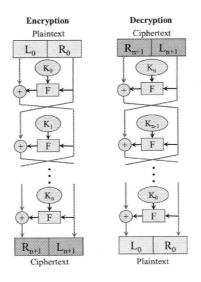

Figure 6.5   The Feistel network with multi-round iterative structure.

The symmetric cipher model is divided into block cipher [245] and sequence cipher [246] according to the processing method of plaintext. The mathematical model of block cipher is to divide the number sequence after encoding the plaintext message into groups of length n (which can be regarded as a vector of length n), and each group is transformed into equal length ciphertext number sequence for output under the control of the key. Horst Feistel is known as the father of block cipher. In 1973, he published the article "Cryptography and Computer Privacy" on Scientific American magazine, in which the Feistel network shown in Figure 2 was proposed. Sequence cipher, also known as stream cipher, refers to the use of a key to generate a key stream, which is used to process the plaintext bit by bit. Commonly used symmetric encryption algorithms include DES, AES, *Rivest Code* (RC) algorithms and their variants.

6.2.1 Data Encryption Standard

DES [247] is a kind of symmetric encryption algorithm, and its encryption principle is as follows: DES uses a 56-bit key and additional 8-bit parity bits to generate 64-bit blocks. It is an iterative block cipher that uses a technique called Feistel , where an encrypted block of text is split in half. Apply a round-robin function to one of the halves using the subkey, then XOR the output with the other half. Then, the two halves are swapped, and the process continues until the last loop (the last loop is not swapped). In general, the DES algorithm is implemented using 16 cycles and four basic operations of XOR, permutation, substitution, and shift.

Fig. 6.6 illustrates the encryption process of the DES. Specifically, it includes the following four steps:

1. **Initial Permutation (IP).** Initial permutation refers to processing the original plaintext through the IP permutation table.

2. **Generate Subkeys.** DES encryption executes 16 iterations in total, and the data length of each iteration is 48bit. Therefore, 16 48-bit subkeys are required for encryption.

3. **Iteration Process.** Fig. 6.10 shows the flow of the i-th round of encryption operation in the DES algorithm. Let L_i (32 bit) and R_i (32 bit) be the left half and right half of the calculation result of the i-th iteration, and the subkey K_i is the 48-bit encryption key of the i-th round. The blue shaded box is the f function for substitution, permutation, XOR and other operations. In encryption,

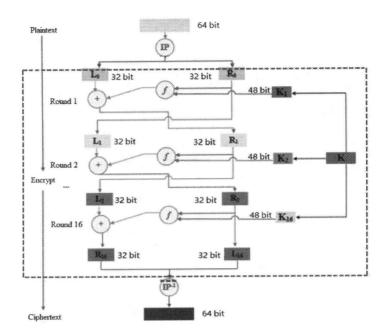

Figure 6.6 The encryption process of the Data Encryption Standard.

the specific process of calculating L_i and R_i is as follows:

$$L_i = R_{i-1}. \tag{6.1}$$

$$R_i = L_{i-1} \oplus f(R_{i-1}, K_i). \tag{6.2}$$

4. **Inverse Permutation (IP^{-1}).** Perform 16 iterations of the initial permutation, that is, perform 16-layer encryption transformation to obtain L_{16} and R_{16}, which are used as input blocks, and perform inverse permutation to obtain the final ciphertext output block. Note that IP^{-1} is the inverse operation of the IP.

In order to further introduce the encryption process of DES in detail, we give a specific instance. In the DES encryption algorithm, plaintext and ciphertext are 64-bit blocks. Suppose the input 64-bit plaintext data M and selected 64-bit key K:

$M = 0110001101101111011011010111000001110101011101000110010101110010$

$K = 0001001100110100010101110111100110011011101111001101111111110001$

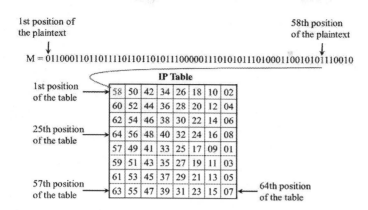

1st position of
the plaintext

58th position
of the plaintext

M = 0110001101101111011011010111000001110101011101000110010101110010

IP Table

1st position
of the table

25th position
of the table

57th position
of the table

64th position
of the table

58	50	42	34	26	18	10	02
60	52	44	36	28	20	12	04
62	54	46	38	30	22	14	06
64	56	48	40	32	24	16	08
57	49	41	33	25	17	09	01
59	51	43	35	27	19	11	03
61	53	45	37	29	21	13	05
63	55	47	39	31	23	15	07

Figure 6.7　Initial Permutation (IP) table in DES.

Note that the total length of the key is 64 bits, and every eighth bit of the key is set as a parity bit, so the actual length of the key is 56 bits.

1. IP

The IP table is in Fig. 6.7. The number in the IP table represents the position before the permutation, and the position of the grid itself represents the position after the permutation. For example, the number 58 in the first row and first column (the 1st position) of the IP table refers to moving the 58th bit in plaintext M to the 1st position. Likewise, the number 60 in the first column and second row (the 9th position) refers to moving the 60th bit in plaintext M to the 9th position. After initial permutation of M, 64-bit M' is obtained:

$M = 1111111110111000011101100101011100000000111111111000001101000011$

Take the first 32 bits of M' as L_0:

$L_0 = 11111111101110000111011001010111$

And take the last 32 bits of M' as R_0, then:

$R_0 = 00000000111111110000011010000011$

2. Generate Subkeys

The process of generating subkeys is shown in Fig. 6.8.

(1) First Round Permutation.

When performing the first round of permutation, the **PC-1** table shown in Table 6.1 is used, and the function of this table is to remove the check digit of the key K. After the permutation operation according to the **PC-1** table, the key:

$K = 0001001100110100001010110111100110011011101111001101111111110001$

becomes 56-bit K':

$K' = 11110000110011001010101011110101010101100110011110001111$

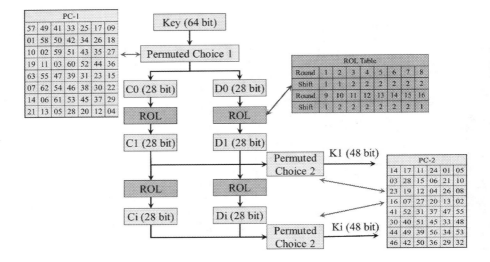

Figure 6.8 The process of generating subkeys.

Take the first 28 bits of K' as C_0, then we have:

$C_0 = 1111000011001100101010101111$

And take the last 28 bits of K' as D_0, then we have:

$D_0 = 0101010101100110011110001111$

After obtaining C_0 and D_0, the left shift operation needs to query the shift table (as shown in Table 6.2) to obtain the number of moves in each round. In the first round, looking at the shift table in Table 6.2, we can see that C_0 is shifted to the left by 1 bit, and C_1 is obtained:

$C_1 = 1110000110011001010101011111$

Table 6.1 The PC-1 Table

57	49	41	33	25	17	09
01	58	50	42	34	26	18
10	02	59	51	43	35	27
19	11	03	60	52	44	36
63	55	47	39	31	23	15
07	62	54	46	38	30	22
14	06	61	53	45	37	29
21	13	05	28	20	12	04

Table 6.2 The Shift Table

Round	1	1	3	4	5	6	7	8
Shift	1	1	2	2	2	2	2	2
Round	9	10	11	12	13	14	15	16
Shift	1	2	2	2	2	2	2	1

D_1 is obtained by shifting D_0 to the left by 1 bit:
$D_1 = 1010101011001100111100011110$

After merging C_1 and D_1, the subkey K_1 is obtained through the permutation operation of the **PC-2** table. Then, 48 bits are selected from the 56-bit keys as the encryption key for the current round. As shown in Fig. 6.9, the size of the **PC-2** table is 6×8 (48 bits in total), removing the 9th, 18th, 22nd, 25th, 35th, 38th, 43rd, 54th bit.

After the permutation by **PC-2**, the 48-bit key K_1 is obtained:
$K_1 = 000110110000001011101111111110001110000001110010$

(2) Second Round Permutation.

C_1 and D_1 are shifted left again. At this time, it is the second round, and the left shift number should be 1 bit from the table lookup. That is, C_1 and D_1 are shifted left by 1 bit to get C_2 and D_2:

$C_2 = 1100001100110010101010111111$
$D_2 = 0101010110011001111000111101$

C_2 and D_2 are combined into 56 bits, and 48-bit key K_2 is obtained after permutation according to **PC-2** table.

$K_2 = 011110011010101110110111011110010011100111100101$

By analogy, C_3-C_{16} and D_3-D_{16} are calculated by moving the appropriate bits to the left according to Fig. 6.9, and then subkeys K_3-K_{16} are obtained. $C_3(28bit) = 0000110011001010101011111111$

$D_3(28bit) = 0101011001100111100011110101$
$K_3(48bit) = 010101011111100100010100100001011001111100011001$
$C_4(28bit) = 0011001100101010101111111100$
$D_4(28bit) = 0101100110011110001111010101$
$K_4(48bit) = 011100101010110111010110110110110011010100011101$
$C_5(28bit) = 1100110010101010111111110000$
$D_5(28bit) = 0110011001111000111101010101$
$K_5(48bit) = 011111001110110000000111111010110101001110101000$
$C_6(28bit) = 0011001010101011111111000011$
$D_6(28bit) = 1001100111100011110101010101$
$K_6(48bit) = 011000111010010100111110010100000111101100101111$
$C_7(28bit) = 1100101010101111111100001100$

PC-1 Table						
57	49	41	33	25	17	09
01	58	50	42	34	26	18
10	02	59	51	43	35	27
19	11	03	60	52	44	36
63	55	47	39	31	23	15
07	62	54	46	38	30	22
14	06	61	53	45	37	29
21	13	05	28	20	12	04

49	41	33	25	17	09	01
58	50	42	34	26	18	10
02	59	51	43	35	27	19
11	03	60	52	44	36	57
55	47	39	31	23	15	07
62	54	46	38	30	22	14
06	61	53	45	37	29	21
13	05	28	20	12	04	63

PC-2 Table					
14	17	11	24	01	05
03	28	15	06	21	10
23	19	12	04	26	08
16	07	27	20	13	02
41	52	31	37	47	55
30	40	51	45	33	48
44	49	39	56	34	53
46	42	50	36	29	32

Figure 6.9 Conversion process from PC-1 table to PC-2 table.

$D_7(28bit) = 0110011110001111010101010110$
$K_7(48bit) = 111011001000010010110111111101100001100010111100$
$C_8(28bit) = 0010101010111111110000110011$
$D_8(28bit) = 1001111000111101010101011001$
$K_8(48bit) = 111101111000101000111010110000010011101111111011$
$C_9(28bit) = 0101010101111111100001100110$
$D_9(28bit) = 0011110001111010101010110011$
$K_9(48bit) = 111000001101101111101011111011011110011110000001$
$C_{10}(28bit) = 0101010111111110000110011001$
$D_10(28bit) = 1111000111101010101011001100$
$K_{10}(48bit) = 101100011111001101000111011101001000110010011111$
$C_{11}(28bit) = 0101011111111000011001100101$
$D_{11}(28bit) = 1100011110101010101100110011$
$K_{11}(48bit) = 001600010101111111010011111011110110100111000011 0$
$C_{12}(28bit) = 0101111111100001100110010101$
$D_{12}(28bit) = 0001110101010101100110011001111$
$K_{12}(48bit) = 011101010111000111110101100101000110011111101001$
$C_{13}(28bit) = 0111111110000110011001010101$
$D_{13}(28bit) = 0111101010101011001100111100$
$K_{13}(48bit) = 100101111100010111010001111110101011101001000001$
$C_{14}(28bit) = 1111111000011001100101010101$
$D_{14}(28bit) = 1110101010101100110011110001$
$K_{14}(48bit) = 010111110100001110110111111100101110011100111010$
$C_{15}(28bit) = 1111100001100110010101010111$
$D_{15}(28bit) = 1010101010110011001111000111$
$K_{15}(48bit) = 101111111001000110001101001111010011111100001010$

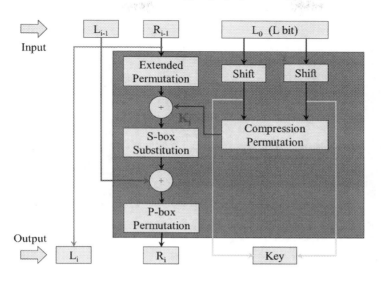

Figure 6.10 The flow of the i-th round of encryption operation in the DES algorithm.

$C_{16}(28bit) = 1111000011001100101010101111$
$D_{16}(28bit) = 0101010101100110011110001111$
$K_{16}(48bit) = 110010110011110110001011000011100001011111110101$

3. Iteration Process.

Fig. 6.10 illustrates the entire iterative process. Let L_i (32-bit) and R_i (32-bit) be the left half and right half of the calculation result of the i-th iteration, and the subkey K_i is the 48-bit encryption key of the i-th round. Define the operation rules: $L_i = R_{i-1}$ and $R_i = L_{i-1} \oplus f(R_{i-1}, K_i)$.

(1) E-box Expansion Permutation.

The right half R_i is 32 bits, while the key K_i is 48 bits. In order to ensure that R_i and K_i can perform XOR operation, it is necessary to expand the bits of R_i. The extended permutation table E is shown in Table 6.3. Fig. 6.10 illustrates the entire iterative process: As an example, the L_0 and R_0 of 32 bits are:

$L_0 = 11111111101110000111011001010111$
$R_0 = 00000000111111110000011010000011$

According to the extended permutation table E, the 32-bit R_0 becomes 48-bit after extended permutation:

$E(R_0) = 100000000001011111111110100000001101010000000110$

Table 6.3 The Extended Permutation Table E

32	01	02	03	04	05
04	05	06	07	08	09
08	09	10	11	12	13
12	13	14	15	16	17
16	17	18	19	20	21
20	21	22	23	24	25
24	25	26	27	28	29
28	29	30	31	32	01

Since we have calculated:

$K_1 = 000110110000001011101111111111000111000001110010$

The 48-bit $E(R_0)$ and the 48-bit K_1 perform the XOR operation to obtain:

$E(R_0) \oplus K_1 = 100110110001010100010001011111001010010001110100$

(2) S-box Substitution.

The substitution operation is performed by 8 different substitution boxes (S-boxes). Each S-box has 6 bits of input and 4 bits of output. The substitution operation flow is shown in Fig. 6.11. We take an example to introduce the calculation rules of the S-box. For example: if the input of the first S-box (S_1) is 110111, the first and last bits form 11, and the corresponding decimal value is 3, which corresponds to the third row. The middle 4 bits are 1011 and the decimal value is 11, which corresponds to the 11th column. According to the calculation process of the S-box, the result of $E(R_0) \oplus K_1$ is substituted by the S-box and the output is 32-bit 10001011110001000110001011101010.

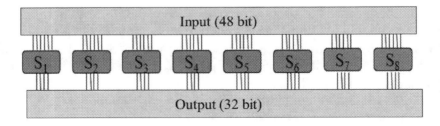

Figure 6.11 The schematic diagram of S-box.

	14	04	13	01	02	15	11	08	03	10	06	12	05	09	00	07
S_1	00	15	07	04	14	02	13	01	10	06	12	11	09	05	03	08
	04	01	14	08	13	06	02	11	15	12	09	07	03	10	05	00
	15	12	08	02	04	09	01	07	05	11	03	14	10	00	06	13
	15	01	08	14	06	11	03	04	09	07	02	13	12	00	05	10
S_2	03	13	04	07	15	02	08	14	12	00	01	10	06	09	11	05
	00	14	07	11	10	04	13	01	05	08	12	06	09	03	02	15
	13	08	10	01	03	15	04	02	11	06	07	12	00	05	14	09
	10	00	09	14	06	03	15	05	01	13	12	07	11	04	02	08
S_3	13	07	00	09	03	04	06	10	02	08	05	14	12	11	15	01
	13	06	04	09	08	15	03	00	11	01	02	12	05	10	14	07
	01	10	13	00	06	09	08	07	04	15	14	03	11	05	02	12
	07	13	14	03	00	06	09	10	01	02	08	05	11	12	04	15
S_4	13	08	11	05	06	15	00	03	04	07	02	12	01	10	14	09
	10	06	09	00	12	11	07	13	15	01	03	14	05	02	08	04
	03	15	00	16	10	01	13	08	09	04	05	11	12	07	02	14
	02	12	04	01	07	10	11	06	08	05	03	15	13	00	14	09
S_5	14	11	02	12	04	07	13	01	05	00	15	10	03	09	08	06
	04	02	01	11	10	13	07	08	15	09	12	05	06	03	00	14
	11	08	12	07	01	14	02	13	06	15	00	09	10	04	05	03
	12	01	10	15	09	02	06	08	00	13	03	04	14	07	05	11
S_6	10	15	04	02	07	12	09	05	06	01	13	14	00	11	03	08
	09	14	15	05	02	08	12	03	07	00	04	10	01	13	11	06
	04	03	02	12	09	05	15	10	11	14	01	07	06	00	08	13
	04	11	02	14	15	00	08	13	03	12	09	07	05	10	06	01
S_7	13	00	11	07	04	09	01	10	14	03	05	12	02	15	08	06
	01	04	11	13	12	03	07	14	10	15	06	08	00	05	09	02
	06	11	13	08	01	04	10	07	09	05	00	15	14	02	03	12
	13	02	08	04	06	15	11	01	10	09	03	14	05	00	12	07
S_8	01	15	13	08	10	03	07	04	12	05	06	11	00	14	09	02
	07	11	04	01	09	12	14	02	00	06	10	13	15	03	05	08
	02	01	14	07	04	10	08	13	15	12	09	00	03	05	06	11

Figure 6.12 Details of the eight S-boxes.

Table 6.4 The P-box Permutation Table

16	07	20	21	29	12	28	17	01	15	23	26	05	18	31	10
02	08	24	14	32	27	03	09	19	13	30	06	22	11	04	25

(3) P-box Permutation.

The output of the S-box substitution is used as the input for the P-box permutation. The P-box permutation table is shown in Table 6.4. The output of the S-box 10001011110001000110001011101010 (32 bits) is permuted by the P-box, and the output of the P-box is 01001000101111110101010110000001 (32 bits). Function f consists of E-box extended permutation, S-box substitution and P-box permutation. The first iteration process $f(R_0, K_1)$ is:

$f(R_0, K_1) = 01001000101111110101010110000001$

Calculate $L_1 = R_0 = 00000000111111110000011010000011$ (32 bits)

The 32-bit R_1 is obtained by performing the XOR operation in Eq. 6.3.

$$R_1 = L_0 \oplus f(R_0, K_1)$$
$$= 11111111101110000111011001010111 \oplus 01001000101111110101010110000001$$
$$= 10110111000001110010001111010110$$

(6.3)

Taking L_1 and R_1 as input, the iterative process f continues to be executed until the outputs L_{16} and R_{16} are computed.

Perform 16 iterations of the IP, that is, perform 16-layer encryption transformation to obtain L_{16} and R_{16}, which are used as input blocks, and perform IP^{-1} to obtain the final ciphertext output block. Inverse permutation is the inverse operation of the initial permutation. It can be seen from the initial permutation rule that the 1st position of the original data is changed to the 40th position, and the 2nd position is changed to the 8th position. Inverse permutation is to change the 40th position to the 1st position and the 8th position to the 2nd position. By analogy, the inverse permutation rule table is shown in Table 6.5. Fig. 6.13 illustrates the inverse permutation process intuitively. The L_{16} and R_{16} are formed into 64-bit data, and the output ciphertext through the inverse permutation table is: 0101100000001000011000000001011110011011101011000011000011101000.

Finally, Alg. 1 presents the implementation of the DES algorithm.

Table 6.5 The Inverse Permutation Table (IP^{-1})

40	08	48	16	56	24	64	32
39	07	47	15	55	23	63	31
38	06	46	14	54	22	62	30
37	05	45	13	53	21	61	29
36	04	44	12	52	20	60	28
35	03	43	11	51	19	59	27
34	02	42	10	50	18	58	26
33	01	41	09	49	17	57	25

6.2.2 Advanced Encryption Standard

The key length of DES is 56 bits, so that the theoretical security strength of the DES algorithm is 2^56. However, in the middle and late 20th century, it was the stage of rapid development of computers. The advancement of component manufacturing technology made the processing power of computers stronger and stronger, and DES gradually failed to provide sufficient security. Although the 3DES encryption method has appeared, its encryption time is more than three times that of the DES algorithm [248], and the 64-bit packet size is relatively small, so that it still cannot meet the security requirements. On January 2, 1997, the NIST announced that it hoped to solicit the AES [249] to replace DES.

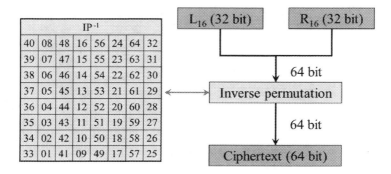

Figure 6.13 Process diagram of inverse permutation IP^{-1}.

Algorithm 1 Data Encryption Standard (DES) Algorithm

1: private static final String ALGO = "DES";
/* DES Encryption Algorithm*/

2: **function** ENCRYPT(byte[] src, String password)

3:    SecureRandom random = new SecureRandom();

4:    DESKeySpec desKey = new DESKeySpec(password.getBytes());

5:    SecretKeyFactory   keyFactory   =   SecretKeyFactory.getInstance(ALGO);

6:    SecretKey securekey = keyFactory.generateSecret(desKey);

7:    Cipher cipher = Cipher.getInstance(ALGO);

8:    cipher.init(Cipher.ENCRYPT_MODE, securekey, random);

9:    **return** cipher.doFinal(src);

10: **end function**
/*DES Decryption Algorithm*/

11: **function** DECRYPT(byte[] src, String password)

12:    SecureRandom random = new SecureRandom();

13:    DESKeySpec desKey = new DESKeySpec(password.getBytes());

14:    SecretKeyFactory   keyFactory   =   SecretKeyFactory.getInstance(ALGO);

15:    SecretKey securekey = keyFactory.generateSecret(desKey);

16:    Cipher cipher = Cipher.getInstance(ALGO);

17:    cipher.init(Cipher.DECRYPT_MODE, securekey, random);

18:    **return** cipher.doFinal(src);

19: **end function**

In the call for cryptographic standards, all AES candidate submissions are required to meet the following criteria:

- A block cipher with a block size of 128 bits.

- Support 128-bit, 192-bit, and 256-bit cipher standards.

- The designed algorithm is more secure than the other algorithms submitted.

- The designed algorithm is efficient in both software and hardware implementations.

AES has received responses from many cryptographic workers around the world, and many people have submitted their own algorithms. There are 5 candidate algorithms entering the final round: Rijndael, Serpent,

Twofish, RC6 and MARS. Finally, after strict steps such as security analysis, software and hardware performance evaluation, Rijndael algorithm wins.

The block size of the plaintext and ciphertext of AES is fixed at 16 bytes, and the key supports 16 bytes, 24 bytes, and 32 bytes. The plaintext of each group is arranged from top to bottom and from left to right according to the sequence of bytes, and the ciphertext is read in the same order as above. It is equivalent to restoring the array to a string, and then decrypting it again according to the 4×4 array. AES mainly has five kinds of operation processing, namely Add Round Key, Substitute Bytes, Shift Rows, Mix Columns and Expand Key.

- **Round Key Addition**. In the encryption process, XOR operation is performed on the input of each round and the round key, that is, the bitwise XOR is performed on part of the current block and extended key. Since the result of continuous XOR of a binary number is unchanged, the input can be recovered by XORing the key of the round during decryption.

- **Substitute Bytes**. The main function of byte substitution is to complete the mapping from one byte to another byte through the S-box. Figs. 6.14 and 6.15 illustrate the byte substitution rules in the S-box and inverse S-box (denoted as S^{-1}) of the AES algorithm, respectively. Furthermore, as shown in Fig. 6.16, we give a concrete example to make the process of byte substitution clearer and more intuitive. For instance, the mapped value of the first byte 19 is $S[1][9] = D4$; the value before a replacement can be obtained by S^{-1}, that is, $S^{-1}[D][4] = 19$.

- **Shift Rows**. The function of row shift is to realize the permutation between the internal bytes of a 4×4 matrix. The operation of row shifting is as follows: The first row remains unchanged, the second row is rotated to the left by one byte; the third row is rotated to the left by two bytes; and the fourth row is rotated to the left by three bytes. Fig. 6.17 shows an example of row shifting.

- **Mix Columns**. Fig. 6.18 illustrates the principle of column mixing operation in AES algorithm. Column mixing is the most complex section of the AES algorithm, which belongs to the diffusion layer. It obfuscates each column of the input matrix, so that each byte of the input affects 4 bytes of the output. According to the multiplication of the matrix, in the process of column mixing (using a

	0	1	2	3	4	5	6	7	8	9	A	B	C	D	E	F
0	63	7C	77	7B	F2	6B	6F	C5	30	01	67	2B	FE	D7	AB	76
1	CA	82	C9	7D	FA	59	47	F0	AD	D4	A2	AF	9C	A4	72	C0
2	B7	FD	93	26	36	3F	F7	CC	34	A5	E5	F1	71	D8	31	15
3	04	C7	23	C3	18	96	05	9A	07	12	80	E2	EB	27	B2	75
4	09	83	2C	1A	1B	6E	5A	A0	52	3B	D6	B3	29	E3	2F	84
5	53	D1	00	ED	20	FC	B1	5B	6A	CB	BE	39	4A	4C	58	CF
6	D0	EF	AA	FB	43	4D	33	85	45	F9	02	7F	50	3C	9F	A8
7	51	A3	40	8F	92	9D	38	F5	BC	B6	DA	21	10	FF	F3	D2
8	CD	0C	13	EC	5F	97	44	17	C4	A7	7E	3D	64	5D	19	73
9	60	81	4F	DC	22	2A	90	88	46	EE	B8	14	DE	5E	0B	DB
A	E0	32	3A	0A	49	06	24	5C	C2	D3	AC	62	91	95	E4	79
B	E7	C8	37	6D	8D	D5	4E	A9	6C	56	F4	EA	65	7A	AE	08
C	BA	78	25	2E	1C	A6	B4	C6	E8	DD	74	1F	4B	BD	8B	8A
D	70	3E	B5	66	48	03	F6	0E	61	35	57	B9	86	C1	1D	9E
E	E1	F8	98	11	69	D9	8E	94	9B	1E	87	E9	CE	55	28	DF
F	8C	A1	89	0D	BF	E6	42	68	41	99	2D	0F	B0	54	BB	16

Figure 6.14 The S-box of the Advanced Encryption Standard (AES) algorithm.

	0	1	2	3	4	5	6	7	8	9	A	B	C	D	E	F
0	52	09	6A	D5	30	36	A5	38	BF	40	A3	9E	81	F3	D7	FB
1	7C	E3	39	82	9B	2F	FF	87	34	8E	43	44	C4	DE	E9	CB
2	54	7B	94	32	A6	C2	23	3D	EE	4C	95	0B	42	FA	C3	4E
3	08	2E	A1	66	28	D9	24	B2	76	5B	A2	49	6D	8B	D1	25
4	72	F8	F6	64	86	68	98	16	D4	A4	5C	CC	5D	65	B6	92
5	6C	70	48	50	FD	ED	B9	DA	5E	15	46	57	A7	8D	9D	84
6	90	D8	AB	00	8C	BC	D3	0A	F7	E4	58	05	B8	B3	45	06
7	D0	2C	1E	8F	CA	3F	0F	02	C1	AF	BD	03	01	13	8A	6B
8	3A	91	11	41	4F	67	DC	EA	97	F2	CF	CE	F0	B4	E6	73
9	96	AC	74	22	E7	AD	35	85	E2	F9	37	E8	1C	75	DF	6E
A	47	F1	1A	71	1D	29	C5	89	6F	B7	62	0E	AA	18	BE	1B
B	FC	56	3E	4B	C6	D2	79	20	9A	DB	C0	FE	78	CD	5A	F4
C	1F	DD	A8	33	88	07	C7	31	B1	12	10	59	27	80	EC	5F
D	60	51	7F	A9	19	B5	4A	0D	2D	E5	7A	9F	93	C9	9C	EF
E	A0	E0	3B	4D	AE	2A	F5	B0	C8	EB	BB	3C	83	53	99	61
F	17	2B	04	7E	BA	77	D6	26	E1	69	14	63	55	21	0C	7D

Figure 6.15 The inverse S-box (S^{-1}) of the Advanced Encryption Standard (AES) algorithm.

Figure 6.16 An example of byte substitution in Advanced Encryption Standard (AES) algorithm.

Figure 6.17 An example of shifting row in Advanced Encryption Standard (AES) algorithm.

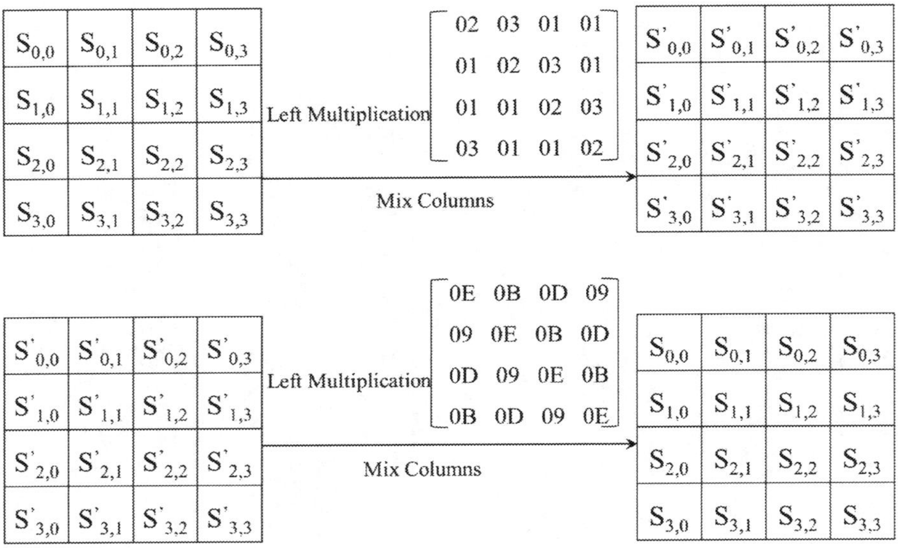

Figure 6.18 The principle of mixing columns in Advanced Encryption Standard (AES) algorithm.

substitution of the arithmetic properties on the field $GF(2^8)$), the value corresponding to each byte is only related to the 4 values of the column. The multiplication and addition here need to pay attention to the following points:

1. The result of multiplying the value corresponding to a byte by 2 is to shift the binary bit of the value one bit to the left. When the highest bit of the result is 1 (indicating that the value is not less than 128), it is need to further perform the XOR operation on the shifted result and 00011011.

2. Multiplication satisfies the distributive law for addition. Eq. 6.4 shows an example of the distributive law.

$$07 \cdot S_{0,0} = (01 \oplus 02 \oplus 04) \cdot S_{0,0} \quad = S_{0,0} \oplus (02 \cdot S_{0,0}) \oplus (04 \cdot S_{0,0}). \tag{6.4}$$

3. Note that matrix multiplication here is different from matrix multiplication in the general sense. Specifically, modulo-2 addition (XOR operation) is adopted when adding each value.

D4	E0	B8	1E
BF	B4	41	27
5D	52	11	98
30	AE	F1	E5

04	E0	48	28
66	CB	F8	06
81	19	D3	26
E5	9A	7A	4C

Figure 6.19 An example of mixing columns in AES algorithm.

The output after performing column mixing is shown in Fig. 6.19.

It can be seen from Eq. 6.5 that the two matrices in Fig. 6.18 are mutually inverse. When decrypting, the original text can be recovered after one reverse column mixing.

$$
\begin{bmatrix} 0E & 0B & 0D & 09 \\ 09 & 0E & 0B & 0D \\ 0D & 09 & 0E & 0B \\ 0B & 0D & 09 & 0E \end{bmatrix}
\begin{bmatrix} 02 & 03 & 01 & 01 \\ 01 & 02 & 03 & 01 \\ 01 & 01 & 02 & 03 \\ 03 & 01 & 01 & 02 \end{bmatrix}
=
\begin{bmatrix} 01 & 00 & 00 & 00 \\ 00 & 01 & 00 & 00 \\ 00 & 00 & 01 & 00 \\ 00 & 00 & 01 & 01 \end{bmatrix}
\tag{6.5}
$$

- **Expand Key**. The complexity of the key is an important part of ensuring the security of the algorithm. When both the block length and the key length are 128 bits (16 bytes), the AES encryption algorithm iterates 10 rounds in total, so that 10 subkeys are required. The purpose of AES key expansion is to expand the input 128-bit key into 11 128-bit subkeys. The key expansion algorithm of AES uses words (one word is 4 bytes) as a basic unit, which is exactly one column of the key matrix. Therefore, the 4-word key needs to be expanded into 11 subkeys, for a total of 44 words.

Fig. 6.20 illustrates the complete encryption process of the AES. The encryption process begins with the round key addition. The reason for using round key addition at the beginning and end of the AES algorithm is that if other stages that do not require a key are placed at the beginning and end, the reverse process can be completed without a key, which

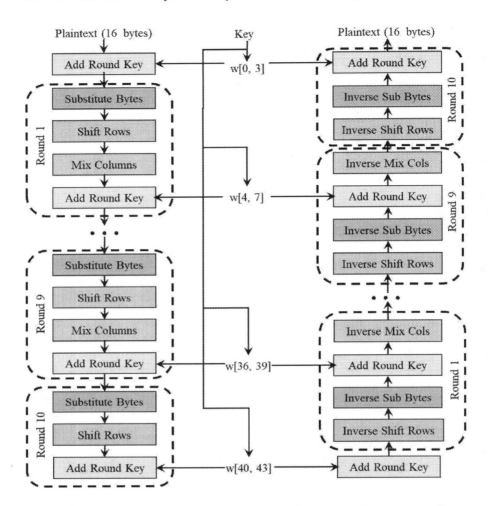

Figure 6.20 The encryption process of the Advanced Encryption Standard.

reduces the security of the algorithm. In terms of processing rounds, we only consider 10 rounds of processing for 128-bit keys. The first 9 rounds of encryption are the same, and the last round of encryption has no column mixing. Finally, Alg. 2 presents the implementation of the AES algorithm.

Algorithm 2 Advanced Encryption Standard (AES) Algorithm

```
1: private static final String ALGO = "AES/ECB/PKCS5Padding";
   /* AES Encryption Algorithm*/
2: function ENCRYPT(String data, Key key)
3:     Cipher cipher = Cipher.getInstance(ALGO);
4:     cipher.init(cipher.ENCRYPT_MODE, key);
5:     return cipher.doFinal(data.getBytes());
6: end function
   /*AES Decryption Algorithm*/
7: function DECRYPT(byte[] result, Key key)
8:     Cipher cipher = Cipher.getInstance(ALGO);
9:     cipher.init(Cipher.DECRYPT_MODE, key);
10:    return cipher.doFinal(result);
11: end function
   /*Generate Key*/
12: function CREATEKEY
13:    KeyGenerator keyGenerator;
14:    keyGenerator = KeyGenerator.getInstance("AES");
15:    keyGenerator.init(128);
16:    SecretKey secretKey = keyGenerator.generateKey();
17:    byte[] keyBytes = secretKey.getEncoded();
18:    return SecretKeySpec(keyBytes, "AES");
19: end function
```

6.3   ASYMMETRIC CIPHER MODEL

Asymmetric cipher model (also known as public-key cipher model) is proposed to solve the two most difficult issues in symmetric cipher model. One is the key distribution problem. In symmetric cipher model, the encryption key and decryption key are the same. Anyone who obtains the encryption key can decrypt the ciphertext to obtain the plaintext. When using symmetric cipher model for secure communication, the key cannot be disclosed, so that it need to be transmitted to the legitimate receiver through a secure channel. When there are n people in the network who want to communicate with each other confidentially, each person needs to save another $(n-1)$ keys, so there will be $n \times (n-1)/2$ keys in the network. In addition, for security reasons, the keys need to be changed frequently. Therefore, when n is relatively large, the generation, distribution and replacement of a large number of keys are very difficult, that is,

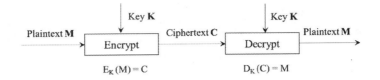

Figure 6.21   Encryption and decryption under Asymmetric Cipher Model.

key management becomes very complicated. The second problem is that symmetric cipher model cannot achieve digital signatures, so it cannot verify the authenticity of information.

The development of public-key cipher model is a revolution in the history of cryptography, and it has an extremely important historical milestone. Most of the cryptosystems (such as DES, AES) before the emergence of public-key cryptosystems are based on basic permutation and substitution operations. Unlike previous approaches, public-key cipher models are usually based on a special mathematical function. Fig. 6.21 illustrates the principle of the asymmetric cipher model as well as the encryption and decryption process. In the asymmetric cipher model, encryption and decryption use two different keys, namely, public key and private key. The public key and the private key are a pair. If the data is encrypted with the public key, it can only be decrypted with the corresponding private key. The public key is publicly known within the system, and the private key is used privately and secretly by each user. The private key is generally used to protect data in asymmetric cipher model, and the public key can be publicly transmitted in the network, which solves the problem of insecure key distribution. Assuming that two users want to encrypt and exchange data, the two parties first exchange public keys. Then, one party uses the other party's public key to encrypt, and the other party can decrypt it with its own private key. Asymmetric algorithms are generally used to encrypt sensitive information such as keys or identity information. Common asymmetric cipher models include DH, RSA, DSA (for digital signatures), ECC (for mobile devices), etc.

6.3.1   Dieffie-Hellman Algorithm

In 1976, Diffie and Hellman first proposed the idea of public-key cipher model in the paper "New Direction in Cryptography" [250], that is, assigning two matching and independent keys (called public key and private key) to both users. The public keys of all users are registered in a key book similar to a telephone directory. When sending encrypted information to user A, first look up user A's public key in the key book, then encrypt the information, and finally send it to user A. User A receives the ciphertext and decrypts it with his private key to obtain the plaintext. The essence of the DH algorithm is to allow two parties to exchange keys in insecure public channels [251], so as to facilitate information encryption. Note that the DH algorithm is not an encryption method, and secret keys need to be used in conjunction with other encryption algorithms.

The effectiveness of the Diffie-Hellman key exchange algorithm depends on the difficulty of computing discrete logarithms. Briefly, discrete logarithms can be defined as follows: First define a primitive root of a prime number p, yielding all integer roots from 1 to p-1 for each power of it. That is, if a is a primitive root of a prime p, then the numbers $(a \bmod p, a^2 \bmod p, \cdots, a^{p-1} \bmod p)$ are distinct integers that form all integers from 1 to p-1 in a certain arrangement. For an integer b and a primitive root a of the prime p, a unique exponent i can be found such that Eq. 6.6 holds.

$$b = a^i \bmod p, 0 \le i \le p - 1. \tag{6.6}$$

The exponent i is called the discrete logarithm or exponent of b modulo p in base a, denoted as $ind a, p(b)$.

Based on the above background knowledge, the DH key exchange algorithm can be defined as follows.

1. There are two globally exposed parameters, a prime number q and an integer a, where a is a primitive root of q.

2. Suppose users A and B wish to exchange a key, user A chooses a random number $X_A < q$ as the private key, and calculates the public key $Y_A = a^{X_A} \bmod q$. User A keeps the value of X_A secretly and makes Y_A publicly available to User B. Similarly, user B chooses a private random number $X_B < q$, and calculates the public key $Y_B = a^{X_B} \bmod q$. User B keeps the value of X_B secretly and makes Y_B publicly available to User A.

3. The calculation method for user A to generate the shared secret key is $K = (Y_B)^{X_A} \bmod q$. Likewise, the computation method for

user B to generate the shared secret key is $K = (Y_A)^{X_B} mod q$. As can be seen from Eq. 6.7, the above two calculations yield the same result.

$$
\begin{aligned}
K &= (Y_B)^{X_A} mod q \\
&= (\alpha^{X_B} mod q)^{X_A} mod q \\
&= (\alpha^{X_B})^{X_A} mod q \\
&= \alpha^{X_B X_A} mod q \\
&= (\alpha^{X_A})^{X_B} mod q \\
&= (\alpha^{X_A} mod q)^{X_B} mod q \\
&= (Y_A)^{X_B} mod q
\end{aligned}
\tag{6.7}
$$

Since $(Y_B)^{X_A} mod q = K = (Y_A)^{X_B} mod q$, it is equivalent that both parties have exchanged the same key.

4. X_A and X_B are kept secret, and parameters available to the adversary are q, a, Y_A, and Y_B. Thus the adversary is forced to take discrete logarithms to determine the key. For example, to obtain the key of user B, the adversary needs to first calculate Eq. 6.8, and then calculate K in the same way as user B does.

$$
X_B = ind a, q(Y_B). \tag{6.8}
$$

The Diffie-Hellman key exchange algorithm's security depends on the fact that computing discrete logarithms is exceedingly difficult whereas finding exponents modulo a prime number is comparatively simple. It is practically hard to compute the discrete logarithm for large prime values.

6.3.2 Rivest-Shamir-Adleman

In 1978, Ron Rivest, Adi Shamirh and Len Adleman of the Massachusetts Institute of Technology proposed the first public-key cryptography algorithm, named RSA according to their names. The RSA algorithm is regarded as one of the milestones in the history of cryptography. Before formally introducing the RSA algorithm, it is necessary to know two definitions and three theorems in elementary number theory as the basis for comprehending RSA.

Definition 6.2 *Euler's Totient Function. Assuming $n \in Z$ and $n > 1$, the number of positive integers less than n and co-prime to n is called the Euler's totient function of n, denoted by $\varphi(n)$.*

Algorithm 3 RSA Algorithm (Par I)

1: private final static String ALGORITHM_RSA = "RSA";
/* Generate objects of public keys and private keys */
2: **function** GETRSAKEYOBJECT(int modulus)
3:     List<Key> keyList = new ArrayList<>(2);
4:     KeyPairGenerator keyPairGen = KeyPairGenerator.getInstance(ALGORITHM_RSA);
5:     keyPairGen.initialize(modulus);
6:     KeyPair keyPair = keyPairGen.generateKeyPair();
7:     keyList.add(keyPair.getPublic());
8:     keyList.add(keyPair.getPrivate());
9:     **return** return keyList;
10: **end function**
/*Generate the string of public and private keys*/
11: **function** GETRSAKEYSTRING(int modulus)
12:     List<String> keyList = new ArrayList<>(2);
13:     KeyPairGenerator keyPairGen = KeyPairGenerator.getInstance(ALGORITHM_RSA);
14:     keyPairGen.initialize(modulus);
15:     KeyPair keyPair = keyPairGen.generateKeyPair();
16:     String publicKey = Base64.getEncoder()
17: .encodeToString(keyPair.getPublic().getEncoded());
18:     String privateKey = Base64.getEncoder()
19: .encodeToString(keyPair.getPrivate().getEncoded());
20:     keyList.add(publicKey);
21:     keyList.add(privateKey);
22:     **return** keyList;
23: **end function**

Definition 6.3 *Multiplicative Inverse Modulo*. Let $a, n \in Z$ and $n > 1$, if there exists $b \in Z$ such that $ab \equiv 1 \bmod n$, then a and b are called the multiplicative inverses of each other modulo n, denoted as $b \equiv a^{-1} \bmod n$.

Theorem 6.1 Let $m_1, m_2 \in N$, $\gcd(m_1, m_2) = 1$, then $\varphi(m_1 m_2) = \varphi(m_1)\varphi(m_2)$. Note that the gcd function returns the greatest common divisor of two or more integers. The greatest common divisor is the largest integer that can divide each parameter, separately.

Theorem 6.2 If p is a prime number, then $\varphi(p) = p - 1$.

Algorithm 3 RSA Algorithm (Par II)

/*Use X509EncodedKeySpec in Java to generate the RSA public key*/

24: **function** GETPUBLICKEY(String publicKey)

25: KeyFactory keyFactory = KeyFactory.getInstance(ALGORITHM_RSA);

26: byte[] keyBytes = Base64.getDecoder().decode(publicKey);

27: X509EncodedKeySpec spec = new X509EncodedKeySpec(keyBytes);

28: **return** (RSAPublicKey) keyFactory.generatePublic(spec);

29: **end function**

/*Use PKCS8EncodedKeySpec in Java to generate an RSA private key*/

30: **function** GETPRIVATEKEY(String privateKey)

31: KeyFactory keyFactory = KeyFactory.getInstance(ALGORITHM_RSA);

32: byte[] keyBytes = Base64.getDecoder().decode(privateKey);

33: PKCS8EncodedKeySpec spec = new PKCS8EncodedKeySpec(keyBytes);

34: **return** (RSAPrivateKey) keyFactory.generatePrivate(spec);

35: **end function**

Theorem 6.3 *Euler Theorem*. *Let m be a positive integer and $gcd(a, m) = 1$, then $a^{\varphi(m)} \equiv 1 \, mod \, m$.*

Fig. 6.22 illustrates the principle and processing of the RSA algorithm. The specific description of the RSA algorithm is as follows.

1. **Key Generation.**

   - Randomly select two large prime numbers p and q, and then calculate Eq. 6.9 and Eq.6.10 .

$$n = pq. \tag{6.9}$$

$$\varphi(n) = (p - 1)(q - 1). \tag{6.10}$$

   - Choose a random number e $(1 < e < \varphi(n))$ that satisfies $gcd(e, \varphi(n)) = 1$, and calculate Eq. 6.12.

$$d = e^{-1} mod \varphi(n). \tag{6.11}$$

   - The public key is n, e and the private key is n, d.

Algorithm 3 RSA Algorithm (Par III)

/*Public key encryption*/

36: **function** ENCRYPTBYPUBLICKEY(String data, RSAPublicKey publicKey)

37:     Cipher cipher = Cipher.getInstance(ALGORITHM_RSA);

38:     cipher.init(Cipher.ENCRYPT_MODE, publicKey);

39:     int modulusSize = publicKey.getModulus().bitLength() / 8;

40:     int maxSingleSize = modulusSize - 11;

41:     byte[][] dataArray = splitArray(data.getBytes(), maxSingleSize);

42:     ByteArrayOutputStream out = new ByteArrayOutputStream();

43:     **for** byte[] s : dataArray **do**

44:         out.write(cipher.doFinal(s));

45:     **end for**

46:     **return** Base64.getEncoder().encodeToString(out.toByteArray());

47: **end function**

/*Private key decryption*/

48: **function** DECRYPTBYPRIVATEKEY(String data, RSAPrivateKey privateKey)

49:     Cipher cipher = Cipher.getInstance(ALGORITHM_RSA);

50:     cipher.init(Cipher.DECRYPT_MODE, privateKey);

51:     int modulusSize = privateKey.getModulus().bitLength() / 8;

52:     byte[] dataBytes = data.getBytes();

53:     byte[] decodeData = Base64.getDecoder().decode(dataBytes);

54:     byte[][] splitArrays = splitArray(decodeData, modulusSize);

55:     ByteArrayOutputStream out = new ByteArrayOutputStream();

56:     **for** byte[] arr : splitArrays **do**

57:         out.write(cipher.doFinal(arr));

58:     **end for**

59:     **return** new String(out.toByteArray());

60: **end function**

2. **Encryption Process.** For plaintext m (m|n), the corresponding ciphertext calculation process is shown in Eq. 6.12.

$$c = m^e mod\, n. \tag{6.12}$$

3. **Decryption Process.** For the ciphertext c, the corresponding plaintext calculation process is shown in Eq.6.13.

$$m = c^d mod\, n. \tag{6.13}$$

Algorithm 3 RSA Algorithm (Par IV)

/*Divide the array by the specified length*/
61: **function** SPLITARRAY(byte[] data,int len)
62: int dataLen = data.length;
63: **if** dataLen ≤ len **then**
64:   return new byte[][]data;
65: **end if**
66: byte[][] result = new byte[(dataLen-1)/len + 1][];
67: int resultLen = result.length;
68: **for** int i = 0; i < resultLen; i++ **do**
69:   **if** i == resultLen - 1 **then**
70:    int slen = dataLen - len * i;
71:    byte[] single = new byte[slen];
72:    System.arraycopy(data, len * i, single, 0, slen);
73:    result[i] = single;
74:    break;
75:   **end if**
76:   byte[] single = new byte[len];
77:   System.arraycopy(data, len * i, single, 0, len);
78:   result[i] = single;
79: **end for**
80: **return** result;
81: **end function**

In order to explain the RSA algorithm more clearly, a specific example of the calculation process is given below. Suppose there are two prime numbers $p = 11$ and $q = 13$. According to Eq. 6.9, calculate $n = pq = 11 \times 13 = 143$. According to Eq. 6.10, calculate $\varphi(143) = (11 - 1)(13 - 1) = 120$. Randomly find a number $e = 7$ that is coprime with $f(n)$. According to Eq. 6.12, calculate $d = 7^{-1}mod\varphi(143) = 103$. From the above calculation process, the public key is $143, 7$, and the private key is $143, 103$.

The mathematical basis of RSA is Euler theorem (shown in Theorem 6.3), and the security of which is built on the difficulty of factoring large integers. Specifically, it is easy to find the product of two large prime numbers, but it is difficult to decompose the product of two large prime numbers and find its prime factors. This is an NP-complete problem, and there is no effective algorithm so far. The RSA algorithm is a type of block cipher. Plaintext and ciphertext are integers between 0 and n-1,

Algorithm 3 RSA Algorithm (Par V)

```
     /*Test the RSA algorithm*/
82:  function MAIN(String[] args)
83:      List<Key> keyList = RSAUtils.getRSAKeyObject(1024);
84:      RSAPublicKey puk = (RSAPublicKey) keyList.get(0);
85:      RSAPrivateKey prk = (RSAPrivateKey) keyList.get(1);
86:      String message = "messageplaintext";
87:      String encryptedMsg = RSAUtils.encryptByPublicKey(message,
     puk);
88:      String decryptedMsg = RSAUtils.decryptByPrivateKey(encryptedMsg,
     prk);
89:      System.out.println("object key ! message == decryptedMsg ? "
     + message.equals(decryptedMsg));
90:      List<String> keyStringList = RSAUtils.getRSAKeyString(1024);
91:      String pukString = keyStringList.get(0);
92:      String prkString = keyStringList.get(1);
93:      System.out.println("public key:" + pukString);
94:      System.out.println("private key:" + prkString);
95:      puk = RSAUtils.getPublicKey(pukString);
96:      prk = RSAUtils.getPrivateKey(prkString);
97:      encryptedMsg = RSAUtils.encryptByPublicKey(message, puk);
98:      decryptedMsg = RSAUtils.decryptByPrivateKey(encryptedMsg,
     prk);
99:      System.out.println"string key ! message == decryptedMsg ? " +
     message.equals(decryptedMsg));
100:     return new String(out.toByteArray());
101: end function
```

usually the size of n is 1024 bits in binary or 309 bits in decimal. As far as the computing power of the current computer is concerned, it is safe to take 1024 bits of n, and it is absolutely safe to take 2048 bits.

The advantages of RSA are summarized as follows:

- The RSA algorithm is an international standard algorithm and is one of the relatively popular mainstream algorithms. If the reader needs to learn the specific theory of asymmetric cipher models, the RSA algorithm is strongly recommended.

- The RSA algorithm is widely compatible and can be applied to various systems. Compared with certain novel algorithms today,

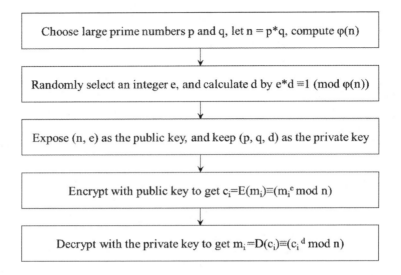

Figure 6.22 The principle and process of RSA algorithm.

the compatibility of the RSA algorithm makes it more convenient in the process of actual use, so that there will be no various restrictions.

- The RSA algorithm composition is relatively simple, not as complicated as other novel algorithms.

Disadvantges of RSA are also summarized as follows:

- The RSA algorithm is slow (100 times slower than the DES algorithm) and is generally used for small amounts of data encryption.

- It is troublesome to generate secret keys. Due to the limitation of prime number generation technology, it is difficult to achieve one-time pad.

- If the block size is k, the number n needs to satisfy: $2^k < n < 2^{k+1}$. In order to ensure security, it is necessary to make n as large as possible, and the block length k also increases, which is not only expensive for computation, but also unfavorable for the standardization of data format.

Finally, Alg. 3 presents the implementation of the RSA algorithm.

6.4 ACCESS CONTROL TECHNIQUES

6.4.1 Concepts and Elements of Access Control

The method by which the system limits a user's access to data resources based on their identity and the specified policy groups to which they belong is known as access control [252]. System administrators typically use it to limit user access to network resources like servers, directories, and files. The fundamental tactic for preventing network security and protecting resources is considered to be the subject's access to the object itself or its resources with varying authorization in accordance with some control policies or permissions. Access control technology is typically created to block unauthorized access to resources so that computers can only be used within certain parameters.

In order to achieve the above goals, the access control policy needs to complete two tasks. The first is to identify and authenticate users accessing the system. The second is to decide what type and level of access the user can have to a system resource.

Access control [253] includes three elements: subject, object and control strategy.

1. Subject refers to a specific request to access resources. It is the initiator of an operation action, but not necessarily the executor of the action. It may be a user, or a process, service, or device initiated by the user.

2. The object refers to the entity of the accessed resource. All information, resources, and objects that can be manipulated can be called objects. The object can be a collection of information, files, records, etc., or it can be a hardware facility on the network, a terminal in infinite communication, or even another object.

3. The control strategy refers to the set of relevant access rules for the subject to the object, that is, the set of attributes. The access policy embodies an authorization behavior, and it is also the default behavior of the object for some operations of the subject.

Main functions of access control include: ensuring that legitimate users can access protected network resources, preventing illegal subjects from entering protected network resources, or preventing legitimate users from unauthorized access to protected network resources.

First, access control needs to verify the legitimacy of user identities, and use control policies for selection and management at the same time.

After user identity and access rights are verified, unauthorized operations also need to be monitored. Therefore, the content of access control includes authentication, control policy [254] implementation and security audit.

1. **Authentication.** The identification of the subject to the object and the inspection and confirmation of the object to the subject.

2. **Control Policy.** The set of control rules is reasonably set to ensure the legitimate use of information resources by users within the scope of authorization. It is not only necessary to ensure the reasonable use of authorized users, but also to prevent illegal users from infringing into the system and leaking important information resources. In addition, legitimate users cannot perform functions and access scope beyond their authority.

3. **Security Audit.** The system can automatically check and verify the relevant activities or behaviors in the computer network environment systematically and independently according to the user's access rights, as well as make corresponding evaluations and audits.

6.4.2   Common Types of Access Control

6.4.2.1   Discretionary access control

The owner of the object in the *Discretionary Access Control* (DAC) mechanism [255] can arbitrarily modify or grant the corresponding authority to the object. Common operating systems generally adopt this mechanism, which we may be familiar with. For example, in the Windows operating system, a user can freely set the read/write of his user/-group/other owner for all his files or directories. /execute permission. The most obvious feature of discretionary access control is that the owner of the object can grant permissions to any other user, so that other users are also called the owner of the object, and can continue to authorize other users. The advantage of the DAC mechanism is flexibility, and the disadvantage is insecurity. Since permissions can spread uncontrollably, they are easily targeted by attackers (e.g., exploited by Trojans).

6.4.2.2   Mandatory access control

In the *Mandatory Access Control* (MAC) mechanism [256], the owner of the object is not allowed to modify or grant the corresponding rights to the object at will, but to grant the rights to each object separately by means of coercion. Granting permissions is mainly based on the security level of the subject and object, as well as specific policies. Taking the BLP model in mandatory access control as an example, it assigns a security level to each subject and object, and the levels in order from bottom to top include: Unclassified (U), Confidential (C), Secret (S), and Top Secret (TS). At the same time, it follows the access control mode of "read down/write up", that is, for read operations, the subject can only read objects with a lower level than it; for write operations, the subject can only read objects with the same level or higher than it. For example, secret level subjects are prohibited from reading the contents of top secret objects, and are allowed to read secret, confidential and unclassified objects. Secret level subjects are prohibited from writing into confidential and unclassified objects and are allowed to write into secret and top secret objects. SELinux is a typical example of a mandatory access control mechanism. Information will only flow in one direction along $(U) \rightarrow (C) \rightarrow (S) \rightarrow (TS)$, thus ensuring that the system remains in a safe state.

The advantage of mandatory access control is to implement strict centralized permissions management according to the pre-defined security level. Therefore, it is suitable for application environments with high-security requirements and is a very important access control model in the security system of national defense and government agencies. In addition, mandatory access control prevents information from spreading through the one-way flow of information and can effectively defend against attacks on system confidentiality by applications with Trojan horses. The disadvantage of mandatory access control is that the security level is too mandatory, and the change of permissions is very inconvenient. In many cases, the division of the security level of the subject or object cannot be consistent with the actual requirements, resulting in inconvenient system management. Therefore, the mandatory access control model has a narrow application field and is not flexible to use. Generally speaking, it is only suitable for industries or fields with strict confidentiality requirements, such as government agencies and military fields.

6.4.2.3 Role-based access control

The *Role-Based Access Control* (RBAC) model [257, 258] is crucial for object-oriented programming. The RBAC approach establishes a set of roles between the user set and the permission set, and each role corresponds to a certain set of permissions, rather than directly granting specific users the various permissions for system operations. A user will have all the operation permissions associated with a role after it has been assigned to them.

The advantage of the RBAC model is that, as long as the user's appropriate role is assigned, it is not essential to assign rights each time a user is created. Role permission changes are far less frequent than those for users, making it easier to manage user permissions and lowering system overhead. The mechanism of permission inheritance and mutual restraint between roles have gradually been introduced to the RBAC model, making it increasingly appropriate for the actual control requirements of complex business systems and achieving the union of security and flexibility.

The control granularity can be greatly increased by establishing three tiers of users, roles, and permissions. Reducing the complexity of the control job allows for more flexible setting of various control techniques in accordance with the situation at hand.

6.5 ATTACK METHODS IN CRYPTANALYSIS

The main goal of cryptography is to protect the confidentiality of plaintext (or the key) and keep it hidden from listeners, also known as adversaries, attackers, interceptors, intruders, opponents, etc. The study of regaining plaintext without the key is called cryptanalysis. The key or the message's plaintext can be obtained by a successful cryptanalysis.

As well as recovering the key or plaintext, cryptanalysis can used to verify the weaknesses in the cryptosystem. Be aware that the loss of a key by non-cryptanalysis methods is referred to as a compromise and the effort to perform cryptanalysis is referred to as an attack. We should be aware that secrecy and protection cannot be attained when it comes to security management by striving to conceal.

Even if something is kept secret, there will always be insiders who will contact it. Once the secrets are leaked, the loss will be heavy and cannot be discovered in time. Only through reasonable authority and password design, can the issue of effective confidentiality be achieved. Auguste Kerckhoff provides a fundamental assumption about the problem of cryptanalysis, known as the Kerckhoff Principle. **Kerckhoffs's principle:** A cryptosystem should be secure even if everything about the system, except the key, is public knowledge. The Kerckhoffs criterion believes that the algorithm of a secure cryptosystem should be able to withstand public inspection, and its security should be based on the fact that the key is kept secret from the adversary. In other words, the cryptanalyst knows the cryptographic system used by both parties, including the statistical characteristics of plaintext, encryption and decryption systems, and the only thing he does not know is the key. Five commonly used cryptanalytic attacks are listed below, assuming that the cryptanalyst in each type of attack has full knowledge of the encryption algorithm.

6.5.1 Ciphertext-Only Attack

Ciphertext Only Attack (COA) refers to the cryptanalysis method that infers the plaintext or key when only the ciphertext is known [259]. Fig. 6.23 shows the schematic diagram of the COA model. It is assumed that the cryptanalyst possesses the cryptographic algorithm as well as plaintext statistics, and intercepts one or more ciphertexts encrypted with the same key. The COA attack is to obtain the plaintext or key by analyzing these ciphertexts. The cryptanalyst has no information to exploit other than the intercepted ciphertext. The task of the cryptanalyst is to recover as much plaintext as possible, or try to deduce the decryption key, so that the encrypted information can be easily deciphered. The COA can use the exhaustive search method, that is, try all the keys in turn for a certain amount of ciphertexts until a meaningful plaintext is obtained. On the whole, the COA mode has the least known conditions. In this case (just wiretapping), password cracking is the most difficult, and a cryptosystem that cannot withstand this attack is considered completely insecure.

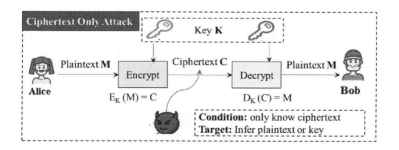

Figure 6.23 The model for Ciphertext Only Attack (COA).

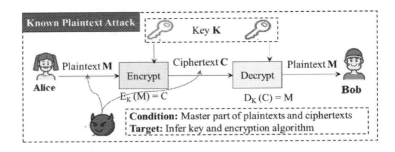

Figure 6.24 The model for Known Plaintext Attack (KPA).

6.5.2 Known Plaintext Attack

Known Plaintext Attack (KPA) [260] means that the cryptanalyst not only has a considerable amount of ciphertext, but also knows certain plain-ciphertext pairs. Fig. 6.24 shows the schematic diagram of the Known Plaintext Attack (KPA) model. The task of the cryptanalyst is to use the ciphertext information to derive a decryption key or an alternative algorithm that can recover the corresponding plaintext from the obtained ciphertext. The basic requirement for modern cryptosystems is to withstand not only ciphertext only attacks, but also known plaintext attacks.

6.5.3 Chosen Plaintext Attack

Fig. 6.25 shows the schematic diagram of the Chosen Plaintext Attack (CPA) model. In the *CPA* [261], a cryptanalyst can not only obtain a certain number of plain-ciphertext pairs, but also obtain the

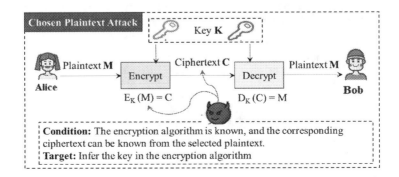

Figure 6.25 The model for Chosen Plaintext Attack (CPA).

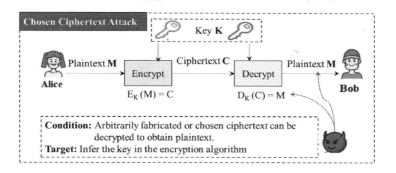

Figure 6.26 The model for Chosen Ciphertext Attack (CCA).

corresponding ciphertext by choosing any plaintext using the same unknown key. In this attack situation, the cryptanalyst often takes temporary control of the encryption machine by some means.

6.5.4 Chosen Ciphertext Attack

Fig. 6.26 shows the schematic diagram of the *Chosen Ciphertext Attack* (CCA) model [262]. The chosen ciphertext attack model means that the attacker can choose the ciphertext for decryption. On the basis of the known plaintext attack, the attacker can arbitrarily create or select some ciphertext and obtain the decrypted plaintext. Chosen ciphertext attack is a stronger attack than the known plaintext attack.

6.5.5 Chosen Text Attack

The *Chosen Text Attack* (CTA) [263] is a combination of chosen plaintext attack and chosen ciphertext attack. Under the premise of mastering the cryptographic algorithm, the cryptanalyst can not only select the plaintext and obtain the corresponding ciphertext, but also select the ciphertext to obtain the corresponding plaintext. This is often the case where the cryptanalyst temporarily controls the encryption and decryption machines by some means. Fig. 6.26 shows the schematic diagram of the CCA model.

From the attacker's perspective, the order of attack difficulty corresponding to the four attack modes is: CTA > CCA > CPA > KPA > COA. From the perspective of cryptographic system security, the security ranking of systems that can resist five attacks is: CTA > CCA >

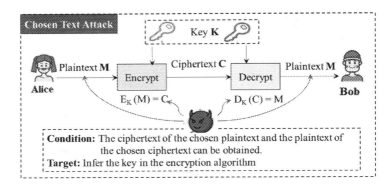

Figure 6.27 The model for Chosen Text Attack (CTA).

CPA > KPA > COA. In other words, a system that is immune to CTA is also immune to the other four attacks.

6.6 SECURITY OF CRYPTOSYSTEM

The security of cryptosystem is divided into unconditional security (also called theoretical security) [264] and conditional security (also called practical security) [265].

6.6.1 Unconditional Security

Assuming that the cryptanalyst has unlimited computing resources and ciphertext, it is still unable to recover the plaintext. According to the information theory, the uncertainty of plaintext before and after the attacker observes the ciphertext is equal, that is, the attacker will not get any information that is conducive to cracking the cryptographic system by observing the ciphertext. In theory, this kind of cryptosystem is not decipherable, or it is said that the cryptosystem has perfect security or unconditional security. Cryptographic algorithms for practical applications are theoretically breakable, simply by trying every possible key one by one and checking whether the resulting plaintext makes sense. The above method is called a brute-force attack. Shannon (known as the father of information theory) has proved that one-time pad is unbreakable. In this case, the key stream is a completely random bit string with the same length as the plaintext, which is unbreakable even given infinite resources. Although the one-time pad has absolute security in theory, considering the cost of key transmission, this method is obviously not practical. At present, there are also opinions that the use of quantum secure communication [266] to transmit the key can realize an absolutely secure one-time pad cryptosystem. This topic is temporarily out of the scope of this book.

6.6.2 Conditional security

Conditional security refers to evaluating the security of a cryptographic system according to the amount of computation required to crack it, including computational security, actual security and provable security.

6.6.2.1 Computational Security

A cryptosystem is said to be computationally secure if it is feasible to crack a cryptosystem, but it is impossible to complete the required amount of computation using known algorithms and existing computing tools. That is to say, the effort required to crack the cryptosystem by the existing best method exceeds the cracking ability of the cracker's time, space or funds.

In theory, only a one-time pad system can truly achieve unconditional security, and other systems can at least be deciphered using the brute-force attack method. In fact, although the brute-force attack method is theoretically feasible, when the key space is large enough, it will be limited by computing conditions and resources. If it cannot be success-fully deciphered within the desired time or under practically possible conditions, the cryptosystem is called computationally unbreakable.

6.6.2.2 Actual security

For cryptosystems in practical applications, since there is at least one deciphering method (ie, brute-force attack method), they cannot sat-isfy unconditional security and only provide computational security. To achieve practical security, a cryptographic system needs to meet the fol-lowing criteria:

1. The actual computational effort (including computation time or expense) to break the cryptosystem is so enormous that it is prac-tically impossible.

2. The time to break the cryptosystem exceeds the valid lifetime of the encrypted information. For example, the order to launch a combat attack in a war only needs to be kept secret until the

battle begins. Important news stories are often kept secret before being reported publicly for only a few hours.

3. The cost of breaking the cryptosystem exceeds the value of the encrypted information itself.

A cryptosystem can be considered practically secure if it can satisfy one of the above criteria, which is unbreakable in current practice. Most of the symmetric and asymmetric cryptographic schemes in practice today belong to this category.

6.6.2.3 Provable security

Provable security is to attribute the security of a cryptosystem to solving a mathematical problem that has been deeply studied but not yet solved. However, the problem of this judgment method only shows that the security of the cryptosystem is related to a certain mathematical problem, and does not fully prove the security of the problem itself. It can be seen that if a cryptosystem is practical, the following basic principles need to be followed:

1. The security of the cryptosystem depends on the security of the key, and the cryptographic algorithm is public.

2. Cryptographic algorithms have no security weaknesses, that is, cryptanalysts cannot find a better attack method than an exhaustive search attack.

3. The key space should be large enough that an attack that attempts to exhaustively search the key space is computationally infeasible.

4. Cryptosystems are both easy to implement and easy to use, mainly referring to the efficient implementation of both encryption and decryption algorithms.

6.7 SUMMARY

In this chapter, we start with the cybersecurity and provide a systematic introduction to basic knowledge about modern cryptosystems. In Section 6.1, the concept and importance of cybersecurity are first introduced, and then the development and classification of cryptosystems are presented in detail. According to the development process, cryptosystems are divided into classical cryptosystems and modern cryptosystems, and the latter is further divided into symmetric cipher models and asymmetric cipher models according to the number of keys. The concept and characteristics of symmetric cipher model are introduced in Section 6.2, and principles and implementations of two typical symmetric encryption algorithms, DES and AES, are systematically given. In addition, in Section 6.3, we focus on the DH and RSA algorithms in asymmetric cipher models. Furthermore, another important technical field in information security, access control technique, is illustrated in Section 6.4. Finally, we outline five commonly used attack methods in modern cryptography and introduce the security of cryptosystems in Sections 6.5 and 6.6, respectively. After reading the content of this chapter, we have provided some exercises in Section 6.8 to facilitate readers to consolidate and self-check.

6.8 EXERCISES

After completing this chapter, please answer the following questions. Suggested answers are also listed below.

1. Modern cryptosystems can be divided into symmetric cipher models and asymmetric cipher models. Please explain the characteristics of each type of cipher model and list the common encryption algorithms.

    SOLUTION. The comparison iS illustrated in Table 6.6.

2. Given plaintext $m = computer$, key $k = program$, the corresponding ASCII representation is as follows:
   $m = 01100011$ 01101111 01101101 01110000
   01110101 01110100 01100101 01110010
   $k = 01110000$ 01110010 01101111 01100111
   01110010 01100001 01101101
   K is 56 bits, excluding 8-bit parity bits. Please calculate the ASCII representation of the ciphertext encrypted by DES.
   SOLUTION. L_0 and R_0 are obtained after initial permutation (IP) of m:
   $L_0 = 11111111101110000111011001010111$
   $R_0 = 00000000111111110000011010000011$
   The key k is permuted to obtain C_0 and D_0:
   $C_0 = 1110110010011001000110111011$
   $D_0 = 1011010001011000100011100110$

TABLE 6.6   Comparison of Symmetric and Asymmetric Encryption

Cipher Model	Advantages	Disadvantages	Usage Case	Representative Algorithms
Symmetric cipher model	Simple and efficient, low system overhead, suitable for encrypting a large amount of data	Difficulty in key management and poor scalability	Encrypt large amounts of data	DES, 3DES, AES, SM1, SM4, etc.
Asymmetric cipher model	It is not possible to derive one key from another; information encrypted with the public key can only be decrypted with the private key.	The complexity of the algorithm leads to a long time to encrypt a large amount of data, and the long ciphertext is not conducive to network transmission.	Encrypt sensitive information such as keys or identity information.	DH, RSA, DSA, ECC, etc.

Rotate the above result by one bit to the left, and then perform compressed permutation to obtain a 48-bit subkey K_1:

$K_1 = 001111011000111111001101001101000011111101001000$

The 48-bit sequence $E(R_0)$ obtained by R_0 through expanded permutation:

$E(R_0) = 100000000001011111111110100000001101010000000110$

Perform XOR operation with $E(R_0)$ and K_1, the result obtained is:

$E(R_0) \oplus K_1 = 101111011001100000110011101101111110101101111110$

Divide the obtained results into 8 groups:

101111   011001   100000   110011   101101   111110   101101   001110

After processing through 8 S-boxes, the 32-bit sequence obtained is:

01110110001101000010011010100001

Perform P-box permutation on the output sequence of the S-box to obtain:

01000100001000001001111010011111

After the above operations, the result of the first round of encryption is:

000000001111111100000110100000111011101110011000111010001100100

The above encryption process is carried out for 16 rounds, and the final ciphertext is obtained as:

0101100010101000010000011011100001101001111111101010111000110011.

3. In the RSA algorithm, it is assumed that the prime numbers p=47, q=71, and e=79 are selected. Please calculate the public key and private key, respectively.

SOLUTION. First, calculate n = pq = 47 × 71 = 3337,

$\varphi(n) = (p\text{-}1)(q\text{-}1) = 46 \times 70 = 3220$.

Second, select e = 79 to make gcd(e, 3220) = 1.

Third, we solve for d according to the equation ed ≡ 1 (mod $\varphi(n)$), that is, 79d ≡ 1 mod 3220. According to the Euclidean algorithm, we know that:

3220 = 40 × 70 + **60**

79 = 1 × 60 + **19**

60 = 3 × 19 + **3**

19 = 6 × 3 + 1

Then we can get:

1 = 19 - 6 × **3**

= 19 - 6 × (60 - 3 × 19) = 19 × **19** - 6 × 60

= 19 × (79 - 1 × 60) - 6 × 60 = 19 × 79 - 25 × **60**

= 19 × 79 - 25 × (3220 - 40 × 79)

= 1019 × 79 - 25 × 3220.

Perform the remainder operation on the modulo 3220 on both sides at the same time to obtain

1019 × 79 ≡ 1 mod 3220

From the above formula, we can get d = 1019. Finally, the public key is P_k = e, n = 79, 3337 and the private key is S_k = d, p, q = 1019, 47, 71.

4. Under the conditions of the first question, assuming that the message is m=6882326879666683, and the packet size is 3, please give the encryption process, the obtained ciphertext, and the decryption process.

   SOLUTION. Since the block size is 3, we can get $m_1 = 688$, $m_2 = 232$, $m_3 = 687$, $m_4 = 966$, $m_5 = 668$, $m_6 = 003$.

   The encryption process is as follows:

   Since $c_i = E(m_i) \equiv m_i^e mod N$, so the ciphertext of m_1 can be calculated as:

   $c_1 \equiv 688^{79} mod 3337 \equiv 1570 mod 3337 = 1570$.

   Similar calculations are performed sequentially from m_2 to m_6, and the final ciphertext can be obtained as:

   $c = \underline{1570275620912276158}$. The decryption process is as follows:

   Since $m_i = D(c_i) \equiv c_i^d mod N$, so the plaintext of c_1 can be calculated as:

   $m_1 \equiv 1570^{1019} mod 3337 \equiv 688 mod 3337 = 688$.

   Similar calculations are performed sequentially from c_2 to c_6, and the final plaintext can be obtained as:

   $m = \underline{6882326879666683}$.

5. What are the attack methods of cryptanalysis in modern cryptography? What are the characteristics and difficulty of these attacks?

   SOLUTION.

   Different horizontal attacks in modern cryptography include: *Ciphertext Only Attack* (COA), *Known Plaintext Attack* (KPA), *Chosen Plaintext Attack* (CPA), *Chosen Ciphertext Attack* (CCA), and *Chosen Text Attack* (CTA). The five different levels of attack are explained next.

   - **COA**. COA refers to the cryptanalysis method that infers the plaintext or key when only the ciphertext is known. It is assumed that the cryptanalyst possesses the cryptographic algorithm as well as plaintext statistics, and intercepts one or more ciphertexts encrypted with the same key. The COA attack is to obtain the plaintext or key by analyzing these ciphertexts.

   - **KPA**. KPA means that the cryptanalyst not only has a considerable amount of ciphertext, but also knows certain plain-ciphertext pairs. The task of the cryptanalyst is to use the ciphertext information to derive a decryption key or an alternative algorithm that can recover the corresponding plaintext from the obtained ciphertext. The basic requirement for modern cryptosystems is to withstand not only ciphertext only attacks, but also known plaintext attacks.

- **CPA**. In CPA scenario, a cryptanalyst can not only obtain a certain number of plain-ciphertext pairs, but also obtain the corresponding ciphertext by choosing any plaintext using the same unknown key. In this attack situation, the cryptanalyst often takes temporary control of the encryption machine by some means.

- **CCA**. The CCA model means that the attacker can choose the ciphertext for decryption. On the basis of the known plaintext attack, the attacker can arbitrarily create or select some ciphertext and obtain the decrypted plaintext. Chosen ciphertext attack is a stronger attack than the known plaintext attack.

- **CTA**. The CTA is a combination of chosen plaintext attack and chosen ciphertext attack. Under the premise of mastering the cryptographic algorithm, the cryptanalyst can not only select the plaintext and obtain the corresponding ciphertext, but also select the ciphertext to obtain the corresponding plaintext. This is often the case where the cryptanalyst temporarily controls the encryption and decryption machines by some means.

From the attacker's perspective, the order of attack difficulty corresponding to the four attack modes is: Chosen Text Attack (CTA) > Chosen Ciphertext Attack (CCA) > Chosen Plaintext Attack (CPA) > Known Plaintext Attack (KPA) > Ciphertext Only Attack (COA).

GLOSSARY

Asymmetric Cipher Model: is proposed to solve the two most difficult issues in symmetric cipher model.

Chosen Ciphertext Attack: can arbitrarily create or select some ciphertext and obtain the decrypted plaintext.

Chosen Plaintext Attack: can not only obtain a certain number of plain-ciphertext pairs, but also obtain the corresponding ciphertext by choosing any plaintext using the same unknown key.

Chosen Text Attack: can not only select the plaintext and obtain the corresponding ciphertext, but also select the ciphertext to obtain the corresponding plaintext.

Ciphertext: refers to the messages and signals generated by the cryptosystem, which are output through some kind of disguise or transformation of the plaintext.

Ciphertext Only Attack: refers to the cryptanalysis method that infers the plaintext or key when only the ciphertext is known.

Conditional Security: refers to evaluating the security of a cryptographic system according to the amount of computation required to crack it.

Confusion: refers to complicating the relationship between the key and the ciphertext, thereby increasing the difficulty of attacking through statistical methods.

Cryptographic Algorithm: refers to a set of operational rules or procedures that describe the cryptographic processing (encryption and decryption), which is the basis of a cryptographic protocol.

Cryptography: is the core technology for ensuring the security of cyberspace including the cyberspace of the Internet of Things.

Decryption: refers to the process of restoring ciphertext to plaintext using the corresponding algorithm or key.

Diffusion: refers to rearranging or spreading each bit in a message, applying the influence of each bit of plaintext or key to more bits of output ciphertext as quickly as possible.

Discretionary Access Control: can arbitrarily modify or grant the corresponding authority to the object.

Encryption: refers to processing the original plaintext information into incomprehensible ciphertext according to a certain algorithm or rule, so as to protect the data from being illegally stolen and read.

Initial Permutation: refers to processing the original plaintext through the IP permutation table.

Known Plaintext Attack: means that the cryptanalyst not only has a considerable amount of ciphertext, but also knows certain plain-ciphertext pairs.

Mandatory Access Control: the owner of the object is not allowed to modify or grant the corresponding rights to the object at will, but to grant the rights to each object separately by means of coercion.

Plaintext: refers to messages waiting to be disguised or encrypted, and in communication systems may be bit streams, such as text, bitmaps, digitized speech, images, and video, etc.

Provable Security: is to attribute the security of a cryptosystem to solving a mathematical problem that has been deeply studied but not yet solved.

Role-Based Access Control: various permissions for system opera-tions are not directly granted to specific users, but a set of roles is established between the user set and the permission set, and each role corresponds to a corresponding set of permissions.

Symmetric encryption: means that the sender and receiver use the same key to encrypt and decrypt data.

III

Security Solutions in the Internet of Things

CHAPTER 7

Wireless Network Security

Wireless security protects wireless networks, devices, and data from unauthorized access, theft, and malicious attacks. It involves a set of measures and technologies designed to ensure the confidentiality, integrity, and availability of wireless networks and their data. Wireless security threats can come from various sources, including eavesdropping, spoofing, hacking, and denial-of-service attacks. Wireless security technologies and practices such as encryption, authentication, access control, intrusion detection and prevention, and regular security updates should be implemented to mitigate these threats. Effective wireless security is crucial for protecting sensitive information and ensuring the proper functioning of wireless networks.

7.1 BACKGROUND OF WIRELESS NETWORKS

Wireless networks have become an integral part of our daily lives, allowing us to access information, communicate with others, and connect to the internet without the need for physical cables. A wireless network [267] is a computer network that uses radio waves to transmit and receive data between devices. These networks have revolutionized how we interact with technology, enabling us to acc,ess information and stay connected while on the go.

Wireless networks are used in various applications, from home and office networks to public Wi-Fi hotspots and cellular networks. They have become increasingly popular due to their convenience, flexibility, and mobility. Wireless networks provide several benefits over wired

DOI: 10.1201/9781032694818-7

networks, including the ability to connect devices without the need for physical cables, the ability to access the internet from anywhere within range, and the ability to set up and reconfigure networks easily.

A wireless network's basic components include routers, access points, and network adapters. Wireless routers are a central hub for wireless devices to connect to the internet, while access points allow wireless devices to connect to a wired network. Network adapters enable devices to connect to a wireless network and typically support one or more wireless networking standards, such as Wi-Fi or Bluetooth.

Wireless networks use radio waves to transmit data between devices. Radio waves are electromagnetic radiation that travels through the air at the speed of light. The frequency of the radio waves determines the speed and range of the wireless network. Higher frequencies provide faster data rates but a shorter range, while lower frequencies provide slower data rates but a longer range.

Wireless networks use wireless networking standards, including Wi-Fi, Bluetooth [268], Zigbee [269], and NFC [270]. Wi-Fi is the most common wireless networking standard for internet access in homes, businesses, and public spaces. Bluetooth is short-range wireless communication [271] between smartphones, headphones, and speakers. Zigbee is used for home automation and IoT devices, while NFC is used for contactless payments and data transfer.

Wireless networks [272, 273] have several advantages over wired networks. They are more flexible and can easily be set up and reconfigured without physical cables. They also enable mobility, allowing devices to connect to the network anywhere within range. Wireless networks are also more convenient for devices that do not have built-in Ethernet ports, such as smartphones and tablets.

However, wireless networks also have some disadvantages. They are more susceptible to interference from other wireless devices, such as microwaves and cordless phones. Wireless networks are also more vulnerable to security threats such as hacking and data theft, as the wireless signal can be intercepted by unauthorized parties if the network is not properly secured.

Several security measures are typically employed to ensure wireless networks' security. These include encryption, firewalls, and network segmentation. Encryption is used to protect data as it is transmitted over the wireless network, while firewalls are used to block unauthorized access to the network. Network segmentation separates the wireless network from the wired network, ensuring that unauthorized access to the wireless network does not lead to access to the wired network.

7.1.1 Basic Concepts

What is a wireless network? In general, Wireless Local Area Network (WLAN) can be classified into general and specific networking.

Specific Networking

A specific wireless network is a wireless local area network based on the IEEE 802.11 standard. It uses radio wave technology to connect various network devices in a computer network. It has the advantages of mobility, easy installation, high flexibility, and high scalability, but the coverage range is small (5–30 meters). The essential feature of a wireless network is that it no longer uses communication cables to connect computers to the network but instead uses wireless connections, making network construction and terminal mobility more flexible. The emergence and development of wireless networks allow people to move freely within wireless coverage while enjoying network resources without being limited by traditional wired networks.

General Networking

The general wireless network includes three aspects: Wireless Personal Area Network (WPAN) , WLAN, and Wireless Wide Area Network (WWAN) .

1. WPAN: a personal area network that uses wireless connections. It is used for communication between digital devices such as phones, computers, peripherals, and small areas (usually within 10 meters) of personal area networks.

   The technologies that support WPAN include Bluetooth, ZigBee, Ultra-Wideband (UWB) [274], Infrared Data Association (IrDA) [275], and Home Radio Frequency (HomeRF) , among which Bluetooth technology is the most widely used WPAN. Each technology can only play its best role when used for specific purposes, applications, or fields. In addition, although some technologies are considered to compete with each other in the WPAN space in some aspects, they are often complementary to each other.

   WPAN is positioned as short-distance wireless communication technology, but it is divided into high-speed (HR-WPAN)

[276, 277]and low-speed (LR-WPAN) [278] according to different application scenarios. From the perspective of network composition, WPAN is located at the bottom of the entire network architecture and is used for wireless connections between terminals within a minimal range, point-to-point short-distance connections. WPAN is a dedicated network based on computer communication, working in a personal operating environment and forming a network of devices that need to communicate without central management devices or software.

2. WLAN: the "specific wireless network" as described above.

3. WWAN: a digital mobile communication network for telecommunications operators' mobile phone and data services. The connection capability of wireless wide-area networks can cover a relatively wide geographical area. However, the data transmission rate is low, only 115 kbit/s, which is far behind other regional wireless technologies. Currently, global wireless wide area networks mainly use GSM and CDMA technologies, and others include 3G or 3.5G technologies.

7.1.2 Wireless Local Area Network Topology

Regardless of the transmission technology used in WLANs, their topology can be divided into two basic types: centralized and decentralized. Generally speaking, the decentralized topology is also known as an infrastructure-less WLAN or wireless LAN without infrastructure, while the centralized topology is known as an infrastructure WLAN.

1. **Point-to-point Mode**

   The typical networking method for a decentralized or infrastructure-less WLAN is the point-to-point mode, also known as ad-hoc mode, peer-to-peer mode, or self-organizing/mobile ad-hoc network (MANET). This type of network topology cannot be connected to a wired network and can only be used independently without needing an Access Point (AP) . Security and other functions are maintained by each client independently. Mobile ad-hoc networks use a non-centralized MAC protocol.

   Advantages of mobile ad-hoc networks:
   Flexible and fast networking, widely used in temporary communication environments.

Disadvantages of mobile ad-hoc networks:

(a) When the number of users in the network is too large, channel competition will seriously affect network performance;

(b) Routing information will rapidly increase with the increase in the number of users, which can seriously hinder data communication;

(c) A node must be able to "see" any other node in the network simultaneously. Otherwise, the network is considered disconnected; and

(d) Only suitable for networking a small number of networks.

2. **Infrastructure Mode**

The infrastructure mode is composed of an AP, wireless workstations, and a Distributed System Service (DSS), which covers the area known as the Basic Service Set (BSS).

The wireless workstation and the AP are associated with the AP's BSSID (Basic Service Set Identifier). In the IEEE 802.11 standard, the BSSID is the MAC address of the AP. The infrastructure network also uses a non-centralized MAC protocol. However, due to the poor anti-destructive capability of the central network topology, a failure of the AP can easily lead to the paralysis of the entire network.

3. **Multi-AP Mode** Multi-AP mode is the infrastructure mode composed of multiple APs and the DSS that connects them. Each AP is an independent BSS, and multiple BSSs form an Extended Service Set (ESS). All APs in the ESS share the same Extended Service Set Identifier (ESSID).

Multi-AP mode is also called "multi-cell structure". There should be a 15% overlap between each cell to facilitate the roaming of wireless workstations. When roaming, switching between different AP access points is necessary. Switching can be centralized through switches or non-centralized by controlling the signal strength of mobile and monitoring nodes.

4. **Relay Mode**

The relay mode is a function of wireless APs in network connections, which can relay and amplify signals to extend the coverage of wireless networks. In the Wireless Distributed System (WDS), the wireless relay mode allows wireless APs to bridge and relay wireless signals between each other without affecting their wireless coverage capabilities, providing a new wireless networking mode. The wireless distributed system links two AP devices through a wireless radio interface. This link can relay the communication traffic from an AP without an Ethernet connection to another AP with an Ethernet connection. WDS allows up to four point-to-point links to be configured between access points. A central AP can generally support up to four remote wireless relay mode APs.

Although the wireless relay mode makes wireless coverage more accessible and flexible, it requires high-end AP support, and if the central AP fails, the entire WLAN will be paralyzed, and redundancy cannot be guaranteed. Therefore, the most common application is "wireless roaming mode". In contrast, the "relay mode" is only used in exceptional cases where network cabling is not possible, such as large open office areas, warehouses, docks, etc., where it is challenging to lay Ethernet cables. In addition, if the distance between two networks is too far and the network signal cannot be transmitted, a relay AP can be set up in the middle to act as a relay only.

5. **Mesh structure**

The Mesh structure, also known as a wireless mesh network, allows each node in the network to send and receive signals. The wireless Mesh network is also called a "multi-hop" network. The IEEE 802.16-2004 standard defines two network topologies: a cellular network structure from Point-to-Multipoint (PMP) and a Mesh structure.

The Mesh structure consists of a group of wireless APs distributed in a mesh pattern and the APs are interconnected through wireless relay links in a point-to-point manner, expanding traditional wireless "hotspots" into truly large-area wireless "hot zones".

In a Mesh network, APs communicate wirelessly with each other without the need for wired relays. It also has the function of broadband wireless aggregation connection, effective routing, and fault discovery features, making it more suitable for large-scale wireless network configurations. Compared with traditional switched networks, Mesh networks do not require cabling but still have distributed networks' redundancy mechanism and re-routing capability.

Advantages of Mesh networks:

(a) Quick deployment and easy installation. Because cabling is unnecessary, device installation is very fast and simple. The device configuration and network management functions are the same as traditional WLAN, which can greatly reduce Total Ownership Costs (TCO) and installation time.

(b) Non-line-of-sight (NLOS) transmission. The wireless interconnection between APs, effective routing discovery characteristics, and the nature of a "multi-hop" network provide wireless broadband access capabilities to adjacent users who do not have direct line-of-sight with users who do.

(c) Robustness. In the Mesh network, each site has one or more paths for transmitting data, so if a node fails or is interfered with, the data will automatically route to a backup link.

(d) Flexible structure. In a multi-hop network, devices can connect to the network through different nodes simultaneously, so it does not reduce system performance.

(e) Greater redundancy and communication load balancing capabilities. Each device has multiple transmission paths available, and the network can dynamically allocate routes based on the load of each node to avoid congestion.

(f) High bandwidth. A relay between nodes shortens the communication distance between adjacent nodes, resulting in higher bandwidth for wireless communication.

(g) Low power consumption. The short distance between adjacent nodes means less signal power is required, and the wireless signal interference between nodes is correspondingly less.

Mesh network shortcomings:

(a) **Interoperability** Current Mesh network products do not have a unified technical standard, and users must consider compatibility issues when choosing products.

(b) **Communication latency** Due to the multi-hop nature of network data transmission, communication data transmission over long distances has a greater delay.

(c) **Security** The multi-hop nature of the network exposes too much data to the public environment, which puts more demands on data security.

7.1.3 Wireless Network Classification

Wireless networks can be classified according to coverage, communication technology, and other dimensions.

1. Classification based on coverage: Wireless networks can be divided into various types, such as WLAN, WMAN, and WWAN, to meet different communication needs.

   - WLAN: generally used for wireless communication between areas with a small coverage area. Representative technologies include the IEEE 802.11 series and HomeRF technology. The data transmission rate is between 11 and 56Mbps or even higher.

   - WMAN: mainly for mobile data communication through mobile phones or vehicle devices, which can cover most areas in the city. The representative technology is the IEEE 802.20 standard proposed in 2002, mainly for Mobile Broadband Wireless Access (MBWA) technology.

   - WWAN: mainly refers to data communication through mobile communication satellites with the largest coverage area. Representative technologies include 3G and future 4G, with data transmission rates generally above 2Mbps.

   - WPAN: the wireless transmission distance is generally around 10 meters, with typical technologies such as IEEE 802.15 (WPAN), Bluetooth, and ZigBee technology. The data transmission rate is above 10Mbps, and the wireless connection distance is around 10 meters.

   - Wireless Body Area Network (WBAN): represented by wireless medical monitoring and entertainment, and military applications, it mainly refers to communication between sensors attached to or implanted in the human body. From the definition, WBAN is closely related to WPAN, but its communication distance is shorter, usually 0–2 meters. Therefore, the physical layer characteristic of WBAN is a very short transmission distance.

2. Classification based on communication technology: Wireless networks can be divided into WLAN, Bluetooth, mobile communication, and other types to meet different communication needs.

- Wi-Fi: uses radio waves to provide wireless high-speed internet and network connections.
- Bluetooth: a short-range wireless technology used for transferring data between devices.
- Cellular Networks: wireless networks that use cellular technology to provide voice, data, and internet services.

3. Classification based on application: Wireless networks can also be classified based on their application or intended use.

- WSN: used for monitoring and controlling physical or environmental conditions, such as temperature, humidity, pressure, and light. It consists of small, low-power devices equipped with sensors that collect information about the environment. WSNs are commonly used in areas such as environmental monitoring, industrial automation, and healthcare.
- WPAN: used for connecting personal devices, such as smartphones, laptops, and wearable devices. WPANs use short-range wireless technologies, such as Bluetooth and Zigbee, to enable communication between devices within a distance of 10 meters or less. They are commonly used for data transfer, device synchronization, and remote control.

7.1.4 Wireless Network Protocol Standards

802.11 is a wireless LAN standard announced by IEEE (The Institute of Electrical and Electronics Engineers) in 1997, which applies to communication connections between wired stations and wireless users or between wireless users. It defines the MAC and Physical layer standards. Among them, the physical layer defines two wireless frequency modulation methods and one infrared transmission method that works at 2.4GHz, with a transmission speed of 2Mbps. The MAC layer supports Ad-hoc communication mode and AP-coordinated communication mode. Currently, this series of WLAN standards include IEEE

TABLE 7.1   IEEE 802.11 Series Standards and Specifications

Standards	Descriptions
802.11	In 1997, the original standard (2Mbps, working at 2.4GHz).
802.11a	In 1999, the physical layer was supplemented (54Mbps, working at 5GHz).
802.11b	In 1999, the physical layer was supplemented (11Mbps, working at 2.4Hz)
802.11c	Compliant with 802.1D medium access control layer bridging (MAC Layer Bridging)
802.11d	Adjusted according to the radio regulations of each country.
802.11e	Support for Quality of Service (QoS).
802.11f	IEEE revoked the inter-Access Point Protocol (Inter-Access Point Protocol) of base stations in February 2006.
802.11g	In 2003, the physical layer was supplemented (54Mbps, working at 2.4GHz).
802.11h	In 2004, the adjustment of wireless coverage radius, indoor (indoor), and outdoor (outdoor) channels (5GHz frequency band).
802.11i	In 2004, the security aspects of wireless networks were added.
802.11n	In September 2009, the official standard was passed, and the transmission rate of WLAN was increased by 350Mbps or even 475Mbps from 54Mbps and 108Mbps provided by 802.11a and 802.11g.
802.11p	In 2010, this agreement was mainly used in the wireless communication of vehicle electronics.
802.11ax	In 2019, WIFI6, the highest speed is 11Gbps.

802.11, IEEE 802.11b, IEEE 802.11a, IEEE 802.11g, IEEE 802.11d, IEEE 802.11e, IEEE 802.11f, IEEE 802.11h, IEEE 802.11i, IEEE 802.11j, etc., each of which has its advantages and disadvantages. The specific standards and their descriptions are shown in Table 7.1.

Below is a brief introduction to four IEEE 802.11 series standards related to the physical layer: IEEE 802.11, IEEE 802.11a, IEEE 802.11b, and IEEE 802.11g.

1. IEEE 802.11 is the earliest wireless LAN network specification, released by IEEE in June 1997, which works at the 2.4GHz ISM

frequency band. Its physical layer uses infrared, Frequency-Hopping Spread Spectrum (FHSS), or Direct-Sequence Spread Spectrum (DSSS) technology, with a maximum data transfer rate of 2Mbps. It is mainly used to solve the wireless access problem of user terminals in office LANs and campus networks.

When using FHSS technology, the 2.4GHz channel is divided into 75 sub-channels of 1MHz each. When the receiver and the transmitter negotiate a frequency-hopping pattern, the data is sent on each sub-channel according to the sequence, and each session on the IEEE 802.11 network may use a different hopping mode.

Using this frequency-hopping method avoids two transmission endpoints using the same sub-channel at the same time, while DSSS technology divides the 2.4GHz frequency band into 14 sub-bands of 22MHz each, and data is transmitted on one of the 14 frequency bands without hopping between sub-bands.

Due to overlapping adjacent frequency bands, only three of the 14 sub-bands of IEEE 802.11 do not overlap. Due to limitations in data transfer rates, IEEE 802.11 also introduced an improved version, IEEE 802.11b, in 2000. However, with the development of networks, especially the need for high-bandwidth network applications such as IP voice and video data streams, the data transfer rate of 11Mbps of IEEE 802.11b cannot meet actual needs. Therefore, the high-speed IEEE 802.11a and IEEE 802.11g, with data transfer rates of up to 54Mbps, were also introduced one after another.

2. IEEE 802.11a works in the 5GHz frequency band in China but in the U-NII frequency band in the United States, covering three frequency bands of 5.15–5.25GHz, 5.25–5.35GHz, and 5.725–5.825GHz. Its physical layer rate can reach 54Mbps, and the transmission layer can reach 25Mbps. The physical layer of IEEE 802.11a can also work in the infrared frequency band with a wavelength of 850–950 nanometers, with a signal transmission distance of about 10 meters.

IEEE 802.11a uses Orthogonal Frequency-Division Multiplexing (OFDM) unique spread spectrum technology. It provides a wireless ATM interface with a speed of 25Mbps and an Ethernet wireless frame structure interface with a speed of 10Mbps, supporting voice, data, and image services. IEEE 802.11a uses OFDM technology to increase the transmission range and uses data encryption with 152-bit WEP.

From a technical perspective, the difference between IEEE 802.11a and IEEE 802.11b mainly lies in the working frequency band. Since IEEE 802.11a works in a different 5GHz frequency band than IEEE 802.11b, it avoids many wireless electronic products' heavily-used 2.4GHz frequency band. Hence, its products are much less interfered with during wireless communication, and its anti-interference performance is better than that of IEEE 802.11b. The real significance of IEEE 802.11a lies in its data transfer bandwidth of up to 54Mbps. When IEEE 802.11b meets the needs of general Internet browsing, data exchange, and shared peripherals with its data transfer rate of 11Mbps, IEEE 802.11a has already prepared for the high data transfer requirements of future wireless broadband networks. From a long-term development perspective, its competitiveness is self-evident.

In addition, IEEE 802.11a's wireless network products have lower power consumption than IEEE 802.11b, which also has significant practical value for mobile devices such as laptops and PDAs. However, the popularization of IEEE 802.11a also needs to improve. First, there is pressure from manufacturers. IEEE 802.11b has matured, and many manufacturers with IEEE 802.11b products are conservative about IEEE 802.11a. From the current situation, because these two technology standards are incompatible, many manufacturers have directly made their products "a+b" to balance market demand. Although this approach solves the "compatibility" problem, it also increases costs.

Secondly, the 5GHz frequency band cannot be approved and recognized in all countries worldwide due to the restrictions of relevant laws and regulations. Although the 5GHz frequency band provides a low-interference environment for devices based on IEEE 802.11a, its disadvantages are also. Because thousands of artificial satellites in space communicate with ground stations using the 5GHz frequency band, interference between them is inevitable. In addition, the European Union has also used the 5GHz frequency for its own HiperLAN wireless communication standard.

3. IEEE 802.11b, or Wi-Fi, is the most popular and widely used wireless standard. IEEE 802.11b works in the 2.4GHz frequency band and supports two physical layer speeds, 5.5Mbps and 11Mbps. The transmission rate of IEEE 802.11b varies due to environmental interference or transmission distance and switches between 1Mbps, 2Mbps, 5.5Mbps, and 11Mbps. It is also compatible with IEEE 802.11 at 1Mbps and 2Mbps speeds. IEEE 802.11b uses DSSS technology and provides data encryption using up to 128-bit Wired Equivalent Privacy (WEP) protocol. However, IEEE 802.11b is incompatible with the later IEEE 802.11a standard that works on the 5GHz frequency.

Regarding operation, IEEE 802.11b has two working modes: point-to-point mode and infrastructure mode. Point-to-point mode refers to the communication between wireless network cards. That is, a computer with a wireless network card can communicate with another computer with a wireless network card. For small-scale wireless networks, this is a very convenient interconnection solution. Infrastructure refers to the communication mode for expanding the wireless network or coexisting with wired and wireless networks. This is also the most commonly used connection mode for IEEE 802.11b. In this working mode, a computer with a wireless network card needs to connect to another computer through a "wireless access point", and the access point is responsible for frequency band management and other work. In the case of allowed bandwidth, an access point can support up to 1,024 wireless nodes to access. The network access speed will slow down when the number of wireless nodes increases. Adding the number of access points can effectively control and manage the frequency band.

The maturity of IEEE 802.11b technology has greatly reduced the cost of network products based on this standard. Whether for home or corporate users, they can build a complete wireless LAN without investing too much money. Of course, IEEE 802.11b is imperfect and has drawbacks. The highest transmission speed of 11Mbps cannot meet users' high data transfer needs. Therefore, its application is limited when high bandwidth is required. However, it can be a good supplement to wired networks.

4. IEEE 802.11g is a high-speed physical layer extension of IEEE 802.11b. It also works in the 2.4GHz frequency band and uses DSSS technology for the physical layer. Additionally, it uses OFDM technology, which allows wireless network transmission rates of up to 54Mbps and is fully compatible with IEEE802.11b. The design of IEEE802.11g is almost the same as that of IEEE802.11a.

The emergence of IEEE 802.11g provides another communication technology choice for the wireless sensor network market, but it also brings controversy, which revolves around IEEE 802.11g and IEEE 802.11a. Like IEEE 802.11a, IEEE 802.11 g also uses OFDM technology so that data transmission can reach 54Mbps. However, unlike IEEE 802.11a, the working frequency band of IEEE 802.11g is not the 5GHz frequency band of IEEE 802.11a but the same 2.4GHz frequency band as IEEE 802.11b. Therefore, IEEE 802.11g is used to solve the compatibility problem faced by users of products based on IEEE 802.11b technology.

From a particular perspective, IEEE 802.11b can be replaced by IEEE 802.11a, so is the introduction of IEEE 802.11g redundant? The answer is undoubtedly negative. In addition to high data transmission rates and compatibility advantages, IEEE 802.11g's signal attenuation in the 2.4GHz frequency band is not as severe as that of IEEE 802.11a in the 5GHz frequency band. Additionally, IEEE 802.11g has better "penetration" capabilities and can achieve good communication effects in complex usage environments. However, the working frequency band of IEEE 802.11g is 2.4GHz, which makes it vulnerable to interference from devices such as microwaves and cordless phones, just like IEEE 802.11b. Furthermore, the signal coverage range of IEEE 802.11g is much smaller than that of IEEE 802.11b, and users need to add more wireless access points to meet the signal coverage of the original usage area.

WiFi Encryption Protocols

WiFi is a wireless communication protocol widely used in WLANs and WWANs. It is a radio-based communication protocol suitable for communication between devices equipped with WiFi modules.

The IEEE Standards Development Committee and IEEE 802.11 Committee initially developed the WiFi protocol in 1997. It defines the specifications for wireless local area networks' physical and data link layers to achieve data transmission and communication between devices. The IEEE 802.11 standard has undergone multiple revisions and extensions, with the latest version being IEEE 802.11-2016, released in 2016. The frequency bands 2.4GHz and 5GHz are commonly used by the Industrial, Scientific, Medical (ISM) as the WiFi protocol. Its communication distance is usually within 30 meters, but with the continuous development of technology, the transmission distance of WiFi is also constantly expanding.

The working principle of WiFi protocol is to convert the data of the wired network into wireless signals through the base station (router) and then receive the wireless signals through the receiving end (WiFi card) and convert them into data of the wired network. The base station and the receiving end communicate through radio frequency signals, which can pass through physical obstacles such as walls and floors so that WiFi can communicate between different rooms and floors.

WiFi protocol supports various application scenarios, including personal use, enterprise office, public transportation, schools, hospitals, airports, etc. Nowadays, WiFi devices usually support different encryption protocols, such as WiFi Protected Access (WPA), WiFi Protected Access 2 (WPA2), and WEP, to protect the security of the network. Wireless passwords are the most basic encryption method in wireless security, and choosing the appropriate encryption level is the most important. Wireless security protocols prevent random people from connecting to wireless networks and encrypt private data from radio waves. Most wireless APs can enable one of the following three wireless encryption standards:

1. **WEP**

   An old encryption method that uses IEEE 802.11 technology. Therefore, when using WEP encryption, it will affect the transmission speed of wireless devices. If the old device only supports IEEE 802.11, then any encryption can be compatible, which has little effect on wireless transmission speed.

   Authentication type: Share requires key authentication before allowing the connection, and Open does not require authentication for an association, but the key must still be correct to connect normally.

Key format: For 64-bit encryption, the key is ten hexadecimal characters (0–9, A-F) or 5 ASCII characters. Sometimes it is 40-bit encryption. For 128-bit encryption, the key is 26 hexadecimal characters or 13 ASCII characters. Sometimes it is called 104-bit encryption.

2. *WPA-PSK/WPA2-PSK (WPA-Preshared, WPA Shared Secret Key)*

WPA-PSK/WPA2-PSK is a common set encryption type nowadays, a simplified version of WPA/WPA2. Based on the shared key of WPA mode, it has high security and is relatively easy to set up. Temporal Key Integrity Protocol (TKIP) is an old encryption standard. The key length used in the password of TKIP is 128 bits. AES has better security than TKIP and can be encrypted using 128, 192, or 256 bits.

Comparison:

(a) Transmission speed: AES uses higher encryption technology than TKIP, and network transmission speed is faster.

(b) Security performance: TKIP must run on existing hardware and cannot use advanced encryption algorithms.

(c) Applicable situations: TKIP is suitable for the 802.11x wireless transmission protocol, and the AES encryption algorithm is suitable for the 802.11n wireless transmission protocol.

3. *WPA/WPA2 (WiFi Protected Access)*

WPA/WPA2 is the most secure encryption type, which requires authentication through a RADIUS server and obtains the WPA/WPA2 security mode key. Since it requires a dedicated authentication server, the cost is relatively high, and maintenance is more complicated. Ordinary users will not use it. Generally, enterprise users will use this encryption method for high data security requirements.

7.2 WIRELESS NETWORK VULNERABILITIES

7.2.1 Overview

A wireless network is based on radio technology, and its transmission medium is electromagnetic waves in the air. It offers advantages such as wireless connectivity, flexibility, and portability. Wireless networks are communication technology that does not require physical connections and can transmit data through wireless signals. The basic principle of a wireless network is to convert digital information into electromagnetic wave signals, transmit them through wireless channels to the receiving end, and then convert them back into digital information. The components of a wireless network include wireless transmitters, receivers, channels, access points, and terminal devices.

With the widespread use of wireless networks, network vulnerabilities have become increasingly prominent. Wireless network vulnerabilities refer to security loopholes and weaknesses in the design, deployment, and operation of wireless networks, which attackers can easily exploit to cause losses and risks. These loopholes and weaknesses may originate from deficiencies or design flaws in the technologies and protocols used in wireless networks or may be caused by environmental factors faced by wireless networks (such as electromagnetic wave interference or insufficient signal coverage).

Wireless network vulnerabilities can be traced back to early wireless communication technologies such as radio and television broadcasting. These technologies used the radio spectrum to transmit information but lacked security mechanisms such as encryption and authentication, making them vulnerable to hackers and other criminals. Due to the broadcast nature of wireless signals and the open transmission medium, wireless networks are more vulnerable to attacks and interference than wired networks. This vulnerability is becoming increasingly apparent in modern society as wireless networks become integral to our lives and work.

The data transmission of wireless networks is carried out through wireless signals, making this vulnerability challenging to avoid and significantly impacting network security. Hackers can exploit the vulnerability of wireless networks to carry out various attacks. For example, hackers can eavesdrop on wireless signals to obtain transmitted data or interfere with signals to prevent data transmission. In addition, hackers can also exploit the vulnerabilities of wireless networks to attack wireless networks, such as tricking users into inputting personal information or passwords utilizing phishing so that hackers can obtain users' sensitive information.

The vulnerability of wireless networks can also lead to network instability. Because wireless signals are susceptible to interference, network connections may be unstable, resulting in disconnection of the network connection or failure of data transmission, affecting the user experience.

Wireless network vulnerabilities may also result in the interruption of network services. If a hacker successfully launches an attack on a network, they may be able to shut down or interrupt the service, making users unable to access the network. A hacker attack can take many forms, such as eavesdropping, data interception, injection of malicious code, or denial of service attacks. Eavesdropping involves listening in on wireless signals to gain access to data being transmitted. Data interception involves intercepting and modifying data being transmitted. Injection of malicious code involves inserting malicious code into a network to cause damage or steal information. DoS attacks involve flooding a network with traffic to overload it and make it inaccessible to users. In any case, a hacker attack aims to gain unauthorized access to a network, its data, and its resources. This action can adversely affect the daily processes of businesses and individuals.

The OSI model is introduced to better analyze the vulnerability of wireless networks. The OSI is a reference model that divides the network communication process into seven layers, each responsible for a specific network function. It is also necessary to divide the communication process into different levels in a wireless network to facilitate network design and optimization.

The Relationship Between Wireless Networks and the OSI Model:

1. **Physical Layer:** In the OSI model, the physical layer converts digital signals into electrical signals and transmits them through physical media (such as cables and optical fibers). In wireless networks, the physical layer is also responsible for converting digital information into electromagnetic wave [279] signals and transmitting them through wireless channels.

2. **Data Link Layer:** In the OSI model, the data link layer divides raw data into frames and adds control information. This is to ensure data transmission at the physical layer is correct. In wireless networks, the data link layer must divide data into frames and add control information such as Cyclic Redundancy Check (CRC) to ensure reliable data transmission.

3. **Network Layer:** In the OSI model, the network layer is responsible for transmitting data from the source host to the destination host, using routing and packet forwarding technologies to achieve data transmission. In wireless networks, the network layer must also be responsible for routing and packet forwarding to achieve data transmission.

4. **Transport Layer:** [280] In the OSI model, the transport layer is responsible for providing reliable end-to-end data transmission services, using protocols such as Transmission Control Protocol (TCP) and User Datagram Protocol (UDP) to achieve data transmission. The transport layer must also provide reliable data transmission services in wireless networks, using protocols such as TCP and UDP to achieve data transmission.

5. **Session Layer:** In the OSI model, the session layer establishes, maintains, and terminates sessions between two applications. In wireless networks, the session layer must also establish, maintain, and terminate sessions between applications.

6. **Presentation Layer:** In the OSI model, the presentation layer is responsible for converting application layer data formats into network formats and processing data encryption and compression. In wireless networks, the presentation layer must also convert application layer data formats into wireless network formats and process data encryption and compression.

7. **Application Layer:** In the OSI model, the application layer provides network services like file transfer and email. The application layer must also provide network services like web browsers, online videos, and audio streams in wireless networks.

It should be noted that wireless networks are designed only partially according to the OSI model. Some layers may be combined or split, and special issues such as the unreliability of wireless channels, interference, and multipath propagation need to be considered in wireless network design and optimization. At the same time, some unique protocols and technologies in wireless networks, such as WiFi, Bluetooth, LTE, and 5G, involve functions across multiple OSI layers in their implementation.

The OSI model provides a universal design framework and reference model for wireless networks. In the following sections, we will discuss the vulnerabilities of wireless networks in detail from the perspectives of the physical layer, data link layer (primarily at the MAC layer), and network layer.

7.2.2 Physical Layer Vulnerabilities

Wireless networks are a type of network that transmits data through wireless signals. Wireless signals are radio waves that transmit data through the air. In wireless networks, signals are transmitted from one device to another to achieve wireless communication.

The basic principle of wireless signals is based on radio waves. Radio waves are a type of electromagnetic wave that can propagate in the air. The characteristics of radio waves include frequency, amplitude, and phase. In wireless communication, frequency is the carrier of information, and amplitude and phase are used to modulate the signal to carry data. Different transmission methods are suitable for different scenarios and requirements.

However, signal propagation in wireless networks is highly uncertain. This is because signal propagation in the air is affected by multiple factors. These factors include signal frequency, transmission distance, antenna height and direction, obstacles, etc. Due to the uncertainty of these factors, signal propagation in wireless networks often produces phenomena such as attenuation, reflection, diffraction, and scattering, which affect the quality and reliability of the signal. This makes wireless networks vulnerable in the physical layer. In the physical layer of wireless networks, data is transmitted through electromagnetic waves. These electromagnetic waves can be interfered with, attenuated, or reflected, leading to unreliable data transmission.

In the physical layer of wireless networks, multiple sources of interference have different effects on wireless networks' transmission quality and stability. The following sections will provide detailed introductions to the vulnerabilities of wireless networks caused by different sources of interference.

1. **Multipath effect** refers to the effect of multiple propagation paths formed by electromagnetic waves due to reflection, refraction, diffraction, and other factors during transmission. The multipath effect can cause signal attenuation and time delay spread, thereby affecting the quality and stability of the signal. The multipath effect is a common interference source in wireless networks, especially in indoor environments.

2. **Spectrum pollution** refers to the interference of wireless signals during transmission caused by other signals with similar frequencies, affecting the signal's quality and stability. Spectrum pollution can be caused by other wireless networks, television, radar, and other wireless devices, as well as by human activities, such as using electromagnetic solid interference devices.

3. **Weather effects** refer to the influence of meteorological factors on the transmission of wireless signals. For example, strong winds, rain, snow, lightning, and other weather conditions can affect the propagation and reception of electromagnetic waves, thereby affecting the quality and stability of wireless signals.

4. **Shadow effect** refers to the impact of obstacles on wireless signal transmission, which prevents the signal from directly reaching the receiver. For example, buildings, trees, mountains, and other obstacles can obstruct and shield wireless signal transmission, affecting the quality and stability of wireless signals. Such interference results in the signal being weakened or lost.

5. **Co-channel interference** refers to the interference between signals from different terminals or different base stations in a wireless network. For example, when multiple wireless networks use the same frequency, their signals interfere, affecting the quality and stability of wireless signals. The consequences of this interference cause signal degradation and instability.

Signal attenuation is inevitable in wireless networks. Attenuation refers to the weakening of signal strength with increasing transmission distance. Different attenuation methods in the physical layer have different effects on the performance of wireless networks. The following are several common attenuation methods and their effects on wireless networks:

1. **Free space propagation attenuation** is an ideal method, which refers to the quadratic attenuation of wireless signals with increasing distance in unobstructed space. This attenuation method has a relatively small impact on wireless networks because wireless signals can travel a long distance and cover a large area in unobstructed space.

2. **Multipath attenuation** refers to signal interference and attenuation caused by multiple paths' length, shape, refraction, and other factors when the signal is transmitted through multiple paths. This attenuation method can cause signal distortion, jitter, and other problems, thereby affecting the performance of wireless networks.

3. **Shadow attenuation** refers to the signal being partially or entirely blocked due to obstructing buildings, terrain, and other objects. This attenuation method can cause the signal strength to decrease rapidly or even be lost completely, affecting wireless networks' coverage range and transmission quality.

4. **Atmospheric attenuation** refers to signal attenuation caused by weather, season, and other factors. This attenuation method can cause the transmission distance of the signal to be shortened and the signal strength to be reduced, thereby affecting the coverage range and transmission quality of wireless networks.

Different attenuation methods have different effects on wireless networks. To improve the performance and reliability of wireless networks, suitable technologies, and strategies should be chosen according to the actual situation to reduce the impact of signal attenuation.

Wireless networks face various vulnerabilities at the physical layer, including signal attenuation, multipath effect, shadow effect, weather effects, interference, and security issues. These issues may cause a decline in the quality, loss, interference, distortion, vulnerabilities, blind spots, and other issues of wireless signals, thereby reducing the transmission performance, coverage range, security, and stability of the network. To improve the reliability and security of wireless networks, corresponding technologies and measures, such as signal enhancement, interference elimination, encryption authentication, backup redundancy, etc., should be adopted to cope with these vulnerabilities.

7.2.3 MAC Layer Vulnerability

A wireless network is a type of network that connects devices without the need for wired cables. In a wireless network, wireless devices communicate using wireless signals. To ensure orderly communication between different devices, a MAC protocol is used. The MAC protocol is used to control access among different devices and ensure the normal operation of the network.

The basic principle of the MAC protocol is to control access between different devices through certain rules. In a wireless network, access between different devices is completed through channels. To prevent access conflicts between different devices, the MAC protocol introduces a technique called Carrier Sense Multiple Access (CSMA) , which means that before accessing a channel, a device will first listen to the channel. If the channel is idle, the device will start accessing the channel.

The MAC protocol operates in two ways: distributed protocol and centralized protocol.

1. **Distributed protocol** refers to a protocol in which each node in the network has the same rights and can send data packets simultaneously. The principle of this protocol is based on a competition mechanism. Before sending data packets, each node needs to listen to the channel to ensure that no other node is sending data and then send its data packet. If two or more nodes send data packets simultaneously, a collision will occur, and the nodes need to wait for some time before resending the data packet.

   Standard distributed protocols include Carrier Sense Multiple Access/Collision Avoidance (CSMA/CA) and CSMA/CD. CSMA/CA is wireless networks' most commonly used protocol. It avoids conflicts between nodes by listening to the channel, ensuring the efficiency and reliability of the network. In the CSMA/CA protocol, each node has a fixed time window to listen to the channel and send data packets. If a node detects that another node is sending data packets on the channel before sending its data packet, it will wait some time before trying again.

2. **Centralized protocol** refers to a protocol in which a central node in the network coordinates communication between all nodes and decides when each node should send data packets. The central node is usually a wireless access point or router in this protocol.

   There are a few common centralized protocols, which include Time Division Multiple Access (TDMA) and Frequency Division Multiple Access (FDMA) . TDMA is a time allocation technology that divides time into several time slots, and each node can only send data packets in its allocated time slot. FDMA is a frequency allocation technology that divides frequency into several frequency bands, and each node can only send data packets in its allocated frequency band.

By controlling the MAC protocol, access between different devices in a wireless network can be orderly, ensuring the regular operation of the network.

The MAC layer is an essential component of wireless networks. It coordinates data transmission between nodes in the wireless network and determines when, where, and how nodes access the wireless channel. In a wireless network, the MAC layer faces multiple vulnerabilities, which will be analyzed from the following aspects in this section.

In wireless networks, the MAC layer is the fundamental protocol layer responsible for coordinating the transmission of data frames between multiple terminals. Routing protocols are important for data forwarding in wireless networks, transmitting packets to their destinations through topology detection and packet transmission selection. Regarding the vulnerability of wireless networks, different MAC protocols have different impacts on wireless network vulnerability. Here are some common MAC protocols and their impacts on the vulnerability of wireless networks:

1. **802.11b MAC Protocol:** 802.11b is one of the earliest wireless local area network protocols, and its MAC protocol is based on a collision detection mechanism. This mechanism can lead to a large amount of broadcast traffic in the network, increasing the risk of network delay and decreased throughput. In addition, the 802.11b protocol does not provide encryption and security mechanisms, making it susceptible to eavesdropping and tampering attacks.

2. **802.11g MAC Protocol:** 802.11g is an upgraded version of 802.11b, and its MAC protocol is based on MIMO technology, which can provide higher data transmission speeds and better coverage. However, the 802.11g protocol also has vulnerabilities, such as susceptibility to channel interference and signal attenuation, leading to decreased network performance.

3. **802.11n MAC Protocol:** 802.11n is one of the latest wireless local area network protocols, and its MAC protocol is based on MIMO technology and channel aggregation. The 802.11n protocol can provide higher data transmission speeds and better coverage

while enhancing network robustness and security. However, the 802.11n protocol also has some vulnerabilities, such as susceptibility to signal interference and channel interference, leading to decreased network performance.

4. **802.11ac MAC Protocol:** 802.11ac is one of the latest wireless local area network protocols, and its MAC protocol is based on the Wi-Fi Alliance's MU-MIMO technology. The 802.11ac protocol can provide higher data transmission speeds and better coverage while enhancing network robustness and security. Compared to the 802.11n protocol, the 802.11ac protocol has fewer vulnerabilities because it uses more efficient encoding and decoding technologies, reducing the impact of signal interference and channel interference.

Different MAC protocols have different impacts on the vulnerability of wireless networks. The 802.11b MAC protocol suffers from a large amount of broadcast traffic and lacks security mechanisms, making it susceptible to eavesdropping and tampering attacks. The 802.11g MAC protocol suffers from channel interference and signal attenuation, making network performance vulnerable. The 802.11n MAC protocol provides higher data transmission speeds and better coverage but can also be susceptible to signal and channel interference, leading to decreased network performance. The 802.11ac MAC protocol has better robustness and security but requires more technical support and higher costs. Therefore, when selecting a MAC protocol, it is necessary to weigh the specific situation and application scenario.

On the other hand, the following are common security issues and attack methods of the MAC layer in wireless networks:

1. Sniffing attack: A sniffer attack is a way for attackers to eavesdrop on data packets in a wireless network to obtain sensitive information. Attackers can use tools such as wireless network cards to monitor the wireless channel, thereby stealing transmitted data information, leading to information leakage in wireless networks.

2. Spoofing attack: A spoofing attack is a way for attackers to forge data packets in a wireless network to deceive the receiving end of the network, making it accept and execute the attacker's instructions. Attackers can achieve attacks and control of wireless networks by forging information such as the source and destination addresses of data packets.

3. Man-in-the-middle attack: A man-in-the-middle attack is a way for attackers to intercept communication between two parties in a wireless network, allowing them to tamper with, delete, or inject malicious code into the communication content. Attackers can deceive the receiving end of the network, making it believe that the attacker is a legitimate communication party, thereby achieving attacks and control of wireless networks.

4. Denial-of-service attack: A denial-of-service attack is a way for attackers to consume the resources of a wireless network, making it unable to work normally and causing the wireless network to be paralyzed. Attackers can send many invalid data packets to the wireless network, causing the network to be overloaded and ultimately causing the wireless network to crash.

In order to ensure the correctness and integrity of data frames during transmission and to avoid the loss or error of data frames, collision avoidance technology has been developed. Collision avoidance technology is important for achieving the data link layer task, which can help ensure that multiple data frames do not collide during transmission, thereby avoiding the loss or error of data frames. Wireless networks use different collision avoidance technologies. The following are several common collision avoidance technologies and their impacts on the vulnerability of wireless networks:

1. Traditional collision avoidance technology: This includes CCK, DFS, TBTT, etc. These technologies optimize the transmission time of the transmitter to avoid signal collisions on the same channel. Traditional collision avoidance technology improves the vulnerability of wireless networks to some extent. However, there are still some problems, such as the risk of signal collision when the channel is blocked.

2. Dynamic collision avoidance technology: This includes DCF, DCF/OFDMA, and HSSD of 802.11n, etc. These technologies are based on dynamic channel allocation, which can effectively utilize channel resources while minimizing signal collisions. Dynamic collision avoidance technology can better cope with channel blocking and load balancing issues, improving wireless network performance.

3. Secure collision avoidance technology: Secure collision avoidance technology includes encryption technologies such as WPA, WPA2, AES, and security protocols such as TKIP and AES of 802.11i. These technologies are designed to reduce the impact of signal collisions and eavesdropping attacks on network security. Secure collision avoidance technology can improve the security of wireless networks and reduce the risk of network attacks.

In summary, different collision avoidance technologies have different impacts on the vulnerability of wireless networks. Traditional collision avoidance technology can reduce the risk of signal collision, but there are still some problems yet to discover. Dynamic collision avoidance technology can better cope with channel blocking and load balancing issues, improving wireless network performance. Secure collision avoidance technology can improve the security of wireless networks and reduce the risk of network attacks. Therefore, designing wireless networks requires choosing collision avoidance technologies suitable for specific situations and application scenarios to meet different needs and scenarios. At the same time, these technologies also have some limitations and disadvantages. For example, traditional collision avoidance technology still has the risk of signal collision when the channel is blocked; dynamic collision avoidance technology requires more channel resources, which may affect network throughput; secure collision avoidance technology requires encryption and authentication operations, which may increase network latency and overhead. Therefore, in practical applications, it is necessary to comprehensively consider network requirements, performance, security, and other factors and choose appropriate collision avoidance technologies.

7.2.4 Network Layer Vulnerabilities

The network layer is responsible for data transmission and routing selection in wireless networks. At this layer, wireless networks face various vulnerabilities that may cause network congestion, packet loss, delay, security problems, etc. This article will introduce the vulnerabilities of wireless networks at the network layer from the aspects of routing selection, network congestion, packet loss, security issues, and mobility.

Routing Options

In wireless networks, routing selection is critical because wireless signals are often affected by interference, attenuation, and obstruction, resulting in the distance and signal strength changes between nodes. These changes can result in changes in the network topology, thereby affecting the efficiency of routing selection and data transmission. The following are some typical routing protocols and their impact on wireless networks:

1. Neighbor Tables-Based Routing Protocol

    The neighbor table-based routing protocol is one of the simplest and most common. Its working principle is to maintain the neighbor table of each node. When a data packet needs to be transmitted, the node transmits the data packet to the neighbor node that selects the best path and eventually transmits the data packet to the destination node.

    Advantages: The neighbor table-based routing protocol has the advantages of simplicity, practicality, and ease of implementation. It can quickly respond to changes in the network topology and is suitable for small wireless networks.

    Disadvantages: The neighbor table requires a huge storage space and is unsuitable for large networks. Also, nodes must constantly maintain the neighbor table, increasing the network load.

2. Distance Vector-Based Routing Protocol

    The distance vector-based routing protocol is a classical routing protocol. Its working principle is that each node maintains distance information from all other nodes and exchanges distance information with adjacent nodes. By constantly updating the distance vector, the shortest path is eventually found.

    Advantages: The distance vector-based routing protocol has good adaptability, can adapt to changes in the network topology, and can quickly recover from network failures. It is suitable for medium-sized wireless networks.

    Disadvantages: The distance vector-based routing protocol requires frequent exchange of distance vector information, which increases network load and delay. It is not suitable for large networks.

3. Link State-Based Routing Protocol

    The link state-based routing protocol is more complex. Its working principle is constructing the entire network topology by actively sending link state information from each node and using the shortest path algorithm to calculate the best path.

Advantages: The link state-based routing protocol has good network performance, can find the global optimal solution, and is suitable for large wireless networks.

Disadvantages: The link state-based routing protocol requires more computing and communication resources. Nodes must frequently exchange link state information, increasing network load and delay. Also, path recalculation is required when the network topology changes, which may cause network jitter.

4. Hybrid Routing Protocol

The hybrid routing protocol is a routing method that combines multiple routing protocols. Better network performance and adaptability can be achieved by using different routing protocols at different network layers.

Advantages: The hybrid routing protocol can meet the needs of different scenarios. Different routing protocols can be selected according to network scale, topology structure, and other factors to improve network performance.

Disadvantages: The implementation of the hybrid routing protocol is relatively complex and requires adaptation and optimization for different scenarios.

Different routing protocols have different effects on wireless networks. The neighbor table-based routing protocol is simple and practical, suitable for small networks but not large ones. The distance vector-based routing protocol is adaptable and suitable for medium-sized networks. The link state-based routing protocol can find the global optimal solution and is suitable for large networks but requires more computing and communication [281] resources.

However, in wireless networks, the complexity and difficulty of routing selection are much greater than in wired networks. This is because the transmission rate and quality of wireless signals are affected by many factors, such as signal attenuation, blocking, and interference. In addition, node mobility and joining/leaving the network can also cause changes in the network topology, leading to changes in routing selection. These issues make the routing selection algorithm in wireless networks more complex, difficult, and prone to errors and mistakes.

Network congestion is one of the common problems in wireless networks. When the data packet traffic in the network exceeds the network's processing capacity, network congestion occurs, leading to a decrease in network performance and packet loss. Network congestion is a more serious because wireless signal transmission rates and quality are limited. Network congestion is more likely to occur when there are too many data packets, leading to decreased network performance and packet loss.

Network congestion is a common problem caused by several factors, including excessive nodes, high data packet traffic, and incorrect routing selection. Measures like traffic control, congestion control, and load balancing are recommended to mitigate this issue. However, these measures face challenges in wireless networks due to the unstable transmission rate and quality of wireless signals. As a result, special measures are necessary to ensure network efficiency and reliability.

Packet loss is another prevalent issue in wireless networks. The packet loss rate is higher in wireless networks than in wired networks due to unstable transmission rates and the quality of wireless signals. Packet loss can reduce network performance, application errors, and data loss. Reasons for packet loss in wireless networks include signal attenuation, blocking, interference, and re-transmission. These issues can lead to packet loss, negatively impacting network performance and reliability.

Adaptive re-transmission, link quality estimation, and multipath transmission are technologies used in wireless networks to address packet loss. These technologies help increase the success rate of packet transmission and reduce the packet loss rate. However, these technologies are also subject to signal interference, node mobility, and routing selection in wireless networks. Hence, optimizing and adjusting these technologies in practical applications is necessary to ensure network efficiency and reliability.

Wireless signal transmission is vulnerable to eavesdropping, interference, and tampering. In addition, the large number of nodes in wireless networks and their uneven location and density make them susceptible to various attacks and threats. Security issues can cause problems such as data leakage, system crashes, and user privacy [282] breaches.

The number of nodes in wireless networks, node mobility, and joining/leaving the network can affect the network topology and routing selection. Node mobility can lead to network instability and performance degradation. In the case of mobile nodes, the transmission path of wireless signals may change, leading to signal attenuation, blocking, and interference. These issues can cause packet loss and network congestion, affecting performance and reliability.

Power consumption is a critical issue since batteries power nodes in wireless networks. Node power consumption can cause nodes to malfunction or even lead to system crashes. Node power consumption is related to node workload, wireless signal transmission distance and quality, and mobility. Optimizing network topology, routing selection, and energy management can address node power consumption issues.

Wireless networks are fragile due to multiple factors, including signal interference, channel capacity, packet loss, security issues, mobility, and power consumption. These issues affect network performance, reliability, security, and user experience. Wireless networks require technologies and strategies like adaptive adjustment, routing selection, energy management, and encryption authentication to overcome these challenges.

7.3   WLAN AND INHERENT INSECURITY

Wireless Local Area Networks (WLANs) have become ubiquitous in our daily lives, providing us with the convenience of wireless connectivity and enabling us to work or access information from anywhere within the range of an access point. However, with this convenience comes inherent security risks that must be addressed to ensure the safety and protection of users and their data. We will explore the inherent security vulnerabilities of WLANs and the measures that can be taken to mitigate these risks. We will examine the various types of attacks that WLANs are susceptible to, and discuss the security protocols commonly used to protect WLANs, including Wired Equivalent Privacy (WEP), Wi-Fi Protected Access (WPA), and WPA2. By understanding the inherent security risks of WLANs and implementing best practices for secure WLAN use, users and organizations can minimize the risk of security breaches and protect sensitive information from unauthorized access and theft.

7.3.1   Infrastructure Attacks

WLAN Frames

The 802.11 protocol defines the data link layer, which can be divided into the logical link control sublayer and the media access control layer. The main functions of the logical link control sublayer are to ensure transmission reliability and control, segment and reassemble data packets, and transmit data packets in order. The media access control layer defines how data packets are transmitted on the medium, providing functions such as line control and traffic control. The 802.11 frame uses four address fields to have multiple functionalities, with different types of frames using different address fields.

Frame Control: The interpretation of the four address fields is affected by the ToDS and FromDS fields. Type indicates the type of frame, with 00 for management frames, 01 for control frames, and 10 for data frames. The SubType field indicates the subtype of the frame.

Duration: Records the network allocation vector, with the value representing the estimated number of microseconds of medium used for the current transmission.

Address: Address1, Address2, Address3, and Address4 are all MAC identifiers with different meanings in different network types. Address1 usually represents the address of the receiving end. Still, the receiving end may not necessarily be the destination address and may be an intermediate station responsible for processing the frame. Address2 represents the address of the sender. Address3 is used for access points and distributed system filtering, depending on the network type. Address4 is relatively rare and only used in wireless bridges.

Sequence Control: This field is used to reassemble fragments and discard duplicates. It comprises a 4-bit fragment number and a 12-bit sequence number (SN). A sequence number is assigned when delivered to the MAC layer from the upper layer. The value of this field is the counter of the delivered frames modulo 4096, with a maximum value of 4095. The counter's value is incremented by 1 for each upper-layer packet processed. If an upper-layer packet is segmented, the sequence numbers of the frame fragments are the same. This field is important in detecting fake APs in attack detection systems.

Frame Body: Carries data and transmits upper-layer payloads between stations. Frames are usually not padded to the minimum length.

FCS: Verifies all fields and the body of the MAC header. As mentioned above, there are three types of 802.11 frames: management, control, and data. Each frame type can be divided into multiple subtypes, with the Type and SubType fields in the MAC header distinguishing between them.

As mentioned above, there are three types of 802.11 frames: management, control, and data. Each frame type can be divided into multiple subtypes, which are differentiated by the Type and SubType fields in the MAC header.

Wireless LAN sniffing technique:

1. According to the TCP/IP protocol, data packets are encapsulated before being sent. Communication between two computers relies on MAC addresses rather than IP addresses, and the MAC address of the target computer is obtained through ARP protocol broadcasting and saved in the MAC address table, which is periodically updated. During this period, the computer will not broadcast address information to obtain the target MAC address, which gives intruders an opportunity.

2. When a computer wants to send data to another, it first searches its ARP address table based on the IP address. If there is no MAC information for the target computer, it triggers an ARP broadcast to address the data until the target computer returns its address message. Once the MAC information for the target computer is in the address table, the computer directly encapsulates the data link layer of the Ethernet address header and sends it out. The system clears the MAC address table to prevent incorrect data from being present in the MAC address table after a specified period. It broadcasts to obtain a new address list. Additionally, new ARP broadcasts can unconditionally overwrite the original MAC address table.

Assuming that two computers, A and B, communicate on a local area network, and computer C wants to obtain the communication data between them as an eavesdropper, it must find a way to insert itself into the data transmission line between the two computers. In a one-to-one exchange network, computer C must act as an intermediate device to allow the data to pass through it. To achieve this goal, computer C must forge false ARP packets.

There are two types of ARP addressing packets: ARP query packets, used to send addressing information, which the source machine uses to broadcast addressing information, and ARP response packets from the target machine, which are used to respond to the source machine with its MAC address. In the presence of eavesdropping, if computer C wants to eavesdrop on the communication between computer A and computer B, it forges a false ARP response packet with an IP address of computer B and a MAC address of computer C and sends it to computer A. This

action resulted in computer A's MAC address table updating incorrectly
to associate computer B's IP address with computer C's MAC address.
As a result, the system obtains computer C's MAC address using the IP
address, and the data is sent to computer C, which is now in a listening
role. However, this will cause a situation where computer B, the original
target, will not receive data. Therefore, computer C, which acts as a
fake data receiver, must also act as a forwarding agent to return the
data sent from computer A to computer B, allowing the communication
between the two computers to proceed normally. Thus, computer C forms
a communication link with computers A and B. For computers, A and
B, computer C always exist transparently, and they do not know that
computer C is eavesdropping on their data transmission. As long as
computer C timely forges false ARP response packets before computer
A sends ARP query packets again, it can maintain this communication
link and obtain continuous data recording. At the same time, it will not
cause communication anomalies for the eavesdropped parties.

The behavior of computer C in eavesdropping on the data communication between computers A and B is called "ARP spoofing" or "ARP
attacking". In a real environment, ARP spoofing and sniffing computer
A's data usually also sniffs computer B's data. As long as computer C
sends a forged ARP response packet disguised as computer B to computer A while sending a forged ARP response packet disguised as computer A to computer B, it can act as a two-way proxy and insert itself
into the communication link between the two computers.

7.3.2 DoS Attack

DoS is a typical attack that disrupts service availability. It is not aimed
at gaining system privileges. According to NIST SP 800-61, denial of
service is a behavior that uses system resources such as CPU, memory,
bandwidth, or disk space to prevent or weaken the authorized use of a
network, system, or application.

Denial of service attacks usually exploit weaknesses in transmission protocols, system vulnerabilities, or service vulnerabilities to launch
large-scale attacks on target systems, consuming available system resources, bandwidth resources, etc., with a massive amount of reasonable
request packets that exceed the target's processing capacity, causing
program buffer overflow errors, making it unable to handle legitimate
user requests, unable to provide normal services, and ultimately causing network services to collapse or even systems to crash. Early denial

Table 7.2 State Description, Client Behavior, Remarks

State	Description	Client Behavior	Remarks
1	Unauthenticated, unassociated	Initial state, it has not passed the verification or established an association with the AP.	The wireless client searches and tries to connect to the AP.
2	Authenticated, unassociated	Passed the authentication, but not associated with the AP.	Wireless clients are allowed to connect (AP automatically assigns address).
3	Authenticated and associated	Passed the verification and has been associated with the AP.	The wireless client has entered the correct connection password while waiting

of service attacks mainly exploited the defects of TCP/IP protocols or applications, causing the target system or application to crash. Current denial-of-service attacks attempt to exhaust system resources to prevent the target system from providing services to authorized users.

In wireless networks, DoS attacks can attack clients and access points by sending special packets to change the association status between clients and access points. Ultimately, DDoS causes legitimate clients to be unable to establish normal communication connections with access points. IEEE 802.11 defines a client-state machine with four states representing client authentication and association status, as shown in Table 7.2. Clients can only communicate on the wireless network after successfully entering state three by completing the association. Clients in states one and two can only join the wireless network for wireless communication after passing authentication and association.

There are several types of denial-of-service attacks in WLAN-based wireless networks:

1. De-authentication Flood Attack. The attack involves sending de-authentication frames to the client's unicast address, which deceives the client and turns it into an unassociated/unauthenticated state, quickly interrupting the connection between the access point and the client. The attacker usually sends continuous de-authentication frames to keep the client disconnected.

2. Authentication Flood Attack. This attack targets clients that have already authenticated and established a connection with the access point and causes them to disconnect. Since the number of client connections to a wireless access point is limited, when the number of connected clients exceeds the maximum value, the access point will refuse connection requests from other clients.

3. Beacon Flood Attack. This attack involves forging many beacon frames, with SSID and MAC information being forged and the attacker broadcasting these beacon frames. When a client attempts to establish a connection with an access point, it cannot find the truly available access point from many beacon frame information, causing it to fail to connect to the local area network.

4. Disassociation Flood Attack. This attack is different from the de-authentication flood attack. Instead, it deceives the client by sending disassociation frames to the client's unicast address, forcing the client into an unassociated/unauthenticated state. The attacker must continue the attack to keep the client in this state.

7.3.3 Confidence Attack

A confidence attack is a social engineering attack in which an attacker gains access to sensitive or confidential information by pretending to be someone authorized to access such information. The goal of a confidence attack is to exploit the trust and confidence of the victim to trick them into revealing information that they should not disclose. There are several types of confidence attacks, including:

1. Phishing: In a phishing attack, an attacker sends an email that appears to be from a legitimate source (such as a bank or a social media platform) and asks the victim to click on a link or provide sensitive information such as login credentials or credit card details.

2. Spear Phishing: Similar to phishing, the attacker targets a specific individual or organization with customized emails that appear to be from a trusted source.

3. Pretexting: In a pretexting attack, the attacker creates a fake scenario or pretext to trick the victim into revealing sensitive information. For example, an attacker might pretend to be a customer

service representative and ask the victim for their account information to resolve a supposed issue.

4. Baiting: Baiting involves offering the victim something they want (such as a free USB drive) in exchange for sensitive information.

5. Tailgating: In a tailgating attack, the attacker follows the victim into a secure area (such as an office building) by pretending to be an authorized person or simply asking the victim to hold the door open.

6. Impersonation: In an impersonation attack, the attacker pretends to be someone the victim knows and trusts (such as a colleague or a friend) and asks for sensitive information.

These attacks can be conducted through various channels, such as email, phone calls, text messages, and social media. It is essential to be aware of these attacks and to take appropriate precautions to protect sensitive information.

7.3.4 Other WLAN Security Threats

APT Attacks

APT attacks are targeted attacks for commercial or political purposes. They aim to obtain important information from an organization or country, especially targeting critical infrastructure and units, such as energy, power, finance, and defense industries. APT attacks often use various techniques, including some of the most advanced methods and social engineering, and penetrate the network for a long time to gradually gain internal network permissions. They then lurk in the internal network for a long time, constantly collecting various information until they can steal important intelligence.

The most authoritative definition of APT attacks comes from the NIST in the United States, which defines the four elements of APT attacks as follows:

- **Attacker:** An adversary with advanced expertise and abundant resources.

- **Attack Purpose:** To disrupt an organization's critical infrastructure or hinder a particular mission.

- **Attack Method:** To use various methods to establish and extend footholds on the target infrastructure to obtain information.

- **Attack Process:** To lurk in the target network for a long time, repeatedly attacking the target while adapting to the defenses and maintaining high-level interaction to achieve the attack purpose.

The APT attack process can generally be summarized into three stages: the pre-attack preparation stage, the attack intrusion stage, and the persistent attack stage, which can be further divided into five steps: intelligence gathering, breach of defenses, channel establishment, lateral infiltration, information collection, and ex-filtration.

1. **Information Gathering** Before launching an attack, attackers gather extensive information on the target organization's network systems and employees. Various methods are used for information gathering, including search engines, web crawlers, network stealth scanning, social engineering, and other methods. Information sources include employees' microblogs, blogs, social networking sites, company websites, and even purchasing relevant information (such as company directories) through certain channels. By analyzing this information, attackers can understand the applications and defense software the target uses, the internal organization structure and personnel relationships, and the location of core assets.

   Attackers then search for vulnerabilities in the specific application software used by the target (usually internal employees) and design specific Trojans/malware to bypass defenses in combination with the antivirus software and firewall used by the target. At the same time, attackers set up intrusion servers and perform technical preparations.

2. **Breach of Defenses** After completing information gathering and technical preparations, attackers start to use Trojans/malware to attack specific employees' personal computers, mainly through the following methods:

   (a) **Social engineering methods**, such as email attacks. Attackers steal the email accounts of people related to specific employees (such as leaders, colleagues, friends, etc.) and pretend to send emails with malicious code attachments to the employee. Once the attachment is opened, the employee's computer is infected with malware.

(b) **Remote vulnerability attack methods**, such as website Trojan attacks. Attackers place a Trojan on a website that employees frequently visit. When the employee visits the website again, the personal computer is attacked by web page code. Since these malicious software targets unknown system vulnerabilities and is specially processed, existing antivirus software and firewalls cannot detect them. Attackers can gradually gain personal computer permissions and eventually control them.

3. **Channel Establishment:** After breaking through the defenses and controlling the employee's computer, attackers establish command and control channels between the employee's computer and the intrusion server. Command and control channels typically use protocols such as HTTP/HTTPS to bypass security devices such as firewalls. Once attackers establish the channel, they send control commands to check whether the implanted malware has been detected and upgrade the malware version before it is detected by the security software, reducing the likelihood of being discovered.

4. **Lateral Infiltration:** Intruding and controlling employees' personal computers is not the ultimate goal of attackers. Attackers will use various penetration methods, such as password eavesdropping and vulnerability attacks, to further invade more personal computers and servers inside the organization while continually elevating their permissions to control more computers and servers. This continues until they gain control of core computers and servers.

5. **Information Collection and Ex-filtration:** Attackers often lurk for a long time and continuously perform lateral infiltration within the network, using methods such as port scanning to obtain valuable information on servers or devices and commands to obtain document list information on personal computers. Attackers use a particular server as a temporary storage server for data and then use the established covert communication channel to transmit information by organizing, compressing, encrypting, and packaging it. After obtaining this information, attackers analyze and identify

the data and make final judgments, even implementing network attacks to cause damage.

APT attacks have five significant characteristics different from traditional network attacks: strong targeting, strict organization, long duration, high concealment, and indirect attacks.

1. Strong targeting

   APT attacks must have clear targets. Most organizations possess rich data/intellectual property, and the data obtained is usually commercial secrets, national security data, intellectual property, etc. Compared with traditional attacks that steal personal information, APT attacks only focus on pre-designated targets, and all attack methods are only aimed at specific targets and specific systems with strong targeting.

2. Strict organization

   APT attacks can bring huge business benefits when successful. Therefore, attackers usually exist in an organized form, formed by skilled hackers to form a group, cooperate and plan long-term attacks. They have sufficient resources in economics and technology and the conditions and abilities to focus on APT research for a long time.

3. Long duration

   APT attacks have strong persistence. After a long period of preparation and planning, attackers usually lurk in the target network for several months or even years and launch continuous attacks through repeated penetrations, constantly improving attack paths and methods, such as zero-day vulnerability attacks.

4. High concealment

   APT attacks can bypass the target network's defense system based on the target's characteristics and steal data or covertly cause damage. In the information gathering stage, attackers often use search engines, advanced crawlers, and data leaks to penetrate, making it difficult for the victim to detect continuously. In the attack stage, based on the results of sniffing the target, attackers design and develop highly targeted Trojan horses and other malicious software to bypass the target network defense system and launch a covert attack.

5. Indirect attacks

APT attacks are different from traditional network attacks in their direct attack methods. They usually use third-party websites or servers as springboards to deploy malicious programs or Trojan horses to penetrate the target. The malicious program or Trojan horse lurks in the target network and can be remotely controlled by the attacker or inadvertently triggered and launched by the victim.

Ad Hoc

Wireless communication networks have two primary networking modes: infrastructure and Ad Hoc. Infrastructure mode integrates existing wired networks with wireless LAN architecture, enabling mobile devices to access the wired network infrastructure through the nearest base station or access point in the communication range to achieve device interconnection. The infrastructure mode requires a central control node with router functions to handle routing and switching between other devices, while ordinary nodes do not have routing functions. This method is widely used today, with mobile cellular networks and wireless LANs belonging to this type of wireless network.

However, the infrastructure mode network has limitations when it comes to special situations that require rapid and temporary networking without network infrastructure support, such as battlefield military communication, fieldwork, crisis relief, and temporary networking. A special communication technology called Ad Hoc wireless self-organizing network communication technology has been developed to address this matter. Unlike infrastructure mode, Ad Hoc networks do not rely on network infrastructure and are composed of mobile devices. Nodes in Ad Hoc networks can directly interconnect without the need for routers or APs. Moreover, the Ad Hoc network is a multi-hop network, and each device node in the network is a host and a router, completing the functions of running various applications and discovering and maintaining routes to other nodes. If a device node needs to communicate with other nodes outside its coverage range, it requires the relay of intermediate nodes. Even if a node fails, it will not affect the normal communication of other nodes, and the entire network can still operate normally.

Ad Hoc networks can support mobile node communication as an independent network and can be combined with other networks. For example, nodes in an Ad Hoc network can communicate with Internet network nodes through Internet gateway nodes, effectively extending Internet services to areas without infrastructure. Ad Hoc's characteristics effectively compensate for the shortcomings of infrastructure networks, providing a reliable and flexible alternative for temporary and emergency communication needs.

Wireless Fake AP Attacks

With the increasing popularity of wireless networks, various types of attacks have emerged. The most prominent problem is the fake AP attack. This attack installs an AP in the network without the administrator's permission. The fake AP has the identical SSID as the real AP, and if the attacker wants to simulate more realistically, they can also forge MAC and channel information. When users access the wireless network, they need to provide a password. According to the 802.11 protocol, users only need a password when connecting to the network. When they connect later, the client device will automatically select and connect to the network based on the connection history and signal strength. During a fake AP attack, malicious attackers collect enough information about the legitimate AP, establish a fake access point with the identical SSID and MAC as the legitimate access point, and to attract users to connect to it, the attacker can set the encryption authentication method of the fake access point to an open state or a more robust signal strength. Wireless client devices are highly likely to connect to this type of network when automatically selecting a network connection, which is automatically completed, and users usually do not receive prompts.

Once users connect to the fake AP, all traffic generated will be forwarded by the fake AP. Data such as usernames, passwords, credit card information, images, and web pages browsed by users during internet access will be intercepted by malicious attackers. If there is unencrypted data, attackers can directly obtain it. Moreover, attackers can tamper with this information, intercept the information submitted by the user, modify it, and then send it. More professional attackers can also manipulate domain name resolution servers, control routers, and perform other network phishing attacks. For example, attackers can forge online payment web pages, which are incredibly harmful.

Meanwhile, conducting fake AP attacks is very simple for attackers. Various software can achieve this function; even people without professional skills can quickly learn it under guidance. A low-specification device is sufficient to conduct AP attacks: a laptop, router, or any specific device can be used. If a laptop is used, the attacker must install special software with two network cards: one card is used for ordinary work to access the Internet, and the other is used to simulate the access point and emit signals to attract victims to connect. At the same time, the laptop needs to set up the corresponding domain and dynamic host configuration service, open traffic forwarding, so that when the victim connects to this network, an IP address can be assigned to the victim. Attackers can also directly use routers for forgery and change the router's MAC to the same as the device to be forged.

7.4 COMMON WIRELESS NETWORK SECURITY TECHNOLOGIES

Wireless networks have become an essential part of our daily lives, providing us with the convenience of wireless connectivity and enabling us to work or access information from anywhere within the range of an access point. However, as wireless networks become more ubiquitous, they become more vulnerable to security threats. Therefore, organizations and individuals must implement effective security measures to protect their wireless networks and the sensitive data transmitted over them. Many wireless network security technologies are being deployed, including encryption protocols, authentication mechanisms, and intrusion detection and prevention systems. By understanding these technologies, users can effectively secure their wireless networks and minimize the risk of security breaches.

7.4.1 Hidden Service Set Identifier

What is SSID?

A WLAN network is identified by its Service Set Identifier (SSID) , which sets it apart from neighboring networks. Wireless networks have a special identity, known as the SSID, much like people have names. BSSID and ESSID are two different types of the SSID. The BSSID is mainly concealed from end users and is used for administration and maintenance purposes. The ESSID, on the other hand, is the SSID that users often use and recognise when joining to a network. Network administrators can divide a wireless LAN into numerous sub-networks that each require independent identity verification by defining different SSIDs. As a result, the user experience, flexibility, and security within the WLAN network are all enhanced.

Why do we need SSID?

For end users, a well-configured SSIDs can optimize the user's internet experience:

1. When users search for accessible wireless networks, they can see a list of SSIDs. Just as we would add a contact name to a difficult-to-remember phone number in our address book, a clear and understandable SSID can help end users find the network they want to connect to more quickly. In a WLAN network, assigning the same SSID to numerous APs might give users the ability to roam freely inside these APs' coverage areas without disrupting network services.

For network administrators, configuring different SSIDs can enhance the flexibility and security of the WLAN network:

1. Dividing a WLAN into sub-networks with different SSIDs configurations allows users with different identities to access the corresponding networks based on different SSIDs, thereby achieving differentiation of access rights and network functions. For example, in an enterprise, administrators can provide different network services for employees and visitors through multiple SSIDs, with the employee SSID as "employee" and the visitor SSID as "guest".

BSSID and ESSID

SSID has two types: BSSID and ESSID, which are used to identify the BSS and ESS, respectively.

For end users, the name of the wireless network they find is the ESSID, which we usually refer to as the SSID. BSSID is typically not perceived by end users and is mainly used for managing and maintaining wireless networks and locating problems.

The 802.11 protocol standard stipulates that the minimum unit of a wireless LAN is the BSS, which represents the coverage area of an AP. Within a BSS service area, STAs can communicate with each other.

Each BSS has a BSSID. The BSSID is the AP's wireless radio's MAC address (48 bits). In a multi-SSID scenario, multiple Virtual Access Points (VAPs) can be created on a single AP to provide wireless network access services with different SSIDs for each VAP. In this case, the BSSID is the MAC address of each VAP on the AP. The BSSID corresponds to each VAP, and the specific VAP can be quickly located based on the BSSID.

Application of SSID

1. Sub-network division based on multiple SSIDs

   Early 802.11 chips only supported APs to create a single SSID, which provided users with a single WLAN network. However, as the number of WLAN users increased, a single network could not meet the needs of users with different identities.

   Current APs typically support multi-SSID functionality: multiple VAPs can be created on a single AP, each VAP setting a different SSID for specific user groups and configuring different security policies, access authentication, rate limiting, access control, MU-MIMO, OFDMA, etc. In this case, a WLAN network is divided into multiple sub-networks with different SSIDs, each sub-network providing "customized" services for its user group.

   For example, different sub-networks can be configured for employees and visitors in an enterprise:

   - Employee network SSID is "employee": the hidden SSID function is enabled, so only wireless users who know the network name can connect to this wireless network; authentication is required when accessing.

   - Visitor network SSID is "guest": the SSID is not hidden; no authentication is required when accessing.

2. Roaming capability based on SSID

   Since the coverage area of a single AP is limited, an enterprise's WLAN network generally provides roaming capability to end users by configuring multiple APs with identical SSID. There is usually some overlap between the signal coverage areas of each AP to ensure uninterrupted communication among users. The following example illustrates the roaming process of an employee's mobile phone in an enterprise:

   - The wireless network is covered in the company, and the employee uses his/her mobile phone to search for and connect to the wireless network with the SSID "employee" in the front lobby. Currently, the ESSID is "employee", and the BSSID is the MAC address of the VAP on the front lobby AP.

- As the employee moves towards the office, the mobile phone enters the coverage area of the office AP.

- When the signal strength meets the requirements, the device automatically roams to the new AP's "employee" network based on the SSID, achieving smooth switching of user services. Currently, the ESSID remains "employee", but the BSSID changes to the MAC address of the VAP on the office AP.

7.4.2   Wireless Network Physical Address Filtering

Wireless MAC address filtering function allows or denies computers in the wireless network to access the WAN based on their MAC addresses, effectively controlling the Internet access permissions of users in the wireless network. Select Wireless Settings - Wireless MAC Address Filtering from the menu to view or add MAC address filtering entries for the wireless network. The wireless MAC address filtering function allows or denies computers in the wireless network to access the WAN based on their MAC addresses, effectively controlling the Internet access permissions of users in the wireless network. The Add New Entry button can add new filtering rules or edit or delete old filtering rules using the Edit and Delete links.

1. MAC address filtering function: Please select whether to enable the router's wireless network MAC address filtering function here.

2. Filtering rules: Please select the MAC address filtering rules that apply to the MAC address entry list below.

3. MAC address: Refers to the host's MAC address in the wireless network that needs access restriction.

4. Status: This item displays the status of the MAC address filtering entry. "Enabled" means that the setting entry is enabled, and "Disabled" means the setting entry is not enabled.

5. Description: This item displays a brief description of the host.

6. Add new entry: Click on this item to add a new MAC address filtering entry in the subsequent interface.

7. Enable all entries: Click this button to enable all entries in the table.

8. Disable all entries: Click this button to disable all entries in the table.

9. Delete all entries: Click this button to delete all entries in the table.

7.4.3 Wired Equivalent Privacy

WEP is a security protocol or algorithm created for Wi-Fi or IEEE 802.11 wireless networks. Wireless is a protocol in which electromagnetic signals transmit data through the air. Since everyone nearby can access the air, anyone can easily access signals and data by sniffing the air. WEP is a wireless LAN security mechanism for access control, data encryption, and data integrity detection. However, there are security vulnerabilities, and it can only achieve one-way identity authentication between the AP and the terminal.

WEP was part of the IEEE 802.11 standard passed in September 1999, using Rivest Cipher (RC4) stream encryption technology for confidentiality and CRC-32 for data integrity. The standard 64-bit WEP uses a 40-bit key connected to a 24-bit Initialization Vector (IV) for the key used in RC4. When drafting the original WEP standard, the US government limited the length of keys in output restrictions on encryption technology. Once this restriction is lifted, all the prominent vendors shall implement a 128-bit WEP extension agreement using a 104-bit key. The method for users to enter a 128-bit WEP key is usually to use a string of 26 hexadecimal numbers (0–9 and A-F) to represent each character representing 4 bits in the key, $4 \times 26 = 104$ bits, plus 24 bits of IV, which becomes the so-called "128-bit WEP key". Some vendors also provide 256-bit WEP systems. As mentioned earlier, 24 bits are IV, and 232 are used for protection. The typical approach uses 58 hexadecimal numbers to enter ($58 \times 4 = 232$ bits) + 24 IV bits = 256 WEP bits.

Key length is not the main factor in WEP security. Cracking longer keys requires intercepting more packets, but some active attacks can generate the required traffic. Many WEP systems require keys to be specified in hexadecimal format, and some users may choose keys that can be spelled out in English words using the limited hexadecimal character set of 0–9 A-F, such as C0DE C0DE C0DE C0DE. Such keys are easy to guess.

In August 2001, Fluhrer et al. published a WEP cryptanalysis using RC4 encryption and IV usage characteristics. After eavesdropping on the network for a few hours, the RC4 key could be cracked. This attack was quickly implemented, and automated tools were also released. This attack can be carried out using a personal computer, off-the-shelf store hardware, and free software.

WEP security provides different functions like confidentiality, integrity, and encryption. WEP uses RC4 for confidentiality and encryption and CRC-32 for integrity. The standard 64-bit WEP uses a 40-bit key contaminated by a 23-bit initialization vector or IV.

7.4.4 Other Security Technologies

WAPI technology

Wireless LAN Authentication and Privacy Infrastructure (WAPI) is a wireless LAN authentication and privacy infrastructure, a security protocol, and a mandatory security standard for wireless LANs in China. The State Key Laboratory of Integrated Services Networks of Xidian University proposed it.

Like infrared, Bluetooth, GPRS, CDMA1X and other protocols, WAPI is a wireless transmission protocol, but it is only a transmission protocol in WLAN, and it is a technology in the same field as the 802.11 transmission protocol.

WAPI includes two parts: WLAN Authentication Infrastructure (WAI) and WLAN Privacy Infrastructure (WPI). WAI and WPI implement user identity authentication and encryption of business data transmission. WAI uses a public key password system and public key certificates to authenticate STAs and APs in the WLAN system. WPI uses symmetric encryption algorithms to implement encryption and decryption operations on MAC layer MSDUs.

1. **WAPI access control entities**

   WAPI access control includes the following four entities.

   - Authentication Service Unit (ASU): The basic function is to manage user certificates and authenticate user identity. It is a crucial component of the WAI authentication infrastructure based on public key cryptography. The certificates managed by ASU include the public key and signature of the certificate issuer, and the signature of the certificate holders, STA and AP, using WAPI's unique digital signature algorithm.

- Authenticator Entity (AE): Provides authentication operations to the authentication requester entity before accessing services. This entity resides in an AP device or AC device.

- Authentication SUpplicant Entity (ASUE): The entity that requests authentication operation before accessing services. This entity resides in the STA.

- Authentication Service Entity (ASE): Provides mutual authentication services for the authenticator and the requester entities. This entity resides in the ASU.

2. **WAPI Information Elements**

To enable an STA to recognize the WAPI wireless security mechanism, WAPI information elements are carried in beacon frames, association request frames, reassociation request frames, and probe request frames. For an AP, it is necessary to include the corresponding WAPI information elements in the beacon frame and probe response frame based on the current WAPI configuration on the AP. At the same time, association request frames and reassociation request frames are parsed, and subsequent negotiations with the STA can only be carried out if they comply with the current WAPI configuration on the AP.

3. **WAPI Authentication and Key Negotiation**

There are two ways to authenticate and manage keys in WAPI: certificate-based and Pre-Shared Key (PSK)-based. The entire process includes certificate authentication, unicast key negotiation, and multicast key announcement if certificate-based authentication is used. If PSK-based authentication is used, the process only involves unicast key negotiation and multicast key announcement.

4. **WAPI Message Encapsulation and Encryption/Decryption**

The WPI confidentiality infrastructure performs encryption and decryption processing on the MAC sublayer's MPDU but does not perform encryption and decryption processing on the WAI protocol group.

Virtual Private Network

A VPN is a technology that establishes a secure private network over the Internet or other public networks. VPNs can achieve remote access, encrypted communication, and other functions in enterprise or personal networks.

VPN technology uses encryption and tunneling protocols to ensure security and privacy. Encryption converts data into an unintelligible form to ensure the confidentiality of transmitted data. Tunneling protocols establish a communication tunnel on the public network, and data is transmitted through this tunnel.

The main types of VPN technology include remote-access VPNs and site-to-site VPNs. Remote access VPNs are used to establish remote work, remote education, remote diagnosis, and other applications over the Internet, and users can connect remotely through VPN client software. Site-to-site VPNs are used to establish private networks between enterprises, branches, and headquarters and have the advantages of high security and fast transmission speed. In site-to-site VPNs, the data center usually serves as the core of the VPN network, and VPN services are implemented by coordinating devices and protocols.

VPN technology has the following advantages:

1. High security. VPN technology ensures the security of data transmission through encryption and tunneling protocols, providing privacy protection and data confidentiality.

2. Flexibility. VPN technology can be customized according to different needs, such as establishing remote access VPNs, site-to-site VPNs, etc. and can quickly establish secure connections in different scenarios.

3. Remote access: VPNs enable remote access to corporate networks, allowing employees to work from home or on the go. This can increase productivity and flexibility while maintaining a secure connection to the corporate network.

4. Cost-effectiveness. Through VPN technology, enterprises and individuals can establish private networks on public networks without investing in expensive dedicated network equipment, reducing network equipment's purchase and maintenance costs.

VPN technology is a secure and reliable Internet communication solution suitable for individuals, enterprises, organizations, and other scenarios.

Port Access Control Technology

Port access control restricts access to specific ports on a computer or network. Each network application uses specific ports to communicate with clients, and port access control technology can restrict which computers or devices can access these specific ports.

1. Port classification: Each application on the network uses different ports for communication, such as web applications that use port 80/443, SMTP that uses port 25, SSH that uses port 22, etc. Port access control technology can classify each port and control access to each port.

2. Port Access Control List (PACL): Port access control technology uses a PACL to control which computers or devices can access ports. The PACL is a network security control mechanism based on ACLs, consisting of rules to control port access.

3. Rule matching: PACL rules filter network access requests based on conditions such as source IP address, destination IP address, source port, and destination port. When a network access request is matched to a rule, the PACL controls whether the request can pass based on the specified action (allow or deny).

4. Range control: In addition to individual ports, PACL can also control access requests within a range of ports. This approach can provide more detailed access control rather than limiting it to a single port.

5. Access logs: Port access control technology can capture and record information about access requests for auditing and security analysis. Access logs can record information such as source address, destination address, timestamp, action, and rule for each access request, providing necessary log information for security personnel.

   The port access control technology is a crucial network security measure that can restrict access to specific ports on a network, protecting the network from malicious attacks.

Pre-Shared Key Technology

PSK technology refers to assigning a shared key to participants in advance for authentication and encrypted communication during network communication [283]. This method has the advantages of high security and fast communication speed compared to traditional public key infrastructure.

The principle of PSK technology is that before the network is established, all participants need to negotiate a shared key and distribute it to all participants. In subsequent communication, participants use this key for encryption and decryption to ensure the confidentiality and integrity of communication content.

PSK technology is mainly used in scenarios where data is transmitted, such as WLANs and VPNs, for data encryption and authentication. In WLANs, PSK refers to a key shared between the device connecting to the WLAN through the WiFi hotspot and the WiFi hotspot itself, for instance WiFi-Protocol Access (WPA/WPA2). In VPNs, PSK refers to a key shared by all participants when establishing a VPN connection.

The pre-shared key should be kept confidential and only known by authorized parties who are involved in the communication. The key should be resistant to guessing and brute-force attacks to maintain security in communication channel. They key safety and distribution is relying on the security of PSK technology. If the key is intercepted during transmission, network security will be threatened. Therefore, when using PSK technology, appropriate key length and unpredictable random number generators should be used, and the key should be distributed securely to ensure that only legitimate participants can obtain the key.

7.5 SUMMARY

This chapter introduced wireless network, WLAN topology, wireless network classification, and standards. In Section 7.2, we take an overview of wireless network vulnerabilities. Different layer vulnerabilities, such as physical, MAC, and network, are introduced. In Section 7.3, we explained the attacks of WLAN and inherent insecurity. Finally, in Section 7.4 we discussed common wireless network security technologies, such as SSID, WEP.

7.6 EXERCISES

1. Advanced Persistent Threat (APT) attacks are a type of cyber attack characterized by their persistence, sophistication, and stealth. Effective defense against APT attacks requires a combination of advanced security technologies, threat intelligence, and best practices in security operations and incident response. Here are the five significant characteristics that make APT attacks different from traditional network attacks:

   - Targeted: APT attacks focus on specific organizations, individuals, or assets. The attackers typically conduct extensive reconnaissance to identify vulnerabilities and weaknesses in their target before launching the attack.

   - Advanced: APT attacks are highly sophisticated, using advanced techniques such as zero-day exploits, custom malware, and social engineering to evade detection and gain access to the target's network.

   - Persistent: APT attacks are persistent, meaning the attackers maintain a long-term presence in the target's network. They may use multiple attack vectors and techniques to maintain access, such as backdoors, command and control servers, and compromised user accounts.

   - Coordinated: APT attacks are often part of a coordinated campaign, with multiple attackers working together to achieve a common goal. The attackers may use different techniques and attack vectors to achieve their objectives, making detecting and defending against the attack challenging.

   - Stealthy: APT attacks are designed to be stealthy, with the attackers taking steps to avoid detection and remaining undetected for as long as possible. They may use encryption, obfuscation, and other techniques to disguise their activities and evade detection by security systems and personnel.

2. What is APT, and what are the characteristics that make it different than normal cyber attacks?

   Advanced Persistent Threats (APTs) are a form of cyber attack that differs from conventional attacks in numerous ways. APTs are generally conducted by well-financed and highly skilled attackers with a specific objective and willing to commit substantial amounts of time and resources to achieve it. APTs are distinguished by their covert nature and persistence since they commonly involve a series of planned attacks over an extended period to acquire sensitive data or damage a targeted organization. This academic paper intends to offer a research-based explanation of APTs by analyzing their features, the methods employed by the attackers, and their effects on organizations.

APT attacks have five clear characteristics, namely:

- Strong targeting

  APT attacks have clear targets and often use multiple attack vectors, including social engineering, spear phishing, and exploitation of vulnerabilities in software and hardware. They have sufficient resources in economics and technology to focus on targets for a long period of time. Preparation before the attack may take longer, and the attack target methods are only aimed at specific targets and specific systems with strong targeting.

- Strict organization

  The tactics attackers use in APTs often differ from those used in traditional cyber attacks. APTs are typically carried out by well-resourced and highly skilled attackers motivated by specific goals. Attackers often know the target organization's infrastructure, systems, and employees extensively. This allows them to develop a targeted attack strategy tailored to the specific organization.

- Long duration

  APT attacks have strong persistence. After a long period of preparation and planning, attackers usually lurk in the target network for several months or even years and launch continuous attacks through repeated penetrations, constantly improving attack paths and methods, such as zero-day vulnerability attacks.

- Hard to discover

  APTs can be difficult to detect and mitigate, as attackers often use advanced techniques to remain undetected. Victims find it hard to know they are under attack as they may bypass the organization's defense system, steal data, or covertly cause damage. The information-gathering stage is the hardest duration to detect by the victims that are being targeted, not even during the attack launched, but only during being penetrated by the attackers.

- Indirect attack

  The attackers will use third-party websites or servers as stepping stones to deploy malicious programs, such as Trojan horses, to penetrate the target. The victims sometimes do not pay attention to Trojan horses' presence until being exploited.

3. What is the difference between BSSID and ESSID?

   BSSID (Basic Service Set Identifier) is a unique identifier assigned to each wireless access point (AP) in a wireless network. It is a 48-bit address used to identify individual APs within a wireless network. Wireless clients use the BSSID to identify the AP they want to connect to, and network administrators also use it to manage and troubleshoot wireless networks.

   ESSID (Extended Service Set Identifier) is the name assigned to a wireless network. It is a character string used to identify a wireless network and is typically chosen by the network administrator. Wireless clients use the ESSID to identify the network they want to connect to. Multiple APs can have the same ESSID if they are part of the same wireless network, allowing wireless clients to roam between different APs without reconnecting to a new network.

4. What are the entities included in WAPI access control?

   WAPI (WLAN Authentication and Privacy Infrastructure) access control involves several entities, including:

   - Station (STA): A wireless device communicating with an access point (AP) over a wireless network.
   - Access Point (AP): The wireless network device that provides wireless connectivity to STAs.
   - Authentication Server (AS): The server authenticates STAs before allowing them to access the wireless network.

- Key Management Server (KMS): The server responsible for managing keys used for encryption and decryption of wireless communication.

- Certificate Authority (CA): The entity responsible for issuing digital certificates for authentication and wireless communication encryption.

- Policy Decision Point (PDP): The entity responsible for enforcing access control policies for STAs attempting to access the wireless network.

5. VPN is an established secure network over the internet and public network. Explain what are the advantages of deploying a VPN.

There are several advantages of deploying a Virtual Private Network (VPN):

- High security: VPNs provide a high level of security for internet communication by encrypting data and establishing secure tunnels for communication. This ensures that sensitive data is protected from unauthorized access, interception, and malicious attacks.

- Privacy: VPNs offer privacy protection by masking the user's IP address and location, making it difficult for others to track their online activities. This is particularly important for users who are concerned about their privacy and want to protect their personal data.
Flexibility. VPN technology can be customized according to different needs, such as establishing remote access VPNs, site-to-site VPNs, etc. and can quickly establish secure connections in different scenarios.

- Remote access: VPNs enable remote access to corporate networks, allowing employees to work from home or on the go. This can increase productivity and flexibility while maintaining a secure connection to the corporate network.

- Cost-effective: VPNs are a cost-effective solution for businesses that need to establish secure connections between remote locations or employees. They eliminate the need for expensive dedicated lines and hardware, reducing costs and increasing efficiency.

GLOSSARY

Centralized protocol: refers to a protocol in which a central node in the network coordinates communication between all nodes and decides when each node should send data packets.

Co-channel interference: refers to the interference between signals from different terminals or different base stations in a wireless network.

Confidence Attack: is a social engineering attack in which an attacker gains access to sensitive or confidential information by pretending to be someone authorized to access such information.

Distributed protocol: refers to a protocol in which each node in the network has the same rights and can send data packets simultaneously.

Multi-AP Mode: is the infrastructure mode composed of multiple APs and the DSS that connects them.

Multipath: effect refers to the effect of multiple propagation paths formed by electromagnetic waves due to reflection, refraction, diffraction, and other factors during transmission.

Pre-Shared Key Technology: refers to assigning a shared key to participants in advance for authentication and encrypted communication during network communication.

Service Set Identifier: identifies a WLAN network used to differentiate it from other WLAN networks.

Shadow effect: refers to the impact of obstacles on wireless signal transmission, which prevents the signal from directly reaching the receiver.

Spectrum pollution: refers to the interference of wireless signals during transmission caused by other signals with similar frequencies, affecting the signal's quality and stability.

Weather effects: refer to the influence of meteorological factors on the transmission of wireless signals.

Wireless LAN Authentication and Privacy Infrastructure: is a wireless LAN authentication and privacy infrastructure, a security protocol, and a mandatory security standard for wireless LANs in China.

Wireless Network: is a computer network that uses radio waves to transmit and receive data between devices.

CHAPTER 8

Infrastructure and Hardware Security

Computer infrastructure security plays a crucial role in today's digital age. With the rapid development of digitization, our society relies on various computer systems and networks to support critical businesses and infrastructure. However, this comes with growing threats and risks. This article focuses on exploring computer infrastructure security and how to ensure its safety and stability. Firstly, the importance of computer infrastructure will be discussed. Infrastructure such as power grids, transportation systems, and communication networks rely on computer systems for support and management. The security of these critical systems directly impacts the normal functioning of society and the quality of people's lives. Therefore, protecting the security of computer infrastructure is vital for social stability and economic prosperity. However, computer infrastructure faces various security threats. Network attackers and malicious actors utilize various techniques to disrupt and infiltrate computer systems, steal sensitive information, or cripple critical infrastructure. These threats include computer viruses, malware, phishing attacks, ransomware, and more. Additionally, hardware devices used in infrastructure may also have security vulnerabilities, making them susceptible to attacks. Hence, a series of measures need to be taken to safeguard the security of computer infrastructure. Establishing a robust cybersecurity framework is key to ensuring computer infrastructure security. This includes employing technologies such as firewalls, intrusion detection systems, and security authentication to monitor and prevent potential attacks. Regular vulnerability scanning and security assessments are essential to patch security loopholes and reduce the chances of attacks. Strengthening employee security awareness through training is also crucial since many security incidents result from social engineering and human errors. Encryption technology plays a vital role in securing computer infrastructure. By encrypting data, sensitive information can be protected from theft and tampering. Additionally, implementing flexible access control mechanisms ensures that only authorized personnel can access critical systems and data.

8.1   CURRENT DEVELOPMENT STATUS OF COMPUTER HARDWARE

8.1.1   Concept of Hardware Security

For a significant period, hardware has been recognized as the trusted component that provides support to the entire computer system. It is commonly acknowledged as the abstraction layer responsible for executing instructions received from the software layer. Consequently, research related to hardware security often focuses on the implementation of cryptographic algorithms, utilizing hardware to enhance the computational performance and efficiency of cryptographic applications. The notion of hardware security gained prominence following the emergence of hardware Trojan Horses and the subsequent efforts to mitigate or prevent such threats. Initially, hardware security primarily centered around the design, classification, detection, and isolation of hardware trojans, with untrusted foundries being identified as the main threat. Consequently, the development of hardware Trojan detection methods has typically emphasized the post-silicon stage, aiming to enhance the security of existing testing approaches.

Hardware security has expanded beyond the realm of hardware Trojan Horse detection and now encompasses formal verification methods. While formal methods have long been employed for ensuring security in software programs, they have also proven effective in verifying the security of hardware code, typically written in Hardware Description Language (HDL). These methods have been instrumental in providing advanced security assurances for hardware designs, even in scenarios where attackers may have access to the original design. Moreover, formal methods address the limitations of gold model requirements found in many other hardware detection approaches. However, the construction of security attributes remains an ongoing challenge that hardware security researchers are actively working to resolve. Recent developments in hardware security research have shifted focus from solely detecting hardware Trojan Horses to establishing trusted hardware as a foundation for establishing trust roots. In this context, secure applications leverage the inherent characteristics of hardware devices, despite the potential negative impact on circuit performance.

A growing trend in hardware security involves the development of hardware infrastructures that provide enhanced device protection. There is an urgent need to integrate security, protection, and authentication mechanisms into a new dedicated hardware foundation through a specialized Toolchain. Numerous security-enhanced architectures are currently being developed to address these requirements.

8.1.2 Principles and Strategies of Computer Hardware Security

In a network environment, computer system equipment includes CPUs, storage devices, computer hard drives for data encryption, wireless routers, etc. to ensure the security of computer system equipment. Only when the computer is in a good office environment can the computer system machines and equipment operate reliably. Otherwise, in a network environment with security risks, the safe operation of the computer system machines and equipment cannot be guaranteed. In addition, temperature and environmental humidity, Electrostatic induction problems, magnetic fields and radio waves will cause special hazards to the machinery and equipment of computer systems. If the machinery and equipment of the computer system are in a high-temperature natural environment, it is easy to cause errors or errors in the relevant performance parameters of the hardware configuration of the machinery and equipment, and when the electronic computers are working normally, otherwise it may lead to sudden logical errors or even damage. The key part of electronic computers. When the machinery and equipment of the computer system are in an extremely cold natural environment, some water vapor molecular structures will solidify on the internal circuit board and cable of the computer, which is easy to cause electrochemical corrosion and rust, cable corrosion and short circuit. If the hardware configuration machine equipment is damaged, the computer will not operate normally. In addition, excessive dust in the air can reduce the resistance of circuit boards, and one of the common faults of computers is the charging and discharging of components. In addition, magnetic fields, radio waves, and excessive radiation sources generated in daily natural environments may affect the normal operation of computer system machinery and equipment. In more severe cases, common malfunctions in hardware configuration machinery and equipment can even cause computer paralysis.

1. Principles of Ensuring Computer Hardware Security

   - *From outside to inside:* In general, if there is a malfunction in the external hardware device of a computer, it is easy to find and troubleshoot. Simply test the external hardware device of the computer based on the actual fault situation, and finally test the host hardware device.

   - *From first to last:* In daily maintenance, maintenance personnel often overlook computer power supply failures, but power supply issues pose a major safety threat to computers. When the power supply is low, the computer is prone to multiple failures. Therefore, the computer power supply equipment was first tested.

   - *From first to last:* In daily maintenance, maintenance personnel often overlook computer power supply failures, but power supply issues pose a major safety threat to computers. When the power supply is low, the computer is prone to multiple failures. Therefore, the computer power supply equipment was first tested.

   - *From simple to complex:* When testing computer hardware devices, it is necessary to first check for simple defects. This is because most computer hardware devices have relatively simple defects. Check for other hardware devices, such as poor contact with network card slots, excessive dust inside the host, etc.

2. Strategies for Ensuring Computer Hardware Security

   - *Security microprocessor:* Security microcontrollers are an important component of computer system security protection equipment and are also important for ensuring the security of computer software. When the security microcontroller receives a system software program flow command for data encryption, it will immediately decrypt the command and execute it according to the decrypted command rules. Electronic computer microcontrollers (intermediate control components) can obtain operational code for data encryption and perform decryption and command execution tasks within a specific time range. A secure microcontroller can prevent external intruders from monitoring the microcontroller's purge of program flow, as it is not easy to display system software program flow commands after decrypting the login password. In addition, the data information parsed by the security microcontroller has been encrypted once before being stored. Although electronic computers can grant access restrictions to clients, secure microcontrollers can prevent authorized clients from forging the system bus. The system software application software must transmit encrypted data to the network information security microcontroller to perform data information decryption. The decrypted data information can only be transmitted to the authenticated website program process and ultimately stored in the protected storage area of the electronic computer to prevent other system software program processes from being browsed or activated.

- *Fully encrypted hard drive:* Computer hard disk with full data encryption function is a key component of computer system security protection equipment. Its function is to encrypt all data information on the computer's hard drive. Electronic computers have complete data encryption functions to prevent external personnel from browsing data information on disk drives. It can be encrypted based on file encryption software or hard drive hardware.

- *Maintain network environment:* Maintaining the network environment is one of the important ways to ensure the safe operation of computer hardware. In the current network environment, many network viruses enter computer systems through various channels. Therefore, in order to ensure the security of computer hardware, relevant personnel should pay high attention to the protection of the network environment. At present, relevant personnel can use various means to monitor the network environment accordingly. For example, through network monitoring methods, they can monitor the data interaction in the current operating network environment, and also conduct corresponding troubleshooting on all data. They can timely discover files with viruses, thereby informing users and allowing them to delete these files in a timely manner. In addition, in addition to network monitoring methods, relevant personnel can also use some software to directly delete files with viruses. However, in order to avoid accidentally deleting important files, relevant technical personnel use certain means to notify users after finding the files with viruses, and the users decide whether to delete them at their own discretion.

- *Accelerate the development of Antivirus software:* At present, many Antivirus software is widely used in computer hardware security. In fact, no matter what kind of virus it is, it is actually a kind of program code, which enables users to check the files inside the computer through effective Antivirus software, so as to eliminate virus attacks. At present, the Antivirus software applied in the market can mainly achieve two purposes, one is to check the files inside the computer in time, and the other is to remove the files carrying viruses. The computer file check function can help relevant users find files with viruses in a timely manner. Compared with manual search, it is more accurate, faster, and easier to operate. Therefore, many people will download certain Antivirus software after purchasing computers. Virus program code cleaning can promptly delete files found to carry viruses, thereby ensuring that computer hardware is not affected by virus attacks.

- *Enhance user security awareness:* In order to ensure the security of computer hardware, computer users must continuously improve their security awareness, so that they can take effective security measures to maintain computer hardware security in their daily lives. For many enterprise users, specialized departments will be established to ensure the safe use of the company's computers. However, individuals, due to a lack of security awareness during the use of computers, are vulnerable to various viruses. In addition, during the storage process of computers, it is necessary to maintain a dry and low-temperature environment as much as possible, so as to ensure that the computer is stored in a safe and scientific environment.

- *Computer Encryption:* Many network viruses use illegal operations to control personal computers during the attack on computer hardware and obtain user information by browsing internal files of the computer. Therefore, users should pay attention to computer encryption in their daily use. By encrypting their own files, the computer system can generate significant resistance even when it is invaded by viruses, and strive for the corresponding time to eliminate viruses in a timely manner. Therefore, relevant users need to place important files in specific folders during the use of computers, and by setting passwords, they can effectively prevent virus intrusion and avoid personal privacy leakage.

8.1.3 Security Threats of Computer Hardware

Threat Analysis

Threat analysis is a cyberspace security technique that looks at a company's security protocols, processes, and procedures to find threats and vulnerabilities as well as to acquire information in advance of future assaults. Security teams can better understand the complexity of threats targeting enterprises, vulnerability exploitation strategies, and areas in the enterprise's security situation that may be vulnerable to these threats by conducting in-depth research on the various threats that target enterprises.

In the area of IT cyberspace security, threat analysis is categorized as a reactive technique since businesses evaluate risks to their security boundaries in real-time. Even though this tactic depends on attacks against the company, when effectively implemented, it can significantly lessen the amount of losses brought on by unforeseen network attacks.

Numerous threats that may exist within the company might be found using a sound threat analysis method. The following categories apply to some threats:

- *Unexpected threat:* Unfortunately, one of the main causes of today's network attacks is the exploitation of vulnerabilities brought on by human mistake, whether it be due to incorrect configuration of security processes or accidents that expose businesses to hazards. Threat analysis allows businesses to identify unanticipated faults and correct them before hostile attackers have a chance to take advantage of them.

- *Intentional threats:* Intentional threats are the threat that all businesses are concerned about. Threats that are intended to harm a company are those that are used by malicious parties in an effort to gain access to sensitive information and profit from it.

● *Internal threats:* This could be the most worrying risks. Typically, businesses worry about external threats and construct intricate security architectures to thwart malevolent attackers, but the true issue is with the enterprise's security parameters. Employees may have easier access to sensitive information, which, regrettably, can have disastrous results when they decide to act maliciously.

Advantages of Threat Analysis

Cyber threats are constantly evolving and it is crucial to stay one step ahead of malicious entities. One of the best ways to stay ahead of these attackers is to have a detailed understanding of their vulnerability exploits. Let's take a look at the three major advantages of incorporating threat analysis strategies.

● *Continuous updates on threat modeling:* Building efficient and current threat models is one of the most crucial components of a solid cyberspace security strategy. The goal of the threat model is to have a thorough understanding of the present state of network threats. Of course, threat models are swiftly evolving to keep up with these changes due to the quick evolution of today's network threat situation. In other words, every new product or service introduced to the market may potentially present security threats or new attack surfaces for hackers to take advantage.

● *Reduce attack surface:* Companies will gain from a significantly smaller attack surface when they invest in strong threat analysis procedures. However, the reason for this is that threat analysis businesses frequently update the list of threats that have been found. As a result, security teams can fortify their individual security borders, decreasing the attack surface.

● *Latest risk profile:* Continuously assessing and classifying threats using internal repositories or risk management systems to obtain the most recent risk profile is a security feature that significantly enhances the enterprise's security status. The most recent risk profile can be used to conduct internal audits, evaluate security policies and procedures, and support ongoing risk reduction plan improvement within the firm. All of these have tremendous value for businesses looking to enhance their safety position.

Execution Methods for Threat Analysis

Threat analysis can be done in a variety of ways based on the specific security requirements specified by the company, however practically all threat analyzes follow the same four basic steps. The majority of threat analysis methodologies include the following four standard steps:

- *Define the scope of threat assessment:* Establishing the scope is the first step in an effective threat assessment. By establishing the goals, the material that will be covered by the threat assessment, and the material needed for a successful execution of the threat assessment, the scope of the assessment can lay the groundwork for success. A comprehensive roadmap outlining each stage's responsibilities and what constitutes a successful threat analysis should be provided during the pre-planned stage.

- *Build the processes and procedures required for conducting threat assessments:* It should be simple to put processes and procedures in place if the scope is well defined, goals are specified, and the content to be covered and the content needed to satisfy these analysis goals. As a result of the roadmap's stated scope, processes and procedures improve this approach by undertaking threat assessments using practical tools, processes, and procedures.

- *Defining a rating system for threats:* Establishing a scoring system for dangers found through threat analysis aids in making clear to all important stakeholders the seriousness of threats, hazards, and vulnerabilities. Additionally, after doing threat analysis, businesses can classify, report, and monitor risks for a considerable amount of time by developing a rating system that is widely accepted throughout the organization and adheres to precise rating criteria.

Perform Threat Analysis

Finally, once the scope, processes, procedures, and rating system are in place, it is time to perform threat analysis. Here, enterprises can utilize the professional skills of internal security teams or personnel to perform threat analysis or hire third-party assistance to conduct threat analysis.

Man-in-the-middle attack

1. The concept of Man-in-the-middle attack

A network attack known as a man-in-the-middle (sometimes abbreviated as MITM or MiM) hijacks sessions. Hackers, often acting as eavesdroppers or assuming the identities of others, snoop on information given online. This kind of attack is quite risky since it can result in a number of hazards, like information theft or fake communication, which are sometimes challenging to spot because this situation appears to be entirely normal to legitimate users.

A MITM attack happens when a third-party listens in on a digital conversation without the intended recipient being aware of it. One human user, one computer system, or two computers can all participate in this discourse. Attackers can simply listen in on talks in any of these scenarios to get information (such as login passwords, private account information, etc.), or they can pose as other users to influence dialogues. In the latter scenario, the attacker might disseminate fake information or harmful links that could bring down systems or invite other network intrusions. Typically, it takes a long time for legitimate users to realise that they are truly speaking with unreliable third parties before any harm is done. A session hijacking example is an MITM attack. Cross-site scripting, session side hijacking, session fixation, and brute force attacks are other forms of session hijacking attacks.

2. Principle of MITM attack

MITM attack requires hackers to gain access to user connections. One of the most common methods is to create a public WiFi hotspot where anyone nearby can join without requiring a password. Once users join this network, hackers can access all their digital communication and even record keystrokes, acting as intermediaries.

The public wifi example is the most common and easiest way to launch a MITM attack, but it is not the only way. Other common methods include:

- *Sending users to fake websites:* By using DNS or IP spoofing, hackers can direct people away from their intended websites and onto false ones. DNS spoofing happens when hackers get access to DNS servers and alter the DNS records of websites, whereas IP spoofing happens when hackers alter packet headers in IP addresses. Even though it seems very genuine, users will eventually go on a bogus website run by hackers (where they can steal all the information).

- *Reroute data transmission:* By engaging in ARP spoofing, hackers can change the path communications take. This circumstance arises when hackers link their MAC address to an IP address that belongs to one of the authorized users taking part in the connection. Hackers have access to any information used to identify legitimate user IP addresses once they have established a connection.

3. Types of Man in the Middle Attack

There are various types of MITM attacks, each of which may have different consequences for the victim. Common types of MITM attack include:

- *Eavesdropping to obtain information:* Hackers are always able to eavesdrop on conversations to collect data for later use. They don't necessarily need to alter their communication in any way, but if they have access to the shared information, they can always find out about sensitive data or get access to login information.

- *Changing communication methods:* Hackers can impersonate another user to change communication using strategies like SSL hijacking. Consider the scenario when Alice and Bob believe they are speaking to one another. In that situation, hackers might intervene in the discussion and alter the messages the parties exchange. With this technique, it's possible to provide misleading information, disseminate harmful links, and even intercept crucial information, such users' bank account and routing codes for deposits.

- *Guide users to fake websites:* Hackers can direct consumers to fake websites that are identical to the ones they planned to visit (phishing scams are a common example). With this setting, they are able to collect any data users provide to reputable websites, including login information and account information. On the other hand, hackers can use this information to pose as legitimate users on real websites in order to gain access to financial data, alter specific information, and even send bogus messages.

4. Potential risks of MITM attack (MITM)

MITM attack will lead to various negative consequences. In fact, an MITM attack is usually the stepping stone for hackers to launch larger and more influential attacks. Considering this, some of the biggest potential risks of MITM attack include:

- *Fraudulent transactions:* MITM attack may lead to fraudulent transactions, such as collecting login and account information through eavesdropping or transferring money through re-routing. In most cases, this applies to financial transactions made directly from banks or through credit card payments.

- *Stolen confidential information:* Confidential information can be stolen through eavesdropping on emails, capturing users' login credentials, and forwarding them to phoney websites. This is especially concerning for major organizations that defend intellectual property rights or gather private information like Social Security Numbers (SSN) or consumer health records. The requirement for different businesses to protect the client information they manage is a problem with the proliferation of privacy legislation.

- *Accessing other systems:* By using an MITM attack to steal user login information, hackers can get access to numerous additional systems. The implication of this is that even if only one system is weak, it might make other, more secure systems weaker to attacks. The organization's security team must make sure there are no weak connections in this situation, regardless of how little any particular connection point may seem. Widespread attacks facilitated by rogue software: Malware can be distributed to consumers by hackers using

MITM attacks. On the other hand, such malware may result in pervasive attacks, such as bringing down the entire system or granting ongoing access to data or systems to carry out long-term attacks.

5. Protective measures against MITM attack

- Insecure connection points, such as public WiFi, are one of the most popular ways for hackers to carry out MITM attacks. As a result, users must utilise the connecting points with particular caution. This entails staying away from public WiFi (and, if the machine is linked to one, not logging into any systems) and utilizing a VPN to encrypt network connections. Another typical way for an MITM attack to start is with a phishing attempt, and the best ones may be quite convincing. Users can detect attack attempts and prevent becoming victims of attacks by being informed about these attacks and how they have evolved.

- A best practise that can help prevent successful phishing and other typical tactics for launching MITM attacks by leading users to bogus websites or embedding malware is to navigate a website by typing the URL rather than clicking a link. This can stop hackers from transmitting marginally altered links, which would otherwise invite attacks.

- Users should make sure that every website they visit has this degree of security by including HTTPS in the URL address when entering it. Before providing important information to a website, it can be quite helpful to evaluate its legality and security by looking at the HTTPS protocol, which may appear straightforward.

- Users must follow the instructions to log into the website for a number of recent MITM attacks. Despite the fact that they appear to be completely legal, these steps are not actually a part of the typical login process. Users who have been given instructions on what to do and what not to do throughout the typical login process may find it easier to recognise odd circumstances.

- Understanding individuals' typical login behaviors might assist security teams quickly spot any unusual trends. For instance, if most people typically check in on weekdays but there is a dramatic increase in activity on the weekend, this may be concerning and necessitate more examination.

- Requiring users to use multiple authentication login can provide another layer of protection to prevent MITM attack, even if hackers try to obtain user name/password combinations, they are also unable to access their account without other forms of authentication (such as codes sent through text messages). Although this two-layer approach is not impeccable, because some MITM attacks have passed through these two layers recently, it does provide more protection.

- It's crucial to require users to check out after finishing a secure session because doing so will end both authorized and unauthorized access to the session. In other words, the chance that a hacker will be able to access it in different ways increases the longer the session is open.

- Strong PKI software is essential for establishing trust and encrypting communication between users (people and machines). The best practise PKI strategy necessitates a highly adaptable system that can handle the exponentially increasing number of identities, completely and consistently implement security rules, and routinely update encryption keys to eliminate dangers like key propagation.

Information leakage

The hardware of a PC is easy to install and disassemble, and the hard drive is prone to theft, making the information in it naturally unsafe. Moreover, the files stored on the hard drive have almost no protection measures, and the storage structure and management methods of DOS file system are almost well-known. The additional security attributes of files, such as hidden, read-only, archive, etc., are easily modified, and modifications to the disk file directory area are neither software nor hardware protected. People who master disk management tools can easily change the directory area of disk files, causing information chaos in the entire system.

The residual magnetic information on the magnetic medium surface of a hard disk or floppy disk is also an important channel for information leakage. The file deletion operation only marks the file directory and does not delete the data storage area of the file itself. Experienced users can easily recover deleted files. The data stored on a floppy disk is also prone to being unreadable due to accidental scratches, various hard objects being damaged, or being affected by moisture and mold. There is no protection mechanism between memory spaces. Even if there is no simple boundary register, there is no monitoring program or privileged instruction that can only be used by the operating system. Anyone can program to access any area of memory, and even the system work area (such as the system's Interrupt vector area) can be modified. The user's data area cannot be guaranteed by the hardware. Some software includes user identity authentication functions, such as passwords, software dogs, etc., which are easily bypassed or modified by experienced programmers. Although some microcomputer processor chips provide hardware protection functions, these functions have not yet been effectively utilized by the operating system.

The external devices of a computer are not under the security control of the operating system, and anyone can use the output commands provided by the system to print file content. The output device is the most likely place to cause information leakage or theft. The display, CPU, and bus components in a computer can radiate electromagnetic waves to the outside during operation, which reflect changes in the internal information of the computer. After actual instrument testing, the information displayed on the display can be received and reproduced at a distance of several hundred meters, and the information on the computer screen can be leaked out without the owner's knowledge. Computer electromagnetic leakage is a serious way of information leakage.

8.2 COMPUTER HARDWARE SECURITY ASSURANCE METHODS

Computer hardware security assurance methods are critical in ensuring the integrity, confidentiality, and availability of computer systems. Hardware security aims to protect against a wide range of attacks, including physical tampering, theft, and unauthorized access. As computer hardware becomes more complex and integrated into our daily lives, the need for effective hardware security measures becomes increasingly important. This section provides an overview of common security issues which will compromise computer hardware security.

8.2.1   Influencing Factors of Hardware Security

Operating environment issues

The operation and application process of computer hardware will be affected by the natural environment. The specific environment will directly affect the operation of computer equipment, such as temperature factors. If the ambient temperature is too high, the relevant technical parameters of the computer hardware are prone to errors or deviations, and even burn out computer electrical components. Too low ambient temperature will affect the service life and shorten the hard disk. Lithium battery life, and if the temperature is too low, the LCD screen may not work. In addition, the ambient humidity also has an important impact on the hardware system. If the air in the operating environment of computer hardware equipment is too humid, it will cause damage to hardware circuit boards and burnt wires. Too much dust in the environment may block the CPU fan, cause the fan to stop, cause the CPU to overheat and burn out, affect the contact between the circuit boards, and may also cause the circuit board to corrode. The interference of electromagnetic waves and electromagnetic fields will also affect the transmission of electrical signals, causing computer hardware equipment to malfunction.

Computer virus

Hidden network viruses have the characteristics of being difficult to find, difficult to remove, and slow to affect. In the network environment, many network viruses have strong concealment capabilities. When there is no special protection for this virus, it usually disguises itself as other files and enters the computer system, then lurks, and then gradually erodes the computer system. At this time, when a hidden network virus erodes a process that manages computer hardware, it will cause the computer hardware to fail to operate normally. With regard to the transmission route and form of covert network viruses, such viruses are generally hidden in carriers such as web pages and data packets, and then when users download the carrier, they will passively enter the computer along with the data flow. In addition, some covert network viruses are actively spreading, that is, after invading a certain computer, they will actively infect other computers along the network structure, which depends on the form of the network structure.

Immediately effective network virus attacks are characterized by instantaneousness, difficulty to remove, easy discovery, and strong destructive power. There are many transmission channels for instant-effective network viruses. In addition to the above-mentioned covert network transmission channels, some active means can also be used to complete the transmission, such as active pop-up windows. If users accidentally click on such pop-up windows, it may Malicious attacks by instant network viruses. When the instant network virus enters the computer, it will attack the related processes of the computer hardware in a short time, which may directly cause the system to be paralyzed, and the user cannot operate the computer, so it is difficult to remove the virus. In addition, due to the obvious characteristics of instant-effective network viruses and quick effect, they are easy to be discovered by users, but due to their strong destructive power, more precautions should be taken.

Burst-type network viruses have the characteristics of the above two viruses, which can be latent and concealed or take effect immediately, but they are more inclined to immediate-effect network viruses, because once they break out, burst-type network viruses will also attack the virus in a short time. The computer hardware process is destroyed, causing the computer to be paralyzed. Burst-type network viruses have the characteristics of being difficult to find, difficult to remove, and the speed of impact is variable. Therefore, among the three types of viruses, burst-type network viruses are the most difficult to deal with. Specifically, sudden network viruses also rely on the above-mentioned various transmission channels to enter the computer, and then they may lie dormant for a period of time. During the dormant process, they will monitor computer resources and files. When the attack conditions are met, they will It will instantly attack the computer and adversely affect the computer hardware.

Security awareness issues

The network topology is very large, but computer security testing and construction are still relatively backward. Some enterprises do not have good methods and measures to prevent network congestion and various counterfeit IP locations for network and computer applications, nor do they have better strict network access and control methods. Some enterprises set login passwords for special network application systems, but do not set authorization restrictions and strict password controls for other information logins. All of these are great security problems in network applications and operations.

8.2.2 Principles and Steps for Hardware Security Maintenance

Maintenance principles

When a computer is in operation, it starts from the operation of the basic equipment to the operation of the main equipment. However, whether it is basic equipment or core equipment, there may be security problems, which will affect the operation of computer software and hardware equipment to a certain extent, and then cause malfunctions, which will affect the smooth and effective operation of the computer. Therefore, for various problems in computer hardware, it needs to be implemented gradually from simple to complex, from basic to core equipment. Do you need to test and inspect the basic equipment first, and effectively confirm the basic equipment. If there is no problem, it can work normally, then detect complex and core equipment, and then gradually discover various problems.

Comprehensive testing and maintenance principles from outside to inside

During the operation of computer hardware, various problems often occur. Computers run on the network for a long time, and there will be various viruses in them, and then they will be attacked by them, which will have a certain impact on computer hardware. Therefore, when people use computers, they must carefully maintain their hardware equipment and do not disassemble mechanical equipment at will. If there is a problem, it needs to be effectively repaired by professionals at a specific location. Make an accurate judgment to distinguish whether there is an internal or external failure. Usually, the external failure will be obvious. If no external equipment and line problems are found, it can basically be judged to be an internal problem. Then carry out a careful internal inspection and carry out detailed maintenance. Carry out careful and thoughtful inspections, and then clearly state the problems that arise, and implement targeted repairs.

8.2.3 From Static to Dynamic Maintenance Principles

For the computer hardware device inspection, the static state and the dynamic state are two states of power off and power on. Static inspection is the inspection and maintenance performed without power on. This process is relatively simple, and it can handle the corresponding hardware problems well. And dynamic maintenance is to carry out the detection of computer hardware equipment failure under the situation of power supply, which needs to spend a long time, and the maintenance after finding the problem is also not very convenient. Therefore, in the maintenance of computer hardware security, a maintenance process from static to dynamic is required, which can shorten the maintenance time as much as possible, and effectively improve the quality and efficiency of hardware equipment maintenance.

Maintenance strategy

In order to ensure the normal life, study, and work of computer users, and to maintain the basic settings of the computer system to the greatest extent, it must be maintained through four aspects: secure microprocessor, isolated memory area, fully encrypted hard disk, and data bus encryption. In computer hardware maintenance, it is mostly used in computer rooms and laboratories with high frequency and large usage. The hardware maintenance used in these places is the hard disk protection card. In order to prevent a large number of operations such as writing, deleting, and modifying the hard disk, the computer system user can restore it to the original state of the system after exiting the system.

Secure Microprocessor

The most critical part of the computer hardware security device is the security microprocessor, which is the core part of the computer system. When the secure microprocessor receives the fully encrypted system program instructions, it immediately decrypts these instructions and executes the instructions according to the decrypted instructions. The computer microprocessor , also known as the central processing unit, can extract and process the encrypted operation code, and complete the decryption and instruction execution operations within the specified time. And because the safety microprocessor will not leak the decrypted system program instructions, it can also prevent external personnel from invading the confidential files in the computer or tampering with the programs in the microprocessor. Therefore, the processed data information must be encrypted before being entered and stored by a secure microprocessor. At the same time, the computer can authorize access to the user, but the authorized user will tamper with it. Therefore, the system application program needs to decrypt the encrypted data through the computer security microprocessor. The decrypted data can only be transmitted in the authenticated site program, and its final storage point is in the computer isolation memory area, which is In order to prevent other programs in the system from accessing or calling the data.

Isolated memory area

The isolated memory area is also a major component of computer security equipment. In this area, a memory area that is safely isolated from the outside world and stores sensitive data can be formed, which can more effectively keep the user's personal privacy confidential. The data information stored in this isolated memory area can only be accessed by the program to which it belongs, and other applications have no right to initiate access to it. The safe and high-level source program codes in the computer system can be stored in this isolated memory area, and other external devices of the computer have no way to call out data from this isolated area, so the safe and stable operation of computer applications can be guaranteed.

Fully encrypted hard disk

A fully encrypted hard disk is an important part of computer hardware security equipment, which encrypts every byte of data in the hard disk. Computer fully encrypted hard disks can not only prevent access to data in the hard disk but also ensure computer security in the network environment through encryption software or disk hardware. However, the disadvantage of a fully encrypted hard disk is that it does not encrypt all data, and can only fully encrypt the hard disk area partitioned by the computer operating system. However, the fully encrypted hard disk realized by the disk hardware can not only fully encrypt the computer system partition hard disk, but also fully encrypt the system boot partition, which can also better protect computer user data from being processed quickly.

Data bus encryption

Computer data bus encryption refers to the use of a key to encrypt data on the data bus when encrypting relevant instructions including system application programs and ordinary data information. However, data bus encryption has certain limitations and can only be applied in computer systems with a higher security level, such as military communication equipment, automatic teller machine equipment, etc. And data bus encryption must require that one computer processor interacts with another computer processor through the data bus before data can be encrypted.

8.3   COMPUTER HARD DRIVE SECURITY MAINTENANCE

8.3.1   Causes of Hard Disk Failure and Data Loss

Computer hard disk is an important part of a computer and one of the main devices for storing data in a computer. With the continuous development of computer technology, the storage capacity of computer hard disk is getting larger and faster, and the reliability is also improving. The safe maintenance of computer hard drives is an important measure to ensure the safety of computer data and the long-term stable operation of hard drives.

The following will introduce the basic concepts and roles of computer hard disks, as well as the importance and purpose of secure maintenance. First, we will discuss the basic concepts and roles of computer hard disks, including the physical structure, data storage principles, and working methods of hard disks. Then, we will discuss the importance and purpose of hard disk security maintenance, as well as the causes of hard disk failure and data loss. Finally, we will introduce the basic principles and strategies of hard disk security maintenance to set the stage for the specific content of the subsequent chapters.

Computer hard disks are an important part of computer storage devices that can hold and read large amounts of data. Computer hard drives are often referred to as hard drives, hard disks, disks, etc. In computers, a hard disk usually refers to a mechanical hard disk, that is, one that uses mechanical mechanisms and magnetic materials to store data. The counterpart is the Solid-State Drive (SSD), which uses flash memory technology to store data.

Computer hard drives usually consist of one or more platters, each of which has two sides, or top and bottom. The platters are made of magnetic material, they are mounted on the spindle of the hard drive and can be read and written to by magnetic heads. The head is the device responsible for reading and writing data and it is located on the read/write arm of the hard drive. The read-write arm of the hard disk can move within the radius of the hard disk platter so that the head can read and write data on the surface of the platter.

The data storage principle of the hard disk is realized based on the properties of magnetic materials. The magnetic material can be magnetized into north and south poles, and this magnetic polarity can represent the 1s and 0s of binary data. the surface of the platter on the hard drive is divided into many magnetic areas, and each magnetic area can be magnetized into 1s or 0s to represent the data. The magnetic head interprets the data by changing the magnetic material as it is read and converts it into an electrical signal.

As technology evolves, the storage capacity of hard disks continues to increase, which also requires them to be increasingly dense. To increase the storage density of hard drives, hard drive manufacturers have used many technologies to increase the storage capacity of each platter, such as multi-layer platters, magnetic perpendicular recording, and thermally assisted magnetic recording. Hard drives are controlled by a hard drive controller on the computer's motherboard. The hard drive controller is responsible for sending commands to the hard drive to control its read-and-write operations and data transfer. When the computer needs to read the data on the hard disk, the hard disk controller sends a read command to the hard disk and specifies the location of the data to be read. The read/write arm of the hard disk moves to the specified location and uses the head to read the data and then transmits the data to the hard disk controller. When the computer needs to write data, the hard drive controller sends a write command to the hard drive and transmits the data to the hard drive. After the hard drive writes the data to the specified location, it returns a write complete signal to the hard drive controller.

Computer hard drives store important user data, including documents, photos, videos, music, software programs, and more. In order to protect this data, the computer hard drive must be maintained securely. The main purpose of security maintenance is to ensure the long-term stable operation of computer hard drives and to prevent data loss, leakage, and damage by malicious software. Hard drive failure is one of the common computer hardware failures and one of the main causes of data loss. Hard drive failure can be caused by damage to the mechanical components inside the hard drive, damage to the electronic components, damage to the magnetic media, etc. Hard drive failure may cause data to be unreadable or unwritten, resulting in data loss. To prevent hard drive failure and data loss, you need to regularly check the health status of your hard drive to identify and resolve hard drive failures promptly.

Data stored on the hard drive may be illegally stolen or leaked, which will seriously affect the privacy and security of the user. Common ways of data leakage and theft include hacking, virus infection, phishing, spyware, etc. In order to protect the data, you need to strengthen the security of your computer, such as using anti-virus software, setting up a firewall, and enhancing password security. Malware is those programs that intentionally damage computer systems and data, including viruses, Trojan horses, worms, etc. This malware may damage the data on the hard disk and even cause the hard disk to not work properly. In order to prevent damage by malware, you need to strengthen your computer's security and regularly check and remove malware from your computer.

8.3.2   Basic Principles of Hard Drive Security Maintenance

The hard drive is one of the most important components of a computer system that stores computer system and user data. However, hard drive failures and data loss problems occur for a variety of reasons. To reduce the occurrence of these problems, several measures must be taken to perform secure hard drive maintenance. This section will introduce the basic principles of hard drive security maintenance, including data backup, regular hard drive cleaning, hard drive partitioning and formatting, and the use of hard drive maintenance tools.

- *Data Backup:* Data backup is one of the basic principles of hard drive security maintenance, which ensures that in the event of a hard drive failure or data loss, data can be recovered quickly and the impact of data loss on users can be reduced. Data backup can be achieved in several ways: backing up data to a local hard drive or an external hard drive is a simple and fast way to backup. Users can use the backup tool that comes with the operating system or third-party backup software to back up important data to another hard drive. The backup drive should be placed in a safe place so that the backup drive is not lost or damaged. Backing up data to cloud storage can make the data more secure and reliable, and users can access the backup data via the Internet. Many cloud storage providers offer free or paid backup services, and users can choose the backup solution that suits their needs.

- *Clean your hard drive regularly:* The continuous reduction of hard drive storage space can affect system performance and even cause system crashes. Therefore, regular hard drive cleanup is another important principle for safe hard drive maintenance. Regular hard drive cleanup can be achieved in several ways: Operating systems and applications generate a large number of temporary files and log files during use, which can take up hard drive space and affect system performance. Users can delete these unwanted files through the disk cleanup tools that come with the operating system or third-party cleanup tools. Users install many applications while using the computer, but not all of them need to be kept. Users can uninstall unwanted applications through the uninstaller that comes with the operating system or a third-party uninstaller tool to free up hard disk space.

- *Hard Disk Partitioning and Formatting:* Hard drive partitioning and formatting is another important principle of safe hard drive maintenance. Hard drive partitioning allows a hard drive to be divided into multiple logical areas, each of which can be used independently, thus allowing more flexibility in the use of the hard drive. Hard drive formatting erases the data on the drive and divides the drive into the logical structures needed for the file system so that the drive can be used by the operating system. Partitioning and formatting a hard disk can be done in several ways: operating systems usually come with partitioning and formatting tools that users can use to partition and format the hard disk. For example, Windows operating systems come with disk management tools that can partition and format hard disks. In addition to the tools that come with the operating system, there are many third-party partitioning and formatting tools available. These tools usually offer more features and options that can better meet the needs of users. For example, tools such as MiniTool Partition Wizard and EaseUS Partition Master allow for more detailed partitioning and formatting of hard drives.

- *Use of hard disk maintenance tools:* Hard drive maintenance tools are another important tool for safe hard drive maintenance. These tools can check the health status of the hard drive, fix hard drive errors, optimize the performance of the hard drive, etc. Here are a few common hard drive maintenance tools: Hard drive health check tools can detect the health status of the hard drive, including its temperature, life span, read and write errors, etc. For example, CrystalDiskInfo is a free hard drive health check tool that displays the indicators of the hard drive and gives a health status score. Hard drive error repair tools can detect and repair errors on the hard drive, including bad sectors, partition table corruption, etc. For example, the chkdsk tool that comes with the Windows operating system can detect and repair errors on the hard drive. Hard disk performance optimization tools can optimize the read-/write speed and response time of the hard disk, thus improving the performance of the hard disk. For example, Disk Defragmenter is a disk defragmentation tool that comes with the Windows operating system and optimizes the read and write speed of the hard disk.

The basic principles of safe hard drive maintenance include data backup, regular hard drive cleaning, hard drive partitioning and formatting, and the use of hard drive maintenance tools. Following these principles can protect the data security of the hard drive, extend the life of the hard drive, and improve the performance and stability of the hard drive. In practice, users can choose a hard drive security maintenance method that suits their needs.

The following points also need to be noted when performing hard drive security maintenance:

- Data backup is an important tool for hard drive security maintenance, but the frequency of backup data needs to be appropriate. If the frequency of backups is too low, it may lead to greater loss of data loss; if the frequency of backups is too high, it may affect the normal use of the hard drive. It is generally recommended that users back up their data in a timely manner after performing important data operations.

- The storage method of backup data also needs attention. Generally speaking, backup data should be stored in another hard drive, U disk, CD-ROM, cloud storage and other reliable media to avoid backup data being deleted or lost by mistake as well.

- Partitioning and formatting operations need to be done carefully to avoid data loss due to mishandling. Before partitioning and formatting, you should back up important data and make sure your operation is error-free before proceeding.

- When choosing and using maintenance tools, you need to pay attention to the reliability and applicability of maintenance tools. Some unreliable maintenance tools may misjudge the health of the hard drive, which can lead to wrong operations and even cause hard drive damage. Therefore, when choosing a maintenance tool, users should select a well-known and tested tool and read the tool's instructions carefully.

- In addition to the above software-level security maintenance, you also need to pay attention to the physical protection of the hard drive. Hard drives need to avoid damage from physical impacts and vibrations during use, as well as damage to the hard drive from excessive temperature and humidity.

Hard drive security maintenance is an important part of computer use and requires users to pay attention to maintaining and protecting the hard drive in daily use so as to ensure the data security, performance and stability of the hard drive.

8.3.3 Secure Maintenance of Computer Processors

8.3.3.1 Overview of computer processors

The processor is one of the most central components in a computer and is also known as the CPU. The main role of the processor is responsible for interpreting and executing instructions in the computer to control various operations of the computer. It understands and executes the instructions in the computer program, performs arithmetic and logical operations, and controls and manages peripherals. The processor is one of the most important components of a computer in terms of performance, and its performance directly determines the overall performance of the computer.

The development of processors can be traced back to the 1950s, when computer processors were still very simple and could only execute some simple instructions. By the 1960s, the first commercially available processor, IBM's System/360, appeared. in the 1970s, as computers became more popular, processor speeds began to increase. in the mid-1980s, Intel released the first processor of the x86 architecture, one of the most widely used processor architectures in modern personal computers. In the mid-1990s, the number of processor cores began to increase and multicore processors became popular. in the early 21st century, with the rise of mobile devices and cloud computing [284], low power consumption and high performance became the focus of processor design.

Processor performance can be measured by several metrics, and common processor performance metrics are described in detail below.

- The clock frequency of a processor refers to the number of clock cycles the processor can execute per second. The higher the clock frequency, the more instructions the processor can execute per second, thereby increasing the processing speed of the computer. However, clock frequency is not the only factor that determines processor performance; other factors such as instruction set and number of cores can also affect processor performance.

- A processor's instruction set determines which instructions it can execute. Different instruction sets support different operations, such as integer operations, floating point operations, vector operations, etc. Currently, common instruction sets include x86, ARM, MIPS, etc.

- The number of cores in a processor refers to the number of cores integrated in the processor. Multi-core processors can execute multiple threads at the same time, thus increasing the parallel processing capability of the computer. However, the performance of a multi-core processor is also limited by factors such as the level of support for multithreaded applications and the memory bandwidth of the processor.

- The processor's cache is a temporary memory used to store the data exchanged between the processor and memory. The larger the size of the cache, the more data the processor can cache, thereby reducing the number of accesses to memory and increasing the speed of the computer.

- Floating-point operations are a common type of operation in processors, especially in areas such as scientific computing and graphics processing. The floating-point performance of a processor refers to the number of floating-point operations that the processor can perform per second. This metric is important for applications that require a large number of floating-point operations.

- The manufacturing process of the processor affects the power consumption and performance of the processor. As the process continues to be upgraded, the processor can work more efficiently and at the same time be more energy efficient. Currently, the manufacturing process of processors has been upgraded to sub-7nm, which is an important reason why modern processors are able to achieve high performance and low power consumption.

Processor performance indicators are multifaceted, and different indicators can reflect the performance of the processor in different application scenarios. In the processor selection and purchase, you need to consider a variety of indicators, and according to the specific application requirements to choose the right processor.

8.3.3.2 Working principle of computer processors

Structure of a computer processor

A CPU is the core component of a computer system, responsible for executing instructions, processing data, and controlling various operations of the computer.

The operator is the core component of the CPU and is responsible for performing various arithmetic operations, including addition, subtraction, multiplication, division, and bitwise operations. It consists of an Arithmetic Logic Unit (ALU) and a status flag register. The ALU is the arithmetic logic unit in the processor, which is responsible for executing various arithmetic operations and storing the results in a specified register. The status flag register is the register that stores the CPU status flag, which is used to record status information such as whether the result of an operation is zero or negative.

The controller is the instruction execution component of the CPU, which is responsible for reading instructions, decoding them, and executing them. The controller includes Instruction Register (IR), Program Counter (PC), and instruction decoder; IR is the register for storing the current instruction and PC is the register for storing the address of the next instruction. The instruction decoder is responsible for parsing the instruction and sending the corresponding control signal to the operator to complete the execution of the instruction.

There are many kinds of registers in the CPU, including general-purpose registers, special registers, segment registers, and so on. General registers are mainly used to store data, special registers are mainly used to store control information, and segment registers are mainly used to store memory addresses.

Instruction set and instruction cycle

The instruction set and instruction cycle of a computer processor is an important part of the CPU, which determines which instructions the CPU can execute and how long the instructions take to execute. When the CPU executes instructions, each instruction needs to go through an instruction cycle, which includes four stages: fetching, decoding, executing, and storing the result.

The instruction set is the set of instructions that the CPU can execute. The instruction set can be divided into two types: Complex Instruction Set Computer (CISC) and Reduced Instruction Set Computer (RISC), which contain a large number of complex instructions and can perform more complicated operations, but also lead to a more complex CPU design and lower execution efficiency. The RISC instruction set contains fewer simple instructions, which improves CPU execution efficiency but requires more assembly code to complete complex operations.

The instruction cycle is the time period for the CPU to execute instructions, which includes four phases: instruction fetching, instruction decoding, instruction execution, and result storage. The CPU clock speed determines the length of each instruction cycle, and the faster the clock speed, the more efficient the CPU execution.

The fetch and decode phases of the instruction cycle are the front end of the CPU, while the execute and store results phases are the back end of the CPU. The front end is responsible for instruction fetching and parsing, while the back end is responsible for instruction execution and storage of results. To improve the execution efficiency of the CPU, modern CPUs use pipelining technology, which divides the instruction cycle into multiple phases and executes multiple instructions simultaneously. This allows multiple instructions to be executed in the same time cycle, improving the CPU's execution efficiency.

Computer memory and cache

Computer memory and cache are important peripherals of the CPU that are responsible for storing data and instructions, as well as providing access interfaces [285] to data and instructions. There is a hierarchy between memory and cache, which can be divided from high to low into cache, primary cache, secondary cache, main memory, and secondary memory.

The cache is a type of high-speed memory integrated within the CPU to store data and instructions that are frequently used by the CPU. The cache has a small capacity but is extremely fast to access and can effectively improve the execution efficiency of the CPU. The cache is divided into multiple levels, and the speed and capacity vary between different levels of the cache.

Level 1 cache, also known as L1 cache, is a small cache inside the CPU that stores the most frequently used data and instructions of the

CPU. The Level 1 cache is slightly slower than the cache in terms of access speed but has more capacity to store more data and instructions.

Level 2 cache, also known as L2 cache, is a medium capacity, medium speed cache that is typically shared by the CPU and motherboard. The L2 cache has a larger capacity than the Level 1 cache but is slightly slower and can store more data and instructions.

The main memory is the main memory in a computer and is used to store programs and data. The main memory has a larger capacity but is slower and takes longer to access. The main memory usually uses Dynamic Random Access Memory (DRAM) or Static Random Access Memory (SRAM) as the storage unit, and each memory unit can store one bit of data.

The secondary memory is the external memory in the computer, usually a hard disk, CD-ROM, etc. Auxiliary memory has a large capacity but is very slow to access and takes a long time to read or write data. Memory and cache play an important role in the work of the CPU, which needs to constantly read data and instructions from memory or cache, and write computation results back to memory or cache. The speed of memory and cache directly affects the execution efficiency of the CPU, so optimizing the access speed of memory and cache is the key to improving computer performance.

We discuss in depth the working principle of computer processors from three perspectives: the basic structure of the CPU, the instruction set and instruction cycle, and computer memory and cache. An in-depth understanding of the working principle of the CPU, as the core component of a computer, is important for computer optimization, performance improvement, and application development.

First of all, the basic structure of the CPU includes registers, an arithmetic logic unit, a control unit, and clock components. Among them, registers are one of the most important components of the CPU, which can store and access data quickly and provide basic support for CPU operations. Meanwhile, ALU and control unit together form the computation and control functions of the CPU and realize the basic operations of the computer.

Second, the instruction set and instruction cycle are key components of the CPU. The instruction set is the collection of instructions that the CPU can execute, which determines the functions and capabilities of the CPU. The instruction cycle is the process of instruction execution by the CPU, including instruction fetching, instruction decoding, instruction execution, and result writing back. An in-depth understanding of the instruction set and instruction cycle helps programmers optimize their program design and improve the execution efficiency of the CPU.

Finally, computer memory and cache are important paths for the CPU to access data and instructions. Memory is the main storage medium for the CPU, and the cache is a kind of high-speed memory set up to increase the access speed. the CPU reads data and instructions from memory, and the calculation results also need to be written back to memory or cache. Therefore, the speed of memory and cache directly affects the execution efficiency of the CPU, and their optimization is one of the important ways to improve computer performance.

The computer processor is one of the most important components of a computer, and its working principle involves several aspects, including the basic structure of the CPU, instruction set, and instruction cycle, as well as computer memory and cache. An in-depth understanding of how processors work is important for improving the performance of computers and application development.

Security risks and threats of computer processors

Computer processors are the core components in computer systems, undertaking important functions such as computing, control, and storage, and their security is directly related to the stability and security of the entire computer system. This chapter will focus on the security risks and threats of computer processors from four perspectives: electromagnetic interference and electrostatic discharge, excessively high and low temperature, computer viruses and malware, and network attacks and remote control.

Electromagnetic interference refers to the action of electromagnetic fields that cause computer processors to make errors or produce random operations. There are many causes of electromagnetic interference, such as power cables, cables in the chassis, radio waves, etc., which may generate electromagnetic interference. Electrostatic discharge is the accumulation of too much charge inside the processor due to static electricity during the operation of the processor, which leads to abnormal operation of the processor. In order to avoid the impact of electromagnetic interference and electrostatic discharge on the computer processor, we need to take some preventive measures.

First, to do a good job of chassis grounding, to ensure that all the internal parts of the chassis can be well grounded to reduce the impact of electromagnetic interference and electrostatic discharge. Secondly, we should choose suitable power cables and cables inside the chassis, these cables should have good shielding performance, which can effectively reduce electromagnetic radiation and electromagnetic interference. Finally, during the operation of the processor, the accumulation of static electricity should be avoided, such as before using the computer should first contact the grounder to discharge the static electricity on the body.

Both too-high or too-low temperatures can have a significant impact on the operation of the computer processor. When the temperature is too high, the circuitry and components inside the processor will be affected by thermal expansion and thermal stress, which will cause the performance of the computer system to degrade or malfunction. When the temperature is too low, the circuitry and components inside the processor will be affected by cold expansion and cold contraction, which will also affect the performance and stability of the computer system.

In order to avoid the impact of high and low temperatures on the computer processor, we need to take some precautions. First, a suitable cooling system should be selected to ensure that the processor can operate within the appropriate temperature range. The cooling system includes fans, heat sinks, heat pipes, etc., which can effectively reduce the temperature of the processor. Second, pay attention to the ventilation inside the case to ensure air circulation and avoid heat stagnation inside the case. In addition, you can also set up a temperature monitoring system to monitor the processor's temperature in real time, and take timely measures to avoid damaging the processor once abnormal temperatures are detected.

Computer viruses and malware are malicious programs that spread through computer networks and infect computer systems, thereby disrupting the normal operation of the system. Computer viruses can be spread in various ways, such as through email, P2P networks, malicious websites, etc. Once a computer is infected with a virus, it will lead to many problems in the computer system, such as abnormal program operation, data loss, system crashes, etc. In order to protect the security of computer systems, we need to take some measures to prevent the attack of computer viruses and malware.

Firstly, we should install antivirus software and update the virus database in time to ensure that the computer system can identify and remove viruses in time. Secondly, we should regularly scan the whole computer system and find viruses and malware to remove them in time. In addition, be careful not to download and install software and files from unknown sources at will to avoid infection with viruses and malware.

Network attack and remote control refer to hackers attacking computer systems through the Internet to gain control of the system or steal sensitive information from the system. There are various ways of cyber attacks and remote control, such as phishing emails, hacking attacks, denial of service attacks, etc. Once a computer system is attacked, it can lead to serious consequences such as system paralysis and data leakage. In order to prevent network attacks and remote control, we need to take some preventive measures.

Firstly, we need to harden the computer system and close unnecessary services and ports to prevent hackers from using loopholes to attack. Secondly, we should regularly update the patches of operating systems and applications to patch the vulnerabilities of the system and improve the security of the system. In addition, network security devices, such as firewalls and intrusion detection systems, can be used to monitor and filter network traffic and prevent network attacks. In addition, it is also necessary to improve users' security awareness by not clicking on email attachments and downloading software from unknown sources at will to avoid being infected by malware.

The security risks and threats of computer processors is an issue that needs to be given high priority. During the use of computers, attention needs to be paid to various security issues such as electromagnetic interference and electrostatic discharge, high and low temperatures, computer viruses and malware, network attacks, and remote control. Only by taking effective security measures can we ensure the normal operation of the computer system and the security of the user's information.

8.3.3.3 Computer processor security maintenance principles

The computer processor is the core component of the computer, and its security maintenance is one of the keys to ensuring the normal operation of the computer and data security. The following will introduce the security maintenance principles of computer processors from two perspectives: hardware maintenance and software maintenance.

The processor is one of the core components of the computer, and to ensure its normal operation, it needs to be cleaned and maintained regularly. The surface of the processor should be wiped frequently with a soft cloth to keep it clean and to avoid dust and dirt from entering the processor's interior and affecting its heat dissipation and operational efficiency. In addition, the processor's heat sink and fan also need to be cleaned and maintained regularly to avoid dust and debris from blocking airflow and causing the processor to overheat.

The processor generates a lot of heat when it is running, and if it does not dissipate heat in time, it will lead to high processor temperature, which will affect its operational efficiency and lifetime. Therefore, the temperature control and heat dissipation of the processor is very important. The usual method used is through heat sinks and fans to dissipate the heat and keep the processor temperature within the normal range. In addition, technologies such as liquid cooling can be used to further improve the efficiency of heat dissipation.

The operating system is the core software of the computer and plays a vital role in the security and maintenance of the processor. Therefore, it is very important to update and maintain the operating system regularly. Operating system updates can fix known vulnerabilities and security issues and improve system stability and security. In addition, regular cleaning of system junk and useless files can effectively improve system operation efficiency and stability.

Each hardware device of the computer needs drivers to control it, therefore, the security maintenance for the processor also needs to pay attention to the installation and update of drivers. Installing and updating the correct drivers can ensure the proper operation of hardware devices, as well as fix known security problems and vulnerabilities.

Security software is one of the keys to securing your computer, including anti-virus software, firewalls, anti-spyware, etc. It is also very important for the security maintenance of the processor to install and update security software. Security software protects the computer and data from viruses, malware and hacker attacks. Also, regular updates of security software can fix known security vulnerabilities and improve the security of your computer.

In addition to the above, the following points need to be noted:

- *Don't overclock:* Overclocking is a situation where the operating frequency of a processor is increased beyond its default frequency. While overclocking can improve the performance of your computer, it can also increase the processor's operating temperature and voltage, which in turn can reduce its lifespan. Therefore, overclocking the processor is not recommended.

- *Avoid using illegitimate software and websites:* Using illegitimate software and visiting unsafe websites increases the risk of your computer being attacked by viruses, malware, and hackers. Therefore, you should avoid using illegitimate software and visiting unsafe websites.

- *Pay attention to the power supply:* Power supply problems can also have an impact on the security maintenance of the processor. Unstable voltage or insufficient power supply can affect the stability and security of the computer. Therefore, you should choose a stable and reliable power supply and ensure that the power supply is sufficient.

In short, the security maintenance of computer processors is one of the keys to ensuring the normal operation of computers and data security. By regularly performing hardware maintenance and software maintenance, avoiding overclocking, using illegal software and visiting unsafe websites, and paying attention to the precautions of power supply, we can effectively improve the security and stability of the computer and protect the security of the computer and data.

8.3.4 Safe Maintenance of Computer Memory Devices

8.3.4.1 Basic knowledge of computer memory

In a computer system, memory is a very important component. It is the computer's storage medium, capable of temporarily storing data and programs and providing the necessary support for the proper operation of the computer. The following will introduce the basics of computer memory from the perspectives of the definition and function of memory, an overview of memory types, units, and representation of memory size, and how memory works.

Memory is the component of a computer system that is used to store data and programs. It stores data and programs temporarily and reads and writes data quickly when needed. The main functions of memory include:

- *Storing data and programs.* Memory is the primary storage medium in a computer system that temporarily stores running programs and related data.

- *Speeds up computer operation.* Memory can read and write much faster than external storage devices such as hard disks and CD-ROMs, which can speed up computer operation.

- *Support system startup.* The computer's operating system and various applications need to be loaded into memory in order to run.

- *Supports multitasking.* Memory can store multiple programs and data at the same time, allowing the computer to handle multiple tasks simultaneously.

Memory can be categorized into different types based on how it is stored and how fast it can be accessed. Common types of memory include:

- *Random Access Memory (RAM).* RAM is a volatile memory device that can read and write data in random order and is the most common type of memory used in computer systems.

- *Read-Only Memory (ROM).* ROM is a type of memory that can only be read but not written to and is often used to store basic programs and data that are needed when a computer system starts up.

- *Cache.* Cache is a cache memory device that sits between the processor and RAM to speed up the processor's access to data in RAM.

- *Virtual Memory.* Virtual memory is a hard disk-based memory management technology that expands the memory capacity of a computer system by storing a portion of the data and programs in RAM that are temporarily unneeded on the hard disk.

The capacity of computer memory usually uses bytes (byte) as the basic unit. Common memory size units include:

- *Byte (byte):* A byte is equal to 8 binary bits and is usually used to represent some very small data and programs.

- *Kilobyte (KB):* a kilobyte is equal to 1024 bytes, usually used to represent some relatively small programs and data.

- *Megabyte (MB):* A megabyte is equal to 1024 kilobytes, usually used to represent medium-sized programs and data.

- *Gigabyte (GB):* a gigabyte is equal to 1024 megabytes, usually used to represent large programs, databases and multimedia files, and other large amounts of data.

- *Terabyte (TB):* One terabyte is equal to 1024 gigabytes and is usually used to represent storage requirements in areas such as ultra-large-scale data centers, cloud computing, scientific research, and high-performance computing.

There are usually two ways to represent the size of memory: decimal and binary. In the decimal representation, 1KB represents 1024 bytes, 1MB represents 1024 kilobytes, and so on. In binary representation, 1KB means 1000 bytes, 1MB means 1000 kilobytes, and so on. Therefore, the size of memory is usually smaller in binary representation than in decimal representation.

The working of memory can be simply summarized as two processes: reading and writing. When reading data, the computer sends the address on the address line to the memory controller, which reads the data onto the data line and passes it to the processor for processing. When writing data, the computer sends the address and data on the address line to the memory controller, which writes the data to the corresponding address in memory.

The speed of memory reading and writing is one of the important factors of computer system performance. In order to improve memory read and write speed, memory is usually optimized using the following techniques:

- *Caching techniques.* Commonly used data and programs are stored in the cache to increase the read speed.

- *Dual channel technology.* Setting up two channels in memory allows the computer to perform two memory read and write operations at the same time to improve read and write efficiency.

- *ECC technology.* Uses error detection and correction techniques to prevent errors in data in memory.

Memory, as an important part of a computer system, plays an important role in the performance and stability of the computer. By understanding the basics of memory, you can better understand how a computer system works and thus provide help to better use the computer system.

8.3.4.2 Overview of memory security threats

Memory vulnerabilities are flaws or errors in program design and coding that result in problems such as memory access exceptions or out-of-bounds access during program operation. Memory vulnerabilities include the following major types:

- Buffer overflow. Refers to writing data to an already filled buffer, thereby overwriting adjacent memory areas and causing out-of-bounds memory accesses.

- Stack overflow. When the return address of a function, local variables, function parameters, and other data exceeds the range of space allocated in the stack frame, resulting in the return address being modified, causing a program crash or malicious code execution.

- Formatted string vulnerability. When a program does not properly handle formatted strings entered by the user, but instead directly outputs them to memory using a formatted string function, it can lead to actions such as a malicious user entering a specific formatted string, modifying internal program variables, or executing malicious code.

- Null pointer reference vulnerability. A null pointer reference vulnerability occurs when a program uses a null pointer for memory operations, and this vulnerability can easily lead to program crashes or cause security problems.

A memory attack is the act of using a memory vulnerability to perform an attack. Types of memory attacks include the following:

- Buffer overflow attacks. An attacker takes control of the program flow and commits a malicious act by inputting specific data into the buffer and overwriting the return address stored in the program.

- Stack overflow attack. An attacker controls the program flow and commits malicious behavior by inputting specific data into the program and modifying the return address in the stack.

- Formatted string attack. An attacker controls the program output by inputting a specific formatted string into the program to perform malicious behavior.

- Memory allocation attack. An attacker commits a malicious act by using a memory allocation function to allocate a larger block of memory than is actually needed, thereby overwriting an adjacent memory area.

- Null pointer reference attack. An attacker commits a malicious act by using a null pointer to perform memory operations and thus control the program flow.

The purposes of memory attacks include the following:

- Stealing sensitive information. Attackers use memory vulnerabilities to steal sensitive information from programs, such as passwords, certificates, private keys, etc.

- Disrupting system functionality. Attackers use memory vulnerabilities to disrupt system functionality, such as tampering with system configuration, deleting critical files, etc.

- Control the system. Attackers use memory vulnerabilities to control the system, thereby gaining system privileges or executing malicious code and other actions.

- Denial of Service Attack. Attackers use memory vulnerabilities to execute denial-of-service attacks, resulting in system paralysis or failure to function properly.

Memory security threats are an important issue in computer systems and require us to strengthen security measures in the design, coding and operation, and maintenance processes to avoid the creation of memory vulnerabilities and the implementation of memory attacks.

8.3.4.3   Methods to prevent memory security threats

Memory security threat refers to the attacker's use of program vulnerability or operating system vulnerability to steal memory data or modify memory data while the program is running, to achieve an attack or control of the computer system. Since memory is a key resource for program execution, memory security threat is a very important issue in the field of computer security. In the following, we will introduce the prevention methods of memory security threats from three perspectives: the patching methods of memory security vulnerabilities, the detection and defense methods of memory attacks, and the overview and application of memory encryption.

Patching Methods for Memory Security Vulnerabilities

Memory security vulnerabilities usually include buffer overflow, stack overflow, format string vulnerabilities, etc., through which attackers can conduct memory attacks. Therefore, patching memory security vulnerabilities is the first step to preventing memory attacks. The methods for patching memory security vulnerabilities include the following:

- using secure programming languages and programming paradigms, such as Rust, Go, etc. These programming languages and paradigms have built-in memory security mechanisms that can avoid common memory security vulnerabilities.

- Perform strict checks and filters on input data to avoid buffer overflows, formatted string vulnerabilities, and other vulnerabilities.

- Use memory security tools, such as AddressSanitizer, Valgrind, etc., to analyze programs dynamically or statically to discover and fix memory security vulnerabilities promptly.

- Apply patches and updates provided by the operating system or application for known memory security vulnerabilities promptly to avoid attackers from using known vulnerabilities to attack the system.

Memory attack detection and defense methods

A memory attack refers to an attacker taking control of a computer system by modifying data in the program's memory or executing malicious code by using vulnerabilities during the program's operation. To prevent memory attacks, we need to use the following methods:

- Memory isolation. Memory isolation can isolate different modules or threads of a program, thus reducing the chance of attackers using program vulnerabilities to conduct memory attacks. Memory isolation includes both hardware isolation and software isolation.

- Memory protection. Memory protection prevents an attacker from modifying data in the program memory or executing malicious code. ASLR can randomly allocate program memory addresses so that attackers cannot accurately predict the program's memory layout; DEP can distinguish between data and code areas in memory to prevent attackers from executing malicious code in data areas; stack protection can detect and prevent stack Stack protection can detect and prevent the occurrence of stack overflow vulnerabilities.

- memory monitoring. Memory monitoring can monitor the memory access behavior of programs, detect memory attacks in time, and stop the attacks. Memory monitoring includes both static analysis and dynamic analysis.

- Strengthen the user rights management. User privilege management can limit the access of non-privileged users to system memory, thus reducing the opportunity for attackers to exploit memory vulnerabilities.

Overview and application of memory encryption

Memory encryption refers to the encryption of data in memory while the program is running to prevent attackers from stealing the data in memory. Memory encryption can be implemented through hardware, software, and other methods. The application of memory encryption includes the following aspects:

- Protecting sensitive data. Memory encryption can protect sensitive data in memory while the program is running, such as passwords, encryption keys, etc., to prevent attackers from stealing these data.

- Prevent memory attacks. Memory encryption can prevent attackers from using memory vulnerabilities to carry out memory attacks, thus improving the security of the system.

- Enhance program security. Memory encryption can enhance the security of programs, thus improving their trustworthiness and reliability.

Memory security threats are a very important issue in computer systems and require effective preventive measures. This chapter provides a detailed introduction to the prevention methods of memory security threats from three perspectives: the repair methods of memory security vulnerabilities, the detection and defense methods of memory attacks, and the overview and application of memory encryption. Through reasonable preventive measures, we can effectively prevent the occurrence of memory security threats and improve the security and stability of computer systems.

8.3.4.4 Security maintenance of memory

Memory is an important component of a computer system and has a significant impact on the stability and security of the system. During the operation of a computer system, memory needs to be regularly maintained, monitored, and diagnosed, as well as backed up and restored. The following is a detailed introduction to memory security maintenance from three perspectives: regular memory maintenance, memory monitoring and diagnosis, and memory backup and recovery.

Regular maintenance of memory

Regular maintenance of memory refers to the regular cleaning and optimization of memory to ensure the stability and performance of the system. Regular memory maintenance includes the following aspects:

- memory defragmentation. Memory fragmentation refers to the space in memory that is not fully utilized. Too much fragmentation will reduce the efficiency of memory usage. Memory defragmentation can organize and merge the fragmented space to improve the efficiency of memory utilization.

- Memory cleanup. During program operation, memory leaks and memory leaks may occur, resulting in excessive memory usage and reducing system stability and performance. Memory cleanup can periodically clean up memory space that is no longer in use and release memory resources, thus ensuring system stability and performance.

- Memory optimization. Memory optimization can improve the efficiency and performance of memory usage by adjusting memory parameters and optimizing memory usage, thus ensuring system stability and performance.

Memory Monitoring and Diagnosis

Memory monitoring and diagnosis refers to the monitoring and diagnosis of memory to find and solve memory problems in time to ensure system stability and security. Memory monitoring and diagnosis include the following aspects:

- Memory leak detection. Memory leak refers to the memory space allocated during program operation that has not been released, resulting in excessive memory occupation. Memory leak detection can be done through memory monitoring tools and other means to detect and solve memory leak problems promptly to avoid excessive memory occupation, resulting in system crashes.

- Memory error detection. Memory error refers to the program running process, accessing an illegal memory address, or using an uninitialized memory space, which leads to program crashes or security problems. Memory error detection can be used to detect and solve memory error problems in a timely manner, such as through memory detection tools, to ensure the stability and security of the system.

- Memory performance monitoring. Memory performance monitoring can be done through memory monitoring tools and other means to monitor. Memory performance monitoring can monitor the usage of memory, including memory occupation, memory usage efficiency, etc. Through the monitoring of memory performance, it is possible to find out the situation of excessive memory usage or inefficient usage in time, make timely adjustment and optimization, and improve the performance of the system.

Memory backup and recovery

Memory backup and recovery refers to the backup and recovery of memory for system crashes, failures, and other situations. Memory backup and recovery includes the following aspects:

- Memory snapshot backup. Memory snapshot backup refers to taking snapshots of memory and saving the current memory state to disk for backup in case of system failure. Memory snapshot backup can quickly restore the system to the state it was in at the time of backup, ensuring system availability and data security.

- Memory data backup. Memory data backup refers to the backup of data in memory in case of data loss, corruption, etc. Memory data backup can be done by regularly backing up memory data to disk, etc. to ensure data availability and security.

- Memory recovery. Memory recovery refers to the recovery by memory backup to ensure system availability and data security in case of system failure, crash, etc. Memory recovery can be done through memory snapshot recovery, memory data recovery, etc. to quickly restore the system to normal operation.

Memory is an important component of a computer system and has a significant impact on the stability and security of the system. In order to ensure the safe maintenance of memory, regular maintenance, monitoring, and diagnosis of memory are required, as well as backup and recovery. Regular maintenance of memory can be done through memory defragmentation, memory cleaning, memory optimization, etc. to improve the efficiency and performance of memory usage; memory monitoring and diagnosis can be done through memory leak detection, memory error detection, memory performance monitoring, etc. to find and solve memory problems in time; memory backup and recovery can be done through memory snapshot backup, memory data backup and memory recovery, etc. to ensure system The backup and recovery of memory can be done through memory snapshot backup, memory data backup and memory recovery to ensure system availability and data security.

8.4 CLASSIFICATION OF INFRASTRUCTURE AND HARDWARE SECURITY ISSUES

Hardware security measures refer to various technical means and measures adopted at the hardware level of computer systems to ensure the security of computer systems. The implementation of hardware security measures can effectively prevent Computer viruses, hacker intrusion, Data breaches, and other security issues, and protect the confidentiality, integrity, and availability of the computer system.

8.4.1 Physical Security

Physical security, also known as physical security, is a measure or process that protects computer equipment and facilities (including networks) from earthquakes, floods, fires, harmful gases, and other environmental accidents (such as electromagnetic pollution). Physical security mainly considers the security of the environment, site and equipment, Physical access control, emergency response plan, etc. Physical security technology mainly refers to the security measures taken for the environment, site, equipment, personnel, etc. of computer and network systems. Physical security includes environmental security, equipment security, power system security, and communication line security.

Environmental security: The operating environment of computer network communication systems should be designed and implemented in accordance with relevant national standards, and should have fire alarms, safety lighting, uninterrupted power supply, temperature and humidity control systems, and anti-theft alarms to protect the system from water, fire, harmful gases, earthquakes, and static electricity hazards.

Equipment security: including ensuring that the hardware is in good working condition at all times and establishing equipment operation logs. At the same time, it also includes the security of storage media (anti theft, anti damage, and anti mold).

Power system safety: including power energy supply, transmission line safety, maintaining power supply stability, etc.

Communication line security: including preventing electromagnetic information leakage, line interception, and resisting electromagnetic interference. The installation of communication equipment and communication lines should be stable and reliable, with a certain ability to resist natural and personal factors.

Physical security includes the following main contents:

- The site environment of a computer room and the impact of various factors on computing equipment.

- Safety requirements for computer rooms.

- Physical access control of computers.

- Fire prevention and waterproofing of computer equipment and premises.

- Electrostatic protection of computer systems.

- Anti-theft and damage measures for computer equipment, software, and data.

- Issues related to the processing, storage, and processing procedures of magnetic media for important information in computers.

In computer systems, physical security faces various threats, including threats from non-human factors such as natural, environmental, and technological failures, as well as threats from human errors and malicious attacks. These threats threaten the security of information systems by disrupting their confidentiality (such as electromagnetic leakage threats), integrity (such as various natural disaster threats), and availability (such as technological failure threats). The factors that pose a threat can be divided into human factors and environmental factors. According to the motivation of the threat, human factors can be further divided into two types: malicious and non-malicious. Environmental factors include uncontrollable factors in nature and other physical factors. The main threats to physical security include:

1. Natural disasters: Mainly including rodent and ant pests, floods, fires, earthquakes, etc.

2. Electromagnetic environment impact: Mainly including power outage, voltage fluctuation, static electricity, electromagnetic interference, etc.

3. Physical environmental impact: Mainly including dust, humidity, temperature, etc.

4. Software and hardware impact: The impact on the security and availability of information systems due to device hardware failures, communication chain interruptions, system or software defects.

5. Physical attacks: Physical contact, physical damage, theft.

6. No action or operational error: The impact on the information system caused by the failure to perform corresponding actions or unintentional execution of incorrect actions that should have been performed.

7. Inadequate management: Physical security management cannot be implemented or in place, resulting in non-standard or chaotic physical security management, thereby disrupting the normal and orderly operation of information systems.

8. Exceeding authority or abuse: By adopting measures that exceed one's own authority to access resources that one does not have access to, or by abusing one's authority to engage in behavior that damages information systems, such as illegal device access or device external connections.

9. Design and configuration defects: There are obvious system availability vulnerabilities during the design phase, such as system failure to configure correctly and effectively, and errors caused by

system expansion and adjustment. In response to the potential threats mentioned above, physical security can be generally protected from the following aspects.

- Environmental safety: Ensure that sufficient measures are taken and ensured to prevent the impact of environmental factors. For data centers, only waterless fire extinguishing systems can be used, and backup batteries can be provided for computers to provide sufficient power.

- Facility and equipment security: Equipment management is strictly prohibited from purchasing and using other information security products that have not been recognized by national information security evaluation institutions. Equipment can only be purchased after meeting the system selection requirements and obtaining approval; Equipment safety mainly includes anti-theft, destruction prevention, electromagnetic information radiation prevention, line interception prevention, electromagnetic interference resistance, and power supply protection.

- Media security: For damage, remote disaster recovery methods can be adopted. For leakage, preventive measures include: shielding the host room and important information storage and transmission departments, resisting the conducted radiation of local network and local area network transmission lines, and preventing radiation from terminal equipment. Take contingency plans for unexpected errors to guide work.

8.4.2 Email and Network Communication Security

In today's world where instant messaging tools such as Whatapps, Telegram, Line, QQ and WeChat are widely used, email, as the oldest and most widely used form of information communication on the internet, still retains its charm. With the continuous strengthening of email storage and business functions, email will continue to be a simple, fast, reliable, and cost-effective modern means of communication between many individuals and enterprises. Many network users even view email as an "online safe" for storing personal information. However, as businesses and individuals transmit more and more important information through email, a series of updated and more complex attack methods such as viruses, Trojans, spam, worms, and spyware make email communication a risky behavior.

From the process of email message transmission, it can be seen that email messages exist in clear text during the transmission process from one network to another, and from one computer to another. The transmission of unencrypted data on the network is not secure, and any node on the physical link through which emails pass can intercept and modify emails, and may even forge others' emails. The security risks of the email include the following aspects:

Due to the inherent security risks of email transmission protocols, such as SMTP not being encrypted, content can be intercepted. Due to design flaws in the email receiving client software, such as security risks in Outlook and the threat of virus trojans running automatically due to specific encoding. Security hazards are caused by the personal reasons of users.

- E-mail virus: E-mail can carry viruses because it can carry attachments such as Word documents or EXE executable files. Word documents may carry Macro viruses, and EXE files may carry more types of viruses. Therefore, when binary data is transmitted with attachments, the transmitted data may contain viruses.

- Malicious code in MIME header: When the MIME header is read into memory, its length is not checked. By adding malicious code to attachments, attackers can overflow emails from the receiving client program's buffer.

- Email leakage: MIME cannot solve the problem of email theft, as anyone with access to emails can read them, which leads to the issue of email leakage.

- Email Bomb: Email Bomb refers to the sender of an email, who uses certain special email software to continuously mail large amounts of emails to the same recipient in a short period of time. The capacity of user email is generally limited, overwhelmed by these thousands of large capacity letters, ultimately leading to resource exhaustion and "explosion".

- Spam: Users may be forced to receive unwanted emails, such as certain commercial advertisements, mailing lists, electronic publications, and website promotions.

The following measures can be taken for security protection against email insecurity:

- Using secure email: Secure email uses digital certificates to digitally sign and encrypt emails, ensuring their authenticity and preventing them from being stolen by others. To use secure email, you need to obtain a digital ID first.

- Perform virus protection on email and its systems: Firstly, choose a reliable antivirus software, borrow the real-time email monitoring function from the antivirus software, and perform virus scanning during the email receiving process to effectively prevent the intrusion of email viruses. For antivirus software, it is important to regularly upgrade and update it, otherwise, it will be difficult to detect and kill new viruses. Secondly, to understand the broad commonalities of some email viruses in order to identify them, when receiving an email, first check the size of the email. If there is no content or attachment in the email, and the email itself is large, it may contain viruses. If the suffix name of the attachment is a double suffix, it is highly likely to be a virus. Simply delete it. In addition, due to the fact that some client programs have always been the focus of attention for hackers, and there are some security vulnerabilities in these programs, it is necessary to update email client programs and download upgrade patches in a timely manner.

- Set mailbox filtering: The email filter allows users to set filtering rules based on the source, recipient, subject, and length of the email. The filter can be set at the local email client level or directly through the browser within the POP3 mailbox. When setting, pay attention to the "size of received mail" option. It is recommended to control this Numerical control to about 1/3 of the e-mail capacity. If the size of sent mail exceeds this value, it will be considered a mail bomb and will be rejected by the system directly. Email filtering can not only prevent spam but also filter out some emails with viruses, so that they do not enter the inbox, reducing the chance of virus infection.

- Email security precautions in public places: People often need to receive and send emails in public places such as internet cafes, school public computer rooms, and units. As other people have the opportunity to access your email sending and receiving machine, emails are easily stolen by others, so special attention should be paid to the security of emails in public places.

- Email security precautions in public places: People often need to receive and send emails in public places such as internet cafes, school public computer rooms, and units. As other people have the opportunity to access your email sending and receiving machine, emails are easily stolen by others, so special attention should be paid to the security of emails in public places.

- Pay attention to encrypting your email: If using an email client program to send and receive emails, be sure to encrypt your email. Otherwise, others can directly view the emails you receive and send, or you can completely delete the emails after checking them. Be sure to clear the deleted emails from the trash to prevent others from accessing your emails. Because public computer rooms are often located in a local area network environment, using client programs to connect to OR/send emails can easily result in others intercepting data packets and obtaining your password. Therefore, it is best to receive/send emails through the web and delete the cache file of the browser before shutting down the computer and leaving. Otherwise, others can view the content of the letters you browse using the web browser by calling the browser's cache.

- Change the opening method of sensitive attachment types: Viruses spread through email, with a large portion spreading through email attachments.

Nowadays, the speed of information development is rapid, and the connection between our communication and the network is becoming increasingly close. In this situation, it has to some extent promoted the rapid development of the network. It is undeniable that in today's increasingly prosperous network communication, its security issues have gradually received attention from consumers, and the pressure on maintaining network communication security is also increasing. The natural attribute of network communication is openness, and at the same time, the existence of openness has also led to many security vulnerabilities. With the deteriorating internal and external security environment, activities such as information theft or network attacks have gradually become rampant. At the same time, the trend of malicious behavior on the internet has gradually become apparent, which to some extent has fully attracted our attention. The existence of many organized groups or hacker attacks seriously affects the communication security of China's network. Network communication faces various threats, as follows:

- Information replay: Without sufficient security measures, it is easy to be subjected to MITM deception attacks using illegal APs. For this type of attack behavior, even with protective measures such as VPN, it is difficult to avoid. MITM attack dupes the authorized client and the AP to steal and tamper with information.

- WEP cracking: It is now common on the Internet to have some illegal programs that can capture data packets located in the AP signal coverage area, collect sufficient WEP weak key encrypted packets, and analyze them to recover WEP keys. According to the speed of the machine monitoring wireless communication and the number of wireless hosts transmitting signals within the WLAN, the WEP key can be broken within two hours at the fastest.

- Network eavesdropping: Generally speaking, most network communication appears in plaintext (non-encrypted) format, which allows attackers within the coverage range of wireless signals to monitor and crack (read) communication. Due to the fact that intruders do not need to physically connect eavesdropping or analysis devices to the eavesdropped network, this threat has become one of the biggest problems faced by wireless local area networks.

- Counterfeiting attack: An entity pretends to access a wireless network as another entity, known as a phishing attack. This is the most common method of invading a security line. In wireless networks, there are no fixed physical links between mobile stations, network control centers, or other mobile stations. Mobile stations must transmit their identity information through wireless channels, and identity information may be eavesdropped during transmission. When attackers intercept the identity information of a legitimate user, they can use that user's identity to invade the network, known as an identity impersonation attack.

- MAC address spoofing: By using network eavesdropping tools to obtain data and further obtain a static address pool that AP allows communication, unscrupulous individuals can use MAC address spoofing and other means to access the network reasonably.

- Denial of service: Attackers may conduct flooding attacks on APs, causing them to refuse service, which is the most serious attack. In addition, attacking a node within the mobile mode, causing it to continuously provide services or forward packets, causing it to run out of energy and be unable to continue working, is commonly referred to as an energy consumption attack.

- Post service repudiation: Post service repudiation refers to one party in a transaction denying their participation in the transaction after it is completed, which is a common threat in network communication.

It is precisely because the functions of communication networks are becoming increasingly powerful, and our daily lives are increasingly inseparable from them. Therefore, we must take a series of effective measures to minimize the risks of the network. The main measures for network communication security protection include:

- Physical secure transmission medium: Using optical fiber to transmit data in the network can prevent information from being stolen. To ensure the security of the communication network, a secure transmission medium can be chosen.

- Encryption of transmission data: confidential data shall be encrypted during data communication, including link encryption and End-to-end encryption. In most cases, password technology is the most effective means of network security, which can prevent unauthorized users from stealing and also effectively prevent malicious attacks.

- Firewall technology: Generally, the firewall technology used for network external interfaces can generate certain control over data, information, and other aspects during network layer access. By identifying and restricting or changing various data flows that pass through firewalls, network security protection can be achieved, which can greatly prevent hackers from appearing in the network. To a certain extent, it can prevent these hackers from maliciously changing or arbitrarily moving important network information. The existence of firewalls can prevent the spread of unsafe factors in the internet and is a more effective security mechanism. Therefore, firewalls can be said to be an indispensable part of network security.

- Identity authentication technology: Authenticated technology can ensure the integrity and confidentiality of information to a certain extent.

- Intrusion detection technology: General firewall knowledge protects the internal network from external attacks, and the level of monitoring illegal activities in the internal network is not enough. Intrusion systems exist to compensate for this. It can actively provide real-time protection against internal and external attacks, and intercept information before the network is compromised, which can improve the security of information.

- Vulnerability scanning technology: When facing the constantly complex and changing situation of the network, relying on relevant network administrators for security vulnerability and risk assessment is obviously not feasible. Only relying on network security scanning tools can eliminate security vulnerabilities and hidden dangers under optimized system configuration. In some low security situations, hacker tools can be used to simulate network attacks, which can expose network vulnerabilities at a certain level.

- Virtual private network technology: A secure and temporary link is established by an internet, which is a stable and secure channel through a chaotic public network.

8.4.3 Cloud Security

"Cloud Security" is an important application of "cloud" technology after "cloud computing" and "cloud storage". It is an extension of the traditional IT security concept in the cloud computing era. It has been widely used in anti-virus software and has played a good role. In the technological competition between viruses and antivirus software, antivirus software has taken the lead. The most recent example of information security in the network era is the "Cloud Security" plan. It incorporates cutting-edge ideas and technology like parallel processing, grid computing, and viral behavior analysis. It gathers the most recent information on trojans and malicious software on the Internet and transmits it to the server for automatic analysis and processing. It also distributes virus and Trojan solutions to every client. It keeps an eye on the strange behavior of software in the network through a large number of mesh clients. The emergence and organic evolution of distributed computing technologies like P2P, the grid, and cloud computing has led to the development of cloud security technology.

In short, cloud computing is an emerging way of utilizing computing resources. Cloud computing service providers turn basic IT resources into freely schedulable resource pools through virtualization of hardware resources, thereby achieving on-demand allocation of IT resources and providing customers with paid for use cloud computing services. Users can dynamically adjust their required resources based on business needs, and cloud service providers can improve their resource utilization efficiency, reduce service costs, and provide users with support for computing, storage, and data business through various types of service methods.

Where there is information transmission, there are security issues, and cloud security is a security issue faced in cloud computing environments. On the one hand, security problems in the traditional environment still exist in the cloud environment, such as SQL injection, internal ultra vires, Data breach, data tampering, web page tampering, vulnerability attacks, etc. On the other hand, a bunch of new security problems continue to emerge in the cloud environment. The following will analyze the security challenges in the cloud computing environment from the two dimensions of management and use and business security protection.

The needs and challenges faced by the use of security management dimensions:

- Difficulty in deploying cloud security: Cloud computing has broken the network boundaries of traditional IT environments, and users' business is deployed on the cloud. Traditional hardware boxes are no longer able to be deployed to users' virtual networks, and cannot meet their cloud security needs.

- Secure on-demand self-service: The business of each user on the cloud is very different, and the security requirements are also different. The traditional mode of pre-planning security devices to protect specific business systems in the traditional environment is no longer applicable to the cloud computing environment, but the on-demand self-service application for security resources and the realization of security services out of the box mode has become the basic demand of cloud security for cloud users.

- Secure on-demand metering and billing: In the cloud environment, users use IT resources like water and pay on demand. However, in traditional environments, the performance and usage period of security equipment models are fixed, which clearly does not meet the needs of cloud users for security resources. Security resources also need to meet the principle of on-demand billing.

- Autoscaling of security resources: The business scale on the user's cloud will scale Autoscaling with the development of the business, so the security resources also need to scale and expand with the business, that is, the security on the cloud needs to have the characteristics of Autoscaling of the security resource pool.

- Unified operation and maintenance management: There may be many types of security services adopted by cloud users, and if each security service is operated and managed separately, it will bring great challenges to users' daily security operations. Therefore, unified security operation and maintenance management is a major pain point that cloud security solutions need to address.

The needs and challenges faced by business security protection:

- Virtual Machine Escape: Cloud computing enables the sharing of host resources. Ideally, programs running in one virtual machine cannot affect other virtual machines. However, in some cases, programs running on virtual machines may bypass the underlying layer to control the host. Once the host is controlled, other users' businesses will face huge security threats.

- East-west safety protection: The business of cloud users may be deployed in multiple virtual machines, and once a single virtual machine is controlled or infected with a virus, the impact on the entire business system is also catastrophic. Therefore, east-west protection is one of the main requirements for cloud security.

- Data leakage: The foundation of cloud computing is massive data, and if massive data is leaked, the losses caused will be much greater than in traditional environments. In cloud environments, multi-user data is shared and stored on the cloud. If a user's application has vulnerabilities, it may lead to the disclosure of data from other customers. Malicious hackers can use viruses, Trojan horses, or direct attack methods to permanently delete cloud data to endanger cloud system security.

- Cloud Platform Security Audit: The business of users relies on the cloud, and data is also stored in the cloud. Compliance and security audits of the cloud platform itself are also major challenges faced by cloud users.

8.4.4 IoT Security

IoT Architecture

The general architecture of the IoT system is mainly divided into three parts: the perception layer, the network layer, and the application layer.

The perception layer corresponds to various IoT devices. The device collects application scene information in real time through sensors and sends it to the application layer, or receives application layer instructions and executes corresponding actions. The internal architecture of the device can be divided into hardware layer, system layer, and user layer. Among them, the hardware layer includes various hardware modules (such as network modules, sensor modules, etc.), processors, peripheral circuits, etc. that support device functions; the system layer is loaded with firmware programs, including operating systems and application programs, responsible for device Realization of functions; the user layer mainly provides the user with an operation interface for displaying data and receiving input.

The network layer corresponds to the communication between devices and the three types of entities: devices, cloud platforms, and mobile apps. Devices can form self-organizing networks (such as industrial equipment networks, and drone clusters) through lightweight protocols such as ZigBee and Z-Wave [286]; devices can also form local area networks (such as smart home networks) after being connected by routers. There are two ways for the device to connect to the router: one is to connect directly through Wi-Fi; the other is to connect to the gateway device (such as a hub) through ZigBee, Z-Wave, and other protocols, and then communicate with the router through Wi-Fi through the gateway.

There are three types of communication [287] between entities: communication between devices and Apps. Devices can be directly connected to mobile phones through Bluetooth (such as wearable devices, and vehicle system networks), or communicate with mobile phones through local area network Wi-Fi (such as smart home networks); The device communicates with the cloud platform, and the device relies on the router to forward the request and receive the response, while the communication between the router and the cloud platform is mainly realized by the traditional TCP/IP network architecture; the communication between the mobile phone and the cloud platform: the mobile app can pass through the 4G/5G network or the local area network Wi-Fi connects to the cloud platform.

The application layer mainly corresponds to the cloud platform and the mobile app. The cloud platform is mainly composed of various application services deployed by manufacturers on the cloud, responsible for managing devices and users, processing data collected by devices, or sending remote control commands to devices. According to the functions provided by the cloud platform, it can be divided into three types: device access platform, service linkage platform, and voice assistant platform. The device access platform provides actual device access and management functions, such as Samsung SmartThings, Google Home, Philips Hue, Xiaomi Mijia, etc. The service linkage platform does not connect real devices but connects the functions of other platforms. Provide "condition-action" automatic execution rule services, such as the IFTTT platform, etc. The voice assistant platform provides voice control services to users through smart speakers, and the voice commands issued by users can be connected to other functions or services of control devices after being processed by the voice platform Together, such as Amazon Alexa and more. In addition, different cloud platforms can also execute device control by calling API (application programming interface) each other after authorization. The mobile app can be regarded as the control terminal provided by the cloud platform to the user. It is mainly used to provide the user with a device-related functional interface, which can visually display the device status or execute control commands.

System threats

1. Cloud platform access control flaws

   Access control is a crucial requirement for the cloud platform to run normally. Many devices that are intimately tied to humans are connected to the IoT cloud platform. The cloud platform will turn into a potent tool for attackers if authentication or permission management have flaws. Existing research shows that the access control problem of cloud platforms is prominent, and the threats of authority management can be divided into two types: intra-platform and inter-platform according to the type of authorization.

   First of all, some platforms have loopholes in the permission management design of internal applications or services. SmartThings and IFTTT are popular cloud platforms around the world, with a large user base and connected to a large number of devices and services. However, some studies have found that these two platforms have adopted coarse-grained control over the applications or services connected to devices. In the permission division method, an application or service can obtain permissions beyond the scope of its application, so that attackers can use this flaw to easily initiate information monitoring or over-authorization control on other people's devices. Secondly, there are also design loopholes in the process of mutual authorization between cloud platforms. At present, most cloud platforms allow users to connect devices registered under other manufacturers' platforms to their own platforms after "cloud authorization". However, in the absence of a unified inter-platform authorization standard, even if the manufacturer has done a security audit within its own scope, new loopholes may be exposed due to asymmetric authorization requirements between platforms during authority transfer. Some scholars have conducted systematic research on such security issues and found security loopholes in the authorization process between many world-renowned cloud platforms. These security loopholes allow attackers to bypass the protection of the device's own platform through the proxy platform. mechanism to initiate illegal access to the device.

2. Malicious applications on the cloud platform

The cloud platform provides various device-oriented applications, and users can realize rich control functions through the applications. However, the current security review of cloud platforms for applications is not perfect, resulting in the presence of malicious applications. This section introduces several forms of malicious applications on cloud platforms.

Some cloud platforms are completely closed to users. Users cannot obtain the logic or code of the application and can only install the application package by the cloud platform or automatically execute rules. Although some platforms hide the underlying operating mechanism from users, they will open a series of basic design functions (such as API or programming framework) to users, and users can write and publish applications by themselves. Such platforms include SmartThings, IFTTT, Alexa, etc. Although they provide a richer and more flexible application ecosystem, they provide attackers with opportunities to implement malicious applications. A number of studies on the SmartThings platform have proved that the platform's application openness and imperfect audit mechanism are very easy to introduce malicious applications. Among the publicly released applications (such as SmartApp in Smart-Things), nearly 2/3 have the ability to leak device privacy risks. On the IFTTT platform, researchers found that nearly 30 percent of the services in the market (such as Applet in IFTTT) have security risks. The malicious link embedded in the code by the attacker will send the private information entered by the user to the attacker's server. In addition, the form of malicious code in the voice platform is a skill with malicious intentions. An attacker can upload a malicious skill to secretly hijack normal voice commands or replace the function of a real skill without the user being aware of it.

3. Communication protocol loopholes

The IoT system communication integrates the traditional TCP/IP protocol, as well as the common underlying protocols and private protocols in the IoT system. Threats against traditional protocols will be introduced into the IoT. Defects in the design and implementation of the IoT system protocol It also creates new security holes. This section focuses on two types of protocols that are closely related to IoT systems: IoT common protocols and proprietary protocols.

The first is the commonly used protocols of the Internet of Things, such as MQTT (message queuing telemetry transport), CoAP, Zig-Bee, Bluetooth low energy, etc. Although this type of protocol is not specially designed for IoT systems, it is favored by many IoT systems due to its characteristics of adapting to low-power devices and low bandwidth requirements, so it is widely used in IoT systems. rate, but it is not designed for adversarial application scenarios, so it lacks built-in security mechanisms, and manufacturers tend to ignore the consideration of security attributes when applying and implementing these protocols. Researchers have found flaws in the implementation of the MQTT protocol in the IoT platforms of many world-renowned manufacturers, which may lead to large-scale distributed denial of service, remote device hijacking, user privacy theft, and other attacks after being exploited by attackers. Bluetooth's low energy consumption is currently the main channel for wearable devices to communicate with mobile apps, but threats such as privacy leaks and device hijacking have been discovered during the application of the protocol.

The second is the private protocol of the Internet of Things. This type of protocol refers to the protocol type customized by the manufacturer, which is usually only applicable to the communication of devices under its platform, and the implementation details are generally not open to the outside world. However, attackers can still obtain communication details through reverse engineering. If the manufacturer has flaws in the design of private protocols, it may also be exploited by attackers to launch attacks. Current research has proved that after the private protocols of many well-known Internet of Things manufacturers in the world are successfully parsed, their vulnerabilities in device authentication and authorization checks will be immediately exposed to attackers.

4. Attacks based on voice channels

Voice assistant devices (such as smart speakers) are in the control center of the Internet of Things system. Users can control other devices through voice assistant devices, so attacks on voice devices will threaten all devices controlled by them.

First, some attack techniques can hide voice signals that are undetectable to humans but recognizable to devices in the voice channel. Researchers have studied several methods for constructing voice commands that can be interpreted by speech recognition systems but not detected by humans while demonstrating that these commands can spy on users' privacy and open phishing websites by themselves. Afterward, many studies have discovered the carrier of transmitting voice commands, for example, modulating voice signals into high-frequency ultrasonic signals that humans cannot recognize or embedding voice commands into music; there are also studies that use solid voice equipment as a medium, through Solid vibration frequencies are used to transmit voice commands. The common feature of the above attacks is that voice devices can normally receive and interpret such signals, but it is difficult for humans to perceive the interaction process.

In addition, hidden speech signals face challenges of propagation distance and noise influence during transmission, but such difficulties are proven to be overcome. For example, by extracting the factors affecting signal distortion caused by hardware structure and channel frequency as one of the factors for generating speech signal adversarial samples, it can effectively overcome the influence of noise in propagation and improve the success rate of speech signal recognition.

Protective measures

1. Fine-grained cloud platform access control

   The main reason for the access control problem of the Internet of Things cloud platform is that the cloud platform fails to follow the principle of least privilege when implementing functions. Therefore, the current research uses the characteristics of the cloud platform to design a fine-grained access control mechanism.

   For the SmartThings platform, the current research extracts the real-time context of the application running process from the SmartApp to provide fine-grained reference information for whether the current operation complies with the access control policy. For example, ContextIoT expresses the context information when the application executes operations by extracting information such as the execution path, data dependencies, real-time variable values, and environmental parameters inside the SmartApp, and then actively solicits user authorization before the operation is executed. Only operations are authorized by the user to continue execution. SmartAuth uses natural language processing technology to extract the information about the operation in the text description of SmartApp's functions and then uses the taint analysis technology to obtain the real operation when the application is running and compares whether the real operation is consistent with the text description. If it is inconsistent, it will actively notify the user to ask for authorization. Both of these two schemes can accurately prevent privacy leakage generated by malicious applications in practical applications but inevitably increase user operations.

   For the service rules based on access token linkage in IFTTT, the researchers proposed an optimization scheme for authority management to address the problems existing in the token management model. The token disperses the centralized permission management model into distributed management with application agents as the unit, which can effectively solve the problems of centralized management and coarse-grained tokens.

In addition, some research is oriented to special application scenarios in the Internet of Things. Based on theories in other fields, such as SDN (software-defined network), smartphone access control, etc., proposing a new access control model, but its implementation requires special architecture support.

2. Secure communication protocol

In order to ensure the communication security of the IoT system, a robust security mechanism needs to be added to the commonly used protocols of the IoT. However, the formulation and improvement of the protocol is a process of multi-party participation and long-term evolution. Strict checks are enforced on the identity and authority of communicating entities. For example, in view of the lack of security attributes in the MQTT protocol model, communication session management mechanisms, message-oriented access control mechanisms, and functional scope restrictions on wildcards should be added; in view of the inherent defects of the ZigBee protocol, devices should be enhanced when they join the network and communicate normally. The level of encryption for these 2 stages. In addition, some studies have designed a secure communication protocol based on the characteristics of the Internet of Things system. For example, Alshahrani et al. proposed a model of mutual authentication and key exchange between devices based on ZigBee communication, which can enhance the robustness of the ZigBee protocol in adversarial environments.

There are also some studies that design a new type of secure pairing protocol for short-distance communication between devices, which can overcome the problems of key information being easily stolen and requiring manual participation in traditional pairing protocols. For example, Han et al. based on the fact that adjacent smart devices have consistent perception of physical activities in the same time period, using the physical perception parameters in the same time period to generate a symmetric key can effectively resist device masquerading and MITM attacks. Jin et al. designed a new pairing scheme for wearable devices by taking advantage of the highly random and unpredictable characteristics of the signal characteristics generated when radio frequency signal noise propagates in different media (such as the surface of the human body and the air).

3. Voice attack defense

Aiming at malicious voice attack samples hidden in various media of voice channels and undetectable by users, some studies have proposed corresponding defense schemes:

- The first solution is to add an interaction mode based on security prompts and voice confirmation in the interaction process of voice devices. Users need to actively confirm sensitive operations to improve security, but this method will bring additional usability overhead and confirmation Operations are easily overlooked by users.

- The second solution is to filter voice signals with special signal characteristics (such as high-frequency ultrasonic waves) by adding dedicated hardware modules or physically isolating the direct contact between voice equipment and hardware media such as desktops, but the former requires special hardware support, while the latter Adds a burden to the usability of voice equipment.

- The third solution is to affect the recognition rate of the speech recognition system for malicious commands by increasing noise interference or reducing the sampling frequency of the input audio, but this solution will also affect the recognition rate of normal speech.

- The fourth option is to implement voiceprint recognition through machine learning algorithms to distinguish between human and machine-generated voices, but this will cause additional operating overhead for the voice recognition system.

In addition, since the artificially generated voice commands lack the wireless signal interference caused by humans speaking on the spot, this feature can be used to distinguish hidden voice commands. For example, researchers can accurately distinguish generated malicious voice signals from real human voices by using the Wi-Fi channel state information change patterns caused by human pronunciation and the correlation of voice signals. However, this solution currently relies on an environment with strong Wi-Fi signal coverage, and the recognition process is sensitive to signal fluctuations. If the speaker is too far away from the signal-receiving antenna, the recognition cannot be performed because the signal disturbance cannot be captured.

8.5 SUMMARY

This chapter introduced the concept, principles, and strategies of computer hardware security. Security threats of computer hardware are also mentioned. In Section 8.2, we discuss the influencing factors, principles and steps of hardware security. Computer hard drive security maintenance, such as causes of hard disk failure and data loss, secure maintenance of computer processors, are listed in Section 8.3. Finally, in Section 8.4 we explained the classification of infrastructure and Hardware Security. Issues

8.6 EXERCISES

1. List and explain some threats faced by computer hardware security, such as resource abuse, privacy breaches, service manipulation, and MITM attacks:

2. What is a secure microprocessor? How does it enhance the security of computer systems?

3. Why is maintaining the network environment crucial for computer hardware security?

4. Explain the principles of computer hardware security and describe the strategies to ensure computer hardware security.

   There are several concepts related to settings:

   - What is network setup? Network setup involves configuring and adjusting computer networks. It includes setting up network connections, IP addresses, subnet masks, gateways, DNS, and other network parameters to ensure that computers can communicate and access resources within the network.

   - What is the setting process? The setting process refers to the procedure and steps followed to configure and prepare devices, systems, or environments. It includes hardware installation, software configuration, network connectivity, and other necessary operations to ensure that the device or system functions properly.

- What is hardware setup? Hardware setup involves the installation and configuration of hardware devices. It includes connecting hardware components to computer systems or other devices and performing necessary physical adjustments and settings to ensure that the hardware devices work properly.

- What is system configuration? System configuration refers to the process of configuring and adjusting computer systems. It includes selecting and setting up operating systems, installing and configuring drivers, performing system optimization, and security settings to ensure that computer systems function properly.

GLOSSARY

Computer memory and cache: are important peripherals of the CPU that are responsible for storing data and instructions, as well as providing access interfaces to data and instructions.

Data Backup: is one of the basic principles of hard drive security maintenance, which ensures that in the event of a hard drive failure or data loss, data can be recovered quickly and the impact of data loss on users can be reduced.

Data bus encryption: refers to the use of a key to encrypt data on the data bus when encrypting relevant instructions including system application programs and ordinary data information.

Fully encrypted hard disk: is an important part of computer hardware security equipment, which encrypts every byte of data in the hard disk.

Isolated memory area: is safely isolated from the outside world and stores sensitive data can be formed, which can more effectively keep the user's personal privacy confidential.

Physical security: is a measure or process that protects computer equipment and facilities (including networks) from earthquakes, floods, fires, harmful gases, and other environmental accidents (such as electromagnetic pollution).

Secure Microprocessor: can extract and process the encrypted operation code, and complete the decryption and instruction execution operations within the specified time.

Threat Analysis: is a cyberspace security strategy aimed at evaluating a company's security protocols, processes, and procedures to identify threats and vulnerabilities, and even gather relevant knowledge before potential attacks occur.

CHAPTER 9

Secure Distributed Data Storage and Processing

Distributed systems are characterized by their decentralized nature and the need for secure authentication and authorization mechanisms. Instead of redundantly implementing authentication and authorization logic in each service, independent authentication services can handle system-wide authentication and authorization requests, including for third-party systems. This approach promotes code reusability, simplifies maintenance, and ensures consistent security policies across the system. This chapter outlined the concepts and principles of distributed systems, distributed data storage and processing. An overview of the latest techniques and practices in secure distributed computing is discussed, including secure Moore's Law, heterogeneous CMP, distributed computing algorithm, and distributed data storage algorithm. The chapter also highlights the importance of secure data storage and processing in modern society and offers insights into future trends and developments in the field.

9.1 DISTRIBUTED SYSTEM SECURITY

9.1.1 Identity Authentication and Authorization

Every service in a distributed system requires identity authentication and authorization. It would be redundant if each service implemented its authentication and authorization logic individually. Considering the shared nature of distributed systems, it is necessary to have an independent system to handle authentication and authorization requests. Considering the openness of distributed systems, authentication is provided for internal services and third-party systems. The requirements for distributed authentication are as follows:

1. *Unified authentication and authorization*

    An independent party provides authentication service to handle authentication and authorization uniformly.

    Regardless of the type of users or clients (web, H5, APP), a consistent authentication, permission, and session mechanism should be used to achieve unified authentication and authorization.

    The existing authentication method must be scalable to get unified. It can support various authentication requirements, such as username and password, SMS verification code, QR code, face recognition, and other authentication methods, and be interchangeable.

2. *Application access authentication*

    The system should possess expansion and openness capabilities, a secure mechanism for docking with other systems, and provide access to some APIs for third-party applications. A unified mechanism should be deployed to ensure seamless integration and consistent access to internal system services and third-party applications. This will help to promote interoperability, enhance security, and facilitate collaboration between different systems and applications.

The two main distributed authentication solutions are as follows. The two authentication methods are to trust all requests that it received from a user.

1. *Session-based authentication method*

    Session-based authentication in a distributed environment often encounters challenges. In this scenario, each application service must store the user's identity information in the session, and the session information must be carried over when the local request is redirected to another application service through load balancing. Failure to do so may result in re-authentication, which can cause interruptions to the user experience and impact system performance. There are three solutions:

    (a) Session replication: Synchronize sessions between multiple application servers to keep them consistent and transparent to the outside world.

(b) Session stickiness: After the user accesses a server in the cluster, all subsequent requests are forced to be directed to this machine.

(c) Centralized session storage: Store sessions in distributed caches, and all server application instances uniformly store and retrieve sessions from distributed caches.

2. *Token-based authentication method*

   Based on this method, the server does not need to store authentication data, which is easy to maintain and has robust scalability. A token is a tampered-proof file. The client can store the token anywhere, and a unified authentication mechanism for the web and app can be achieved. However, its drawbacks are also prominent. Due to the self-contained information of the token, the data volume is generally large, and it needs to be transmitted with every new request, which occupies more bandwidth. In addition, the signature verification operation of the token will also bring an additional processing burden to the CPU.

3. *System suits unified authentication*

   To achieve unified authentication, it is essential that the client, first-party application, and third-party application all adopt a consistent authentication mechanism. This ensures that all parties adhere to the same standards, promoting interoperability and enhancing security. The token authentication method is more suitable for third-party application access because it is more open and can use popular protocols such as OAuth2.0 and JWT. In general, the server does not need to store session information, reducing the pressure on the server. The distributed authentication flow is as follows:

   (a) The user logs in through the accessing party (application), and the accessing party authenticates in the unified Authentication Service (UAA) in the OAuth2.0 manner.

   (b) The UAA verifies the legality of the user's identity and obtains the user's permission information.

   (c) The UAA obtains the access party's permission information and verifies whether the accessing party is legal.

(d) If both the logged-in user and the accessing party are legal, the authentication service generates a JWT token. It returns it to the access party, including the user and access party permissions.

(e) Subsequently, the accessing party carries the JWT token to access microservice resources in the API gateway.

(f) The API gateway parses the token and verifies whether the access party's permissions can access the microservice requested in this request.

(g) If there are no issues with the access party's permissions, the API gateway attaches the parsed plaintext token to the original request header and forwards the request to the microservice.

(h) The microservice receives the request, and the plaintext token contains the login user's identity and permission information. Therefore, the microservice can do two things by itself in the future:

- User authorization interception (to see if the current user has the right to access the resource)
- Store user information in the current thread context (it is helpful for subsequent business logic to obtain current user information at any time).

9.1.2 Secure Communication and Transport Protocols

1. Secure Socket Layer Protocol

    SSL protocol , and its successor TLS protocol, is a secure protocol that provides security and data integrity for network communication. TLS and SSL encrypt network connections at the transport layer to ensure the security of network data transmission. Data encryption technology ensures that data cannot be intercepted or eavesdropped during network transmission. The SSL protocol has become a global standard, and all major browsers and web server programs support it. SSL protocol can be activated by installing an SSL certificate.

    (a) SSL Protocol Structure

        The SSL protocol provides security assistance for data transfer by sitting between the TCP/IP protocol and different application layer protocols. There are two layers to the SSL protocol:

- **SSL Record Protocol:** The data stream is divided into pieces, each of which is safeguarded and transferred independently. To guarantee data integrity, the MAC of the data must be determined before transmission of data pieces. To create a record of the actual material transferred, the header data is joined with the encrypted data fragments and MAC. For SSL connections, the SSL Record Protocol offers the two services of message integrity and secrecy. All sent data in the SSL protocol is included into records. The record consists of record data (length not equal to 0) and record header. The SSL Record layer, which includes higher-level handshake protocols, alert protocols, and change cypher standard protocols, is used in all SSL communication. Record headers and record data formatting are supported by the SSL Record Protocol. Above some trustworthy transport protocols (like TCP) for encapsulating various higher-level protocols, the SSL Record Protocol specifies the data format to be transferred. Message authentication, encryption, compression, and grouping are the major tasks it completes.

- **SSL Handshake Protocol:** In the SSL protocol, the SSL Handshake Protocol is used by the client and server to obtain a key through a handshake process. Subsequently, this key is used in the Record Protocol to encrypt communication information between the client and server. The handshake process first uses asymmetric encryption to exchange information, allowing the server to obtain the pre-master secret provided by the client. Then, the server and client use this pre-master secret to generate a session key.

- **SSL Change Cipher Spec Protocol:** It is one of the three specific protocols of the SSL higher-level protocol that uses the SSL Record Protocol service and is also the simplest one. The protocol consists of a single message containing only a single byte with a value of 1. The only function of this message is to replicate the pending state as the current state and update the password group used for the current connection. To ensure the security of SSL transmission, both parties should change the encryption specification every so often. The SSL Change Cipher Spec Protocol is one of the three specific high-level protocols and the simplest one. After the client and server complete the handshake protocol, it needs to send a related message to the other party (this message only contains a single byte with a value of 1), notifying the other party that subsequent data will be processed using the password specification algorithm and associated key just negotiated, and responsible for coordinating the local module to work according to the negotiated algorithm and key.

- **SSL Alert Protocol:** It communicates alerts relating to SSL across peer entities and is also known as the SSL Alerting Protocol or SSL Warning Protocol. One side is required to notify the other party if it notices any anomalies during communication. Alerts pertaining to SSL are transmitted between peer organizations via the SSL Alert Protocol. One side is required to notify the other party if it notices any anomalies during communication. There are two different kinds of warning messages: fatal errors, such as MAC errors discovered during data transmission, call for an immediate session termination and the deletion of the corresponding session records from each party's buffers; and warning messages, in which case both parties typically only record logs without interfering with communication. The server and client can negotiate precise encryption, MAC methods, and secret keys to safeguard data delivered in SSL records using the SSL Handshake Protocol after authenticating one another.

(b) SSL Handshake Process

- In order to recognize each other, the client and server need to exchange X.509 certificates. During this process, the entire chain of verification can be exchanged, or only select a few underlying certificates. Certificate verification includes checking validity dates and verifying the signature authority of the certificate.

- The client randomly generates keys for message encryption and MAC calculation. The server's public key encrypts these keys before sending to the server. Four keys are used for communication from the server to the client and from the client to the server.

- The encryption algorithm (for encryption) and a hash function (to ensure message integrity) are used together. Netscape's SSL implementation scheme is as follows: the client lists all the algorithms it supports, and the server selects the most effective password. Server administrators can use or prohibit specific passwords.

With the presence of SSL Handshake Protocol, SSL Cipher Suite, SSL Alert Protocol, and SSL Record Protocol, the security of the SSL can be achieved. We can use these methods for web security because their security technologies are reliable.

2. Transport Layer Security Protocol

TLS, the successor to SSL, is an encryption protocol that provides a confidential, secure channel on the Internet for data transmissions such as websites, email, and file transfers. Although there are slight differences between SSL 3.0 and TLS 1.0, the specifications are roughly the same.

TLS uses cryptographic algorithms to provide endpoint authentication and communication confidentiality on the Internet, it was based on PKI. However, in typical implementations, only network servers are reliably authenticated, while their clients may not be. This is because PKI is generally commercial, and electronic signature certificates are expensive and difficult for the general public to purchase. The protocol design can prevent eavesdropping, tampering, and message forgery in client/server application communication.

TLS consists of three basic stages:

(a) Negotiation of supported key algorithms

In the first stage, the client and server negotiate the cryptographic algorithm. The currently widely used algorithm options are as follows:

- Public Key Encryption Systems: RSA, Diffie-Hellman, DSA, and Fortezza
- Symmetric Key Systems: RC2, RC4, IDEA, DES, Triple DES, and AES
- One-way Hash Functions: MD5 and SHA

(b) Exchange of symmetric keys based on public key encryption and identity authentication based on certificates

(c) Confidential data transmission based on symmetric keys

The working principle of TLS is the SSL handshake process with mutual certificate authentication. First, the Record layer of TLS is used to encapsulate higher-layer protocols such as HTTP. The Record layer data can be compressed, encrypted, and packaged with a MAC at will. Each Record layer packet has a `content_type` segment to record the protocol used by the higher layer.

The client sends and receives several handshake signals: it sends a `ClientHello` message, indicating the list of supported cryptographic algorithms, compression methods, and the highest protocol version. It also sends a random number that will be used later. Then it receives a `ServerHello` message, which contains the connection parameters selected by the server, derived from the `ClientHello` provided by the client initially. When both parties know the connection parameters, the client and server exchange certificates (using the selected public key system), these certificates are usually based on X.509. However, there are draft specifications that support certificates based on OpenPGP. The server can request the client's certificate and achieve mutual identity authentication. The client and server negotiate a standard "Master Key" through an encrypted channel (the client and server calculate random numbers), implemented using a carefully designed pseudorandom number function. The result may use Diffie-Hellman exchange or simple public key encryption, and each party decrypts with its private key. The encryption of all other critical data uses this "Master Key". All Record layer data is numbered, and the sequence number is used in the MAC.

3. Secure Shell Protocol (SSH)

   SSH, or Secure Shell Protocol, is an encrypted network transmission protocol that provides a secure transmission environment for network services in an insecure network. It creates a secure tunnel in the network to connect SSH clients and servers. In the early days of Internet communication, communication was in plaintext, and the content would be exposed once intercepted.

The IETF standardization organization developed the SSH protocol, one of the most widely deployed network security protocols, similar to TLS and IPSec. It was initially designed to replace remote login protocols such as Telnet, which send unprotected information over the network. Since then, SSH has become a universal tool for ensuring internet transmission security. Currently, SSHv2 is the latest specification of SSH, defined in RFC 31. Due to its popularity and the insecurity of other remote login protocols, some organizations only allow users to use SSH to access their facilities remotely.

When using FTP or Telnet, every time you enter your account and password, it is sent in plaintext, there will be the risk of the content being revealed to attackers. However, SSH has no such concern considering that it has strong authentication and secure channel transmission mechanisms. Since SSH is an open protocol, it has been widely recognized in the Linux and Unix worlds. Developers and anyone can freely improve performance or add new features. It uses mature security systems in cryptography to enhance channel transmission's confidentiality and identity authentication. Optional encryption algorithms include IDEA, 3DES, DES, RC4, and TSS. Due to SSH being easy to install, use, and relatively common, most Unix, Linux, and FreeBSD systems come with application packages that support SSH.

Currently, the SSH protocol has two versions: SSHv1 and SSHv2. SSHv1 uses symmetric cryptographic mechanisms such as DES, 3DES, Blowfish, and RC4 to ensure channel transmission security, and the symmetric cryptographic mechanism key is negotiated using asymmetric cryptographic mechanisms. SSHv1 uses a CRC to ensure data integrity. Later, some security vulnerabilities were discovered in the SSHv1 protocol, such as using CRC to ensure data transmission integrity, but CRC has a compensatory attack detection vulnerability. SSHv2 corrected some security issues in SSHv1, such as adding a MAC and fixing the CRC compensatory attack detection vulnerability. In addition, based on SSHv1, SSHv2 also added security mechanisms such as algorithm negotiation and user dual authentication to improve the protocol's security. SSHv2 uses the DH key exchange algorithm instead of RSA to exchange symmetric keys for encrypted sessions. In addition, SSHv2 also introduces symmetric encryption algorithms such as AES and Twofish and supports the Secure File Transfer Protocol (SFTP). SSHv1.99 supports both SSHv1 and SSHv2. The appearance of this version increased the universality of the protocol but also provided vulnerabilities to attackers.

The process of establishing a secure SSH connection is as follows:

1. Version negotiation phase:

   After the TCP connection is established, both parties must send their version strings to each other, including the SSH protocol version number, software version number, etc., which together form a string like "SSH-<major protocol version>.<minor protocol version>-<software version>m". The version string can be up to 255 bytes long. The server sends its version string to the client first. When the client receives the server's message, it checks the version number. If the server's version number is higher, the client sends its lower version number. When the server receives the client's message, it compares the version numbers with its own to determine compatibility. If they are not compatible, the TCP connection is disconnected. If they are compatible, both sides work with a lower protocol version. At this stage, the data packet is transmitted in plaintext.

2. Algorithm negotiation phase:

   After the version negotiation, the server sends a packet to the client, including the host key's public key, the service key's public key, the minor protocol version flag, the good password algorithm, the authentication method, and a 64-bit cookie. This packet is not encrypted. The client selects various algorithms as follows: matching the supported algorithm with the algorithm sent by the server in turn, and if successful, selecting this algorithm as the negotiated algorithm for both sides. If none of the algorithms are successful, the algorithm negotiation fails.

3. Key negotiation phase:

   After the algorithm negotiation is successful, both parties enter the key negotiation phase. This phase involves client authentication of the server. The SSH protocol supports server authentication to prevent server impersonation. The client checks the host list to see if the host key received from the server is in the list. It is added to the list if it is not on the list.

4. User authentication phase:

This phase is the server authentication of the client. The client sends a request authentication message to the server. The authentication request contains the username, authentication method, and other related content, and the server starts the authentication process for the client user. SSH provides two authentication methods: password authentication and public key authentication.

5. Session interaction phase:

Next, the client can request a session from the server. After the session request is successful, both parties enter the interaction mode. In this mode, encrypted data is transmitted bi-directionally. When the client requests to close the session, the server allows the request, the connection terminates, and the session interaction phase ends.

The existing implementations and applications of the SSH protocol mainly include the following aspects:

1. **Open Secure Shell (OpenSSH)** is a free and open-source implementation of the SSH protocol, an open-source alternative to the commercial version SSH Communications Security provides. It is currently a more authoritative implementation of SSH. OpenSSH software is generally installed on Linux distribution versions, and the ssh server daemon `sshd` is started by default. OpenSSH supports clients and servers and can be used for remote login, backup, or file transfer through `scp` or `sftp`. Modifying the corresponding configuration files can enable other features, such as data compression and proxy forwarding.

2. **PuTTY** is a remote connection software that combines Telnet, SSH, and log in. Earlier versions only supported the Windows platform, but recent versions have begun to support various Unix platforms and are intended to be ported to MacOSX. In addition to the official version, many third-party groups or individuals have ported PuTTY to other platforms, such as mobile phones based

on Symbian. PuTTY is an open-source software mainly maintained by Simon Tatham and is licensed under the MIT license.

3. **WinSCP** is an open-source graphical SFTP client for SSH in the Windows environment, supporting the Secure Copy Protocol (SCP). WinSCP can connect to an SSH server that provides SFTP or SCP services. Its main function is to copy files between local and remote computers securely, and it can also directly edit files.

9.1.3 Security Routing and Topology Control

1. Cryptographic-based Security Routing Protocol

   This technology mainly uses cryptographic techniques to sign, authenticate, and verify the integrity of routing control information (such as routing requests, routing replies, and routing invalidation information) to ensure a normal and stable operation of routing protocols. In this method, the distribution and management of keys and certificates are the prerequisites of security policies, representing protocols such as SMOR, SRP, and SOLAR.

   The Multi-path On-demand Routing (SMOR) protocol implements signature and encryption on routing control information based on identity-based cryptography. It can construct preventive mechanisms before attacks occur and effectively respond to various routing security issues caused by external network attacks. The on-demand routing strategy is a reactive dynamic routing technology that searches for routing only when data needs to be sent, which can avoid the complex process of establishing, maintaining, and updating routing tables and reduce routing overhead. At the same time, in the process of on-demand routing establishment, a combination of "tight constraints" and "loose constraints" is used to reduce the scope of routing control information diffusion and effectively reduce routing maintenance overhead.

   The SMOR protocol uses an identity-based signature and encryption scheme, which no longer requires the maintenance of public key certificates. This method can significantly simplify the key management aspects of traditional public key cryptographic systems and is more suitable for spatial conditions with limited computing and storage resources. However, there are several issues with this protocol. Firstly, the reliability and scalability still need to be improved when the number of network nodes is relatively fixed. Secondly, the protocol is designed for a single-layer LEO network, and the extension to a multi-dimensional space network still needs to consider the management relationship and information interaction process among different layers of satellites. Thirdly, this protocol's signature and encryption scheme is built on the Diffie-Hellman problem, which requires complex bi-linear pairing operations on the routing information received or sent by nodes, which poses requirements on the computing and storage capabilities of space nodes.

Similarly, based on the identity-based signature and encryption strategy, including a satellite network Security Routing Protocol (SRP) based on identity-based signature and encryption, it draws on the dynamic construction and maintenance of routing information in the wireless sensor network AODV protocol. It ensures network information security during routing through the identity-based signature and encryption strategy. SRP adopts a dynamic isolation mechanism to effectively respond to complex threats caused by network internal node attacks. That is, when the private key generation center PKG discovers that a previously legitimate node has performed an attack behavior on other nodes and is no longer trustworthy, the PKG generates a notification message, encrypts it, and broadcasts it to other nodes in the network. The receiving nodes will delete the routing information containing the untrusted node, thereby achieving timely isolation of the untrusted node and ensuring that the network can resist destruction and provide uninterrupted network services after suffering internal attacks by quickly isolating the corresponding attacking nodes.

However, the On-demand Routing protocol (LAOR) did not consider security measures such as user terminal identity authentication and network node entity authentication in the design, making the routing process vulnerable to black hole attacks, impersonation, denial of service attacks, Byzantine attacks, and routing replay attacks, which severely affect the network operation and service guarantees. With the above considerations, a secure routing protocol based on identity-based cryptographic systems (S-LAOR) was derived based on the LAOR protocol. Similar to SMOR, it uses an identity-based cryptographic system to encrypt and authenticate routing control packets in the network, effectively ensuring the integrity and confidentiality of routing information and ensuring the secure operation of the routing protocol. However, S-LOAR inherits the characteristics of LOAR and is mainly designed for polar LEO constellations, and its scalability still needs to be further considered.

2. Reputation-based Security Routing Protocol

The reputation-based security mechanism timely judges malicious behavior of nodes and isolates harmful nodes based on changes in the reputation of network nodes. An effective trust management mechanism can enable nodes in the network to perform distributed collaboration and detect harmful behavior of nodes. The adjacent nodes are quantified into a trust value. The trust value is a comprehensive evaluation index of the behavior of nodes, such as forwarding packets, discarding packets, and discovering routes. If there are nodes with a trust value greater than the specified value, it can participate in routing, otherwise, it will be excluded from participating in routing. These security routing protocols include SODV, PW, TARP-HL, and RELAODV.

The security routing design by using a dynamic routing algorithm based on security mechanisms was to introduce a node trust mechanism based on reputation. The algorithm uses a complementary mechanism of static policies and dynamic allocation to achieve the periodic update of routing information and on-demand real-time updates. Thereby, it adapts the network routing algorithm with smaller computational or storage overhead and better meets the problem of limited computing or storage capabilities in the spatial.

However, TARP-HL also has some drawbacks. Firstly, it does not consider the issue of nodes with restored reputations rejoining the network. Secondly, the routing control information needs to be encrypted and decrypted at each step during transmission, which undoubtedly increases the routing establishment time and causes a loss of network performance. Thirdly, similar to traditional authentication and signature mechanisms based on certificates, it requires complex certificate storage and management and is challenging to adapt to space networks' weak computing and storage capabilities.

3. Multi-Strategy-Based Security Routing Protocol

Most of the research on security routing technology in space networks adopts cryptographic-based strategies to control routing information to ensure reliable end-to-end information transmission and achieve proactive defense of network security; or uses a reputation-based security evaluation system to isolate network nodes that generate suspicious behavior to ensure the continuous and stable operation of the network and achieve reactive defense of network security. Some researchers have proposed combining the above two security strategies to form a security routing protocol that combines active and passive defense. Such security routing protocols mainly include S-ALBR, TSRP, etc.

The dynamic routing protocol based on mobile agents (ALBR) can use the static agents carried on satellites to collect satellite positions, link delays, and other information for route table construction and use mobile agents to autonomously migrate, collect routing information, detect path information, and obtain real-time network status information to support routing decision-making, effectively ensuring network security directly. Based on this, a dynamic security routing protocol based on mobile agents (S-ALBR) is proposed, which introduces authentication technology to achieve trusted authentication when satellite or agent nodes communicate, introduces encryption technology to ensure the secure transmission of routing control information, and introduces a reputation-based security strategy to exclude misbehaving satellite nodes from the scope of routing decision-making and guide traffic away from untrusted nodes. The security routing protocol for multi-layer satellite networks - Trusted Secure Routing Protocol (TSRP) simplifies the routing design complexity by considering the periodic changes in the topology of satellite nodes. Regarding node security, trusted mutual authentication is achieved between source and destination nodes through identity authentication systems, effectively resisting DoS attacks. Digital encryption technology is used in transmission security, and the use of signature, timestamp, and routing maintenance technologies, are introduced to achieve reliable end-to-end information security transmission and resist possible replay, selfish behavior, and black hole attacks in the network. At the same time, through the real-time evaluation of network node behavior and dynamic reputation adjustment based on the reputation-based security mechanism, security isolation of abnormal nodes is achieved.

9.1.4   Security Fault Tolerance and Recovery

The term is used in many fields, it is crucial for data storage and the architecture of information technology. Fault tolerance in this context refers to a computer system's or storage subsystem's capacity to continue operating in the face of hardware or software problems without halting operations, losing data, or jeopardising security. The complete data storage platform, including HDD and SSD hard drives, RAID and NAS, can be fault tolerant in a system. Despite its many difficulties, fault tolerance is ultimately intended to provide security protection, which is more difficult to achieve.

Fundamentally, single points of failure can be removed from a system to add fault tolerance. Fault-tolerant features must be implemented since if one component failed, it may cause the entire system to shut down. The Power Supply Unit (PSU), which transforms AC power into various voltages of DC power to supply various components, is a typical single point of failure in a conventional system. All of the components that the PSU supports would fail if it malfunctioned, frequently resulting in a catastrophic system failure. When a fault-tolerant system fails, it may still operate normally without affecting throughput, response time, or other performance parameters. When inevitable breakdowns take place, others' performance may suffer from "functional degradation". In other words, a failure's effect on system performance will be proportionate to how serious it is. Because of this, modest failures will have a proportionately minor impact as opposed to a huge one and won't bring down the entire system. Highly fault-tolerant systems will continue to function despite one or more major failures.

To avoid (or at least to reduce as much as possible) the potential that the system's functionality may become unavailable owing to a breakdown in one or more of its components is the core goal of fault tolerance.

Systems needed to safeguard human safety (such as air traffic control hardware and software systems) and systems relying on security, data protection and integrity, and high-value transactions must also have fault tolerance.

Redundancy is a concept that fault-tolerant systems use to get rid of single points of failure and provide fault-tolerant functionality. In essence, this entails giving the system one or more redundant supplementary PSUs that won't be needed to supply power when the main PSU is operating regularly. However, if the primary PSU malfunctions (or detects a defect, like overheating, suggesting an impending failure), the service may be interrupted and the redundant PSU may be turned on to ensure continuity of the entire system's operation.

Several key elements of fault-tolerant systems are:

1. Hardware Systems

   Typical computer systems or data storage systems include a CPU, RAM, auxiliary storage systems such as hard drives, PSUs, network interfaces, and motherboards. Fault-tolerant computers or data storage systems can use various components to provide fault tolerance. This includes CPU replication, redundant PSUs and memory, hard drives configured in some form of RAID array including redundancy and replication, and power diversity providing backup generators.

   Fault-tolerant networks can be provided by redundant Network Interface Cards (NICs) and/or network options such as wired LAN NICs and wireless LAN adapters.

2. Software Systems

   The software can be fault-tolerant to continue running even when encountering errors, exceptions, or invalid inputs, as long as it is designed to handle these errors rather than defaulting to reporting errors and stopping.

   In particular, protocols such as TCP/IP have been explicitly developed to create fault-tolerant networks. TCP/IP can continue to operate in environments where individual network links or nodes may become unexpectedly unavailable. It can adapt to different conditions to send packets to their destination through any available route. Software systems can also use replication to provide fault-tolerant functionality. A highly critical database can be continuously replicated to another server so that operations can be immediately redirected to the replica database if the server hosting the primary database fails.

Alternatively, some services (especially web servers) can be placed behind a load balancer so that multiple servers provide the same service. If one server fails, the load balancer sends all web requests to other servers until the fault is repaired.

Of course, this raises the question of what happens if the load balancer fails. The answer is usually a failover system that immediately transfers web requests to a server elsewhere. Since the resources at this failover location may differ from those at the primary data center, this may result in a normal degradation until normal operations are restored.

3. Power

   Many fault-tolerant systems include multiple PSUs to provide redundancy in case of PSU failure. Since redundant primary power supplies are typically unavailable, most organizations rely on forms of power from alternative sources. This is often a generator that automatically starts up in case of a power failure to ensure that IT hardware, storage devices, HVAC, and other systems have the required power.

4. High Availability and Fault Tolerance

   There is often some confusion between high availability and fault tolerance concepts. At the most basic level, high availability refers to systems that experience minimal service interruption, while fault-tolerant systems are designed such that the service will not experience interruptions. In practice, the difference between the two may be small. The goal of many high-availability systems is what is known as "five nines", or 99.999% uptime, which translates to only a few minutes of downtime per year.

However, the principles governing these two concepts are very different. Fault-tolerant systems are designed to detect and fix faults (possibly by swapping out redundant components) without interruption. In contrast, high-availability systems typically use standard hardware and are designed to restore service after an interruption quickly.

High availability is often considered acceptable rather than fault-tolerant by cost: building fault-tolerant facilities into a system may be much more expensive than occasional brief interruptions. Many organizations combine these two approaches: fault-tolerant systems for the most critical activities and high availability for less essential activities.

9.2   DISTRIBUTED SECURE DATA STORAGE

9.2.1   Moore's Law and Heterogeneous Systems

Moore's Law

Moore's Law states that the number of transistors integrated into a computer chip of the same area doubles every 18 months, doubling the chip's processing speed and processing power while halving the cost. Since Thomson confirmed the existence of electrons by the end of the 19th century, humans have made great efforts to utilize electronics. In the early 20th century, the invention of vacuum tubes allowed electrons to move in a vacuum, creating the radio. In the mid-20th century, Shockley and others invented the transistor, marking the beginning of the microelectronics era. With the development of point-contact transistors and silicon planar transistor technology, Kilby invented the integrated circuit in 1958. As the number of transistors on integrated circuits continued to increase, integrated circuits' functionality and processing speed continued to accelerate. In 1959, the American company Fairchild Semiconductor introduced planar transistors. In 1961, it introduced planar integrated circuits, mainly using photolithography to form components such as diodes, transistors, resistors, and capacitors on a finely ground silicon wafer. This photolithography technology and the development of planar integrated circuits provided a solid technical foundation for Moore's Law.

With the increasing popularity of personal computers, the scope of Moore's Law has also been extended from describing the density and number of transistors in integrated circuits to describing the leading indicators and coefficients of computers. It consists of CPU speed, hard disk capacity, and memory size, all of which are developing at a rate of doubling every 18 months while costs are halved. In the entire computer industry, Moore's Law is regarded as a hard-and-fast rule and axiom for industry and enterprise development. If technology cannot be upgraded every 18 months, for twice the performance and half the cost, it may mean being abandoned by competitors and industry development and falling into decline. It is precisely in this panic and background that the entire personal computer industry has achieved rapid development in the past 20 to 30 years. Not only have the performance of computers, such as operating speed, storage space, and memory size that have developed rapidly, but, with the continuous development of various technologies, the cost has been reduced for of various technologies. Consequently, the price of personal computers constantly decreasing, which significantly promotes the popularity of personal computers worldwide. In turn, the popularity of personal computers is more conducive to the scale effect of the research, development, and production of major components and whole machines of computers, further promoting the price reduction and popularity of personal computers.

Heterogeneous Systems

Heterogeneous [288–291] systems refer to computing systems composed of different types of computer hardware or software components that may be heterogeneous. Heterogeneous systems refer to a system from different manufacturers or use different operating systems, programming languages, or protocols. Compared to homogeneous systems, the components of heterogeneous systems have higher diversity and complexity and require specific protocols or interfaces for communication and collaboration.

The advantage of heterogeneous systems is that they can achieve resource sharing and task allocation between different types of hardware and software, thereby improving the efficiency and performance of the system. For example, compute-intensive tasks can be assigned to high-performance GPUs in a heterogeneous system. In contrast, data processing tasks can be assigned to efficient CPUs, and different devices can be connected through a network for data sharing and transfer. This distributed computing method may generate a more parallel and scalable system, while reducing the burden on individual hardware devices and improving the fault tolerance and stability of the entire system.

However, due to heterogeneous systems' higher complexity and heterogeneity, more factors and challenges must be considered in their design, deployment, and maintenance. For example, how to design practical communication protocols and interfaces, handle data formats and compatibility between different devices, and perform task allocation and resource scheduling, among others. Therefore, designing and managing heterogeneous systems requires higher technical skills and professional knowledge.

In summary, heterogeneous systems are computing systems composed of different types of computer hardware or software components, with higher diversity and complexity, but also capable of achieving resource sharing and task allocation, improving the efficiency and performance of the system. Although heterogeneous systems have significant advantages in distributed computing and large-scale data processing, their design and management require more factors and challenges to be considered.

9.2.2 Combining MRAM and SRAM in On-Chip Memory

SRAM

SRAM is a type of random-access memory. The term "static" refers to the fact that this type of memory can maintain its stored data as long as it is powered on, without periodic updates like those required by DRAM.

Basic SRAMs can generally be divided into five main parts: the core cell array, the row or column address decoder, the sense amplifier, the control circuit, and the buffer/drive circuit (FFIO). SRAM is a static storage method that uses bistable circuits as storage units. Unlike DRAM, SRAM does not require constant refreshing and has a faster operating speed. However, its integration density is relatively low, and its power consumption is higher due to more storage unit devices.

SRAM is mainly used for Level 2 Cache and uses transistors to store data. Compared to DRAM, SRAM is faster, but its capacity is smaller than other types of memory in the same area. SRAM is fast but expensive, so small-capacity SRAM is generally used as a cache between higher-speed CPUs and lower-speed DRAM. There are also many types of SRAM, such as AsyncSRAM (Asynchronous SRAM), Sync SRAM (Synchronous SRAM), PBSRAM (Pipelined Burst SRAM), etc.

MRAM

Magnetoresistive Random Access Memory (MRAM) is a non-volatile magnetic random-access memory type. It has the high-speed read and writes capabilities of SRAM and the high integration density of DRAM and allows for unlimited rewriting.

MRAM based on the Spin-Transfer Torque (STT) effect and pure current writing is called STT-MRAM. The STT-type writing method can be described as follows: when current flows through the free layer toward the reference layer (with the direction of electron motion opposite to that of the current), the electrons passing through the reference layer are spin-polarized by the reference layer magnetization. It forms a spin current in the same direction as the reference layer magnetization injected into the free layer, causing the free layer's magnetization to align with that of the reference layer. When the current flows through the reference layer towards the free layer, the electrons passing through the free layer cannot generate a spin current sufficient to change the reference layer's magnetization direction due to the free layer's weaker magnetization.

However, when the electrons reach the surface of the reference layer, the stronger magnetization of the reference layer will reflect the spin state opposite to its magnetization direction (note that it is only the spin state of the electron that reflects, not the electron itself), forming a spin current injected into the free layer with the opposite direction to the reference layer magnetization, causing the magnetization of the free layer to tend to align with the opposite direction to that of the reference layer. The writing current of the STT effect can be reduced as the size of the Magnetic Tunnel Junction (MTJ) is reduced. Moreover, the writing operation based on this effect does not require a pre-reading process. It can directly overwrite the previous data, making STT-MRAM the mainstream MRAM technology currently being industrialized.

The main structure of MRAM is composed of a three-layer MTJ: a free layer, a fixed layer, and a tunneling oxide layer. The materials of the free layer and the fixed layer are CoFeB and MgO, respectively. The STT-MTJ uses the magnetization direction of the free layer and the fixed layer to store information, with the parallel state having a low resistance and the anti-parallel state having a high resistance. The memory read circuit judges the output current by loading the same voltage to determine the memory information. A zero (0) represents the anti-parallel state, and one (1) represents the parallel state.

The most common internal combination of STT-MRAM storage today is the 1T-1MTJ (one transistor, one magnetic tunnel junction) unit given that it has the advantages of small size, low manufacturing cost, and good integration with CMOS technology. When a current flows through the MTJ junction, it exhibits different resistance values depending on the stored information. An NMOS transistor controls the current flowing through the MTJ, and the word line is connected to the gate of the NMOS, which functions similarly to traditional SRAM. When writing or reading is needed, the NMOS is opened. The source of the NMOS is connected to the source line, and the bit line is connected to the free layer of the MTJ. Due to the shorter read and write times of STT-MRAM, it will replace SRAM as the main storage medium for the cache.

SSRAM-MRAM Hybrid Structure

Researchers have proposed a hybrid structure of SRAM-MRAM to replace pure MRAM memory, where SRAM only accounts for a small part. The main purpose is to concentrate as many write operations as possible on the SRAM and reduce the number of write operations in the MRAM.

The researchers reduced some of the MRAM, replaced it with SRAM, and grouped all SRAM cells to form several complete SRAM groups on the processor layer. The SRAM groups are placed in the center of the processor layer instead of being scattered, which increases the area of the processor layer and reduces the area of the high-speed cache layer.

The management strategy for the hybrid structure is as follows:

1. The high-speed cache controller needs to know the locations of the SRAM and MRAM. When a write error occurs, the controller prioritizes placing the data in the SRAM.

2. Considering the possibility of the processor repeatedly writing data to the specific cells, if the data is in the MRAM, it needs to be moved to the SRAM. If the data undergoes two consecutive write operations, it needs to be moved to the SRAM.

3. Note that the processor's read operation may also cause data transfer, and the number of reads may be greater than the writes. Therefore, a new data movement strategy is introduced. For traditional management strategies, data is moved to the host group, while the strategy adapted to the hybrid structure moves data to the SRAM.

9.2.3 Heterogeneous SPM Architecture of CMP

Heterogeneous CMP

Heterogeneous CMP refers to a CPU chip containing multiple identical or different processor cores connected through on-chip networks and high-speed transmission buses, enabling communication between different processor cores. Each core is similar to a single-processor system and contains all the hardware required to execute CPU instructions, such as interrupters, arithmetic and control units, and caches so that programs can achieve a full parallel execution. CMP technology has the following advantages:

1. Low cost.

   All cores of the CMP system are distributed on a single CPU chip, so the hardware structure changes are small, and the design cost is low.

2. Parallelism.

   Each processor core of the CMP system can run different tasks simultaneously and transmit data information to each other, achieving true parallelism.

3. On-chip communication.

   Even if the tasks executed on different processor cores require data communication, the interconnect structure between the cores is short, and a specific network structure optimization design is adopted. At the same time, they can share caches, so the communication overhead between the cores is much lower than that of two single processors.

4. Low power consumption.

Due to the CMP system relying on multiple processor cores to execute programs in parallel to obtain a performance boost, it avoids the problem of high power consumption and heat generation caused by a single core's high operating frequency.

At the same time, all cores share peripheral devices, caches, and other hardware resources. Therefore, the power consumption becomes lower.

The CMP hardware architecture includes homogenous CMP and heterogeneous CMP, depending on whether the properties of the cores on the chip are entirely identical. Homogeneous means that many cores on the same chip have equal status, identical properties, and functions. For example, Compaq's Piranha multi-core processor and Stanford's Hydra multi-core processor use a common homogeneous CMP architecture design. Unlike homogeneous CMP, the status of many cores in heterogeneous CMP is standard equal, and most processor cores have different properties and functional characteristics. Heterogeneous CMP usually adopts a "master-slave" design; one central core controls multiple slave cores to perform tasks together. The central core is generally a more common processor, and the slave cores have different functions, such as ARM cores, DSP cores, etc.

Currently, the most widely used heterogeneous platform is the Cell multi-core processor, whose architecture design is shown in the following figure. The Cell architecture includes nine independent cores, a 64-bit microprocessor PPE (PowerPC Processing Element), and eight SPEs (Synergistic Processing Elements) for floating-point calculations. Unlike the SPEs, the PPE has a different performance and structure, but all SPEs have the same performance and structure. PPE and SPE are interconnected through on-chip networks. PPE is responsible for the operating system running and coordinating the control of each SPE's task execution, enabling the SPEs to execute programs with high parallelism.

A heterogeneous CMP can arrange its execution according to the nature of the program and instruction requirements. Due to its unique structure design, the efficiency of running the same task on different cores is not the same. Therefore, through proper software optimization and effective control of task or instruction allocation and execution, the heterogeneity of the platform can be fully utilized to demonstrate its parallel performance better and make resources utilized reasonably and effectively. Therefore, compared with homogeneous CMP, heterogeneous CMP has higher performance improvement and development potential and is also an important research direction of CMP technology.

Symmetrical Multiprocessing architecture

Symmetrical Multiprocessing (SMP) architecture refers to a symmetrical work of multiple CPUs with the same structure in a server without a master-slave or subordinate relationship. Each CPU shares the memory subsystem and bus structure. It is a widely used parallel technology relative to asymmetric multiprocessing. Since each CPU shares physical memory and requires the same amount of time to access the same address in memory, SMP is also referred to as a Uniform Memory Access (UMA) structure. Although the SMP structure uses multiple CPUs simultaneously, it is like a single machine from a management perspective. The system evenly distributes tasks to each CPU, significantly improving the data processing capability of the entire system and distributing the workload across all available processors. Extending the SMP structure processor can include increasing memory, increasing CPUs, expanding I/O, or adding external devices such as disk storage.

The main feature of SMP structure processors is sharing, where all system resources (CPU, memory, I/O, etc.) are shared. Due to this feature, the major problem of SMP processors is their scalability limitation. For SMP processors, each shared link may cause a bottleneck when expanding the SMP processor, and the most limited resource is memory. Since each CPU must access the same memory resources through the same memory bus, as the number of CPUs increases, memory access conflicts will quickly increase, ultimately causing a waste of CPU resources and significantly reducing the effectiveness of CPU performance. Moreover, since multiple processors share one operating system, once the operating system goes wrong, the entire machine will ultimately crash. The practice has proved that the best CPU utilization for SMP structure processors is between 2 and 4 CPUs. We commonly refer to a dual CPU as the most common type of symmetric multiprocessing system, usually called "2-way symmetric multiprocessing". The hardware structure diagram of a simple dual-core SMP architecture is shown.

To conduct an SMP system, the following requirements must be met:

1. Same product model and the same type of CPU core. The running frequency should be the same, and it is best if these CPUs are produced in the same batch.

2. The CPUs that make up the multi-core system must have built-in Advanced Programmable Interrupt Controllers (APIC) units.

CPUs communicate with each other by sending interrupts to each other. Different CPUs can control each other by attaching actions to interrupts. Each CPU has its own local APIC, and there is also an I/O APIC to handle interrupts caused by I/O devices. This I/O APIC is installed on the motherboard, but the APIC on each CPU is indispensable; otherwise, interrupt coordination between multiple CPUs cannot be processed.

9.2.4 Data Allocation Strategy

Data sharding refers to slicing a large table into smaller slices in a data storage system, and the segmented data blocks will be distributed across multiple servers. In a broader sense, data sharding also includes data computation sharding, which routes requests to different servers for data computation processing.

There are many methods for data sharding. The first method is to shard based on the hash value of the keyword. The key's hash value establishes a mapping relationship with several points in the system. A more straightforward method is directly using the modulo operation, where the remainder indicates the position in the node list. The advantage of this method is that it requires less metadata management. However, the disadvantage is also obvious: when a node needs to join or leave, a lot of data movement is required, and hash can cause data skew and hotspots, resulting in uneven load distribution between nodes.

Therefore, a consistent hashing algorithm is proposed: the key is mapped to a ring, and the nodes (hashed by IP address or machine name) are also mapped to this ring. Starting from the position of the key's hash value on the ring, the first node found clockwise is the storage node for that key. When adding or deleting nodes, the data affected by consistent hashing is limited. Another method is to shard based on the hash value range of the keyword, dividing the key space after hashing into different intervals, establishing a mapping between physical nodes and intervals, and each physical node corresponds to one or more intervals.

Sharding by interval requires metadata management, and if each query or data request needs to go through the metadata management node to obtain the current partition location of the key, that node should also ensure high availability and high performance. Distributed systems generally use ZooKeeper or etcd as metadata and configuration storage. To reduce overhead and avoid performance bottlenecks, ideally, it is not necessary to go through etcd for every request. Therefore, metadata information can be cached on each node to reduce access to, etcd. At the same time, the correct operation of the system strictly depends on the correctness of the metadata, which requires that the metadata information cached on each node is strongly consistent with the metadata on etcd and can handle node failures, network interruptions, and other issues.

A reasonable sharding mechanism is required to implement a complete partition sharding system, and a metadata management node and a master node are required for partition-related maintenance. For example, when the system starts, the mapping relationship between partitions and physical nodes is initialized, written to, etcd. When a physical node fails or becomes a hotspot, its partitions must be migrated to other physical nodes. When a new physical node joins the system, its location information is registered in the metadata management node, and the master node schedules sharding to it or re-balances sharding. When the number of physical nodes increases or decreases, or when the system encounters serious data skew or hotspot problems, the mapping of sharding positions needs to be changed. The addition and removal of nodes can be scheduled by the master center management node for sharding. It is necessary to implement the ability of the master to monitor the work status of each worker and to listen to the node list directory of etcd to perceive node changes, offload partitions of failed nodes, and load the partitions on new nodes (or existing nodes that are working normally).

9.3   DISTRIBUTED SECURE DATA PROCESSING

9.3.1   Distributed Computing Models and Algorithms

Overview of Distributed Computing

Modern computer systems are becoming increasingly complex, and the amount of data and computation is snowballing. In order to handle these large-scale data and tasks, distributed computing has become a vital computing model and technology. Distributed computing is a computing model that assigns tasks to multiple computer nodes, physical computers located in different places, virtual machines, or cloud computing instances. This computing model fully utilizes multiple computer resources, improving computing efficiency, reducing costs, and enhancing system reliability.

In this section, we will introduce the basic concepts, goals, and application scenarios of distributed computing and the comparison between distributed computing and traditional computing models. We will also discuss the advantages, disadvantages, and limitations of distributed computing and the challenges and development trends of current distributed computing technology.

Basic Concepts and Goals of Distributed Computing

Distributed computing is a computing model that assigns tasks to multiple computer nodes. In distributed computing, each computer node can independently execute computing tasks and merge the computing results to form the final result. Distributed computing can use various communication mechanisms to coordinate communication and collaboration between nodes, including message passing, shared memory, remote procedure calls, etc.

The main goal of distributed computing is to improve computing efficiency, reduce computing costs, and enhance system reliability. By assigning computing tasks to multiple computer nodes for execution, distributed computing can fully utilize the computing resources of multiple computers, thereby speeding up the computation. In addition, since computing tasks are assigned to multiple computer nodes for execution, distributed computing can reduce computing costs. Finally, since computing tasks in distributed computing can be executed in parallel on multiple nodes, system reliability and fault tolerance can be improved.

Comparison between Distributed Computing and Traditional Computing Models

Compared with traditional computing models, distributed computing has the following characteristics:

1. Scalability: Traditional computing models usually only handle small-scale data and tasks using a single computer. However, in distributed computing, multiple computers can process large-scale data and tasks, making it easy to scale the system's computing capabilities.

2. Reliability: In traditional computing models, the computing task is interrupted if a computer fails or crashes. However, if a computer node fails in distributed computing, the computing task can continue to be executed on other computer nodes, thereby improving system reliability and fault tolerance.

3. High concurrency: In traditional computing models, only one computing task can be executed simultaneously because only one CPU or processor core is available. However, in distributed computing, computing tasks can be assigned to multiple computer nodes for parallel execution, achieving high concurrency and improving computing efficiency.

4. High availability: Distributed computing systems can ensure high availability using backup nodes and redundant computing resources. If a node fails, the backup node can automatically take over its computing tasks, avoiding system downtime.

5. High complexity: The design and implementation of distributed computing systems are more complex than traditional computing models, requiring consideration of communication and collaboration between multiple computer nodes, as well as system reliability and fault tolerance issues.

The advantages, disadvantages, and limitations of distributed computing

Distributed computing has many advantages but also some limitations and disadvantages.

Advantages:

- Improved computing efficiency: Distributed computing can fully utilize the computing resources of multiple computers, process computing tasks in parallel, and thus speed up computing speed.

- Reduced computing costs: Distributed computing can assign tasks to multiple computer nodes for execution, thereby reducing computing costs.

- Enhanced system reliability: Distributed computing can execute computing tasks in parallel on multiple computer nodes, thereby improving system reliability and fault tolerance.

- Scalability: Distributed computing can easily expand the computing capacity of the system and support large-scale computing tasks.

Disadvantages and Limitations:

- High system complexity: The design and implementation of distributed computing systems are more complex than traditional computing models. It requires consideration of communication and collaboration among multiple computer nodes, as well as system reliability and fault tolerance issues.

- Difficult to ensure data consistency: In distributed computing, multiple computer nodes can simultaneously access and modify the same data collection, making it difficult to ensure data consistency.

- High network communication latency: Distributed computing requires frequent network communication among multiple computer nodes, and high network communication latency can become a bottleneck.

- Difficult to debug and maintain: Due to the high complexity of distributed computing systems, debugging and maintenance are also tricky.

Current challenges and trends in distributed computing technology

Although distributed computing has become a vital computing model and technology, some challenges and trends remain.

Challenges:

- Security challenges: Distributed computing systems face various security threats, including network attacks, data leaks, and malicious software. Ensuring the security of distributed computing systems is a critical challenge that requires constant attention and updates.

- Large-scale data processing: With increasingly large-scale data sets, current distributed computing systems face the challenge of processing data efficiently. Finding ways to optimize data processing is a persistent challenge.

- Resource scheduling and management: One of the key challenges of distributed computing systems is to schedule and manage resources dynamically across multiple computer nodes. Efficiently managing these resources is a constant challenge that requires ongoing attention and optimization.

- Interoperability of distributed computing frameworks and platforms: Different distributed computing frameworks and platforms can face interoperability issues, making it difficult to achieve data exchange and communication between them. Overcoming these challenges requires finding ways to ensure compatibility and seamless integration between different platforms.

Development trends:

- Cloud computing and edge computing: The increasing reliance on cloud computing and edge computing technologies will be critical for improving the efficiency of resource management and computing capabilities in distributed computing systems.

- AI and machine learning: Distributed computing systems have the potential to support large-scale AI and machine learning computing tasks, and achieving highly efficient computing capabilities in these areas will be a crucial future direction for distributed computing.

- Blockchain technology: Distributed computing systems can benefit from the security and trust mechanisms provided by blockchain technology. Exploring the potential applications of blockchain technology in distributed computing will also be a promising future development direction.

- Distributed storage: The ability to store and manage large-scale data sets is essential for distributed computing systems. Therefore, achieving efficient distributed storage and management will be a critical development direction for future distributed computing.

Distributed computing algorithms

Distributed computing algorithms refer to algorithms for computing and data processing in distributed computing environments. They usually need to consider the characteristics of distributed computing, such as communication delays between nodes and unreliable networks. Distributed computing algorithms can be divided into two categories: distributed and distributed data processing algorithms.

Distributed algorithms

Distributed algorithms refer to algorithms for computing in distributed computing environments. They usually need to consider the characteristics of communication delays between nodes and unreliable networks. Distributed algorithms can be divided into the following categories:

1. Distributed graph algorithms (DGA)

   DGA refers to algorithms for graph computing in distributed computing environments. They usually need to consider the characteristics of communication delays between nodes and unreliable networks. Distributed graph algorithms can be divided into the following categories:

   - Graph traversal algorithms, such as breadth-first search and depth-first search, are used to traverse all nodes in a graph.
   - Shortest path algorithms, such as Dijkstra's and Floyd's algorithms, calculate the shortest path between two nodes in a graph.
   - Minimum spanning tree algorithms, such as Prim's algorithm and Kruskal's algorithm, are used to generate the minimum spanning tree of a graph.

   The characteristics of distributed graph algorithms are the need to consider communication delays between nodes and unreliable networks and load balancing and node failure recovery issues.

2. Distributed sorting algorithms (DSA)

   DSA refers to algorithms for data sorting in distributed computing environments. They usually need to consider the characteristics of communication delays between nodes and unreliable networks.

Distributed sorting algorithms can be divided into the following categories:

- DSA based on *merge sorting*, such as the sorting algorithm in MapReduce, are used to sort large-scale data.
- DSA based on *bucket sorting*, such as the sorting algorithm in Hadoop, are used to sort large-scale data.
- DSAs based on *quick sortings*, such as the sorting algorithm in Spark, are used to sort large-scale data.

The characteristics of distributed sorting algorithms are the need to consider communication delays between nodes and unreliable networks and load balancing and node failure recovery issues.

3. Distributed machine learning algorithms (DMLA)

DMLAs perform machine learning in distributed computing environments. They usually need to consider the characteristics of communication delays between nodes and unreliable networks. Distributed machine learning algorithms can be divided into the following categories:

- Distributed gradient descent algorithms, such as the gradient descent algorithm in MapReduce, are used for training large-scale data.
- Distributed random forest algorithms, such as the random forest algorithm in Hadoop, are used for the classification and regression of large-scale data.
- Distributed deep learning algorithms, such as the distributed deep learning algorithm in TensorFlow and PyTorch, used for training deep neural networks on large-scale data.

The characteristics of distributed machine learning algorithms are the need to consider communication delays between nodes and unreliable networks and load balancing and node failure recovery issues.

Distributed data processing algorithms

Distributed data processing algorithms are algorithms for processing data in distributed computing environments. They usually need to consider the characteristics of communication delays between nodes and unreliable networks. Distributed data processing algorithms can be divided into the following categories:

1. Distributed data storage algorithms (DDSA)

   DDSAs are algorithms for storing data in distributed computing environments. They usually need to consider the characteristics of communication delays between nodes and unreliable networks. Distributed data storage algorithms can be divided into the following categories:

   - Distributed file systems, such as HDFS, GFS, and Ceph in Hadoop, are used for storing large-scale data.

   - Distributed key-value storage systems, such as Cassandra and Redis, are used for storing and retrieving large-scale data.

   - Distributed databases, such as MySQL Cluster and Oracle RAC, are used for storing and querying large-scale data.

   The characteristics of distributed data storage algorithms are the need to consider communication delays between nodes and unreliable networks and data reliability and scalability.

2. Distributed data processing algorithms (DDPA)

   DDPAs are algorithms for processing data in distributed computing environments. They usually need to consider the characteristics of communication delays between nodes and unreliable networks. Distributed data processing algorithms can be divided into the following categories:

   - Distributed MapReduce algorithms, such as the MapReduce algorithm in Hadoop, are used for processing large-scale data.

   - Distributed stream processing algorithms, such as Storm and Spark Streaming, are used for processing real-time data.

   - Distributed graph processing algorithms, such as GraphLab and Pregel, are used for processing graph data. The characteristics of distributed data processing algorithms are the need to consider communication delays between nodes and unreliable networks and load balancing and node failure recovery issues.

Overall, distributed computing models and algorithms have played an important role in big data processing and analysis while facing some challenges and problems. In the future, with the continuous progress of computing and communication technologies, distributed computing models and algorithms will continue to develop and improve, providing us with more efficient and reliable big data processing and analysis services.

The characteristics of distributed data processing algorithms include considering factors such as communication delays between nodes and unreliable networks and load balancing and node failure recovery issues.

Distributed computing models and algorithms are an effective method for handling large-scale data processing. Distributed computing can utilize the parallel computing capabilities of multiple computing nodes to process data, thereby improving computing speed and efficiency. Distributed computing models and algorithms can be divided into two categories: distributed machine learning algorithms and distributed data processing algorithms.

Distributed machine learning algorithms mainly include distributed data mining algorithms, distributed machine learning algorithms, and distributed deep learning algorithms. These algorithms can process and analyze large-scale data in a distributed computing environment while considering issues such as load balancing and node failure recovery.

Distributed data processing algorithms mainly include distributed data storage algorithms and distributed data processing algorithms. Distributed data storage algorithms are mainly used for storing and managing large-scale data in a distributed computing environment. In contrast, distributed data processing algorithms are mainly used for processing and analyzing large-scale data. These algorithms must also consider communication delays between nodes and unreliable networks, load balancing, and node failure recovery issues.

Overall, distributed computing models and algorithms have played an important role in big data processing and analysis while facing some challenges and problems. In the future, with the continuous advancement of computing and communication technologies, distributed computing models and algorithms will continue to develop and improve, providing us with more efficient and reliable big data processing and analysis services.

9.3.2 Distributed Computing Models and Algorithms

With the rapid development and widespread application of the Internet, distributed systems have been widely used and developed in Internet applications. Distributed computing models and algorithms are critical technologies in distributed systems and are crucial for designing and implementing distributed systems. In this section, we will explore the relevant knowledge of distributed computing models and algorithms from the perspective of distributed system models.

1. Distributed System Models A distributed system is a network system composed of multiple computer nodes that can collectively accomplish complex tasks. In a distributed system, nodes can communicate with each other through a network and achieve distributed processing of tasks through collaboration. According to the characteristics of distributed systems, distributed system models can be divided into three types:

   - Client-server model
     The client-server model is the most common in distributed systems. In this model, the client sends a request to the server, and the server processes the request and returns the result. Communication between the client and server is done through a network. The advantage of this model is its simple implementation and easy management and maintenance. The disadvantage is that the server becomes the system's bottleneck and cannot support large-scale concurrent requests.

   - Peer-to-peer model
     The peer-to-peer model refers to a model in which nodes in a distributed system cooperate equally to complete tasks. In this model, each node has the same status and ability and can communicate and cooperate to complete tasks. The advantage of this model is its high flexibility and ability to support large-scale concurrent requests. The disadvantage is the high cost of management and maintenance.

   - Hybrid model
     The hybrid model is a combination of the client-server model and the peer-to-peer model. Different models can be adopted according to different task requirements. In the hybrid model,

tasks can be divided into different parts and different models can be used to complete the tasks. The advantage of this model is its high flexibility, as the optimal model can be selected based on the characteristics of the task.

2. Distributed Computing Models Distributed computing models refer to dividing and allocating tasks in a distributed system and completing task computation and processing through node collaboration. Different distributed computing models can be used according to the characteristics and requirements of the tasks.

   • Message-passing model The message-passing model refers to communication and collaboration between nodes in a distributed system through messages. In this model, each node can send and receive messages, and tasks can be cooperatively completed through message passing between nodes. The advantage of this model is its high flexibility and ability to support large-scale concurrent requests. The disadvantage is the relatively high cost of communication and collaboration, requiring the design of appropriate message-passing protocols and data structures to ensure reliable message transmission and processing.

   • Shared-storage model The shared-storage model refers to the allocation and computation of tasks in a distributed system by sharing the same storage space among all nodes. In this model, each node can read and write the shared storage, and tasks can be cooperatively completed through shared storage reading and writing between nodes. The advantage of this model is the relatively low cost of communication and collaboration, which can support large-scale concurrent requests. The disadvantage is that shared storage may become the system's bottleneck, requiring appropriate data structures and algorithms to improve its concurrent processing ability.

   • Task-scheduling model The task-scheduling model refers to allocating tasks through a task scheduler in a distributed system and completing task computation and processing through collaboration between nodes. In this model, the task scheduler assigns tasks to different nodes based on the characteristics and requirements of the tasks, and data transmission and collaboration between nodes are carried out to complete the computation and processing of tasks. The advantage of this model is its high flexibility, as it can dynamically adjust and optimize task scheduling based on the characteristics and requirements of the task. The disadvantage is that the task scheduler may become the system's bottleneck, requiring appropriate algorithms and strategies to improve the efficiency and accuracy of task scheduling.

3. Distributed Computing Algorithms Distributed computing algorithms refer to implementing task allocation and computation through appropriate algorithms and strategies in a distributed computing model. Different distributed computing algorithms can be used according to the characteristics and requirements of the tasks.

- MapReduce

  The MapReduce algorithm is a task-scheduling-based distributed computing algorithm widely used for large-scale data processing and analysis. The MapReduce algorithm divides tasks into two stages: Map stage and Reduce stage. In the Map stage, tasks are decomposed into multiple subtasks and assigned to different nodes for computation. In the Reduce stage, the results computed by each node are merged to obtain the final result. The advantages of the MapReduce algorithm are its strong processing capability and scalability, making it suitable for large-scale data processing and analysis. The disadvantage is that the algorithm has high complexity and requires appropriate Map and Reduce functions to ensure correctness and efficiency.

- Paxos

  The Paxos algorithm is a message-passing-based distributed computing algorithm used to solve the consistency problem in distributed systems. In the Paxos algorithm, nodes negotiate and reach a consensus decision result through message passing. Through the phased voting and negotiation process, the algorithm ensures the consistency and reliability of the distributed system. The advantage of the Paxos algorithm is its ability to ensure the consistency and reliability of distributed systems, making it suitable for high-concurrency and high-availability systems. The disadvantage is that the algorithm has high complexity and implementation difficulty.

- Message-Passing Based QuickSort Algorithm

  The message-passing-based QuickSort algorithm is a distributed computing algorithm based on message-passing used to solve large-scale data sorting problems. In this algorithm, data is divided into multiple parts and assigned to different nodes for sorting, and a globally ordered result is obtained through message-passing cooperation. The advantage of this algorithm is its strong processing capability, making it suitable for large-scale data sorting. The disadvantage is that the algorithm has high complexity and requires appropriate message-passing protocols and data structures to ensure correctness and efficiency.

Distributed computing models and algorithms are important components of distributed systems and play an important role in large-scale data processing and high-concurrency computing scenarios. Through the above introduction, we have learned the basic concepts and features of distributed computing models and algorithms, as well as the three commonly used distributed computing models and three distributed computing algorithms. In practical applications, it is necessary to choose appropriate distributed computing models and algorithms based on specific scenarios and requirements and implement and optimize them through appropriate tools and frameworks.

9.3.3 Data Sharing and Distributed Scheduling

Overview of Data sharding

With the rapid development of the Internet and the Internet of Things, the era of big data has arrived. In this context, the processing and analysis of large-scale data have become an indispensable part of various fields. However, due to a single computing node's limited computing and storage capacity, how to efficiently process and analyze large-scale data sets has become an important issue.

Data sharding is a common technique that divides a large-scale data set into multiple smaller data blocks so that each computing node only needs to process a part of the data, reducing the burden on a single computing node and improving the efficiency of data processing and analysis. Data sharding aims to evenly distribute the data to each computing node as much as possible to ensure load balancing. Data sharding typically needs to consider the following factors:

(a) Data size: The size of the data sharding should be reasonable. If it is too small, it will cause too much communication overhead; if it is too large, it will cause an excessive burden on a single computing node.

(b) Data properties: Data sharding needs to consider data properties, such as whether it has temporal and spatial correlation.

(c) Number and performance of computing nodes: Data sharding needs to consider the number and performance of computing nodes to ensure load balancing.

Data Sharding Algorithms

Data-sharding algorithms aim to distribute data to different computing nodes as evenly as possible to achieve load balancing. The following are typical data-sharding algorithms:

(a) Hash-based sharding algorithm

The hash-based sharding algorithm is a standard data sharding algorithm that uses the hash value of data as the sharding basis and divides data with the same hash value into the same shard. The hash-based sharding algorithm ensures the even distribution of data and avoids correlation between data. However, the hash-based sharding algorithm may have hash collision problems, which means that different data can produce the same hash value, thereby affecting the effectiveness of data sharding.

(b) Round-robin sharding algorithm

The round-robin sharding algorithm is a simple data sharding algorithm that assigns data to different shards in sequence, each processing the same amount of data. The round-robin sharding algorithm can ensure the even distribution of data but cannot consider the correlation between data, so it may cause load imbalance in some cases.

(c) Range-based sharding algorithm

The range-based sharding algorithm is based on the range of data attributes. For example, a time-series data set can be divided into shards based on time range. The range-based sharding algorithm can consider the correlation between data, but there may be data imbalance problems, such as in cases where data distribution is uneven.

(d) Sample-based sharding algorithm

The sample-based sharding algorithm is a sharding algorithm based on data sampling. It first randomly selects some samples from the data set and then divides the data into different shards based on the features of the samples. The sample-based sharding algorithm can consider the correlation between data and avoid hash collision problems, but it needs to ensure the representativeness of the samples. Otherwise, it may cause data distribution imbalance problems.

Implementation of Data Sharding

When implementing data sharding, the following factors need to be considered:

(a) Selection of sharding method: Choose the appropriate sharding algorithm according to the actual situation, such as a hash-based sharding algorithm, round-robin sharding algorithm, range-based sharding algorithm, or sample-based sharding algorithm.

(b) Sharding granularity: Choose the appropriate sharding granularity according to the size of the data set and the number of computing nodes to ensure the load balance of computation.

(c) Data synchronization and consistency: Data synchronization and consistency issues must be considered to avoid inconsistent data during the data sharding process.

(d) Dynamic adjustment of sharding: In the case of changes in the number of computing nodes or uneven data distribution, dynamic adjustment is needed to ensure load balancing and data consistency.

(e) Fault tolerance of sharding: In the event of a computing node failure or network anomaly, fault tolerance processing is needed to avoid data loss or interruption of computation.

Applications of Data Sharding

Data sharding technology has been widely used in distributed computing systems like Hadoop, Spark, Flink, etc. Data sharding can significantly improve the efficiency and scalability of distributed computing, thus supporting the processing and analysis of large-scale data. In various application scenarios, data sharding plays an important role, such as:

1. Internet search engine: By sharding massive web page data, distributed computing is implemented to speed up the response speed of search engines and the accuracy of search results.

2. Financial risk management: By sharding transaction data, distributed computing is implemented to analyze transaction behavior, identify potential risks, and thus protect customer funds.

3. IoT data analysis: By sharding sensor data, distributed computing is implemented to monitor and predict various physical phenomena, such as weather changes and earthquake warnings.

4. Medical and health data analysis: By sharding patient data, distributed computing is implemented to diagnose and treat various diseases, such as cancer and cardiovascular disease.

5. Artificial intelligence computation: By sharding large-scale training data, distributed computing is implemented to train deep learning models, such as image and speech recognition.

In summary, data sharding technology is one of the core technologies of distributed computing, providing efficient, scalable, and reliable solutions for processing and analyzing large-scale data. When applying data-sharding technology, issues such as sharding algorithms, sharding granularity, data synchronization and consistency, dynamic adjustment of sharding, and sharding fault-tolerance need to be considered.

Distributed Scheduling

Distributed scheduling refers to assigning distributed computing tasks to different computing nodes for execution. It is one of the key factors in implementing distributed computing, which can fully utilize computing resources, improve computing efficiency and throughput, and improve the reliability and availability of computing systems. This section will introduce the basic concepts of distributed scheduling, standard scheduling algorithms, and implementation methods of distributed scheduling.

1. Basic Concepts

In distributed computing systems, distributed scheduling mainly involves the following concepts:

1. Computing node: A computing node is a node in the distributed computing system that executes a computing task. It can be a physical machine, a virtual machine, a container, or a process.

2. Task: A task refers to a computing work that needs to be executed in the distributed computing system. It can be a standalone program, a data processing process, a model training process, or a task flow.

3. Resource: Resource refers to the computing resources available for scheduling in the distributed computing system, including computing nodes, storage devices, network bandwidth, etc.

4. Scheduler: A scheduler refers to a component in the distributed computing system responsible for scheduling tasks to different computing nodes for execution. It is usually an independent service or module.

2. Common Scheduling Algorithms

In distributed computing systems, standard scheduling algorithms mainly include the following:

1. **Random scheduling algorithm**: This algorithm assigns tasks to available computing nodes for execution. Its implementation is relatively simple, but the scheduling efficiency and quality could be better, and it is not suitable for complex task scheduling scenarios.

2. **Static scheduling algorithm:** The static scheduling algorithm refers to pre-assigning tasks to appropriate computing nodes for execution based on task characteristics, computing node performance, load, and other information. It can improve scheduling efficiency and quality but is unsuitable for dynamic computing loads and resource changes.

3. **Dynamic scheduling algorithm:** The dynamic scheduling algorithm adjusts the task distribution strategy based on real-time computing load and resource changes to achieve the best scheduling effect. Common dynamic scheduling algorithms include load-balancing scheduling algorithms, resource-aware scheduling algorithms, feedback scheduling algorithms, etc.

4. **Hybrid scheduling algorithm:** The hybrid scheduling algorithm combines multiple scheduling algorithms and flexibly selects appropriate scheduling algorithms based on different task characteristics and scheduling strategies.

3. Implementation Methods of Distributed Scheduling

The distributed scheduling implementation methods can be divided into two categories:

1. **Centralized scheduling** refers to managing all scheduling decisions in a scheduling center or scheduler. All tasks must be allocated and scheduled through the scheduling center in centralized scheduling. The scheduling center is responsible for resource allocation, load balancing, task priority management, task status monitoring, and fault recovery. Standard centralized scheduling systems include Hadoop YARN, Apache Mesos, and Kubernetes.

   Taking Hadoop YARN as an example, its centralized scheduling process is as follows:

   (a) The application submits a task request to the resource manager (ResourceManager).
   (b) ResourceManager assigns an ApplicationMaster to the task.
   (c) The ApplicationMaster requests resources from ResourceManager, and ResourceManager assigns available resources.

(d) The ApplicationMaster assigns the task to an available computing node.

(e) The computing node executes the task and returns the result to the ApplicationMaster.

(f) The ApplicationMaster summarizes the task results and returns them to the application.

Centralized scheduling has the advantages of centralized scheduling decisions, high scheduling efficiency, and strong load-balancing capabilities. However, it also has problems such as single-point-of-failure, scheduling center performance bottlenecks, and poor system scalability.

2. **Decentralized scheduling** distributes task allocation and scheduling decisions to multiple computing nodes. Each computing node can decide to execute a task based on its local load and resource situation. In decentralized scheduling, each computing node has a specific capability to allocate and schedule tasks through communication and collaboration with other nodes. Standard decentralized scheduling systems include Apache Hadoop Fair Scheduler and Google Borg.

Taking Apache Hadoop Fair Scheduler as an example, its decentralized scheduling process is as follows:

(a) Each computing node has its scheduler.

(b) After submitting a task, the scheduler adds the task to the pending task queue.

(c) The scheduler allocates and schedules tasks through communication and collaboration with other nodes.

Decentralized scheduling has the advantages of decentralized scheduling decisions, robust system scalability, and system performance independent of the scheduling center. However, it also has problems such as low task scheduling efficiency and weak load balancing capabilities.

Distributed scheduling is a vital component of distributed computing, which can improve the utilization of computing resources and system performance while enhancing system reliability and availability. Standard scheduling algorithms include random, static, dynamic, and hybrid scheduling, each suitable for different scenarios and requirements.

Data sharding is one of the key technologies for implementing distributed computing. It involves partitioning large amounts of data into smaller blocks and distributing them to different computing nodes for processing. Common data sharding algorithms include hash, range, and random sharding, each suitable for different data distributions and access patterns.

The implementation methods of distributed scheduling can be centralized or decentralized, each suitable for different scenarios and requirements. Centralized scheduling has the advantages of centralized scheduling decisions, high scheduling efficiency, and strong load-balancing capabilities. However, it also has issues such as single-point-of-failure, scheduling center performance bottlenecks, and poor system scalability. Decentralized scheduling has the advantages of decentralized scheduling decisions, strong system scalability, and system performance independent of the scheduling center. However, it also has low task scheduling efficiency and weak load-balancing capabilities.

In practical applications, appropriate scheduling and sharding algorithms must be selected based on system requirements and characteristics while also considering system reliability, availability, and performance, to ensure the efficient operation of distributed computing systems.

The Combined Application of Data Fragmentation and Distributed Scheduling

With the continuous increase in data volume and the constant evolution of business scenarios, the traditional single-machine computing model can no longer meet the demands of the big data era. As a result, the distributed computing model has emerged. The distributed computing model is a computing model that decomposes computing tasks into multiple computing units and coordinates their work. In the distributed computing model, each computing unit is an independent computing node communicating with other nodes over a network to exchange data and collaborate on computing. To ensure the efficiency and scalability of the distributed computing model, a series of distributed algorithms are needed to implement the sharding and scheduling of distributed computing tasks.

In distributed computing, data sharding decomposes large datasets into smaller data blocks so that each computing node only needs to process a portion of the data, thus reducing computational complexity and improving computational efficiency. There are multiple ways to shard data, such as by key value or timestamp. Data sharding aims to decompose the computing task into smaller sub-tasks so that each computing node only needs to process a portion of the data, thereby improving computational efficiency.

Distributed scheduling assigns decomposed tasks to different computing nodes for execution and coordinating the computation of results. There are multiple ways to perform distributed scheduling, such as based on data streams or tasks. In distributed scheduling, communication and collaboration between nodes must be considered to ensure computational correctness while maximizing computational efficiency.

Data sharding and distributed scheduling are two critical issues in distributed computing, and their combined application can make distributed computing more efficient and scalable. For example, the data is often extensive in large-scale machine learning tasks and requires a distributed computing model. First, the data set can be decomposed into smaller data blocks so that each computing node only needs to process a portion of the data. Then, the computing tasks are assigned to different computing nodes for execution, and the results are collaboratively computed. The sharding and scheduling strategies must be adjusted continuously to maximize computational efficiency during the computation process.

The distributed computing model and algorithms have many applications in practical scenarios, such as internet search engines, machine learning, and data mining. In Internet search engines, massive web pages must be indexed and sorted, requiring a distributed computing model for computation. Large datasets must be trained and predicted in machine learning, requiring a distributed computing model. Large amounts of data must be mined and analyzed in data mining, which also requires a distributed computing model. In addition to these applications, the distributed computing model and algorithms can also be applied to large-scale scientific computing, social network analysis, image and video processing, and other fields to improve computational efficiency and processing capabilities.

In summary, the distributed computing model and algorithms are key technologies for processing massive amounts of data in the current big data era. Data sharding and distributed scheduling are two core issues in the distributed computing model, and their combined application can make distributed computing more efficient and scalable. With the advent of the big data era, the application of the distributed computing model and algorithms will become increasingly widespread, becoming an important force driving technological progress and social development.

9.3.4 Parallel Computing and Task Coordination

In computer science, as data volume and computational complexity increase, serial computing can no longer meet the demand for computational efficiency. Parallel computing has emerged, which can simultaneously use multiple computing resources to complete a task, significantly improving computational efficiency and performance. At the same time, task coordination has become an important research direction. It involves task scheduling and load balancing in parallel computing, communication, synchronization, and mutual exclusion issues between processes. This section will focus on the basic concepts of parallel computing and task coordination and discuss their importance and application scenarios.

1. Definition of Parallel Computing

   Parallel computing refers to dividing a computing problem into sub-problems, assigning them to multiple processors for simultaneous execution, and coordinating and communicating them through a reasonable mechanism to enable multiple processors to complete the computing task jointly. It can significantly improve computational efficiency and processing capabilities compared to serial computing. Parallel computing is widely used in high-performance computing, data mining, image processing, scientific computing, and artificial intelligence.

2. Importance of Parallel Computing

   The importance of parallel computing lies in its ability to speed up computation, shorten task execution time, and improve processing efficiency. It enables computer systems to simultaneously utilize the computing power of multiple processors, thus meeting higher computational requirements. In addition, parallel computing can reduce costs, improve reliability and scalability, and make the computing system more stable and robust. Therefore, parallel computing is widely used in large-scale, high-performance data mining, machine learning, image processing, biomedical, weather forecasting, and other fields.

3. Definition of Task Coordination

Task coordination refers to the process in which multiple computing nodes work together to complete a task. In parallel computing, task coordination includes assignment, communication, and synchronization. The goal of task coordination is to achieve efficient task execution, thus improving the overall performance of the computing system.

4. Importance of Task Coordination

Task coordination plays a vital role in parallel computing. Task assignment, communication, and synchronization affect computational efficiency and performance in a multi-processor system. Proper task coordination can balance the system load, prevent some processors from idle, and improve overall system efficiency. At the same time, task coordination can also avoid competition and conflict between tasks, ensuring system correctness and reliability. Therefore, task coordination is also an indispensable part of parallel computing.

5. Application Scenarios of Parallel Computing and Task Coordination

Parallel computing and task coordination have a wide range of applications across various fields. Here are some common application scenarios:

(a) **High-Performance Computing** refers to using parallel computing techniques to accelerate the execution of tasks using multiple processors and computing nodes. In high-performance computing, task coordination is critical, including task assignment, communication, and synchronization. High-performance computing is widely used in scientific fields such as weather forecasting, aerodynamics, and molecular simulation and can significantly improve computing efficiency and accuracy.

(b) **Data Mining** refers to mining useful information and knowledge from a large amount of data. In data mining, parallel computing is widely used in data analysis, pre-processing, feature extraction, model training, and other aspects. At the same time, task coordination is also an indispensable part of data mining, which can coordinate the work of multiple processors and improve the system's overall performance.

(c) **Artificial Intelligence** refers to a technology that uses computers to simulate human intelligence. In artificial intelligence, parallel computing and task coordination are widely used in deep learning, machine learning, natural language processing, and other aspects. By using multiple processors for parallel computing, the speed of model training and inference can be accelerated, and the system's overall performance can be improved.

(d) **Image Processing** refers to the process of digital processing and analysis of images. In image processing, parallel computing is widely used in image filtering, image segmentation, image recognition, and other aspects. At the same time, task coordination is also an indispensable part of image processing, which can coordinate the work of multiple processors and improve the system's overall performance.

The basic concepts, importance, and application scenarios of parallel computing and task coordination have been outlined above. Parallel computing can improve computational efficiency and performance. At the same time, task coordination is an indispensable part of parallel computing that can coordinate the work of multiple processors and improve the system's overall performance.

Parallel computing and task coordination are widely used in high-performance computing, data mining, artificial intelligence, and image processing. In practical applications, suitable parallel computing models and task coordination schemes should be selected according to different application scenarios and requirements to achieve optimal computational efficiency and performance.

In the future, with the continuous development of computer hardware technology, the scale and speed of computing resources will continue to increase, which will bring broader development space for parallel computing and task coordination. At the same time, with the development of artificial intelligence, the Internet of Things, big data, and other technologies, the demand for parallel computing and task coordination will continue to grow, further promoting the development of these two fields.

Although parallel computing and task coordination face many challenges and difficulties, such as concurrency control, load balancing, communication overhead, and other issues, they will be effectively addressed with technology's continuous advancement and development. Therefore, in the future, parallel computing and task coordination will become more mature and popular and provide more efficient and reliable computing capabilities for various application scenarios.

(a) **Parallel computing models** describe the structure and computing patterns of parallel computing systems. Ordinary parallel computing models include shared memory models, distributed memory models, message-passing models, data flow models, and others. Different parallel computing models are suitable for different application scenarios and computing requirements.

(b) The **shared memory model** refers to a model in which all processors share the same physical memory. In parallel computing, multiple threads can read and write to the same shared memory to achieve parallel computing. There are two main types of shared memory models: shared memory multiprocessor (SMP) systems and shared memory systems based on virtual memory.

In the shared memory model, all processors share the same physical memory and communicate by accessing memory. Multiple threads can access the same memory address simultaneously, thus achieving data sharing and communication. The shared memory model has the advantages of low communication overhead and simple program writing, making it suitable for parallel computing scenarios where frequent communication is required between computing tasks.

Ordinary programming models for shared memory include OpenMP, Pthreads, and others. OpenMP is a multi-threaded programming model that supports shared memory models and can be used in programming languages such as C, C++, and Fortran. Pthreads is a POSIX standard thread library that can be used on Unix and Linux operating systems, supporting multi-threaded programming.

Distributed Memory Model

The distributed memory model refers to a model in which all processors have their physical memory and communicate with each other through a network. In parallel computing, multiple processes can read and write to different memories to achieve parallel computing. There are two main types of distributed memory models: distributed memory systems based on the Message-Passing Interface (MPI) and distributed memory systems based on Distributed Shared Memory (DSM).

In the distributed memory model, each processor has its physical memory, and processors communicate through a network. Data must be split, transmitted, and recombined during communication, resulting in relatively large communication overhead. The distributed memory model suits scenarios where computing tasks require much computation and communication overhead.

Standard programming models for distributed memory models include MPI, Hadoop, and others. MPI is a message-passing interface standard used in programming languages such as C, C++, and Fortran, supporting parallel computing under distributed memory models. Hadoop is a distributed computing framework that can be used for big data processing and distributed computing on distributed computing clusters.

Message Passing Model

The message-passing model refers to a model in which processors communicate with each other through messages, and processors do not share memory. In parallel computing, the message-passing model can exchange data and synchronize different processors through sending and receiving messages. The message-passing model suits scenarios where computing tasks require much communication and data exchange.

There are two ways of message communication in the message-passing model: synchronous and asynchronous communication. Synchronous communication means that the sending process waits for the receiving process to process the message before execution, while asynchronous communication means the sending process can continue execution without waiting for the receiving process to process the message.

Trivial message-passing programming models include MPI and PGAS. MPI has been introduced in the distributed memory model above, and PGAS will be briefly introduced here. PGAS is a programming model based on distributed shared memory. It divides the global address space into multiple local address spaces and maps the local address space to different processors to achieve distributed computing. PGAS supports synchronous and asynchronous communication and guarantees memory consistency, which can simplify parallel computing programming.

Dataflow Model

The dataflow model refers to a model in which data flows from one computing task to another in parallel computing, and computation is performed through data flow. In the dataflow model, computing tasks are called dataflow graph nodes, and nodes are connected through the data flow. The computation of each node only depends on input data, not the state and time of computation. The dataflow model perfectly works in scenarios where computing tasks have data dependencies and clear data flow.

There are two programming models for the dataflow model: static dataflow model and dynamic dataflow model. The static dataflow model determines the structure of the dataflow graph before program execution, while the dynamic dataflow model can dynamically generate the dataflow graph during program execution.

Typical dataflow programming models include Dataflow and StreamIt. Dataflow is a static dataflow programming language in programming languages such as Java, C++, and Python. StreamIt is a dynamic dataflow programming language that can be used in C++.

In general, parallel computing models can be classified according to the data interaction between computing tasks and the memory relationship between processors. Choosing a suitable parallel computing model can improve the performance and efficiency of parallel computing according to specific application scenarios and computing requirements.

Task Coordination Methods

In parallel computing, task coordination is an important method that can improve the efficiency and reliability of parallel computing. Task coordination refers to multiple tasks cooperating in parallel computing to complete a complex computing task jointly. Task coordination methods can be divided into static task allocation and dynamic task allocation.

Static Task Allocation

Static task allocation refers to the task being assigned to different processors before parallel computing begins, and then the processor independently executes the task. The main advantage of static task allocation is that it can reduce communication and synchronization overhead. Still, some problems exist, such as uneven load balancing between processors and resource waste.

Common methods of static task allocation include:

- Round-robin allocation: tasks are assigned to processors in order, and the load balance between processors is relatively even.

- Uniform allocation: tasks are evenly distributed to processors to achieve a relatively balanced load distribution.

- Divide-and-conquer algorithm: tasks are divided into several subtasks, which are then assigned to different processors for computation.

The main problem with static task allocation is that it is difficult to deal with situations such as processor failure and task changes, so dynamic task allocation is needed.

Dynamic Task Allocation

Dynamic task allocation refers to dynamically assigning tasks to processors during parallel computing based on different task requirements and processor load conditions. The main advantage of dynamic task allocation is that it can deal with different task requirements and processor load conditions, ensuring the efficiency and reliability of computation.

Common methods of dynamic task allocation include:

1. Task allocation based on the work-stealing model: Each processor has its task queue in a task queue, and when a processor completes its task, it can steal tasks from other processors' task queues for computation. The work-stealing model can ensure load balancing between processors and improve computational efficiency.

2. Task allocation based on task graph: It refers to breaking down a complex computing task into several sub-tasks and representing the dependency relationship between sub-tasks as a directed graph. Task allocation based on a task graph can dynamically assign tasks to processors for computation based on different task requirements and processor load conditions.

3. Task allocation based on task queue: It means that tasks are arranged in a particular order, and processors take tasks from the queue for computation. Task allocation based on task queue can dynamically adjust the order of tasks based on different task requirements and processor load conditions to ensure load balancing between processors.

In addition to the standard task coordination methods mentioned above, there are other task coordination methods, such as task coordination based on data flow and task coordination based on message passing.

Dataflow-Based Task Coordination

Dataflow-based task coordination refers to decomposing a computing task into several data flows and then assigning the data flows to different processors for computation. In dataflow computing, each processor can independently compute its data flow and then pass the results to other processors for subsequent computation. Dataflow-based task coordination can improve computational efficiency and reliability, but it also has issues, such as data flow allocation and synchronization between data flows.

Message Passing-Based Task Coordination

Message-passing-based task coordination using message-passing mechanisms to jointly transmit information between different processors to complete a complex computing task. In message-passing-based task coordination, each processor can independently compute its task and then pass the computation results to other processors through message-passing mechanisms for subsequent computation. Message-passing-based task coordination can improve computational efficiency and reliability, but it also has issues, such as message-passing efficiency and synchronization.

Task coordination methods are one of the essential methods in parallel computing, which can improve computational efficiency and reliability. In task coordination, suitable task coordination methods should be chosen based on different task requirements and processor load conditions. Static task allocation can reduce communication and synchronization overhead, but dealing with processor failure and task changes is challenging. Dynamic task allocation can handle task requirements and processor load conditions, ensuring computational efficiency and reliability. Dataflow-based and message-passing-based task coordination can improve computational efficiency and reliability. However, issues such as data flow allocation, synchronization, and message-passing efficiency and synchronization need to be addressed.

9.3.5 Efficient Data Exchange and Transmission

Efficient data exchange and transmission are crucial in distributed secure data processing environments. How to quickly and reliably transmit large amounts of data is a significant challenge modern data processing systems face. This section will introduce how to achieve efficient data exchange and transmission in a distributed environment and explore some related challenges and solutions.

In a distributed system, data exchange and transmission are core issues. Data must often be exchanged and transmitted in a distributed system between different nodes. For example, a large-scale data processing task may need to be collaboratively completed among multiple nodes, with each node processing its responsible data and returning the processing results to other nodes. In this case, the efficiency and reliability of data exchange and transmission directly affect the performance and stability of the entire system.

Due to the large number of nodes in distributed systems and the significant differences in network bandwidth and latency, achieving efficient data exchange and transmission in a distributed environment is a very complex problem. Generally, suitable technologies such as data transmission protocols, compression algorithms, data fragmentation, and transmission parallelization must be selected according to the application scenarios and requirements. Additionally, data caching, pre-fetching, and security issues must be considered.

Challenges and Solutions for Data Transmission

There are many challenges in data transmission in distributed systems. Some of the significant challenges include:

1. Uneven network bandwidth and latency

   In a distributed system, significant network bandwidth and latency differences exist between different nodes. For example, some nodes may be connected by high-speed networks, while others may only be connected by low-speed networks. Therefore, achieving efficient data exchange and transmission in such an environment takes time and effort.

   Data fragmentation and transmission parallelization can solve this problem by improving transmission efficiency. Data fragmentation can divide large data blocks into small ones for individual transmission, reducing network transmission latency. Transmission parallelization refers to dividing data into multiple parts for parallel transmission to utilize network bandwidth fully. These technologies can effectively improve data transmission efficiency and reliability, but additional overhead and burden brought by data fragmentation and parallel transmission also need to be considered and balanced.

Data Compression and Decompression

Data compression can effectively reduce bandwidth consumption and transmission time and improve data transmission efficiency during data transmission. However, distributed systems must also consider data compression and decompression overhead. It may be necessary to compress and decompress large amounts of data for large-scale data processing tasks, which will bring significant computational burdens and additional overhead.

Solving this problem requires choosing suitable compression and decompression algorithms based on the actual situation, existing computing resources, and network bandwidth. At the same time, some optimization techniques for data compression and decompression can be adopted, such as incremental and pre-processing compression, to improve the efficiency of data compression and decompression.

Data Security

In distributed systems, data security is a fundamental issue. Various forms of attacks, such as interception, tampering, and forgery, may occur during data transmission, so ensuring the security of data transmission is a problem that must be considered.

To guarantee the security of data transfer, certain encryption and authentication approaches can be utilized. For instance, digital signatures and other authentication methods can be used to confirm the accuracy and integrity of data, and SSL/TLS encryption protocols can be used to assure the security of data transmission.

Data Transmission Protocols

Choosing the appropriate data transmission protocol is crucial for efficient data exchange and transmission in a distributed environment. Trivial data transmission protocols include TCP, UDP, HTTP, WebSocket, etc. Below, we will introduce these protocols' characteristics and application scenarios, respectively.

1. **TCP Protocol**

   A dependable transmission protocol that is connection-oriented is TCP. A four-way handshake is necessary to end the connection after the transmission of all the data, while a three-way handshake is necessary to establish the connection before data transmission. TCP protocol introduces inevitable overhead but also ensures the dependability of data transport through procedures for packet confirmation and re-transmission.

The TCP protocol is suitable for highly reliable data-transmission scenarios, such as file transfer, database synchronization, etc. During data transmission, TCP protocol ensures the smoothness and fairness of data transmission through flow control and congestion control mechanisms, but it may also bring some delay and bandwidth consumption.

2. UDP Protocol

UDP is a connectionless and unreliable transmission protocol. There is no need to establish a connection or confirm during data transmission, and data packets are not guaranteed to arrive at the receiver in the order they were sent. UDP protocol has a fast data transmission speed but may also encounter problems such as packet loss, duplication, and disorder.

The UDP protocol is suitable for scenarios that require high real-time data transmission, such as video streaming, audio streaming, etc. In these scenarios, real-time data is more important than reliable data, so UDP protocol can be used to achieve efficient data transmission.

3. HTTP Protocol

HTTP is an application-layer protocol based on TCP protocol, usually used for data transmission in web applications. HTTP protocol uses a request-response mode for data transmission, transmitting requests and responses in plaintext. The advantage of HTTP protocol is that it is easy to implement and extend, but the disadvantage is its low efficiency.

The HTTP protocol is suitable for scenarios with a small amount of data to transmit and does not require high transmission speed, such as web browsing, API calls, etc.

4. **WebSocket Protocol**

WebSocket protocol is a bidirectional communication protocol based on TCP protocol, which can achieve real-time bidirectional communication between clients and servers. WebSocket protocol requires a handshake to establish a connection, and data transmission can be performed directly after the handshake is completed.

The WebSocket protocol is suitable for scenarios that require real-time communication, such as online chat, games, etc. Compared with the HTTP protocol, the WebSocket protocol can achieve faster data transmission speed and lower delay.

5. **Considerations for Protocol Selection**

When choosing a data transmission protocol, various factors must be considered comprehensively, including reliability, real-time, transmission volume, transmission speed, delay, etc. Choose the most suitable protocol to achieve data transmission.

For scenarios that require reliable data transmission, TCP protocol can be selected; for scenarios that require high real-time data, UDP protocol can be selected; for scenarios that have a small amount of data to transmit and do not require high transmission speed, HTTP protocol can be selected; for scenarios that require real-time communication, WebSocket protocol can be selected.

In addition, when selecting a protocol, the security of the protocol also needs to be considered. For example, when using HTTP protocol for data transmission, HTTPS protocol must encrypt data transmission to prevent data from being stolen or tampered with.

Data Compression and Encryption

Data compression and encryption are often used to improve transmission efficiency and protect data security during data exchange and transmission.

Data Compression

Data compression can reduce the amount of data transmitted and improve transmission efficiency. Common data compression algorithms include LZ77, LZ78, LZW, Deflate, etc. Among them, Deflate algorithm is a commonly used compression algorithm based on the LZ77 algorithm and Huffman coding.

There are two ways to perform data compression: one is to compress data before transmitting it, and the other is to decompress the transmitted data at the receiving end. The former method can better improve transmission efficiency.

Data Encryption

Data encryption can protect the security of data transmission and prevent data theft and tampering. Common data encryption algorithms include DES, AES, RSA, etc. DES and AES algorithms are symmetric encryption algorithms, and the RSA algorithm is asymmetric.

When performing data encryption, it is necessary to determine the encryption algorithm and key. For symmetric encryption algorithms, the same key is used for encryption and decryption; for asymmetric encryption algorithms, a public key is used for encryption, and a private key is used for decryption.

In addition, when performing data encryption, attention should be paid to key management and the security of key transmission. Key management includes key generation, storage, updating, etc.; a secure and reliable method should be used to manage the keys. Key transmission needs to be encrypted in a secure way to prevent key theft and tampering.

Data Caching and Pre-fetching

Data caching and pre-fetching can improve data access efficiency and reduce data transmission. Common data caching and pre-fetching technologies include local caching, distributed caching, and pre-fetching.

1. Local Caching

   Local caching stores data on local devices to quickly retrieve data during subsequent access. Local caching can reduce data access latency and network transmission volume, improving data access efficiency.

Typical local caching technologies include memory caching and disk caching. Memory caching provides faster data access speed but limited storage capacity, while disk caching provides larger storage capacity but slower data access speed.

2. Distributed Caching

Distributed caching stores data on multiple nodes to increase cache capacity and reliability. Distributed caching can reduce latency and improve data access efficiency by storing data on nearby nodes.

Common distributed caching technologies include Redis, Memcached, etc. These technologies can achieve distributed caching through clustering, increasing data storage capacity and reliability.

3. Data Pre-fetching

Data pre-fetching stores data in the cache before it is requested, making retrieving data during subsequent access quick. Data pre-fetching can reduce data access latency and network transmission volume, improving data access efficiency.

Common data pre-fetching technologies include cache pre-fetching and queue pre-fetching. Cache pre-fetching stores data in the cache for quick retrieval during the subsequent access, while queue pre-fetching stores data in a queue to be processed during the subsequent access.

The above mainly introduces the concepts, architectures, and technologies of distributed secure data processing and efficient data exchange and transmission implementation methods. Distributed secure data processing is a hot topic in the current era of big data and is significant for ensuring data security and value. Efficient data exchange and transmission are vital links in distributed secure data processing, which need to be implemented through network optimization, data compression and encryption, asynchronous message transmission, and data stream processing.

9.4 SECURE DISTRIBUTED APPLICATION CASE STUDIES

9.4.1 Cloud Computing Platform Security

1. Alibaba Cloud Security

   Alibaba Cloud is committed to providing secure and reliable computing and data processing capabilities through online public services, making computing and artificial intelligence a universal technology. In addition, Alibaba Cloud has deployed more than 200 Flying Data Centers for global customers, providing a unique hybrid cloud experience through a unified Flying operating system.

   Alibaba Cloud has established security protection, monitoring, audit, identity authentication, and security operations and maintenance mechanisms for cloud security.

   Regarding the security needs of tenants in the cloud, Alibaba Cloud provides various cloud security service products, such as Cloud Shield, DDoS Protection, Web Application Firewall, Security Center, SSL Certificates, Cloud Firewall, Encryption Service, Real Person Authentication, etc.

2. Tencent Cloud Security

   Tencent Cloud provides a network security protection technology system that includes network security, terminal security, application security, data security, business security, security management, security services, identity authentication, etc. The specific security measures are described as follows:

   (a) Network Security

      - DoS Protection: Provides various solutions such as DDoS Protection Packages and IPs to address DDoS attacks. Combining sufficient and high-quality DDoS protection resources with continuously evolving "self-developed + AI intelligent recognition" cleaning algorithms ensures a user business's stable and secure operation.

      - Cloud Firewall: A SaaS-based firewall for public cloud environments that provides users with network access control for internet and VPC boundaries. Based on traffic embedding, it integrates access control and security defense and achieves integration and automation.

- Network Intrusion Prevention System: Deploying in bypass mode can block network layer four sessions in real-time without changes or intrusions. It also provides full network log storage and retrieval, security alarms, and big visual screens to solve problems such as compliance, log auditing, administrative supervision, and cloud platform management.

- Tencent Cloud Sample Intelligent Analysis Platform: By relying on a self-developed dynamic analysis module, static analysis module, and stable and efficient task scheduling framework in a deep sandbox, it achieves automatic, intelligent, and customizable sample analysis. By constructing a large-scale analysis cluster, including multiple high-coverage malicious sample detection models that cover deep learning, it can obtain basic information, triggered behaviors, security level, and other information about the sample, thereby accurately and efficiently combating malicious samples in the current network.

(b) Terminal Security

    i. Host Security: Based on massive threat data accumulated by Tencent Security and utilizing machine learning, it provides security protection services such as hacker intrusion detection and vulnerability risk warnings for users. The main security features include password-cracking interception, abnormal login reminders, Trojan file killing, high-risk vulnerability detection, etc.

    ii. Tencent Cloud Antivirus Engine: A virus detection program that runs on the terminal, independently developed by Tencent Antivirus Laboratory. It includes both Tencent's local antivirus and cloud-based antivirus engines. It offers multiple functional interface SDKs, supports various platforms, and does not require an internet connection.

iii. Tencent Terminal Security Management System: Based on Tencent's 20-year security accumulation and Tencent PC Manager's product, operation, and technical precipitation for hundreds of millions of users over more than a decade, it applies security technologies and capabilities such as a virus-killing database with billions of records, AI antivirus engines, and big data security analysis engines to internal government and enterprise, creating a new generation of integrated terminal security solutions that include virus killing, desktop control, security operations and maintenance, security detection, and response.

iv. Tencent Cloud Zero Trust Access Control System (ZTAC): Dependent on three core capabilities: terminal security, identity security, and link security, it ensures secure, stable, and efficient access to enterprise resources and data on terminals in any network environment.

v. Mobile Terminal Security Management System: Users can centrally manage, configure, and protect terminal devices, applications, and mobile data according to their needs, improving IT management efficiency and ensuring mobile environment security.

(c) Application Security

i. Tencent Cloud Web Application Firewall: Addresses website and web application security protection problems for Tencent Cloud and external users, including web attacks, intrusion, vulnerability exploitation, hacking, tampering, backdoors, crawlers, domain hijacking, and more.

ii. Tencent Application-Level Intelligent Gateway: Based on zero trust policies, it provides centralized control, unified prevention and control, and unified auditing for enterprise applications and services, ensuring more secure and reliable enterprise applications and services.

iii. Vulnerability Scanning Service: A security service for monitoring website vulnerabilities, providing accurate and comprehensive monitoring services 24/7.

iv. Mobile Application Security: Includes application reinforcement, security assessment, compatibility testing, piracy monitoring, crash monitoring, security components, etc.

v. Mobile Game Security: Has 24-hour security capabilities, supporting rapid response to common game security issues such as cheating, tampering, and cracking for mobile game manufacturers.

(d) Business Security

i. Tencent Anti-Fraud for Lending: Identifies fraud risks in the financial industry, such as banking, securities, and insurance. Using Tencent Cloud's AI and machine learning capabilities, it accurately identifies malicious users and behavior, solves fraud threats that customers encounter in payment, lending, wealth management, risk control, and other business processes, and improves risk identification capabilities.

ii. Insurance Anti-Fraud: Accurately locates fraud threats encountered in business processes such as application, underwriting, and claims using AI risk control models.

iii. Login Protection Service: Real-time detection of malicious login behavior, such as account theft and database attacks in the user login scenarios for websites and apps, reduces the risk of malicious user login.

iv. Tencent Cloud CAPTCHA: Based on ten security barriers, it creates a comprehensive human-machine verification for web pages, apps, and mini-programs to maximize business security in registration, login, activity rush buying, likes and posting, and data protection.

v. Tencent Cloud Anti-Fraud for Activities: A service that prevents malicious behavior such as scalping during promotional activities in e-commerce, O2O, P2P, games, payments, and other industries. The anti-fraud engine accurately identifies malicious behavior and prevents the significant economic losses caused by scalping to businesses.

vi. Registration Protection Service: In the online registration scenarios for websites and apps, it provides a malicious protection engine based on the Tencent DNA algorithm to effectively identify malicious registration behavior from the three dimensions of account, device, and behavior and prevent business risks from the "source".

vii. Marketing Risk Control Service: Quickly identifies malicious requests, precisely combats "scalpers" using Tencent's security risk control model and AI correlation algorithm, improves the effectiveness of funding use, and restores data authenticity.

viii. Text Content Security Service: Uses deep learning technology to effectively identify harmful content such as pornography, politics, and terrorism, supports user-configured dictionaries, and combats custom non-compliant text. The recognition results are divided into regular, suspicious, and non-compliant categories. It is recommended to release typical images, manually review suspicious images, and block non-compliant images, saving human resources costs and improving review efficiency.

ix. Marketing Number Security: Provides a one-stop, accurate number security perception, protection, and prevention service, covering multiple capabilities such as number security protection, risk number identification, and malicious call governance.

x. Business Risk Intelligence: Provides comprehensive, real-time, and accurate business risk intelligence services. Simple API access provides profile data of IP, numbers, apps, URLs, and other business risks for precise assessment, real-time perception, evaluation, response, and loss prevention for business risks and black market attacks.

(e) Data Security

    i. Tencent Cloud Bastion Host: Combines bastion host and artificial intelligence technology to provide enterprises with operation audit for operation and maintenance personnel, alert for abnormal behaviors, and prevent internal data leakage.

    ii. Tencent Cloud Data Security Audit: Based on an AI database security audit system that can mine various potential risks and hidden dangers during the operation of the database and escort the secure operation of the database.

    iii. Data Security Governance Center: Through data asset perception and risk identification, it locates and classifies sensitive data on the cloud for enterprises and helps them set data security policies against risk problems to improve the effectiveness of protection measures.

    iv. Sensitive Data Processing: Provides sensitive data desensitization and watermarking tools and services, which can desensitize sensitive information in data systems and provide traceability evidence in case of leakage.

    v. Cloud Encryption Machine: Based on the Hardware Security Module (HSM) certified by the National Cryptography Administration, it uses virtualization technology to provide elastic, highly available, high-performance data encryption and decryption, key management, and other cloud-based data security services. It meets national regulatory compliance requirements and satisfies the encryption needs of industries such as finance and the Internet, ensuring the privacy and security of business data.

(f) Security Management

    i. **Security Operation Center:** Tencent Cloud's native unified security operation and management platform provides capabilities such as asset automation inventory, internet attack surface mapping, cloud security configuration risk inspection, compliance risk assessment, traffic threat perception, leakage monitoring, log audit, and search investigation, security orchestration and automation response, and security visualization to help cloud users achieve one-stop, visualized, and automated cloud security operation and management that covers security prevention, event monitoring and threat detection, and response and disposal after the fact.

ii. **Security Operation Center:** With security detection as the core, event correlation analysis, Tencent threat intelligence as the focus, 3D visualization as the feature, and reliable services as the guarantee, it can perform in-depth detection for external attacks and potential internal risks faced by enterprises and provide timely security alerts. It is suitable for various security operation and management scenarios. Through massive data, multi-dimensional analysis, and timely warning, it can intelligently dispose of threats promptly, achieving the closed loop of the whole network security situation being known, visible, and controllable.

iii. **Key Management System:** Enables users to create and manage keys, protect the confidentiality, integrity, and availability of keys, and meet the key management needs of users for multiple applications and businesses while complying with regulatory and compliance requirements.

iv. **Credential Management System:** Provides lifecycle management services such as credential creation, retrieval, update, and deletion and quickly realizes unified management of sensitive credentials combined with resource-level role authorization. To address the sensitive credential hard coding that may have leakage risk, users or applications can retrieve credentials by calling the Secrets Manager API, effectively avoiding sensitive information leakage caused by program hard coding and plain text configuration and business risks caused by loss of control over permissions.

(g) Data Security

    i. Tencent Cloud Bastion Host: Combines bastion host and artificial intelligence technology to provide enterprises with operation audit for operation and maintenance personnel, alert for abnormal behaviors, and prevent internal data leakage.

    ii. Tencent Cloud Data Security Audit: Based on an AI database security audit system that can mine various potential risks and hidden dangers during the operation of the database and escort the secure operation of the database.

    iii. Data Security Governance Center: Through data asset perception and risk identification, it locates and classifies sensitive data on the cloud for enterprises and helps them set data security policies against risk problems to improve the effectiveness of protection measures.

    iv. Sensitive Data Processing: Provides sensitive data desensitization and watermarking tools and services, which can desensitize sensitive information in data systems and provide traceability evidence in case of leakage.

    v. Cloud Encryption Machine: Based on the Hardware Security Module (HSM) certified by the National Cryptography Administration, it uses virtualization technology to provide elastic, highly available, high-performance data encryption and decryption, key management, and other cloud-based data security services. It meets national regulatory compliance requirements and satisfies the encryption needs of industries such as finance and the Internet, ensuring the privacy and security of business data.

(h) Security Management

    i. **Security Operation Center:** Tencent Cloud's native unified security operation and management platform provides capabilities such as asset automation inventory, internet attack surface mapping, cloud security configuration risk inspection, compliance risk assessment, traffic threat perception, leakage monitoring, log audit and search investigation, security orchestration and automation response, and security visualization to help cloud users achieve one-stop, visualized, and automated cloud security operation and management that covers security prevention, event monitoring and threat detection, and response and disposal after the fact.

ii. **Security Operation Center:** With security detection as the core, event correlation analysis, Tencent threat intelligence as the focus, 3D visualization as the feature, and reliable services as the guarantee, it can perform in-depth detection for external attacks and potential internal risks faced by enterprises and provide timely security alerts. It is suitable for various security operation and management scenarios. Through massive data, multi-dimensional analysis, and timely warning, it can intelligently dispose of threats promptly, achieving the closed loop of the whole network security situation being known, visible, and controllable.

iii. **Key Management System:** Enables users to create and manage keys, protect the confidentiality, integrity, and availability of keys, and meet the key management needs of users for multiple applications and businesses while complying with regulatory and compliance requirements.

iv. **Credential Management System:** Provides lifecycle management services such as credential creation, retrieval, update, and deletion and quickly realizes unified management of sensitive credentials combined with resource-level role authorization. To address the sensitive credential hard coding that may have leakage risk, users or applications can retrieve credentials by calling the Secrets Manager API, effectively avoiding sensitive information leakage caused by program hard coding and plain text configuration and business risks caused by loss of control over permissions.

(i) Security Services

    i. **Expert Services:** Provided by a professional security expert team, offering services such as security consultation, website penetration testing, emergency response, and compliance.

    ii. **Quantitative Evaluation of Public Internet Threats:** Provides real-time and objective services for quantifying and evaluating network security risks, and through a WeChat mini-program, can intuitively present information such as enterprise network security index, security level, and detailed security issues.

    iii. **Cloud Threat Intelligence Search Service:** Provides threat intelligence (IoC) query service, IP/domain/file reputation query service, and more.

    iv. Network Asset Risk Monitoring System: Conducts regular security scanning, continuous risk warning, and vulnerability detection for the availability, security, and compliance of network devices and application services and provides professional repair suggestions to reduce security risks.

(j) User Identity Verification

Tencent Cloud has a massive data analysis and training set for face and image recognition. Tencent Cloud provides technologies such as identity card OCR, face comparison, and live detection, enabling online user identity confirmation in seconds, effectively solving complex offline identity verification problems in high-risk industries, and meeting the high requirements of business scenarios for identity verification.

3. Huawei Cloud Security

Huawei Cloud provides IT infrastructure cloud services such as cloud computing, cloud storage, cloud networking, cloud security, cloud databases, cloud management, and application deployment. Huawei Cloud has built a security protection technology system for chips, platforms, systems, applications, data, development, ecology, and privacy to protect cloud security.

(a) Chip-level Trusted Computing and Security Encryption
Huawei has launched a trusted server and cloud platform solution supporting national cryptography algorithms. Using a trusted computing module chip, Huawei Cloud can measure the integrity of cloud platform hosts and provide more security features, reducing the risk of software and hardware tampering with cloud hosts and meeting higher security requirements.

(b) Platform Security
Huawei Cloud's Unified Virtualization Platform (UVP) runs directly on top of physical servers, building multiple simultaneously running, mutually isolated virtual machine execution environments on a single physical server by abstracting physical server resources. UVP provides virtualization capabilities based on hardware-assisted virtualization technology, providing efficient operating environments for virtual machines and ensuring that virtual machines run in legal spaces, avoiding unauthorized access by virtual machines to UVP or other virtual machines.

(c) System Security
Huawei EulerOS has passed the fourth-level certification of the Ministry of Public Security Information Security Technology Operation System Security Technology Requirements. EulerOS can provide configurable hardening strategies, kernel-level OS security capabilities, and other security technologies to prevent intrusion and ensure customer system security.

(d) Application Security
Each application provides standardized integrated interfaces to customers through Huawei's self-developed API gateway, with strict identity authentication and authorization, transmission encryption protection, granular traffic control, and

other security capabilities to prevent data theft and sniffing. Furthermore, Huawei Cloud utilizes technologies such as deep learning, runtime application protection, decentralized authentication, and more to develop further advanced security capabilities such as user behavior profiling and business risk control, monitoring and intercepting abnormal behaviors in real-time to protect application service security and stable operation.

(e) Data Security

Huawei Cloud has built secure protection capabilities for the full data lifecycle. Through research and application of multiple technologies such as automated sensitive data discovery, dynamic data desensitization, high-performance and low-cost data encryption, fast abnormal operation auditing, and data security destruction, data is controlled in the creation, storage, use, sharing, archiving, and destruction stages to ensure cloud data security. Specific data security mechanisms include data isolation, encryption, and redundancy.

(f) Development Security

Huawei Cloud manages the full software and hardware lifecycle end-to-end through perfect systems and processes and automated platforms and tools, including security design, security coding, and testing, security acceptance and release, vulnerability management, and more.

(g) Eco-Security

Based on strict access and wide use, Huawei Cloud ensures the secure introduction and use of open-source and third-party software. Huawei Cloud has established explicit security requirements and sound process control plans for introduced open source and third-party software, implementing strict controls in selection and analysis, security testing, code security, risk scanning, legal review, software application, and software exit.

(h) Privacy Security

The design of Huawei Cloud's various service products follows the "Privacy Protection Design Specification", which establishes a privacy baseline, maintains privacy integrity, guides privacy risk analysis, formulates corresponding measures, and incorporates them into service product development and design processes. In addition, to meet the security needs of cloud users, Huawei Cloud provides security services such as DDoS protection, Anti-DDoS traffic cleaning, Database Security Services (DBSS), data encryption services, enterprise host security, container security services, expert security services, SSL certificate management, cloud bastion hosts, vulnerability scanning services, Web Application Firewalls (WAF), and more.

4. Microsoft Azure Cloud Security

Microsoft Azure's main network security measures in cloud security are described as follows:

(a) Data storage security: All customer data, applications processing the data, and data centers hosting Century Internet online services are located within China.

(b) Business continuity guarantee: Data centers in East and North China are geographically separated by over 1000km and provide remote replication, ensuring business continuity support for Azure services and reliable data storage.

(c) Physical environment security: All data centers select the item-level data centers of domestic telecommunications operators and adopt N+1 or 2N uninterrupted power supply protection. In addition, high-power diesel generators provide backup power for data centers, with on-site diesel storage and nearby refueling stations.

(d) Privacy protection: Customers have full control over their customer data and permissions and can decide where to store their data. No one is allowed to use customer data without authorization.

(e) Compliance: Meets international and industry-specific standards ISO/IEC 27001, the third-level record of the Ministry of Public Security Information System Security Level Protection Evaluation, and multiple trusted cloud service certifications.

(f) Infrastructure security: Helps ensure customer data security through encrypted communication, threat management, and mitigation practices (including regular penetration testing).

9.4.2 IoT Data Security

1. Information Leakage

On March 27, 2014, CCTV reported the high-security risks of home surveillance cameras, causing widespread public concern. In recent years, home surveillance cameras have become increasingly popular and are widely used by ordinary citizens to prevent home security risks.

The revelation that these cameras are being monitored on a large scale undoubtedly causes great panic and poses incalculable threats to personal and property safety. Hackers can easily control the entire camera through these vulnerabilities to achieve the purpose of spying. Moreover, hackers can deceive users into always seeing a static image rather than the real on-site environment when remotely viewing the surveillance camera footage of their own homes. Even more frightening is that surveillance cameras with security risks are not limited to home surveillance cameras but also pose privacy risks when used in other public places, banks, offices, prisons, and other locations.

2. Device Attacks

Symantec researchers recently discovered a new Linux worm virus that can infect home routers, set-top boxes, security cameras, and other internet-connected home devices. This worm virus, called LinuxDarlloz has been classified as a low-security risk because the current version can only infect X86 platform devices. However, after some modifications, variants of this virus can threaten devices using ARM chips, as well as PPC, MIPS, and MIPSEL architectures. This worm virus exploits device vulnerabilities, generates a random IP address, enters a specific path in the machine through commonly used IDs and passwords, and sends HTTP POST requests. If the target is not patched, it will continue downloading the worm from the malicious server while searching for the next target. Although Linux. Darlloz has not caused significant harm worldwide; it exposes a major flaw in most internet-connected devices. They mostly run on Linux or other outdated open-source systems.

3. Network Attacks

An Italian security company claims that attackers have begun using the recently exposed Shellshock vulnerability to build a zombie network. The network runs on Linux servers and can infect other servers automatically using the Bash Shellshock bug. One of the active zombie networks is Wopbot, which scans the internet to find systems with vulnerabilities, including scanning the IP address range 215.0.0.0/8 of the US Department of Defense. Wopbot launched a distributed denial-of-service attack on CDN service provider Akamai.

9.4.3 Blockchain Technology Security

Blockchain is a decentralized distributed ledger built on a model providing absolute security and trust. In encryption technology, each transaction is publicly recorded with a unique timestamp and linked to the previous block. Most importantly, these digital "blocks" can only be updated with the agreement of all participants, making data theft, tampering, and deletion almost impossible. Since reaching the peak of the Gartner "hype cycle" in 2016, blockchain has been a focus of attention for industry leaders, especially in the financial, energy, and manufacturing industries. Bitcoin payment verification may be the most commonly cited blockchain application case. However, the technology is not limited to Bitcoin and can be extended to applications such as content delivery networks and smart grid systems.

Blockchain technology has enormous potential for enhancing data integrity, preserving digital identities, and securing IoT devices to fend off DDoS attacks. Blockchain technology has the potential to improve system resilience, confidentiality, integrity, and availability while also strengthening encryption, auditing, and transparency. Lack of trust and inadequate security implementation leave gaps, which blockchain fills. In 2018, we must encrypt everything at all times. We are unable to confirm the sender's identity or if the emails we receive have been read or altered by others. However, using blockchain methods, we can reasonably verify and sign transactions. Although there is still some hype surrounding cryptocurrency issues, implementing blockchain methods can create a more trusted infrastructure for our digital services. The best application is the transformation of our public utilities sector and the creation of citizen-centric infrastructure. This will give citizens their identities, and every transaction can be verified. We can use smart contracts and signed assertions to develop elements of public services, such as benefit payments, etc. The following are several real-world blockchain applications in the security field:

1. **Protecting Boundary Data Security with Identity Authentication**

    Security is also concerned about this transformation as IT focuses on migrating data and connectivity to "smart" edge devices. After all, network expansion can increase IT efficiency and productivity and reduce power consumption, but it also brings security challenges to CISOs, CIOs, and the entire company. Many companies seek to apply blockchain to protect the security of IoT and IIoT devices because blockchain technology can enhance identity authentication, improve data traceability and liquidity, and assist with record management.

    For example, Xage Security, created at the end of 2017, claims its "tamper-proof" blockchain technology platform can distribute privacy data in bulk and perform identity verification in device networks. The company also claims to support any communication protocol, adapt to irregularly connected edge devices, and protect many heterogeneous industrial systems. The company claims to have worked with ABB Wireless to jointly build an energy and automation project that requires distributed security. It also partnered with Dell to deliver security services to the energy industry on Dell IoT Gateways and its EdgeX platform.

    While testing blockchain technology to see if it can stop IoT devices from being hacked (by giving physical devices a unique identity to confirm their authenticity), the government of the Isle of Man has adopted a different strategy as another example of real-world blockchain applications. The chip level incorporates these enhancements as well. Recently, the startup Filament unveiled a new chip that enables IIoT devices to use various blockchain technologies. The primary goal of its Blocklet chip is to immediately embed Internet of Things sensor data onto the blockchain, creating a secure basis for decentralized iteration and exchange.

2. **Enhancing Confidentiality and Data Integrity**

   Although blockchain was created without a specific access control mechanism (due to its open distribution properties), some blockchain implementations are now addressing data confidentiality and access control issues. In an era where data is easily tampered with or forged, ensuring data confidentiality and integrity is undoubtedly a huge challenge. However, the complete encryption of blockchain data ensures that these data cannot be tampered with by unauthorized parties yet still retain liquidity (with almost no possibility of man-in-the-middle attacks).

   IoT and IIoT are likewise covered by this data integrity. On its Watson IoT platform, which is connected with IBM's cloud services, for instance, IBM provides a choice to manage IoT data with private blockchain ledgers. App developers using the General Electric Predix PaaS platform may access completely auditable, compliant, and trusted data thanks to Ericsson's blockchain data integrity solution.

3. **Protecting Private Messages**

   Blockchain technology is being used by startups like Obsidian to safeguard private information shared on social media and instant messaging platforms. Obsidian employs blockchain to secure user metadata, as opposed to end-to-end encryption used by apps like WhatsApp and iMessage. Because metadata is dispersed at random throughout the ledger and there is no central gathering point, it cannot be compromised.

   In addition, it has been reported that the US Defense Advanced Research Projects Agency (DARPA) is trying to use blockchain to create secure messaging services that foreign attacks cannot penetrate. With blockchain rooted in verified secure communication, privacy message security will mature.

4. Enhancing and Replacing PKI

PKI is a public key encryption system that protects email, messaging applications, websites, and other communication forms. However, most PKI implementations rely on centralized third-party certificate authorities to issue, revoke, and store key pairs, which allows cybercriminals to eavesdrop on encrypted communications and impersonate identities. Publishing keys on the blockchain can eliminate the spread of false keys and enable applications to verify the identity of communication objects.

CertCoin is the first blockchain-based PKI implementation that eliminates the central certificate authority and uses the blockchain as a ledger for distributing domain names and public keys. Additionally, CertCoin provides an auditable and publicly available PKI without a single point of failure.

On the other hand, Startup REMME uses blockchain to assign unique SSL certificates to each device, eliminating the possibility of intruders forging certificates. A blockchain-based PKI that uses the blockchain to record hashed values of issued and revoked certificates has been published by technology research company Pomcor (albeit a CA is still necessary in this situation). If the Estonian data security firm Guardtime can be trusted, its blockchain-based Keyless Signature Infrastructure (KSI), a replacement for PKI, may fully replace PKI. The most prosperous, most populous, and most extensively used blockchain company in the world, Guardtime, obtained the health records of all one million Estonians in 2016.

We rely on PKI to establish a system of confidence, but it is frequently weak, particularly in light of the fact that fraudsters are now producing their own digital certificates. Blockchain technology can be used to sign transactions using identities created by citizens.

5. More Secure DNS

The Mirai botnet showed how simple it was for attackers to interfere with vital internet infrastructure. To disable network access to services like Twitter, Netflix, and other ones, attackers just need to take control of a sizable website's Domain Name System (DNS) service provider. Theoretically, DNS security is improved by storing records on the blockchain because it removes a single point of vulnerability.

Nebulis is a new project exploring the concept of distributed DNS, which can handle access flood requests without crashing due to response overload. Nebulis uses the Ethereum blockchain, the InterPlanetary File System (IPFS), and a distributed replacement protocol for HTTP to register and resolve domain names. Hackers can exploit critical Internet services like DNS to create large-scale outages and attack companies, so using a trusted DNS infrastructure with blockchain methods will significantly enhance the core trust infrastructure of the Internet.

6. **Reducing DDoS Attacks**

Gladius, a blockchain firm, asserts that its decentralized ledger technology aids in thwarting DDoS attacks. This claim is notable given that DDoS attack peak bandwidth has surpassed 100 Gbps. The business asserts that by enabling customers to access adjacent protection resource pools and fending off DDoS attacks, its decentralized system may offer greater protection and expedite client content.

It's interesting to note that Gladius asserts its decentralized network enables people to rent out their unused bandwidth to make some additional cash, and the extra bandwidth is assigned to website nodes that are under DDoS attack to ensure they can weather the attack. The Gladius network functions as a content delivery network to speed up internet connection during less busy times (when there isn't a DDoS attack).

However, blockchain is not a panacea. From technical complexity and system quantity to implementation, blockchain cannot guarantee 100% security. Limitations on transaction speed and debates about whether information should be saved on the blockchain are also concerns for the technology's security applications.

9.4.4 Security of Large-Scale Data Analysis and Mining

Network security issues have grown more sensitive as a result of the extensive usage of networks and the speedy development of information technology. A substantial amount of data is transmitted across networks. Due to the constant updating and alteration of network attack techniques, traditional defense strategies are no longer able to keep up with the speedy detection and processing of new attacks. Data mining technologies can analyze and mine a substantial amount of network data in this scenario to establish the attacker's attack path, attack target, and attack method. This will make it possible to maintain network security and to apply defense measures quickly.

1. Big Data Analysis Platform Architecture

   The Big Data analysis platform, also referred to as the Big Data deployment platform supported by data center technology, is a comprehensive platform that integrates a variety of data sources, classification, labeling, intelligent analysis, intelligent query, semantic inference, and other technologies in the network security field. Its primary objective is to meet the customers' needs by detecting threats such as false positives, load dragging, and business interruption within a limited time frame. By providing a unified and efficient solution, the Big Data analysis platform plays a vital role in ensuring the security of network systems.

2. Network Attack Detection Based on Multidimensional Mining

   The algorithm based on multidimensional overlay analysis is an effective method for detecting and identifying network attacks. This algorithm combines multiple indicator dimensions to analyze network attackers' behavior and attack methods with good detection results. The basic steps to achieve this goal shall include data source collection, feature extraction, model construction, model validation, and model evaluation.

3. Network Attack Recognition Based on Machine Learning

   Network attack recognition based on machine learning is a data-based method that uses machine learning algorithms to train a large amount of data to determine whether it is a network attack accurately. Common machine learning algorithms include support vector machines, random forests, decision trees, and naive Bayes. Training a large amount of data can improve the recognition rate of network attacks, effectively ensuring network security.

9.5 SUMMARY

The chapter provides a comprehensive overview of the concepts and principles related to secure distributed computing. The chapter begins by delving into the latest techniques and practices in secure distributed systems, including authentication and authorization method. These techniques enable secure computation on distributed data without revealing sensitive information to unauthorized parties. The chapter also discusses the design principles of secure distributed data, such as the type of hardware, secure network, and architecture to secure the infrastructure for handling distribution data. Then, the protocol commonly used to encrypt communication channels and how this communication channel is established has been discussed in detail, for instance, TLS, SSL, and SSH. Finally, the chapter offers insights into existing case studies in cloud computing, IoT, blockchain and large-scale data analysis in leveraging distributed data. This chapter is a valuable resource for researchers and practitioners who aim to develop secure distributed systems for processing and storing sensitive data.

9.6 EXERCISES

1. What are the secure communication and transport protocols available in the market?

- Secure Socket Layer protocol (SSL): is a security protocol used to establish an encrypted link between a web server and a web browser. It uses a combination of public and private keys to encrypt data transmitted over the internet, preventing unauthorized access to sensitive information such as passwords, credit card numbers, and other personal data. SSL is widely used to secure online transactions, such as online banking, e-commerce, and email. In 2015, SSL was replaced by TLS (Transport Layer Security), which offers improved security and performance over SSL. Today, SSL/TLS encryption is considered a standard practice for securing sensitive data online and is widely adopted by websites and web-based services to ensure the privacy and security of their users.

- Transport Layer Security protocol (TLS): is a cryptographic protocol used to secure communications over the internet. It provides privacy and data integrity between two communicating applications by encrypting the data that is transmitted between them. TLS is widely used to secure sensitive information such as passwords, credit card numbers, and other personal data in online transactions. TLS operates at the transport layer of the internet protocol (IP) stack and uses symmetric and asymmetric encryption to secure data. It is the successor to SSL (Secure Sockets Layer) and is widely adopted by websites and web-based services to ensure the privacy and security of their users.

- Secure Shell protocol (SSH): is a cryptographic network protocol used to secure remote access to networked devices. It provides secure encrypted communications between two untrusted hosts over an insecure network, such as the Internet. SSH gives users the option of using a command-line interface or a graphical user interface (GUI) to remotely access and administer devices including servers, routers, and switches. SSH establishes a safe, encrypted connection by authenticating the remote device using public-key cryptography. It also provides secure file transfer capabilities and can be used to create secure tunnels for other applications, such as web browsing and email. SSH is widely adopted in enterprise environments and a standard practice for securing remote access to networked devices.

2. What are the common types of faults can occur in distributed data systems?

several common types of faults can occur in distributed data systems, including:

- Network failures: These can occur due to network congestion, hardware failures, or software errors. Network failures can cause nodes to become unavailable, resulting in data loss or decreased system performance.

- Server failures: These can occur due to hardware or software errors, power outages, or other issues. Server failures can lead to data loss or downtime until the server is repaired or replaced.

- Storage failures: These can occur due to hardware or software errors, disk failures, or other issues. Storage failures can cause data loss or decreased system performance until the data is restored from backup or recovered.

- Software errors: These can occur due to bugs, configuration errors, or other issues in the software used to manage the distributed data system. Software errors can cause data corruption or system crashes.

- Security breaches: These can occur due to unauthorized access, malware, or other security threats. Security breaches can compromise the data's confidentiality, integrity, and availability in the distributed data system.

- Human errors: These can occur due to mistakes made by operators, administrators, or other personnel responsible for managing the distributed data system. Human errors can cause data loss, system downtime, or other issues that affect system availability and performance.

3. What is the IoT data security that requires our concerns in today's development?

- Information Leakage: Information leakage occurs when IoT devices transmit sensitive information to unauthorized parties. This can occur due to vulnerabilities in the communication protocols used by IoT devices or due to poor security practices in the design and implementation of IoT devices. Information leakage can be prevented by implementing strong encryption and access control measures to protect sensitive data from unauthorized access.

- Device Attacks: Device attacks are attacks that target IoT devices directly. These attacks can take many forms, including denial-of-service (DoS) attacks, malware infections, and physical attacks. DoS attacks can overload IoT devices with traffic, causing them to crash or become unavailable. Malware infections can compromise the security of IoT devices and allow attackers to gain control of them. Physical attacks can involve the theft or destruction of IoT devices. Device attacks can be prevented by implementing strong access control measures, keeping firmware and software up-to-date, and using secure communication protocols.

- Network Attacks: Network attacks are attacks that target the communication channels used by IoT devices. These attacks can take many forms, including man-in-the-middle (MITM) attacks, eavesdropping, and packet injection. MITM attacks involve intercepting and modifying data transmitted between IoT devices and their servers, potentially allowing attackers to steal sensitive data or inject malicious code. Eavesdropping involves intercepting and reading data transmitted between IoT devices and their servers, potentially allowing attackers to steal sensitive data. Packet injection involves injecting malicious data into the communication channels used by IoT devices. Network attacks can be prevented by implementing strong encryption and authentication measures to protect data in transit, using secure communication protocols, and monitoring network activity for suspicious behavior.

4. What are some common security threats to distributed data systems, and how can they be mitigated?

   Some common security threats to distributed data systems include:

   - Unauthorized access: This can occur when an attacker gains access to sensitive data by exploiting vulnerabilities in the system. To mitigate this threat, access control mechanisms such as authentication, authorization, and encryption should be implemented.

- Malware: This can include viruses, worms, and other types of malicious software that can infect systems and compromise data. To mitigate this threat, anti-malware software, firewalls, and intrusion detection systems can be used.

- Denial-of-service attacks: These attacks are designed to overwhelm a system with traffic or requests, making it unavailable to legitimate users. To mitigate this threat, load balancing, traffic filtering, and other techniques can be used.

- Data breaches: These occur when sensitive data is accessed or stolen by unauthorized users. To mitigate this threat, data encryption, access control, and data backup procedures should be implemented.

- Insider threats: These can include malicious insiders who intentionally or unintentionally compromise the security of the system. To mitigate this threat, access control policies, monitoring systems, and user training programs can be used.

5. How decentralized scheduling works compared with centralized scheduling

Decentralized scheduling and centralized scheduling are two different approaches to managing and scheduling resources, such as computing resources or network bandwidth.

In centralized scheduling, a central scheduler or central authority is responsible for managing and allocating resources to different tasks or users. The central scheduler maintains a global view of the available resources and makes decisions based on that information. The central scheduler is responsible for monitoring resource usage, detecting bottlenecks and making decisions about how resources should be allocated.

Decentralized scheduling involves distributing the responsibility for resource management across multiple nodes or devices in a network. In a decentralized scheduling system, each node makes decisions about how to allocate its own resources based on local information. There is no central authority that makes decisions about resource allocation.

There are some significant advantages over centralized scheduling:

- Fault Tolerance: Decentralized scheduling is more resilient to failures or attacks that target the central authority or central scheduler.

- Scalability: Decentralized scheduling can scale more easily than centralized scheduling since each node can make decisions based on local information rather than relying on a central scheduler to make decisions.

- Flexibility: Decentralized scheduling allows for more flexibility and adaptability since each node can make decisions based on local conditions and requirements.

- Lower Latency: Decentralized scheduling can reduce latency since decisions can be made locally without the need for communication with a central authority.

Decentralized scheduling also has some disadvantages:

- Coordination: Decentralized scheduling requires coordination between nodes to ensure that resources are allocated efficiently and effectively.

- Complexity: Decentralized scheduling can be more complex to implement and manage than centralized scheduling.

- Inefficiency: Decentralized scheduling may lead to suboptimal resource allocation decisions if nodes are not properly coordinated.

6. How can blockchain networks enhance the confidentiality and data integrity of the ledger?

Blockchain networks can enhance the confidentiality and data integrity of the ledger through several key mechanisms:

- Encryption: Blockchain networks safeguard transactions and prevent unauthorized access to sensitive data using public and private key encryption. This makes sure that only individuals with permission can access and change the ledger.

- Consensus algorithms: Consensus algorithms are used in blockchain networks to verify transactions and make sure that everyone in the network agrees on the ledger's current state. This helps maintain data integrity by preventing hostile actors from altering or interfering with the ledger.

- Immutability: It is impossible to change or remove a transaction once it has been approved and uploaded to the blockchain. This guarantees that the ledger is impenetrable and that its integrity will endure.

- Smart contracts: Blockchain networks can use smart contracts to enforce rules and automate transactions, reducing the risk of errors or fraud. Smart contracts can also enhance confidentiality by ensuring that sensitive data is only revealed to authorized parties.

- Privacy features: Some blockchain networks provide privacy features like ring signatures and zero-knowledge proofs that can be used to safeguard the integrity of the ledger while preserving the confidentiality of sensitive data.

7. Name security protection available in Tencent Cloud.

- Network security: DoS protection, cloud firewall, network IPS, sample analysis platform

- Terminal security: hacker intrusion detection and vulnerability risk warnings, login reminders, Trojan file killing, antivirus, zero trust access control system

- Application security: application reinforcement, security assessment, vulnerability scanning service, unified prevention and control, unified auditing, an application firewall for Tencent Cloud and external users

- Business security: anti-fraud, login protection, CAPTCHA, marketing risk control service, text content security service

- Data security: bastion host and AI technology to provide operation audit, sensitive data processing, cloud encryption machine based on Hardware Security Module (HSM)

8. Explain data security in IoT.

   In IoT data security, *information leakage* refers to the unauthorized access of sensitive data from IoT devices or networks, which can lead to privacy violations and data breaches. *Device attacks* involve exploiting vulnerabilities in IoT devices, such as weak passwords or outdated software, to gain unauthorized access or control. *Network attacks* target IoT networks by intercepting or manipulating data traffic, disrupting service availability, or launching denial-of-service (DoS) attacks. All these security threats pose a significant risk to the confidentiality, integrity, and availability of IoT data and require comprehensive security measures such as encryption, access controls, and intrusion detection/prevention systems to mitigate them.

GLOSSARY

Dataflow Model: refers to a model in which data flows from one computing task to another in parallel computing, and computation is performed through data flow.

Data sharding: refers to slicing a large table into smaller slices in a data storage system, and the segmented data blocks will be distributed across multiple servers.

Distributed graph algorithms: refer to algorithms for graph computing in distributed computing environments.

Distributed machine learning algorithms: perform machine learning in distributed computing environments.

Distributed Memory Model: refers to a model in which all processors have their physical memory and communicate with each other through a network.

Distributed sorting algorithms: refer to algorithms for data sorting in distributed computing environments.

Dynamic Task Allocation: refers to dynamically assigning tasks to processors during parallel computing based on different task requirements and processor load conditions.

Fault Tolerance: refers to the ability of a computer system or storage subsystem to continue working without interrupting service and without losing data or compromising security when hardware or software failures occur.

Heterogeneous CMP: refers to a CPU chip containing multiple identical or different processor cores connected through on-chip networks and high-speed transmission buses, enabling communication between different processor cores.

Heterogeneous Systems: refer to computing systems composed of different types of computer hardware or software components that may be heterogeneous.

MapReduce: is a task-scheduling-based distributed computing algorithm widely used for large-scale data processing and analysis.

Message Passing Model: refers to a model in which processors communicate with each other through messages, and processors do not share memory.

Multi-path On-demand Routing: implements signature and encryption on routing control information based on identity-based cryptography.

Open Secure Shell: is a free and open-source implementation of the SSH protocol, an open-source alternative to the commercial version SSH Communications Security provides.

Parallel Computing: refers to dividing a computing problem into sub-problems, assigning them to multiple processors for simultaneous execution, and coordinating and communicating them through a reasonable mechanism to enable multiple processors to complete the computing task jointly.

Reputation-based Security Routing: judges malicious behavior of nodes and isolates harmful nodes based on changes in the reputation of network nodes.

Secure Shell Protocol: is an encrypted network transmission protocol that provides a secure transmission environment for network services in an insecure network.

Secure Socket Layer Protocol: is a secure protocol that provides security and data integrity for network communication.

Static Task Allocation: refers to the task being assigned to different processors before parallel computing begins, and then the processor independently executes the task.

Symmetrical Multiprocessing Architecture: refers to a symmetrical work of multiple CPUs with the same structure in a server without a master-slave or subordinate relationship.

Task Coordination: refers to multiple tasks cooperating in parallel computing to complete a complex computing task jointly.

Transport Layer Security Protocol: is an encryption protocol that provides a confidential, secure channel on the Internet for data transmissions such as websites, email, and file transfers.

IV

Next Generation of Cybersecurity in the Internet of Things

CHAPTER 10

Digital Twin Optimization in the Internet of Things

The integration of Artificial Intelligence (AI) technology has emerged as a crucial driving force in the edge computing domain, particularly in enhancing the capabilities of complex systems like smart critical infrastructure. The convergence of physical and cyberspaces necessitates the utilization of digital twin technology, which enables AI-driven solutions to optimize various operational tasks in the physical realm.

However, implementing task allocation in the digital twin setting presents multiple challenges, including the simultaneous fulfillment of energy-saving, efficiency, and accuracy requirements. In this chapter, we propose a solution empowered by Digital Twin (DT) technology to optimize the efficiency of IoT (Internet of Things) systems. Specifically, our approach focuses on enhancing the training accuracy of AI tasks while considering the constraints of training time and energy consumption.

The contents of this chapter are based on our previous publication, where we delve into the details and implications of employing DT-enabled solutions for improving the performance of IoT systems [292].

10.1 DIGITAL TWIN (DT) AND IOT

DT technology enhances the connectivity and potential of both physical and digital domains [293]. It plays a crucial role in enabling interconnectivity and optimizing productivity, particularly in the era of 5G and the industrial Internet. DT has become a vital asset in supporting various advanced and intricate systems, including critical infrastructure management, aerospace, industrial manufacturing, supply chain operations, and healthcare. The utilization of DT in these sectors aims to maximize productivity and efficiency, leveraging the potential of interconnected physical and digital spaces. The significance of DT technology continues to grow as it becomes an essential component in driving advancements and improvements across a wide range of industries [294–298]. DT technology can be described as a simulation process combining various disciplines, physical quantities, scales, and probabilities. It leverages the capabilities of physical models, sensor data updates, operational history, and other relevant data to create a virtual representation that mirrors the entire life cycle process of the corresponding physical equipment. This integration of diverse simulation processes allows for a comprehensive understanding and mapping of the physical equipment within a virtual space. In essence, DT technology maximizes the use of available data and captures the holistic life cycle of the equipment in a simulated environment.

Adopting decentralized *AI*-based methods have emerged as a prominent technical trend in addressing complex big data processing tasks across extensive networks. DT exhibits remarkable capabilities in aligning with distributed computing scenarios when combined with edge computing. This is primarily due to its decentralized nature and ability to sense and process data effectively. By leveraging these features, DT demonstrates strong functionality in handling distributed computing tasks, making it a valuable tool in managing and analyzing large-scale data within network environments [299].

Even while DT-edge-based may make AI technology more widely adopted, we can still find that some AI solutions run on conventional clouds are frequently prone to network delays and availability. In this chapter, we present a practical solution to the problem mentioned above, one that involves moving computation from centralized clouds to decentralized edge devices [300].

Edge AI is a conceptual, technical phrase that elucidates and highlights the necessity of incorporating AI in edge environments. The fundamental concept of Edge AI revolves around efficiently assigning AI computing tasks to edge devices. In scenarios like smart critical infrastructure, the close proximity of edge devices and equipment to the source of data generation offers benefits such as reducing the workload and cost associated with data transmission, including delays and energy consumption [301]. In other words, the objective of edge AI is to enable the simultaneous execution of multiple computing tasks on edge networks in a parallel manner.

This chapter presents a novel edge AI mechanism called Digital Twin-Enabled Edge AI (DTE2AI), proposed in our previous study [292]. This mechanism aims to offer an efficient approach to enhancing critical infrastructure management. It encompasses various functionalities such as production coordination/cooperation, comprehensive life-cycle management, parallel composition, and intelligent manufacturing [302, 303]. By leveraging the capabilities of DTE2AI, organizations can effectively upgrade their critical infrastructure operations and leverage the benefits of advanced management techniques in diverse aspects of their processes [302, 303]. Edge AI systems assist task allocation to guarantee that computing jobs are dispersed optimally, as opposed to executing AI algorithms on individual edge devices [304].

An AI system typically consists mostly of training and prediction procedures. For instance, the training step involves extensive computer and storage resources, whereas the prediction process relies on a well-fitted model to infer data. The following issues must be resolved.

The first obvious obstacle is offering real-time service while retaining accuracy. The overall latency is influenced by the computation and communication times. Communication delay is influenced by network bandwidth and data volume being transferred. The size of the calculation model and the edge devices' computing power affect how quickly calculations are completed. As the need for precise prediction increases, the model's size steadily increases, making real-time performance ineffective.

The restricted adoption is frequently constrained by dispersed resource constraints, such as computation, storage, and energy usage, as opposed to large-scale server clusters (such as cloud data centers) [305]. Large quantities of energy are used in the calculation and communication phases of decentralized AI model training. Energy efficiency is influenced by the size of the target training model and the edge device resources.

Unlike massive server clusters (such as those found in cloud data centers), distributed resource constraints, such as computing, storage, and energy usage, typically hampered the adoption. Decentralized AI model training's computation and communication steps consume much energy. The target training model's size and the resources available to edge devices impact energy efficiency.

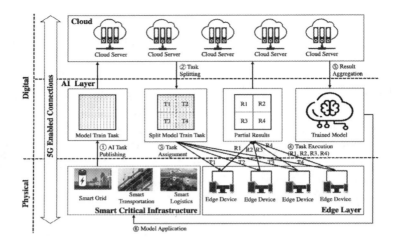

Figure 10.1 The high-level architecture of the Digital Twin-Enabled Edge AI (DTE2AI).

Finally, the problem of uneven storage also presents a problem. For instance, huge amounts of data are required to support AI algorithms that handle data-driven problems. Even though data is dispersed across many edge devices, an inadequate dataset may lower the accuracy of outputs.

10.2 BACKGROUND

Efficiency improvement, energy conservation, and storage consumption are three main issues with AI work allocation.

On one hand, most work allocation strategies become exponentially more complex as the problem grows; on the other hand, the ability of some algorithms to identify sub-optimal solutions is insufficient. A mixed offloading setup on clouds and edges improves AI performance in critical infrastructure management, as shown in Fig. 10.1, which depicts the mechanism's high-level architecture.

In practice, many collaborative computing devices typically have access to all network resources rather than just edge terminals. For instance, large-scale neural network models can boost deep learning's accuracy. In summary, our approach looks at how to upgrade essential infrastructure using distributed AI while considering complexity and adaptability in the context of 5G.

An effective vehicular edge computing network was created in the work of Zhang et al. by integrating adaptive digital twins and multiagent learning algorithms [306]. The complexity of service management can be reduced by using digital twins to identify potential edge service matching among large vehicle pairs. The cars' task offloading tactics were made possible by the learning algorithm. A multiagent learning technique was also designed to optimise edge resource scheduling in physical vehicular networks based on a gravity model created using a vehicle aggregation scheme on the digital twin side. Real traffic datasets were used to test the suggested methods, demonstrating that they were more cost-effective than the benchmarks.

Finding a suitable task allocation mechanism for edge AI systems is a challenging topic in the field [307]. On one side, devices within the same edge network are highly heterogeneous, which may be operated by different organizations [308, 309]. Multiple dimensions, including architecture, interface, computation, storage, and communication capabilities, are heterogeneous [310, 311].

On the other hand, many modern edge devices are incredibly autonomous [311]. The edge network does not include any global variables or data, therefore all authorized edge devices can access the network. There is a pressing need for edge AI systems to have dynamic and reasonable task allocation mechanisms [312, 313]. The foundation for task distribution in edge AI is computational task distribution [314]. Decomposing AI computational workloads into numerous smaller tasks that can be carried out concurrently (by various devices) with a minimum of job duplication is a problem that has to be addressed [315, 316]. Task distribution in edge AI is based on computational task distribution [314]. The problem of breaking down AI computational operations into a number of smaller tasks that may be carried out concurrently (by various devices) with a minimum of job duplication must be addressed [315, 316].

In order to increase the operational efficiency of deep learning algorithms and reduce the time required for model construction, the authors point out that the deep learning computational tasks should be divided according to their difficulty and that the sub-tasks should be carried out using practical computational resources [317]. A computational task allocation strategy for DNN-based robotic image perception situations was proposed by Hadidi et al. to address a related problem [318] . Real-time DNN-based recognition and robot arithmetic aggregation are the goals of this technique. There are two layers at play. Devices are grouped into one layer, which also supplies functions for a certain job slice. These efforts, however, were more concerned with the hardware adaption issue of various computational jobs than with the inference of the task partitioning process.

Traditional approaches to task allocation in edge AI primarily involve centralized planning allocation methods, where a central controller exists within edge devices responsible for managing computing tasks [319]. These global controllers can access comprehensive system-level information, including factors like time overhead and energy consumption [320, 321]. The global controller utilizes this information to define constraints, establish an objective function tailored to the specific edge computing scenario, and search for a task allocation method that maximizes the objective function [322]. In essence, the global controller leverages the available global information to guide the task allocation process and optimize the allocation decisions within the edge computing system.

Centralized allocation methods offer simplicity in implementation and the ability to find optimal global solutions. However, these methods suffer from unstable time complexity. Additionally, the communication pattern in centralized allocation methods tends to be concentrated and potentially frequent, leading to network congestion that hampers efficiency and increases communication costs [323].

The limitations of these algorithms are further exacerbated in 5G communication or future B5G communication scenarios. As the frequency bands used in 5G/B5G increase and transmission distances become more limited [324, 325], each communication in 5G/B5G requires more base stations to relay messages. Consequently, traditional allocation methods in 5G/B5G scenarios increase the burden on the base station network and result in higher energy consumption.

Decentralized task allocation methods have gained popularity in recent times, as they do not rely on a global controller for allocation decisions [326]. Instead, nodes in the system collaborate and share the task allocation process [327]. Through communication in a single channel, each node can negotiate and compete during the allocation process [328]. Alternatively, each device can independently select or dynamically adjust its computational tasks based on its perception of the computing environment [329]. Significant progress has been made in the research of distributed task allocation optimization methods. Bakolas et al. [330] introduced a game theory-based framework for the decentralized dynamic task allocation problem. This framework considers multiple allocation schemes and calculates the benefits and cost consumption for each node under different schemes based on their states. The objective is to ensure maximum benefit for each node and dynamically adjust the task allocation scheme. Numerical simulation experiments have demonstrated the feasibility of this allocation framework.

Otte et al. [331] evaluated three task allocation algorithms based on multi-robot market auctions: Sequential, Parallel, and G-prim auction algorithms. The evaluation involved probabilistic and mathematical-statistical analyzes in various task evaluation scenarios. The results revealed that the G-prim algorithm could involve more nodes or entities when the channel bandwidth between nodes was blocked. In the distance-evaluation scenario, achieving a global optimal task assignment solution proved challenging, regardless of the auction algorithm employed, especially when communications between nodes were weak.

Influenced by the elastic behavior observed in locusts, Kurdi et al. (2018) developed a task allocation method for multi-UAV systems [332]. Each UAV utilizes its sensors to perceive the surrounding environment and dynamically adjusts its execution tasks based on operational status and attributes. Unlike other decentralized task allocation methods, UAVs actively participate in computational tasks linked to specific controllers rather than relying on direct communication with other UAVs.

Schwarzrock et al. proposed an optimization algorithm for collaborative task allocation among multiple UAVs using swarm intelligence technology [333]. Their approach assumed the existence of a task center that broadcasts tasks to each UAV based on their individual status. The method prioritizes task assignments according to the center's defined priority and employs a swarm-GAP algorithm to distribute these assignments. This approach effectively resolves the issue in existing heuristic algorithms, where some tasks may remain unassigned due to resource limitations within the nodes.

In recent years, numerous studies have been conducted to tackle the issue of latency. Zhu et al. [334] introduced a task allocation scheme called Folo, specifically designed for vehicular networks to address concerns such as service latency, data loss, and limited fog capacity. The proposed approach formulates fog allocation as a bi-objective minimization problem that aims to balance minimizing latency and minimizing quality loss.

Similarly, Josilo et al. [335] explored a solution that combines hardware and software properties, such as CPU and memory, to optimize task allocation in static mixed strategies. Their work employed game theory to compute an equilibrium task allocation. They aimed to achieve an efficient and decentralized task allocation mechanism by considering both the physical and computational aspects.

In a coordinated motion target tracking scenario, Jin et al. [336] introduced a task allocation method for multi-robot systems based on competition. This method involved selecting robots to perform tasks based on their individual status and attributes. The allocation decision considered the specific characteristics and capabilities of each robot before assigning them tasks within the system.

In the domain of autonomous driving, a separate study [337] addressed a similar challenge. While this method considered the system's scalability, it still faced difficulties related to frequent communication and high energy consumption in the edge environment.

10.3 CONCEPTS AND KEY DEFINITIONS

10.3.1 Problem Definition

In DTE2AI (Device-to-Edge-to-AI) systems, three important metrics are latency, energy consumption, and accuracy. When the terminal node lacks sufficient processing capacity, the computing tasks are transferred to the edge of the cloud for execution. The total delay is primarily composed of two elements: computing delay, which is influenced by factors such as the computational capability and scale of the computing model, and communication delay, which is influenced by factors such as the size of data transmission and the bandwidth of the network. The issue is that when AI models are trained in a decentralized manner, distributed computing and communication typically need a higher-level cost (energy, time, etc.) when taken into account in the context of smart critical infrastructure.

Although most terminals have energy restrictions. Energy efficiency is largely affected by the dimensions of the target training model and the edge equipment resources.

Hence, combining the accuracy of the computing model with the energy usage of edge nodes is thus a crucial task. The formulation of the problem is given by Definition 10.3.1.

Definition 10.3.1 (TECAMP) Problem with Maximum Time and Energy Constraints

The input includes a set I of edge AI tasks $\{T_i\}$ ($i \in N, 0 < i \leq I$), a set J of available edge devices $\{D_j\}$ ($j \in N, 0 < i \leq J$), a pre-stored table TB recoding all tuples of energy costs, time consumptions, and accuracy $\langle E_{ij}, T_{ij}, A_{ij} \rangle$ where the subscript i and j indicates the assignment of T_i to D_j, a timing constraint T^C, a energy constranint E^C, $J \geq I$.

A mapping table P with recommended task assignments is the output.

Objective: is to find near-optimal strategies for assigning edge AI tasks to the edge devices that can train models with the maximum accuracy ($A_t otal$) while using the least amount of time and energy.

TECAMP is mathematically expressed by Eq. (10.1).

$$A_{total} = MAX\left[\sum A\right] \parallel T^C \geq \sum T \parallel E^C \geq \sum E. \qquad (10.1)$$

In Eq. (10.1), $MAX[\cdot]$ is a function that elects the maximum value from the input. $\sum A$ refers to the total accuracy, $\sum T$ and $\sum E$ are the total cost of execution time and energy. The $\sum A$, $\sum T$, and $\sum E$ are obtained from Eqs. (10.2), (10.3), and (10.4), where $s(\cdot)$ is a determinative function and its output value determines the objective of an edge device; $c(\cdot)$ is a boolean function signifying whether a computing unit is selected. Additionally, $c(i) = 1$ means that the edge device is assigned to a task; $c(i) = 0$ means that the edge device is unassigned.

$$\sum A = \sum_{\substack{a=1}}^{J} \sum_{\substack{s(i)=a \\ c(i)=1 \\ i=1}}^{I} A_i = \sum_{\substack{s(i)=1 \\ c(i)=1 \\ i=1}}^{I} A_i + \sum_{\substack{s(i)=2 \\ c(i)=1 \\ i=1}}^{I} A_i + \cdots + \sum_{\substack{s(i)=J \\ c(i)=1 \\ i=1}}^{I} A_i. \qquad (10.2)$$

$$\sum T = \sum_{\substack{a=1}}^{J} \sum_{\substack{s(i)=a \\ c(i)=1 \\ i=1}}^{I} T_i = \sum_{\substack{s(i)=1 \\ c(i)=1 \\ i=1}}^{I} T_i + \sum_{\substack{s(i)=2 \\ c(i)=1 \\ i=1}}^{I} T_i + \cdots + \sum_{\substack{s(i)=J \\ c(i)=1 \\ i=1}}^{I} T_i. \qquad (10.3)$$

$$\sum E = \sum_{\substack{a=1}}^{J} \sum_{\substack{s(i)=a \\ c(i)=1 \\ i=1}}^{I} E_i = \sum_{\substack{s(i)=1 \\ c(i)=1 \\ i=1}}^{I} E_i + \sum_{\substack{s(i)=2 \\ c(i)=1 \\ i=1}}^{I} E_i + \cdots + \sum_{\substack{s(i)=J \\ c(i)=1 \\ i=1}}^{I} E_i. \qquad (10.4)$$

Theorem 10.3.1 (Hardess of the TECAMP) *The problem of TECAMP is NP-hard.*

Proof 10.1 (*Proof*) *For the TECAMP problem, assume that there are* **m** *edge devices, and each edge device has different computing resources. There are* **n** *edge artificial intelligence sub-tasks that need to be assigned to these* **m** *devices, and the accuracy of performing each sub-task is different for different devices (due to energy and device data limitations). It is necessary to find a suitable allocation to maximize the training accuracy of the total task, and to ensure that the time and energy consumption are within a certain limit. Then the problem can be reduced to the generalized knapsack problem.* **m** *edge devices can be compared to* **m** *backpacks, while* **n** *sub-tasks can be compared to* **n** *different items, each with different quality (time and energy limitations) and value (task training accuracy). The problem is to maximize the total value of the objects put into the backpack without exceeding the capacity of each backpack (the highest training accuracy of the total task). The GAP problem has been proven to be a NP-hard problem. Because the constraint condition is stronger than the ordinary GAP problem, the complexity of the TECAMP problem will be higher than that of the ordinary GAP problem. Therefore, the TECAMP problem is also an NP-hard problem.*

10.3.2 System Design

10.3.2.1 Overview of the system

The main function of the system is to divide the task of training large-scale neural network models into a number of more manageable sub-tasks and assign each sub-task to the appropriate edge device/equipment. Three essential elements – clients, edge devices, and cloud servers – are included in the smart critical infrastructure as depicted in Fig. 10.2, align with smart critical infrastructure. Due of their limited computational capacity, clients are thought to be incapable of performing sophisticated training tasks. In comparison to clients, edge devices have a limited amount of compute power and can only complete a tiny percentage of the task at hand. The large task must be broken up into a number of smaller sub-tasks, and the cloud server must assign the smaller sub-tasks to the appropriate edge devices in accordance with the allocation strategy.

The model also uses the quantitative criterion to describe the computational capabilities of edge devices. The model makes use of pre-stored tables to map the precision, efficiency, and energy costs of certain actions at designated edge devices. Because edge devices have unique hardware configurations, the values in tables are often varied. Each edge device in

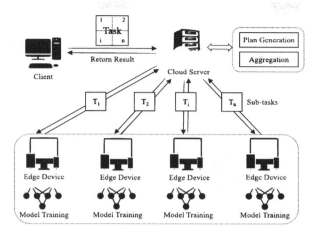

Figure 10.2 The workflow of DTE2AI model.

the pre-stored database can be represented as a 5-tuple using the notations: $\langle T, E, \alpha, \tau, \varepsilon \rangle$. The tuple contains the elements T, which stands for the serial number of tasks, E, which stands for the corresponding edge device for task T, *alpha*, which refers to the accuracy of the task when trained on E, *tau*, which stands for the estimated execution time, and *varepsilon*, which stands for the estimated energy

In the high-level workflow of the model shown in Fig. 10.2, the client sends the task T of training large-scale neural network models to the cloud server due to its poor computing capacity. The cloud server receives the workload-intensive task and then runs algorithms to generate an allocation plan for splitting the large task T into a series of smaller sub-tasks with middle- or light-weighted workloads and delivering to edge devices. These sub-tasks are represented as a set $\{t_i\}$, $i \in N, 0 < i \leq I$, where $\sum_{i=1}^{I} t_i = T$. The cloud server creates a new mapping table with pre-stored tuples regarding incoming tasks before processing task allocations. It does this by retrieving the task header from the job and retrieving it. A task allocations plan that identifies the ultimate destination edge devices for each sub-task is produced using the mapping table, one of the inputs to the algorithms. For the model, the workflow is of utmost importance. To finish the production of allocation plans and aggregate the results of intermediate computing, we present a number of unique techniques.

Due of its inadequate computational capacity, the client transmits the task T of training large-scale neural network models to the cloud server in the high-level workflow of the model shown in Fig. 10.2. After receiving the task with a high workload, the cloud server uses algorithms to create an allocation plan for breaking up the large task T into several smaller subtasks with medium- or light-weight workloads and sending them to edge devices. These subtasks are denoted by the set $\{t_i\}$, $i \in N, 0 < i \leq I$, and $\sum_{i=1}^{I} t_i = T$. The cloud server will obtain the task header before processing task allocations and generate a new mapping table made up of previously stored tuples regarding the incoming job. A task allocations plan that identifies the ultimate destination edge devices for each sub-task is produced using the mapping table, one of the inputs to the algorithms. For the model, the workflow is of utmost importance. To finish the production of allocation plans and aggregate the results of intermediate computing, we present a number of unique techniques.

A cloud server will be given the task of training a neural network model by the client, as shown in Fig. 10.2. The cloud server is in charge of developing the allocation strategy and integrating the outcomes of the intermediate computing from numerous edge devices. The cloud server then distributes tasks to the appropriate edge devices in accordance with the allocation plan after receiving it. Edge devices, which have a restricted compute capacity, can only accomplish a small portion of the whole task. For model training, edge devices will be employed. The final output will then be created by combining all of the intermediate computing results from edge devices on the cloud server. The ultimate result is then sent to the initial client. These procedures combine to provide an operational cycle that allows the system to function properly. The main focus of this work is on task distribution strategies.

10.3.2.2 Task division and allocation procedures

The first step is split up into a number of smaller sub-tasks as the initial stage for the cloud server. The task division process has various requirements. In order to avoid missing any crucial information and having the model provide incorrect results, it must first be ensured that the sum of all subtasks equals the original task. Second, as it is impossible for edge devices to hold all sub-tasks in the same volume, the combined processing power of all edge devices should be greater than the combined computing power required of all sub-tasks. The task division process results in the cloud server receiving a number of subtasks.

The second step for the cloud server is to assign sub-tasks to edge devices that are in charge of developing intermediate outcomes and training neural network models. Two steps make up the main part of the work allocation process. To ensure that the output solution complies with timing constraint T^C and energy constraint E^C, the first phase is to construct a sub-task allocation plan with priorities taking into account the running time and energy cost.

The second step for the cloud server is to allocate sub-tasks to edge devices that are in charge of training neural network models and generating intermediate results. The core of the task allocation procedure lies in two phases. The first phase is to create a sub-task allocation plan with priorities considering the running time and energy cost to make sure that the output solution abides by timing constraint T^C and energy constraint E^C. Due of the greedy algorithm's low computational complexity, we want to implement it at this stage. We choose the greedy approach because, in most cases, the near-optimal solution can only be created within a certain amount of time. So, using a greedy algorithm, we are able to reach an intermediate sub-optimal solution that can be carried out quite quickly.

In order to increase the overall accuracy while still satisfying the timing and energy restrictions, we finally further optimise the intermediate sub-optimal solution. The key to this phase is to use the Hill-climbing mechanism, which transforms a less-than-ideal solution into one that is close to ideal. The sub-optimal answer produced by the greedy algorithm is enhanced with a few tweaking procedures. Following is a list of the adjustment operations.

1. Table Relativiation. Based on accuracy, timing, and energy cost, three relativiation tables will be created from the three mapping tables.

2. Smart Swapping. In this step, all swapping actions based on the relativiation tables will be searched. Additionally, the overall execution time and energy cost will be verified to make sure they both fall inside the TC and EC bounds. If not, the swapping process cannot be carried out.

10.4　OPTIMIZATION ALGORITHMS

To achieve the nearly ideal DTE2AI task *Allocation Table* (AT), we have created a number of fundamental algorithms. Energy-Consuming Table (ECT), Time Consuming Table (TCT), and Training Accuracy Table (TAT) are three variables that algorithms must take into account while calculating the energy used by edge AI jobs, training time, and training accuracy.

Mainly three steps make up the algorithm. A sub-optimal solution is produced at this point, however initially the greedy approach is employed to allocate the appropriate computing node based on the job time. Following this, two specified task computing nodes are exchanged according to the task execution time using Smart Swapping, which lowers total energy consumption. Following that, Smart Swapping operations are carried out based on the distribution findings discovered in the second stage and in accordance with the energy consumption of the task execution. The procedure must ensure that the total execution time does not go beyond the allotted time.

The third stage's distribution findings are then used to determine how to undertake Smart Swapping operations based on task training accuracy. The procedure must make sure that the total execution time and total energy consumption stay under the cap. The Smart Swapping operation is the key step in the suggested algorithm that converts the less-than-ideal solution into a solution that is close to ideal.

It is required to pre-store the time, energy, and training accuracy linked to various types of DTE2AI tasks due to the variety of tasks and compute nodes. Task arrival is a dynamic process. Other jobs will be included in the following round of task assignments when the initial batch is finished. Only the task allocation information pertaining to the recently introduced task has to be calculated by the algorithm; all other table allocation plans do not need to be updated.

10.4.1 Workflow

Two stages make up the workflow. A greedy algorithm first produces a sub-optimal solution, and a Smart Swapping Algorithm (SSA) subsequently produces a solution that is close to ideal. The paper is where the concept for this algorithm originated [338]. The most important stage, the SSA, ensures that the accuracy of the solution is significantly increased while staying within the time frame. An overview of the algorithm flow is shown below.

1. The edge AI tasks that need to be distributed are read, and the TCT is used to determine which node will have the quickest computation time for each work.

2. making the first stage's allocation table relative. Particularly, the data in the TCT and the ECT are altered to the relative value

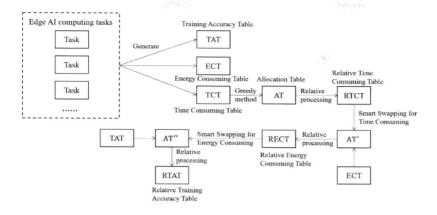

Figure 10.3 The process of a near-optimal algorithm for allocating edge AI computing tasks.

of the chosen calculation node. Here, we obtain the Relative Time Consuming Table (RTCT) and the Relative Energy Consuming Table (RECT).

3. Performing a smart swap operation on the ECT received in the previous stage. Find alternative computing tasks to exchange computing nodes with the node based on the energy requirements of each task. Perform the task exchange operation (swap the compute nodes used by the two tasks) if the overall energy consumption may be lowered after the exchange. Additionally, it's important to make sure that no task's execution time goes beyond a predetermined threshold.

4. Using the ECT collected in the previous stage as the basis for a Smart Swapping operation. Look for additional computing activities to trade computing nodes with the node based on the energy requirements of each work. Exchange the computing nodes used to conduct the two activities if doing so will result in a reduction in overall energy consumption. Furthermore, it's important to make sure that no task's execution time goes beyond a predetermined threshold.

The workflow is shown in Fig. 10.3. Initial job allocation, relative process, and clever swapping operation are the three basic processes that are present. initial assignment of the work is mostly in charge of

Table 10.1 Sample of Time Consuming Table

T＼CN ＼ TK	N_1	N_2	N_3	N_4	N_5
T_1	270	195	237	246	280
T_2	254	232	208	237	267
T_3	175	203	216	227	238
T_4	278	265	254	225	236
T_5	290	285	282	275	249

CN: Computing Nodes; T: Time (counted in seconds); TK: Tasks

creating the initial tasks, such as abstracting the structure and objects the algorithm needs from other jobs. The primary function of the relative process is the relative processing of the initial form, which facilitates future processing. The primary operation of the algorithm, known as the "Smart Swapping Algorithm", is what produces near-optimal solutions.

Greedy-based Allocation Generation Algorithm

Edge AI computing jobs will be delivered to the cloud computing center in a specific order, and the center will utilise the greedy algorithm to instantly distribute these tasks among the computing nodes. Every edge AI computing work is given to the computing node that completes it in the quickest amount of time. Each job is subjected to the greedy procedure, which eventually creates the AT task allocation table. It should be noted that the AT table only has the values 0 and 1. The data at that point is set to 1 if a computing node is chosen, and to 0 otherwise. It should be mentioned that the greedy algorithm only takes the node's execution time into account. An example of TCT is shown in Table 10.1.

There are five edge AI computing tasks (T_1, T_2, T_3, T_4 and T_5) in Table 10.1. Meanwhile, there are five computing nodes (N_1, N_2, N_3, N_4, and N_5). The data in Table 10.1 is the execution time of each task in the corresponding computing node.

In Table 10.2, an ECT example that corresponds to the previous example is displayed. Each task's energy usage in the accompanying computing node makes up the data in ECT. In Table 10.3, the AT produced using the greedy technique is displayed.

Table 10.2 Sample of Energy Consuming Table

E \ CN TK	N_1	N_2	N_3	N_4	N_5
T_1	12	6	10	9	11
T_2	8	13	5	15	14
T_3	6	14	17	11	9
T_4	11	16	19	8	14
T_5	22	25	19	30	15

CN: Computing Nodes; E: Energy; TK: Tasks

It is assumed that there are NT total edge AI computing tasks and NC total computing nodes. Only when $NCgeNT$ is true can any task be carried out. Assuming that in the table, the edge AI computing tasks arrive in the following order: $T_1, T_2, T_3...T_{NT}$, etc. Node N_2 has the shortest execution time for computing task T_1, and node N_3 has the shortest execution time for computing task T_2. The greedy strategy allows for the assignment of all edge AI computing tasks to the appropriate computing nodes. Algorithm 3 displays the greedy algorithm's pseudo-code.

Some key steps are shown below.

1. Putting in place associated data structures like AT, min, and index.

2. Finding the computing node in each row of the TCT that requires the fewest time-consuming traversals.

Table 10.3 Sample of Task Allocation Table (AT)

CN TK	N_1	N_2	N_3	N_4	N_5
T_1	0	1	0	0	0
T_2	0	0	1	0	0
T_3	1	0	0	0	0
T_4	0	0	0	1	0
T_5	0	0	0	0	1

CN: Computing Nodes; TK: Tasks

Algorithm 3 The Greedy-based Allocation Generation Algorithm

Require: TCT, NC, NT
Ensure: AT

 1: Initializing the empty table of AT.
 2: min ← -1
 3: index ← 0
 4: **for** $i = 1 \rightarrow NT$ **do**
 5:    **for** $j = 1 \rightarrow NC$ **do**
 6:       **if** $TCT[i][j] < min$ **then**
 7:          $min \leftarrow TCT[i][j]$
 8:          $index \leftarrow j$
 9:       **end if**
10:    **end for**
11:    $AT[i][index] \leftarrow 1$
12: **end for**
13: **return** AT

---

3. Look for the computer node that can do the work in the shortest amount of time.

4. AT is updated after traversing every row. The last AT is returned following the traversal process.

In Algorithm 3, the TCT denotes the time consumed in transfer, the NC denotes the total number of computing nodes, the NT denotes the total number of edge AI computing tasks. The algorithm uses a two-layer loop to traverse all elements in the TCT table, the time complexity of the algorithm is $O(NT*NC)$.

In the Algorithm 3, the TCT stands for "time consumed in transfer", the NC for "number of computing nodes overall", and the NT for "number of edge AI computing tasks overall". The temporal complexity of the algorithm is $O(NT*NC)$ and it employs a two-layer loop to explore every element in the TCT table.

10.4.2   Tables Relativization Algorithm

We use Table Relativization Algorithm (TRA) to relativize TCT, ECT, and TAT. We got the sub-optimal AT from The Greedy-based Allocation Generation Algorithm. The three tables after relativization will become RTCT, RECT, and RTAT. The subsequent algorithm continue to optimize AT based on RTCT, RECT, and RTAT, the allocation plan will continue to reduce energy and time, it can also improve task training accuracy. RTCT, RECT, and RTAT are tables based on AT, TCT, ECT, and TAT.

TCT, ECT, and TAT are relativized using the Table Relativization Algorithm (TRA). The Greedy-based Allocation Generation Algorithm provided the less-than-ideal AT for us. The three tables will change into RTCT, RECT, and RTAT following relativization. The following algorithm keeps improving AT based on RTCT, RECT, and RTAT; the allocation plan keeps reducing energy and time; it can also increase task training accuracy. Tables RTCT, RECT, and RTAT are derived from AT, TCT, ECT, and TAT.

Here is a basic explanation of relativization's mechanism. The energy, time, or training accuracy generated by the computing node that was selected for an edge AI computing task is subtracted from the energy, time, or training accuracy generated by the computing node that was selected for that work. Take the TCT, for instance. As an illustration, consider the TCT.

Assuming that the currently processed computing task is T_i, the greedy algorithm allocates T_i to the computing node N_s for processing. Then the i-th row of RTCT can be obtained by the Eq. (10.5). We provide the pseudo codes in Algorithm 3.

The greedy method assigns T_i to the computing node N_s for processing, assuming that T_i represents the computing task that is currently being worked on. Then, using Eq. (10.5), one can determine the i-th row of RTCT. The pseudo codes are provided in Algorithm 3.

$$RTCT_i = \underset{j=1 \rightarrow NC}{TCT_{ij}} - \underset{s=1 \rightarrow NC}{TCT_{is}} \qquad (10.5)$$

In the same way, we can get the i-th row of RECT as shown in the Eq. (10.6).

$$RECT_i = \underset{j=1 \rightarrow NC}{ECT_{ij}} - \underset{s=1 \rightarrow NC}{ECT_{is}} \qquad (10.6)$$

The loop in the TRA has three layers. Depending on the number of computing nodes, each edge AI computing work will go through a two-time loop. This algorithm's complexity is $O(NT * NC^2)$.

10.4.3 Time-Based Smart Swapping Algorithm

The key algorithm, SSA, is in charge of optimizing the results of the allocation process that the greedy algorithm produces. The overall task

---

Algorithm 3 Tables Relativization Algorithm

Require: TCT, ECT, TAT, AT
Ensure: $RTCT$, $RECT$, $RTAT$

 1: Initializing i, j.
 2: **for** $i = 1 \rightarrow NT$ **do**
 3:     Getting index of the AT[i][index] is equal to 1.
 4:     **for** $j = 1 \rightarrow NC$ **do**
 5:         $RTCT[i][j] \leftarrow TCT[i][j] - TCT[i][index]$
 6:         $RECT[i][j] \leftarrow ECT[i][j] - ECT[i][index]$
 7:         $RTAT[i][j] \leftarrow TAT[i][j] - TAT[i][index]$
 8:     **end for**
 9: **end for**
10: **return** RTCT, RECT, RTAT

---

execution time, total energy consumption, and accuracy of AI task training will all be reduced specifically by SSA by swapping out computing nodes for different activities. Following the relativization operation, the data of the previously selected computing node will become 0 for the RTCT and RECT, whilst the data of the previously unselected computing node may become negative.

The only distinction is that ESSA needs to be limited by deadlines. To update RTAT and RECT, we first run the TSSA algorithm for RTCT, then update AT to AT', and then update RECT.

Both the ESSA and the TSSA are connected. The only difference is that time limits are mandated by ESSA. We first perform the TSSA algorithm for RTCT, update AT to AT', and then update RECT and RTAT.

If the task T_i selects the computing node N_s, when the relative value of the calculation time generated by the other unselected computing node N_j is a negative number ($TCT_{ij} - TCT_{is} < 0$), the computing node N_j can generate shorter calculation time ($TCT_{ij} < TCT_{is}$). Therefore, it is a better choice for T_i to choose N_j as the computing node.

In particular, if another task T_k has selected the N_j node, the overall calculation time must be assessed to determine whether it has lowered after the two computing nodes are switched. The condition $RTCT_{ij} + RTCT_{ks} < 0$ indicates that the overall task execution time has decreased, making it advantageous to change the computing nodes of the two jobs. If not, there is no exchange and the operation continues on the next compute node.

Algorithm 3 Time-based Smart Swapping Algorithm

Require: *AT*, *RTCT*, *RECT*, *RTAT*
Ensure: *AT'*, *RTCT*, *RECT*, *RTAT*

1: Initializing i, j, k, s.
2: **for** $i = 1 \rightarrow NT$ **do**
3:     **for** $j = 1 \rightarrow NC$ **do**
4:         **if** RTCT[i][j] < 0 **then**
5:             **if** RTCT[i][j] + RTCT[k][s] < 0 **then**
6:                 *Swapping the AT[i][s] and AT[k][s].*
7:                 *Swapping the AT[i][j] and AT[k][j].*
8:                 Renew the RTCT and RECT.
9:             **end if**
10:         **end if**
11:     **end for**
12: **end for**
13: $AT' \leftarrow AT$
14: **return** AT', RTCT, RECT, RTAT

The method will traverse all the elements in the RTCT table once, and then return the changed AT, RTCT, RECT, and RTAT. The algorithm used by the TSSA to traverse the RTCT is *O(NT*NC)* complicated. The TSSA pseudocodes are shown by algorithm 3.

The method will return the modified AT, RTCT, RECT, and RTAT after traversing all of the RTCT table's elements once. The complexity of the TSSA's algorithm, which traverses the RTCT, is *O(NT*NC)*. Algorithm 3 displays the TSSA pseudocodes.

The method will traverse all the elements in the RTCT table once, and then return the changed AT, RTCT, RECT, and RTAT. The TSSA's algorithm, which traverses the RTCT, is *O(NT*NC)* complex. The pseudocodes for the TSSA algorithm are shown.

10.4.4 Energy-Based Smart Swapping Algorithm

An exchange system for RECT is called ESSA. After each exchange operation, it is important to check to see if the task's execution time has over the $\mathcal{T}^{\sigma}$ barrier. The present compute node is kept in place if the time exceeds the limit. ESSA is more complex than TSSA but still follows the same basic processes. These are ESSA's fundamental steps.

1. Using the modified RETC, A', and RTCT as input, iterate through each row in the table.

Algorithm 3 Energy-based Smart Swapping Algorithm

Require: AT', $RTCT$, $RECT$, $RTAT$, $\mathcal{T}^\sigma$
Ensure: AT'', $RTCT$, $RECT$, $RTAT$

1: Initializing i, j, k, s.
2: Initializing $\mathcal{T}^{sum}$ to store the sum of tasks execution time.
3: **for** $i = 1 \to NT$ **do**
4: **for** $j = 1 \to NC$ **do**
5:   **if** RECT[i][j] < 0 **then**
6:    **if** RTCT[i][j] + RTCT[k][s] < 0 **then**
7:     *Swapping the $AT'[i][s]$ and $AT'[k][s]$.*
8:     *Swapping the $AT'[i][j]$ and $AT'[k][j]$.*
9:     Renew $\mathcal{T}^{sum}$.
10:     **if** $\mathcal{T}^{sum} \leq \mathcal{T}^\sigma$ **then**
11:      Renew the RTCT, RECT and RTAT.
12:     **else**
13:      Revoking the operations.
14:     **end if**
15:    **end if**
16:   **end if**
17: **end for**
18: **end for**
19: $AT'' \leftarrow AT'$
20: **return** AT'', RTCT, RECT, RTAT

---

2. If a negative value is found for any RECT element, then attempt exchanging computing nodes performing associated tasks.

3. Continue to the next element if the overall energy consumption decreases after the exchange and the total task execution time is below the $\mathcal{T}^\sigma$ criterion.

4. Continue to the next element and skip this exchange procedure if the overall energy usage doesn't drop.

Because the same size table is traversed, ESSA and TSSA have the same temporal complexity, which is $O(NT*NC)$. The Algorithm 3 displays ESSA pseudocodes.

10.4.5 Accuracy-Based Smart Swapping Algorithm

The accuracy of each node training task needs to be optimized using SSA once the task execution time and energy usage are optimized. The work allocation is still optimized using an Accuracy-based Smart Swapping

Algorithm 3 Accuracy-based Smart Swapping Algorithm

Require: AT'', $RTCT$, $RECT$, $RTAT$, $\mathcal{T}^\sigma$, $\mathcal{E}^\sigma$
Ensure: AT_f, $RTCT$, $RECT$, $RTAT$

1: Initializing i, j, k, s.
2: Initializing $\mathcal{T}^{sum}$ to store the sum of tasks execution time.
3: Initializing $\mathcal{E}^{sum}$ to store the sum of tasks consumed energy.
4: **for** $i = 1 \rightarrow NT$ **do**
5:     **for** $j = 1 \rightarrow NC$ **do**
6:         **if** RTAT[i][j] > 0 **then**
7:             **if** RTAT[i][j] + RTAT[k][s] < 0 **then**
8:                 *Swapping the $AT''[i][s]$ and $AT'[k][s]$.*
9:                 *Swapping the $AT''[i][j]$ and $AT'[k][j]$.*
10:                 Renew $\mathcal{T}^{sum}$.
11:                 Renew $\mathcal{E}^{sum}$.
12:                 **if** $\mathcal{T}^{sum} \leq \mathcal{T}^\sigma \&\&\mathcal{E}^{sum} \leq \mathcal{E}^\sigma$ **then**
13:                     Renew the RTCT, RECT and RTAT.
14:                 **else**
15:                     Revoking the operations.
16:                 **end if**
17:             **end if**
18:         **end if**
19:     **end for**
20: **end for**
21: $AT_f \leftarrow AT'$
22: **return** AT_f, RTCT, RECT, RTAT

Algorithm (ASSA). Each computer node that can train for various types of edge AI computing jobs has its training accuracy saved on the cloud computing center server. In contrast to energy and time consumption, task allocation is better the greater the value of training accuracy. SSA must be changed as a result.

After relativization, we must take into account that the positive number in the result is a better solution, after which we must exchange the calculation nodes that correspond to these positive values. The total execution time of all jobs must not exceed the thresholds of $\mathcal{T}^\sigma$ and $\mathcal{E}^\sigma$ while transferring compute nodes. ASSA has the same temporal complexity as TSSA and ESSA, which is $O(NT*NC)$. Algorithm 3 provides the corresponding ASSA pseudocodes.

The following are the basic steps of ASSA.

1. Using the modified A'', RTCT, RECT, and RTAT as input, iterate through each row of the table one at a time.

2. Try exchanging compute nodes with tasks that are related for each element in RTCT if the value is negative.

3. If the overall accuracy decreases following the exchange and the sum of the job execution time and energy spent does not exceed the threshold, then move on to the following item.

4. Continue to the following element and skip this exchange procedure if the overall accuracy does not drop.

10.5 EVALUATIONS

We introduce the approach's implementation in this part and use simulations to assess its effectiveness. We'll describe the specific experimental conditions and findings in the subsections that follow. On a computer with an Intel(R) Core(TM) i5-10400 CPU running at 2.90GHz and 16GB of memory, all trials were conducted.

10.5.1 Configuration

An experiment simulation programme was created using Java. By adjusting different network parameter settings during the experiment, we assess the performance of our technique. We do this by selecting a range of edge AI algorithms that deliver various time, energy consumption, and training accuracy metrics. For the experiment, we created a number of setups to accurately replicate the real-world environment of the edge AI.

We model the processing delays brought on by different workload scenarios and job assignments, as well as the network transmission delays brought on by the physical locations of cloud center and edge devices. In terms of energy usage, we create a suitable figure based on the scope of the task and the edge device. On various cutting-edge pieces of equipment, different tasks have varying levels of training accuracy. Our experiment focuses on how quickly the allocation scheme may be generated and how accurate it is throughout training.

We make use of a range of experimental settings to imitate the actual application environment. In our experiment, we take into account the impact of various job numbers and various edge device counts on the test findings and get to a persuasive conclusion by using numerous combinations of various parameters. In Table 10.4, the parameter settings

Table 10.4 Parameter Settings

Parameter	Values
Task numbers	[20, 30, 40, 50, 60, 70, 80, 90, 100]
Edge devices	[5, 10, 15]

are displayed. In addition, we contrast our method with a few others, particularly the ECWO [339] and AGADA [340].

The financial sector's heterogeneous cloud computing server workloads are predicted by ECWO using greedy programming. Efficiency-Aware Task Assignment (EATA) Algorithm and Task Mapping Algorithm (TMA) are the two primary algorithms employed in the suggested paradigm. With just slight time and space overhead, AGADA can find close to ideal solutions. Dynamic programming for data allocation causes significant time and space consumption, which is solved via a genetic algorithm. Contrary to ECWO and AGADA, the DTE2AI provided by EAHAS is more concerned with optimizing the training accuracy of AI tasks within the constraints of training time and energy consumption and takes into account the allocation policy generation time.

The issue is that distributed computing and communication typically need a higher-level cost (energy, time, etc.) when AI models are trained in a decentralized method, especially when taking into account the context of smart critical infrastructure. But the majority of terminals have energy limitations. A vital factor to take into account is the interaction between the computational model's accuracy and the energy usage of edge nodes. The effectiveness and stability of the method should also be taken into account. As a result, we evaluated the performance of EAHAS, ECWO, and AGADA in five aspects, namely the total execution time for all tasks completed, the total energy consumed, the average accuracy, the generating time of the allotted plan, and the training accuracy distribution under 10,000 trials.

10.5.2 Results

The results of the comparison experiment allowed us to draw some significant conclusions, which can be shown in Fig. 10.4. We discovered that

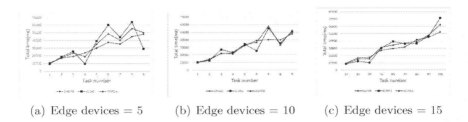

(a) Edge devices = 5   (b) Edge devices = 10   (c) Edge devices = 15

Figure 10.4   Comparisons on total execution time of all tasks.

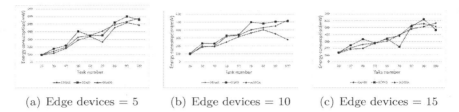

(a) Edge devices = 5   (b) Edge devices = 10   (c) Edge devices = 15

Figure 10.5   Comparisons on total energy consumption of all tasks.

when the overall job count rises, our EAHAS would slowly lengthen the execution time of the overall task, and for the most part, the consumed time won't surpass the average of two other related approaches (ECWO and AGADA).

Our method generates time that is gradually less than that produced by the other two related ways as the number of edge devices gradually grows (from Fig. 10.4(a) to Fig. 10.4(c)). The time generated by the task allocation of our method is reduced by 28.6% compared to ECWO and 14.5% compared to AGADA when the number of edge devices is 15 and the number of training tasks is 100 (Fig. 10.4(c)).

We discovered that the proposed technique uses less energy overall than ECWO and AGADA (Fig. 10.5). Although time is a factor in our strategy, which is based on energy optimization job allocation, the result is still below average compared to the other two ways. As can be seen from Fig. 10.5(a) to Fig. 10.5(c), our method's energy usage rises steadily as the number of tasks rises. In particular, 10 edge computing devices are shown in Fig. 10.5(b), and our solution uses less energy than ECWO and AGADA in 91% of the instances. Our approach is quite scalable, and work distribution will gradually utilise more energy.

The disparity in accuracy between the three approaches is depicted in Fig. 10.6. Since our task allocation is for edge AI training scenarios, as

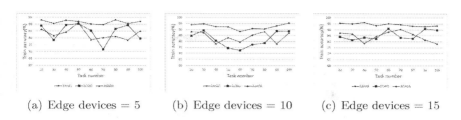

(a) Edge devices = 5   (b) Edge devices = 10   (c) Edge devices = 15

Figure 10.6 Comparisons on average accuracy of task training.

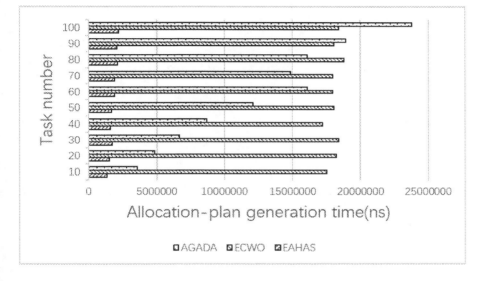

Figure 10.7 Allocate-plan generation time for five edge devices.

opposed to task allocation in cloud computing, accuracy is the primary index. In terms of accuracy, it is intuitively obvious that the proposed strategy is superior to the other two in terms of distribution of edge AI jobs. As the number of tasks rises in all three instances, our method's accuracy surpasses that of ECWO and AGADA.

In Fig. 10.6, our method produces accuracy that is approximately 10.8% (Fig. 10.6(a)), 13.5% (Fig. 10.6(b)), and 10.5% (Fig. 10.6(c)) higher than the highest accuracy values of the other two methods.

We see that while using dynamic programming, it typically takes a while to build the ideal answer. One of the most important aspects of our experiment is therefore assessing the generation time of the allocation technique. In the cases of five edge devices and ten edge devices, respectively, Figs. 10.7 and 10.8 illustrate the effects of various job numbers on

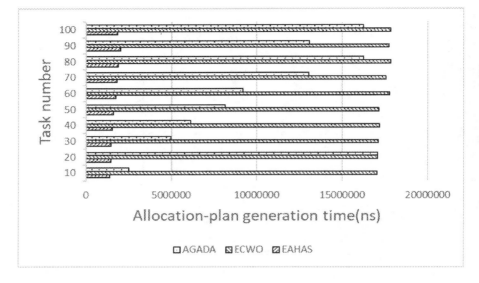

Figure 10.8 Allocate-plan generation time for ten edge devices.

the generation time of allocation method. It is clear that the allocation policy is generated by EAHAS significantly faster than it is by the other two approaches.

The average amount of time spent by EAHAS to develop allocation plans is only 10% of the time spent by ECWO; the average amount of time spent by EAHAS to generate allocation plans is only 14% of the time spent by AGADA. Furthermore, the time required by EAHAS to develop the allocation method does not vary significantly as the number of tasks rises. This demonstrates that EAHAS is effective at adapting to the edge AI setting with a changeable number of tasks and that it is effective at producing allocation plans.

After completing edge AI tasks using the allocation strategies created by the three techniques in 10,000 tests, the distribution of model training accuracy is shown in Fig. 10.9. The figure shows that, in comparison with ECWO and AGADA, the model's training accuracy is higher and the distribution is more uniform after conducting edge AI tasks in accordance with the allocation strategy produced by EAHAS. The model's training accuracy is typically distributed between 90% and 100% when using the EAHAS allocation technique.

However, the distribution of the model's training accuracy under the ECWO and AGADA allocation plans is quite dispersed, and the total

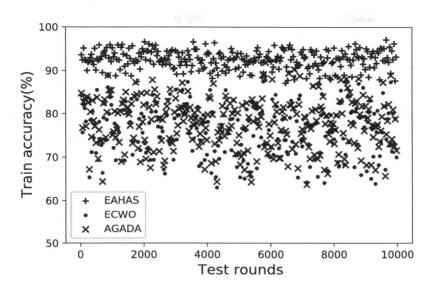

Figure 10.9 Distribution of training accuracy for each scheme across 10,000 tests.

training accuracy is not particularly high. The reason for this outcome is that EAHAS prioritises model training accuracy while not exceeding the time and energy consumption limitation, and works to identify the plan that satisfies the conditions and has the highest model training accuracy. ECWO and AGADA, however, do not specifically take the model training accuracy as the standard for the generation of allocation plan, so the performance of the generated allocation plan in model training accuracy is subpar.

In conclusion, this section only included a portion of the experimental findings. The findings shown indicate that, in comparison to other approaches, our methodology takes less time to generate the allocation strategy and has a greater model training accuracy of the generation strategy. Experimental findings demonstrate that our procedure outperforms the measured ones. When it comes to the time needed to produce allocation plans, ECWO and AGADA both take longer than EAHAS on average (10% and 14% more time). Our technique outperforms ECWO and AGADA's greatest accuracy values for the train by 13.5% and 10.5%, respectively. The evaluation demonstrated the superiority of our strategy for allocating edge AI tasks.

10.6 SUMMARY

This chapter provides an energy-aware, high precision edge AI technique that is ideal for work allocation. It is supported by DT technology. Through the use of a heuristic algorithm, the plan approach offers a nearly optimal work allocation method for edge AI and achieves improved model training accuracy while requiring little latency and little energy. DTE2AI may be used to power distributed AI in a real-world production scenario because it also offers quick and efficient strategy creation.

GLOSSARY

Digital Twin: is a technology that powers up the interconnectivity and capability between physical and digital spaces.

Bibliography

[1] K. Gai, M. Qiu, L. Tao, and Y. Zhu. Intrusion detection techniques for mobile cloud computing in heterogeneous 5G. *Security and Communication Networks*, 9(16):3049–3058, 2016.

[2] K. Gai, M. Qiu, and H. Hassan. Secure cyber incident analytics framework using Monte Carlo simulations for financial cybersecurity insurance in cloud computing. *Concurrency and Computation: Practice and Experience*, 29(7):1–13, 2016.

[3] CISA. Cybersecurity Insurance Reports, 2020, https://www.cisa.gov/resources-tools/resources/cybersecurity-insurance-reports.

[4] S. Elnagdy, M. Qiu, and K. Gai. Understanding taxonomy of cyber risks for cybersecurity insurance of financial industry in cloud computing. In *The 2nd IEEE International Conference of Scalable and Smart Cloud*, pages 295–300. IEEE, 2016.

[5] S. Elnagdy, M. Qiu, and K. Gai. Cyber incident classifications using ontology-based knowledge representation for cybersecurity insurance in financial industry. In *The 2nd IEEE International Conference of Scalable and Smart Cloud*, pages 301–306. IEEE, 2016.

[6] K. Gai, M. Qiu, and S. Elnagdy. Security-aware information classifications using supervised learning for cloud-based cyber risk management in financial big data. In *The 2nd IEEE International Conference on Big Data Security on Cloud*, pages 197–202, New York, USA, 2016.

[7] K. Gai, M. Qiu, and S. Elnagdy. A novel secure big data cyber incident analytics framework for cloud-based cybersecurity insurance. In *The 2nd IEEE International Conference on Big Data Security on Cloud*, pages 171–176, New York, USA, 2016.

[8] L. Zhu, H. Dong, M. Shen, and K. Gai. An incentive mechanism using shapley value for blockchain-based medical data sharing. In *5th IEEE International Conference on Big Data Security on Cloud, IEEE International Conference on High Performance and Smart Computing, and IEEE International Conference on Intelligent Data and Security, BigDataSecurity/HPSC/IDS 2019, May 27-29, 2019*, pages 113–118, Washington, DC, USA, 2019. IEEE.

[9] G. Alipui, L. Tao, K. Gai, and N. Jiang. Reducing complexity of diagnostic message pattern specification and recognition on inbound data using semantic techniques. In *The 2nd IEEE International Conference of Scalable and Smart Cloud*, pages 267–272. IEEE, 2016.

[10] S. Jayaraman, L. Tao, K. Gai, and N. Jiang. Drug side effects data representation and full spectrum inferencing using knowledge graphs in intelligent telehealth. In *The 2nd IEEE International Conference of Scalable and Smart Cloud*, pages 289–294. IEEE, 2016.

[11] R. DeStefano, L. Tao, and K. Gai. Improving data governance in large organizations through ontology and linked data. In *The 2nd IEEE International Conference of Scalable and Smart Cloud*, pages 279–284. IEEE, 2016.

[12] C. Asamoah, L. Tao, K. Gai, and N. Jiang. Powering filtration process of cyber security ecosystem using knowledge graph. In *The 2nd IEEE International Conference of Scalable and Smart Cloud*, pages 240–246. IEEE, 2016.

[13] M. Sette, L. Tao, K. Gai, and N. Jiang. A semantic approach to intelligent and personal tutoring system. In *The 2nd IEEE International Conference of Scalable and Smart Cloud*, pages 261–266. IEEE, 2016.

[14] Google Cloud. Google infrastructure security design overview, 2017. url=https://cloud.google.com/security/security-design/.

[15] K. Gai, M. Qiu, X. Sun, and H. Zhao. Smart data deduplication for telehealth systems in heterogeneous cloud computing. *Journal of Communications and Information Networks*, 1(4):93–104, 2016.

[16] H. Zhao, M. Qiu, and K. Gai. Empirical study of data allocation in heterogeneous memory. In *Smart Computing and Communication - Second International Conference, SmartCom 2017*, volume 10699, pages 385–395. Springer, 2017.

[17] K. Gai, M. Qiu, M. Liu, and Z. Xiong. In-memory big data analytics under space constraints using dynamic programming. *Future Generation Computer Systems*, 83:219–227, 2018.

[18] R. Ottis and P. Lorents. Cyberspace: Definition and implications. In *International Conference on Cyber Warfare and Security*, page 267. Academic Conferences International Limited, 2010.

[19] R. Langner. Stuxnet: Dissecting a cyberwarfare weapon. *IEEE Security & Privacy*, 9(3):49–51, 2011.

[20] M. Abomhara and G. M. Køien. Cyber security and the internet of things: vulnerabilities, threats, intruders and attacks. *Journal of Cyber Security and Mobility*, pages 65–88, 2015.

[21] M. Nawir, A. Amir, N. Yaakob, and O. B. Lynn. Internet of things (iot): Taxonomy of security attacks. In *2016 3rd International Conference on Electronic Design (ICED)*, pages 321–326. IEEE, 2016.

[22] S. Kumar and D. Agarwal. Hacking attacks, methods, techniques and their protection measures. *International Journal of Advance Research in Computer Science and Management*, 4(4):2253–2257, 2018.

[23] Y. Ye, T. Li, D. Adjeroh, and S. S. Iyengar. A survey on malware detection using data mining techniques. *ACM Computing Surveys (CSUR)*, 50(3):1–40, 2017.

[24] I. Andrea, C. Chrysostomou, and G. Hadjichristofi. Internet of things: Security vulnerabilities and challenges. In *2015 IEEE Symposium on Computers and Communication (ISCC)*, pages 180–187. IEEE, 2015.

[25] D. E. Denning. Framework and principles for active cyber defense. *Computers & Security*, 40:108–113, 2014.

[26] O. A. Hathaway, R. Crootof, P. Levitz, H. Nix, A. Nowlan, W. Perdue, and J. Spiegel. The law of cyber-attack. *California Law Review*, pages 817–885, 2012.

[27] S. Aggarwal, S. Houshmand, and M. Weir. New technologies in password cracking techniques. In *Cyber Security: Power and Technology*, pages 179–198. Springer, 2018.

[28] A. L. Han, D. F. Wong, and L. S. Chao. Password cracking and countermeasures in computer security: A survey. *arXiv preprint arXiv:1411.7803*, 2014.

[29] L. Zhu, K. Gai, and M. Li. *Blockchain Technology in Internet of Things*. Springer, 2019.

[30] T. Wu, W. Wang, C. Zhang, W. Zhang, L. Zhu, K. Gai, and H. Wang. Blockchain-based anonymous data sharing with accountability for internet of things. *IEEE Internet Things J.*, 10(6, March 15):5461–5475, 2023.

[31] Y. Xu, Z. Lu, K. Gai, Q. Duan, J. Lin, J. Wu, and K. R. Choo. BESIFL: blockchain-empowered secure and incentive federated learning paradigm in iot. *IEEE Internet Things J.*, 10(8, April 15):6561–6573, 2023.

[32] B. Gates, N. Myhrvold, P. Rinearson, and D. Domonkos. *The Road Ahead*. Viking New York, 1995.

[33] K. Gai, M. Qiu, and X. Sun. A survey on fintech. *Journal of Network and Computer Applications*, 103:262–273, 2018.

[34] K. Gai, K. R. Choo, M. Qiu, and L. Zhu. Privacy-preserving content-oriented wireless communication in internet-of-things. *IEEE Internet Things J.*, 5(4):3059–3067, 2018.

[35] Itu internet reports 2005: The internet of things, 2005. url=https://www.itu.int/dms_pub/itu-s/opb/pol/S-POL-IR.IT-2005-SUM-PDF-E.pdf.

[36] A smarter planet: The next leadership agenda, 2008. url=https://www.ibm.com/ibm/cioleadershipexchange/us/en/pdfs/SJP_Smarter_Planet.pdf.

[37] R. Xu, L. Zhu, A. Wang, X. Du, K. R. Choo, G. Zhang, and K. Gai. Side-channel attack on a protected RFID card. *IEEE Access*, 6:58395–58404, 2018.

[38] Y. Zhang, K. Gai, J. Xiao, L. Zhu, and K. R. Choo. Blockchain-empowered efficient data sharing in internet of things settings. *IEEE Journal on Selected Areas in Communications*, 40(12):3422–3436, 2022.

[39] K. Gai, Q. Xiao, M. Qiu, G. Zhang, J. Chen, Y. Wei, and Y. Zhang. Digital twin-enabled AI enhancement in smart critical infrastructures for 5g. *ACM Transactions on Sensor Networks*, 18(3):45:1–45:20, 2022.

[40] C. A. Repec. Epc tag data standard. url=https://www.gs1.org/sites/default/files/docs/epc/GS1_EPC_TDS_i1_11.pdf.

[41] K. Gai, H. Tang, G. Li, T. Xie, S. Wang, L. Zhu, and K. R. Choo. Blockchain-based privacy-preserving positioning data sharing for iot-enabled maritime transportation systems. *IEEE Transactions on Intelligent Transportation Systems*, 24(2):2344–2358, 2023.

[42] X. Wang, L. Wang, Y. Li, and K. Gai. Privacy-aware efficient fine-grained data access control in internet of medical things based fog computing. *IEEE Access*, 6:47657–47665, 2018.

[43] Y. Yan, K. Gai, P. Jiang, L. Xu, and L. Zhu. Location-based privacy-preserving techniques in connected environment: A survey. In *IEEE International Conference on Smart Cloud, SmartCloud 2019, December 10-12, 2019*, pages 156–162, Tokyo, Japan, 2019. IEEE.

[44] J. He, Z. Zhang, L. Zhu, Z. Zhu, J. Liu, and K. Gai. An efficient and accurate nonintrusive load monitoring scheme for power consumption. *IEEE Internet Things J.*, 6(5):9054–9063, 2019.

[45] J. Guo, K. Gai, L. Zhu, and Z. Zhang. An approach of secure two-way-pegged multi-sidechain. In *Algorithms and Architectures for Parallel Processing - 19th International Conference, ICA3PP 2019, December 9-11, 2019*, volume 11945, pages 551–564, Melbourne, VIC, Australia, 2019. Springer.

[46] A. Odiljon and K. Gai. Efficiency issues and solutions in blockchain: A survey. In *Smart Blockchain - Second International Conference, SmartBlock 2019, October 11-13, 2019*, volume 11911, pages 76–86, Birmingham, UK, 2019. Springer.

[47] Keke Gai and Meikang Qiu. Optimal resource allocation using reinforcement learning for iot content-centric services. *Applied Soft Computing*, 70:12–21, 2018.

[48] Yang Yu, Rui Jin, Hao Yin, Keke Gai, and Zijian Zhang. A searchable re-encryption-based scheme for massive data transactions. In *2022 IEEE 9th International Conference on Cyber Security and Cloud Computing (CSCloud)/2022 IEEE 8th International Conference on Edge Computing and Scalable Cloud (EdgeCom)*, pages 135–140. IEEE, 2022.

[49] Wan Haslina Hassan et al. Current research on internet of things (iot) security: A survey. *Computer Networks*, 148:283–294, 2019.

[50] Li Fusheng, Li Ruisheng, and Zhou Fengquan. Composition and classification of the microgrid. *Microgrid Technology and Engineering Application*, pages 11–27, 2016.

[51] Axel Daneels and Wayne Salter. What is scada? 1999.

[52] Geeta Yadav and Kolin Paul. Architecture and security of scada systems: A review. *International Journal of Critical Infrastructure Protection*, 34:100433, 2021.

[53] Manar Alanazi, Abdun Mahmood, and Mohammad Jabed Morshed Chowdhury. Scada vulnerabilities and attacks: A review of the state-of-the-art and open issues. *Computers & Security*, 125:103028, 2023.

[54] Chih-Yuan Lin and Simin Nadjm-Tehrani. Protocol study and anomaly detection for server-driven traffic in scada networks. *International Journal of Critical Infrastructure Protection*, 42:100612, 2023.

[55] Amir Sinaeepourfard, Jordi Garcia, Xavier Masip-Bruin, and Eva Marín-Torder. Towards a comprehensive data lifecycle model for big data environments. In *Proceedings of the 3rd IEEE/ACM International Conference on Big Data Computing, Applications and Technologies*, pages 100–106, 2016.

[56] Mohammed Ghouse, Manisha J Nene, and C Vembuselvi. Data leakage prevention for data in transit using artificial intelligence and encryption techniques. In *2019 International Conference on Advances in Computing, Communication and Control (ICAC3)*, pages 1–6. IEEE, 2019.

[57] Yuri Shapira, Bracha Shapira, and Asaf Shabtai. Content-based data leakage detection using extended fingerprinting. *arXiv preprint arXiv:1302.2028*, 2013.

[58] Wei-Min Ouyang, Hong-Liang Xin, and Qin-Hua Huang. Privacy preserving sequential pattern mining based on data perturbation. In *2007 International Conference on Machine Learning and Cybernetics*, volume 6, pages 3239–3243. IEEE, 2007.

[59] Manik Lal Das. Two-factor user authentication in wireless sensor networks. *IEEE Transactions on Wireless Communications*, 8(3):1086–1090, 2009.

[60] Binod Vaidya, Dimitrios Makrakis, and Hussein Mouftah. Two-factor mutual authentication with key agreement in wireless sensor networks. *Security and Communication Networks*, 9(2):171–183, 2016.

[61] Christian Esposito, Aniello Castiglione, and Kim-Kwang Raymond Choo. Encryption-based solution for data sovereignty in federated clouds. *IEEE Cloud Computing*, 3(1):12–17, 2016.

[62] MR Sumalatha, S Hemalathaa, R Monika, and C Ahila. Towards secure audit services for outsourced data in cloud. In *2014 International Conference on Recent Trends in Information Technology*, pages 1–6. IEEE, 2014.

[63] K. R. Choo, K. Gai, L. Chiaraviglio, and Q. Yang. A multidisciplinary approach to internet of things (iot) cybersecurity and risk management. *Computers & Security*, 102:102136, 2021.

[64] Peter Mell and Timothy Grance. The nist definition of cloud computing. NIST recommendation, NIST, 2011.

[65] Devyani Patil and Nilesh Mahajan. An analytical survey for improving authentication levels in cloud computing. In *2021 International Conference on Advance Computing and Innovative Technologies in Engineering (ICACITE)*, pages 6–8. IEEE, 2021.

[66] Lalit Mohan, Richa Pandey, Sanjeev Bisht, and Janmejay Pant. A comparative study on saas, paas and iaas cloud delivery models in cloud computing. *International Journal on Emerging Technologies*, 8(1):158–160, 2017.

[67] Robail Yasrab. Platform-as-a-service (paas): the next hype of cloud computing. *arXiv preprint arXiv:1804.10811*, 2018.

[68] HA Dinesha and Vinod Kumar Agrawal. Multi-level authentication technique for accessing cloud services. In *2012 International Conference on Computing, Communication and Applications*, pages 1–4. IEEE, 2012.

[69] Daniela Pöhn and Wolfgang Hommel. An overview of limitations and approaches in identity management. In *Proceedings of the 15th International Conference on Availability, Reliability and Security*, ARES '20, New York, NY, USA, 2020. Association for Computing Machinery.

[70] Ishaq Azhar Mohammed. Factors affecting user adoption of identity management systems: An empirical study. *International Journal of Innovations in Engineering Research and Technology*, 8(1):104–110, 2021.

[71] K. Gai, Y. Zhang, M. Qiu, and B. Thuraisingham. Blockchain-enabled service optimizations in supply chain digital twin. *IEEE Transactions on Services Computing*, 16(3):1673–1685, 2023.

[72] Matthias Hummer, Sebastian Groll, Michael Kunz, Ludwig Fuchs, and Günther Pernul. Measuring identity and access management performance-an expert survey on possible performance indicators. In *ICISSP*, pages 233–240, 2018.

[73] Michael Kunz, Ludwig Fuchs, Michael Netter, and Günther Pernul. Analyzing quality criteria in role-based identity and access management. In *2015 International Conference on Information Systems Security and Privacy (ICISSP)*, pages 1–9. IEEE, 2015.

[74] Steven Tuecke, Rachana Ananthakrishnan, Kyle Chard, Mattias Lidman, Brendan McCollam, Stephen Rosen, and Ian Foster. Globus auth: A research identity and access management platform. In *2016 IEEE 12th International Conference on e-Science (e-Science)*, pages 203–212. IEEE, 2016.

[75] Xiaoyang Zhu and Youakim Badr. A survey on blockchain-based identity management systems for the internet of things. In *2018 IEEE International Conference on Internet of Things (iThings) and IEEE Green Computing and Communications (GreenCom) and IEEE Cyber, Physical and Social Computing (CPSCom) and IEEE Smart Data (SmartData)*, pages 1568–1573. IEEE, 2018.

[76] Celia Paulsen and Robert Byers. Nistir 7298 rev 3 glossary of key information security terms. W3C recommendation, W3C, November 2019.

[77] Celia Paulsen and Robert Byers. Y.2702(09/2008) authentication and authorization requirements for ngn release 1. ITU recommendation, ITU, November 2008.

[78] Rohan H. Shah and D. P. Salapurkar. A multifactor authentication system using secret splitting in the perspective of cloud of things. In *2017 International Conference on Emerging Trends & Innovation in ICT (ICEI)*, pages 1–4, 2017.

[79] Lawrence O'Gorman. Comparing passwords, tokens, and biometrics for user authentication. *Proceedings of the IEEE*, 91(12):2021–2040, 2003.

[80] Jesus Carretero, Guillermo Izquierdo-Moreno, Mario Vasile-Cabezas, and Javier Garcia-Blas. Federated identity architecture of the european eid system. *IEEE Access*, 6:75302–75326, 2018.

[81] Paul Grassi, Elaine Newton, Ray Perlner, Andrew Regenscheid, William Burr, Justin Richer, Naomi Lefkovitz, Jamie Danker, Yee-Yin Choong, Kristen Greene, and Mary Theofanos. Digital identity guidelines: Authentication and lifecycle management, 2017-06-22 2017.

[82] Divya Hadke and Rajesh Babu. Privacy-preserving and public auditing for regenerating-code-based cloud storage using finger print authentication. In *2020 Fourth International Conference on I-SMAC (IoT in Social, Mobile, Analytics and Cloud)(I-SMAC)*, pages 1284–1288. IEEE, 2020.

[83] Kalyani Pendke, Shivam Singh, Nihar Dhoble, Shubham Kewat, and Snehal Patil. Privacy-preserving of data using bio-metric in cloud storage. 2019.

[84] Hakan Yildiz, Christopher Ritter, Lan Thao Nguyen, Berit Frech, Maria Mora Martinez, and Axel Küpper. Connecting self-sovereign identity with federated and user-centric identities via saml integration. In *2021 IEEE Symposium on Computers and Communications (ISCC)*, pages 1–7. IEEE, 2021.

[85] A. Butowsky, K. Gai, M. Coakley, M. Qiu, and C. C. Tappert. City of white plains parking app: Case study of a smart city web application. In *IEEE 2nd International Conference on Cyber Security and Cloud Computing, CSCloud 2015*, pages 278–282, New York, NY, USA, 2015. IEEE Computer Society.

[86] Shamini Emerson, Young-Kyu Choi, Dong-Yeop Hwang, Kang-Seok Kim, and Ki-Hyung Kim. An oauth based authentication mechanism for iot networks. In *2015 International Conference on Information and Communication Technology Convergence (ICTC)*, pages 1072–1074. IEEE, 2015.

[87] Jan De Clercq. Single sign-on architectures. In *International Conference on Infrastructure Security*, pages 40–58. Springer, 2002.

[88] V Radha and D Hitha Reddy. A survey on single sign-on techniques. *Procedia Technology*, 4:134–139, 2012.

[89] Yassine Sadqi, Yousra Belfaik, and Said Safi. Web oauth-based sso systems security. In *Proceedings of the 3rd International Conference on Networking, Information Systems & Security*, NISS2020, New York, NY, USA, 2020. Association for Computing Machinery.

[90] Stefano Calzavara, Riccardo Focardi, Matteo Maffei, Clara Schneidewind, Marco Squarcina, and Mauro Tempesta. {WPSE}: Fortifying web protocols via browser-side security monitoring. In *27th {USENIX} Security Symposium ({USENIX} Security 18)*, pages 1493–1510, 2018.

[91] Daniel Fett, Ralf Küsters, and Guido Schmitz. A comprehensive formal security analysis of oauth 2.0. In *Proceedings of the 2016 ACM SIGSAC Conference on Computer and Communications Security*, CCS '16, page 1204–1215. New York, NY, USA, 2016. Association for Computing Machinery.

[92] Nitin Naik and Paul Jenkins. Securing digital identities in the cloud by selecting an apposite federated identity management from

saml, oauth and openid connect. In *2017 11th International Conference on Research Challenges in Information Science (RCIS)*, pages 163–174. IEEE, 2017.

[93] K. Wierenga, E. Lear, and S. Josefsson. Rfc 6595: A simple authentication and security layer (sasl) and gss-api mechanism for the security assertion markup language (saml), 2012.

[94] Viral Parmar, Harshal A Sanghvi, Riki H Patel, and Abhijit S Pandya. A comprehensive study on passwordless authentication. In *2022 International Conference on Sustainable Computing and Data Communication Systems (ICSCDS)*, pages 1266–1275. IEEE, 2022.

[95] E Praveen Kumar and S Priyanka. A password less authentication protocol for multi-server environment using physical unclonable function. *The Journal of Supercomputing*, pages 1–33, 2023.

[96] Mohammed Aziz Al Kabir and Wael Elmedany. An overview of the present and future of user authentication. In *2022 4th IEEE Middle East and North Africa COMMunications Conference (MENA-COMM)*, pages 10–17. IEEE, 2022.

[97] Mahdi Fotouhi, Majid Bayat, Ashok Kumar Das, Hossein Abdi Nasib Far, S Morteza Pournaghi, and Mohammad-Ali Doostari. A lightweight and secure two-factor authentication scheme for wireless body area networks in health-care iot. *Computer Networks*, 177:107333, 2020.

[98] Wenting Li and Ping Wang. Two-factor authentication in industrial internet-of-things: Attacks, evaluation and new construction. *Future Generation Computer Systems*, 101:694–708, 2019.

[99] SungJin Yu, KiSung Park, and YoungHo Park. A secure lightweight three-factor authentication scheme for iot in cloud computing environment. *Sensors*, 19(16):3598, 2019.

[100] Laura Vegh. Cyber-physical systems security through multi-factor authentication and data analytics. In *2018 IEEE International Conference on Industrial Technology (ICIT)*, pages 1369–1374. IEEE, 2018.

[101] Ignacio Velásquez, Angélica Caro, and Alfonso Rodríguez. Authentication schemes and methods: A systematic literature review. *Information and Software Technology*, 94:30–37, 2018.

[102] Gueltoum Bendiab, Stavros Shiaeles, Samia Boucherkha, and Bogdan Ghita. Fcmdt: A novel fuzzy cognitive maps dynamic trust model for cloud federated identity management. *computers & security*, 86:270–290, 2019.

[103] Bandar Omar ALSaleem and Abdullah I. Alshoshan. Multi-factor authentication to systems login. In *2021 National Computing Colleges Conference (NCCC)*, pages 1–4. IEEE, 2021.

[104] Yue Guo, Yuan Liang, Yan Zhuang, Rongtao Liao, Liang Dong, Fen Liu, Jie Xu, Xian Luo, Xiang Li, Wangsong Ke, et al. A security protection technology based on multi-factor authentication. In *2022 IEEE 2nd International Conference on Mobile Networks and Wireless Communications (ICMNWC)*, pages 1–5. IEEE, 2022.

[105] Official legal text, Sep 2022.

[106] Christopher F Mondschein and Cosimo Monda. The eu's general data protection regulation (gdpr) in a research context. *Fundamentals of Clinical Data Science*, pages 55–71, 2019.

[107] Mohammed El Arass, Iman Tikito, and Nissrine Souissi. Data lifecycles analysis: towards intelligent cycle. In *2017 Intelligent Systems and Computer Vision (ISCV)*, pages 1–8. IEEE, 2017.

[108] Hanae Elmekki, Dalila Chiadmi, and Hind Lamharhar. Open government data: Towards a comparison of data lifecycle models. In *Proceedings of the ArabWIC 6th Annual International Conference Research Track*, pages 1–6, 2019.

[109] Alex Ball. *Review of Data Management Lifecycle Models*. Citeseer, 2012.

[110] L. Zhu, Y. Wu, K. Gai, and K. R. Choo. Controllable and trustworthy blockchain-based cloud data management. *Future Generation Computer Systems*, 91:527–535, 2019.

[111] K. Gai and M. Qiu. Reinforcement learning-based content-centric services in mobile sensing. *IEEE Network*, 32(4):34–39, 2018.

[112] H. Zhao, M. Qiu, K. Gai, J. Li, and X. He. Cost reduction for data allocation in heterogenous cloud computing using dynamic programming. In *Smart Computing and Communication - First International Conference, SmartCom 2016*, volume 10135, pages 1–11. Springer, 2016.

[113] K. Gai, L. Zou, and L. Zhu. Ontology-based personalized telehealth scheme in cloud computing. In *Web Services - ICWS 2018 - 25th International Conference, Held as Part of the Services Conference Federation, SCF 2018*, volume 10966, pages 49–64, Seattle, WA, USA, 2018. Springer.

[114] M. Qiu, K. Gai, H. Zhao, and M. Liu. Privacy-preserving smart data storage for financial industry in cloud computing. *Concurrency and Computation: Practice and Experience*, 30(5), 2018.

[115] K. Gai, K. R. Choo, and L. Zhu. Blockchain-enabled reengineering of cloud datacenters. *IEEE Cloud Computing*, 5(6):21–25, 2018.

[116] K. Gai, M. Qiu, H. Zhao, and W. Dai. Anti-counterfeit scheme using monte carlo simulation for e-commerce in cloud systems. In *IEEE 2nd International Conference on Cyber Security and Cloud Computing, CSCloud 2015*, pages 74–79, New York, NY, USA, 2015. IEEE Computer Society.

[117] H. Li, K. Gai, Z. Fang, L. Zhu, L. Xu, and P. Jiang. Blockchain-enabled data provenance in cloud datacenter reengineering. In *Proceedings of the 2019 ACM International Symposium on Blockchain and Secure Critical Infrastructure, BSCI 2019, July 8, 2019*, pages 47–55, Auckland, New Zealand, 2019. ACM.

[118] United States Codes. United states code, 2006 edition, supplement 5, title 44 - public printing and documents. GovInfo recommendation, U.S. Government Publication Office, 2011.

[119] Eric Ke Wang, Yunming Ye, Xiaofei Xu, S. M. Yiu, L. C. K. Hui, and K. P. Chow. Security issues and challenges for cyber physical system. In *2010 IEEE/ACM Int'l Conference on Green Computing and Communications & Int'l Conference on Cyber, Physical and Social Computing*, pages 733–738, 2010.

[120] L. Ma, L. Tao, Y. Zhong, and K. Gai. Rulesn: Research and application of social network access control model. In *2nd IEEE*

International Conference on Big Data Security on Cloud, Big-DataSecurity 2016, IEEE International Conference on High Performance and Smart Computing, HPSC 2016, and IEEE International Conference on Intelligent Data and Security, IDS 2016, pages 418–423, New York, NY, USA, 2016. IEEE.

[121] X. Li, Z. Zhang, J. Liu, and K. Gai. A new complex network robustness attack algorithm. In *Proceedings of the 2019 ACM International Symposium on Blockchain and Secure Critical Infrastructure, BSCI 2019 July 8, 2019,* pages 13–17, Auckland, New Zealand, 2019. ACM.

[122] K. Gai, M. Qiu, M. Liu, and H. Zhao. Smart resource allocation using reinforcement learning in content-centric cyber-physical systems. In *Smart Computing and Communication - Second International Conference, SmartCom 2017,* volume 10699, pages 39–52. Springer, 2017.

[123] Radhakisan Sohanlal Baheti and Helen Gill. Cyber-physical systems. *2019 IEEE International Conference on Mechatronics (ICM),* 2019.

[124] Yiwen Wu, Ke Zhang, and Yan Zhang. Digital twin networks: A survey. *IEEE Internet of Things Journal,* 8(18):13789–13804, 2021.

[125] Edward A Lee. Cyber physical systems: Design challenges. In *2008 11th IEEE International Symposium on Object and Component-oriented Real-Time Distributed Computing (ISORC),* pages 363–369. IEEE, 2008.

[126] Faisal Alrefaei. The importance of security in cyber-physical system. In *2020 IEEE 6th World Forum on Internet of Things (WF-IoT),* pages 1–3, June 2020.

[127] Veronika Lesch, Marwin Züfle, André Bauer, Lukas Ifflländer, Christian Krupitzer, and Samuel Kounev. A literature review of iot and cps—what they are, and what they are not. *Journal of Systems and Software,* 200:111631, 2023.

[128] Arda Goknil, Phu Nguyen, Sagar Sen, Dimitra Politaki, Harris Niavis, Karl John Pedersen, Abdillah Suyuthi, Abhilash Anand,

and Amina Ziegenbein. A systematic review of data quality in cps and iot for industry 4.0. *ACM Computing Surveys*, 2023.

[129] Jacob Morgan. A simple explanation of'the internet of things'. *Retrieved November*, 20:2015, 2014.

[130] Ying Tan, Steve Goddard, and Lance C Perez. A prototype architecture for cyber-physical systems. *ACM Sigbed Review*, 5(1):1–2, 2008.

[131] Goran D Putnik, Luis Ferreira, Nuno Lopes, and Zlata Putnik. What is a cyber-physical system: Definitions and models spectrum. *Fme Transactions*, 47(4):663–674, 2019.

[132] K. Gai, L. Qiu, M. Chen, H. Zhao, and M. Qiu. SA-EAST: security-aware efficient data transmission for ITS in mobile heterogeneous cloud computing. *ACM Transactions on Embedded Computing Systems*, 16(2):60:1–60:22, 2017.

[133] M. Qiu and K. Gai. Heterogeneous assignment of functional units with gaussian execution time on A tree. In *20th IEEE International Conference on High Performance Computing and Communications; 16th IEEE International Conference on Smart City; 4th IEEE International Conference on Data Science and Systems, HPCC/SmartCity/DSS 2018*, pages 22–29, Exeter, United Kingdom, 2018. IEEE.

[134] S. Ding, X. He, J. Wang, B. Qiao, and K. Gai. Static node center opportunistic coverage and hexagonal deployment in hybrid crowd sensing. *Journal of Signal Processing Systems* , 86(2-3):251–267, 2017.

[135] Tomas Fencl, Pavel Burget, and Jan Bilek. Network topology design. *Control Engineering Practice*, 19(11):1287–1296, 2011.

[136] Young-Sik Jeong, Hyun-Woo Kim, and Haeng Jin Jang. Adaptive resource management scheme for monitoring of cps. *The Journal of Supercomputing*, 66(1):57–69, 2013.

[137] Aditya Gupta and Amritpal Singh. A comprehensive survey on cyber-physical systems towards healthcare 4.0. *SN Computer Science*, 4(2):199, 2023.

[138] Homa Alemzadeh, Catello Di Martino, Zhanpeng Jin, Zbigniew T Kalbarczyk, and Ravishankar K Iyer. Towards resiliency in embedded medical monitoring devices. In *IEEE/IFIP International Conference on Dependable Systems and Networks Workshops (DSN 2012)*, pages 1–6. IEEE, 2012.

[139] Shah Ahsanul Haque, Syed Mahfuzul Aziz, and Mustafizur Rahman. Review of cyber-physical system in healthcare. *International Journal of Distributed Sensor Networks*, 10(4):217415, 2014.

[140] Huda M Abdulwahid and Alok Mishra. Deployment optimization algorithms in wireless sensor networks for smart cities: A systematic mapping study. *Sensors*, 22(14):5094, 2022.

[141] Jin Wang, Hassan Abid, Sungyoung Lee, Lei Shu, and Feng Xia. A secured health care application architecture for cyber-physical systems. *arXiv preprint arXiv:1201.0213*, 2011.

[142] Insup Lee, Oleg Sokolsky, Sanjian Chen, John Hatcliff, Eunkyoung Jee, BaekGyu Kim, Andrew King, Margaret Mullen-Fortino, Soojin Park, Alexander Roederer, et al. Challenges and research directions in medical cyber-physical systems. *Proceedings of the IEEE*, 100(1):75–90, 2011.

[143] Sadhana Tiwari and Sonali Agarwal. Data stream management for cps-based healthcare: A contemporary review. *IETE Technical Review*, pages 1–24, 2021.

[144] Yin Zhang, Meikang Qiu, Chun-Wei Tsai, Mohammad Mehedi Hassan, and Atif Alamri. Health-cps: Healthcare cyber-physical system assisted by cloud and big data. *IEEE Systems Journal*, 11(1):88–95, 2015.

[145] Bikash Guha, Sean Moore, and Jacques M Huyghe. Conceptualizing data-driven closed-loop production systems for lean manufacturing of complex biomedical devices—a cyber-physical system approach. *Journal of Engineering and Applied Science*, 70(1):50, 2023.

[146] Flavio Tonelli, Melissa Demartini, Massimo Pacella, and Roberta Lala. Cyber-physical systems (cps) in supply chain management: from foundations to practical implementation. *Procedia CIRP*, 99:598–603, 2021.

[147] Kyoung-Dae Kim and PR Kumar. An overview and some challenges in cyber-physical systems. *Journal of the Indian Institute of Science*, 93(3):341–352, 2013.

[148] Mohamed Ben-Daya, Elkafi Hassini, and Zied Bahroun. Internet of things and supply chain management: a literature review. *International Journal of Production Research*, 57(15-16):4719–4742, 2019.

[149] Damian Pokorniecki and Kartikeya Acharya. Experiment to scope low carbon electricity based additive manufacturing with iot. In *Global IoT Summit*, pages 411–420. Springer, 2022.

[150] Xiaokang Zhou, Xuesong Xu, Wei Liang, Zhi Zeng, Shohei Shimizu, Laurence T Yang, and Qun Jin. Intelligent small object detection for digital twin in smart manufacturing with industrial cyber-physical systems. *IEEE Transactions on Industrial Informatics*, 18(2):1377–1386, 2021.

[151] Premkumar Murugiah, Akila Muthuramalingam, and S Anandamurugan. A design of predictive manufacturing system in iot-assisted industry 4.0 using heuristic-derived deep learning. *International Journal of Communication Systems*, 36(5):e5432, 2023.

[152] Muhammad Shoaib Farooq, Shamyla Riaz, Adnan Abid, Kamran Abid, and Muhammad Azhar Naeem. A survey on the role of iot in agriculture for the implementation of smart farming. *IEEE Access*, 7:156237–156271, 2019.

[153] Wan-Soo Kim, Won-Suk Lee, and Yong-Joo Kim. A review of the applications of the internet of things (iot) for agricultural automation. *Journal of Biosystems Engineering*, 45:385–400, 2020.

[154] Khaled Obaideen, Bashria AA Yousef, Maryam Nooman AlMallahi, Yong Chai Tan, Montaser Mahmoud, Hadi Jaber, and Mohamad Ramadan. An overview of smart irrigation systems using iot. *Energy Nexus*, page 100124, 2022.

[155] Vippon Preet Kour and Sakshi Arora. Recent developments of the internet of things in agriculture: a survey. *IEEE Access*, 8:129924–129957, 2020.

[156] Lui Sha, Sathish Gopalakrishnan, Xue Liu, and Qixin Wang. Cyber-physical systems: A new frontier. In *2008 IEEE International Conference on Sensor Networks, Ubiquitous, and Trustworthy Computing (sutc 2008)*, pages 1–9. IEEE, 2008.

[157] You Li and Javier Ibanez-Guzman. Lidar for autonomous driving: The principles, challenges, and trends for automotive lidar and perception systems. *IEEE Signal Processing Magazine*, 37(4):50–61, 2020.

[158] Krishna Sampigethaya and Radha Poovendran. Aviation cyber–physical systems: Foundations for future aircraft and air transport. *Proceedings of the IEEE*, 101(8):1834–1855, 2013.

[159] Fengzhong Qu, Fei-Yue Wang, and Liuqing Yang. Intelligent transportation spaces: vehicles, traffic, communications, and beyond. *IEEE Communications Magazine*, 48(11):136–142, 2010.

[160] Yuchen Jiang, Shen Yin, and Okyay Kaynak. Data-driven monitoring and safety control of industrial cyber-physical systems: Basics and beyond. *IEEE Access*, 6:47374–47384, 2018.

[161] Belma Memić, Adisa Hasković Džubur, and Elma Avdagić-Golub. Green iot: sustainability environment and technologies. *Science, Engineering and Technology*, 2(1):24–29, 2022.

[162] Md Abdur Rahim, Md Arafatur Rahman, Md Mustafizur Rahman, A Taufiq Asyhari, Md Zakirul Alam Bhuiyan, and D Ramasamy. Evolution of iot-enabled connectivity and applications in automotive industry: A review. *Vehicular Communications*, 27:100285, 2021.

[163] Christopher Turner, O Okorie, Christos Emmanouilidis, and John Oyekan. Circular production and maintenance of automotive parts: An internet of things (iot) data framework and practice review. *Computers in Industry*, 136:103593, 2022.

[164] K. Gai, Y. Wu, L. Zhu, K. R. Choo, and B. Xiao. Blockchain-enabled trustworthy group communications in UAV networks. *IEEE Transactions on Intelligent Transportation Systems*, 22(7):4118–4130, 2021.

[165] X. Yu, X. Li, J. Li, and K. Gai. A geographical behavior-based point-of-interest recommendation. In *5th IEEE International Conference on Big Data Security on Cloud, IEEE International Conference on High Performance and Smart Computing, and IEEE International Conference on Intelligent Data and Security, Big-DataSecurity/HPSC/IDS 2019, May 27-29, 2019*, pages 166–171, Washington, DC, USA, 2019. IEEE.

[166] Jixiang Gan, Lei Zeng, Qi Liu, and Xiaodong Liu. A survey of intelligent load monitoring in iot-enabled distributed smart grids. *International Journal of Ad Hoc and Ubiquitous Computing*, 42(1):12–29, 2023.

[167] Alireza Ghasempour. Internet of things in smart grid: Architecture, applications, services, key technologies, and challenges. *Inventions*, 4(1):22, 2019.

[168] Mahmoud Amin, Fayez FM El-Sousy, Ghada A Abdel Aziz, Khaled Gaber, and Osama A Mohammed. Cps attacks mitigation approaches on power electronic systems with security challenges for smart grid applications: A review. *IEEE Access*, 9:38571–38601, 2021.

[169] Gu Chaojun, Panida Jirutitijaroen, and Mehul Motani. Detecting false data injection attacks in ac state estimation. *IEEE Transactions on Smart Grid*, 6(5):2476–2483, 2015.

[170] Zhenyong Zhang, Ruilong Deng, Youliang Tian, Peng Cheng, and Jianfeng Ma. Spma: Stealthy physics-manipulated attack and countermeasures in cyber-physical smart grid. *IEEE Transactions on Information Forensics and Security*, 18:581–596, 2022.

[171] K. Gai, Y. Wu, L. Zhu, L. Xu, and Y. Zhang. Permissioned blockchain and edge computing empowered privacy-preserving smart grid networks. *IEEE Internet of Things Journal*, 6(5):7992–8004, 2019.

[172] K. Gai, X. Sun, and Y. Li. An approach of fog detecting magnitude using referenceless perceptual image defogging. In *5th IEEE International Conference on Cyber Security and Cloud Computing, CSCloud 2018 / 4th IEEE International Conference on Edge Computing and Scalable Cloud, EdgeCom 2018*, pages 58–63, Shanghai, China, 2018. IEEE Computer Society.

[173] K. Gai, M. Qiu, and M. Liu. Privacy-preserving access control using dynamic programming in fog computing. In *4th IEEE International Conference on Big Data Security on Cloud, IEEE International Conference on High Performance and Smart Computing, and IEEE International Conference on Intelligent Data and Security, BigDataSecurity/HPSC/IDS 2018*, pages 126–132, Omaha, NE, USA, 2018. IEEE.

[174] K. Gai, Y. Ding, A. Wang, L. Zhu, K. R. Choo, Q. Zhang, and Z. Wang. Attacking the edge-of-things: A physical attack perspective. *IEEE Internet of Things Journal*, 9(7):5240–5253, 2022.

[175] K. Gai, Z. Fang, R. Wang, L. Zhu, P. Jiang, and K. R. Choo. Edge computing and lightning network empowered secure food supply management. *IEEE Internet of Things Journal*, 9(16):14247–14259, 2022.

[176] K. Gai, L. Zhu, M. Qiu, K. Xu, and K. R. Choo. Multi-access filtering for privacy-preserving fog computing. *IEEE Transactions on Cloud Computing*, 10(1):539–552, 2022.

[177] K. Gai, Z. Lu, M. Qiu, and L. Zhu. Toward smart treatment management for personalized healthcare. *IEEE Network*, 33(6):30–36, 2019.

[178] L. Zhu, B. Zheng, M. Shen, S. Yu, F. Gao, H. Li, K. Shi, and K. Gai. Research on the security of blockchain data: A survey. *CoRR*, abs/1812.02009, 2018.

[179] Eric Newcomer. *Understanding Web Services: XML, Wsdl, Soap, and UDDI*. Addison-Wesley Professional, 2002.

[180] Paul Adamczyk, Patrick H Smith, Ralph E Johnson, and Munawar Hafiz. Rest and web services: In theory and in practice. *REST: from Research to Practice*, pages 35–57, 2011.

[181] Jaideep Roy and Anupama Ramanujan. Understanding web services. *IT Professional*, 3(6):69–73, 2001.

[182] H. Guo, H. Zheng, K. Xu, X. Kong, J. Liu, F. Liu, and K. Gai. An improved consensus mechanism for blockchain. In *Smart Blockchain - First International Conference, SmartBlock 2018*, volume 11373, pages 129–138, Tokyo, Japan, 2018. Springer.

[183] Sungchul Lee, Ju-Yeon Jo, and Yoohwan Kim. Authentication system for stateless restful web service. *Journal of Computational Methods in Sciences and Engineering*, 17(S1):S21–S34, 2017.

[184] Sungchul Lee, Ju-Yeon Jo, and Yoohwan Kim. Method for secure restful web service. In *2015 IEEE/ACIS 14th International Conference on Computer and Information Science (ICIS)*, pages 77–81. IEEE, 2015.

[185] Harihara Subramanian and Pethuru Raj. *Hands-On RESTful API Design Patterns and Best Practices: Design, develop, and deploy highly adaptable, scalable, and secure RESTful web APIs*. Packt Publishing Ltd, 2019.

[186] Todd Fredrich. Restful service best practices. *Recommendations for Creating Web Services*, pages 1–34, 2012.

[187] Mark Nottingham and Roy Fielding. Additional http status codes. Technical report, 2012.

[188] Imam Ahmad, Emi Suwarni, Rohmat Indra Borman, Farli Rossi, Yessi Jusman, et al. Implementation of restful api web services architecture in takeaway application development. In *2021 1st International Conference on Electronic and Electrical Engineering and Intelligent System (ICE3IS)*, pages 132–137. IEEE, 2021.

[189] Ian Hopkinson, Steven Maude, Marco Rospocher, et al. A simple api to the knowledgestore. In *ISWC (Developers Workshop)*, pages 7–12, 2014.

[190] Festim Halili, Erenis Ramadani, et al. Web services: a comparison of soap and rest services. *Modern Applied Science*, 12(3):175, 2018.

[191] Christian Werner, Carsten Buschmann, and Stefan Fischer. Wsdl-driven soap compression. *International Journal of Web Services Research (IJWSR)*, 2(1):18–35, 2005.

[192] Robert Richards. Universal description, discovery, and integration (uddi). In *Pro PHP XML and Web Services*, pages 751–780. Springer, 2006.

[193] Billy Lim and H Joseph Wen. Web services: An analysis of the technology, its benefits, and implementation difficulties. *Information Systems Management*, 20(2):49–57, 2003.

[194] Amy W Ray and Julian J Ray. Strategic benefits to smes from third party web services: An action research analysis. *The Journal of Strategic Information Systems*, 15(4):273–291, 2006.

[195] Michael C Daconta, Leo J Obrst, and Kevin T Smith. *The Semantic Web: a Guide to the Future of XML, Web-Services, and Knowledge Management*. John Wiley & Sons, 2003.

[196] Jagdeep Singh and Sunny Behal. Detection and mitigation of ddos attacks in sdn: A comprehensive review, research challenges and future directions. *Computer Science Review*, 37:100279, 2020.

[197] Paul Ferguson and Daniel Senie. Network ingress filtering: Defeating denial of service attacks which employ ip source address spoofing. Technical report, 1998.

[198] Jing Liu, Yang Xiao, Kaveh Ghaboosi, Hongmei Deng, and Jingyuan Zhang. Botnet: classification, attacks, detection, tracing, and preventive measures. *EURASIP Journal on Wireless Communications and Networking*, 2009:1–11, 2009.

[199] Theerasak Thapngam, Shui Yu, Wanlei Zhou, and Gleb Beliakov. Discriminating ddos attack traffic from flash crowd through packet arrival patterns. In *2011 IEEE Conference on Computer Communications Workshops (INFOCOM WKSHPS)*, pages 952–957. IEEE, 2011.

[200] Angelos D Keromytis, Vishal Misra, and Dan Rubenstein. Sos: An architecture for mitigating ddos attacks. *IEEE Journal on Selected Areas in Communications*, 22(1):176–188, 2004.

[201] Mitko Bogdanoski, Tomislav Suminoski, and Aleksandar Risteski. Analysis of the syn flood dos attack. *International Journal of Computer Network and Information Security (IJCNIS)*, 5(8):1–11, 2013.

[202] Nazrul Hoque, Dhruba K Bhattacharyya, and Jugal K Kalita. Botnet in ddos attacks: trends and challenges. *IEEE Communications Surveys & Tutorials*, 17(4):2242–2270, 2015.

[203] Ying Xing, Hui Shu, Hao Zhao, Dannong Li, and Li Guo. Survey on botnet detection techniques: Classification, methods, and evaluation. *Mathematical Problems in Engineering*, 2021:1–24, 2021.

[204] Yichen An, Shuichiro Haruta, Sanghun Choi, and Iwao Sasase. Traffic feature-based botnet detection scheme emphasizing the importance of long patterns. In *Image Processing and Communications: Techniques, Algorithms and Applications 11*, pages 181–188. Springer, 2020.

[205] Esraa Alomari, Selvakumar Manickam, Brij Bhooshan Gupta, Shankar Karuppayah, and Rafeef Alfaris. Botnet-based distributed denial of service (ddos) attacks on web servers: classification and art. *arXiv preprint arXiv:1208.0403*, 2012.

[206] An Wang, Wentao Chang, Songqing Chen, and Aziz Mohaisen. Delving into internet ddos attacks by botnets: characterization and analysis. *IEEE/ACM Transactions on Networking*, 26(6):2843–2855, 2018.

[207] Satish Pokhrel, Robert Abbas, and Bhulok Aryal. Iot security: botnet detection in iot using machine learning. *arXiv preprint arXiv:2104.02231*, 2021.

[208] Lei Zhang, Shui Yu, Di Wu, and Paul Watters. A survey on latest botnet attack and defense. In *2011IEEE 10th International Conference on Trust, Security and Privacy in Computing and Communications*, pages 53–60. IEEE, 2011.

[209] K Munivara Prasad, A Rama Mohan Reddy, and K Venugopal Rao. Dos and ddos attacks: defense, detection and traceback mechanisms-a survey. *Global Journal of Computer Science and Technology*, 14(7-E):15, 2014.

[210] M Ghil and Carla Taricco. Advanced spectral-analysis methods. In *Past and Present Variability of the Solar-Terrestrial System: Measurement, Data Analysis and Theoretical Models*, pages 137–159. Ios Press, 1997.

[211] Narmeen Zakaria Bawany, Jawwad A Shamsi, and Khaled Salah. Ddos attack detection and mitigation using sdn: methods, practices, and solutions. *Arabian Journal for Science and Engineering*, 42:425–441, 2017.

[212] Philippe Golle and Nicolas Ducheneaut. Preventing bots from playing online games. *Computers in Entertainment (CIE)*, 3(3):3–3, 2005.

[213] Rebecca Gurley Bace, Peter Mell, et al. Intrusion detection systems. 2001.

[214] Kelly M Kavanagh, Oliver Rochford, and Toby Bussa. Magic quadrant for security information and event management. *Gartner Group Research Note*, 2015.

[215] Mark Nicolett and Kelly M Kavanagh. Magic quadrant for security information and event management. *Gartner RAS Core Reasearch Note (May 2009)*, 2011.

[216] Milad Ghaznavi, Elaheh Jalalpour, Mohammad A Salahuddin, Raouf Boutaba, Daniel Migault, and Stere Preda. Content delivery network security: A survey. *IEEE Communications Surveys & Tutorials*, 23(4):2166–2190, 2021.

[217] Behrouz Zolfaghari, Gautam Srivastava, Swapnoneel Roy, Hamid R Nemati, Fatemeh Afghah, Takeshi Koshiba, Abolfazl Razi, Khodakhast Bibak, Pinaki Mitra, and Brijesh Kumar Rai. Content delivery networks: State of the art, trends, and future roadmap. *ACM Computing Surveys (CSUR)*, 53(2):1–34, 2020.

[218] Mohamed Haddadi and Rachid Beghdad. A confidence interval based filtering against ddos attack in cloud environment: A confidence interval against ddos attack in the cloud. *International Journal of Information Security and Privacy (IJISP)*, 14(4):42–56, 2020.

[219] Katerina J Argyraki and David R Cheriton. Active Internet Traffic Filtering: Real-time response to denial-of-service attacks. In *USENIX Annual Technical Conference, General Track*, volume 38, 2005.

[220] Zulfikar Sembiring. Stuxnet threat analysis in scada (supervisory control and data acquisition) and plc (programmable logic controller) systems. *Journal of Computer Science, Information Technology and Telecommunication Engineering*, 1(2):96–103, 2020.

[221] Jue Tian, Rui Tan, Xiaohong Guan, Zhanbo Xu, and Ting Liu. Moving target defense approach to detecting stuxnet-like attacks. *IEEE Transactions on Smart Grid*, 11(1):291–300, 2019.

[222] Agathe Blaise, Mathieu Bouet, Vania Conan, and Stefano Secci. Detection of zero-day attacks: An unsupervised port-based approach. *Computer Networks*, 180:107391, 2020.

[223] Nadine Kashmar, Mehdi Adda, and Mirna Atieh. From access control models to access control metamodels: A survey. In *Advances in Information and Communication: Proceedings of the 2019 Future of Information and Communication Conference (FICC), Volume 2*, pages 892–911. Springer, 2020.

[224] Emmanuel Bertin, Dina Hussein, Cigdem Sengul, and Vincent Frey. Access control in the internet of things: a survey of existing approaches and open research questions. *Annals of Telecommunications*, 74:375–388, 2019.

[225] Zoran Barać and Daniel Scott-Raynsford. Configuring transparent data encryption to bring your own key. In *Azure SQL Hyperscale Revealed: High-performance Scalable Solutions for Critical Data Workloads*, pages 171–186. Springer, 2023.

[226] Ruchi Soni. Managing accounts and security. In *Snowflake SnowPro™ Advanced Architect Certification Companion: Hands-on Preparation and Practice*, pages 173–188. Springer, 2023.

[227] Manish Saraswat and RC Tripathi. Cloud computing: Comparison and analysis of cloud service providers-aws, microsoft and google. In *2020 9th International Conference System Modeling and Advancement in Research Trends (SMART)*, pages 281–285. IEEE, 2020.

[228] Paola Pierleoni, Roberto Concetti, Alberto Belli, and Lorenzo Palma. Amazon, google and microsoft solutions for iot: Architectures and a performance comparison. *IEEE Access*, 8:5455–5470, 2019.

[229] Deepti Gupta, Smriti Bhatt, Maanak Gupta, Olumide Kayode, and Ali Saman Tosun. Access control model for google cloud iot. In *2020 IEEE 6th Intl Conference on Big Data Security on Cloud (BigDataSecurity), IEEE Intl Conference on High Performance and Smart Computing, (HPSC) and IEEE Intl Conference on Intelligent Data and Security (IDS)*, pages 198–208. IEEE, 2020.

[230] Hongzhi Guo, Jingyi Li, Jiajia Liu, Na Tian, and Nei Kato. A survey on space-air-ground-sea integrated network security in 6g. *IEEE Communications Surveys & Tutorials*, 24(1):53–87, 2021.

[231] Zhijie Zhang, Huazhu Fu, Hang Dai, Jianbing Shen, Yanwei Pang, and Ling Shao. Et-net: A generic edge-attention guidance network for medical image segmentation. In *Medical Image Computing and Computer Assisted Intervention–MICCAI 2019: 22nd International Conference, Shenzhen, China, October 13–17, 2019, Proceedings, Part I 22*, pages 442–450. Springer, 2019.

[232] Amit Kumar Singh and Anand Mohan. *Handbook of Multimedia Information Security: Techniques and Applications*. Springer, 2019.

[233] Pan Yang, Naixue Xiong, and Jingli Ren. Data security and privacy protection for cloud storage: A survey. *IEEE Access*, 8:131723–131740, 2020.

[234] Pawan Kumar and Ashutosh Kumar Bhatt. Enhancing multi-tenancy security in the cloud computing using hybrid ecc-based data encryption approach. *IET Communications*, 14(18):3212–3222, 2020.

[235] Vasantha Lakshmi. Beginning security with microsoft technologies. *Beginning Security with Microsoft Technologies*, 2019.

[236] Shulei Xu, S Mahdieh Ghazimirsaeed, Jahanzeb Maqbool Hashmi, Hari Subramoni, and Dhabaleswar K Panda. Mpi meets cloud: Case study with amazon ec2 and microsoft azure. In *2020 IEEE/ACM Fourth Annual Workshop on Emerging Parallel and Distributed Runtime Systems and Middleware (IPDRM)*, pages 41–48. IEEE, 2020.

[237] M. Bianucci, T. Mahesh, J. Mallory, J. Tsoi, and J. Warren. Computer crimes. *Am. Crim. L. Rev.*, 59:511, 2022.

[238] Y. Lu and L. Da Xu. Internet of things (iot) cybersecurity research: A review of current research topics. *IEEE Internet of Things Journal*, 6(2):2103–2115, 2018.

[239] Z. Ma, J. Wang, K. Gai, P. Duan, Y. Zhang, and S. Luo. Fully homomorphic encryption-based privacy-preserving scheme for cross edge blockchain network. *J. Syst. Archit.*, 134:102782, 2023.

[240] M. N. Alenezi, H. Alabdulrazzaq, and N. Q. Mohammad. Symmetric encryption algorithms: Review and evaluation study. *International Journal of Communication Networks and Information Security*, 12(2):256–272, 2020.

[241] G. S. Poh, J. Chin, W. Yau, K. R. Choo, and M. S. Mohamad. Searchable symmetric encryption: designs and challenges. *ACM Computing Surveys (CSUR)*, 50(3):1–37, 2017.

[242] K. Gai, M. Qiu, Y. Li, and X. Liu. Advanced fully homomorphic encryption scheme over real numbers. In *4th IEEE International Conference on Cyber Security and Cloud Computing, CSCloud 2017*, pages 64–69, New York, NY, USA, 2017. IEEE Computer Society.

[243] K., Y. Wu, L. Zhu, and M. Qiu. Privacy-preserving data synchronization using tensor-based fully homomorphic encryption. In *17th IEEE International Conference On Trust, Security And Privacy In Computing And Communications / 12th IEEE International Conference On Big Data Science And Engineering, Trust-Com/BigDataSE 2018*, pages 1149–1156, New York, NY, USA, 2018. IEEE.

[244] Y. Dodis, M. Stam, J. Steinberger, and T. Liu. Indifferentiability of confusion-diffusion networks. In *Annual International Conference on the Theory and Applications of Cryptographic Techniques*, pages 679–704. Springer, 2016.

[245] L. R. Knudsen and M. Robshaw. *The Block Cipher Companion*. Springer Science & Business Media, 2011.

[246] Y. Tsunoo, T. Saito, M. Shigeri, H. Kubo, and K. Minematsu. Shorter bit sequence is enough to break stream cipher lili-128. *IEEE Transactions on Information Theory*, 51(12):4312–4319, 2005.

[247] M. Matsui. Linear cryptanalysis method for des cipher. In *Workshop on the Theory and Application of of Cryptographic Techniques*, pages 386–397. Springer, 1993.

[248] K. Furkan Altınok, A. Peker, C. Tezcan, and A. Temizel. Gpu accelerated 3des encryption. *Concurrency and Computation: Practice and Experience*, 34(9):e6507, 2022.

[249] J. Daemen and V. Rijmen. Aes proposal: Rijndael. 1999.

[250] W. Diffie and M. E. Hellman. New directions in cryptography. In *Democratizing Cryptography: The Work of Whitfield Diffie and Martin Hellman*, pages 365–390. 2022.

[251] U. M. Maurer and S. Wolf. The diffie–hellman protocol. *Designs, Codes and Cryptography*, 19(2):147–171, 2000.

[252] J. Qiu, Z. Tian, C. Du, Q. Zuo, S. Su, and B. Fang. A survey on access control in the age of internet of things. *IEEE Internet of Things Journal*, 7(6):4682–4696, 2020.

[253] Y. Li, K. Gai, Z. Ming, H. Zhao, and M. Qiu. Intercrossed access controls for secure financial services on multimedia big data in cloud systems. *ACM Trans. Multim. Comput. Commun. Appl.*, 12(4s):67:1–67:18, 2016.

[254] K. Thakur, M. Liakat Ali, K. Gai, and M. Qiu. Information security policy for e-commerce in saudi arabia. In *2nd IEEE International Conference on Big Data Security on Cloud, BigDataSecurity 2016, IEEE International Conference on High Performance and Smart Computing, HPSC 2016, and IEEE International Conference on Intelligent Data and Security, IDS 2016*, pages 187–190, New York, NY, USA, 2016. IEEE.

[255] N. Li and M. V. Tripunitara. On safety in discretionary access control. In *2005 IEEE Symposium on Security and Privacy (S&P'05)*, pages 96–109. IEEE, 2005.

[256] H. Lindqvist. Mandatory access control. *Master's Thesis in Computing Science, Umea University, Department of Computing Science, SE-901*, 87, 2006.

[257] D. F. Ferraiolo, S. Sandhu, R.and Gavrila, and R. Kuhn, D. R.and Chandramouli. Proposed nist standard for role-based access control. *ACM Transactions on Information and System Security (TISSEC)*, 4(3):224–274, 2001.

[258] R. S. Sandhu, E. J. Coyne, H. L. Feinstein, and C. E. Youman. Role-based access control models. *Computer*, 29(2):38–47, 1996.

[259] W. Li, L. Liao, D. Gu, C. Li, C. Ge, Z. Guo, Y. Liu, and Z. Liu. Ciphertext-only fault analysis on the led lightweight cryptosystem in the internet of things. *IEEE Transactions on Dependable and Secure Computing*, 16(3):454–461, 2018.

[260] M. Mangia, F. Pareschi, R. Rovatti, and G. Setti. Low-cost security of iot sensor nodes with rakeness-based compressed sensing: Statistical and known-plaintext attacks. *IEEE Transactions on Information Forensics and Security*, 13(2):327–340, 2017.

[261] H. A. Bergen and J. M. Hogan. A chosen plaintext attack on an adaptive arithmetic coding compression algorithm. *Computers & Security*, 12(2):157–167, 1993.

[262] R. Cramer and V. Shoup. Design and analysis of practical public-key encryption schemes secure against adaptive chosen ciphertext attack. *SIAM Journal on Computing*, 33(1):167–226, 2003.

[263] Y. Desmedt and A. M. Odlyzko. A chosen text attack on the rsa cryptosystem and some discrete logarithm schemes. In *Conference on the Theory and Application of Cryptographic Techniques*, pages 516–522. Springer, 1985.

[264] C. Cachin and U. Maurer. Unconditional security against memory-bounded adversaries. In *Annual International Cryptology Conference*, pages 292–306. Springer, 1997.

[265] N. Koblitz and A. J. Menezes. Another look at "provable security". *Journal of Cryptology*, 20(1):3–37, 2007.

[266] A. Kumar and S. Garhwal. State-of-the-art survey of quantum cryptography. *Archives of Computational Methods in Engineering*, 28(5):3831–3868, 2021.

[267] M. Qiu, K. Gai, and Z. Xiong. Privacy-preserving wireless communications using bipartite matching in social big data. *Future Gener. Comput. Syst.*, 87:772–781, 2018.

[268] Pravin Bhagwat. Bluetooth: technology for short-range wireless apps. *IEEE Internet Computing*, 5(3):96–103, 2001.

[269] Hossein Pirayesh, Pedram Kheirkhah Sangdeh, and Huacheng Zeng. Securing zigbee communications against constant jamming

attack using neural network. *IEEE Internet of Things Journal*, 8(6):4957–4968, 2020.

[270] Younghwan Choi, Yunchul Choi, Dongmyoung Kim, and Jungsoo Park. Scheme to guarantee ip continuity for nfc-based iot networking. In *2017 19th International Conference on Advanced Communication Technology (ICACT)*, pages 695–698. IEEE, 2017.

[271] K. Gai, M. Qiu, Z. Xiong, and M. Liu. Privacy-preserving multi-channel communication in edge-of-things. *Future Gener. Comput. Syst.*, 85:190–200, 2018.

[272] K. Gai, K. Xu, Z. Lu, M. Qiu, and L. Zhu. Fusion of cognitive wireless networks and edge computing. *IEEE Wirel. Commun.*, 26(3):69–75, 2019.

[273] H. Zhao, M. Qiu, K. Gai, and X. He. Optimal solution to intelligent multi-channel wireless communications using dynamic programming. *J. Supercomput.*, 75(4):1894–1908, 2019.

[274] G Roberto Aiello and Gerald D Rogerson. Ultra-wideband wireless systems. *IEEE Microwave Magazine*, 4(2):36–47, 2003.

[275] Henning Helmers, Cornelius Armbruster, Moritz von Ravenstein, David Derix, and Christian Schöner. 6-w optical power link with integrated optical data transmission. *IEEE Transactions on Power Electronics*, 35(8):7904–7909, 2020.

[276] Dong-Keun Jeon and Yeonwoo Lee. Performance evaluation of ship area network with tdma-based hr-wpan for an m2m application. In *2014 8th International Conference on Future Generation Communication and Networking*, pages 13–16. IEEE, 2014.

[277] H. Zhao, K. Gai, J. Li, and X. He. Novel differential schema for high performance big data telehealth systems using pre-cache. In *17th IEEE International Conference on High Performance Computing and Communications, HPCC 2015, 7th IEEE International Symposium on Cyberspace Safety and Security, CSS 2015, and 12th IEEE International Conference on Embedded Software and Systems, ICESS 2015*, pages 1412–1417, New York, NY, USA, 2015. IEEE.

[278] S Jayalekshmi and R Leela Velusamy. Gsa-rpi: Gsa based rendezvous point identification in a two-level cluster based lr-wpan for uncovering the optimal trajectory of mobile data collection agent. *Journal of Network and Computer Applications*, 183:103048, 2021.

[279] Y. Li, K. Liang, X. Tang, and K. Gai. Cloud-based adaptive particle swarm optimization for waveband selection in big data. *J. Signal Process. Syst.*, 90(8-9):1105–1113, 2018.

[280] J. Wu, X. Cui, W. Hu, K. Gai, X. Liu, K. Zhang, and K. Xu. A new sustainable interchain design on transport layer for blockchain. In *Smart Blockchain - First International Conference, SmartBlock 2018*, volume 11373, pages 12–21, Tokyo, Japan, 2018. Springer.

[281] Z. Li, C. Huang, K. Gai, Z. Lu, J. Wu, L. Chen, Y. Xu, and K. R. Choo. Asyfed: Accelerated federated learning with asynchronous communication mechanism. *IEEE Internet Things J.*, 10(10):8670–8683, 2023.

[282] K. Gai, Y. Wu, L. Zhu, M. Qiu, and M. Shen. Privacy-preserving energy trading using consortium blockchain in smart grid. *IEEE Trans. Ind. Informatics*, 15(6):3548–3558, 2019.

[283] Lein Harn, Chingfang Hsu, and Zhe Xia. Lightweight group key distribution schemes based on pre-shared pairwise keys. *IET Communications*, 14(13):2162–2165, 2020.

[284] K. Gai, M. Qiu, and H. Zhao. Privacy-preserving data encryption strategy for big data in mobile cloud computing. *IEEE Trans. Big Data*, 7(4):678–688, 2021.

[285] S. Li, A. Leider, M. Qiu, K. Gai, and M. Liu. Brain-based computer interfaces in virtual reality. In *4th IEEE International Conference on Cyber Security and Cloud Computing, CSCloud 2017*, pages 300–305, New York, NY, USA, 2017. IEEE Computer Society.

[286] Y. Li, K. Liang, X. Tang, and K. Gai. Waveband selection based feature extraction using genetic algorithm. In *4th IEEE International Conference on Cyber Security and Cloud Computing, CSCloud 2017*, pages 223–227, New York, NY, USA, 2017. IEEE Computer Society.

[287] K. R. Choo, K. Gai, and L. Chiaraviglio. Blockchain-enabled secure communications in smart cities. *J. Parallel Distributed Comput.*, 152:125–127, 2021.

[288] H. Zhao, M. Qiu, M. Chen, and K. Gai. Cost-aware optimal data allocations for multiple dimensional heterogeneous memories using dynamic programming in big data. *J. Comput. Sci.*, 26:402–408, 2018.

[289] W. Wang, G. Li, K. Gai, Y. Tang, B. Yang, and X. Si. Modelization and analysis of dynamic heterogeneous redundant system. *Concurr. Comput. Pract. Exp.*, 34(12), 2022.

[290] S. Tang, X. Du, Z. Lu, K. Gai, J. Wu, P. C. K. Hung, and K. R. Choo. Coordinate-based efficient indexing mechanism for intelligent iot systems in heterogeneous edge computing. *J. Parallel Distributed Comput.*, 166:45–56, 2022.

[291] K. Gai, X. Qin, and L. Zhu. An energy-aware high performance task allocation strategy in heterogeneous fog computing environments. *IEEE Trans. Computers*, 70(4):626–639, 2021.

[292] K. Gai, Q. Xiao, M. Qiu, G. Zhang, J. Chen, Y. Wei, and Y. Zhang. Digital twin-enabled ai enhancement in smart critical infrastructures for 5G. *ACM Transactions on Sensor Networks (TOSN)*, 18(3):1–20, 2022.

[293] F. Tao, H. Zhang, A. Liu, and A.Y. Nee. Digital twin in industry: State-of-the-art. *IEEE Transactions on Industrial Informatics*, 15(4):2405–2415, 2018.

[294] Princess Adjei and Reza Montasari. A critical overview of digital twins. *International Journal of Strategic Engineering (IJoSE)*, 3(1):51–61, 2020.

[295] E. Glaessgen and D. Stargel. The digital twin paradigm for future nasa and us air force vehicles. In *53rd AIAA/ASME/ASCE/AHS/ASC Structures, Structural Dynamics and Materials Conference 20th AIAA/ASME/AHS Adaptive Structures Conference 14th AIAA*, page 1818, Honolulu, Hawaii, 2012. AIAA.

[296] Q. Qi and F. Tao. Digital twin and big data towards smart manufacturing and industry 4.0: 360 degree comparison. *IEEE Access*, 6:3585–3593, 2018.

[297] K. Park, Y. Son, and S. Noh. The architectural framework of a cyber physical logistics system for digital-twin-based supply chain control. *International Journal of Production Research*, 1:1–22, 2020.

[298] Y. Liu, L. Zhang, Y. Yang, L. Zhou, L. Ren, F. Wang, R. Liu, Z. Pang, and M. Deen. A novel cloud-based framework for the elderly healthcare services using digital twin. *IEEE Access*, 7:49088–49101, 2019.

[299] K. Gai, M. Qiu, H. Zhao, L. Tao, and Z. Zong. Dynamic energy-aware cloudlet-based mobile cloud computing model for green computing. *Journal of Network and Computer Applications*, 59:46–54, 2016.

[300] K. Gai, M. Qiu, and H. Zhao. Energy-aware task assignment for mobile cyber-enabled applications in heterogeneous cloud computing. *Journal of Parallel and Distributed Computing*, 111:126–135, 2018.

[301] Z. Zhou, X. Chen, E. Li, L. Zeng, K. Luo, and J. Zhang. Edge intelligence: Paving the last mile of artificial intelligence with edge computing. *Proc. IEEE*, 107(8):1738–1762, 2019.

[302] X. Wang, Y. Han, C. Wang, et al. In-edge ai: Intelligentizing mobile edge computing, caching and communication by federated learning. *IEEE Network*, 33(5):156–165, 2019.

[303] Y. Shi, K. Yang, T. Jiang, et al. Communication-efficient edge ai: Algorithms and systems. *IEEE Communications Surveys & Tutorials*, 22(4):2167–2191, 2020.

[304] Z. Zhou, X. Chen, E. Li, et al. Edge intelligence: Paving the last mile of artificial intelligence with edge computing. *Proceedings of the IEEE*, 107(8):1738–1762, 2019.

[305] Y. Liu, X. Yuan, Z. Xiong, J. Kang, X. Wang, and D. Niyato. Federated learning for 6G communications: Challenges, methods, and future directions. *China Communications*, 17(9):105–118, 2020.

[306] Ke Zhang, Jiayu Cao, and Yan Zhang. Adaptive digital twin and multi-agent deep reinforcement learning for vehicular edge computing and networks. *IEEE Transactions on Industrial Informatics*, 18(2):1405–1413, 2022.

[307] T. Hao, Y. Huang, X. Wen, et al. Edge aibench: towards comprehensive end-to-end edge computing benchmarking. In *International Symposium on Benchmarking, Measuring and Optimization*, pages 23–30, Seattle, WA, USA, 2018. Springer.

[308] M. Satyanarayanan. The emergence of edge computing. *Computer*, 50(1):30–39, 2017.

[309] W. Khan, E. Ahmed, H. Saqib, et al. Edge computing: A survey. *Future Generation Computer Systems*, 97:219–235, 2019.

[310] N. Abbas, Y. Zhang, A. Taherkordi, et al. Mobile edge computing: A survey. *IEEE Internet of Things Journal*, 5(1):450–465, 2017.

[311] Y. Mao, C. You, J. Zhang, et al. A survey on mobile edge computing: The communication perspective. *IEEE Communications Surveys & Tutorials*, 19(4):2322–2358, 2017.

[312] X. Zhang, Y. Wang, S. Lu, et al. Openei: An open framework for edge intelligence. In *2019 IEEE 39th International Conference on Distributed Computing Systems (ICDCS)*, pages 1840–1851, Dallas, TX, USA, 2019. IEEE.

[313] W. Zhang, Z. Zhang, S. Zeadally, et al. Masm: A multiple-algorithm service model for energy-delay optimization in edge artificial intelligence. *IEEE Transactions on Industrial Informatics*, 15(7):4216–4224, 2019.

[314] Q. Zhang, L. Gui, F. Hou, et al. Dynamic task offloading and resource allocation for mobile-edge computing in dense cloud ran. *IEEE Internet of Things Journal*, 7(4):3282–3299, 2020.

[315] A. Dutta, V. Ufimtsev, and A. Asaithambi. Correlation clustering based coalition formation for multi-robot task allocation. In *Proceedings of the 34th ACM/SIGAPP Symposium on Applied Computing*, pages 906–913, Limassol, Cyprus, 2019. ACM.

[316] S. Alirezazadeh and L. Alexandre. Optimal algorithm allocation for single robot cloud systems. *IEEE Transactions on Cloud Computing*, 1(1):1–1, 2021.

[317] J. Dean, G. Corrado, R. Monga, et al. Large scale distributed deep networks. *Advances in Neural Information Processing Systems*, 25:1223–1231, 2012.

[318] R. Hadidi, J. Cao, M. Woodward, et al. Distributed perception by collaborative robots. *IEEE Robotics and Automation Letters*, 3(4):3709–3716, 2018.

[319] K. Sato and T. Fujii. Radio environment aware computation offloading with multiple mobile edge computing servers. In *2017 IEEE Wireless Communications and Networking Conference Workshops (WCNCW)*, pages 1–5, San Francisco, CA, USA, 2017. IEEE.

[320] B. Guo, Y. Liu, L. Wang, et al. Task allocation in spatial crowdsourcing: Current state and future directions. *IEEE Internet of Things Journal*, 5(3):1749–1764, 2018.

[321] Z. Wang, J. Hu, R. Lv, et al. Personalized privacy-preserving task allocation for mobile crowdsensing. *IEEE Transactions on Mobile Computing*, 18(6):1330–1341, 2018.

[322] T. Dinh, J. Tang, Q. La, et al. Offloading in mobile edge computing: Task allocation and computational frequency scaling. *IEEE Transactions on Communications*, 65(8):3571–3584, 2017.

[323] J. Wang, F. Wang, Y. Wang, et al. Hytasker: Hybrid task allocation in mobile crowd sensing. *IEEE Transactions on Mobile Computing*, 19(3):598–611, 2019.

[324] S. Li, L. Da, and S. Zhao. 5g internet of things: A survey. *Journal of Industrial Information Integration*, 10:1–9, 2018.

[325] L. Chettri and R. Bera. A comprehensive survey on internet of things (iot) toward 5g wireless systems. *IEEE Internet of Things Journal*, 7(1):16–32, 2019.

[326] Q. Chen, Z. Zheng, C. Hu, et al. On-edge multi-task transfer learning: Model and practice with data-driven task allocation. *IEEE Transactions on Parallel and Distributed Systems*, 31(6):1357–1371, 2019.

[327] S. Mahmood, S. Anwer, M. Niazi, et al. Key factors that influence task allocation in global software development. *Information and Software Technology*, 91:102–122, 2017.

[328] S. Yang, F. Li, M. Shen, et al. Cloudlet placement and task allocation in mobile edge computing. *IEEE Internet of Things Journal*, 6(3):5853–5863, 2019.

[329] M. Li, C. Liu, K. Li, et al. Multi-task allocation with an optimized quantum particle swarm method. *Applied Soft Computing*, 96:106603, 2020.

[330] E. Bakolas and Y. Lee. Decentralized game-theoretic control for dynamic task allocation problems for multi-agent systems. In *2021 American Control Conference (ACC)*, pages 3228–3233, New Orleans, LA, USA, 2021. IEEE.

[331] M. Otte, M. Kuhlman, and D. Sofge. Multi-robot task allocation with auctions in harsh communication environments. In *2017 International Symposium on Multi-Robot and Multi-Agent Systems (MRS)*, pages 32–39, California, CA, USA, 2017. IEEE.

[332] H. Kurdi, E. Aloboud, M. Alalwan, et al. Autonomous task allocation for multi-uav systems based on the locust elastic behavior. *Applied Soft Computing*, 71:110–126, 2018.

[333] J. Schwarzrock, I. Zacarias, A. Bazzan, et al. Solving task allocation problem in multi unmanned aerial vehicles systems using swarm intelligence. *Engineering Applications of Artificial Intelligence*, 72:10–20, 2018.

[334] C. Zhu, J. Tao, G. Pastor, et al. Folo: Latency and quality optimized task allocation in vehicular fog computing. *IEEE Internet of Things Journal*, 6(3):4150–4161, 2018.

[335] S. Jošilo and G. Dán. Decentralized algorithm for randomized task allocation in fog computing systems. *IEEE/ACM Transactions on Networking*, 27(1):85–97, 2018.

[336] L. Jin, S. Li, H. La, et al. Dynamic task allocation in multi-robot coordination for moving target tracking: A distributed approach. *Automatica*, 100:75–81, 2019.

[337] Z. Su, Y. Hui, and T. Luan. Distributed task allocation to enable collaborative autonomous driving with network softwarization. *IEEE Journal on Selected Areas in Communications*, 36(10):2175–2189, 2018.

[338] K. Gai, M. Qiu, H. Zhao, and L. Qiu. Smart energy-aware data allocation for heterogeneous memory. In *The 18th IEEE International Conference on High Performance Computing and Communications*, pages 136–143, Sydney, Australia, 2016.

[339] K. Gai, Z. Du, M. Qiu, and H. Zhao. Efficiency-aware workload optimizations of heterogenous cloud computing for capacity planning in financial industry. In *The 2nd IEEE International Conference on Cyber Security and Cloud Computing*, pages 1–6, New York, USA, 2015. IEEE.

[340] M. Qiu, Z. Chen, and M. Liu. Low-power low-latency data allocation for hybrid scratch-pad memory. *IEEE Embedded Systems Letters*, 6(4):69–72, 2014.

Index